HANDBOOK OF DEVELOPMENTS IN CONSUMER BEHAVIOUR

To David (VKW)
To Jean (GRF)

Handbook of Developments in Consumer Behaviour

Edited by

Victoria Wells

Durham Business School, Durham University, UK

Gordon Foxall

Cardiff Business School, Cardiff University, UK

Edward Elgar
Cheltenham, UK • Northampton, MA, USA

Published by
Edward Elgar Publishing Limited
The Lypiatts
15 Lansdown Road
Cheltenham
Glos GL50 2JA
UK

Edward Elgar Publishing, Inc.
William Pratt House
9 Dewey Court
Northampton
Massachusetts 01060
USA

A catalogue record for this book
is available from the British Library

Library of Congress Control Number: 2012930572

ISBN 978 1 84980 244 4 (cased)

Typeset by Servis Filmsetting Ltd, Stockport, Cheshire
Printed and bound by MPG Books Group, UK

Contents

v

Contributors

Paul J. Albanese (PhD Economics, Harvard) is an Associate Professor of Marketing at Kent State University. Dr Albanese conducts research on personality and consumer behaviour and is the author of *The Personality Continuum and Consumer Behavior* (2002). The Personality Continuum is an integrative framework for the interdisciplinary study of consumer behaviour. Currently his research is focused on the areas of compulsive buying behaviour and the unconscious processing of information. Dr Albanese is active in presenting his research at conferences of the Association of Consumer Research, Society for the Advancement of Behavioral Economics, International Association for Research in Economic Psychology, Consumer Personality and Research Methods, and the International Society for the Scientific Study of Subjectivity. Dr Albanese primarily teaches courses on Consumer Behavior.

Russell Belk is Professor of Marketing at York University, Toronto, is a past president of the International Association of Marketing and Development and is a fellow and past president of the Association for Consumer Research. He initiated the Consumer Behavior Odyssey, the Association for Consumer Research Film Festival, and the Consumer Culture Theory Conference. His awards include the Paul D. Converse Award and the Sheth Foundation/*Journal of Consumer Research* Award for Long Term Contribution to Consumer Research. His research involves the meanings of possessions, collecting, gift-giving, materialism, and global consumer culture. He is currently Professor of Marketing and Kraft Foods Canada Chair in Marketing at the Schulich School of Business, York University in Toronto, Canada and holds honorary professorships in North America, Europe, Asia, and Australia. He has more than 475 publications.

C. Samuel Craig is the Catherine and Peter Kellner Professor, Professor of Marketing and International Business and Director of the Entertainment, Media and Technology Program at New York University's Stern School of Business. He received his PhD from the Ohio State University. Prior to joining New York University, Professor Craig taught at Cornell University. Professor Craig is co-author of *Consumer Behavior: An Information Processing Perspective* (Prentice Hall), *Global Marketing Strategy* (McGraw-Hill) and *International Marketing Research*, 3rd edition (Wiley). His research has appeared in the *Journal of Marketing Research, Journal of Marketing, Journal of Consumer Research, Journal of International Business Studies, Columbia Journal of World Business, International Journal of Research in Marketing, Journal of International Marketing, International Marketing Review* and other publications. His research interests focus on the entertainment industry, global marketing strategy and methodological issues in international marketing research.

Susan P. Douglas was the Paganelli-Bull Professor of Marketing and International Business at New York University's Stern School of Business. She received her PhD from the University of Pennsylvania. Prior to joining New York University, Professor Douglas taught at Centre-HEC, Jouy-en-Josas, France, and was a faculty member of the European Institute for Advanced Studies in Management in Brussels. Professor Douglas was elected as a fellow of the Academy of International Business in 1991 and was made a fellow of the European Marketing Academy in 2002. She was a leading scholar in international marketing and passed away suddenly in January 2011.

Professor Douglas was co-author of *Global Marketing Strategy* (McGraw-Hill) and *International Marketing Research*, 3rd edition (Wiley). Her research has appeared in the *Journal of Marketing, Journal of Consumer Research, Journal of Marketing Research, Journal of International Business Studies, Columbia Journal of World Business, International Journal of Research in Marketing, International Marketing Review, Journal of International Marketing* and other publications.

Gordon R. Foxall is Distinguished Research Professor and Professor of Economic Psychology at Cardiff University where he is the Director of the Consumer Behaviour Analysis Research Group at Cardiff Business School. His chief research interests lie in psychological theories of consumer choice and consumer innovativeness and their relationships to marketing management and strategy. He has published some 20 books and over 250 articles and papers on these and related themes and has previously held professorial appointments at the Universities of Strathclyde, Birmingham and Keele. His books include the popular text *Consumer Psychology for Marketing* (co-authored with Ron Goldsmith and Stephen Brown), which has been translated into Korean, Russian, Polish and Chinese, and monographs such as *Consumer Choice* and *Marketing Psychology*. In addition, he has published in numerous scholarly journals including *Journal of Consumer Research, Journal of Business Research, International Journal of Research in Marketing, Psychology and Marketing, Journal of the Experimental Analysis of Behavior, Behavioural Processes*, and *Journal of the Academy of Marketing Science*. His undergraduate work and early research career were undertaken at the University of Salford and he is also a graduate of the Universities of Birmingham (PhD industrial economics and business studies) and Strathclyde (PhD psychology). In addition, he holds a higher doctorate of the University of Birmingham (DSocSc). He is a Fellow of both the British Psychological Society (FBPsS) and the British Academy of Management (FBAM) and was recently elected an Academician by the Academy of Social Sciences (AcSS). He is particularly concerned with the development and evaluation of consumer behaviour analysis, which systematically relates consumer choice to the situational contexts in which it arises. This work began with an analysis of the empirical evidence for attitude–behaviour relationships, a mainstay of consumer and marketing research, which showed that the expected consistency between cognitive and behavioural measures was rarely demonstrated in empirical research. Both psychologists and marketing scientists agreed that situational influences must be taken into consideration in order to predict behaviour accurately from attitude measures. Nevertheless, neither group had produced a model of situational influences on consumer behaviour that served this purpose. (See the books *Consumer Choice* and *Marketing Psychology*.) The Behavioural Perspective Model makes possible an eightfold classification of consumer situations, and recent empirical research involving both English- and Spanish-speaking consumers demonstrates that attitude–behavioural consistency is high when the situational contexts derived from the model are taken into consideration. In addition, the empirical research that has stemmed from the model suggests practical solutions to problems of retail design and the management of consumer situations. Further empirical research funded by grants from the Nuffield Foundation is concerned with the nature of consumers' brand choices and the decision processes that underlie them. The theoretical and empirical scope of consumer behaviour analysis is apparent from a three-volume set that Gordon has just edited for Routledge: *Consumer Behaviour Analysis: Critical Perspectives in Business and Management* (2002) which deals comprehensively with the philosophical background to the behavioural perspective, its empirical basis, and its managerial implications.

Ronald E. Goldsmith, PhD, is the Richard M. Baker Professor of Marketing in the College of Business at Florida State University where he teaches consumer behavior and marketing research. Most of his research focuses on personality's role in consumer behavior and measurement issues, especially in the areas of diffusion of innovations, consumer involvement, and services marketing. Since 1991 he has been a co-editor (North America) for the *Service Industries Journal*. He has published over 160 articles in such journals as the *Journal of Services Marketing, Journal of Consumer*

Behaviour, Journal of Advertising, European Journal of Marketing, Journal of Social Psychology, Journal of the Academy of Marketing Science, and *Journal of Business Research*. His book co-authored with Gordon Foxall entitled *Consumer Psychology for Marketing* was first published in 1994 and appears in Chinese, Polish, Russian, and Korean editions.

Leonard Green received his undergraduate degree from the City College of New York (CCNY) and his PhD from the State University of New York at Stony Brook. After completing post-doctoral research, Green joined the faculty of Washington University in St. Louis where he is Professor of Psychology and Director of Undergraduate Studies. Green's research concerns choice and decision-making in rats, pigeons, and humans, with a particular interest in models of self-control, impulsivity, choice and decision-making, and basic learning processes. In addition, he is one of the developers of 'behavioral economics,' a transdisciplinary field that combines the experimental methodology of psychology with the theoretical constructs of economics. He has published over 150 articles and book chapters, is co-author of *Economic Choice Theory: An Experimental Analysis of Animal Behavior* (Cambridge University Press), and editor of *Advances in Behavioral Economics*, the third volume of which is subtitled *Substance Use and Abuse*. He was Associate Editor and later Editor of the *Journal of the Experimental Analysis of Behavior*, Associate Editor of the *Pavlovian Journal of Biological Science*, is a Consulting Editor for *Behavior and Philosophy*, and on the Advisory Board of *The Psychological Record*. Green's research has been funded by the National Institutes of Health, National Institute on Aging, and the McDonnell Center for Higher Brain Function. He has served on the Executive Board of the Society for the Quantitative Analysis of Behavior (SQAB) and was President of the Society for the Experimental Analysis of Behavior (SEAB). Green is a Fellow of the Association for Behavior Analysis International (ABAI) and the Association for Psychological Science (APS).

Charles S. Gulas is a Professor of Marketing in the Raj Soin College of Business at Wright State University in Dayton Ohio USA. He earned his PhD in marketing at the University of Massachusetts Amherst. Chuck has published articles in the *Journal of Advertising, Journal of Current Issues and Research in Advertising, Journal of Business and Psychology, Journal of Business Ethics, Advances in Consumer Research* and other business publications. He and Marc Weinberger are the co-authors of *Humor in Advertising: A Comprehensive Analysis* published by M.E. Sharpe. He has previous work experience as a regional sales representative, founder and owner of small business, and co-founder and former president of a not-for-profit corporation. He has worked as a consultant for government agencies, small businesses, advertising agencies, and Fortune 1000 firms. He is currently on the advisory boards of two small businesses.

Donald A. Hantula (BA, Emory University; PhD University of Notre Dame), is an organizational psychologist, associate professor of Psychology, member of the Interdisciplinary Masters Program in Applied Behavior Analysis and director of the Decision Laboratory at Temple University, Philadelphia. Previous positions include occupational health promotion at the Johns Hopkins University School of Medicine, appointments in business schools at King's College and St. Joseph's University, and as a visiting scholar in Behavior Analysis at University of Nevada-Reno. He is the past Executive Editor of the *Journal of Social Psychology*. Currently he serves as Associate Editor of the *Journal of Organizational Behavior Management*, where he recently guest edited two special issues on Consumer Behavior Analysis. He has also edited special issues of other journals on topics such as: experiments in e-commerce, evolutionary perspectives on consumption (*Psychology & Marketing*), and Darwinian Perspectives on Electronic Communication (*IEEE Transactions*). Professor Hantula served on the National Science Foundation's Decision Risk and Management Sciences review panel and remains an ad hoc reviewer for government and private research funding agencies. He has published in many high impact journals including the *Journal of the American Medical Association, Journal of Applied Psychology, Journal of Economic Psychology, Organizational Behavior and Human Decision Processes* and *Behavior Research Methods*. His research in evolutionary behavioral economics combines behavior analytic and Darwinian theory to focus on questions in financial and consumer decision making and escalation of commitment. He also maintains active research and application projects in performance improvement and human/technology interactions. He has published over 80 articles and book chapters, authored or edited 10 books, manuals, and technical reports, made over 150 presentations at national and international scientific meetings, and is a busy researcher, consultant and speaker.

Mirja Hubert is a PhD student in Marketing at Zeppelin University, Germany. Her overall research interest is consumer behaviour, consumer neuroscience, and neuroeconomics. Her work has been published among others in the *Journal of Economic Psychology, Journal of Consumer Behaviour* and *Advances in Consumer Research*.

Uzma Javed is an assistant professor at COMSATS Institute of Information Technology, Islamabad. She earned her PhD in Human Resource Management (HRM) at Cardiff Business School in 2010. Her PhD research primarily investigated the impact of work environment characteristics, as perceived by employees, on their attitudes, wellbeing and behaviour. This research was grounded in the theories and methods from sociology and psychology with an application to the field of HRM. Her research interests include work psychology, wellbeing, emotions and attitudes, meta-analysis, structural equation modeling, internet addiction and consumer behaviour.

Peter Kenning is a professor of Marketing at Zeppelin University, Germany. His overall research interest is consumer behaviour, consumer neuroscience, neuroeconomics, and marketing management. His work has been published widely in outlets including *Management Information Systems Quarterly*, *Management Decisions*, *Journal of Consumer Behaviour*, *Journal of Economic Psychology*, and *Advances in Consumer Research*, as well as in the *Journal of Neuroimaging*, *Neuroreport*, and *Brain Research Bulletin*. He has presented papers at a number of conferences including the AMA Conference, the EMAC and ACR. He has received several best-paper awards and grants from the German government. Since 2011, Peter Kenning is a member of the Scientific Advisory Board on Consumer and Food Policies at the Federal Ministry of Food, Agriculture and Consumer Protection in Germany.

Marc Linzmajer is a PhD student in Marketing at Zeppelin University, Germany. His overall research interest is consumer behaviour, consumer neuroscience, and neuroeconomics. His work has been published in *Advances in Consumer Research* and *Journal of Consumer Protection and Food Safety*. He has presented papers at a number of conferences including the Conference of the Society for Neuroeconomics.

Luís L. Oliveira is a PhD student at Washington University, St Louis, USA and earned his bachelor's degree in Psychology and a master's degree in Cognitive Sciences from the University of Minho (Portugal) under the supervision of Dr Armando Machado. During this time, his research focused on comparing the predictions of two major models of timing, SET and LeT. In 2008, Luís entered the doctoral program in psychology at Washington University in St Louis under the supervision of Dr Leonard Green. He has been pursuing comparative studies that investigate probability and delay discounting in animals and humans, the discounting of token reinforcers in pigeons, and extensions of the hyperboloid model of discounting. Luís recently was awarded a doctoral fellowship from the Foundation for Science and Technology (FCT, Portugal) and was the recipient of the Experimental Analysis of Behavior Fellowship from the Society for the Advancement of Behavior Analysis (SABA).

Ken Peattie is Professor of Marketing and Strategy at Cardiff Business School and Director of the ESRC-funded BRASS Research Centre based at Cardiff, which specialises in research into business sustainability and corporate social responsibility. Before working as an academic he worked in marketing and strategic planning in an American paper multinational and a UK electronics company. His research interests focus on the impact of sustainability concerns on marketing and corporate strategy making; social marketing for healthy and sustainable lifestyles; social enterprise; corporate social responsibility; and education for sustainable development. He has published three books and numerous book chapters on these topics, and has published in journals including *California Management Review*, *Journal of Business Research*, *Journal of Marketing Management*, *Public Policy and Marketing*, and *European Management Journal*. His most recent book, *Sustainability Marketing: A Global Perspective*, coauthored with Frank-Martin Belz, won the 2010 Business Book of the Year Award of the German Business Research Association.

Don Ross is Professor of Economics and Dean of Commerce at the University of Cape Town, and Research Fellow in the Center for Economic Analysis of Risk at Georgia State University. Until 2010 he was Professor of Philosophy and Professor of Economics at the University of Alabama at Birmingham. He is Canadian, and holds a PhD in Philosophy of Science from the University of Western Ontario. His main research interests are the microeconomics of addiction and other impulsive consumption, game theoretic models of human sociality, unification of sciences, and trade and industry policy in Africa. He is the author or editor of 12 books, recently including *The Oxford Handbook of Philosophy of Economics*, which he co-edited with Harold Kincaid, and numerous articles. He is Director of Research for the National Responsible Gambling Programme of South Africa, and former Director of the SABITA Infrastructure Development Assessment Project.

Harry Timmermans is Professor of Urban Planning and Director of Research, Eindhoven University of Technology, the Netherlands. He holds a PhD degree in Geography/Urban and Regional Planning. He studied at the Catholic University of Nijmegen, the Netherlands. His dissertation concerned a theory of the functional and spatial structure and the dynamics of central place systems. Since 1976 he has been affiliated with the Faculty of Architecture, Building and Planning of the Eindhoven University of Technology, the Netherlands, first as an Assistant Professor of Quantitative and Urban Geography, later as an Associate Professor of Urban Planning Research. In 1986 he was appointed chaired professor of Urban Planning at the same institute. In 1992 he founded the European Institute of Retailing and Services Studies (EIRASS) in Eindhoven, the Netherlands (a sister-institute of the Canadian Institute of Retailing and Services Studies). His main research interests concern the study of human judgement and choice processes, mathematical modelling of urban systems and spatial interaction and choice pattens, and the development of decision support and expert systems for application in urban planning. He has published several books and many articles in journals in the fields of Marketing, Urban Planning, Architecture and Urban Design, Geography, Environmental Psychology, Transportation Research, Urban and Regional Economics, Urban Sociology, Leisure Sciences and Computer Science.

Rodoula H. Tsiotsou is currently an Assistant Professor of Services Marketing at the Department of Marketing & Operations Management, University of Macedonia, Greece where she teaches services marketing, consumer behavior, tourism marketing and sports marketing. She obtained her Master's degree from Ohio University and her PhD from Florida State University. Dr Tsiotsou is also a Visiting Assistant Professor at the Athens University of Economics and Business (Master's Program in Services Management), Greece. Dr Tsiotsou has published in a variety of international scientific journals such as *The Service Industries Journal, Journal of Marketing Management, International Journal of Retail and Distribution Management, Applied Financial Economics Letters, Journal of Vacation Marketing, Journal of Hospitality and Leisure Marketing, International Journal of Nonprofit and Voluntary Sector Marketing, Journal of Travel & Tourism Marketing,* and *International Journal of Sport Marketing and Sponsorship.* Dr Tsiotsou serves at the editorial board of the *International Review on Public and Nonprofit Marketing* and is an ad hoc reviewer for the *Journal of the Academy of Marketing Science, European Journal of Marketing, Journal of Business and Industrial Marketing, Journal of Strategic Marketing, Computers in Human Behavior* and other marketing journals. Dr Tsiotsou's research interests include services marketing, brand management, nonprofit marketing, and e-marketing.

Marc G. Weinberger is Professor of Marketing at the University of Massachusetts, Amherst where his marketing work has examined negativity effects and his advertising papers have explored the use of humour and other message devices in magazines, television and radio. His most recent book is *Humour in Advertising: A Comprehensive Analysis.* His articles have appeared in the *Journal of Marketing, Journal of Advertising Research, Journal of Advertising, European Journal of Marketing, Journal of the Academy of Marketing Science,* and *International Journal of Advertising,* among others.

Michelle F. Weinberger is an Assistant Professor at Northwestern University in the Medill School's Integrated Marketing Communications department. Her research on consumer culture takes a sociological perspective, examining topics such as the resource value of experiences, non-participation in dominant consumption rituals, collective gift giving, and the role of cultural knowledge in the activation and use of resources. She has presented work at the Association for Consumer Research, Consumer Culture Theory, and American Sociological Association conferences.

Victoria K. Wells is senior lecturer in marketing at Durham Business School. Previously she was lecturer in marketing and strategy and research associate at Cardiff Business School as well as a research assistant and graduate teaching assistant at Keele University. Prior to her academic position she has also worked in retail and communications. As an account executive she was involved with a wide range of companies developing advertising and communications solutions, marketing plans, PR development and event development and management.

Jochen Wirtz holds a PhD in services marketing from the London Business School and has worked in the field of services for over 20 years. He is a tenured Associate Professor of Marketing at the National University of Singapore (NUS), where he teaches service marketing in executive, MBA, and undergraduate programs. Professor Wirtz's research focuses on service marketing and has been published in over 80 academic journal articles, 100 conference presentations, and some 40 book chapters. His more than ten books include *Services Marketing – People, Technology, Strategy* (Prentice Hall, 7th edition, 2011), co-authored with Professor Lovelock; *Essentials of Services Marketing* (co-authored with Lovelock and Chew, Prentice Hall, 2009), and *Flying High in a Competitive Industry: Secrets of the World's Leading Airline* (co-authored with Heracleous and Pangarkar, McGraw Hill, 2009). Professor Wirtz was the winner of the inaugural Outstanding Service Researcher Award 2010 and the Best Practical Implications Award 2009, both by Emerald Group Publications. He serves on the editorial review boards of over ten academic journals, including the *Journal of Service Management, Journal of Service Research, Journal of Service Science* and *Cornell Hospitality Quarterly*, and is an ad hoc reviewer for the *Journal of Consumer Research* and *Journal of Marketing*.

Mirella Yani-de-Soriano is a lecturer in marketing at Cardiff Business School, Cardiff University, UK. She has managerial and consultancy experience, working for international organisations such as Gillette before coming into academia. She holds a PhD from Keele University, UK and an MBA from Bryant College, USA. She teaches consumer behaviour to postgraduate students at Cardiff Business School, and her research focuses on consumer behaviour, particularly in the areas of emotions, online behaviour, consumer culture, anticonsumption, ethical marketing/ branding and cross-cultural research. She has published her work in a number of publications, including *Journal of Business Research, Journal of Applied Social Psychology, Psychology & Marketing, Journal of Marketing Management, Journal of Retailing and Consumer Services, Journal of Consumer Behaviour*, and *Journal of Management History*.

Shumaila Y. Yousafzai is lecturer in marketing and consumer behaviour at Cardiff Business School, Cardiff University, UK. She holds a PhD from Cardiff University and an MSc in E-Commerce from Coventry University. Her research specialism is in the field of adoption and diffusion of innovation, ethical consumption, online additions, and consumer behaviour in the financial service sector. She has published in various international journals including *Psychology & Marketing, Technovation, Services Industries Journal*, and *Journal of Applied & Social Psychology*.

Judith Lynne Zaichkowsky is Professor of Marketing and Communications at Copenhagen Business School, Denmark. She is currently at the Beedle School of Business, Simon Fraser University Vancouver, Canada. She received her PhD in marketing from University of California, Los Angeles in 1984. Her dissertation, 'Conceptualizing and Measuring the Involvement Construct', was completed under the supervision of Hal Kassarjian. The measurement part of the dissertation was published in 1985 in the *Journal of Consumer Research* and has become one of the top cited articles from the journal. Her other research interests have led to monographs on Brand Imitation (1995) and Trademark Infringement and Counterfeiting (2006). Her main academic goal these days is to help young researchers publish.

1 Developments in consumer behaviour
Gordon R. Foxall and Victoria K. Wells

1.1 SOME WORDS OF EXPLANATION

Research on consumer behaviour provides a focus of theorisation and empirical investigation for a wide range of social and natural sciences and as a result often reflects the aspirations and ideologies of its authors and sponsors. So much consumer research appears nowadays to regard consumer behaviour as no more than an application area or testing ground for theories and methodologies, speculations and vested interests, that arise elsewhere. To the extent that consumer behaviour proves amenable to these broader perspectives, its validity as a field of investigation is safeguarded, but there are numerous alternative foci for empirical research should it disappoint. Whether these interests are managerial or scholarly, they do little to advance genuine understanding of consumer behaviour as a defining characteristic of much of humankind.

We have sought as far as possible in editing this volume to make disinterested curiosity the central motivation for an examination not of 'current trends' in consumer research but of perspectives which promise to develop into new directions for the discipline, and new opportunities to comprehend the nature of consumer choice per se. We have sought, therefore, to embody work that reflects a passion to understand consumer choice as a phenomenon in its own right. We have been inspired to some degree by the development of the scientific study of animal behaviour as a science that has several parallels with that of consumer research. Both are comparatively recent as social sciences, both are multi-disciplinary studies striving to be interdisciplinary, both are capable of revolutionising how humans regard themselves. Each has an applied aspect, each is amenable to technological development, each can serve interests beyond those of the academy.

Like ethology, the analysis of consumer behaviour is now a well-established discipline with its own journals and learned societies. Like ethology, consumer research incorporates perspectives from a spectrum of long-established sciences: psychology, economics and sociology amongst the most common in consumer research; biology and especially ecology more to the fore in the case of ethology. The chapters that comprise this handbook similarly strive to incorporate a multitude of sources of thought and learning, adding geography, neuroscience, ethics and behavioural ecology, among others, to this list. There is an interesting tension within consumer research between the pursuit of scholarship in and of itself and the pursuit of managerial concerns. Ken Peattie notes in his chapter that consumer behaviour research can tend towards myopia by over-emphasising those aspects of the behaviour that marketers find most interesting. The research utilised for his own chapter comes largely from non-consumer behaviour journals or researchers whose primary focus is not consumer behaviour. This is a tendency found in all of the chapters we have included. All seek, albeit in varying degrees, to encompass multiple perspectives, en route to the interdisciplinarity without which our understanding of consumer choice is impoverished.

Two other points about our general orientation deserve to be briefly made. First, despite what we have said about the pursuit of narrow instrumental concerns, we recognise that consumer behaviour, in all economies that operate beyond the level of subsistence, influences and is influenced by the behaviour of producers, suppliers and marketers. These interactions are part of the subject matter of marketing and consumer research. Such subjects as new product development, marketing communication and retail response to consumer preferences are not only essential to understanding the nature of consumer behaviour, they present intriguing intellectual challenges in their own right. We have sought therefore to present developments in consumer behaviour from the perspective they afford. Second – and this is the major thrust of our observations on ethology – we have striven to encompass the deep feeling for our subject matter that we mentioned earlier by inviting scholars with a passion for knowing about consumers. Reading the live histories of those biologists who established ethology during the middle and later decade of the last century, one is struck by the abiding excitement, even obsession, with animal behaviour, what animals do, how it can be explained. Many students of animal behaviour began as amateur ornithologists in their teens, for example, and despite the eminence of their later contributions to science never lost their passion for bird watching (Dewsbury, 1985). Without patronising them or aggrandising our own efforts, we maintain that consumer researchers forget their original motivations only at some cost to the development of their discipline.

We took the view at an early stage that we wanted authors to provide a deeper understanding of the subjects on which they are experts than they might otherwise have the opportunity to do. This has led inevitably to fewer, longer chapters; moreover, it has not been possible to include every theme that is currently promising and which may well turn out to be important. But it has the advantage of permitting the authors to enlarge upon the linkages between their subjects and the disciplinary bases on which further development depends. Many current foci of research are nevertheless picked out: while, for instance, there is no chapter on online behaviour, its influence recurs. Likewise, waste disposal, which does not warrant its own chapter, is discussed in a chapter on ethical consumption. Branding, a marketing issue affecting consumer behaviour in numerous ways, is discussed in a variety of places.

In developing themes, deciding on the sectionalisation of the book, and inviting authors to produce chapters, we have arrived at an anthology that stretches from cultural interactions with consumer choice (I. Consumer Culture), through contextual spheres (II. Consumers in Context), and the impulsivity inherent in much consumer choice (III. Consumer Impulsivity, Compulsiveness and Beyond), to the role of neuroscience in explaining consumer behaviour (IV. Neuroscience and Consumer Choice), and finally back to environmental influences in the form of an ecological–behavioural standpoint (V. Consumer Behaviour in Evolutionary Perspective). If this appears to be a contrived continuum, that is inadvertent on our part. The aim has been to reflect developments that are taking place and likely to continue while encouraging the interaction of all of these themes.

While influences on consumer behaviour research have changed over the years, so have the subjects that consumer behaviouralists have chosen to study. In 2004 the *Journal of Consumer Research*, one of the most respected consumer behaviour journals, published a subject index covering the thirty years since its inception. This provides an authoritative overview of the development and popularity of topics within consumer research. Some popular themes attracted publications across the whole period since 1974, including Advertising/Advertising Effects, Attitudes, Charity and Gift Giving, Cross-Cultural Research, Information Processing/Search, Involvement and Persuasion. Some of these are central to the discipline and have been included in other hand-books as formative. Some are also included and elaborated in this hand-book: Advertising is represented by the chapter by Weinberger, Gulas and Weinberger, which concentrates on humour in advertising; Charity and Gift-Giving are covered by Peattie's chapter on the unselfish consumer; Cross-cultural research is covered by the chapters by Weinberger, Gulas and Weinberger, and Craig and Douglas; and Involvement is the subject of the chapter by Zaichowsky. The *JCR* subject index also highlights areas that have become more popular in consumer research since the year 2000. These include Aesthetic/Hedonic consumption, Affect/Emotions/ Mood, Communication, Diffusion/Innovation/Technology, Perceptual Processes, Satisfaction and Shopping Behaviour amongst others. Again, a range of these is represented within this handbook: Emotion is a strong theme of the chapter by Foxall, Yani-de-Soriano, Yousafzai and Javed; diffusion of Innovations is explored by Goldsmith. Satisfaction is a key concept in services marketing and is therefore also a key concept within the chapter by Tsiotsou and Wirtz on services consumer behaviour.

However, *JCR* is a mainstream journal and consumer behaviouralists do not, mainly because of the multi discipline nature of the subject area, restrict themselves to the mainstream. Notable contributions to the history and philosophy of science such as those by Kuhn (1970), Lakatos (1978) and Feyerabend (1975), all emphasise the role of competing paradigms or research programmes in the growth of knowledge. Paradigms which do not underlay the normal science component of a discipline often come to the fore through unconventional media. We have not therefore restricted our selection to mainstream consumer research. While *JCR* and other leading journals in the field are justly highly respected, good ideas can be published in any journal and the excellence of an idea should not necessarily be judged on the basis of its origin.

1.2   THE THEMES

1.2.1   Consumer Culture

Part I of the handbook concentrates on culture. The first chapter, by Russell Belk, provides an overview and comment on both people and things they own, consume and use. The second chapter is a comprehensive overview of the state of culture research in consumer behaviour, while the third chapter is much narrower in focus, concentrating on advertising humour and consumers' cultural reactions to it.

Belk ('People and Things'), presents a fascinating discussion of the links between and definitions of both people and things. Assessing the distinguishing features between people and things as well as discussion overlaps in terms of robotics and virtual lives, he presents an increasing blurring of people and things. He then discusses the role of things in our lives as the extended self and the potential associations between them. He deals in particular with magical and sacred objects as well as ordinary and extraordinary things, drawing on many aspects of consumer research including culture, religion and gift giving.

Craig and Douglas ('Culture and Consumer Behavior: Contextual and Compositional Components'), present a thorough and substantial discussion of various aspects of culture, the merits of studying them, and their limitations. Presenting both contextual and compositional components that have generally been used to explore culture as well as the context and social implications of culture they provide a detailed and full presentation of the state of culture research. They also note how the contextual and compositional elements of culture interact and the evolution of this is examined. Also of central interest is the increasingly virtual context of culture and its effects on the culture of groups and subcultures and research associated with it. The authors complete the chapter by calling for development of a better understanding of culture's influence and for the study of culture to be less fragmented: instead of concentrating on one contextual or compositional element, a more rounded and integrated cultural model should be assessed.

Weinberger, Gulas and Weinberger ('The role of culture in advertising humor') present a model, the challenge model, of advertising humour, and consumer responses to it, highlighting the importance of culture in the way in which consumers respond positively or negatively to advertising humour. They also discuss how the behaviour of consumers and changing culture affect the humour used in advertising and the interpretation of it. While culture has always been a part of advertising humour, their chapter contends that culture is being seen as more central than previously and is hence gaining increased attention. The chapter presents two particular cases of advertising that are subjected to detailed scrutiny: outdoor/billboard advertising and the changing role of males within all types of advertising.

1.2.2 Consumers in Context

Part II deals with applications of consumer research in specific contexts. There are four chapters in this part. The first highlights spatial and retail contexts of consumer behaviour. The second discusses consumer behaviour within services, and the third chapter looks at consumer behaviour in green and ethical terms by highlighting the role of the unselfish consumer. The fourth chapter explores developments in diffusion of innovations theory. The first chapter is motivated by studying consumers in a particular physical environment. The second chapter is also motivated by the study of consumers within physical environments, but also, like the nature of services marketing itself, it is motivated by studying consumers who choose services remotely (online) and the social interactions of consumers. The third chapter is motivated by consumers' reactions to certain social and ethical dimensions such as patriotism, frugality and citizenship, and the fourth chapter concentrates on the purchasing of new and innovative products.

Timmermans ('Retail and spatial consumer behaviour') draws on a number of spatial disciplines including urban planning and geography to study the behaviour of consumers in choosing, travelling to and using physical consumption locations. He presents a view of modelling in retail choice behaviour from these spatial dimensions. Discussing the development of models to take into account a number of features of retail choice, he notes the general absence of behavioural, or more marketing variables in these current approaches. He reports the most recent attempts to develop a framework in which psychometric indicators are more closely combined with observed choice data to predict choice behaviour. Finally, he suggests the benefits of further integrations between these approaches to the study of retail and store choice behaviour.

In the second chapter in this part ('Consumer behavior in a service context'), Tsiotsou and Wirtz present a comprehensive overview of services consumer behaviour, breaking the literature and buying process into three stages: pre-purchase, the service encounter stage and the post encounter stage. The chapter provides highlights and new developments from across the whole range of services consumer behaviour, highlighting recent developments in service dominant logic, remote services consumer behaviour and dysfunctional behaviour amongst others. The growth in services consumer behaviour is strongly linked to the growth in services research itself, an area which has gained increasing attention over the last 10 years.

Peattie ('Researching the unselfish consumer') argues that many consumption behaviours and practices are increasingly motivated by social, ethical and environmental concerns. In doing this he highlights different types of unselfish consumers, from the pious consumer to the patriotic consumer to the green consumer, as well as a number of others. He also discusses the issue of sustainability and looks in detail at different forms of pro sustainability behaviour as well as influences on it, implications of it and the modelling of it, highlighting the importance of context.

Goldsmith tackles 'New developments in the diffusion of innovations'. Describing it as a fragmented area, he makes clear that a chapter could only focus on a few of the main and developing themes in the area of innovation diffusion. In concentrating on three areas of recent development and addition, he also decides to assess and present research that makes a contribution to the theory of adoption/diffusion rather than work that has added to its practical implications. Goldsmith therefore concentrates on (1) the conceptualisation and measurement of innovativeness, (2) innovation resistance and (3) diffusion network and adoption models. In doing so Goldsmith articulates both the origins of these areas (and more broadly of innovation adoption and diffusion) as well as the latest developments in the areas. This involves the response of the area to major technological changes affecting social networks and communications methodologies. Goldsmith also notes the increasingly important nature of evolutionary psychology in making fundamental insights into the characteristics of innovators and adoption. While noting the continuing fragmentation of the area, Goldsmith uses this as a footing for how to reintegrate the study of innovation and more importantly the potential role of future research in doing so.

1.2.3 Consumer Impulsivity, Compulsiveness and Beyond

Part III takes us away from the more mainstream areas of consumer behaviour and instead concentrates on some of the more extreme aspects of consumers' behaviour. Other parts of the handbook concentrate on the day to day behaviour of normal consumers. While these normal everyday behaviours have attracted a great deal of attention within consumer behaviour research, a growing area of interest is those behaviours on the extremes and at the edges of our understanding. The first chapter in this section highlights impulsivity and discounting behaviour, the second concentrates on addictive, impulsive and counter-normative behaviour. While impulse and discounting behaviour can be seen in many normal consumers, these chapters highlight the points at which these behaviours become problematic or even destructive. The third chapter provides a specific case of a compulsive buyer, Lois, and relates her behaviour to personality work.

Oliveira and Green ('Discounting and Impulsivity: overview and relevance to consumer choice') explore the area of choice and decision making and in particular aspects of uncertainty in it based on different models of discounting and impulsivity. Different types of discounting are discussed within the chapter as well as the question of impulsivity as a trait or traits. Aspects of commitment are also discussed. The chapter ends with two consumer related applications, the first to food consumption and obesity and the second to credit cards and consumer contracts.

Ross provides a fascinating and wide ranging review of work on 'Addictive, impulsive and other counter-normative consumption'. The chapter takes an economic rather than psychological perspective and spends time concentrating on the recent developments and historical background in the specific areas of drug addiction and problem gambling, while also providing a wider context of and discussion surrounding 'what is counter-normative consumption?'. While concentrating on economic approaches the review also covers areas as wide ranging as contingency based behaviour, discounting, neuroscience, clinical approaches and screeners and 'the self'.

Albanese ('A template matching technique of personality classification for the study of consumer behaviour') presents new developments in the application of personality to consumer behaviour and in particular a case study of one buyer – Lois. While Albanese concentrates on compulsive consumption he clearly communicates other aspects of consumer behaviour and differing types of personality. The chapter takes a balanced methodological approach using quantitative measurements, qualitative exploration and a case study, highlighting the usefulness of all methods and a multi-method approach overall. The work, unlike much modern marketing and consumer behaviour research, also uses a small number of subjects, finally looking in detail at a single subject, Lois, through a case study. This, like much recent consumer behaviour research, is starting to explore the extremes of behaviour, that is, the anti-social and compulsive behaviour of consumers (see also the chapters by Ross and Tsiotsou and Wirtz). The work also tends to move away from marketing and its applications and instead integrates the expertise of clinical psychologists, psychiatrists and counsellors to study the behaviour of consumers. Rather than giving an overview of all aspects of personality and consumer behaviour, the chapter concentrates on one very specific 'development' in consumer behaviour.

1.2.4   Neuroscience and Consumer Choice

Part IV contains three chapters that explore the relevance of biology and, in particular, neuroscience to consumer research. While the first chapter (Kenning, Hubert and Linzmajer) provides an overview of the use of neuroscience in consumer behaviour, highlighting future potential, the two following chapters (Foxall, Yani-de-Soriano, Yousafzai and Javed, and Zaichkowsky) highlight long standing areas which have had recent developments in the neuroscience area of work.

Kenning, Hubert and Linzmajer provide a comprehensive overview of consumer neuroscience and provide a great starting point for those completely unfamiliar with the area of neuroscience. They position consumer neuroscience as a sub discipline of neuroeconomics with research taking place at the nexus of neuroscience, psychology and marketing. They start the chapter by discussing the history of neuroscience, describing the brain and nervous system and areas used in the research before discussing the tools and theories of neuroscience, methodologies and ethics of the approach. They overview the findings related to both marketing and consumer behaviour using the traditional marketing-mix elements as well as branding before discussing the limitations of the approach.

The chapter by Foxall, Yani-de-Soriano, Yousafzai and Javed ('The role of neurophysiology, emotion and contingency in the explanation of consumer choice') highlights the role of neurophysiology, emotion and contingency in the explanation of consumer choice. The Behavioural Perspective Model (BPM) has proved a valuable means of predicting and explaining aspects of consumer behaviour such as consumers' choices of products, brands and stores. It has linked well with the prediction of consumer behaviour on the basis of the substitutability, independence and complementarity of the commodities purchased, and has shown that the value consumers accord brands with particular functional and symbolic characteristics varies with the pattern of reinforcement each provides. There are limits however to the explanation provided by an extensional model of this kind. The chapter therefore argues that intentional constructs such as emotional feelings must be incorporated in a second version of the model and discusses in detail how this might be accomplished and justified. The neurophysiological basis of consumer choice plays a large role in this epistemological task.

In 'Consumer involvement: review, update and links to decision neuroscience', Zaichkowsky reviews the large body of research related to the concept of involvement and its most recent developments in the area of neuroscience. The chapter reviews not only the history and background of involvement, from Zaichkowsky's unique knowledge of the subjects, but also the background and history of neuroscience research, which can be read in parallel with the Kenning et al. chapter above. After discussing some of the applications of involvement including innovations (see also the Goldsmith chapter) and meat consumption amongst many others, she considers the most up to date research, bringing together involvement and neuroscience as well as exploring the role of emotions.

1.2.5   Consumer Behaviour in Evolutionary Perspective

The final part of the handbook explores the use of evolutionary and ecology perspectives on consumer behaviour.

Hantula ('Consumers are foragers, not rational actors: towards a behavioral ecological of consumer choice') presents an approach to the consumer based on foraging and evolutionary theory. The chapter presents an overview of foraging theory describing consumers as foragers rather than the rational actors they are often assumed to be in traditional consumer research. Hantula looks at foragers as financiers and at information foraging theory and also applies foraging behaviour to diet and nutrition behaviour.

1.3   FINAL COMMENTS

The focus of each of the chapters is consumer behaviour but they vary in scope, some looking more broadly by encompassing a wide ranging view of a number of aspects of consumer choice while others focus more on specific aspects. For example Kenning, Hubert and Linzmajer in their chapter on consumer neuroscience look very broadly at the subject. In comparison both Foxall, Yani-de-Soriano, Yousafzai and Javed, and Zaichkowsky employ the theme of neuroscience when seeking to understand specific aspects of consumer choice: involvement and emotions and contingency, respectively. It might be stated that neuroscience is the most recent development in these areas and that it has reinvigorated them.

As noted above there are areas of overlap and interactions between subject areas, and these types of interactions can also be seen in the chapters themselves. Obvious interactions and overlaps come in each of the parts of the handbook with each chapter building on the others in the part. This can be seen strongly within the culture section where, for example, the ideas regarding individualistic and collectivist societies are commented on in multiple chapters. Part III contains a number of overlaps especially when it comes to the study of compulsive consumers, but each chapter approaches this subject from a different background and viewpoint. Part IV also contains interactions. Whilst the first chapter (Kenning, Hubert and Linzmajer) provides a broad overview of the use and potential use of neuroscience within consumer behaviour research, the following two chapters (Foxall, Yani-de-Soriano, Yousafzai and Javed, and Zaichkowsky) highlight a continuing field of consumer behaviour enquiry (emotions and the BPM in the case of Foxall et al., and involvement in Zaichkowsky) and not only highlight developments in these but also discuss the potential and future work linking these areas with neuroscience. There are also overlaps across parts, some explicit, some less so or implicit. For example, both the chapters on foraging (Hantula) and the unselfish consumer (Peattie) contain references towards and suggestions for social policy. The issue of hedonic and utilitarian consumption is also highlighted in both the Timmermans and Foxall et al. chapters.

The chapters and research within them also highlight different units of analysis. Many of the chapters concentrate on the individual consumer, as is the case for much consumer behaviour research, but some of the chapters extend beyond this by looking at social groups (either enforced or natural) (Goldsmith), retail stores and shopping centres (Timmermans), from a company viewpoint (Weinberger et al.) and society as a whole (see Part I). Peattie's chapter also highlights the idea of 'Collective consumption' where consumers purchase together. It should also be noted that the approach used by Albanese in his study of one single consumer is unusual, with many (but certainly not all) of the other research reported relying on a number of individuals.

The chapters, and research reported within them, also demonstrate a wide range of methodologies. While most, in reviewing a whole area of study, report both qualitative and quantitative approaches, some of the chapters concentrate more quantitatively (for example Timmermans) and some more qualitatively (for example Peattie) in terms of methodology but also the way they report the subjects. A case study approach is also used by Albanese.

Many of the chapters also contain, either as their central purpose or as a part, a review of the area of interest. In doing this many of the chapters actively highlight gaps in the literature and research and thus provide a number of future research ideas and developments. In addition, the disciplinary perspectives on which the international authors who have contributed to this volume draw are legion: psychology, behavioural economics, anthropology, psychoanalysis, geography, sociology, philosophy, neuro-biology . . . no one can accuse consumer research of being a parochial field of intellectual endeavour! We hope that our suggestions for future research agendas and the expert treatment they receive in the chapters that follow will interest established researchers in these fields, others who are interested in moving into one of these areas, and especially those just starting their research careers.

REFERENCES

Dewsbury, D.A. (1985), *Studying Animal Behavior: Autobiographies of the Founders*, Chicago: Chicago University Press.

Feyerabend, P. (1975), *Against Method*, London: NLB.

Kuhn, T.S. (1970), *The Structure of Scientific Revolutions*, Chicago: Chicago University Press.

Lakatos, I. (1978), *The Methodology of Scientific Research Programmes: Philosophical Papers Volume 1*, Cambridge: Cambridge University Press.

PART I

CONSUMER CULTURE

2 People and things
Russell Belk

In Western languages we are taught that nouns consist of persons, places, and things. In the study of consumer behaviour we focus on the various ways in which these three types of nouns are related. Of the various combinations, we have been most apt to focus on people and the ways in which they regard and interact with various things. For example recent treatments have highlighted *The Social Life of Things* (Appadurai 1986b), *The Sex of Things* (de Grazia 1996), *Wild Things* (Attfield 2000), *The Value of Things* (Cummings and Lewandowska 2000), *The Order of Things* (Foucault 1970), *A Sense of Things* (Brown 2003), *Living with Things* (Gregson 2007), *The Comfort of Things* (D. Miller 2008), *The Meaning of Things* (Csikszentmihalyi and Rochberg-Halton 1981), *History From Things* (Lubar and Kingery 1995), and *The Nature of Things* (L. Watson 1990). In other vocabularies we have focused our attention on consumers and their "stuff" (e.g., Frost and Steketee 2010; Gosling 2008; D. Miller 2010), "objects" (e.g., Akhtar 2005; Forty 1986; Freund 1995; Kirkham 1996; Turkle 2007), "possessions" (e.g., Belk 1988; Dittmar 1992; Miller 2001a; Rudmin 1991), or "property" (e.g., Doyle 1999; Hann 1998; Verdery and Humphrey 2004). And at a somewhat more abstract level, we have studied commodification (e.g., Carrier 1995; Cook 2004; Ertman and Williams 2005; Radin 1996; Scheper-Hughes and Wacquant 2002), materialism (e.g., Belk 1985; Kasser 2002; Richins and Dawson 1992; Twitchell 1999; Wuthnow 1995), material culture (e.g., D. Miller 1998; Tilley et al. 2006), and consumer culture (e.g., Brewer and Trentmann 2006; Dittmar 2008; Kasser and Kanner 2004; Sassatelli 2007; Scanlon 2000; Slater 1997), each of which concerns the relationships between people and things. Lash and Lury (2007) refer to the "thingification of media", which they illustrate through such transformations as movies that become computer games and cartoon characters that become collectibles and costumes. In other words, through cross-marketing, monetizing virtual assets, and tangiblizing intangible properties, more and more of what we took as ephemeral culture is being made manifest in things. As a result of such processes as well as the growth of the global economy, the proliferation of cheap production through outsourcing and offshoring, and the general increase in the size of the global middle class, there is more and more stuff to desire, consume, and dispose of.

Given the nature of the contemporary marketplace, the brand is a seemingly obvious omission from the preceding enumeration of the various perspectives from which we might examine people and things. To be sure brands are critical to contemporary marketing and consumption (e.g., Arvidsson 2006; Danesi 2006; Holt 2004; Lury 2004; Schroeder and Salzer-Mörling 2006; Twitchell 2004). And to be sure there is often a special relationship between groups of consumers and brands as implied by concepts like brand communities (McAlexander et al. 2002; Muñiz and O'Guinn 2001), brand cults (e.g., Belk and Tumbat 2005; Chadha and Husband 2006; Kahney 2004, 2005), brand subcultures (Martin et al. 2006; Schouten et al. 2007; Schouten and McAlexander 1995), and brand tribes (e.g., Cova and Cova 2001; Cova et al. 2007; Maffesoli 1996). But what I mostly wish to focus on here is an equally intense, but more private and personal relationship between people and things. I focus primarily on things that have become singular possessions (Appadurai 1986a; Kopytoff 1986) rather than merely members of a category like a brand. There is a passage in *The Little Prince* (Saint Exupéry 2000) when the Little Prince meets a fox who explains such singularity:

> For me you're only a little boy just like a hundred thousand other little boys. And I have no need of you. And you have no need of me, either. For you I'm only a fox like a hundred thousand other foxes. But if you tame me, we'll need each other. You'll be the only boy in the world for me. I'll be the only fox in the world for you. (p. 59)

Later, when the Little Prince learns that the rose he has been caring for is not the only one on the planet, he applies a similar logic. Confronting a field of roses he addresses them:

> Of course, an ordinary passerby would think my rose looked just like you. But my rose, all on her own, is more important than all of you together, since she's the one I've watered. Since she's the one I put under glass. Since she's the one I sheltered behind a screen. Since she's the one for whom I killed the caterpillars (except the two or three for butterflies). Since she's the one I listened to when she complained, or when she boasted, or even sometimes when she said nothing at all. Since she's *my* rose. (p. 63)

This is thus a more specific relationship between people and things than is encompassed by brand loyalty. Thus rather than focusing on the brand loyalty of a consumer to a particular make of automobile, I am more interested here in the relationship between a particular consumer and the particular car that this person drives. In the process of examining the special relationships that bond people with specific things I wish to first separate them and distinguish what makes a person a person and a thing a thing. As we shall see, this is not as simple as it may seem.

2.1 PEOPLE AND THINGS: DISTINGUISHING BETWEEN THEM

In a recent book on technology and human relationships, Sherry Turkle (2011) describes being interviewed by a journalist who was researching an article on robots. He asked her what she thought of the possibility of a human marrying and mating with a robot, something that D. Levy (2007) advocated in a recent book. When Turkle strenuously rejected this proposition, the reporter suggested that her attitude displayed the same prejudice exhibited by those who oppose allowing gay marriage. Turkle strongly objected and argued that what distinguishes intimacy with a machine from intimacy with a person is the emotional authenticity of the experience. To love a robot would bastardize the concept of love in her view. This argument raises some basic questions about what keeps a thing from being a person. In Turkle's view it is the inability of things to feel emotion. A person may love a robot, but a robot cannot love a person. Nevertheless, suppose a robot could make us *believe* that it loved and cared for us? In the view of many of those Turkle interviewed for her book, this would make the robot "human enough" to provide genuine satisfaction. Such a litmus test would be a more sophisticated version of the test proposed by Albert Turing (1950) for artificial intelligence. For Turing it would be sufficient if, in exchanging messages between a machine and a human interrogator, the human was unable to determine that the machine was a machine. While some programs like ELIZA (Weizenbaum 1966) showed promise of achieving this, ultimately all AI devices have failed the Turing Test and are likely to do so for the foreseeable future. Although the notion of artificial emotion is an even higher standard than artificial intelligence, and one that Turkle is convinced an android could never pass, it is one on which her informants were willing to compromise. If a Furby, Tamagotchi, or AIBO was considered alive enough for its owner to care for it, appreciate its maturation, and mourn its death, this suggests at least that it was "alive enough" to develop a genuine relationship with. The next generation of robots studied by Turkle, including My Real Baby, Cog, and Kismet, displayed "emotion enough" toward those possessing them that they or their successors could be seen as playing a legitimate future role in caring for children and the elderly.

There are older precedents for the willing suspension of disbelief that things are alive or human. In 270 BCE, Ctesibius reportedly enthralled viewers with water-driven automata that included blackbirds singing and figures that drank and moved (Thorndike 1958). As During (2002) chronicles, Jean-Eugène Robert-Houdin became the most famous magician in nineteenth-century Europe with his trick and nontrick automata that astonished crowds who witnessed mechanical trapeze artists, acrobats, and pastry cooks. Predecessor marvels of the eighteenth century were no less mesmerizing (Buchner 1978; Taussig 1993). Baudelaire ([1845]1995) traces our fascination with the possibility of "machines as human" to the child's desire to find the souls of their dolls, toys, and playthings. But it goes both ways. We are equally fascinated to see statue-like mimes who pretend to be mechanical devices, blurring the line between people and things in the other direction (Schwartz 1998). The influence of the machine and the computer on the ways we think about human behaviour are also telling. For example, we refer to ourselves in computer-like terms when we network or interface with people, when something does not compute, when we process information, or when we talk about being hard-wired to do something. Turkle (1984) found that computer engineers in Silicon Valley (itself a telling metaphor) sometimes referred to their spouses as "lousy peripherals".

The darker side of treating people as things, property, and commodities is found in slavery, rape, involuntary prostitution, child pornography, and the sale of children (e.g., Epele 2002; Hernández 2005; A. Lucas 2005; Zelizer 1985). When those providing care and affection for older or dying partners are named in a contested will, the courts are often faced with decisions to uphold or break the will based on whether they conclude that these services were provided for love or were more about the money the caregiver expected to inherit (Zelizer 2005). But even in the case of paid professional care providers, it is rare that they and those they care for remain in purely commoditized relationships devoid of love (Stone 2005). Perhaps when Turkle's (2011) robot care givers come into being we will be closer to dealing with a purely person–thing (i.e., person–robot) relationship in care giving. But for the time being even the most monetized and commodified care relationships seem almost unavoidably to be interpersonal (i.e., person–person) relationships.

The sinister side to conflating the human and the non-human is also seen in Mary Shelley's ([1818]1999) *Frankenstein* critique of the industrial revolution and Fritz Lang's (Lang and von Harbou 1926) *Metropolis* critique of Fordism. In the former the result was a monstrous half-machine that acted like a pseudo-human, while in the latter the result was emasculated humans who were forced to act as pseudo-machines. More recent evidences of our fascinated love/hate relationship with human-like machines include HAL, the computer in *2001: A Space Odyssey* (Kubrick 1968), R2-D2 and C-3PO in *Star Wars* (G. Lucas 1977), *Robocop* (Verhoeven 1987), *The Terminator*

(Cameron 1984), and Lieutenant Commander Data in *Star Trek: The Next Generation* (Roddenberry 1987). In one episode of *Star Trek: The Next Generation* called "The Measure of a Man," a Starfleet legal hearing must determine whether Lieutenant Commander Data is a thing that is the property of Star Fleet and therefore able to be shut down and disassembled, or whether Data is a sentient being with intelligence, self-awareness and emotions (http://en.wikipedia.org/wiki/The_Measure_of_a_Man_(Star_Trek:_ The_Next_Generation). We might also consider the alter-egos found in our avatars (Bélisle and Bodur 2010) in virtual worlds such as *Second Life* (Boellstorff 2008) and online games such as *World of Warcraft* (Bessière et al. 2007). Some of these blurred person–thing visions are positive and others are negative, but all seem to captivate us.

Freud (1953) explains part of our fascination with such challenges to the boundary between people and things as instances of encountering the "uncanny." The uncanny involves things long taken to be familiar suddenly becoming unfamiliar, as with machines that act like humans or humans who act like machines. Anthropologists are more apt to regard such confusions as instances of anthropomorphism, animism, or totemism (Belk et al. 1989). A related concept shared by Freudianism and anthropology as well as Marxism, is that of fetishism. Although we are used to thinking of these three different disciplinary concepts of the fetish as being unrelated, Ellen (1988) shows that there is a common core to all three. This core consists of the elements of personification, concretization, conflation of the signifier and the signified, and ambiguity about whether the person controls the fetish object or the fetish object controls the person. Yet all of these perspectives are pejorative and come from an earlier era in which there was an attempt to distinguish a primitive, superstitious, or unhealthy "them" from a civilized, scientific, and healthy "us". Much as we might wish to think so, we are hardly immune from such phenomena. For example we talk about a computer's memory, language, and its crashing and dying. Although we indeed continue to fetishize and anthropomorphize certain inanimate objects (Aggarwal and McGill 2007; Kniazeva and Belk 2010), this acts as more of a demonstration of our fascination with the distinction between people and things rather than offering an explanation for this fascination.

In critiquing the tendency of artists to render inanimate objects as if they possessed human thought and emotion, John Ruskin (1856) labelled this practice the pathetic fallacy. He suggested that it is the artist's or poet's own passion and reason that is being inappropriately projected onto the inanimate object in such cases. The pathetic fallacy label has since been used more broadly to characterize any attempt to treat mere objects as if they had a will and feelings of their own. An explanation for this pejorative label may lie in our preference for clear binary categories, especially when they distinguish our species, group, or sex from others'. Even non-human life forms are often regarded as dirty, polluting, disgusting, or taboo if they seem to mix categories (Douglas 1966; I. Miller 1997). Thus to the Lele people in what is now the Democratic Republic of the Congo, the pangolin is regarded as anomalous because it has scales like a fish but climbs trees (Douglas 1966, pp. 168–74). Likewise malformed or sexually ambiguous humans are seen as abnormal, quasi-human, and monstrous (Shildrick 2002). They are boundary-spanning or liminal beings who threaten the security of our categories and remind us of our own vulnerability. In a less politically correct era, these liminal people were labelled "freaks" and were often exhibited to the morbid curiosity of paying onlookers (Adams 2001; Bogdan 1988; Fiedler 1978). Such exhibitions were not limited to the physically deformed or to carnival sideshows, but also included living villages of "primitive" people brought to World's Fairs for the amusement of "civilized" fairgoers (Rydell 1984, 1993) as well as tours of Bedlam (Bethlem), the mental asylum in London, where guests once marvelled at the "crazy people" (Arnold 2010; Chambers 2009). As the one-time popularity of such now cruel-seeming exhibitions suggests, we display a fascination with the liminal, the other, and the category-challenging. This can also be seen in our continuing fascination with the life and death straddling forms we entertain ourselves with on Halloween, in horror films, and in related invocations of the "grotesque body" (Bakhtin 1968; Belk 1994; Skal 2002). A popular monster film motif continues to be the "undead" or the "living dead" of zombies, vampires, werewolves, and other monstrous liminal creatures that defy the simple binaries of living and dead, human and non-human, person and thing.

If automata, mimes, cyborgs, avatars, freaks, and monsters do not sufficiently problematize the distinction between people and things, consider our companion animals or pets. Although Descartes ([1637]1976) described non-human animals as dumb machines to which we owe no more feeling and allegiance than a clock, this is not the way that we treat our pets (Belk 1996a). We instead treat them as a part of self, as engaging playthings, and as members of the family; they are given names, participate in our family rituals, and often act as surrogate children for empty nest households (Belk 1996a; Curasi et al. 2001; Ridgeway et al. 2008). Once we have acquired a pet it is singular and unique; it is no longer fungible with its littermates, no matter how similar they may appear to others (c.f., the earlier quotes from *The Little Prince*). After having spent time with our pets we believe we can communicate with them. We have seen them mature, although they may be seen to remain perpetually "childlike". We love them and we believe that they love us. We may spend considerable sums of money on sick pets and when they die some of us invest in funerals and burials in pet cemeteries. We mourn their death much as we mourn the death of a family member (Carmack 1985; Cowles 1985; Kay et al. 1984; Stewart 1983). At an objective level, we know that animals are not human. But as our behaviour suggests, we are loathe to regard our pets as mere things. It is not unusual for many people to have stronger relationships with their pets than with other people (Cameron and Mattson 1972; Lawrence 1995; Szasz 1968). Although none of these behaviours make our pets truly human, they do give us pause to consider whether our pets are not, for all intents and purposes, much closer to being regarded as people than an objective appraisal would suggest that they are.

Although those who do not own pets may dismiss such anthropomorphic affection for animals as misplaced, it is unlikely today that we regard it as bizarre or deviant. In Bauman's (2000) view, we live in a postmodern world of blurred boundaries, liquid category memberships, and disappearing classifications. Although Bauman's (2000, 2003, 2007) perspective on liquid categories focuses on the fluid boundaries in contemporary views of identity, family, social class, and relationships, there is also a technological sense in which the boundaries between people and things may be blurring. In one vocabulary, we are becoming posthuman (e.g., Campbell et al. 2005; Giesler et al. 2009; Giesler and Venkatesh 2005; Hayles 1999; Venkatesh et al. 2002). Some of the evidence of our posthumanity is found in our increasing use of plastic surgery, our use of age-defying chemicals like Botox and Viagra, and our acceptance of such biotechnological advances as pacemakers and computerized mechanical limbs. Some of this blurring of people and things is also due to the increasing use of powerful electronic prosthetic devices like smart phones, computers, Internet searches, and portable entertainment devices that allow us to "know" and do far more than we could ever know and do without them (e.g., Tian and Belk 2005). For example, Gordon Bell, a Microsoft engineer, is conducting a personal experiment by digitizing and storing every possible aspect of his life, including his encounters with other people (Bell and Gemmell 2009). If he wants to remember the name of someone he met at a conference in 1997, he merely does a quick search on the virtual memory of his personal data base and pulls up images of the business cards he obtained at the conference. Clicking on the business card can then bring up a photo of the person taken on the spot and link to records of any other contacts they have may have had before or since. Although such reliance on technology has its detractors (e.g., Carr 2010; Jackson 2009; Mayer-Schönberger 2009; Siegel 2008), it is neither new nor restricted to electronic and digital technologies. Within consumer research such mergers of people and things have been regarded as instances of the extended self (Belk 1988).

2.2   PEOPLE, THINGS, AND THE EXTENDED SELF

Samuel Butler (1872) observed that when someone digs with a spade, the implement becomes an elongated extension of the forearm with the handle fused to an iron plate in such a way that feats of earth cultivation become feasible that would have been quite impossible for the unaided hand. Indeed the construction and use of tools is one of the features distinguishing contemporary humans from most of our non-human forebears. Not only tools for manual labour, but also instruments for making music, technologies for communicating, devices for making pictures and writing, and devices for transporting ourselves more efficiently all act as extensions of our body, mind, and soul. Not only do such objects do things *for* us, they are often perceived as being a *part* of us. Increasingly you are not only what you eat, but what you drive, what you wear, what you read, what you listen to, where you live, and what you own (Belk 1988; Rentfrew and Gosling 2007; Gosling 2008).

These self-identifying inferences about things are easily made when automobiles replace feet, telescopes and radar extend our vision, telephones amplify our hearing capacity, and computers take on brain functions. But things also become a part of us because they express our aspirations, make status claims, show our affiliations with other people and groups (what Douglas and Isherwood (1979) call marker goods), are the objects of our attention and psychic energy (what Freud calls cathexis—see Rook 1985), and simply imprint themselves upon us by their co-presence in our lives (what Sartre (1943) refers to as knowing them). Sartre (1943) also specifies that we may identify with certain objects through our mastery of them. It is not enough to merely own a pair of skis, a clarinet, or a book; to really cathect it requires developing a certain skill or knowledge in or from using it (Belk 1988).

Once we come to regard an object as a part of the self, it may also be regarded by others as an extension of us. This association can lead to possibilities of de facto ownership, contagion, and sympathetic magic. De facto ownership is illustrated by the co-presence of students and specific unassigned classroom chairs that come together in each class such that a given chair comes to be regarded as so-and-so's chair. This claim is recognized by others in the class who also have "their own" seats. Similarly, the new owners of a house previously owned by the Smiths may be referred to for some time as living in the Smiths' house. Daniel Miller (2001b) attributes the idea that houses are occupied by ghosts to the fact that houses outlive people. And Grant McCracken (1988) details divestment rituals involving overly thorough scrubbing and cleaning to try to remove symbolic traces of the old owner of an object like a previously occupied house or a used car. Such rituals are not unlike exorcisms to drive evil spirits out of a body. They are transformative purification rituals.

As I have suggested (Belk 1988), the principle at work in such cases is that of contagion whereby the essence of the owner of an object is thought to magically merge with or contaminate the object. In Walter Benjamin's ([1955]1969) words the object becomes infused with its former owner or creator's "aura." It is likely due to this sort of reasoning that grave goods consisting of the possessions of the dead began to be buried with people very early in the prehistory of humankind (Alekshin 1983; Leaky 1981). We may now be more apt to retain or attempt to give away or resell the possessions of the dead, but this does not remove their associations with former owners. Sometimes this is a positive contagion, as seen in the importance of the provenance of art works and antiques owned by famous people (Akhtar 2005; van der Grijp 2006). But often the association with a deceased prior owner is seen as tainting former possessions such as clothing, making it virtually unsaleable, especially in the case of objects like shoes, underwear, pipes, or cigarette holders that have been in close proximity with the now deceased person (Gregson and Crew 2003; Petit 2006). This trace can be made more palpable by any lingering stain, odour, or visible evidence of the former owner such as teeth marks (Douglas 1966; Gregson and Crew 2003).

The association of people with their possessions is not simply an inference made by others. The possessor or owner of an object may also become quite attached to certain objects as well (e.g., Belk 1992a; Kleine and Baker 2004). This is a psychological attachment more than a physical attachment. Thus we can be psychically attached to a place from which (or a person from whom) we are physically detached. We can be attached to prior experiences and even beliefs (Abelson 1986). We can also be quite attached to a television series, a sports team, or a musical group (e.g., Crawford 2004; Gray et al. 2007; Hills 2002; Sandvoss 2005). These people and things are no less a part of the extended self because of our normal inability to physically possess them. When we revere posters, pennants, videos, or even bobble-head dolls of our heroes and heroines we engage in acts of sympathetic magic based on similarity. By invoking the image we feel we are somehow controlling or making contact with the person these things represent. In some cases this can lead to developing one-way para-social relationships whereby we feel we personally know those whom we have seen only at a distance (Horton and Wohl 1976).

Classroom desks and celebrities are not the only un-owned objects to which we may feel attached. The trait or value of materialism and the sub-trait of possessiveness are related to our degree of attachments to tangible things (Belk 1985; Richins and Dawson 1992), but may not apply as readily to attachments to people and things that are not typically individually owned or possessed (Van Boven et al. 2010). However, materialists appear to have a greater tendency to tangibilize such objects of affection with souvenirs, mementos, photographs, and similar evidences of our identification and affection (Ger and Belk 1996). Furthermore, because certain people and even communities may be a part of our extended self, collective possessions shared with these others can also be regarded as a part of the extended self (Belk 1992a). This can result in even non-fans basking in the reflected glory of a winning sports team from our city, university, or country (Cialdini et al. 1976).

One consequence of our regarding certain possessions as a part of our extended selves is that when these things are lost, damaged, or stolen, we take these losses much harder than if the objects were merely functional things to which we were not attached. Thus victims of burglaries report the experience of having some stranger go through their things as being akin to rape (e.g., Korosec-Serfaty 1984; Maguire 1980). The mere presence of the burglar is felt as polluting and contaminating the extended self. And when these things are stolen or damaged a loss of self is often reported and a process of grief and mourning ensues (Young and Wallendorf 1989). Similar feelings can occur with the loss of collective possessions that comprise the aggregate extended self, as with the loss of neighborhood or community (Fried 1963; Sayre 1994; Wolfenstein 1957).

Because there is a feeling of loss of self when possessions critical to the extended self are lost or stolen, Wicklund and Gollwitzer (1982) theorize that there may be an attempt to restore feelings of self integrity through symbolic self completion. For instance, they found that MBAs who were less secure in their job prospects were more apt to adopt consumption items that they associated with successful businesspersons than were those who perceived that they had better job prospects. Solomon and Anand (1985) report similar results and note that this pattern is like the use of magical amulets, talismans, and totemic emblems in traditional societies. In bringing these objects from the commoditized marketplace into the singular wardrobes of their new owners, there are also rituals of possession (McCracken 1988) and grooming (Rook 1985) by which consumers hope to extract these new items' meanings and promises and thereby secure their blessings. These rituals may be as simple as trying out the clothes or grooming products and modeling them before a mirror or they may be as elaborate as having them tailored, having our monogram placed on them, or otherwise customizing them for our personal use.

2.3 MAGICAL AND SACRED OBJECTS

2.3.1 The Magical

As the preceding characterization suggests, finding or investing magical powers in things is by no means a practice restricted to traditional people. I have suggested that:

> We more often than not wear magic clothes, jewels, and perfumes. We drive magic cars. We reside in magic places and make pilgrimages to even more magical places. We eat magic foods, own magic pets, and envelop ourselves in the magic of films, television, and books. We court magic in a plethora of material loci that cumulatively compel us to conclude that the rational possessor is a myth that can no longer be sustained. It fails because it denies the inescapable and essential mysteriousness of our existence. (Belk 1991b, pp. 17–18)

Although it would seem that people have agency and things do not, we have already seen possible exceptions with robots and pets. It has been suggested that even without magic, certain objects have agency (e.g., Latour 2005; Pottage 2001). But I am concerned with the agency of things in ways that go beyond Latour's examples of kettles boiling water, knives cutting meat, hammers hitting nails, and baskets holding provisions. Although we fuse with our tools and become hybrids like human power-drills doing things in the world we could not do separately (Shove et al. 2007), it is still us who decide to do these things, not the tools. Although it would indeed be difficult to accomplish these actions without the appropriate objects, it would be equally or more difficult for the objects to accomplish them without humans setting these actions in motion. Furthermore, when it comes to imparting meaning to possessions rather than simply using them to do something, it requires a possessor or an observer to create these meanings; things have no meanings without humans actively engaging them. A book that I have not read or an e-mail that I have not opened has no meaning for me beyond its title and author or subject line and sender.

The magical meaning making that sometimes goes on in verbal communication, occurs with equal potential force nonverbally. As Douglas and Isherwood (1979) elaborate in their preface, Henry James was a master of creating portraits of people based largely on their possessions in novels like *The Ambassadors* and *The Bostonians*. However, possessions move from background props to foreground narrative devices in other James novels like *Portrait of a Lady*, *The American Scene*, *The Spoils of Poynton*, and *The Golden Bowl*. These novels helped mark the shift in American culture from a culture of character to a culture of consumption (Agnew

1983; Lears 1981). For example, in *Portrait of a Lady*, Madame Merle helps instruct the young American Isabel Archer:

> When you've lived as long as I you'll see that every human being has his shell and that you must take the shell into account. By the shell I mean the whole envelope of circumstances. There's no such thing as an isolated man or woman; we're each of us made up of some cluster of appurtenances. What shall we call our "self"? Where does it begin? Where does it end? It overflows into everything that belongs to us—and then it flows back again. I know a large part of myself is in the clothes I choose to wear. I've a great respect for *things*! One's self—for other people—is one's expression of one's self; and one's house, one's furniture, one's garments, the books one reads, the company one keeps—these things are all expressive. (Henry James 1881, p. 247)

Nine years later, Henry's brother, the psychologist William James, said something that initially appears quite similar:

> . . . a man's Self in the sum total of all that he CAN call his, not only his body and his psychic powers, but his clothes and his house, his wife and children, his ancestors and friends, his reputation and works, his lands, and yacht and bank-account. All these things give him the same emotions. If they wax and prosper, he feels triumphant; if they dwindle and die away, he feels cast down,—not necessarily in the same degree for each thing, but in much the same way for all. (William James 1890, pp. 291–2)

However, there is one key difference between these two portrayals of the relationship between people and things. Whereas William is talking about possessions and property as assets and fungible commodities, Henry is talking about possessions as vessels of meaning that are indelibly imprinted on their owners and are no longer fungible. In *The Spoils of Poynton*, for example, Mrs. Gareth struggles mightily with her son to retain ownership of the antiques that she has lovingly collected rather than have them liquidated and dispersed. It is the specific objects rather than their generic or monetary equivalents that are at stake here. What's more, in *The Spoils of Poynton* the precious antiques themselves exhibit prosopopeia and ultimately disappear (Tintner 1984).

We can also see in Henry James' novels the inversion that Karl Marx (1990) warned of involving the personification of things and the reification of people (Brown 2003, pp. 114, 178). This takes us back to our fascination with the blurred boundaries between people and things discussed earlier. In this case it is as though people have been drained of personality and things have become endowed with the personalities that have been evacuated from people. A recent case in point is the Japanese pop star Hatsune Miku. She is a 16-year-old, 158 cm, 42 kg singer who packs sold out auditoriums where she sings her hit songs. She is also not a person. She is instead a clever anime hologram whose singing comes from a voice synthesizer made by Yamaha. In addition to seeing her in concert, for about $200 fans can acquire the software to have Miku come to their computers and sing whatever lyrics the fan creates for her. She has a distinct personality and routinely outsells and outdraws flesh and blood singers in Japan (Graham 2010).

But we do not need such an extreme example as Miku to demonstrate the magical blurring of people and things. A pervasive example is the use of celebrity advertising in which the characteristics of the celebrity spokesperson become the characteristics of the brand that he or she promotes. Boon (2010) sees this as an act of sympathetic magic and illustrates it with a Louis Vuitton ad:

> A famous 2005 ad for Louis Vuitton features the actress Uma Thurman lounging on a stone structure, her arms above her head, her body somewhat exposed but her hands coiled around a monogram bag which sits in front of her. Thurman looks at the camera with a casual but powerful neutrality, the whole image radiating a strange mixture of exhibitionism, confidence, and security. By touching the bag (the gesture is repeated again and again in Vuitton campaigns), Thurman confers on it the power of her celebrity. (p. 34)

While McCracken (1989) sees this as a two-step meaning transfer process in which the attributes of the celebrity are detached from her person, attached to the brand, and subsequently extracted by the consumer, a more direct association is equally likely in which the brand *is* the celebrity and the celebrity *is* the brand. They each gain prestige from one another and become a singular fused entity. And the person in the ad need not be a celebrity or even a spokesperson for the brand for this to occur. The people shown in an ad for Coca Cola, Calvin Klein, or Apple, for all intents and purposes, become these brands and impart their (positive) image to the brand (Belk and Pollay 1985; Pavitt 2000). Or take the larger than life retail personifications shown in Figure 2.1. These models are not only the face of Armani, for consumers they *are* Armani—the perfect blend of the thing and the person. If the brand possessions of a person form their extended self, we might think of these personifications through advertising celebrities and models as the 'extended brand'.

2.3.2   The Sacred

As Mauss (2001), Durkheim (1995), and Sheffield (2006) concur, a key factor differentiating the magical from the sacred is that the magical is individual in its manifestations whereas the sacred is communally constituted. Not only is there ample evidence of the presence of magic in our

Photo: Russell Belk

Figure 2.1   Store front in Honolulu

regard for things, there is also ample evidence of communities of fellow believers who constitute the sacred through their aggregate reverence (Belk and Tumbat 2005; Belk et al. 1989; Muñiz and Schau 2005). Eliade (1959) maintains that one of the purposes of the sacred is to transcend the mundane secular world and to find the sublime. Among the properties of the sacred that help achieve transcendence is hierophany—". . . the act of manifestation of the sacred . . . i.e., that something sacred shows itself to us" (Eliade 1958, p. 7). In the view of Stivers (2001, p. 39) one of the functions of certain technological consumer goods is exactly this—they act as hierophanies or manifestations of the sacred. As a number of analyses have concluded, the Apple iPod may be a perfect example (Bull 2007; Kahney 2005; S. Levy 2006). The iPod allows us to transcend the here and now and to transport ourselves to another world through music. Its mysticism (another property of the sacred—Belk et al. 1989) is increased by its shuffle and genius modes, which some early adopters took to be mysterious forces in the devices that sensed their moods and programmed the musical selections accordingly or that counter-programmed according to a perverse trickster spirit (S. Levy 2005).

Another object that partakes of many evidences of the sacred is money (Belk and Wallendorf 1990). Money—not just paper and electronic money but *all* money—has value only because we have faith in it. Unlike many other things in the world, money has no inherent use value without our leap of faith to believe that it is so valuable that we will work all our lives for it. It is a mysterious substance that is not well understood by those who use it. It is marked with images of supreme rulers, nations, and strange symbols and mottos (e.g., a pyramid with an eye atop it and "In God We Trust" on the American dollar bill). Yet money brings wealth, prestige, and power. It is seemingly the one substance that can bring us all the good things in life. In times of difficulty, it can be our salvation, and when we lack it we feel cursed. Through certain rituals, investments, and sacrifices our money can grow and become greater. The financiers, brokers, and bankers who perform these secretive rituals can well be thought of as the high priests of money. The institutions in which they carry out these ceremonies are virtual temples with impressive, if not awe-inspiring, appearances, even when they are presented virtually (Schroeder 2003). Yet our faith is put to the test in bad economic times when forces we do not understand and cannot control threaten to enslave us for the sin of excessive debt. The recent financial meltdown suggests that our high priests of finance have begun to be perceived as black priests of the black Sabbath. Both greed and lack of generosity are other monetary sins for which we may be condemned. To a visitor from another universe, it would be apparent that we worship money. It is a sacred substance that guides our lives and is the focus of our prayers, hopes, and fears.

The mysteries of money are also apparent in its use. Although it would seem to be a completely fungible and interchangeable thing, it is not. Like the anthropological notion of "special monies" that can only be used for certain purposes like bride purchase and blood atonement, we also reserve monies for special purposes (Zelizer 1994). Thus, for instance, money that is received as an inheritance from our parents should be spent for special purchases and not frittered away on everyday expenses. Similarly, life insurance proceeds, windfall income, gift money, and money received in rites of passage such as marriage should not be used in the same manner as money earned as income. Food stamps and welfare payments are also often restricted to certain types of uses. And money can be tainted if it has been obtained illegally, as seen in expressions such as blood money, blood diamonds, and ill-gotten gains. Deservingness is also invoked in referring to the curse of poverty, the blessings of wealth, and monies earned by the sweat of the brow. The fact that we can quantitatively count as well as count *on* money for financial security does little to take away from its more qualitative and sacred qualities of being the one substance on which we all depend. For many, it has become our holy grail.

2.4   ORDINARY AND EXTRAORDINARY THINGS

Despite our regard for certain possessions as being magical or sacred, in an affluent society many of the things in our lives seem quite ordinary while others stand out as bearing extraordinary meanings. In this final section I wish to consider what makes some things "special" to us (Belk 1991b; Csikszentmihalyi and Rochberg-Halton 1981; Mehta and Belk 1991; D. Miller 2008; Turkle 2007; Wallendorf and Arnould 1988). I have suggested five characteristics that imply that an object has obtained a special place in our life:

1. Unwillingness to sell for market value
2. Willingness to buy with little regard for price
3. Non-substitutability
4. Unwillingness to discard
5. Feelings of elation or depression due to the object (Belk 1991b, pp. 35–36).

A possession need not meet all of these criteria to occupy a special place in our lives, but the more of these criteria an object meets the more certain we can be that it is, to us, an extraordinary thing. As Csikszentmihalyi and Rochberg-Halton (1981) found in a three-generation study of Chicago families, the particular possessions held to be special differ by age. Young people were more apt to cite possessions with which they could do things, such as musical instruments and sports equipment. Members of the older generation were more likely to focus on possessions like gifts and photographs that were linked to and that reminded them of other family members and friends. And the middle generation was most inclined to treasure possessions like sculptures and paintings that provided aesthetic pleasures.

Cultural differences have also been found. For example, men in Niger were especially likely to treasure religious objects and souvenirs like those representing the hajj to Mecca (Wallendorf and Arnould 1988). While South Asian Indians in North America frequently cited objects that represented their Indian homeland as favorite objects, those in India showed no special fondness for Indian objects (Mehta and Belk 1991). It is not necessary to signal or cling to your cultural identity when you are living it on a daily basis. Contact between cultures can also bring special attention to particular objects like clothing that outwardly differentiate between "us" and "them" (Comaroff 1996; Sobh et al. forthcoming). And moving between locations and cultures often thrusts possessions into the spotlight as links between the old life and the new life (Belk 1992b; Marcoux

2001). Moving and re-situating these things can also involve using them as transitional objects, much like a child's blanket or other soft object that may help to ease the trauma of separating from mother (Gulerce 1991; Winnicott 1953). Familiar objects over which we can exert order and control can also provide a sense of being at home, even in strange places (Bardhi and Askegaard 2009; D. Miller 2008).

Another instance in which objects become special is when we give them as gifts. While not all gifts are treasured, many are kept more as mementos of those who have given them than for any utilitarian value they offer (Jacobson 1985). They serve as reminders of our links to others and to our past and present (Belk 1991a; Komter 2005). The gift economy operates by different rules from the monetary economy (Cheal 1988; Godbout and Caillé 1998). Gifts are typically more luxurious objects than we would buy for ourselves and may involve a sacrifice by the giver; they are ideally chosen solely to please the recipient who is surprised and delighted by them; and they are wrapped and ceremoniously presented, often on special occasions, with the price tags and store insignias of the marketplace carefully removed (Belk 1996b; Hendry 1993). Although gift certificates and cards are growing in popularity, money is generally not an acceptable gift and if it is given, it too is specially wrapped and ceremoniously presented, often with a special paper gift wallet (Cameron 1989; Webley et al. 1983). Gifts are singular (Appadurai 1986a) and we make a sharp distinction between gifts and commodities (Carrier 1991, 1995; Gregory 1982). Just as there is special purpose money that should not be treated as a fungible commodity, gifts are separated from commodities and are not to be traded, discarded, or sold because this would betray their sentimental, mnemonic, and non-utilitarian character.

A further case in which objects are taken out of the money economy and held up as objects of special scrutiny and meaning is when they enter a collection. As I have defined it, collecting is "the process of actively, selectively, and passionately acquiring and possessing things removed from ordinary use and perceived as part of a set of non-identical objects or experiences" (Belk 1995, p. 67). This definition distinguishes collecting from hoarding (which would not object to identical objects—Cherrier and Ponner 2010), accumulating (which would not involve the perception of a set—Frost and Steketee 2010), as well as from assembling an inventory (which would neither object to identical objects nor take things out of ordinary use). It also distinguishes the active acquisitive pursuit of collecting from the possessive and more passive curation of an existing collection.

Danet and Katriel (1989) distinguish the Type A or taxonomic collector from the Type B or aesthetic collector. An example of the Type A collector is a stamp or coin collector who knows precisely which stamps or coins are needed to complete a collection. A Type B collector is exemplified by an art collector for whom there is no finite set of works that comprise a complete set. Even if the category is twenty-first century Chinese Cynical Realist art, there is no way to assemble a definitive collection, especially as the sphere of such art continues to expand. For both the Type A and the Type B collector, once an object enters a collection, it is considered part of a sacred set and should not be sold or traded unless that part of the collection is being upgraded or improved (Belk et al. 1991). The permanence or immortality of the objects in a collection is even more fixed when the collector is a museum (Pearce 1992). Museums of various types are our societal statements of what objects are truly extraordinary.

On the one hand, collecting might be seen as an extremely materialistic pursuit. It involves the perpetual pursuit of inessential luxury goods. If the collection ever nears completion, leaving the collector only a curatorial role, the collector is apt to switch to another collection that he or she can pursue as avidly as the former, now complete, collection (Belk 1995). But on the other hand, the collector often regards him or herself as the noble savior of objects that others fail to adequately appreciate (Belk 1998). They may see themselves as contributing in some uncertain but important way to the advancement of art or science, even with objects as seemingly humble and unimportant as beer cans, elephant replicas, or dirt from various parts of the world (Belk 1995). In this role, the collector may sacrifice mightily for the sake of building the collection and make a heroic effort to find a suitable caring heir for the collection. This selfless dedication and sacrifice is often seen by collectors as the very antithesis of materialism. The objects are seen as more important than the collector and as worthy of preservation for future more appreciative audiences. Recently the rise of the Internet and eBay have made it possible for collectors to find such appreciative audiences as well as potential additions to their collections much more readily (Hillis and Petit 2006).

There are many more types of things that are neither gifts nor parts of a collection, but that nevertheless take on extraordinary special meanings for people. I have suggested that they commonly include perfume, jewelry, clothing, hair and other body parts, special foods, our homes and vehicles, religious icons and relics, amulets, talismans, and totems, drugs and medicines, family photographs, souvenirs, mementos, heirlooms, antiques, monuments, treasure, art, celebrities and their relics, quintessential corporate icons, certain high tech goods, and sexual pornography (Belk 1991b). If many of these objects seem fetishistic in nature, it is appropriate to ask what things were special to the two most prominent theorists of the fetish: Sigmund Freud and Karl Marx. Freud spent most of his adult life after his father died collecting antique statues from ancient civilizations (S. Barker 1996; Gamwell and Wells 1989). He exhibited a dozen or so of these rather phallic looking objects on his desk as he was consulting with patients and reportedly often fondly stroked them. He also had a collection of stone penises broken off by Christian iconoclasts. Many of these objects can be seen in the Freud museums in Vienna, Austria and Hampstead Heath, England.

Marx had a different sort of fetish—his overcoat (Stallybrass 1998). While he was writing *Capital* in the Reading Room of the British Museum, his family ran out of money. After going through his wife Jenny's family fortune and selling or pawning her jewelry and clothing, they would periodically pawn the children's clothing, precluding them from attending school. Karl himself would periodically take jobs as a journalist to support them. But the last item to be pawned was his precious overcoat. For he felt it necessary to appear a proper English gentleman and would stop his writing in the Reading Room when the coat was in hock. For someone who wrote only of the congealed labor of the workers who produced an object as constituting the commodity fetish, Marx's overcoat is a rather good case study of *consumer* fetishization of things.

2.5   TRUE AND FALSE THINGS

If things can be magical, sacred, and extraordinary, one final consideration is what difference it makes whether an object is an original or a copy, authentic or inauthentic, genuine or counterfeit, real or virtual, true or false. Although these are all somewhat different binaries, they all speak of a sharp value dichotomy in which one member of a pair of similar appearing objects is seen as possessing value and sincerity while the other is seen as lacking both and as merely imitating the other object. For example spectacles such as Hawaiian hula performances for tourists are described as presenting only "staged authenticity" in place of more organic cultural events (MacCannell 1976; Desmond 1999). In a similar vein, others have disparaged pseudo-events (Boorstin 1964), hyperreality (Eco 1986; Baudrillard 1988), simulacra (Baudrillard 1994), artificialization (Belk 2005), forgeries (Lessing 1965; Dutton 1983), piracy (Johns 2009), intellectual property theft (Choate 2005), and unreasonable facsimiles (Schwartz 1998). The common idea here is that these things are pretending to be something they are not and are thereby somehow cheating by imitating something else.

Yet some have begun to challenge these distinctions as being elitist, exploitative, superficial, selfish, disingenuous, harmful to creativity, and as themselves artificial (e.g., Boon 2010; Bruner 2005; Hyde 2010; Lessig 2004; Shenkar 2010; Vaidhyanathan 2001). Boon (2010) also notes that there are cultural determinants of regard for copies and that copying in Buddhist tradition is a noble undertaking. Furthermore it is not necessarily seen as copying because things are seen to appear only as essences which either remain fixed in the original object or do not really exist at all. Mass production introduces a further irony. We revere the original and then seek to make an endless number of copies of it. Abbas (2002) offers an interesting take on this fact:

> The "designer watch" is already, in a sense, a fake. There is a relation therefore between taste-as-ignorance and the culture of the fake . . . Part of the animus directed against the fake, especially on the part of the producers of taste, comes we might suspect from the fact that it threatens to expose such goods themselves to the charge of fakery. (Abbas 2002, pp. 316–17)

This charge was heard from the participants in an eight-country consumer ethics study who responded to scenarios involving buying a fake Louis Vuitton roll-on bag or wallet (Belk et al. 2005; Eckhardt et al. 2010). A common response was that it was the company itself that was behaving unethically in charging outrageous prices for their products. Like the magical value imparted by Vuitton celebrity associations and its famous brand name, we do not replicate essences as much as the magical auras that shape the thing's meaning as we perceive it in our particular socially constructed world.

Boon (2010) takes the point farther and argues that copying is an unavoidable and desirable part of being human. It is the expansion of both intellectual property laws and enhanced digital copying potential in recent decades that is the source of friction. Hyde (2010) questions whether intellect is really the source of all that has been claimed as intellectual property:

> Does it make sense . . . to say that "intellect" is the source of the "properties" in question? A novel like *Ulysses*, the know-how for making antiviral drugs, Martin Luther King, Jr.'s "Dream" speech, the poems of Rimbaud, Andy Warhol screen prints, Mississippi Delta blues, the source code for electronic voting machines: who could name the range of human powers and historical conditions that attends such creations? (Hyde 2010, p. 5)

Companies like Disney skillfully extract property rights from formerly free folk cultural tales and give nothing back that is not copyright protected. As I have suggested (Belk 2007; 2010; Belk and Sobh 2007; Belk and Llamas forthcoming), at stake here is the culture of sharing that has sustained humankind for several hundred thousand years.

2.6 CONCLUSION

In this chapter I have hopefully done more to whet the appetite for considering the various relationships between people and things than to provide any comprehensive treatment to such a vast topic. I have focused especially on areas touched by my own work and have attempted to paint with a broad interpretive brush that creates detail in only a few areas, while leaving vast areas of the canvas untouched or little more than roughly sketched. I have not even sketched the various perspectives from which our obsession with things might be critiqued (e.g., Badiner 2002; Barber 2007; Benson 2000; Hammerslough 2001; Haug 1986; Kaza 2005; Klein 1999; Mauch 1983; Schor 1998; Steffen 1993; Wachtel 1989; Whybrow 2005). I have largely failed to bring up gender differences in the meanings of things (e.g., Costa 1994; de Grazia 1996; Martinez and Ames 1997; Saisselin 1985; Sparke 1995; Wardlow 1996). And I have neglected the historical developments that have brought us to our current fascination with objects acquired in the marketplace in the West (e.g., Brewer and Porter 1993; Brewer and Trentmann 2006; Campbell 1987; Cohen 2003; Cross 2000; Domosh 2006; Glickman 1999; Goodwin et al. 1997; Leach 1993; Lears 1994; Mukerji 1983; Schama 1987; Schor and Holt 2000; Strasser et al. 1998) as well as elsewhere (e.g., Alsharekh and Springborg 2008; A. Barker 1999; Croll 2006; Davis 2000; Dikötter 2006; Drakulić 1996; Farquhar 2002; Gerth 2003; Kemper 2001; Mathews and Lui 2001; Mazzarella 2003; Pinches 1999; Stan 1997; Stearns 2001; Wang 2008; J. Watson 1997; Yeh 2007).

Still, it should be evident that the relationship between people and things goes far beyond the merely functional and utilitarian. The latest technological inventions, far from banishing the magical and the sacred have made them increasingly relevant to re-enchanting a disenchanted world (Ritzer 1999). Even the distinction between people and things is now blurring such that it makes sense to talk of the extended self, the extended thing, and hybrid, prosthetic, and posthuman entities. That we cannot (yet) mass produce or digitally copy people remains one of the characteristics distinguishing people and things.

I have tried to be expansive with references in the hope that the interested reader may have a beginning in pursuing the surfaced topics in greater detail. Much remains to be done in order to understand the various relationships between people and things. Consumer research is poised to make a real contribution by seeking to understand these relationships during a key period in human history when much of the world is turning to anticipated material pleasures from goods acquired in the marketplace. In a world of rapidly dwindling natural resources and rapidly increasing gaps between the haves and have-nots of the world, the most basic question we can ask is what all this stuff means to us.

REFERENCES

Abbas, Ackbar (2002), 'Theory of the fake', in *HK Lab*, Laurent Gutierrez, Ezio Manzini, and Valérie Portefaix (eds), Hong Kong: Map Book Publishers, pp. 312–323.

Abelson, R.P. (1986), 'Beliefs are like possessions', *Journal for the Theory of Social Behavior*, **16** (3), 223–250.

Adams, Rachel (2001), *Sideshow USA: Freaks and the American Cultural Imagination*, Chicago: University of Chicago Press.

Aggarwal, P. and A. McGill (2007), 'Is that car smiling at me? Schema congruity as a basis for evaluation of anthropomorphized products', *Journal of Consumer Research*, **34** (December), 468–479.

Agnew, J.-C. (1983), 'The consuming vision of Henry James', in Richard Wightman Fax and T.J. Jackson Lears (eds), *The Culture of Consumption: Critical Essays in American History 1880–1980*, New York: Pantheon, pp. 67–100.

Akhtar, S. (2005), *Objects of Our Desire: Exploring Our Intimate Connections with the Things Around Us*, New York: Harmony Books.

Alekshin, V.A. (1983), 'Burial customs as an anthropological source', *Current Anthropology*, **24** (April), 137–150.

Alsharekh, Alanoud and Robert Springborg (eds) (2008), *Popular Culture and Political Identity in the Arab Gulf States*, London: The London Middle East Institute.

Appadurai, Arjun (1986a), 'Introduction: commodities and the politics of value', in Arjun Appadurai (ed.), *The Social Life of Things: Commodities in Cultural Perspective*, Cambridge: Cambridge University Press, pp. 3–63.

Appadurai, Arjun (ed.) (1986b), *The Social Life of Things: Commodities in Cultural Perspective*, Cambridge: Cambridge University Press.

Arnold, Catharine (2010), *Bedlam: London and Its Mad*, London: Simon and Schuster UK.

Arvidsson, Adam (2006), *Brands: Meaning and Value in Media Culture*, London: Routledge.

Attfield, Judy (2000), *Wild Things: The Material Culture of Everyday Life*, Oxford: Berg.

Badiner, Allan H. (ed.) (2002), *Mindfulness in the Marketplace: Compassionate Responses to Consumerism*, Berkeley, CA: Parallax Press.

Bakhtin, Mikhail (1968), *Rabelais and His World*, trans. Helene Iswolsky, Cambridge, MA: MIT Press.

Barber, Benjamin R. (2007), *Consumed: How Markets Corrupt Children, Infantilize Adults, and Swallow Citizens Whole*, New York: W.W. Norton.

Bardhi, Fleura and Søren Askegaard (2009), 'Home away from home: home-as-order and dwelling in mobility', in John H. Sherry, Jr. and Eileen Fischer (eds), *Explorations in Consumer Culture Theory*, London: Routledge, pp. 83–97.

Barker, Adele Marie (ed.) (1999), *Consuming Russia: Popular Culture, Sex, and Society Since Gorbachev*, Durham, NC: Duke University Press.

Barker, Stephen (ed.) (1996), *Excavations and Their Objects: Freud's Collection of Antiquity*, Albany, NY: State University of New York Press.

Baudelaire, Charles ([1845]1995), 'A philosophy of toys', in *The Painter of Modern Life and Other Essays*, 2nd edn, trans. Jonathan Mayne, London: Phaidon Press, pp. 198–204.

Baudrillard, Jean (1988), *America*, London: Verso.

Baudrillard, Jean (1994), *Simulacra and Simulation*, trans. Sheila Faria Glaser, Ann Arbor: University of Michigan Press.

Bauman, Zygmunt (2000), *Liquid Modernity*, Cambridge: Polity.

Bauman, Zygmunt (2003), *Liquid Love: On the Frailty of Human Bonds*, Cambridge: Polity.

Bauman, Zygmunt (2007), *Liquid Times: Living in an Age of Uncertainty*, Cambridge: Polity.

Bélisle, Jean-François and H. Onur Bodur (2010), 'Avatars as information: perception of consumers based on their avatars in virtual worlds', *Psychology and Marketing*, **27** (August), 741–765.

Belk, R.W. (1985), 'Materialism: trait aspects of living in the material world', *Journal of Consumer Research*, **12** (December), 265–280.

Belk, R.W. (1988), 'Possessions and the extended self', *Journal of Consumer Research*, **15** (September), 139–168.

Belk, R.W. (1991a), 'Possessions and the sense of past', in Russell W. Belk (ed.), *Highways and Buyways: Naturalistic Research From the Consumer Behavior Odyssey*, Provo, UT: Association for Consumer Research, pp. 114–130.

Belk, Russell W. (1991b), 'The ineluctable mysteries of possessions', *Journal of Social Behavior and Personality*, **6** (June), 17–55.

Belk, R.W. (1992a), 'Attachment to possessions', in Irwin Altman and Setha Low (eds), *Human Behavior and Environment: Advances in Theory and Research, Vol. 12, Place Attachment*, New York: Plenum Press, pp. 37–62.

Belk, R.W. (1992b), 'Moving possessions: an analysis based on personal documents from the 1847–1869 Mormon migration', *Journal of Consumer Research*, **19** (December), 339–361.

Belk, Russell W. (1994), 'Carnival, control, and corporate culture in contemporary Halloween celebrations', in Jack Santino (ed.), *Halloween and Other Festivals of Death and Life*, Knoxville, TN: University of Tennessee Press, pp. 105–132.

Belk, Russell W. (1995), *Collecting in a Consumer Society*, London: Routledge.

Belk, R.W. (1996a), 'Metaphoric relationships with pets', *Society and Animals*, **4** (2), 121–145.

Belk, Russell W. (1996b), 'The perfect gift', in Cele Otnes and Richard F. Beltramini (eds), *Gift Giving: A Research Anthology*, Bowling Green, OH: Bowling Green University Popular Press, pp. 59–84.

Belk, R.W. (1998), 'The double nature of collecting: materialism and antimaterialism', *Etnofoor*, **11** (1), 7–20.

Belk, Russell W. (2005), 'Artificialization', *Ethnologia Europaea*, **35** (1–2), 103–106.

Belk, R.W. (2007), 'Why not share rather than own?', *Annals of the American Academy of Political and Social Science*, **611** (May), 126–140.

Belk, R.W. (2010), 'Sharing', *Journal of Consumer Research*, **37** (February), 715–734.

Belk, Russell and Rosa Llamas (forthcoming), 'The nature and effects of sharing in consumer behavior', in David Mick, Connie Pechmann, Julie Ozanne, and Simone Pettigrew (eds), *Transformative Consumer Research for Human and Earthly Welfare: Reviews and Frontiers*, London: Routledge.

Belk, R. and R. Pollay (1985), 'Images of ourselves: the good life in twentieth century advertising', *Journal of Consumer Research*, **11** (March), 887–897.

Belk R. and R. Sobh (2007), 'Is sharing an alternative to private ownership?', *International Review of Business Research Papers*, **3** (November), 78–87.

Belk, R. and G. Tumbat (2005), 'The cult of Macintosh', *Consumption, Markets and Culture*, **8** (September), 205–218.

Belk, R. and M. Wallendorf (1990), 'The sacred meanings of money', *Journal of Economic Psychology*, **11** (March), 35–67.

Belk, R., M. Wallendorf, and J.F. Sherry, Jr. (1989), 'The sacred and the profane in consumer behavior: theodicy on the Odyssey', *Journal of Consumer Research*, **15** (June), 1–38.

Belk, Russell, Melanie Wallendorf, John Sherry, and Morris Holbrook (1991), 'Collecting in a consumer culture', in Russell W. Belk (ed.), *Highways and Buyways: Naturalistic Research From the Consumer Behavior Odyssey*, Provo, UT: Association for Consumer Research, pp. 178–215.

Belk, R.W., T. Devinney, and G. Eckhardt (2005), 'Consumer ethics across cultures', *Consumption, Markets & Culture*, **8** (September), 275–290.

Bell, Gordon and Jim Gemmell (2009), *Total Recall: How the E-Memory Revolution Will Change Everything*, New York: Dutton.

Benjamin, Walter ([1955]1969), 'The work of art in the age of mechanial reproduction', in

Hannah Arendt (ed.), *Illuminations*, trans. Edward Jephcott and K. Shorter, New York: Shocken, pp. 271–251.
Benson, April L. (ed.) (2000), *I Shop, Therefore I am: Compulsive Buying and The Search for Self*, Northvale, NJ: Jason Aronson.
Bessière, Katherine, A. Flemming Seay, and Sara Kiesler (2007), 'The ideal elf: identity exploration in World of Warcraft', *CyberPsychology and Behavior*, **10** (August), 530–535.
Boellstorff, Tom (2008), *Coming of Age in Second Life: An Anthropologist Explores the Virtually Human*, Princeton, NJ: Princeton University Press.
Bogdan, Robert (1988), *Freak Show: Presenting Human Oddities for Amusement and Profit*, Chicago: University of Chicago Press.
Boon, Marcus (2010), *In Praise of Copying*, Cambridge, MA: Harvard University Press.
Boorstin, Daniel (1964), *The Image: A Guide to Pseudo-Events in America*, New York: Harper.
Brewer, John and Roy Porter (eds) (1993), *Consumption and the World of Goods*, London: Routledge.
Brewer, John and Frank Trentman (eds) (2006), *Consuming Cultures, Global Perspectives*, Oxford: Berg.
Brown, Bill (2003), *A Sense of Things: The Object Matter or American Literature*, Chicago: University of Chicago Press.
Bruner, Edward M. (2005), *Culture on Tour: Ethnographies of Travel*, Chicago: University of Chicago Press.
Buchner, Alexander (1978), *Mechanical Musical Instruments*, trans. I. Urwin, Westport, CT: Greenwood Press.
Bull, Michael (2007), *Sound Moves: iPod Culture and the Urban Experience*, London: Routledge.
Butler, Samuel (1872), *Erewhon*, Harmondsworth, Middlesex: Penguin.
Cameron, James, dir. (1984), *The Terminator*, Hollywood, CA: MGM, 107 minutes.
Cameron, Paul and M. Mattson (1972), 'Psychological correlates of pet ownership', *Psychological Reports*, **30**, 286.
Cameron, S. (1989), 'The unacceptability of money as a gift and its status as a medium of exchange', *Journal of Economic Psychology*, **10** (June), 253–255.
Campbell, Colin (1987), *The Romantic Ethic and the Spirit of Modern Consumerism*, Oxford: Blackwell.
Campbell, N., A. O'Driscoll, and M. Saran (2005), 'Cyborg consciousness—a visual culture approach to the technologized body', *European Advances in Consumer Research*, **7**, 355–351.
Carmack, Betty J. (1985), 'The effects on family members and functioning after the death of a pet', in Marvin B. Sussman (ed.), *Pets and the Family*, New York: Haworth, pp. 149–162.
Carr, Nicholas (2010), *The Shallows: What the Internet is Doing to Our Brain*, New York: W.W. Norton.
Carrier, J. (1991), 'Gifts in a world of commodities: the ideology of the perfect gift in American society', *Social Analysis*, **29**, 19–37.
Carrier, James (1995), *Gifts and Commodities: Exchange and Western Capitalism Since 1700*, London: Routledge.
Chadha, Radha and Paul Husband (2006), *The Cult of the Luxury Brand: Inside Asia's Love Affair with Luxury*, London: Nicholas Brealey International.
Chambers, Paul (2009), *Bedlam: London's Hospital for the Mad*, Hersham, UK: Ian Allan.
Cheal, David (1988), *The Gift Economy*, London: Routledge.
Cherrier, H. and T. Ponner (2010), 'A study of hoarding behavior and attachment to material possessions', *Qualitative Market Research*, **13** (1), 8–23.
Choate, Pat (2005), *Hot Property: The Stealing of Ideas in an Age of Globalization*, New York: Alfred A. Knopf.
Cialdini, R., R. Borden, A. Thorne, M. Walker, S. Freeman, and L. Sloan (1976), 'Basking in reflected glory: three (football) field studies', *Journal of Social Psychology and Personality*, **34** (3), 366–375.

Cohen, Lizbeth (2003), *Consumers' Republic: The Politics of Mass Consumption in Postwar America*, New York: Vintage.

Comaroff, Jean (1996), 'The empire's old clothes: fashioning the colonial subject', in David Howes (ed.), *Cross-Cultural Consumption*, London: Routledge, pp. 19–38.

Cook, Daniel Thomas (2004), *The Commodification of Childhood: The Children's Clothing Industry and the Rise of the Child Consumer*, Durham, NC: Duke University Press.

Costa, Janeen (ed.) (1994), *Gender Issues and Consumer Behavior*, Thousand Oaks, CA: Sage.

Cova, B. and V. Cova (2001), 'Tribal marketing: the tribalization of society and its impact on the conduct of marketing', *European Journal of Marketing*, **36** (5/6), 595–620.

Cova, Bernard, Robert V. Kozinets, and Avi Shankar (2007), *Consumer Tribes*, Burlington, MA: Butterworth-Heinemann.

Cowles, Kathleen V. (1985), 'The death of a pet: human responses to the breaking of the bond', in Marvin B. Sussman (ed.), *Pets and the Family*, New York: Haworth, pp. 135–148.

Crawford, Garry (2004), *Consuming Sport: Fans, Sport and Culture*, London: Routledge.

Croll, Elizabeth (2006), *China's New Consumers: Social Development and Domestic Demand*, London: Routledge.

Cross, Gary (2000), *An All-Consuming Century: Why Commercialism Won in Modern America*, New York: Columbia University Press.

Csikszentmihalyi, Mihalyi and Eugene Rochberg-Halton (1981), *The Meaning of Things: Domestic Symbols and the Self*, New York: Cambridge University Press.

Cummings, Neil and Marysia Lewandowska (2000), *The Value of Things*, Basel: Birkhäuser.

Curasi, Carolyn Folkman, Margaret K. Hogg and Pauline Maclaran (2001), 'Entering the empty nest stage: a multi-method exploration of women's life experiences and coping strategies in periods of life stage transition', in Andrea Groeppel-Klien and Frank-Rudolf Esch (eds), *European Advances in Consumer Research*, Volume 5, Provo, UT: Association for Consumer Research, pp. 260–267.

Danesi, Marcel (2006), *Brands*, New York: Routledge.

Danet, Bernda and Tamar Katriel (1989), 'No two alike: the aesthetics of collecting', *Play and Culture*, **2** (3), 253–277.

Davis, Deborah S. (ed.) (2000), *The Consumer Revolution in Urban China*, Berkeley, CA: University of California Press.

De Grazia, Victoria (ed.) (1996), *The Sex of Things: Gender and Consumption in Historical Perspective*, Berkeley, CA: University of California Press.

Descartes, René ([1637]1976), 'Animals are machines', in Tom Regan and Peter Singer (eds), *Animal Rights and Human Obligations*, Englewood Cliffs, NJ: Prentice-Hall, pp. 60–66.

Desmond, Jane C. (1999), *Staging Tourism: Bodies on Display from Waikiki to Sea World*, Chicago: University of Chicago Press.

Dikötter, Frank (2006), *Exotic Commodities: Modern Objects and Everyday Life in China*, New York: Columbia University Press.

Dittmar, Helga (1992), *The Social Psychology of Material Possessions: To Have is To Be*, New York: St. Martin's Press.

Dittmar, Helga (2008), *Consumer Culture, Identity and Well-Being: The Search for the 'Good Life' and the 'Body Perfect'*, East Sussex, UK: Psychology Press.

Domosh, Mona (2006), *American Commodities in an Age of Empire*, London: Routledge.

Douglas, Mary (1966), *Purity and Danger: An Analysis of the Concepts of Pollution and Taboo*, London: Routledge and Kegan Paul.

Douglas, Mary and Baron Isherwood (1979), *The World of Goods: Towards an Anthropology of Consumption*, New York: W.W. Norton.

Doyle, Kenneth O. (1999), *The Social Meanings of Money and Property: In Search of a Talisman*, Thousand Oaks, CA: Sage.

Drakulić, Slavenka (1996), *Café Europa: Life After Communism*, New York: W.W. Norton.

During, Simon (2002), *Modern Enchantments: The Cultural Power of Secular Magic*, Cambridge, MA: Harvard University Press.

Durkheim, Emile (1995), *The Elementary Forms of Religious Life*, trans. Karen E. Fields, New York: The Free Press.

Dutton, Denis (ed.) (1983), *Artistic Crimes: The Forger's Art, Forgery and the Philosophy of Art*, Berkeley, CA: University of California Press.

Eckhardt, G., R. Belk, and T. Devinney (2010), 'Why don't consumers consume ethically?', *Journal of Consumer Behaviour*, **9** (December), 426–436

Eco, Umberto (1986), *Travels in Hyper-Reality*, London: Picador.

Eliade, Mircea (1958), *Patterns in Comparative Religion*, London: Sheed and Ward.

Eliade, Mircea (1959), *The Sacred and the Profane: The Nature of Religion*, trans. Willard R. Trask, New York: Harper and Row.

Ellen, Roy (1988), 'Fetishism', *Man*, **21** (June), 213–235.

Epele, María E. (2002), 'Excess, scarcity and desire among drug-using sex workers', in Nancy Scheper-Hughes and Loïc Wacquant (eds), *Commodifying Bodies*, London: Sage, pp. 151–180.

Ertman, Martha M. and Joan C. Williams (eds) (2005), *Rethinking Commodification: Cases and Readings in Law and Culture*, New York: New York University Press.

Farquhar, Judith (2002), *Appetites: Food and Sex in Post-Socialist China*, Durham, NC: Duke University Press.

Fiedler, Leslie (1978), *Freaks: Myths and Images of the Secret Self*, New York: Anchor.

Forty, Adrian (1986), *Objects of Desire: Design and Society from Wedgewood to IBM*, New York: Pantheon Books.

Foucault, Michel (1970), *The Order of Things: An Archaeology of Human Sciences*, New York: Pantheon.

Freud, Sigmund (1953), 'The uncanny', in James Strachey and Anna Freud (eds), *The Standard Edition of Sigmund Freud*, Vol. 17, London: Hogarth Press, pp. 219–256.

Freund, Thatcher (1995), *Objects of Desire: The Lives of Antiques and Those Who Pursue Them*, New York: Penguin.

Fried, Marc (1963), 'Grieving for a lost home', in Leonard J. Duhl (ed.), *The Urban Condition: People and Policy in the Metropolis*, New York: Basic Books, pp. 151–171.

Frost, Randy O. and Gail Steketee (2010), *Stuff: Compulsive Hoarding and the Meaning of Things*, Boston: Houghton Mifflin Harcourt.

Gamwell, Lynn and Richard Wells (1989), *Sigmund Freud and Art: His Personal Collection of Antiquities*, Binghamton, NY: State University of New York Press.

Ger, G. and R. Belk (1996), 'Cross-cultural differences in materialism', *Journal of Economic Psychology*, **17** (1), February, 55–78.

Gerth, Karl (2003), *China Made: Consumer Culture and the Creation of the Nation*, Cambridge, MA: Harvard University Press.

Giesler, M. and A. Venkatesh (2005), 'Reframing the embodied consumer as cyborg: a posthuman epistemology of consumption', *Advances in Consumer Research*, **31**, 661–669.

Giesler, M., M. Luedicke, and B. Ozergin (2009), 'Self-enhancement culture and the cyborg consumer: consumer identity construction beyond the dominance of authenticity', *Advances in Consumer Research*, **36**, 72–75.

Glickman, Lawrence B. (ed.) (1999), *Consumer Society in American History: A Reader*, Ithaca, NY: Cornell University Press.

Godbout, Jacques T. and Alain Caillé (1998), *The World of the Gift*, Montreal: McGill-Queen's University Press.

Goodwin, Neva R., Frank Ackerman, and David Kiron (eds) (1997), *The Consumer Society Reader*, Washington, DC: Island Press.

Gosling, Sam (2008), *Snoop: What Your Stuff Says About You*, New York: Basic Books.

Graham, Nicholas (2010), 'Hatsune Miku: Japanese HOLOGRAPH plays sold-out concerts; science fiction comes to life', *Huffington Post*, 11 November, http://www.huffingtonpost.com/2010/11/11/hatsune-miku-japanese-holograph-_n_782442.html.

Gray, Jonathan, Cornel Sandvoss, and C. Lee Harrington (eds) (2007), *Fandom: Identities and Communities in a Mediated World*, New York: New York University Press.

Gregory, Christopher A. (1982), *Gifs and Commodities*, London: Academic Press.

Gregson, Nicky (2007), *Living with Things: Ridding, Accommodation, Dwelling*, Wantage, UK: Sean Kingston Publishing.

Gregson, Nicky and Louise Crewe (2003), *Second-Hand Cultures*, Oxford: Berg.

Grijp, Paul van der (2006), *Passion and Profit: Towards an Anthropology of Collecting*, Berlin: LIT Verlag.

Gulerce, A. (1991), 'Transitional objects: a reconsideration of the phenomenon', *Journal of Social Behavior and Personality*, **6** (June), 187–208.

Hammerslough, Jane (2001), *Dematerializing: Taming the Power of Possessions*, Cambridge, MA: Perseus Books.

Hann, C.M. (ed.) (1998), *Property Relations: Renewing the Anthropological Tradition*, Cambridge: Cambridge University Press.

Haug, W.F. (1986), *Critique of Commodity Aesthetics: Appearance, Sexuality and Society in Capitalist Society*, Minneapolis, MN: University of Minnesota Press.

Hayles, N. Katherine (1999), *How We Became Posthuman: Virtual Bodies in Cybernetics, Literature, and Informatics*, Chicago: University of Chicago Press.

Hendry, Joy (1993), *Wrapping Culture: Politeness, Presentation, and Power in Japan and Other Societies*, Oxford: Oxford University Press.

Hernández, Tanya Kateri (2005), '"Sex in the [Foreign] City": commodification and the female sex tourist', in Martha Ertman and Joan Williams (eds), *Rethinking Commodification: Cases and Readings in Law and Culture*, New York: New York University Press, pp. 222–242.

Hillis, Ken and Michael Petit (eds) (2006), *Everyday eBay: Culture, Collecting, and Desire*, New York: Routledge.

Hills, Matt (2002), *Fan Cultures*, London: Routledge.

Holt, Douglas (2004), *How Brands Became Icons: The Principles of Cultural Branding*, Boston: Harvard Business School Press.

Horton, Donald and R. Richard Wohl (1976), 'Mass communication and para-social interaction: observations on intimacy at a distance', in James Coombs (ed.), *Drama in Life: The Uses of Communications in Society*, New York: Hastings House, pp. 212–228.

Hyde, Lewis (2010), *Common as Air: Revolution, Art, and Ownership*, New York: Farrar, Straus and Giroux.

Jackson, Maggie (2009), *Distracted: The Erosion of Attention and the Coming Dark Age*, Amherst, NY: Prometheus Books.

Jacobson, Stuart E. (1985), *Only the Best: A Celebration of Gift Giving in America*, New York: Abrams.

James, Henry (1881), *Portrait of a Lady*, Cambridge, MA: Riverside.

James, William (1890), *The Principles of Psychology*, Vol. 1, New York: Basic Books.

Johns, Adrian (2009), *Piracy: The Intellectual Property Wars from Gutenberg to Gates*, Chicago: University of Chicago Press.

Kahney, Leander (2004), *The Cult of Mac*, San Francisco: No Starch Press.

Kahney, Leander (2005), *The Cult of iPod*, San Francisco: No Starch Press.

Kasser, Tim (2002), *The High Price of Materialism*, Cambridge, MA: MIT Press.

Kasser, Tim and Allen D. Kanner (2004), *Psychology and Consumer Culture: The Struggle for a Good Life in a Materialistic World*, Washington, DC: American Psychological Association.

Kay, William, Herbert A. Nieberg, Austin H. Kutscher, Ross M. Grey, and C.E. Fudin (eds) (1984), *Pet Loss and Human Bereavement*, Ames, IA: Iowa State University Press.

Kaza, Stephanie (ed.) (2005), *Hooked! Buddhist Writings on Greed, Desire, and the Urge to Consume*, Boston: Shambhala.

Kemper, Steven (2001), *Buying and Believing: Sri Lankan Advertising and Consumers in a Transnational World*, Chicago: University of Chicago Press.

Kirkham, Pat (ed.) (1996), *The Gendered Object*, Manchester: Manchester University Press.

Klein, Naomi (1999), *No Logo: Taking Aim at the Brand Bullies*, New York: Picador.

Kleine, Susan Schultz and Stacey Menzel Baker (2004), 'An integrative review of material possession attachment', *Academy of Marketing Science Review*, **1**, 1–39.

Kniazeva, M. and R. Belk (2010), 'If this brand were a person, or anthropomorphism of brands through packaging stories', *Journal of Global Academy of Marketing Science*, **20** (2), 1–8.

Komter, Aafke E. (2005), *Social Solidarity and the Gift*, Cambridge: Cambridge University Press.

Kopytoff, Igor (1986), 'The cultural biography of things: commoditization as process', in Arjun Appadurai (ed.), *The Social Life of Things: Commodities in Cultural Perspective*, Cambridge: Cambridge University Press, pp. 64–91.

Korosec-Serfaty, P. (1984), 'The home from cellar to attic', *Journal of Experimental Psychology*, **4** (2), 303–321.

Kubrick, Stanley (1968), *2001: A Space Odyssey*, Hollywood, CA: Warner Brothers, 141 minutes.

Lang, Fritz and Thea von Harbou, dir. (1926), *Metropolis*, Berlin: UFA, 96 minutes.

Lash, Scott and Celia Lury (2007), *Global Culture Industry*, Cambridge: Polity Press.

Latour, Bruno (2005), *Reassembling the Social: An Introduction to Actor-Network Theory*, Oxford: Oxford University Press.

Lawrence, E.A. (1995), 'Cultural perceptions of differences between people and animals: a key to understanding human-animal relationships', *Journal of American Culture*, **18**, 75–82.

Leach, William (1993), *Land of Desire: Merchants, Power, and the Rise of a New American Culture*, New York: Vintage.

Leaky, Richard E. (1981), *The Making of Mankind*, New York: E. Po. Dutton.

Lears, T.J. Jackson (1981), *No Place of Grace: Antimodernism and the Transformation of American Culture, 1880–1920*, Chicago: University of Chicago Press.

Lears, Jackson (1994), *Fables of Abundance: A Cultural History of Advertising in America*, New York: Basic Books.

Lessig, Lawrence (2004), *Free Culture: The Nature and Future of Creativity*, London: Penguin.

Lessing, A. (1965), 'What's wrong with forgery?', *Journal of Aesthetics and Art Criticism*, **23** (Summer), 461–471.

Levy, David L. (2007), *Love and Sex with Robots: The Evolution of Human–Robot Relationships*, New York: Harper Collins.

Levy, S. (2005), 'Does your iPod play favorites?', *Newsweek*, **31** (January), 10.

Levy, Steven (2006), *The Perfect Thing: How the iPod Shuffles Commerce, Culture, and Coolness*, New York: Simon and Schuster.

Lubar, Steven and W. David Kingery (eds) (1995), *History from Things: Essays on Material Culture*, Washington, DC: Smithsonian Institution Press.

Lucas, Ann (2005), 'The currency of sex: prostitution, law, and commodification', in Martha Ertman and Joan Williams (eds), *Rethinking Commodification: Cases and Readings in Law and Culture*, New York: New York University Press, pp. 248–270.

Lucas, George, dir. (1977), *Star Wars*, Hollywood, CA: Twentieth Century Fox, 121 minutes.

Lury, Celia (2004), *Brands: The Logos of the Global Economy*, London: Routledge.

MacCannell, Dean (1976), *The Tourist: A New Theory of the Leisure Class*, New York: Shocken.

Maffesoli, Michel (1996), *The Time of the Tribes: The Decline of Individualism in Mass Society*, London: Sage.

Maguire, M. (1980), 'The impact of burglary upon victims', *British Journal of Criminology*, **20** (July), 261–275.

Marcoux, Jean-Sébastien (2001), 'The refurbishment of memory', in Daniel Miller (ed.), *Home Possessions*, Oxford: Berg, pp. 69–86.

Martin, D.M., J.W. Schouten, and J.H. McAlexander (2006), 'Claiming the throttle: multiple femininities in a hyper-masculine subculture', *Consumption, Markets and Culture*, **9** (3), 171–205.

Martinez, Katherine and Kenneth L. Ames (eds) (1997), *The Material Culture of Gender: The Gender of Material Culture*, Winterthur, DL: Henry Francis du Point Winterthur Museum.

Marx, Karl (1990), *Capital*, Vol. 1, New York, Penguin.

Mathews, Gordon and Tai-lok Lui (eds) (2001), *Consuming Hong Kong*, Hong Kong: University of Hong Kong Press.

Mauch, Charles (1983), *Too Much of Everything: A Plan for Living Better without Wealth or Excessive Material Possessions*, Dallas, TX: Moderation Press.

Mauss, Marcel (2001), *A General Theory of Magic*, trans. Robert Brain, London: Routledge.

Mayer-Schönberger, Viktor (2009), *Delete: The Virtue of Forgetting in the Digital Age*, Princeton, NJ: Princeton University Press.

Mazzarella, William (2003), *Shovelling Smoke: Advertising and Globalization in Contemporary India*, Durham, NC: Duke University Press.

McAlexander, J.H., J.W. Schouten, and H.J. Koening (2002), 'Building brand community', *Journal of Marketing*, **66** (January), 38–54.

McCracken, Grant (1988), *Culture and Consumption: New Approaches to the Symbolic Character of Consumer Goods and Activities*, Bloomington, IN: Indiana University Press.

McCracken, G. (1989), 'Who is the celebrity endorser? Cultural foundations of the endorsement process', *Journal of Consumer Research*, **16** (December), 310–321.

Mehta, R. and R. Belk (1991), 'Artifacts, identity, and transition: favorite possessions of Indians and Indian immigrants to the U.S.', *Journal of Consumer Research*, **17** (March), 398–411.

Miller, Daniel (ed.) (1998), *Material Cultures: Why Some Things Matter*, Chicago: University of Chicago Press.

Miller, Daniel (ed.) (2001a), *Home Possessions*, Oxford: Berg.

Miller, Daniel (2001b), 'Possessions', in Daniel Miller (ed.), *Home Possessions*, Oxford: Berg, 107–121.

Miller, Daniel (2008), *The Comfort of Things*, Cambridge: Polity.

Miller, Daniel (2010), *Stuff*, Cambridge: Polity Press.

Miller, Ian (1997), *The Anatomy of Disgust*, Cambridge, MA: Harvard University Press.

Mukerji, Chandra (1983), *From Gravel Images: Patterns of Modern Materialism*, New York: Columbia University Press.

Muñiz, A.M., Jr. and T.C. O'Guinn (2001), 'Brand community', *Journal of Consumer Research*, **27** (4), 412–432.

Muñiz, A.M., Jr. and H.J. Schau (2005), 'Religiosity in the abandoned Apple Newton brand community', *Journal of Consumer Research*, **35** (March), 737–747.

Pavitt, Jane (ed.) (2000), *Brand.New*, London: V&A Publications.

Pearce, Susan M. (1992), *Museum Objects and Collections: A Cultural Study*, Leicester, UK: Leicester University Press.

Petit, Michael (2006), '"Cleaned to eBay standards": sex panic, eBay, and the moral economy of underwear', in Ken Hillis and Michael Petit (eds), *Everyday eBay: Culture, Collecting, and Desire*, London: Routledge, pp. 267–281.

Pinches, Michael (ed.) (1999), *Culture and Privilege in Capitalist Asia*, London: Routledge.

Pottage, Alain (2001), 'Persons and things: an ethnographic analogy', *Economy and Society*, **30** (February), 112–138.

Radin, Margaret Jane (1996), *Contested Commodities: The Trouble with Trade in Sex, Children, Body Parts, and Other Things*, Cambridge, MA: Harvard University Press.

Rentfrew, P.J. and S.D. Gosling (2007), 'The content and validity of stereotypes of fans of 14 music genres', *Psychology of Music*, **35**, 306–326.

Richins, M. and S. Dawson (1992), 'A consumer values orientation for materialism and its measurement: scale development and validation', *Journal of Consumer Research*, **19**, 303–316.

Ridgeway, N., M. Kukar-Kenney, and K. Monroe (2008), 'Over-spending on pets: the relationship with excessive buying', *European Advances in Consumer Research*, **8**, 216–217.

Ritzer, George (1999), *Enchanting a Disenchanted World: Revolutionizing the Means of Consumption*, Thousand Oaks, CA: Pine Forge Press.

Roddenberry, Gene, dir. (1987), 'Star Trek: The Next Generation', television series, Hollywood, CA: Paramount.

Rook, Dennis (1985), 'Body cathexis and market segmentation', in Michael Solomon (ed.), *The Psychology of Fashion*, Lexington, MA: Lexington Press, pp. 233–242.

Rudmin, Floyd W. (ed.) (1991), *To Have Possessions: A Handbook on Ownership and Property*, Corte Madera, CA: Select Press.

Ruskin, John (1856), 'The pathetic fallacy', in *Modern Painters*, Vol. 3, see http://www.our-civilisation.com/smartboard/shop/ruskinj/.

Rydell, Robert W. (1984), *All the World's a Fair*, Chicago: University of Chicago Press.

Rydell, Robert W. (1993), *World of Fairs: The Century-of-Progress Expositions*, Chicago: University of Chicago Press.

Saint-Exupéry, Antoine de (2000), *The Little Prince*, trans. Richard Howard, San Francisco, CA: Harcourt.

Saisselin, Rémy G. (1985), *Bricabracomania: The Bourgeois and the Bibelot*, London: Thames and Hudson.

Sandvoss, Cornell (2005), *Fans*, Cambridge: Polity Press.

Sartre, Jean-Paul (1943), *Being and Nothingness: A Phenomenological Essay on Ontology*, New York: Philosophical Library.

Sassatelli, Roberta (2007), *Consumer Culture: History, Theory and Politics*, London: Sage.

Sayre, S. (1994), 'Possessions and identity in crisis: meaning and change for victims of the Oakland firestorm', *Advances in Consumer Research*, **21**, 109–114.

Scanlon, Jennifer (ed.) (2000), *Gender and Consumer Culture Reader*, New York: New York University Press.

Schama, Simon (1987), *The Embarrassment of Riches: An Interpretation of Dutch Culture in the Golden Age*, New York: Aldred A. Knopf.

Scheper-Hughes, Nancy and Loïc J.D. Wacquant (eds) (2002), *Commodifying Bodies*, London: Sage.

Schor, Juliet B. (1998), *The Overspent American: Upscaling, Downshifting, and the New Consumer*, New York: Basic Books.

Schor, Juliet B. and Douglas B. Holt (eds) (2000), *The Consumer Society Reader*, New York: The New Press.

Schouten, J.W. and J. McAlexander (1995), 'Subcultures of consumption: an ethnography of the new bikers', *Journal of Consumer Research*, **11** (June), 43–61.

Schouten, John W., Diane M. Martin, and James McAlexander (2007), 'The evolution of a subculture of consumption', in Bernard Cova, Robert Kozinets, and Avi Shankar (eds), *Consumer Tribes: Theory, Practice, and Prospects*, London: Elsevier/Butterworth-Heinemann.

Schroeder, Jonathan (2003), 'Building brands: architectural expression in the electronic age', in Linda M. Scott and Rajeev Batra (eds), *Persuasive Imagery: A Consumer Response Perspective*, Mahwah, NJ: Lawrence Erlbaum, pp. 349–382.

Schroeder, Jonathan E. and Miriam Salzer-Mörling (eds) (2006), *Brand Culture*, New York: Routledge.

Schwartz, Hillel (1998), *The Culture of the Copy: Striking Likenesses, Unreasonable Facsimiles*, New York: Zone Books.

Sheffield, Tricia (2006), *The Religious Dimensions of Advertising*, New York: Palgrave Macmillan.

Shelley, Mary Wollstonecraft ([1818]1999), *Frankenstein, or, The Modern Prometheus*, David Lorne Macdonald and Kathleen Scherf (eds), 2nd edn, Petersborough, ON: Broadview Press.

Shenkar, Oded (2010), *Copycats: How Smart Companies Use Imitation to Gain a Strategic Edge*, Cambridge, MA: Harvard Business Press.

Shildrick, Margrit (2002), *Embodying the Monster: Encounters with the Vulnerable Self*, London: Sage.

Shove, Elizabeth, Mathew Watson, Martin Hand, and Jack Ingram (2007), *The Design of Everyday Life*, Oxford: Berg.

Siegel, Lee (2008), *Against the Machine: How the Web is Reshaping Culture and Commerce—and Why it Matters*, New York: Spiegel and Grau.

Skal, David J. (2002), *Death Makes a Holiday: A Cultural History of Halloween*, New York: Bloomsbury.

Slater, Don (1997), *Consumer Culture and Modernity*, Cambridge: Polity.

Sobh, Rana, Russell Belk, and Justin Gressel (forthcoming), 'Conflicting imperatives of modesty and vanity among young women in the Arabian Gulf', *Advances in Consumer Research*.

Solomon, Michael and Punam Anand (1985), 'Ritual costumes and status transition: the female business suit as totemic emblem', *Advances in Consumer Research*, **12**, 315–318.

Sparke, Penny (1995), *As Long as it's Pink: The Sexual Politics of Taste*, London: Pandora.

Stallybrass, Peter (1998), 'Marx's overcoat', in Patricia Spyer (ed.), *Border Fetishisms: Material Objects in Unstable Spaces*, New York: Routledge, pp. 183–207.

Stan, Lavinia (ed.) (1997), *Romania in Transition*, Aldershot, UK: Dartmouth Publishing.

Stearns, Peter N. (2001), *Consumerism in World History: The Global Transformation of Desire*, London: Routledge.

Steffen, Jerome (1993), *The Tragedy of Abundance: Myth Restoration in American Culture*, Niwot, CO: University Press of Colorado.

Stewart, M. (1983), 'Loss of a pet—loss of a person: a comparative study of bereavement', in Aaron H. Katcher and Alan M. Beck (eds), *New Perspectives on Our Lives with Companion Animals*, Philadelphia, PA: University of Pennsylvania Press, pp. 390–404.

Stivers, Richard (2001), *Technology as Magic: The Triumph of the Irrational*, New York: Continuum.

Stone, Deborah (2005), 'For love or money: the commodification of care', in Martha Ertman and Joan Williams (eds), *Rethinking Commodification: Cases and Readings in Law and Culture*, New York: New York University Press, pp. 271–290.

Strasser, Susan, Charles McGovern, and Matthias Judt (eds) (1998), *Getting and Spending: European and American Consumer Societies in the Twentieth Century*, Cambridge: Cambridge University Press.

Szasz, Kathleen (1968), *Petishism Pets and Their People in the Western World*, New York: Holt, Rinehart and Winston.

Taussig, Michael (1993), *Mimesis and Alterity: A Particular History of the Senses*, London: Routledge.

Thorndike, Lynn (1958), *A History of Magic and Experimental Science during the First Thirteen Centuries*, Vol. 1, New York: Macmillan, p. 188.

Tian, K. and R. Belk (2005), 'Extended self and possessions in the workplace', *Journal of Consumer Research*, **32** (September), 297–310.

Tilley, Chris, Webb Keane, Susanne Küchler, Mike Rowlands, and Patricia Spyer (eds), (2006), *Handbook of Material Culture*, London: Sage.

Tintner, A.R. (1984), 'The disappearing furniture in Maupassant's "Qui Sait?" and *The Spoils of Poynton*', *The Henry James Review*, **6** (1), 3–7.

Turing, Alan (1950), 'Computing machinery and intelligence', *Mind*, **59** (October), 433–460.

Turkle, Sherry (1984), *The Second Self: Computers and the Human Spirit*, New York: Simon and Schuster.

Turkle, Sherry (2007), *Evocative Objects: Things We Think With*, Cambridge, MA: MIT Press.

Turkle, Sherry (2011), *Alone Together: Why We Expect More from Technology and Less from Each Other*, New York: Basic Books.

Twitchell, James B. (1999), *Lead Us Into Temptation: The Triumph of American Materialism*, New York: Columbia University Press.

Twitchell, James B. (2004), *Branded: The Marketing of Megachurch, College, Inc., and Museum World*, New York: Simon and Schuster.

Vaidhyanathan, Siva (2001), *Copyrights and Copywrongs: The Rise of Intellectual Property and How it Threatens Creativity*, New York: New York University Press.

Van Boven, L., M. Campbell, and T. Gilovich (2010), 'Stigmatizing materialism: on stereotypes and impressions of materialistic versus experiential pursuits', *Personality and Social Psychology Bulletin,* **36**, 551–563.

Venkatesh, A., E. Karababa, and G. Ger (2002), 'The emergence of the posthuman consumer and the fusion of the virtual and the real: a critical analysis of Sony's ad for Memory Stick™', *Advances in Consumer Research*, **29**, 446–452.

Verdery, K. and C. Humphrey (eds) (2004), *Property in Question: Value Transformation in the Global Economy*, Oxford: Berg.

Verhoeven, Paul, dir. (1987), *Robocop*, Hollywood, CA: MGM, 102 minutes.

Wachtel, Paul L. (1989), *The Poverty of Affluence: A Psychological Portrait of the American Way of Life*, Philadelphia, PA: New Society Publishers.

Wallendorf, M. and E.J. Arnould (1988), '"My Favorite Things": a cross-cultural inquiry into object attachment, possessiveness, and social linkage', *Journal of Consumer Research*, **14** (March), 531–547.

Wang, Jing (2008), *Brand New China: Advertising, Media, and Commercial Culture*, Cambridge, MA: Harvard University Press.

Wardlow, Daniel L. (1996), *Gays, Lesbians, and Consumer Behavior: Theory, Practice, and Research Issues in Marketing*, New York: Haworth.

Watson, James L. (ed.) (1997), *Golden Arches East: McDonald's in East Asia*, Stanford, CA: Stanford University Press.

Watson, Lyall (1990), *The Nature of Things: The Secret Life of Inanimate Objects*, London: Hodder and Stoughton.

Webley, P., S. Lea, and R. Portalska (1983), 'The social unacceptability of money as a gift', *Journal of Economic Psychology*, **4** (September).

Weizenbaum, J. (1966), 'ELIZA—a computer program for the study of natural language communication between man and machine', *Communication for the ACM*, **9** (January), 36–45.

Whybrow, Peter C. (2005), *American Mania: When More is Not Enough*, New York: W.W. Norton.

Wicklund, Robert A. and Peter M. Gollwitzer (1982), *Symbolic Self Completion*, Hillsdale, NJ: Lawrence Erlbaum.

Winnicott, D.W. (1953), 'Transitional objects and transitional phenomena', *International Journal of Psychoanalysis*, **34**, 89–97.

Wolfenstein, Martha (1957), *Disaster: A Psychological Essay*, Glencoe, IL: The Free Press.

Wuthnow, Robert (ed.) (1995), *Rethinking Materialism: Perspectives on the Spiritual Dimension of Economic Behavior*, Grand Rapids, MI: William B. Eerdsman.

Yeh, Wen-Hsin (2007), *Shanghai Splendor: Economic Sentiments and the Making of Modern China, 1843–1949*, Berkeley, CA: University of California Press.

Young, Melissa and Melanie Wallendorf (1989), 'Ashes to ashes, dust to dust: conceptualizing dispossession of possessions', *American Marketing Association Winter Educator's Conference Proceedings*, Chicago: American Marketing Association.

Zelizer, Viviana A. (1985), *Pricing the Priceless Child: The Changing Social Value of Children*, New York: Basic Books.

Zelizer, Viviana A. (1994), *The Social Meanings of Money: Pin Money, Paychecks, Poor Relief, and Other Currencies*, New York: Basic Books.

Zelizer, Viviana A. (2005), *The Purchase of Intimacy*, Princeton, NJ: Princeton University Press.

3 Culture and consumer behavior: contextual and compositional components
C. Samuel Craig and Susan P. Douglas

3.1 INTRODUCTION

Cultures around the world are many, diverse, multifaceted, and changing. Certain elements of culture are malleable and others are highly resistant to change. While the pace of change has accelerated due to modern technology and increased mobility, there is an ethnie core (Naroll 1970) that remains more or less constant. This provides an enduring core, although at times it may be obscured by external changes. For example, adoption of Western modes of dress or acceptance of US fast food might suggest an embrace of Western values. However, these external trappings may simply mask deep seated traditional values that are firmly rooted in the culture and highly resistant to change. Thus, the challenge is often to separate extraneous elements and determine culture's role in shaping behavior.

The most visible manifestations of culture are often the cultural artifacts that members of the culture create and consume such as food, clothing, entertainment, housing, and personal possessions. Equally important are the values and beliefs that sustain the culture and the language that facilitates communications and helps bind a particular culture together. Collectively, they create an enduring legacy of traditions and customs handed down from generation to generation. At the same time, members of a particular culture are exposed to elements of other cultures through mass media, the internet, or personal contact. These links to other cultures have the potential to alter an existing culture, either enriching it or diminishing it, depending on one's point of view.

In the exploration of culture and its various manifestations, the country has often been viewed as the relevant unit to study culture and inferences are made about culture based on values, socio-cultural norms, lifestyles, consumption and behavior patterns observed within a country. Equally, prototypical patterns of consumption and purchase decision-making associated with a member of that country have been identified (Barzini 1983). Culture has been viewed in terms of national culture, and cultural boundaries are seen as synonymous with political boundaries (Clark 1990). This raises the question of whether country fully defines culture and the nature of cultural influences. Examination of American culture, for example, neglects regional differences in behavior patterns (Vandello and Cohen 1999), or differences between ethnic subgroups, such as Asian Americans or Hispanic Americans.

In an era of globalization, the patterning of culture and its influences have become increasingly complex. Expanding networks of intra-personal and mass communications, spawned by rapid advances in technology and the internet have changed territorially based notions of culture (Hermans and Kempen 1998). Members of different cultural groupings are moving from one country to another, bringing with them their interests, values, and distinctive behavior patterns and intermingling with each other, thus further clouding the spatial and social boundaries of culture (Andreasen 1990).

As a result, the traditional concept of culture as consisting of static, delimited and homogeneous entities is evolving towards a more fluid concept of culture consisting of geographically dispersed, but interlinked entities (Hermans and Kempen 1998). Cultural interpenetration causes cultural boundaries to be porous and mutable so that geographic locality is less critical in defining cultural groupings. The distinctive traits and artifacts of a culture may become less clearly distinguished and become blended with one another in a process of cultural fusion, leading in some instances to the emergence of a global culture. This also dramatically changes consumption patterns, often resulting in greater similarity, at least among certain groups, e.g. teens.

The increasing complexity of cultural patterning suggests the need for a fresh look at the concept of culture and its various manifestations. This should go beyond traditional perspectives of culture as localized homogeneous sub-groupings or ethnie cores (Hermans and Kempen 1998; Naroll 1970) to a clearer understanding of its multi-faceted, multi-layered character (see also Leung et al. 2005). In particular, greater attention needs to be paid to the distinction between the contextual and compositional components of culture and how they are intertwined and influence behavior, as well as how they are continually changing and evolving. Research typically focuses on examining compositional elements of culture or examining variation in compositional elements as a function of variation in context (see Berry 1975, 2001 and Georgas et al. 2004). On a more macro level, scholars such as Pieterse (2009), Featherstone (1990), and Hermans and Kempen (1998) look broadly at the influence of globalization of culture.

The purpose of this chapter is to develop a more thorough understanding of the complexity of cultural influences in an increasingly multi-cultural environment. First, the way in which culture has been examined in marketing is discussed, together with the implied or underlying concept of culture focusing on the distinction between contextual and compositional views of culture. Next, the various components of culture are discussed, as well as the interaction between contextual and compositional elements. Finally, implications and conclusions are drawn.

3.2 CULTURE AND MARKETING

The most fundamental question is, what is culture? Kroeber and Kluckhohn (1952) in their classic review of culture in the Peabody Papers listed over 160 different definitions of culture, and were sufficiently dissatisfied with all of them to add one of their own. Of all these definitions, perhaps the most widely accepted is that given by E.B. Tylor (1881) who described culture as "that complex whole which includes knowledge, belief, art, morals, law, custom, and any other capabilities and habits acquired by man as a member of society," (p. 1) or as later synthesized by Herskovits (1955), as the man-made part of the environment—i.e. what distinguishes humans from other species. Consumer researchers have largely followed this view of culture. McCracken (1986) adopts an all-encompassing view of culture, defining it as the "lens through which the individual views phenomena" (p. 72). As such, it determines how individuals perceive and interpret phenomena, provides the "blueprint" of human activity, helps determines social action and productive activity, and specifies the behaviors and objects that issue from both.

In marketing, as throughout the social sciences, the study of culture has been approached in a number of different ways. At least six major threads, each incorporating different conceptualizations of culture, can be identified. These differ essentially in terms of their perspective and explicit or implicit definition of culture. They fall into two main categories: contextual and compositional (see Figure 3.1). Contextual perspectives typically view dimensions of culture in terms of physical space with established boundaries that separate cultural entities. Compositional perspectives on the other hand, focus on the components of culture within that physical space. The two views are closely intertwined. The context exerts influence on the composition and the compositional elements are embedded in the context. An element that is compositional in one instance, can become contextual in another. For example, the retail infrastructure provides the context in which purchasing takes place, but its design, form and function can also be interpreted as a compositional element of culture.

Of the six perspectives on culture, the most significant, particularly in studies comparing consumer behavior in different parts of the world, is the view of culture as contextual and synonymous with country. Here, membership in a culture is defined by nationality (Clark 1990; Nakata and

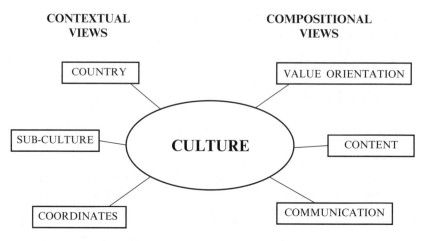

Figure 3.1   Perspectives on culture

Sivakumar 1996; Shimp and Sharma 1987). A second contextual perspective centers on specific cultural groups or market segments, for example, ethnic linguistic or demographic groupings within or across national boundaries (Penaloza 1994; Mehta and Belk 1991; Hassan and Katsansis 1994). The values, attitudes and lifestyle patterns of these groups are viewed as a sub-culture within a larger cultural entity. The third perspective looks at context independent from political boundaries and considers context simply as where people live based on geographic coordinates (Parker 1997; Parker and Tavassoli 2000).

There are also three distinct streams focusing on the compositional elements of culture. Value orientation has been the central construct in understanding and defining culture (Aaker and Maheswaran 1997; Aaker 2000). This perspective, grounded in psychology, has focused on examining cognition and cognitive processes and the universality of models and conceptual frameworks developed in one society or culture in another. Another compositional perspective is rooted in semiotics and anthropological traditions (Tse et al. 1989; Arnould 1989; Holt 1998; Wallendorf and Arnould 1988). This focuses on components of culture, such as consumption rites, cultural symbols, cultural meaning and knowledge. Finally, culture has also been studied as communication, centering on the specific communication systems used within a culture, as well as the role of language (Schmitt and Zhang 1998; Schmitt et al. 1994). Each of these perspectives, focusing either on contextual or compositional elements of culture is rooted in a different research tradition. As such, each provides a unique and distinct perspective and insights into a facet of culture.

3.2.1   Contextual Views of Culture

3.2.1.1   Culture as country

The largest body of research has either explicitly or implicitly viewed culture as synonymous with country, and hence equates cultural boundaries with political entities. In these studies, the country is used as the geographic unit or domain to define the boundaries of cultural context. The country becomes the spatial unit in relation to which samples are drawn, surveys or experiments designed and inferences made about similarities and differences.

As a political and organizational entity, the country provides a practical and convenient unit for data collection. Most secondary and industry data are available on a country-by-country basis. Countries also provide distinctive linguistic entities and have official languages. In addition, as countries are customarily used as the unit of analysis, findings can be related to and interpreted in the light of previous research.

Early comparative studies (Green and Langeard 1975) *implicitly* equated "culture" with country without any explicit operationalization of cultural variables or influences. Without a clear articulation of culture, interpretation of findings is problematic. For example, differences and similarities observed between countries are attributed to "culture" and interpreted in the light of national stereotypes or knowledge about a country or "culture". Results are thus idiosyncratic to the specific countries compared and generalizability to other countries or cultures is problematic.

The country or nation state has been used to define the context of culture and constructs such as national character (Clark 1990), national culture (Nakata and Sivakumar 1996), consumer ethnocentrism (Shimp and Sharma 1987), and animosity (Klein et al. 1998). Alternatively, such variables may be used as a moderating factor on consumer behavior in studies of innovative behavior (Steenkamp et al. 1999) and new product development (Song and Perry 1997).

The concept of national character has its origins in cultural anthropology and personality research (Inkeles and Levinson 1969). In cultural anthropology, interest in the study of deviant behavior led to the recognition that the fulfillment of cultural imperatives was dependent on an individual's internalization of cultural values and his/her learning of appropriate behavior. As a result, an individual's personality came to be seen as an expression of culture, sparking interest in the relation of culture and personality. Benedict (1934) was one of the first to point out the link between culture and personality, arguing that unique cultural configurations produced group and individual personality types. This work received considerable impetus during World War II as anthropologists, psychoanalysts and others attempted to understand the psychology of different nations, and particularly enemies of the US (Adorno et al. 1950). In this tradition, Barzini's (1983) studies in various European countries developed stereotypical portraits of Italians, Germans and French, etc.

Nations are, however, not necessarily comparable entities with regard to aspects such as the nature of their linguistic and cultural heritage, which may influence their cultural patterning. Particularly problematic is the situation where countries appear appropriate entities, for example, in terms of Individualism or Collectivism but are not comparable with regard to another aspect, for example, the degree of linguistic fragmentation or proliferation of ethnic groupings that may influence culture. Many international marketing studies examine attitudes such as nationalism and ethnocentrism within the context of large industrialized countries with large internal markets (Netemeyer et al. 1991; Klein et al. 1998). Findings may not be readily generalized to small open societies, which have high levels of external trade and communication (Nijssen and Douglas 2004).

3.2.1.2   Culture as sub-culture

Sub-cultures, such as ethnic, sociodemographic or other groupings exist within countries and often have their own distinctive interests, consumption and purchasing behavior patterns. For example, Mexican Americans (Penaloza 1994) and Indian immigrants to the US (Mehta and Belk 1991) have all been found to have interest in specific product attributes, brands or product categories, as well as to use different distribution outlets.

In Canada, differences have been identified among different linguistic groupings (Schaninger et al. 1985). Francophones, for example, tend to be more introspective, emotional and humanistic and less materialistic than Anglophones (Heon 1999). Anglophones were also found to be less innovative and fashion conscious, and rely less on opinion leadership, while demonstrating greater price consciousness, and brand loyalty (Hui et al. 1993; Mallen 1977). Differences in search behavior for gifts between Anglophones and Francophones have also been identified (Laroche et al. 2000).

Studies of consumer acculturation of different immigrant groups typically reveal a complex pattern of transition and trade-offs (Penaloza 1994). Mexican immigrants, for example, tend to adopt food, clothing and language of their host culture in certain situational contexts such as at home, at work and in schools, to facilitate assimilation and relations with others. Yet, they also maintain ties to their culture and families through foods they prepare, use of Spanish media and their choice of leisure activities.

Examination of favorite possessions of Indian immigrants and of Italian households in Montreal also illustrates the importance placed on maintaining ties to the home cultures (Mehta and Belk 1991; Joy et al. 1995) For example, Indian household shrines, as well as Indian music and videos serve as a connection to India and provide a sense of cultural identity and security. The favorite possessions of Indian households also emphasize commonality over individuality as seen in family photographs, Indian foods and artifacts from India (Mehta and Belk 1991). At the same time, conspicuous consumption and possession of material goods, such as a large house or car, suggest an emphasis on materialism and material possessions more commonly associated with American values.

These studies typically provide vignettes of the lifestyles and behavior patterns of each sub-culture. While providing a rich description and insights into a particular context, they provide limited ability to generalize to other contexts. In addition, sub-cultures evolve over time as individuals move from one place to another and progress through the life cycle, marrying or interacting with members of other cultures. As a result, boundaries become amorphous and it becomes difficult to define membership in a sub-culture or to isolate the influencing factors.

3.2.1.3 Culture as coordinates

The most direct examination of culture as context is research that examines the effect of geographic location on culture. These studies (Parker 1997; Parker and Tavassoli 2000) consider the role of the physio-economic environment in determining cultural variation in behavior, and particularly consumption patterns. According to this view, the physio-economic environment, which encompasses both abiotic factors, such as climate and terrain, as well as biotic factors, such as flora and fauna, are forces behind physiological and physiographic mechanisms that result in variation from one culture to another. In particular, such mechanisms result in differences in homeothermic consumption such as dressing behavior, caloric intake, energy and architectural design as well as nonhomeothermic consumption such as food, medicine, leisure, art and entertainment. Equally, climate and terrain are viewed as shaping social processes and economic activity that in turn influence cognitive maps and cognitive styles.

This approach is highly consistent with Berry's eco-cultural framework (Berry 1976; Berry 2001), which views cultural adaptation as interacting with both the ecological system and the sociopolitical system (Mishra et al. 1996). Ecological and sociopolitical influences are not deterministic, but rather follow a pattern of mutual adaptation in which changes in one part follow changes in other parts. In essence, the ecological situation and sociopolitical factors affect psychological outcomes through a dual process of acculturation and adaptation. On the one hand, human organisms interact with and adapt to their physical environment in order to satisfy their needs. On the other hand, cultural change occurs through sociopolitical institutions, such as education and employment that alter extant cultural patterns. Physio-economic theory (Parker 2000), on the other hand, appears to neglect this dual process, and especially the role of sociopolitical variables such as education in understanding cultural patterning. As such, it highlights key and often neglected variables, and illustrates the importance of considering the context in which individuals live.

3.2.2   Compositional Views of Culture

3.2.2.1   Culture as value orientation
Culture as value orientation, typically characterized in terms of Individualism/ Collectivism has been the primary focus of a compositional approach that has generated significant amounts of research. This has also been a key theme in cross-cultural research in psychology and social psychology (Triandis 1995; Oysermann et al. 2002). Countries are selected as exemplars of either individualist or collectivist societies and cognitive processes or behavior patterns of respondents in two or more countries compared. A key objective is to determine whether cognitive processes and constructs typically identified in an individualist society, such as the US, can be generalized to collectivist societies such as Hong Kong, Taiwan or Japan. In general, Individualism/Collectivism has been found to have moderate effects on self-concept and relationality and strong effects on attribution and cognitive style (Oysermann et al. 2002).

In marketing, cultural orientation has been studied primarily in relation to marketing communications and cognitive processes to them. Differences have been found between individualist and collectivist societies in relation to the influence of consensus information on product evaluation (Aaker and Maheswaran 1997), information content in advertising (Hong et al. 1987) emotional appeals in advertising (Aaker and Williams 1998) and in the accessibility or diagnosticity of persuasion appeals (Aaker 2000). These studies suggest the existence of major differences in the salience of appeals between individualist and collectivist societies (i.e. importance of the individual relative to the group).

Other scholars have identified specific value orientations in society. In their classic study, Kluckhohn and Strodtbeck (1961) identified four value orientations, man's relation to nature, time dimension, personal activity and others, which form the basis for the development of culture. The work of Hofstede has been particularly influential in the study of values and culture. He developed a schema of national culture based on an extensive study of work related goals and value patterns of managers in a large multi-national company (Hofstede 2001). He identified four dimensions: Power Distance, or acceptance of inequality in power in society; Individualism, or emphasis on self-interest and immediate family vs. collective goals; Uncertainty Avoidance, or society's tendency to cope with unstructured situations by developing strict codes of behavior; and Masculinity vs. Femininity, or the extent to which society values goals perceived as masculine, such as competition, vs. goals perceived as feminine, such as nurturing. These four dimensions are postulated to represent the collective patterning of the mind, and to constitute fundamental value orientations that underlie differences in managerial practices, organizational patterns and decision-making. This was subsequently expanded to a fifth dimension, Long-term Orientation, to encompass elements of Asian culture (Hofstede and Bond 1988).

While cultural value orientations tap a central dimension of cultural variation and provide a highly parsimonious approach to studying culture, they constitute broad societal constructs which do not reflect more nuanced aspects or process-oriented aspects of society or the importance of contextual variables in influencing behavior and cognition (Miller 2002; Oysermann et al. 2002). In particular, they ignore differences among individuals in the extent to which they subscribe to the dominant societal cultural orientation as well as the extent to which cultural influences may be activated in a given situation (Briley et al. 2000). It has, therefore, been argued that a dynamic constructionist view of culture should be adopted, which focuses on identifying specific knowledge structures or implicit cultural theories that mediate social behavior in specific domains (Hong and Chiu 2001).

3.2.2.2 Culture as content

Each culture has its own vision of the world and set of culturally constituted meanings that provide understanding and rules for its members while being unintelligible to others. Within this stream, McCracken's work provides a framework for understanding the cultural meaning of consumer goods and consumption patterns (McCracken 1986; Applebaum and Jordt 1996) and identifies cultural categories of time, space, nature and person as the fundamental coordinates of meaning that organize the phenomenal world. A key mechanism framing interpretation of consumption is advertising in a society, which serves as a conduit through which viewers or readers are informed of the meaning of consumer goods (Tse et al. 1989; Belk and Pollay 1985).

Rituals associated with consumption behavior, or specific consumption occasions provide insights into the way in which consumer goods are embedded in and form an integral part of the cultural fabric of society (Arnould 1989; Belk et al. 1989). For example, rituals and behavior associated with gift-giving are an important element in promoting social ties and bonding between individuals in a culture (Joy 2001; Sherry 1983; Carrier 1991). Studies of diffusion patterns and favorite objectives also underscore differences in preference formation from one culture to another and hence the importance of understanding cultural specific factors underlying diffusion patterns in a society (Wallendorf and Arnould 1988).

These studies generate a rich understanding of consumption phenomena at a particular site, especially in terms of product use and symbolism. However, to the extent that the unit of analysis is a specific cultural context, generalizations to a broader context, and implicit comparisons with regard to other cultures, are difficult to make. As a result, integration of findings relating to specific sites into a broader understanding of cultural influences on consumption, and of the significance and meaning of these influences across multiple sites or cultural contexts is somewhat problematic. Ultimately, much depends on how sites are selected, and the cultural components being studied.

3.2.2.3   Culture as communication

The view of culture as content focuses on interpreting the role of artifacts and the meanings consumers ascribe to them. Closely related to this is research that examines the meaning and implications of language as an interpretation of culture. While both streams may end up examining similar stimuli, the focus is different. Content studies examine the role and meaning of an object as it is used by consumers. For example, favorite objects of specific cultural groups, such as the Hansa, have been studied (Arnould 1989). Communication studies, on the other hand, examine the use of objects and language as conveyors of culture, as for example the use of ideographic writing systems in brand recall (Schmitt et al. 1994).

Language has many facets that relate to the meaning of consumer products. Linguistic structure plays an important role in the formation of cognitive processes, such as perception and hence judgment and choice (Schmitt and Zhang 1998), as well as in brand recall and recognition (Schmitt et al. 1994) and the encoding and recall of information (Tavassoli 1999). Equally, foreign language and loanwords can help in establishing the identity of a local (indigenous) product (Sherry and Camargo 1987). Use of a minority sub-culture's language in advertising (Koslow et al. 1994) has also been found to impact consumer response. Examination of how bilinguals process information in advertisements further demonstrates the importance of language in message recall (Luna and Peracchio 2001). Language is shown to be an important thread of culture not only in communication within a culture, but also in categorizing cultural content and in retaining information relating to that culture.

While language is a key element of culture it provides only one aspect of communication in a culture. In addition, visual expression, gestures and signs are often important elements of communication, particularly in certain types of cultures (Hall 1976). Both language and visual modes of communication play an important role in social communication and issues, such as message interpretation or misinterpretation which merit further attention, particularly in relation to communications between cultures.

Each of the six perspectives provides its own distinctive aperture framed by a different lens into the many intertwined facets of culture. Whether contextual or compositional, each perspective is rooted in a specific research tradition reflecting a concern or focus on a particular aspect of culture. As a result, any one perspective provides only a partial glimpse that fails to capture the full richness of cultural influences. As a consequence, findings are often interpreted in terms of a single perspective, ignoring other possible interpretations or insights. Incorporating both contextual and compositional facets simultaneously is essential to develop a deeper understanding of culture and the myriad ways in which it shapes and influences behavior.

3.3   COMPOSITIONAL AND CONTEXTUAL ELEMENTS OF CULTURE

The numerous ways in which culture has been viewed, the complexity of cultural influences, and the diverse ways in which culture is changing suggest the need to adopt a broader perspective. Specifically, it should be expansive enough to encompass both contextual and compositional elements. This perspective should capture the richness and diversity of these different aspects of culture and their influence, as well as providing a view of culture that can be applied meaningfully to marketing and consumption situations. To begin with, the three main compositional elements of culture should be included: (1) the abstract or intangible elements of culture, such as values and belief systems, (2) the material aspects such as artifacts, symbols and rites, and (3) the communication links which bind and perpetuate a cultural system. At the same time an attempt needs to be made to control for or account for the influence of a particular context as in turn these compositional elements are influenced by the context in which a particular culture exists.

The dual links between the contextual and compositional elements of culture with each influencing the other is shown in Figure 3.2. What is not shown, but can be of great importance, is the impact of the compositional

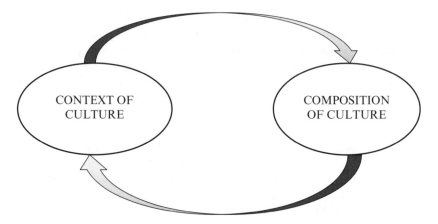

Figure 3.2   Interplay of the context and composition of culture

elements of one culture on the compositional elements of another. This has been examined indirectly in the literature on sub-culture where the changes in the consumption patterns of a particular immigrant population are examined (Penaloza 1994). Also, the role that immigrants play in American culture has been examined, primarily in terms of the immigrants' degree of assimilation and contribution to aspects of society (see Koven 2010). However, more broadly this influence is occurring through mass media, entertainment such as movies and television, travel and the internet. These multiple influences mean that the proximate context continues to exert influence on the compositional elements of culture, but that increasingly a "virtual" context exists. The exact nature of virtual context is more difficult to discern and can be different for individuals living in the same locale depending on their exposure to these different elements.

Differential exposure to compositional elements outside of a particular culture presents both conceptual and methodological issues, particularly when the researcher is attempting to establish reasonably pure measures of culture attributable to a particular locale. On a conceptual level it is difficult to determine whether the responses to survey questions reflect only the values and beliefs historically associated with the indigenous people or also include values and beliefs that have infiltrated the local culture through travel, mass media, entertainment content or the internet. Thus, there is always the possibility that any measures may reflect some degree of contamination from other cultures. The most direct way to deal with the issue is to collect additional information on the degree of exposure to outside influences. This information can then be used to split the sample into two groups, high and low exposure to external influences. If there are significant differences in values and beliefs between the two groups then less confidence can be placed in the purity of the cultural measures obtained. Alternatively, the degree of exposure to external elements can be used directly in the analysis. If the variable is significant, it would suggest that there is cultural contamination as well. Here it is important to add control variables, such as the age of the respondent, to be certain that some other variable is not responsible for the observed difference. Also, in both instances, there may be self-selection issues. Individuals who more strongly hold the traditional values of a particular culture, may avoid exposure to outside influences. At the same time, individuals who feel less strongly about the prevailing cultural values are somewhat more likely to seek and be receptive to outside influences.

Douglas and Craig (1997) suggest a number of approaches to obtain analytically purer measures of cultural values and beliefs or at least identifying whether there are significant external influences. To begin with, the unit of analysis should be a "culti-unit" which is a small, relatively homogeneous unit that is likely to contain the ethnie core of a particular culture. Further, definition of the culti-unit should be consistent with the view that transmission of a collective cultural identity requires a sense of common destiny to endure (Smith 1990). The small nature of the culti-unit helps deal with the problem of within-country heterogeneity, as small proximate units are likely to be more uniform. Conducting multi-site studies with multiple culti-units allows the researcher to compare results across culti-units. Consistent results across multiple sites increases confidence that the results reflect the ethnie core of a culture. While multiple sites within a country help the researcher have more confidence in the results if there is consistency across all the sites, lack of consistency is open to multiple interpretations. It could reflect widespread cultural contamination to varying degrees, making it difficult to tease out the ethnie core. Alternatively, it may reflect contextual differences between culti-unit sites. In large countries such as China, India, Russia and the US, there are marked differences across the countries. Cui and Liu (2000) found significant differences throughout China and identified seven regional markets. While many of the differences related to demographics, leisure pursuits, appliance ownership, and consumption preferences, there were also significant differences in values and beliefs across the seven regions.

A second approach is to conduct studies that focus on assessing external cultural influences. Here context may be held constant and the extent of exposure to the virtual context assessed. The research would determine whether any observed differences appear to be associated with greater exposure to influences from outside the culture being studied. Exposure could be direct, through travel or living in another country for a period of time or indirect through exposure to entertainment, mass media and internet content that originates from outside a specific culture. The same result could be obtained through a longitudinal study, but significantly more time and expense is required to complete the study.

A third way to examine the influence of context is through transitional studies that examine individuals who have moved from their home culture to another macro-culture. Insights can be gained from studying multiple groups of immigrants who settled in different macro-cultures. Similarities in values and beliefs would be attributed to the home context and represent the ethnie core of that culture, while differences would be attributed to the new macro-context. Comparisons could also be made with individuals who remained in the home country. However, those who chose to leave the home country may already be systematically different on a number of attitudinal variables and observed differences may be misleading.

All three approaches start with clearly defined culti-units to reduce heterogeneity and help rule out alternative explanations. By focusing on the culti-unit, insights can be gained into not only the ethnie core of a particular culture, but also the influence of context. Obviously, if the context is static, it is difficult if not impossible to disentangle the impact of context. However, with migration becoming more common and an ever expanding virtual context, there are increasing opportunities to assess the impact of context on culture.

Incorporating context is not the only issue. In the past, the three compositional elements, intangibles, artifacts and communication links have often been examined independently or attention focused on a single element. They are, however, closely intertwined. Communication provides a means of transmitting some of the intangible aspects of culture, such as values and beliefs from one person to another or from one generation to another. This communication process is inherently dynamic and at the same time continually evolving. Artifacts ranging from religious icons to shoes or clothing may also be expressions of intangible beliefs, and at the same time designate membership in a particular culture.

In the global teen culture, media advertising and the internet, as well as movies, music and magazines communicate shared values such as individualism, independence and self-reliance. Items of apparel, such as jeans, athletic shoes, baseball caps, smart phones, jewelry, and watches symbolize their membership in this global culture. At the same time, communications, such as advertising or television shows, will both reflect and influence cultural values. For example, Nike advertising targeted at teens in the US emphasizes sports and stresses individualistic values and competitiveness, core values of US teen culture. The same advertising aimed at teens in collectivist societies that emphasize relations and interaction with others, suggests and instills new values and may gradually change core beliefs to resemble those of their peers in the Western world.

In examining teen or any other culture, it is critical to examine all three elements, intangibles, artifacts and communication in order to understand their interaction and consider the context in which it occurs. Emphasis on a single element, for example artifacts, neglects the critical role of intangibles and communication links in perpetuating and sustaining the essence of a culture. Further, efforts need to be made to expand the notion of context to incorporate the influence of the virtual context.

3.3.1   Cultural Intangibles

The intangible elements of culture incorporate the dominant societal values and belief systems that characterize a society or culture and guide the patterning of behavior in that society. Here, it is important to consider the layering or patterning of beliefs and value-systems as well as their scope or relevance to a particular behavior or consumption situation. Value-systems can be examined at the level of the society, specific groups or organizations within society, as well as at the individual level (i.e. personal values). Equally, values may be general value orientations, relating to time, behavior towards others, concepts of self or alternatively relative to specific areas or domains of life, e.g. work, leisure, relations to others, or to specific consumption or purchase situations, i.e. a gift, a consumer durable, a family purchase, or for oneself.

At the aggregate or societal level, as noted earlier, the most widely cited schema for characterizing values is that developed by Hofstede (2001). An alternative schema, grounded in Rokeach's Value Survey, was developed by Schwarz (1992). Schwarz grouped values into value types according to the underlying motivational goals. Reasoning that basic human values would be found in all cultures, he identified ten value types that formed an integrated motivational structure. He then developed a survey consisting of 56 values tapping into these value types, which after data collection in 54 countries were reduced to 45. These remaining values were then used to form indexes that could be used to measure the importance of each value type in a culture, and also to measure individual differences in values (Schwarz and Bilsky 1996).

At the societal level these value types were grouped into three cultural dimensions: Conservatism vs. Autonomy, Hierarchy vs. Egalitarianism, and Mastery vs. Harmony. While Schwarz viewed his approach as distinctly different from that of Hofstede, there are some strong underlying similarities. The first two dimensions closely resemble the Individualism-Collectivism and the Power Distance value-orientations while Mastery vs. Harmony parallel Hofstede's Masculinity/Feminity dimensions. The similarities between the two-value schemas provide further support for their validity as dominant value structures, which exist across societies. Other approaches have examined a specific value orientation, as for example materialism or time orientation, comparing two or more societies on this dimension (Belk and Pollay 1985). Typically this is then linked to some aspect of behavior, as for example the importance attached to material possessions and lifestyle activities (Dawson and Bamossy 1990).

The GLOBE project (House et al. 2004) involved 170 different researchers in 62 different societies. Data were gathered from 17,300 middle managers in 951 different organizations. The study is the most extensive of its type and provides insights into how leadership varies across cultural contexts. House and his colleagues (House et al. 2004) identified nine underlying cultural values. The nine dimensions are: (1) Power Distance, (2) Uncertainty Avoidance, (3) Humane Orientation, (4) Collectivism I (Institutional Collectivism), (5) Collectivism II (In-group collectivism), (6) Assertiveness, (7) Gender Egalitarianism, (8) Future Orientation, and (9) Performance Orientation. Some of the dimensions correlated with previous cultural studies, for example, Uncertainty Avoidance was correlated (.74) with Schwartz's Embeddedness, and Power Distance was correlated (.61) with Hofstede's Power Distance, although generally the GLOBE dimensions were not highly correlated with previous studies. The research provides insight into how different cultural contexts, defined in terms of national borders, influence leadership styles and effectiveness. The GLOBE study identified some characteristics of good leaders that are universal such as Trustworthy, Honest, and Decisive. Another group of characteristics are viewed as culturally contingent and are valued in certain cultures but not in others, such as Ambitious, Domineering, Risk Taker, and Self-effacing.

Attention has been focused on cultural intangibles at the societal level and their impact on individual behavior, however numerous other intangibles impact individual consumption patterns and ways of behaving. These include ideals and aspirations, role norms and gender ideology, cultural myths, metaphors and signs. Many of these intangibles have been examined, but primarily within a particular culture, not across cultures (see Stern 1995; Thompson 1997, 2004; Arnould and Thompson 2005). However, they do provide an indication of the richness and complexity of the relationship between culture and consumption. While complex and difficult to compare across cultures due to their subjective and existential nature, these are nonetheless key elements of culture that determine the patterning of daily life and of behavior as consumers.

3.3.2   Material Culture

Material culture incorporates the rituals, artifacts, institutions and symbols of a society that bind it together and establish rules and norms for behaving towards others within the society, either in general or on specific occasions, such as weddings, funerals, festivals, etc. The meaning and symbolism attached to individual possessions and goods owned by individuals, families or social groups and the significance attached to gifts and gift-giving rituals are also important elements of material culture. Consumption patterns also demarcate lifestyles and social class (Holt 1998).

The rituals and institutions established by a society are important indicators of the strength of cultural ties and the shared collective programming of a society. In Japan, for example, the existence of formal rituals and customs is an important element binding the society and ensuring harmonious relations among its members. In the US, on the other hand, the broad mix of cultures and national origins results in multiple and diverse cultural traditions and rituals, which often intermingle and blend into each other.

Gift giving has been one of the most extensively studied social rituals (Sherry 1983; Belk 1988a). Here, the practices surrounding the formalized nature of gift giving in Japan have been contrasted with gift-giving practices in other cultures. Equally, study of gift-giving practices in Hong Kong have revealed these to be embedded in particular socio-cultural practices which form a continuum from intimates to acquaintances (Joy 2001). In essence, therefore, each culture develops its own specific gift-giving practices incorporating ties of obligation and reciprocity consistent with the network of social relationships within the culture.

The meaning attached to possessions is another integral component of culture. Wallendorf and Arnould (1988) note "objects serve as the set and props on the theatrical stage of our lives" and as "markers to remind ourselves of who we are" (p. 531). Favorite objects serve as possessions that reflect local cultures, and as such different values and social structure. In the American South West favorite objects represent unique individual expressions of self or personal experiences, while in Niger they are fewer and more likely to represent links with other members of society, either of a co-operative (e.g. Koranic texts), or competitive nature (e.g. horses) (Wallendorf and Arnould 1988). While the specific favorite objects differ between cultures, attachment to objects as distinct from materialism is a pervasive phenomenon in all cultures.

Brands also serve as cultural markers. The meaning and set of associations surrounding a brand name and also a brand category may vary from one culture to another. For example, in some cultures foreign brands are prized as symbols of more affluent cultures, while in others they are viewed as inferior, or poor quality or morally inappropriate purchases (Shimp and Sharma 1987). The image or associations with brand names have also been found to vary from one culture to another (Aaker 2000). While in the US, McDonald's is viewed as ubiquitous low-priced fast food, in other cultures it is viewed as a luxury or treat, and a valued icon of Western lifestyle.

3.3.3   Cultural Links

Modes of communication, both verbal and non-verbal, are an integral part of culture (Hall 1969, 1973, 1976; Samovar and Porter 1994; Whorf 1956) and provide links within and across cultural units. Communication arises from the need to connect and interact with others and unites otherwise isolated individuals. Communication involves messages that are encoded and transmitted to others who decode them and respond accordingly.

Communication is thus a key element of culture as it provides a mechanism for transmitting and interpreting messages relating to the world around an individual. Communication takes place in a physical and social context such as time, location and the social relationship of the participants, as well as in relation to other competing messages (Hall 1973). All these influence and condition how a communication is received. Members of a culture share a common key for interpreting their social surroundings, which establishes rules for governing the interaction. Members of different cultures may not know how to interpret these signs, resulting in miscommunication.

Language is a key component of communication since it provides a mechanism for encoding and decoding messages. A shared language is thus a key factor unifying members of a common culture. Language provides an organizing schema for interpreting and understanding the world. The Sapir Whorf hypothesis, for example, postulates that language plays an important role in the formation of thought patterns and behavioral response as well as in the transmission of cultural norms and behavior patterns from one generation to another (Whorf 1956). For example, Eskimos have several words for snow to reflect different types of snow, and in the UK there are multiple words for different types of rain.

Modes of non-verbal communication such as gestures, posture and movement, use of space or time, and eye contact, are also critical elements of communication and interpretation (Hall 1969, 1973). Often these differ from culture to culture. For example, a smile may be used to hide embarrassment in Asian cultures, rather than indicating pleasure or amusement as in the West. Equally, the appropriate distance for social interaction or personal space is considerably closer in Latin cultures than in the US (Hall 1969).

Language and communication are key threads of culture, which give meaning to objects and symbols for the individual. At the same time, they act as a unifying force binding together the members of a specific society and culture, and facilitating intragroup interaction, while at the same time hindering interaction with members of other societies and culture. Rapid advances in communications technology have dramatically reduced the importance of geographic proximity for communication. Individuals can now be in instant touch with others around the world by voice or written word. Information that once took days or weeks to spread is available immediately. As a result, physical proximity is no longer a key requirement for formation of a cultural entity.

On a macro level these broad issues have been looked at by a number of scholars. Hermans and Kempen (1998) examine the process of globalization and the interconnectedness of cultures across the globe. They argue that culture is increasingly becoming deterritorialized and is not necessarily confined to specific locations. Pieterse (2009) looks at global culture in terms of hybridization of culture. Essentially new forms of culture are being created by the combination of elements from two existing cultures. Rowe and Schelling (1992) give examples of hybridization such as Asian rap, Irish bagels, Chinese tacos, Mardi Gras Indians, and Mexican school girls dressed in Greek togas dancing in the style of Isadora Duncan. While these studies often lack the rigor of more empirically based work, they do offer insights into the changes that are occurring on the global level and suggest the complexity and difficulties involved in disentangling it. Further, they suggest topics that can be researched more extensively. Also, de Mooij (2011) has studied consumption and consumer behavior extensively. She examines the differences in consumer behavior across the globe and generally finds a lack of convergence and suggests the importance of understanding local cultural differences. Her work also looks at the implications for marketers and advertisers (de Mooij 2010). Both books have a strong blend of theory and practice.

3.4   CULTURE AND CONSUMPTION

3.4.1   Interplay of Context and Composition

Culture is a dynamic phenomenon that is continually evolving. The three elements of culture that are typically studied, material artifacts, values and beliefs, and communications, each tap a crucial dimension of culture, but each by itself provides only a partial view. The limited perspective provided by a single view is compounded by the fact that culture is changing dramatically. These changes are precipitated by the constant interplay of the context in which culture exists and the composition of the culture. The compositional elements of culture can change in response to changes in the context, which can include greater economic prosperity. Hofstede's work suggests that as income rises cultures become more individualistic (Hofstede 2001). Cultural influences change and evolve as the cultural context changes, and political, social, economic and technological forces reshape the landscape. The speed of change is also accelerating as technological advances and competitive pressures increase the pace of innovation and shrink the time taken to transmit ideas, information and images across the globe. As a result, it becomes increasingly imperative to take account of the dynamic character of culture and to understand the way the composition of culture is being transformed by global forces.

Cultural boundaries are evolving, changing the context of culture and transforming its composition. Transnational cultures are emerging, linked by global flows diffusing ideas, products and images across the world at amazing speed. As contextual patterns evolve, they change the nature and disposition of compositional elements. The dynamics of this process result in alterations to traditional cultures and the creation of distinctly new consumption patterns (Craig and Douglas 2006). For example, cultural interpenetration takes place as people from one culture enter another, introducing ideas, artifacts and rituals from their own culture to the new culture. People from the penetrated culture may begin to adopt and absorb ideas and objects from the foreign culture into their own. Consumers in the UK, for example, have adopted Indian foods, chutneys and breads into mainstream consumption patterns and preferences. Cultural penetration can also result in cultural pluralism, where an individual may belong simultaneously to more than one culture. For example, the children of Indian or Chinese immigrants to the US may identify with multiple cultures—the Indian or Chinese culture in which they were raised at home, as well as the US teen or youth culture of which they are a part at school or college. Changing contextual patterns thus impact the composition of a culture while changing and creating new compositional elements.

The most profound change is that in many instances culture is no longer associated with a particular locale. Modern communications, particularly the internet, have made it possible for individuals to maintain cultural ties or be exposed to elements of other cultures, even though they are not geographically proximate. This implies that cultures are no longer necessarily tied to specific localities with defined contextual features. While the immediate context continues to exert influence on individuals, changes beyond the local environment can exert influence.

3.4.2 Culture's Context

While culture is often a key variable impacting consumer attitudes and behavior, it is important to recognize that culture's influence does not occur in a vacuum. Numerous other variables (both macro- and micro-environmental) co-exist with and impact culture and hence may affect consumer behavior, both directly and indirectly. Culture may be viewed as the causal factor, but underlying contextual variables, such as the affluence of a society or cultural grouping, level of education, degree of urbanization, the topographical or climatic context, or even the political system, may be at least partially responsible for the observed differences or confound the impact of cultural influences. The context is particularly crucial when cross-cultural comparisons are being made, as not only do the cultures potentially differ, but the contexts invariably do. Failure to take such contextual factors into consideration in cross-cultural research can result in mistaken inferences. Even where contextual effects are subtle, these may still alter observations and relationships.

A wide variety of different contextual factors may be identified which potentially influence values and consumption behavior. These include macro-environmental variables, such as income, economic growth, population, education, health, religion and climate, etc. and micro-environmental variables, such as family, local educational or government institutions, social organizations, population density and other geographic characteristics. Equally, media and distribution infrastructure may help to form consumer attitudes and purchase behavior habits. All of these provide a backdrop or context in which cultural influences play out and may directly or indirectly influence consumer values and behavior. For a more detailed treatment of the effect of context on culture, see Douglas and Craig (2009) and for a discussion of the different level of context see Douglas and Craig (2011).

Berry's eco-cultural or ecosocial model (Berry 1975, 1976, 2001; Georgas and Berry 1995), provides a framework for examining the role of contextual factors in influencing behavior. Human diversity, both cultural and psychological, is viewed as a set of collective and individual adaptations to contextual factors and, more specifically, the ecological and sociopolitical system. Ecological and sociopolitical influences are not seen as deterministic, but rather as following a pattern of mutual adaptation in which changes in one part follow changes in other parts through a dual process of acculturation and adaptation. On the one hand, human organisms interact with and adapt to their physical environment in order to satisfy their needs. On the other hand, cultural change occurs through sociopolitical institutions such as education and employment that alter extant cultural patterns.

Six principal contextual dimensions: ecology, economy, education, mass media, population and religion were identified in a recent study (Georgas et al. 2004) that applied the ecological framework (Berry 1976, 2001) to account for differences in psychological characteristics and, in particular, psychological values across countries and geographic zones. These are considered critical in understanding variation in psychological variables. Following this view, such contextual factors may also be expected to impact consumer values, attitudes and behavior patterns. In particular, three distinct categories of contextual variables relevant to behavior as consumers can be identified: the ecological context; the level of social affluence (i.e. the wealth of a society); and the religious context.

3.4.2.1   Ecological context

Ecology, measured in terms of factors such as monthly levels of precipitation or temperature or climatic zone, influences both values and consumption patterns (Georgas et al. 2004; Parker and Tavasolli 2000). Georgas et al. (2004), for example, found ecological factors to have an important impact on psychological variables such as Involvement, Power Distance and Individualism. Equally, Parker and Tavassoli (2000) found climate to have an important influence on the consumption of pharmacological products such as alcohol, cocoa, coffee, tea and tobacco.

As indicated earlier, according to Parker and Tavassoli (2000) the physio-economic environment encompasses both *abiotic* factors, such as climate, terrain, navigable waterways, access to oceans and rivers, as well as *biotic* factors such as the nature of vegetation and animal life and availability of arable land, water, minerals, and resources to produce food and build lodgings. Such factors result in differences in homeothermic consumption such as dressing behavior, caloric intake, energy and architectural design as well as nonhomeothermic consumption such as food, medicine, leisure, art and entertainment. Equally, climate and terrain are viewed as shaping social processes and economic activity and as particularly important factors in influencing the location of centers of cultural growth.

Climate, for example, is an important factor influencing food and clothing needs as well as housing. Clearly, individuals living in cold climates need warm clothing, such as furs, wool and leather, influencing modes of dressing. Conversely, warmer climates require lighter clothing and use of fabrics such as cotton and silk. In addition to clothing, other important cultural artifacts relate to housing needs. Again, the nature of building is influenced by climate and local vegetation. In Scandinavian countries, where forests are abundant, housing is typically made of wood. In countries where clay is more widely available, houses are more likely to be built of bricks. Climate also has an important impact on temperament. Since most humans tend to respond to light and warmth, people living in warmer climates and those where the hours of light remain the same throughout the year are more likely to be happy and cheerful, and respond and communicate with enthusiasm. Although perhaps somewhat counter intuitively, suicide rates seem to be highest when longer daylight returns. In a study of 19 countries, suicides are highest in May and June in the northern hemisphere and November and December in the southern hemisphere (Petridou et al. 2002). Also, two of the three countries with the highest absolute rates of suicide were on the Mediterranean coast where sunshine is more abundant than in the Northern European countries included in the study.

Climate and terrain influence what crops will grow in a given location, as well as what natural plants and other vegetation exist and whether cattle, sheep or goats can be herded, or fish caught as sources of food. Differences in food consumption patterns are a central element of cultural behavior and influence other factors such as health, energy and sporting activity. In hotter climates people eat less, especially of foods which require high energy to digest, such as meat. In colder climates there is higher consumption of alcoholic beverages (Parker 1997).

This approach emphasizes the role of ecological factors in shaping culture, and ignores the role of sociopolitical and economic factors, such as wealth, education, employment, governmental and social institutions in fostering and filtering adaptation to the physical environment. However, it highlights key and often-neglected physio-economic variables, and illustrates the importance of considering the role of the physical/ecological context in which individuals live, in shaping cultural and consumption patterning.

3.4.2.2   Societal affluence

The affluence of society is another powerful factor impacting culture and mediating its role on consumer behavior. Levels of GDP per capita have, for example, been found to be correlated with national value orientations and, in particular, with Hofstede's measures of Individualism and Collectivism (Hofstede 2001). Highly developed countries are more likely to have high levels of Individualism and to value individualistic values such as personal achievement and ambition. These are often important motivational factors driving the engine of economic growth and entrepreneurship. Furthermore, in poor countries, people depend on support from in-groups, such as families or local communities, but as wealth increases, individuals gain access to resources which enable them to make their own personal choices and spend according to their own individual interests.

The affluence of a society also influences the nature of its material possessions. Most treasured possessions and status symbols depend on the affluence of a culture and hence what an individual can afford to purchase. While in developed countries, possession of an expensive model of car, such as a Mercedes Benz, may be an important status symbol, in Western Africa, possession of a bicycle or a radio may confer similar status. Similarly in developing markets, possession of brands which are perceived as symbols of a Western lifestyle, such as Adidas, Nike and Levi's, is highly valued as well as brands which reflect the local culture (Belk 1988b; Ger et al. 1993).

The level of education in a country measured, for example, in terms of factors such as levels of illiteracy, education or expenditure on R&D, also impacts culturally embedded consumption behavior. Professionals and individuals with high levels of education are more likely to buy products such as books and certain types of entertainment products such as opera, classical music, and classical ballet, as well as to travel to other countries to explore different cultures than those with lower levels of education (Katz-Gerro 1999). Equally, they are more likely to be ecologically concerned and to purchase in environmentally friendly stores, such as The Body Shop or Whole Foods Market, and be more concerned with fitness and health, to exercise regularly and belong to gyms and health spas (Lee and Holden 1999). Also they are more likely to be aware and open to ideas and information from other cultures and be willing to try unfamiliar products from other countries, even if these are relatively expensive, for example exotic foods such as frog's legs, or truffles (Nijssen and Douglas 2008).

Social, economic and political institutions also play an important role in forming and perpetuating cultural patterns and behavior. In some societies there are social hierarchies such as the social class structure typical of certain Western European countries or the caste system in India (Berry 2006). Membership of a given social class, often defined by a combination of occupation, wealth and birth implies a certain social status. Each social class is bound by a system of social norms and obligations and social interaction occurs predominantly within members of the same group, resulting in pressures for social conformity and similar consumption patterns (Berry 2006).

Since wealth and possessions are a key factor defining membership in a given social class, the distribution of wealth is often closely linked to the degree of social stratification and hence variation in consumption patterns within society. Many Latin American countries, with highly skewed income distribution, are also marked by high variation in consumption patterns and price sensitivity. Stratified societies also vary in terms of the extent to which individuals are tightly enmeshed in the social structure or are free to develop their own lifestyles and patterns of social interaction. Conversely, in egalitarian societies, such as the Scandinavian countries, Japan or Iceland, there is substantial social homogeneity and less variation in consumption patterns and behavior.

Former communist societies, such as Eastern Europe and Russia, are also characterized by relatively egalitarian consumption patterns, although in Eastern Europe, privatization of the economy is resulting in the emergence of a middle class who are adopting Western consumer values and behavior patterns and look to the Western consumption society as their model. For example, Central European women's concern about their appearance and hence use of and involvement in cosmetics and branded products has been evolving as these countries transition from socialism to capitalism (Coulter et al. 2003). At the same time in Russia, the emergence of business moguls in the energy and commodity sectors has resulted in the creation of a class of wealthy nouveaux riches engaging in conspicuous consumption.

3.4.2.3 Religious context

Religion is another factor with a strong influence on cultural values and consumption patterns. It is important to note that religion is both a contextual and a compositional element of culture as it is often a central component of the values and beliefs that individuals hold. In Europe and the US, Judeo-Christian values influence aspects of behavior and help establish broad societal norms, even for those who are not active adherents to a particular religion. In the Middle East, Islamic values exert a strong influence on virtually all aspects of life. There are very clearly prescribed rules for consumption behavior, with regard to food, alcohol, interactions with members of the opposite sex, and dress, particularly for women. Strong religious beliefs are typically also associated with conservative traditional values (Spika et al. 1985) with regard to social conformity and social issues such as feminism, divorce and sexuality. These in turn may have either a direct or indirect effect on behavior as consumers and, in particular, responses to certain types of advertising appeals or product positioning strategies.

The religious environment of a nation has been found to influence individual religious beliefs and the extent to which religious beliefs are passed from one generation to another (Kelley and de Graaf 1997).

Individuals living in religious nations are more likely to acquire ortho-dox beliefs than those living in secular nations. In relatively secular nations, family religiosity influences the strength of children's religious belief, while in religious nations, family religiosity has less effect than the national context. In the latter case, contacts with friends outside the family, and with other peer groups, teachers in school or colleagues at work may all become important influences on their lives. These all reflect the national religious context and play a key role in shaping their religious beliefs and values.

In essence, therefore, ecological, social and religious contextual factors play a key role in the formation and perpetuation of cultural values and behavior, as well as directly impacting attitudes and behavior as consumers. Interactions within the family unit, and with friends, with teachers or colleagues at work, or members of other social and religious organizations to which an individual belongs will mediate the impact of macro environmental forces. In some cases, these interactions may reinforce the impact of contextual variables on individuals' behavior. In other cases they may mediate their influence on values, attitudes and behavior, and act as barriers to change, at both a societal and an individual level. Contextual factors are thus important elements influencing consumer attitudes and behavior. Even where their influence is subtle and indirect, they need to be taken into account in studying cultural influences on consumer behavior.

3.4.3   Virtual Context

Most of the discussion and studies referred to so far have focused on culture as being associated with a particular time and place. Increasing flows of people, information, ideas and technology across world markets have resulted in the diffusion of ideas, products and trends across societies worldwide at an amazing speed and on an unprecedented scale. This virtual context both incorporates and obscures the impact of local context insofar as local ideas and trends are rapidly diffused and may become part of a transnational or global context. Individuals are also exposed to information that is external to their own culture in either an active or a passive fashion. In the first case, individuals may actively seek out information, ideas and content from other parts of the world. This may involve travel to other countries, membership in organizations that focus on other cultures, such as the Japan Society or French Institute Alliance Francaise, watching movies and other entertainment from a specific country, or visiting web sites in another country. In the latter case, information and content from other cultures is incorporated into content that is consumed as a part of normal activities. For example, at one time the most highly watched television show around the world was *Dallas*. While it contains entertainment content and themes with universal appeal, such as greed, power, and lust, there are also values contained in the content that reflect to varying degrees American culture (or at least a stereotype of American culture). As individuals in other countries watch American television programs, they may either reject or accept the implicit and explicit messages contained in the content. Value laden content also appears in advertisements, music, and movies. Consequently, the virtual context contains compositional elements from one culture which may influence and ultimately be incorporated into other cultures. The impact of context on culture is ongoing and can be the most difficult to discern (see Craig et al. 2009). The interplay of context, proximate and virtual, with the existing compositional elements of a culture and how it is evolving, can result in a fusion of cultural elements.

Global and local are not necessarily polar opposites, but act as complementary dual forces. Global media flows further reinforce the spread of local trends as they result in increased exposure to products, values and interests from diverse cultures. Consumers in emerging markets may see the lifestyle and products of developed countries and desire products, such as Coca-Cola, Levi's jeans, Apple iPods, and Nike shoes, that they see as symbols of that lifestyle. Equally, individuals may acquire or desire to emulate values such as competitiveness, independence and ambition, which they see reflected in these lifestyles and the advertisements that are used to market these products. Activities of international marketers further change traditional local patterns of behavior as they introduce products, services and ideas typical of one culture or national culture, to another culture or country. Particularly influential is the advertising through traditional and new media, since it can be seen almost anywhere around the world simultaneously.

As a result, a culture has emerged that transcends national boundaries, encapsulating interests and influences that occur at a world or global level (Alden et al. 1999, 2006; Robertson 1990). Icons of this global culture, such as Coca-Cola, iPods, smart phones and Rolex watches, are purchased by those who wish to be identified as members of this culture. Television channels such as MTV and CNN seek to reach these markets and provide a flow of music, entertainment, and information that creates a common link spanning multiple locales. The internet provides access to common information and facilitates communication between members of these communities through blogs, Twitter and Facebook. Collectively, these mechanisms serve to reinforce a sense of belonging to something that transcends national boundaries.

3.5   IMPLICATIONS

3.5.1   Multiplicity of Cultural Influences

The multifaceted nature of culture means that adoption of a particular perspective provides only a partial view of its nature and the complex interplay of context and composition. The six perspectives on culture discussed earlier and the different contextual and compositional aspects of culture need to be taken into consideration to develop a fuller understanding. Focus may be placed on contextual factors and examining their impact on and interaction with compositional elements and consumption behavior. Alternatively, attention may be centered on examining compositional elements and their relation to consumption behavior within a given contextual setting.

At the same time, cultural influences are not independent, but rather interdependent, further adding to the difficulty of isolating and understanding the impact of a single aspect of culture. Cultural influences occur at many different levels of society, creating a multi-layered patterning of values, icons, artifacts and behavior linked together by a complex system of within-culture communication and between-culture communications. Cultural forces impact human behavior on these multiple levels adding complexity to the study of culture's influence. To fully understand the richness of culture's impact on consumer behavior the influences at these different levels must be clearly delineated and examined.

3.5.2   Expanding the Range of Contexts

Extension of the range and diversity of countries and socio-cultural contexts can provide greater understanding of culture and consumption. This is critical in order to understand which compositional elements of culture are universal and which are embedded in a specific culture. It will also aid in studying variation in cultural theories and constructs in different societal contexts. Study of a broader range of socio-cultural contexts, especially where extensive preliminary research is conducted in each case, also helps to identify new concepts and constructs or relevant compositional elements of culture. In addition it enables systematic examination of the impact of specific aspects of the socio-cultural context, such as language, size or geographic scope. This is parallel to the distinction made by Lonner and Adamopoulos (1997) in comparing the impact of cultural context vs. comparing cultures or compositional elements.

Most cross-cultural consumer research published in English has been US-centric—i.e. conducted by US or US-trained researchers (see Craig and

Douglas 2011). Often it has focused on examining the generality of models and theories developed in the US to other countries in Europe or Asia. In particular, focus on Individualism/Collectivism, for example, has resulted in comparison of behavior in the US as an exemplar of Individualism, with that in an Asian country such as China, Taiwan or Hong Kong as an exemplar of Collectivism. Examination of cultural phenomena and cultural traditions in other continents, such as Latin America, Africa or India, would considerably enrich and enhance understanding of the range of culture and its influence. This would also offer greater insight into the impact of different contexts on consumption behavior.

3.5.3   Extending the Time Frame

The dynamic and continually evolving character of cultural phenomena imply that it is important to undertake longitudinal studies in order to understand the process of cultural change. Here it is important to understand both how cultures evolve naturally, and also how they are affected by the introduction of external elements, for example immigrants, products from other countries, and flows from other cultures. Longitudinal research is, however, difficult to design, costly to conduct and requires time to execute. Consequently, few consumer researchers, whether in domestic or cross-cultural research, undertake it. However, given the dynamic nature of cultural influences, it is imperative that longitudinal studies be undertaken.

Such studies might, for example, focus on studying in depth a particular culture over time, examining how values and belief systems evolve, how patterns of communication change and new forms of material artifacts replace the old. At the same time it would be important to monitor changes in contextual variables to be able to observe their impact. Perhaps of even greater salience, given the importance of the global flows of people, products, and ideas, is to examine how such flows impact cultural patterning and the nature of linkages across cultural boundaries. Cultural interpenetration, cultural contamination, cultural pluralism and fusion, while by no means new, have been little studied to date. Examination of such phenomena would undoubtedly provide fruitful avenues for understanding the dynamics of cultural change and the roles that context and composition play in influencing consumption.

3.5.4   Accounting for Virtual Context

The new reality of the global market place is that with few exceptions, in remote areas of the world, individuals have the ability to be exposed to the content of other cultures. This exposure can be fleeting or constant and ultimately will influence aspects of an existing culture. For example, American culture has many facets and manifestations and through various media can reach consumers all over the world. One pervasive influence is US films and television shows which embody US culture to varying degrees. While films from other countries are shown in the US, the dominant pattern is for US films to be shown in other countries. Of the 256 top grossing films of all time in terms of non-US box office (gross revenue of $100 million or more outside the US), all but six were US films and three of these remaining films were from the UK (imbd. com). In aggregate, non-US films accounted for only 2 percent of the total revenue. The pattern is consistent from year to year. For example, in 2002 the top five films in Germany, UK, Australia, Spain, Argentina, The Netherlands, Japan, South Korea, and China were US films, while in Mexico and France, all but one of the top five films were from the US (*Variety* 2003).

In examining the influence of US entertainment in other countries, Craig et al. (2006) found that American movies do better in foreign countries that are culturally closer to the US and that have more McDonald's restaurants per capita. The presence of fast food restaurants in countries outside the US is a function of the profit-motivated ambitions of the parent company and the receptiveness of the indigenous population to new forms of food, which also reflect Western lifestyles. Large numbers of fast food restaurants in a particular country alter the context, but also reflect underlying cultural values. Thus, the extent to which inhabitants of a particular country embrace fast food suggests receptiveness to American movies, although the causal direction may be reversed, or an overarching construct may be driving both. The key thing is the presence of American movies and television shows, creating a virtual context that subtly and often not so subtly brings American values into a country. This can introduce new values and beliefs into a culture and alter existing beliefs, particularly among the young who may have not fully embraced the societal values that their elders adhere to. The virtual context can also be formed through travel and migration, which exposes individuals from one culture to another. Consequently, in studying culture and consumption it is important to account for these influences.

3.6 CONCLUSION

The parallel trends of globalization and multiculturalism make it increasingly important to develop a deeper understanding of culture and its various manifestations. In particular it is important to recognize the complex nature of cultural influences and to distinguish between contextual and compositional elements and their pervasive impact on values, beliefs, and consumption both within and across countries. Contextual influences are changing dramatically, as cultures are no longer dependent on local resources to formulate their characteristic tastes, preferences and behavior, and are increasingly linked across vast geographic distances by modern communication media. Consequently, contextual patterning is becoming increasingly complex as traditional cultural boundaries are eroding and cultural entities themselves become more mobile. Equally, membership in a culture is becoming more fluid as individuals travel freely and both adapt to new cultural contexts while transporting elements of one culture to another.

The interplay between contextual and compositional elements is becoming more active and consequential. Increasingly important is the role of cultural interpenetration (Andreasen 1990) and the virtual context in shaping and altering local culture. While the ethnie core of a particular culture may change, this does not necessarily mean that there is increased homogenization of culture. Rather, elements of different cultures are combining in a process of cultural hybridization (Hermans and Kempen 1998), resulting in new and distinctive forms of cultural expression. As membership in a culture becomes increasingly transitional, compositional elements are less clearly demarcated or distinctive. New hybrid cultures are emerging, blending elements of different origins. At the same time, compositional elements may themselves adapt to a new context, creating new forms and developing new features. The dynamic and evolving character of these contextual and compositional influences greatly complicates research designed to disentangle the meaning of culture and its impact on consumption. For progress to be made, research designs must account for this complexity and span multiple contexts to establish the generality of findings. Also, adequate statistical controls need to be incorporated into the design to insure that valid and meaningful inferences are made. It is critical that consumer researchers recognize the multitude of influences, both within and from outside the culture that shape and change the intangible components of culture. Along with this it is important to determine the material aspects of culture used to express conformity to traditional elements of culture as well as those signifying an adoption on some level of another culture. Finally, communication links that both bind a culture together and serve to limit encroachment from other cultures need to be examined. Collectively, this will result in improved knowledge of culture, its role in molding consumption behavior, and insights into how it is changing.

REFERENCES

Aaker, Jennifer L. (2000), 'Accessibility or diagnosticity? Disentangling the influence of culture on persuasion processes and attitudes', *Journal of Consumer Research*, **24**, 340–357.

Aaker, Jennifer L. and Durairaj Maheswaran (1997), 'The effect of cultural orientation on persuasion', *Journal of Consumer Research*, **24**, 315–328.

Aaker, Jennifer L. and Patti Williams (1998), 'Empathy versus pride: the influence of emotional appeals across cultures', *Journal of Consumer Research*, **25**, 24–261.

Adorno, T.W., Else Frenkel-Brunswick, Daniel J. Levinson and R. Nevitt Sanford (1950), *The Authoritarian Personality*, New York: Harper & Row.

Alden, Dana L., J.B.E.M. Steenkamp and Rajeev Batra (1999), 'Brand positioning through advertising in Asia, North America and Europe: the role of global consumer culture', *Journal of Marketing*, **63** (January), 75–87.

Alden, D.L., J.B. Steenkamp and R. Batra (2006), 'Consumer attitudes towards marketplace globalization: structure, antecedents and consequences', *International Journal of Research in Marketing*, **23** (3), 227–239.

Andreasen, A.R. (1990), 'Cultural interpretation: a critical consumer research issue for the 1990's', in M. Goldberg, G. Gorn and R.W. Pollay (eds), *Advances in Consumer Research*, **17**, Provo, UT: Association for Consumer Research, pp. 847–849.

Applebaum, Kalman and Ingrid Jordt (1996), 'Notes towards an application of McCracken's cultural categories for cross-cultured consumer research', *Journal of Consumer Research*, **23** (December), 204–217.

Arnould, Eric J. (1989), 'Toward a broadened theory of preference formation and the diffusion of innovations: cases from Zinder Province Niger Republic', *Journal of Consumer Research*, **16** (September), 239–267.

Arnould, E.J. and C.J. Thompson (2005), 'Consumer culture theory (CCT): twenty years of research', *Journal of Consumer Research*, **31** (4), 868–882.

Barzini, Luigi (1983), *The Europeans*, New York: Simon and Schuster.

Belk, Russell (1988a), 'Possessions and the extended self', *Journal of Consumer Research*, **15** (September), 39–168.

Belk, Russell W. (1988b), 'Third World consumer culture', in Erdogan Kumcu and A. Fuat Firat (eds), *Marketing and Development: Toward Broader Dimensions*, Greenwich, CT: JAI Press.

Belk, Russell W. and Richard W. Pollay (1985), 'Materialism and status appeals in Japanese and U.S. print advertising', *International Marketing Review*, Winter, 38–47.

Belk, Russell W., Melanie Wallendorf and John F. Sherry Jr. (1989), 'The sacred and profane in consumer behavior: theodicy on the Odyssey', *Journal of Consumer Research*, **16** (June), 1–35.

Benedict, Ruth (1934), *Patterns of Culture*, Boston: Houghton Mifflin.

Berry, J.W. (1975), 'An ecological approach to cross-cultural psychology', *Nederlands Tijdschrift voor de Psycholgie*, **30**, 51–84.

Berry, J.W. (1976), *Human Ecology and Cognitive Style: Comparative Studies in Cultural and Psychological Adaptation*, Sage: Beverly Hills, CA.

Berry, J.W. (2001), 'Contextual studies of cognitive adaptation', in J.M. Collis and S. Messick (eds), *Intelligence and Personality: Bridging the Gap in Theory and Measurement*, Mahwah, NJ: Lawrence Erlbaum.

Berry, J.W. (2006), 'Contexts of acculturation', in D.L. Sam and J.W. Berry (eds), *The Cambridge Handbook of Acculturation Psychology*, Cambridge, UK: Cambridge University Press.

Briley, Donnel A., Michael W. Morris and Itamar Simonson (2000), 'Reasons as carriers of culture: dynamic vs. dispositional models of cultural influences on decision making', *Journal of Consumer Research*, **27**, 157–178.

Carrier, James (1991), 'Gifts in a world of commodities: the ideology of the perfect gift in American society', *Social Analysis*, **29** (January), 19–37.

Clark, Terry (1990), 'International marketing and national character: a review and proposal for an integrative theory', *Journal of Marketing* (October), 66–79.

Coulter, R., L. Price and L. Feick (2003), 'Rethinking the origins of involvement and brand commitment: insights from postsocialist Central Europe', *Journal of Consumer Research*, **30** (2), 151–169.

Craig, C.S. and S.P. Douglas (2006), 'Beyond national culture: implications of cultural dynamics for consumer research', *International Marketing Review*, **23**, 322–342.

Craig, C.S. and S.P. Douglas (2011), 'Assessing cross cultural marketing theory and research: a commentary essay', *Journal of Business Research*, **64**, 625–627.

Craig, C.S., W.H. Greene and S.P. Douglas (2006), 'Culture matters: consumer acceptance of U.S. films in foreign markets', *Journal of International Marketing*, **13** (4), 80–103.

Craig, C.S., S.P. Douglas and A. Bennett (2009), 'Contextual and cultural factors underlying Americanization', *International Marketing Review*, **29**, 90–109.

Cui, G. and Q. Liu (2000), 'Regional market segments of china: opportunities and barriers in a big emerging market', *Journal of Consumer Marketing*, **17** (1), 55–72.

Dawson, Scott and Gary Bamossy (1990), 'Isolating the effect of non-economic factors on the development of a consumer culture: a comparison of materialism in the Netherlands and the United States', in Marvin E. Goldberg, Gerald Gorn and Richard W. Pollay (eds), *Advances in Consumer Research*, vol. XVII, Provo, UT: Association for Consumer Research, pp. 182–185.

De Mooij, M. (2010), *Global Marketing and Advertising*, 3rd edn, Thousand Oaks, CA: Sage Publications.

De Mooij, M. (2011), *Consumer Behavior and Culture*, 2nd edn, Thousand Oaks, CA: Sage Publications.

Douglas S.P. and C.S. Craig (1997), 'The changing dynamic of consumer behavior: implications for cross-cultural research', *International Journal for Research in Marketing*, **14**, 379–395.

Douglas S.P. and C.S. Craig (2009), 'Impact of context on cross-cultural research', in C. Nakata (ed.), *Beyond Hofstede: Cultural Frameworks for Global Marketing and Management*, New York: Palgrave Macmillan, pp. 125–145.

Douglas, S.P. and C.S. Craig (2011), 'Role of context in assessing international marketing opportunities', *International Marketing Review*.

Featherstone, M. (1990), *Global Culture: Nationalism, Globalization and Modernity*, London: Sage.

Georgas, J. and J.W. Berry (1995), 'An eco-cultural taxonomy for cross-cultural psychology', *Cross-Cultural Research*, **29** (2), 121–157.

Georgas, J., F.J.R. van de Vijver and J.W. Berry (2004), 'The ecological framework, ecosocial indices, and psychological variables in cross-cultural research', *Journal of Cross-Cultural Psychology*, **35**, 74–96.

Ger, Guliz, Russell W. Belk and Dana-Nicoleta Lascu (1993), 'The development of consumer desire in marketizing developing economies: the case of Romania and Turkey', in Leigh McAlister and Michael L. Rothchild (eds), *Advances in Consumer Research*, Vol. 20, Provo, UT: Association for Consumer Research, pp. 102–107.

Green, R.E. and E. Langeard (1975), 'A cross-national comparison of consumer habits and innovator characteristics', *Journal of Marketing*, **39** (July), 34–41.

Hall, Edward T. (1969), *The Hidden Dimension*, New York: Anchor Books.

Hall, Edward T. (1973), *The Silent Language*, New York: Anchor Books.

Hall, Edward T. (1976), *Beyond Culture*, Garden City, NY: Doubleday.

Hassan, S.S. and L.P. Katsansis (1994), 'Global market segmentation: strategies and trends', in S.S. Hassan and E. Kaynak (eds), *Globalization of Consumer Markets: Structures and Strategies*, New York: International Business Press.

Heon, E. (1999), 'Excess means success in Quebec market', *Marketing*, August 6.

Hermans, H.J.M. and H.J.G. Kempen (1998), 'Moving cultures: the perilous problems of cultural dichotomies in a globalizing society', *American Psychologist*, **53** (October), 1111–1120.

Herskovits, Melville J. (1955), *Cultural Anthropology*, New York: Knopf.

Hofstede, G. (2001), *Culture's Consequences: Comparing Values, Behaviors, Institutions and Organizations Across Cultures*, Thousand Oaks, CA: Sage.

Hofstede, G. and M.H. Bond (1988), 'The Confucius connection: from cultural roots to economic growth', *Organizational Dynamics*, **16** (4), 4–21.

Holt, D.B. (1998), 'Does cultural capital structure American consumption?', *Journal of Consumer Research*, **25** (June), 1–25.

Hong, J.W., A. Muderrisoglu and G.M. Zinkham (1987), 'Cultural differences and advertising expression: a comparative content analysis of Japanese and US magazine advertising', *Journal of Advertising*, **1** (16), 55–86.

Hong, Y.-Y. and C.-Y. Chui (2001), 'Toward a paradigm shift: from cross-cultural differences in social cognition to social-cognitive mediation of cultural differences', *Social Cognition*, **19** (3), 181–196.

House, R.J., P.J. Hanges, M. Javidan, P.W. Dorfman and V. Gupta (eds) (2004), *Culture, Leadership, and Organizations: The GLOBE Study of 62 Societies*, Thousand Oaks, CA: Sage.

Hui, M., A. Joy, C. Kim and M. Laroche (1993), 'Equivalence of lifestyle dimensions across four major subcultures in Canada', *Journal of International Consumer Marketing*, **5**, 15–35.

Inkeles, Alex and Daniel J. Levinson (1969), 'National character: the study of model personality and sociocultural systems', in G. Lindzey and E. Aronson (eds), *Handbook of Social Psychology*, vol. 4, 2nd edn, Cambridge, MA: Addison Wesley.

Joy, A. (2001), 'Gift-giving in Hong Kong and the continuum of social ties', *Journal of Consumer Research*, **28** (September), 239–256.

Joy, A., M. Hui, C. Kim and M. Laroche (1995), 'The cultural past in the present: the meaning of home and objects in the homes of working class Italian immigrants in Montreal', in J.G. Costa and J. Bamossy (eds), *Marketing in a Multicultural World*, Thousand Oaks, CA: Sage.

Katz-Gerro, T. (1999), 'Cultural consumption and social stratification: leisure activities, musical tastes, and social location', *Sociological Perspectives*, **42** (4), 627–646.

Kelley, J. and N. Dirk de Graaf (1997), 'National context, parental socialization and religious belief: results from 15 nations', *American Sociological Review*, **62** (4), 639–659.

Klein, J.G., R. Ettenson and M. Morris (1998), 'The animosity model of foreign product purchase: an empirical test in the People's Republic of China', *Journal of Marketing*, **62** (January), 89–100.

Kluckhohn, F.R. and F.L. Strodtbeck (1961), *Variations in Value Orientations*, Westport, CT: Greenwood Press.

Koslow, S., P.M. Shamdasani and E.E. Touchstone (1994), 'Exploring language effects in ethnic advertising: a sociolinguistic perspective', *Journal of Consumer Research*, **20**, 575–585.

Koven, S.G. and F. Götzke (2010), 'Immigrant contributions to American culture', in S.G. Koven and F. Götzke (eds), *American Immigration Policy*, Public Administration, Governance and Globalization Series. New York: Springer, pp. 93–122.

Kroeber, A.L. and C. Kluckhohn (1952), 'Culture: a critical review of concepts and definitions', *Papers of the Peabody Museum of American Archaeology and Ethnology*, **47** (1), 1–223, Cambridge, MA: Harvard University.

Laroche, M., G. Saad, C. Kim and E. Brown (2000), 'A cross-cultural study of in-store information search strategies for a Christmas gift', *Journal of Business Research*, **49**, 113–126.

Lee, J.A. and S.J.S. Holden (1999), 'Understanding the determinants of environmentally conscious behavior', *Psychology & Marketing*, **16** (5), 373–392.

Leung, K., R.S. Bhagat, N.R. Buchan, M. Erez and C.B. Gibson (2005), 'Culture and international business: recent advances and their implications for future research', *Journal of International Business Studies*, **36**, 357–378.

Lonner, William J. and J. Adamopoulos (1997), 'Culture as antecedent to behavior', in J.W. Berry, Y.H. Poortinga and J. Pandey (eds), *Handbook of Cross-Cultural Psychology*, 2nd edn, Vol. 1, Chicago, IL: Allyn and Bacon, pp. 43–83.

Luna, D. and L. Peracchio (2001), 'Moderators of language effects in advertising to bilinguals: a psycholinguistic approach', *Journal of Consumer Research*, **28** (September), 284–295.

Mallen, Bruce (1977), *French Canadian Consumer Behavior: Comparative Lessons from the Published Literature and Private Corporate Marketing Studies*, Montreal: Advertising and Sales Executive Club of Montreal.

McCracken, G. (1986), 'Culture and consumption: a theoretical account of the structure and movement of the cultural meaning of consumer goods', *Journal of Consumer Research*, **13**, 71–84.

Mehta, R. and R.W. Belk (1991), 'Artifacts, identity and transition: favorite possessions of Indians and Indian immigrants to the United States', *Journal of Consumer Research*, **17** (March), 398–411.

Miller, J. (2002), 'Bringing culture to basic psychological theory – beyond individualism and collectivism: comment on Oysermann et al.', *Psychological Bulletin*, **128**, 97–109.

Mishra, R.C., D. Sinha and J.W. Berry (1996), *Ecology, Acculturation, and Psychological Adaptation: A study of Adivasis in Bihar*, Thousand Oaks, CA: Sage.

Nakata, C. and K. Sivakumar (1996), 'National culture and new product development', *Journal of Marketing*, **60** (January), 61–72.

Naroll, Raoul (1970), 'The culture-bearing unit in cross-cultural surveys', in Raoul Naroll and R. Cohen (eds), *The Handbook of Method in Cultural Anthropology*, New York: Natural History Press.

Netemeyer, R., S. Durvasula and D.R. Lichtenstein (1991), 'A cross-national assessment of the reliability and validity of the CETSCALE', *Journal of Marketing Research*, **28** (August), 320–327.

Nijssen, E.J. and S.P. Douglas (2004), 'Examining the animosity model in a country with a high level of foreign trade', *International Journal of Research in Marketing*, **21** (January), 23–38.

Nijssen, E.J. and S.P. Douglas (2008), 'Consumer worldmindedness, social responsibility and the impact on store choice', *Journal of International Marketing*, **16** (3), 84–107.

Oysermann, D., H. Coon and M. Kemmelmeier (2002), 'Rethinking individualism and collectivism: evaluation of theoretical assumptions and meta-analyses', *Psychological Bulletin*, **128** (1) (January), 3–72.

Parker, P.M. (1997), *National Cultures of the World: A Statistical Reference*, Westport, CT: Greenwood Press.

Parker, P.M. (2000), *Physioeconomics: The Basis for Long-Run Economic Growth*, Cambridge, MA: The MIT Press.

Parker, P.M. and N.T. Tavassoli (2000), 'Homeostasis and consumer behavior across cultures', *International Journal of Research in Marketing*, **17** (1), 33–53.

Penaloza, L. (1994), 'Altravesando fronteros/border crossings: a critical ethnographic exploration of the consumer acculturation of Mexican immigrants', *Journal of Consumer Research*, **21** (June), 32–54.

Petridou, E., F.C. Papadopoulos, C.E. Frangakis, A. Skalkidou and D. Trichopoulos (2002), 'A role of sunshine in triggering of suicide', *Epidemiology*, **13** (1), 106–109.

Pieterse, J.N. (2009), *Globalization and Culture: Global Mélange*, 2nd edn, Lanham, MD: Rowman & Littlefield.

Robertson, Roland (1990), 'Mapping the global condition: globalization as the central concept', in Mike Featherston (ed.), *Global Culture: Nationalism, Globalization and Modernity*, London: Sage.

Rowe, W. and V. Schelling (1992), *Memory and Modernity: Popular Culture in Latin America*, London: Verso.

Samovar, Larry A. and Richard E. Porter (1994), *Intercultural Communication*, Belmont, CA: Wadsworth.

Schaninger, C.M., J.C. Bourgeois and W.C. Buss (1985), 'French-English Canadian subcultural consumption differences', *Journal of Marketing*, **49**, 82–92.

Schmitt, B. and S. Zhang (1998), 'Language, structure and categorization: a study of classifiers in consumer cognition, judgment and choice', *Journal of Consumer Research*, **25** (September), 108–122.

Schmitt, B.H., Y. Pan and N.T. Tavassoli (1994), 'Language and consumer memory: the impact of linguistic differences between Chinese and English', *Journal of Consumer Research*, **21**, 419–431.

Schwarz, S.H. (1992), 'Universals in the context and structure of values: theoretical advances and empirical tests in 20 countries', in M. Zanna (ed.), *Advances in Experimental Social Psychology*, **25**, Orlando, FL: Academic Press, pp. 1–65.

Schwarz, S.H. and W. Bilsky (1996), 'Towards a theory of the universal structure and content of values: extensions and cross-cultural replications', *Journal of Personality and Social Psychology*, **58**, 878–891.

Sherry, J.F. (1983), 'Gift giving in anthropological perspective', *Journal of Consumer Research*, **10** (September), 157–168.

Sherry, J.F. and E.G. Camargo (1987), 'May your life be marvelous, English language labeling and the semiotics of Japanese promotion', *Journal of Consumer Research*, **14** (September), 174–188.

Shimp, T.A. and S. Sharma (1987), 'Consumer ethnocentrism: construction and validation of the CETSCALE', *Journal of Marketing Research*, **XXIV** (August), 280–289.

Smith, A.B. (1990), 'Toward a global culture?' in M. Featherstone (ed.), *Global Culture: Nationalism, Globalization and Modernity*, London: Sage, pp. 171–192.

Song, M. and M.E. Perry (1997), 'A cross-national comparative study of new product development process: Japan and the United States', *Journal of Marketing* (April), 1–18.

Spika, B., R. Hood and R. Gorsuch (1985), *The Psychology of Religion: An Empirical Approach*, Englewood Cliffs, NJ: Prentice Hall.

Steenkamp, J.B.E.M., Frenkel ter Hofstede and M. Wedel (1999), 'A cross-national investigation into the individual and national cultural antecedents of consumer innovativeness', *Journal of Marketing*, **63**, 55–59.

Stern, B.B. (1995) 'Consumer myths: Frye's taxonomy and the structural analysis of consumption text', *Journal of Consumer Research*, **22** (September), 165–185.

Tavassoli, N. (1999), 'Temporal and associative memory in Chinese and English', *Journal of Consumer Research*, **26** (September), 170–181.

Thompson, C.J. (1997), 'Interpreting consumers: a hermeneutical framework for deriving marketing insights from the texts of consumers' consumption stories', *Journal of Marketing Research*, **34** (4), 438–455.

Thompson, C.J. (2004), 'Marketplace mythology and discourses of power', *Journal of Consumer Research*, **31** (1), 162–180.

Triandis, Harry C. (1995), *Individualism and Collectivism*, Boulder, CO: Westview Press.

Tse, D., R.W. Belk and N. Zhou (1989), 'Becoming a consumer society: a longitudinal and cross-cultural content analysis of print ads from Hong Kong, the People's Republic of China and Taiwan', *Journal of Consumer Research*, **15** (March), 457–472.

Tylor, E.D. (1881), *Anthropology: An Introduction to the Study of Man and Civilization*, New York: D. Appleton.

Vandello, J.A. and D. Cohen (1999), 'Patterns of individualism and collectivism across the United States', *Journal of Personality and Social Psychology*, **77** (2), 279–292.

Variety (2003), 'Media congloms' global grip grows', 14–20 April, p. 4.

Wallendorf, M. and E.J. Arnould (1988), 'My favorite things: a cross-cultural inquiry into object attachment, possession and social linkage', *Journal of Consumer Research*, **14** (March), 531–547.

Whorf, Benjamin (1956), *Language, Thought and Reality*, New York: John Wiley & Sons.

4 The role of culture in advertising humor

*Marc G. Weinberger, Charles S. Gulas and
Michelle F. Weinberger*

Humor has been studied by linguists, philosophers, psychologists, anthropologists, sociologists, and advertising researchers (see Gulas and Weinberger 2006 for a review) and its use in advertising dates back to the very roots of the field. English pub signs dating to the 1500s used incongruity. Puns appeared in print advertising by the 1700s. With the advent of radio advertising in the 1920s and television in the 1950s the acceptance and use of humor became widespread. Virtually all cultures make some use of humor in advertising; however its usage often differs between countries and sub-cultural groups. Paradoxically, while found in every culture, humor is specific to time and context. As a result, the amount and nature of successful humor attempts might also undergo changes based on changing contextual meanings. The focus of this chapter is not only on how contextualized cultural meanings shape perceptions of humor in advertising but also how humorous advertisements reflect and potentially influence cultural norms.

The use of humor in advertising represents an annual global investment of more than $167 billion in campaigns (ZenithOptimedia 2007) and as such it has commanded significant research attention by scholars over the past several decades. It is no surprise that in a world of CNN, Sky News, BBC, YouTube, Al Jazeera, Facebook, Twitter, blogs, and ad campaigns designed to go viral, it is harder to compartmentalize the effects of advertising to the intended country or audience.

Humor is a fundamental ingredient in social communication; it is featured in more than 24 percent of prime television programs in the USA with higher percentages in other countries such as the UK. Often humorous ads are favorites among the judges of the International Advertising Film Festival at Cannes, and various other industry competitions as documented in 62 percent of Clio Award winning radio ads (Murphy et al. 1993). The use of humor in advertising is growing and in events such as the Super Bowl of American football, the percentages are now routinely greater than 70 percent.

The prevalence of advertising humor has attracted substantial research by consumer behavior scholars in recent years, and the result is that quite a bit is known about both the amount and effectiveness of humor and the views of individuals in companies and agencies concerning the use of advertising humor. After studying humor in advertising for many years, it has become increasingly obvious that its use, interpretation and impact are affected by the cultural context of the audience. This cultural context can vary by place, time and media.

4.1   A MODEL OF ADVERTISING HUMOR

To understand humor in advertising we begin with an overall view of it as illustrated in Figure 4.1. This model, from Gulas and Weinberger (2006), is named the Challenge Model, because at its core, humor relies on the departure from expectation that confronts the audience with a challenge to interpret the unexpected. This may play out as an innocent incongruity or a violent physical aggression that is different from norms which an audience expects. Mirth is the end product if the humor is successful, but whether the challenge works depends on the Facilitating Conditions. Culture is an Audience factor that impacts receptivity to the humor attempt. We are increasingly convinced that culture is central to understanding the effectiveness of advertising humor.

In order for an audience member to recognize disparity or incongruity they must have the cultural knowledge and associated schemas to understand the meanings of the 'set-up.' These contextual meanings influence a range of facilitating conditions including Play Signals. Typically

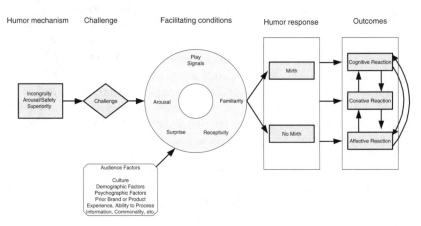

Source: Gulas and Weinberger, 2006.

Figure 4.1   Audience Factors and the Humor Challenge Model

Play Signals use pre-existing schemas to signal to the audience that the situation is not serious and the humor is intended. Play Signals serve to convert a raw aggression into humor. A character being tossed out of a window would not be humorous unless there are signals that the audience recognizes and accepts as playful. This can then result in a positive humor response.

There is considerable agreement that there needs to be a common understanding of the situation (schema familiarity) to decipher the challenge triggered by the message. Schema familiarity explains why some humor developed in one culture falls flat in another where an audience may have no idea of the schema that may be the basis of the challenge.

Another facilitating condition is the audience predisposition toward the humor in a given situation. For example, receptivity to violent, sexual or racial humor can vary over time based on the socio-cultural norms and meanings of the time. In fact, culture plays a crucial role in whether the facilitating conditions (play signals, schema familiarity and executional receptivity) result in the message challenge being deciphered correctly and resulting in a mirth response.

To illustrate and examine the connection between humor and culture, we start by establishing a framework for understanding culture and then present some insights into the issue of humor and culture using three studies. First, we explore humor through a global lens which establishes differences in the use of humor both across and within borders. Second, we examine the evolution of humor in outdoor advertising to demonstrate changes in cultural norms and in the use of humor within a country. Finally, we highlight the recent cultural shift in acceptable humor in American television advertising through an examination of denigration and violence as a prevalent humor genre.

4.2   HUMOR AS SHAPED BY CULTURE

By understanding culture and associated schemas, norms, values, and meanings, we can understand the building blocks of humor, when it works, and why it falls flat. So in this section we focus on culture: what it is and isn't, how it is formed, and most importantly the relationship between culture and people's ability to interpret marketing communications messages, particularly humorous ones.

To be clear, when using the term 'culture' we do not refer to cultural products such as art, music, television, or movies. Nor do we use it only to describe people from one part of the world vs. another part (Chinese culture or American culture) (Hofstede 2001). Instead, we see culture as sociologists and anthropologists, as contextualized systems of meaning housed within individual minds that are drawn on constantly but usually tacitly in daily life (Sewell 1999). Abstractly, culture is the knowledge base that forms values, tastes, and ideologies (Bourdieu 1983; Swidler 1986, 2001). It provides the lens through which people view, categorize, and understand the world but, like one's heartbeat, it is constantly at work in the background.

In psychological terms, this knowledge fills the content of schemas (Anderson 1984; DiMaggio 1997), the networks of information that help people to categorize information as familiar or not, good or bad and of course meaningful. People have schemas for everything they know and this helps them make sense of the world around them. This knowledge, sometimes multiple and conflicting, accretes and layers over time, creating dimension in an ever expanding schematic network.

Swidler describes how all of this organized cultural knowledge builds a metaphorical 'tool kit' or 'bag of tricks,' a set of 'symbols, stories, rituals, and world-views, which people may use in varying configurations to solve different kinds of problems' in daily life (1986, p. 273; 2001, pp. 24–5). This knowledge base is what all people use on a daily basis to make sense of their environments. It guides them in everything from knowing what to wear (and to wear something!) when getting dressed in the morning, to knowing how to eat out at a restaurant, to how to be a good parent in their particular social world, to which style or brand of sneaker/trainer is 'cool.' For marketers and advertisers then, it is of utmost importance to understand this cultural knowledge base.

While each individual has a different set of cultural knowledge that is constantly evolving, this knowledge is also shared by people within particular social fields or contexts (Bourdieu 1984). Those socialized similarly, who have similar experiences and have similar educations have a similar set of cultural knowledge that helps them to understanding meaning in a similar way, and, as much sociological research has shown, is the basis for similar tastes, not only in products and art (Bourdieu 1984; Holt 1997a) but also for the type of humor people understand and prefer (Kuipers 2006).

4.2.1   Learning Culture

All people learn culture in three ways: through childhood socialization, through later life experiences, and through formal education. First and most importantly, people accumulate cultural knowledge when they are children. Through socialization, they simply learn how the world 'is.' Both consciously and without consciously trying, a child learns good and bad, proper and not, rules for acting, behaving and order, acceptable foods, manners, tastes, and linguistic cues from informal daily activity. Culture is taught both actively and passively through daily activity by socializing agents such as parents, teachers, and close family friends who help children to see the world in a particular way (Bourdieu 1983; Martin 1998).

Over time, this knowledge is, what sociologists call, 'embodied': it just becomes seen as natural, the way things should be, what is right (Bourdieu 1983; Giddens 1984; Sewell 1999). It becomes unconsciously integrated and assimilated as what seems normal, framing and directing one's behavior and values (Bourdieu 1984; Holt 1998; Holt 1997b). This shapes an individual's life long perspective (Bourdieu 1984) and forms 'cultured capacities,' the habits, skills, and ideas that are hard to learn and easily taken for granted (Swidler 2001, 73). It allows individuals to act as 'competent social actors,' rendering the world as meaningful, but also delineating what is appropriate within each contextualized environment (Giddens 1984, p. 18).

Secondly, people accumulate cultural knowledge through post-childhood socialization experiences as they live in different places or are exposed to new neighborhoods, clubs, and work environments; this knowledge of cultural meanings can also be embodied over time and integrated into the tool kit of meanings used in different situations. In his research, Wacquant (2004) describes the awkward process of training to become a boxer and the slow embodiment of a mindset, norms, meanings, and skills to make it second nature.

Finally, people learn culture through formal education or codified 'book' knowledge. This cultural knowledge is more fact-based, like reading about art in a book, but it isn't necessarily embodied. Learning through classroom education or through books, videos, and training manuals where the knowledge has been codified is a more formal source of accumulating cultural knowledge. It is what others have called: institutionalized knowledge (Bourdieu 1983), information (Kogut and Zander 1992) or explicit knowledge (Nonaka 1994).

In sum, people learn culture through socialization, experiences, and education. As a result, their social context or social field fundamentally influences their values, norms, and meanings that they use to interpret everything in their environment. By understanding this, we can now focus on the ways cultural knowledge influences an audience's ability to understand a humor attempt and how knowledge of an audience's cultural knowledge can help a communicator successfully deliver the message.

4.2.2 Using Cultural Meanings to Understand Humor

Cultural knowledge bases from which people draw to understand the world around them vary dramatically, causing them to understand the meanings of advertising messages quite differently, even in a networked world. An elderly person might conclude that a teen with dirty, holey pants is homeless or poor because holey-dirty clothing fits into their schema for homeless based on socialization and experiences; however, the teen may have paid a premium for these pants because their schema for these pants is cool or multiple including both cool and homeless, depending on other contextual cues. Similarly, failures in understanding humor often are rooted in failures to understand the meanings behind crucial references (Kuipers 2006) based on inaccurate or incomplete cultural knowledge.

Humor attempts also play off embodied knowledge. For humor based on inconsistency to successfully create mirth, an individual must have the appropriate cultural knowledge or schema to understand the act, context, and messages in the ad. Take for example a recent American Bud Light beer ad where two young men are doing yoga in a class of women. For this to be funny the audience targeted must firstly understand that the contextual cues—the mats, tight clothing, positioning of the people, and contemplative eastern music—are all cues for a schema for yoga. Second though, the audience must also have as part of their schema that men doing yoga is still a norm violation to many in America. This is a mild norm violation, something that happens often in ads as a way to capture attention. However, there is a line. Violations of certain norms, those deemed morally reprehensible, would be seen as offensive. On the opposite end, communicators too may make explicit something that is not a norm violation but something that is so embodied and taken for granted or prototypical that when it is articulated it is funny in a self-conscious way.

In the following sections, we focus on understanding cultural norms and meanings as a tool for understanding humor through the challenge model. While cultural meanings vary at a much deeper level than country of origin, differences at the national and regional levels do exist. We examine the complexities of humorous advertising in the context of attempts to cross 'boundaries' rather than the more common term 'borders' used in many discussions of global advertising. We prefer the term boundaries, because even within borders there are differences in cultural knowledge that require different communication strategies, including humor attempts. These meaning boundaries influence whether the audience is familiar enough with the context to understand the humor, whether the intended play signals are interpreted as play or if the meanings are read as offensive to the audience, and whether there is receptiveness for a humor attempt. Drawing on this understanding of culture, in the following section we detail the mechanics of humor. We then use this cultural perspective to look at how changes in humor genres in outdoor advertising over a 100 year period are a reflection of changing cultural meanings.

Finally, we look in depth at the increasing use of denigration and violent humor in American television advertising as a phenomenon reflecting change in cultural norms.

4.3   HUMOR BACKGROUND

Theories of humor fall broadly into three general categories: Cognitive-perceptual (including the incongruity theories), Superiority (including Disparagement and Affective-Evaluative theories) and Relief or Arousal Safety (including psychodynamic theories) (Speck 1987). Each of these general categories is composed of many variations which devotees often doggedly defend as the key to understanding the topic. In practice, incongruity may be used by itself or in combination with disparagement or arousal safety or both to form different types of humor (Speck 1987).

4.3.1   Humor Style

The general mechanisms thought to generate humor are incongruity, arousal-safety, and disparagement with incongruity (including incongruity-resolution) being the most heavily used form (Speck 1987; Spotts et al. 1997). Incongruity is acknowledged as having a central role in humor. In fact, according to one school of thought, incongruity alone may be a necessary and sufficient condition for producing humor (Koestler 1964; Suls 1977). Following this line of thought, the mere presence of an incongruent image in a playful comical setting could be construed as humorous. Yet what cultural norms are violated through incongruity are determined based on extant socio-historic norms. For example in the 1950s in America and most of the world, images of a female CEO, a female airline pilot, a male nurse, or a stay-at-home dad would all be incongruent. Today, to most Americans, these images would not be incongruent because the norms, values, and meanings associated with women and men have shifted to include those roles.

Suls (1977) formulates a two-stage process in which an incongruity (deviation from expectation) is described followed by a resolution in which the incongruity is understood. Incongruity as a category includes both incongruity (I) and incongruity-resolution (IR). Jokes are often conceived as having both an incongruity and resolution component. The resolution results in greater amusement than just incongruity. The resolution is the punch line that makes the context and setup of the joke make sense. Without the punch line, the story or cartoon may seem odd and mildly funny, but it is closing the loop with an ending or pratfall that provides the resolution to add to the mirth experienced by the audience. In the 1950s, the incongruity of a female CEO might be resolved with an embarrassed male mistaking her for a secretary. Of course concepts that are considered incongruent are largely culturally determined; an incongruence for one social group may not be considered incongruent in another and what was an incongruity in the past may not be an incongruity today.

Superiority in humor, often labeled disparagement, has a long history of proponents dating to Aristotle and Hobbes and is part of a broader class of research that examines the social function of humor. Morreall (1983) believes that this is probably the oldest and most widespread theory of laughter. Zillman (1983) asserts that other essential humor cues must be part of any disparagement for humor to be present. Gruner (1997) a contemporary of many of the other superiority researchers, leaves no doubt that in his view 'superiority theory' is the dominant and only universal thread that is present in all humor. He argues that there is a social inhibition that most of us and probably his colleagues have against believing that humor can be explained in the negative terms of superiority, aggression, hostility, ridicule or degradation. Though superiority has long been recognized as an important component for humor (Zillman et al. 1974), its presence as a necessary condition is what distinguishes Gruner's (1997) work. Historically, advertisers have not employed disparagement frequently perhaps because of a fear of offending the audience.

Different sub-theories of arousal safety have in common a view that there is a physiological release in which humor helps to vent tension. Spencer (1860) was an advocate for this 'safety valve' view of humor. Morreall (1983) summarizes the relationship between arousal-safety and the other theories: 'While superiority theory focuses on emotions involved in laughter, and the incongruity theory on objects or ideas causing laughter, relief theory addresses a question little discussed in the other two theories, viz.: Why does laughter take the physical form it does, and what is its biological function?' (p. 20). Morreall argues that Relief theory may coexist with an incongruity (relief through resolution) or superiority (relief as triumph) situation. The arousal may be triggered by circumstances outside the humor stimulus or be created within it. McGhee concludes that, 'greater amounts of induced arousal are associated with increased enjoyment' (1983, p. 19). Thus, a linear relationship rather than a U-shape is expected between arousal and pleasure. Godkewitsch (1976), also a proponent of arousal as necessary for humor and the linear connection to pleasure, argues that other humor cues that signal play are important for humor and may explain why his work found a linear relationship between arousal and humor response while others found that higher levels of arousal may be dysfunctional. It is not clear after all the research whether the increased enjoyment results from arousal or an arousal-relief mechanism. Much like the incongruity v. incongruity-resolution debate, the superiority advocates and the arousal safety advocates are proponents for their style of humor as a necessary condition to trigger a humor response.

Whether through incongruity, superiority or arousal safety the outcome of amusement generated by humor is believed to result in a positive affect that may benefit the communicator, the message or associated objects. It is generally understood that a number of situational factors may play a role in determining the effectiveness of humor (see Gulas and Weinberger 2006 for complete review). Cho (1995) found that surprise at the punch line or some part of the ad had the highest positive loading on the cognitive humor mechanism and that perceived humor is mainly determined by the cognitive mechanism. For example, response to humor from Incongruity Resolution depends on: '(1) rapid resolution of the incongruity; (2) a "playful" context, i.e., with cues signifying that the information is not to be taken seriously; and (3) an appropriate mood for the listener' (Alden and Hoyer 1993, p. 31).

4.3.2 Perception of Humor

Past research provides empirical evidence suggesting that appreciation of humor does differ. Gender and culture are two broad factors that appear to influence audience appreciation for different types of humor (Madden and Weinberger 1982; Weller et al. 1976; Shama and Coughlin 1979; Whipple and Courtney 1980). Rustogi et al. (1996) concluded that although basic instincts and personal values between cultures are the same, appreciation of humor varies. We discuss appreciation of humor in more detail in the 'Crossing Boundaries' section of this chapter. Further, situational factors such as repetition and the object of the humor can influence whether a humorous attempt is actually perceived by a particular audience as humorous at a particular point in time (Gallivan 1991; Gelb and Zinkhan 1986; Gruner 1991; Weinberger and Gulas 1992; Zhang and Zinkhan 1991).

Because attempts at humor do not always result in a humorous reaction, intended humor is not the same as perceived humor both generally and in advertising. Because an ad intended to be humorous may not always be perceived as such by audiences, it is important to consider potential outcomes of unsuccessful attempts. Humor is strategically risky; the same individual at different times might find a message humorous and not based on the context in which the message is received.

When asked in a survey about the use of humor, ad executives saw humor as harder to create, more risky, and more susceptible to wear out than non-humor (Madden and Weinberger 1984). From the advertiser's perspective what happens when a joke falls flat is of central importance. Does a mere attempt at humor bring positive effects, or must the humor generate mirth in order to benefit the advertiser?

The few studies that had been done on this issue produced mixed findings about whether perceived humor matters. Duncan et al. (1984) found a positive relationship between perceived humor and recall (of a hair care product), and Zhang (1996) found that perceived humor positively impacted attitudes toward the product (a 35 mm camera) and the advertising. In contrast, Gelb and Pickett (1983) found perceived humor had a negative impact on persuasion (to stop smoking).

A study of radio advertising humor (Flaherty et al. 2004) manipulated humor treatments such that the level of perceived humor would vary. The result was that the perception of humor overwhelmed the type of humor tested, meaning that the type of humor was less important than whether the audience perceived any attempt as humorous. Indeed it overwhelmed the effects of both humor type (whether the ad used incongruity or incongruity-resolution) and product risk (high-risk or low-risk). It is surprising that humor with a punch line resolution did not have more of an impact than the same ad without the punch line on attitudes toward the advertising, the brand or toward purchase intent. Perceptions of the humor were quite individual, telling us that a mere attempt at humor is not sufficient to provide the positive benefits of a humorous campaign. To gain a positive impact on attitude toward the ad, attitude toward the brand and purchase intention, the ads must be first seen as humorous regardless of the type of humor being used. This study demonstrated that ads seen as humorous out-performed ads that failed to be seen as humorous.

In an ad designed to be humorous, the audience is usually aware that an attempt at humor has been made but as we see in the Challenge Model without the receptivity, ability to understand the play signals or background to decode the schema, they may not be able to either understand the humor attempt or react to it favorably. The diagnostic analysis in the Flaherty et al. study provides evidence that humor that fails on audiences may irritate them. This irritation may carry over to the lower attitude toward the ad, attitude toward the brand and purchase intention scores. For researchers, the implication is that perceived humor is a dominant factor that needs to be explicitly treated in research designs. A complication of course is that the interpretation of the humor attempt occurs in a context that may be impacted by a global or sub-cultural backdrop. We look now at three detailed examples where culture has influenced the use and interpretation of humor. In the first, Crossing Boundaries, we look at how differences across boundaries can shape the types of humor used, the subject of the humor and the decoding of the humor itself. In the second example, Outdoor Advertising Reflecting Cultural Meanings, we see humor change as cultural norms evolved over the last 100 years in the USA. Finally, we look at an example of Humor, Violence and Gender where major increases are seen in the use of superiority humor using violent and denigrating humor about men.

4.4   CROSSING BOUNDARIES AND HUMOR[1]

Humor is found in every culture throughout history, which might suggest that aspects of humor are universal and are therefore appropriate for international ad campaigns (Alden et al. 1993; Unger 1995). There is considerable practitioner experience and research (Rustogi et al. 1996) which suggests that particular executions of humor are not liked universally. Given the high risk of failed attempts at humor in advertising reported in the Flaherty et al. (2004) study, it is prudent to test any attempt at humor on appropriate target audiences before attempting an international humor campaign. As one of the jurors at the Cannes festival stated, 'Humour travels, but it sometimes gets a bit car sick' (Archer 1994).

Cross-cultural patterns in receptivity to humor messages across both borders and boundaries are identifiable. Alden et al. (1993) conducted a large multi-country investigation of humor in advertising. While the study found use of incongruity in the television advertising in each of the four countries examined, they also found that the use of humor in advertising differed across cultures systematically and varied along major cultural dimensions. For example, Thailand and South Korea are countries that rate high on Hofstede's (2001) power distance dimension, a measure of the degree to which power is distributed unequally. These cultures tend to be hierarchical in nature. This hierarchical cultural dimension was reflected in the nature of humorous advertising employed. Alden et al. (1993) found that 63 percent of the humorous ads in these two countries portrayed characters of unequal status. On the other hand, ads in the United States and Germany, cultures that rate low on the power distance dimension, were significantly less likely to portray characters of unequal status. Indeed 71 percent of the ads in the sample featured equal status characters. Additionally, 75 percent of the sampled ads in Thailand and South Korea, both collectivist cultures, featured three or more characters, while only 26 percent of the ads in the sample from Germany and the USA, both individualized cultures, featured three or more characters. In short, these findings suggest that use of humor in advertising plays off culturally constituted norms and meanings.

Building on the work conducted by Alden et al. (1993), Lee and Lim (2008) examined the interaction between cultural orientation and humor processes. Specifically they examined the humor processes of incongruity-resolution and arousal-safety along with cultural orientations of individualism vs. collectivism and uncertainly avoidance. Uncertainty avoiding respondents were more likely to respond positively to humorous ads that had resolved or safe outcomes. A higher collectivist orientation of the country was found to intensify the effects of safe results for ads using arousal-safety humor. Taken together, these findings suggest that the effectiveness of incongruity resolution humor depends on the recipient's socialized orientation towards uncertainty avoidance, and the effectiveness of arousal-safety humor depends on the cultural group's tolerance for uncertainty and/or its individualist or collectivist orientations.

Lee and Lim's (2008) findings have implications for global businesses conducting international ad campaigns, as is increasingly the case. But perhaps more importantly they have implications for domestic advertising as well. Unlike many studies of cultural orientation, Lee and Lim (2008) did not use an international sampling frame. The participants in the Lee and Lim study were 222 Chinese MBA students, indicating that within-country cultural differences are very important in communications.

Empirical evidence indicates that people of different cultural backgrounds within the same country respond to humor differently. In a sociological study of Dutch audiences from different age groups, social classes, and gender groups, Kuipers (2006) found clear differences in perceptions of humor based on cultural knowledge, the norms, tastes, and preferences formed through socialization and experiences. In particular, he found that those with professional occupations and higher levels of education were receptive to abstract and intellectually grounded humor. This fits with overall understandings of tastes and processes of distinction beyond humor for the upper classes (Bourdieu 1984). Women meanwhile socialized to more collaborative roles and preferred more collaborative jokes, but were also more easily embarrassed, with more stringent policing of moral boundaries.

In an experiment that compared Israeli Jews of Eastern and Western descent, Weller and his colleagues found significant differences in the appreciation for absurd jokes between the two groups (Weller et al. 1976). They posit that these differences are due to 'habits of thought and mental attitudes rooted in cultural backgrounds' (p. 163). Similarly, Nevo (1986) found that Israeli Jews and Arabs differed in their perception of humorous events in a manner consistent with other studies. The traditional majority–minority difference was found in which the majority group (Jews) expressed more aggression in humor (Nevo 1986). These findings imply that jokes may not be easily 'translatable' between cultures even in a given country. Theoretically, this is understandable as the different groups are socialized in different social fields and have different life experiences, developing different knowledge bases from which they draw to make meaning out of the messages in the advertisements.

As electronic communication becomes normalized through removing the past national, regional, and sub-cultural boundaries of communication, advertising campaigns can unintentionally reach the wrong audiences, resulting in potentially negative consequences, and sometimes passionately negative responses to humorous ads. In 2007, Absolut vodka introduced an ad campaign called 'Absolut World.' There have been many different executions of the concept, which implies that in the 'Absolut World' everything is better. In one ad, a politician's nose grows like Pinocchio's when he tells a lie. In another, factory smokestacks produce soap bubbles like a child's toy. Many of these cues have the required 'schema familiarity,' are perceived as 'play signals,' and there is 'receptivity' to what might be universal themes in the ads. However, this is not always the case. In early 2008, an ad in this series featured a redrawn map of North America (see Gulas and Weinberger 2010 for more detailed discussion of the Absolut World campaign). This map shows the border between the USA and Mexico located where it was in 1821 when Mexico received its independence from Spain (see Figure 4.2). For some historic background, in 1854 the USA annexed Texas, which had declared independence from Mexico in 1836. This was viewed as an act of war by the Mexican government resulting in the Mexican–American War. The war ended with the Treaty of Guadalupe Hidalgo. The provisions of this treaty called for Mexico to cede the land of present-day Arizona, California, New Mexico, and parts of Colorado, Nevada and Utah in exchange for fifteen million dollars in compensation and forgiveness of Mexican debt to American citizens. There remains a deep-seated bitterness in some about the aftermath of the Mexican–American War as many Mexicans and Americans of Mexican descent believe that much of the land that comprises the American southwest was stolen from Mexico.

The Absolut ad that features the 1821 map was produced by Teran/ TBWA in Mexico City as a print and outdoor campaign. While the campaign did not run in the USA, it was seen by many Americans and sparked heated discussion on many USA-based websites and inspired several parody ads including one that featured a map with a Nazi flag drawn over the parts of Europe that were captured by Germany during World War II. The company responded to the consumer backlash. Absolut said the ad was designed for a Mexican audience and intended to recall 'a time which the population of Mexico might feel was more ideal. As a global company,

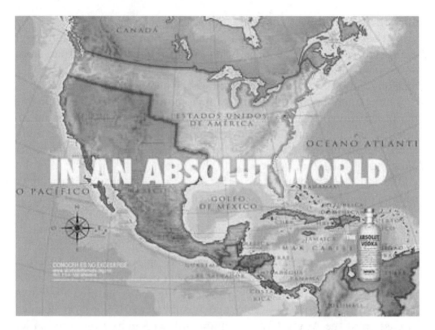

Figure 4.2   Absolut ad, Teran/TBWA, Mexico City 2008

we recognize that people in different parts of the world may lend different perspectives or interpret our ads in a different way than was intended in that market, and for that we apologize' (Associated Press as posted on FoxNews.com, 2008).

This incident is a prime example of variant socio-cultural meanings impacting 'executional receptivity.' While the ad may have triggered a 'mirth' response for many Mexicans in its target audience, the message, despite being in a non-digital medium in a different country, reached and offended many American consumers who did not perceive the humor.

Advertisers are increasingly confronting cross-cultural issues with regard to humorous advertising. In 2010, KFC ran an ad in Australia in which a white Australian cricket fan offers fried chicken to black cricket fans supporting a team from the West Indies. The ad created a furor in the USA after it was posted on YouTube. KFC Australia ultimately pulled the ad since it had been 'misinterpreted by a segment of people in the US as an African-American stereotype' (Mitchell 2010).

To a large extent advertisers are no longer in control over who is exposed to their advertising. Ads intended for one audience can now be seen by audiences who the advertiser never targeted. This has significant implications for advertisers since the cultural norms, values, and meanings that different audiences bring to bear on the ads, including humorous ones, cause them to interpret the ads differently.

4.4.1 Outdoor Advertising Humor Reflecting Cultural Meanings

The changing use of humor in outdoor advertisements provides an archive of changes in American cultural meanings. Outdoor advertising is a medium less affected than other media by editorial context and is unfiltered by selective exposure of audiences through choice of program or publication (Burtt 1938). As such, its analysis in the context of its time and place provides a good indicator of the cycles of socio-cultural meanings over the past hundred years.

The perspective in this study was shaped by McCracken's statement, 'Advertising is a conduit through which meaning constantly pours from the culturally constituted world to consumer goods' (McCracken 1986, p. 74). Similarly, Pollay posited, 'Old magazines provide a fascinating window into our social history, and it is the advertisements that comprise the most interesting pages, displaying behaviors, styles, and roles of diverse objects of our culture' (Pollay 1985, p. 24). While Pollay was discussing print advertising, his commentary is perhaps even more apt for outdoor advertising. Outdoor advertising is a part of the 'visual culture' and literally a part of the landscape like trees, buildings and highways (Jakle and Sculle 2004). Individuals choose which magazines to read, which radio stations to listen to, and which television programs to watch. By virtue of these choices they select, to a certain extent, the ads that they will be exposed to in these media. Individuals do not choose the outdoor advertising to which they will be exposed any more than they choose which buildings they will see on a daily commute. Even in areas with a concentration of certain industries or certain demographic groups, outdoor advertising will reach many people outside of the target audience. Therefore, these ads are a discourse with the general public. Outdoor advertisements are generally written to appeal to a broad audience (Gudis 2004).

Socio-cultural meanings, norms and values influence advertising but advertising also reflects socio-cultural meanings and norms. Both shift over time, sometimes with one nudging the other along. In order to gain a better understanding of how cultural meanings change over time and are expressed through advertising, we explore the evolution of outdoor advertising in the USA. First, we look at examples of outdoor humor from the late 1800s to the mid 1920s, largely from lithographs and black and white photos of posters and billboards published in *The Bill Poster* journal (later *The Poster*) and from Duke University's Hartman Center for Sales, Advertising & Marketing History, which houses the collections

Figure 4.3   c. 1896, from reproduction in The Bill Poster, *Volume 1*

from the Outdoor Advertising Association of America. The second set of advertisements is from award competitions. These collections date from the mid-1920s to the present and are the most consistent and preserved national record of poster advertising spanning 1925–2007, providing 82 years of award winning ads.

In the early 1900s, barely 35 years after the end of slavery, racial segregation was still the norm and even the law in many parts of America. In 1883 the courts had ruled that Congress lacked power to ban segregation by private individuals and organizations. Organizations such as the NAACP opposing such treatment did not form until 1909. The racial power dynamic and associated socio-cultural norms, now regarded nearly universally as racist, were reflected in advertising during this time. A page by page examination of the early *The Bill Poster* and *The Poster* between 1896 and 1920 confirmed the use of racially oriented humor by a number of national brands in America. For example, the poster ad for the Borax Company's White Victor Soap (see Figure 4.3) shows a black male bathing in a wooden tub with the sub-headline 'will whiten anything.' To the white audience the ad was probably viewed as playful and not offensive; however the majority of Americans today would find it offensive.

A second notable example of the use of racial stereotypes in poster

Figure 4.4   c. 1908, from reproduction in The Poster, *1910, 329*

advertising as the basis of humor is the Fairbank Soap Company's use of the Gold Dust Twins. This poster campaign is remarkable not only because Gold Dust used humor early and frequently in its outdoor advertising but also because racial caricatures were central to their advertising. The company featured cartoonish black twins in native skirts using their brand of household cleaning soap as the solution to household cleaning chores. One of the ads connects the product and the Twins to the 1903 flight at Kitty Hawk by the Wright Brothers, with an image of the Twins flying a plane and the slogan, 'The Right Brothers for Cleaning,' a classic play on words (see Figure 4.4). The Gold Dust and Borax ads are examples of what Laird (1998) cites as racial and ethnic caricatures, limericks and cartoons that marked the period, and as we can see humor was marshaled in such efforts.

From the early era of outdoor advertising through the 1920s, writers were cautious about using humor in advertising at all. The prevailing wisdom was that advertising humor was demeaning to the advertiser and not effective. The preferred approach was to focus on the product and reasons to purchase. The sample from this period of outdoor advertising shows just 3.9 percent of the ads employing humor. The view was that humor itself was not culturally acceptable. In the analysis humor was

YOU KNOW	BEFORE I TRIED IT
YOUR ONIONS	THE KISSES
LETTUCE SUPPOSE	I MISSED
THIS BEETS 'EM ALL	BUT AFTERWARD—BOY!
DON'T TURNIP YOUR NOSE	THE MISSES I KISSED
BURMA-SHAVE	BURMA-SHAVE
1935	1938

Figure 4.5   Examples of Burma Shave advertising copy

categorized into five types; 'word play,' 'warmth,' 'nonsense,' 'aggression,' 'sexual.' In this earliest period the majority of the humor employed word play followed by warmth and nonsense. Advertising humor in the early periods used almost no aggression or sex.

There was a four-fold increase of ad humor to over 15 percent from the 1930s through the 1950s. This trend contradicts what might be expected in the Depression era. Instead it reflects a general acceptance of the comic form as evidenced by the widespread popularity of humor on the radio and in newspaper comic strips. Perhaps humor became an acceptable escape for the bad times or it may simply reflect the heightened competition in radio for advertising attention.

During this period the use of warmth as a humor style rose dramatically to a peak of almost 46 percent of the sample. Perhaps warmth such as plays on words reflects a gentle and acceptable use of humor while remaining professional. An example of this style is seen in the popular Burma Shave campaign with its iconic rhyming humor (see Figure 4.5).

Over the next three decades the use of humor rose, reaching nearly 40 percent by 1989. We speculate that the change in competition brought about by television and the creative movement in advertising generally uncorked the use of humor in outdoor advertising at rates similar to that found in television ads of the era. The award winning ads of the time reflect and amplify key socio-cultural tensions that resonated with viewers. Ads making fun of long hair and mocking anti-billboard laws were found

Figure 4.6 Obie Award Winner 2006, courtesy of OAAA

in the late 1960s. For the audience which was part of the cultural establishment, an ad mocking the long hair, anti-war, dope-smoking hippies capitalized on a shared receptivity to ridicule this anti-establishment group with humor. This was a rare use of superiority humor in advertising to put down another group. The disappearance of warmth as a humor style and the rise of aggressive humor in the 1970s seems an apt insight into the mood of this tumultuous decade, in which existing norms were being tested by a large and vocal baby-boom generation and older Americans pushed back against these changes.

Through the 1990s and 2000s the percentage of humor in outdoor advertising again increased by more than 1.5 times with more than 70 percent of award-winning ads employing humor. Non-tendentious humor (warmth and play on words) continued to dominate the humor styles, though it had given way to some subtle and not so subtle changes in aggressive humor, including sexual humor which was rare or non-existent in earlier decades. There is a stark contrast between the gentle innocent humor of the Depression era and the aggressive and edgy humor in outdoor ads of more recent vintage (see Figure 4.6, Figure 4.7 and Figure 4.8). Perhaps advertisers perceive that American audiences shaped by visions of Clinton–Lewinsky sex scandals, erectile dysfunction ads and cable television rife with sexual and aggressive humor are primed to be more receptive to advertising which employs more aggressive and sexual humor. Transit ads also provide evidence to suggest that they also now reflect the more aggressive style seen in outdoor advertising (see Figure 4.9 and Figure 4.10). The warmth style which peaked at 45.6 percent in the 1930–1945 period is virtually non-existent today. A cultural lid seemed to be lifted on sexual, crude and aggressive media discourse which is reflected in the outdoor humor of the day.

Some of what passed for humor in the early days of outdoor advertising humor would disgust the public today. By the same token, some of

Figure 4.7   Obie Award Winner 2007, courtesy of OAAA

*Figure 4.8   Richmond Society for the Prevention of Cruelty to Animals
2005 (Barbara Martin Advertising)*

the suggestive word play and images used in outdoor humor today would have been unacceptable and would have disgusted audiences of the early days. The Gold Dust Twins would be as unlikely a humor strategy in 2012 as the Legal Sea Foods (Figure 4.10) would have been in 1950. In the context of the Challenge Model, cultural norms have shaped the amount and variety of humor used by advertisers and in turn been accepted by audiences. Audience receptivity to view play signals as humorous have changed dramatically. The subtle shift toward more tendentious and provocative humor and away from racist humor and then warm humor by American society represents seismic changes in what is considered acceptable and therefore what is perceived as humorous.

4.5   HUMOR, VIOLENCE AND GENDER[2]

As we saw a shift in the outdoor advertising humor toward more aggression and sex, we also observe a recent shift in American television toward

Figure 4.9   Obie Award Winner 2002, courtesy of OAAA

Figure 4.10   Obie Award Winner 2008, courtesy of OAAA

aggressive advertising humor particularly aimed at men. Advertising reflects and shapes cultural meanings. However, as noted by Pollay (1986), the reflection occurs in a distorted mirror. Yet this incomplete and distorted reflection helps to shape the culture (Pollay 1986). Kilbourne (1999) states, 'advertising often sells a great deal more than products . . . to a great extent, it tells us who we are and who we should be' (p. 74). Advertising is a refracted reflection of culture but its reading by consumers as a cultural text perpetuates and reinforces particular idealistic cultural norms, values, and meanings.

In the 1970s, advertising researchers first began to consider the broader effects of advertising. These researchers examined how women and minorities were portrayed in advertising (Bush et al. 1977; Courtney and Lockeretz 1971; Wagner and Banos 1973). Over time, researchers across a broad range of disciplines began to realize the secondary effects of advertising (e.g. Cortese 2008; Goffman 1979; Kilbourne 1999; Richins 1991), but the focus of the research has been on the portrayal of women, minorities and adolescents. With the exception of Gulas et al. (2010), the portrayal of white males and their role in shaping cultural meanings has been largely overlooked in the advertising literature.

Research on female images in advertising describes that men were historically shown in a dominant role with women in a subordinate or submissive position. In business settings, men were portrayed as leaders and women were portrayed as assistants. In family settings, the father figure played a dominant role. Additionally, men work in empowered, active positions as craftsmen, businessmen, and athletes. During periods of war, it has been common to portray men in ads as heroic figures (Hill 2002).

These advertising images were echoed by popular television shows. Popular television dads included Andy Taylor on the *Andy Griffith Show*, Ward Cleaver on *Leave it to Beaver*, Charles Ingalls on *Little House on the Prairie*; Mike Brady on *The Brady Bunch*, and Cliff Huxtable on *The Cosby Show*. Each of these characters was stable, financially secure, competent, and confident. While there were notable exceptions such as Fred Flintstone, Herman Munster, and Archie Bunker, TV dads generally served as a voice of reason, a source of wisdom and a stabilizing influence on the family. The exemplar of this role was the character Jim Anderson on the aptly named *Father Knows Best*.

The modern era of television is defined by a very different type of dad. This dad is often bumbling, or lazy, or self-centered, or some combination of these. The voice of reason on these shows is nearly always the wife, the children, a neighbor, or some secondary character. These dads include Homer Simpson on *The Simpsons*, Ray Barone and his father Frank Barone on *Everybody Loves Raymond*, Al Bundy on *Married With Children*, Tim Taylor on *Home Improvement*, Peter Griffin on *Family Guy* and Ed Goodson on *$#*! My Dad Says*. From the 1950s through the 1990s the portrayal of the father figure in TV programming changed significantly (Scharrer 2001). An analysis of sitcom characters from the 1950s through the 1990s revealed that female characters tell significantly more jokes at the expense of father characters in later decades than in earlier decades and the overall foolishness of portrayal of the father figure increased significantly in later decades compared to earlier decades (Scharrer 2001).

To more closely examine the portrayal of men in humorous advertising, an analysis of television ads was conducted by Gulas et al. (2010). Their analysis developed through work on other research projects, preparation of class materials, and general exposure to advertising, and was supplemented with ads appearing in the Super Bowls in 1989, 1999, and 2009. Ads for the five most advertised brands on American television in 2008 were also examined.

The analysis reveals two broad themes of violence in the context of humorous advertising. The first is explicit physical violence toward men. The second is denigration, which is a form of psychological violence (Candib 2000; Montminy 2005). Both of these trends represent a departure from past advertising practices. It is likely that it would not have been acceptable to either target and denigrate men or use physical violence in earlier periods in the USA.

Perhaps because it relies on an explicit verbal or physical put down, disparagement (superiority), as we noted earlier, has been used with some caution by advertisers to avoid alienating an audience which may either miss the play signals that help convert raw aggression into mirth, or who empathize with the target of the disparaging humor. However, the analysis suggests that disparagement of male characters now appears in a significant number of television ads. The butt of the joke in current advertising is now typically a male, often a male father figure. The gradual shift toward more aggressive and sexual humor that we recounted in the recent outdoor advertising study is magnified here where superiority humor is now widely employed on American television. There are several subcategories of denigration of men found in the ads in our sample: men are animals, men are childish, patronizing behavior toward men is acceptable, men are lazy, men are incompetent and ignorant, and men have an inflated view of themselves (and therefore deserve scorn). We examine each of the subthemes of denigration found in the ads.

4.5.1 Men are Animals

In an ad for the Sony Cybershot camera the dad is portrayed literally as a horse's ass. In a series of scenes set in and around a suburban house and at a school, a young girl, a young boy, and an adult woman interact with a horse's hindquarters. The children refer to the hindquarters as 'Dad,' and the wife refers to the hindquarters as 'sweetie.' The payoff of the joke is, 'your dad is not a horse's behind. A Sony Cybershot Camera knows this.' The implication is that the family may not know this but the camera does.

In yet another animal portrayal, an overweight slovenly dressed man is lying on the back of a sofa. His wife walks into the room and in a tone of voice that one might use in addressing an infant says, 'Boris, Boris, the neighbors are here.' Boris slumps slowly and awkwardly off of the back of the couch and down into the seat. He asks, 'Did they bring any food?' The wife replies, 'No they just came to visit.' In response, he moans and buries his face into the couch. A voice over then states, 'only cats can be cats, and some cats need to watch their weight.'

In these ads the humor derives from transforming men into animals. As animals, the men lose the right to be treated as humans. This dehumanizing can be used to justify a wide range of behaviors. In wars, propaganda is often used to deny humanity to enemies. Similarly, the Bushmen of the Kalahari refer to themselves as 'the humans' thereby denying human status to all others. Normal rules of humanity do not apply to these others (Watson 1995). We are not suggesting that these ads will lead to the hunting of men, but this type of imagery literally dehumanizes men and lowers their status in society.

4.5.2   Men are Childish

Many humorous ads portray men as children. In a Fidelity ad, a man is shown in a vigorous table-tennis match in a suburban garage. After a smash shot he shouts with glee that he has won the game and runs out of the garage whooping and then struts back into the garage. We then see that his opponent is a very young girl. He mockingly says 'What was that – like five games in a row?' He continues by mocking the girl, making fun of the look on her face when he made his kill shot.

In a Subway ad a man throws a tantrum, including stomping his feet and holding his breath, when his wife refuses to comply with his request to get a Big Philly Cheese Steak sandwich. She responds, 'that's real mature.' His young child joins in the condemnation angrily stating, 'yeah Dad grow up.'

In his discussion of ads that portrayed women as children, Goffman (1979) stated, 'Given the subordinated and indulged position of children in regard to adults, it would appear that to present oneself in puckish styling is to encourage corresponding treatment' (p. 48). A cell phone ad shows exactly this. A man with a cell/mobile phone is eating dinner with a family. He is enamored with the phone's technology and is sending text messages to family members to have them pass food to him. Eventually the wife demands that he give the phone to her in the same way that a mom would demand a toy from an ill-mannered child. He gives her the phone and pouts – just like a child.

4.5.3 Patronizing Behavior Towards Men is Acceptable

In humorous advertising it has become acceptable to patronize men. A Fidelity ad shows a couple speaking to the camera about their retirement planning. The wife says, 'We don't know much about handling money.' The man counters, 'When I switched jobs who handled the turnover?' 'Rollover,' the wife corrects him. She continues that Fidelity did it all. 'They would have signed your name if they could have.' She adds, 'You can't get the dog to roll over.' The man sheepishly replies, 'It's your dog.'

In a Sonic ad, a man and woman are ordering food. The woman says, 'I will have the hickory grilled chicken junior wrap and so will you.' The man replies, 'I really thought I wanted the light ranch grilled chicken.' The characters then begin talking over each other. He says awkwardly, 'I guess I was wrong.' The woman says, 'You don't know what you like.' The man continues, at this point speaking more to himself than to the woman, 'I don't know what to eat ever.'

4.5.4 Men are Lazy

This is the message in many humorous ads. Examples of this include a WKD ad where a man is sitting in a chair watching TV. His wife is hard at work multi-tasking several unpleasant household chores. While sitting in the chair he yells out asking if she needs help. She replies sarcastically, 'Only if it is not too much trouble.' In response, the man yells out the window, 'Mom! Mom! When you are finished out there Maxine needs a hand in the kitchen!' The shot cuts to the elderly mother who is outside struggling to wash a large truck, presumably owned by the man in the chair.

An ad for Brandt appliances shows an overweight, slovenly dressed man lying on a couch with snack bags and other debris scattered near him. The ad contrasts the reliability of Brant appliances with the lack of reliability of lazy men.

In an interesting ad in this genre, a man brings a drinking glass into the kitchen and puts in on the counter, then picks it up and puts it in the dishwasher as his wife looks on in amazement. The tagline is, 'Give that man a Klondike bar.' The clear implication is that the man is so lazy his wife is amazed when he makes even the most modest effort to be helpful. The tag line suggests that men help so little with household chores that this tiny contribution is worthy of a reward.

4.5.5   Men are Incompetent and Ignorant

Many humorous ads portray men as ignorant. For example, in a digital camera ad, a man walks through a grocery store trying to match photos in his hand with items on the shelf. We then see a woman taking pictures of items in the pantry, presumably because the man is incapable of following a list, or making choices on his own. Similarly, in an ad for a minivan, a hapless man fumbles about while trying unsuccessfully to fold a child's stroller. Meanwhile a woman quickly and efficiently reconfigures the minivan's seats. She then confidently takes the stroller from the man and places it in the van in the space she created by folding the seat down while he stands by looking utterly helpless.

In an ad that harkens back to the sexist advertising of earlier decades, albeit with the roles reversed, an Oven Pride oven cleaner ad claims that the product is so easy to use that a man could do it. While this ad appears to target women by making fun of men, the incompetent man execution style is used even for products that are generally targeted at men. For example, in an ad for Ortho weed-killer a woman instructs a man to 'kill the weeds, not the lawn.' The man replies in a tone that suggests he is trying hard to remember this valuable instruction, 'Weeds not lawn, got it.'

In a radio commercial for National Bank and Trust, a man and a woman are talking about online banking services that the company offers. The man seems overwhelmed by the technology. The woman concludes, 'plenty of features for people like me—easy to use for people like you.'

4.5.6   Men have an Inflated View of their Worth and Therefore Deserve Scorn

Another category is defined by the scorn shown to men. In one of these ads a group of people is gathered for a backyard cookout. A woman approaches a charcoal grill. A man urgently calls out, 'Honey, wait!' He explains that lighting charcoal requires a technique. He proceeds to light a match and place it on the pile of charcoal which ignites. The woman mockingly says 'wow.' She then turns to the crowd and proclaims in a mocking manner, 'it's OK everyone.'

Even when a man accomplishes something more significant than parking in a nearly empty lot, he can incur disdain. In an ad for Verizon Wireless, a dad proudly tells his daughters how they can call him as much as they want with the new family plan he has purchased. In response the daughters stare at him vacantly. The mom then says they can also use it to call their friends. This statement generates a very excited reaction. In the excitement the dad asks for a group hug since it is the plan that he purchased that has created the joyous situation but he is completely ignored by the mom and daughters who leave the room.

4.5.7 Violence Against Men is Humorous

Of all the aspects of the negative portrayals of men outlined in this chapter perhaps the most troubling is that violence against men is shown as humorous. There are two subcategories of this type of advertisement. In one type, the violence is of a general nature. In the other, the violence is presented as a reasonable response to something that the man has done.

A mild example of the first type is an ad for Polysporin Complete, an OTC antiseptic and pain treatment. It shows a dad using a water slide toy with kids. His momentum carries him off of the end of the slide and he crashes into the garbage that has been put out to the curb. He moans in pain. An almost identical execution is used in an ad for Country Time Lemonade where again an adult man using a children's water slide appears to get injured. While this is a relatively minor type of slap-stick violence it is unlikely that the ad would present the same fate occurring to a mom – or a child – as a humorous event.

An ad for the Dodge Ram pickup truck shows a wedding scene. As the minister approaches the part of the ceremony where a kiss is customary, the bride chooses instead to head-butt the groom and knocks him unconscious. She then carries him out to her pickup truck. In yet another general violence ad, in an ad for Wellesley Sound Studios a woman wearing boxing gloves appears to be beating a man.

It is most disturbing that violence against men in ads is often 'justified.' For example, in a Visa credit card ad, a woman walks into a room where a man is watching TV and eating popcorn. A children's cartoon is playing on the TV and the man is laughing uproariously and dropping popcorn all over the floor. The woman says that she has bought a new vacuum, but the man is too engrossed in the cartoon to react to her statement. She begins to vacuum the floor. When she gets near his feet he says, 'You missed a spot.' In reaction to his statement she points the vacuum at him and he gets sucked into the machine. She says in a pleased tone, 'it works.' The scene then flashes back to when she bought the machine, and the salesman says the machine will be good for her biggest problem areas.

In a wireless ad a woman is frantically looking for her lost Sprint Blackberry when two male colleagues ask if everything is alright. She then hears the phone ring in one of the colleague's pockets. She gives him an angry look and he replies in a frightened tone that he was just making a joke. The next scene is set in a hospital where the woman is texting the message that Frank might be late. The shot widens to show one of the men being treated by the medical staff and the other man sitting next to the woman. He is holding an ice pack on his head.

Violence (disparagement), albeit a mild form, is also portrayed as justified in an ad for Net Florist. In this ad, a woman wearing rubber gloves and a face mask vigorously scrubs a toilet with a blue toothbrush, which she then places back in the toothbrush holder next to a pink toothbrush. The tag line is, 'whatever you do, don't forget.' The ad then offers a service providing anniversary reminders, birthday reminders etc.

More harsh forms of violence are reserved for men who remember to buy gifts but buy the wrong items. An animated banner ad on the Detroit News website demonstrated that men who buy the wrong Valentine's Day gift might be subject to a beating. A similar, more extreme example of this 'justified' violence is an ad for lxdirect.com. The ad opens in a hospital emergency room. In the background, 'The Twelve Days of Christmas' is playing out of tune as if being played by a child on a recorder. The emergency room is decorated for Christmas. In the waiting area, a man with a black-eye, bloodied face, and possibly broken nose is wiping blood off his face with what appears to be lingerie. Next to him sits a man with a woman's spike-heeled slipper impaled into the top of his shaved head. The man in the next seat has an electric hand mixer impaled into his ear. The whisk part of the blender is sticking out and is still spinning. All three men look to be in pain. A squeaking noise occurs off camera and the three men turn towards it. The squeak is coming from the wheels of a vacuum cleaner. The vacuum is being pushed by a man who is doubled over in pain. The hand wand of the vacuum appears to have been forced up the man's rectum. He greets the other three men. The screen then displays the text, 'How wrong will he get it this year?' As that text fades from the screen, new text appears. 'Vote now for the worst Xmas present ever in our national "What Women Won't Want" survey.' The ad is sponsored by an online retailer.

In all of the ads discussed in this section, the attempted humor derives from violence targeted at men. The most troubling aspect of these ads is that often the violence appears to be justified. This suggests the 'blame the victim' mentality that has been condemned in domestic violence literature for decades.

4.5.8   Prevalence of Male Denigration in Advertising

To examine the prevalence of portrayals such as those described and to ascertain if there has been a change in the portrayal of men in advertising, we examined Super Bowl advertising from 1989, 1999, and 2009. The ads were obtained from the online archive available at AdLand.tv (AdLand 2009).

In 1989 just 13.6 percent of Super Bowl ads using humor involved aggressive or disparaging humor, none of which used physical violence. In 1999, aggression was used in almost a third of the ads using humor, and physical humor mainly aimed at men became more common. In 2009 over 70 percent of the humorous ads in the Super Bowl used some form of aggression (Gulas et al. 2010). More notable is that 13 out of 34 of these ads use males as the victims of physical violence in contrast with only one ad in which women were the victims of physical violence. The advertisers using physical violence with male victims in the 2009 sample include Coke Zero, Audi, Frito Lay, Doritos, Castrol, Sobe and Pepsi Max and Bud Light. In the Pepsi Max ad five different men are the victims of physical violence. In at least two of these violent acts the victim would likely have been hospitalized or killed if the events portrayed had actually happened.

Violent humor has become a significant theme in Bud Light advertising. Thirty-four television ads aired for Bud Light in the USA between January 1, 2009 and December 2, 2009 (AdScope 2009). All of these ads used humor. Of these ads, eight included some form of physical violence. In seven ads the violence is directed against men and often perpetrated by a woman. For example, in one ad a woman breaks up with her boyfriend by pushing him out the door of a moving car. In another Bud Light ad, a woman attaches a boutonniere to a man's tuxedo with seven nails shot from a nail gun. The man grimaces in agony from what would be in reality a life-threatening assault.

Two recent Bud Light ads also 'justify' violence. In one of these ads a female restaurant patron is attempting to get the attention of a waiter who is ignoring her. She eventually gets his attention by tripping him. He falls across a table, where another man is dining, and through a plate glass window almost landing on a third man seated in the patio area of the restaurant. All three men are hit by falling glass. In the Bud Light 'meeting' ad, a man gets thrown out of a third story window for suggesting that the company could save money by cutting back on its beer purchases.

4.5.9   Cultural Implications

Today, males, particularly white males, bear the brunt of humorous attacks of all types. From a cultural perspective these portrayals are understandable. As awareness has increased over domestic violence, the impact of advertising on body image, and the increased prevalence and empowerment of women and minorities, men are the safest target of humor. While norms for women and minorities have changed, there are still much more rigid schemas for what it means to be a man or not that are relatively unquestioned and therefore easier sources of humor through incongruency. Moreover, if a woman was substituted in many ads as the butt of the joke, the ads would often lose humor and become offensive. In ads depicting violence, if the victim were a woman, it is likely that the audience would not perceive a play signal, thus turning comedy into tragedy, particularly if the perpetrator was a man, as schemas of domestic violence would be made salient. Indeed the extreme violence found in some of these attempts at humor is a new phenomenon as evidenced by our examination of Super Bowl ads. Audiences in an earlier era might not have perceived play signals in these ads regardless of the gender of the victim. Nonetheless, the victims in these ads are overwhelmingly, indeed nearly exclusively, male. This says something about norms in the current culture in America and in other countries where this imagery is prevalent.

Humor gives a broad license to the humorist. By means of humor, one can make statements that would not be tolerated if delivered in a serious manner. Even when an individual is personally ridiculed, the options for response to the ridicule are limited. You can disingenuously laugh along; you can try to ignore it; or you can protest and be accused of not having a sense of humor. Therefore, ridicule is often felt to be more humiliating than other forms of interaction, including physical or verbal violence (Kuipers 2006).

The question is whether the use of men as the targets of denigration and sometimes violent humor may be ephemeral. Is it just a passing fad which we will judge as sternly in the future as we do the early racist humor, or is this a permanent change toward more aggressive humor? What is seen as funny is likely to change over time, a fact we were reminded of when examining advertising humor over the past century. In the context of the Challenge Model, the play signals and schemas that are familiar to audiences portray men as lazy, animals, children, ignorant, incompetent and with inflated views of themselves. Somehow advertiser use of and audience receptivity of these contextual cues to create humor has undergone considerable change on American television. The use of violence targeted at men assumes that aggression has play signals that are viewed by audiences as pretend and almost cartoon like. If the violence is wrapped in such play signals the denigration is seen as 'just a joke.'

4.6   CONCLUSION

Advertisers are working in an increasingly global marketplace. In 2010 an ad agency in Amsterdam was charged with creating a humorous campaign for a German company that manufactured an iconic British car that was sold in markets around the world. Yet it is very likely that the Dutch,

German, British and American perceptions of a given humorous execution produced by the Amsterdam agency will vary. It is possible that reactions will also vary by subgroup within each country. This suggests that nuances embedded in cultural norms, expectations and practices present a minefield of potential obstacles for advertisers. The advertiser based in a country or culture needs to create ads that may intentionally be seen or heard in another country. As we saw in the Absolut ad, a company may have their ad unintentionally seen by audiences in other countries with different cultural histories who could be offended by the same ad. It has become clear to us that understanding cultural meanings is essential as advertisers create narratives that are appropriately perceived by audiences. Yet meanings evolve and are constructed over time. As we saw in the outdoor advertising over the past century in America, the use and style of humor changed significantly based on evolving cultural meanings. The more recent shift to denigration and violence toward men in television ads is a further example that the norms shift even within borders, sometimes quite drastically, as advertisements both reflect and influence cultural meanings.

The Challenge Model presented earlier highlights that decoding of advertising humor is shaped by the context of 'Facilitating Conditions'. It is clear that the cultural context sits atop the audience factors that shape the norms that influence perceptions of 'Play Signals', 'Schema Familiarity', and 'Executional Receptivity'. Humor that violates norms or can't be interpreted as humor can be risky and have a negative impact, opposite to that intended. Our contention is that humor is often culturally based, and given the increasingly multicultural consumer markets, it is dangerous to assume that even within a single culture that all audiences will consider a given 'humorous' ad as equally funny.

It is clear the decoding of what generates mirth and its subsequent effects is bounded by the point of view of the society at a point in time. It is most unlikely even in a world homogenized by communication in movies, satellite TV programming and the internet that any one humor attempt in an ad will have universal appeal. It is possible that when crossing cultural and even sub-cultural boundaries that the edgier humor denigrating people, groups or countries is more likely to trigger unwanted responses. The findings reported here strongly suggest that any attempt at humorous advertising be pre-tested on the appropriate target audiences, and that consideration should be given to what might occur if an ad designed for one target audience gets exposed to unintended audiences.

The age-old question that will remain unanswered is whether the racist images of early 1900s outdoor advertising, the raunchy humor of the 1990s, the physically violent advertising on American TV in the 2000s, and the other genres of advertising humor themselves have an impact on our culture. Does more TV ad violence for the sake of a laugh itself change the norm for what is a 'Play Signal' and of the future 'Receptivity' such that it begets more violent ads in order to further surprise audiences? It will be interesting to observe if such forms of more extreme ad humor travel well within and across cultural borders and whether their use expands and becomes more widespread and even more extreme.

NOTES

1. Selected portions of this section drawn from Gulas and Weinberger (2010).
2. Selected portions originally published as Gulas, McKeage, and Weinberger (2010), 'It's just a joke: violence against males in humorous advertising', *Journal of Advertising*, **39** (4) 109–120, used by permission of M.E. Sharpe, Inc.

REFERENCES

AdLand (2009), Super Bowl Archives available online: http://adland.tv/SuperBowlCommer cials accessed 22 December 2008.

AdScope (2009), data acquired from TNS Media Intelligence, http://www.tns-mi.com/

Alden, D.L. and W.D. Hoyer (1993), 'An examination of cognitive factors related to humor-ousness in television advertising', *Journal of Advertising*, **22** (June), 29–37.

Alden, D.L., W.D. Hoyer and C. Lee (1993), 'Identifying global and culture-specific dimen-sions of humor in advertising: a multinational analysis', *Journal of Marketing*, **57** (April), 64–75.

Anderson, R.C. (1984), 'The notion of schemata and the educational enterprise: general discussion of the conference', in R.C. Anderson, R.J. Spiro and W.E. Montague (eds), *Schooling and the Acquisition of Knowledge*, Hillsdale, NJ: Lawrence Erlbaum.

Archer, B. (1994), 'Does humor cross borders?' *Campaign* (17 June), 32–34.

Associated Press (2008), 'Vodka maker apologizes for ad depicting southwest as part of Mexico', Vol. 2008: FoxNews.com.

Bourdieu, P. (1983), 'Handbook of theory and research for the sociology of education: the forms of capital', in J.C. Richards (ed.), New York: Greenwood Press.

Bourdieu, P. (1984), *Distinction: A Social Critique of the Judgment of Taste*, Cambridge: Harvard Press.

Burtt, H.E. (1938), *Psychology of Advertising*, Boston: Houghton Mifflin Company.

Bush, R.F., P.J. Solomon and J.F. Hair (1977), 'More blacks in TV ads', *Journal of Advertising Research*, **17** (February), 21–25.

Candib, L.M. (2000), 'Primary violence prevention', *Journal of Family Practice*, **49** (10), 904–906.

Cho, H. (1995), 'Humor mechanisms, perceived humor and their relationships to various executional in advertising', in F. Kardes and M. Sujan (eds), *Advances in Consumer Research*, **22** (1), 191–197.

Cortese, A.J. (2008), *Provocateur: Images of Women and Minorities in Advertising*, Lanham, MD: Rowman & Littlefield.

Courtney, A.E. and S.W. Lockeretz (1971), 'A woman's place: an analysis of the roles portrayed by women in magazine advertisements', *Journal of Marketing Research*, **8** (1), 92–95.

DiMaggio, P. (1997), 'Culture and cognition', *Annual Review of Sociology*, **23** (1), 263–87.

Duncan, C., J.E. Nelson and N.T. Frontczak (1984), 'The effect of humor on advertising comprehension', in T.C. Kinnear (ed.), *Advances in Consumer Research*, **11**, Provo, UT: Association for Consumer Research.

Flaherty, K., M.G. Weinberger and C.S. Gulas (2004), 'The impact of perceived humor, product type and humor style in radio advertising', *Journal of Current Issues and Research in Advertising*, **26** (1), 25–36.

Gallivan, J. (1991), 'What is funny to whom, and why?', in Ninth International Conference on Humour and Laughter, Brock University, St. Catharines, Ontario, Canada.

Gelb, B.D. and C.M. Pickett (1983), 'Attitude-toward-the-ad: links to humor and to advertising effectiveness', *Journal of Advertising*, **12** (2), 34–42.

Gelb, B.D. and G.M. Zinkhan (1986), 'Humor and advertising effectiveness after repeated exposures to a radio commercial', *Journal of Advertising*, **15** (2), 15–20, 34.

Giddens, A. (1984), *The Constitution of Society*, Berkeley: University of California Press.

Godkewitsch, M. (1976), 'Physiological and verbal indices of arousal in rated humour', in A.J. Chapman and H.C. Foot (eds), *Humour and Laughter: Theory, Research and Application*, London: John C. Wiley & Sons.

Goffman, E. (1979), *Gender Advertisements*, NY: Harper and Row.

Gruner, C.R. (1991), 'On the impossibility of having a taxonomy of humor', paper presented at Ninth International Conference on Humour and Laughter, Brock University, St. Catharine's.

Gruner, C.R. (1997), *The Game of Humor*, New Brunswick and London: Transaction Publishers.

Gudis, C. (2004), *Buyways: Billboards, Automobiles, and the American Landscape*, New York: Routledge.

Gulas, C.S., K.K. McKeage and M.G. Weinberger (2010), 'It's just a joke: violence against males in humorous advertising', *Journal of Advertising*, **39** (4), 109–120.

Gulas, C.S. and M.G. Weinberger (2006), *Humor in Advertising: A Comprehensive Analysis*, Armonk, NY: M.E. Sharpe.

Gulas, C.S. and M.G. Weinberger (2010), 'That's not funny here: Humorous Advertising across boundaries', in D. Chiaro (ed.), *Translation, Humour and the Media*, London: Continuum Books, pp. 17–33.

Hill, D.D. (2002), *Advertising to the American Woman*, Columbus: Ohio State University Press.

Hofstede, G. (2001), *Culture's Consequences*, 2nd edn, Thousand Oaks: Sage Publications.

Holt, D.B. (1997a), 'Distinction in America? Recovering Bourdieu's theory of tastes from its critics', *Poetics*, **25** (November), 93–120.

Holt, D.B. (1997b), 'Poststructuralist lifestyle analysis: conceptualizing the social patterning of consumption in postmodernity', *Journal of Consumer Research*, **23** (4), 326–50.

Holt, D.B. (1998), 'Does cultural capital structure American consumption?', *Journal of Consumer Research*, **25** (June), 1–25.

Jakle, J.A. and K.A. Sculle (2004), *Signs in America's Auto Age: Signatures of Landscape and Place*, Iowa City: University of Iowa Press.

Kilbourne, J. (1999), *Deadly Persuasion: Why Women and Girls Must Fight the Addictive Power of Advertising*, New York: The Free Press.

Koestler, A. (1964), *The Act of Creation*, New York: Macmillan.

Kogut, B. and U. Zander (1992), 'Knowledge of the firm, combinative capabilities, and the replication of technology', *Organization Science*, **3** (3), 383–97.

Kuipers, G. (2006), *Good Humor, Bad Taste: A Sociology of the Joke*, Berlin: Walter de Gruyter.

Laird, P.W. (1998), *Advertising Progress: American Business and the Rise of Consumer Marketing*, Baltimore: Johns Hopkins University Press.

Lee, Y.H. and E.A.C. Lim (2008), 'What's funny and what's not', *Journal of Advertising*, **37** (2), 71–83.

Madden, T.J. and M.G. Weinberger (1982), 'The effects of humor on attention in magazine advertising', *Journal of Advertising*, **11** (3), 8–14.

Madden, T.J. and M.G. Weinberger (1984), 'Humor in advertising: a practitioner view', *Journal of Advertising Research*, **24** (4), 23–29.
Martin, K.A. (1998), 'Becoming a gendered body: practices of preschools', *American Sociological Review*, **63** (4), 494–511.
McCracken, G. (1986), 'Culture and consumption: a theoretical account of the structure and movement of the cultural meaning of consumer goods', *Journal of Consumer Research*, **13** (June), 71–84.
McGhee, P.E. (1983), 'The role of arousal and hemispheric lateralization in humor', in P.E. McGhee and J. Goldstein (eds), *Handbook of Humor Research: Basic Issues*, New York: Springer-Verlag.
Mitchell, P. (2010), 'KFC Australia pulls "racist" ad after US anger', available online http://www.news.com.au/world/kfc-australia-pulls-racist-ad-after-us-anger/story-e6frfkyi-12258169698952010. Accessed 11 November 2010.
Montminy, L. (2005), 'Older women's experiences of psychological violence in their marital relationships', *Journal of Gerontological Social Work*, **46** (2), 3–22.
Morreall, J. (1983), *Taking Laughter Seriously*, Albany, NY: State University of New York Press.
Murphy, J.H., D.K. Morrison and M. Zahn (1993), 'A longitudinal analysis of the use of humor in award winning radio commercials: 1974–1988', in E. Thorson (ed.), *Proceedings of the 1993 Conference of The American Academy of Advertising*, Columbia, MO: School of Journalism, University of Missouri-Columbia.
Nevo, O. (1986), 'Humor diaries of Israeli Jews and Arabs', *Journal of Social Psychology*, **126** (3), 411–13.
Nonaka, I. (1994), 'A dynamic theory of organizational knowledge creation', *Organization Science*, **5** (February), 14–37.
Pollay, R.W. (1985), 'The subsiding sizzle: a descriptive history of print advertising, 1900–1980', *Journal of Marketing*, **49** (3), 24–37.
Pollay, R.W. (1986), 'The distorted mirror: reflections on the unintended consequences of advertising', *Journal of Marketing*, **50** (2), 18–36.
Richins, M.L. (1991), 'Social comparison and the idealized images of advertising', *Journal of Consumer Research*, **18** (1), 71–83.
Rustogi, H., P.J. Hensel and W.P. Burgers (1996), 'The link between personal values and advertising appeals: cross-cultural barriers to standardized global advertising', *Journal of Euromarketing*, **5** (4), 57–79.
Scharrer, E. (2001), 'From wise to foolish: the portrayal of the sitcom father, 1950s–1990s', *Journal of Broadcasting & Electronic Media*, **45** (1), 23–40.
Sewell, W.H. (1999), 'The concept(s) of culture', in V.E. Bonnell and L. Hunt (eds), *Beyond the Cultural Turn*, Berkeley: University of California Press.
Shama, A. and M. Coughlin (1979), 'An experimental study of the effectiveness of humor in advertising', in N. Beckwith (ed.), *Educators' Conference Proceedings*, Chicago: American Marketing Association.
Speck, P.S. (1987), 'On humor and humor in advertising', unpublished doctoral dissertation, Texas Tech University.
Spencer, H. (1860), 'The physiology of laughter', *Macmillan's Magazine*, **1**, 395–402.
Spotts, H.E., M.G. Weinberger and A.L. Parsons (1997), 'Assessing the use and impact of humor on advertising effectiveness: a contingency approach', *Journal of Advertising*, **26** (3), 17–32.
Suls, J.M. (1977), 'Cognitive and disparagement theories of humor: a theoretical and empirical synthesis', in A.J. Chapman and H.C. Foot (eds), *It's a Funny Thing Humour*, Oxford: Pergamon Press.
Swidler, A. (1986), 'Culture in action: symbols and strategies', *American Sociological Review*, **51** (April), 273–86.
Swidler, A. (2001), *Talk of Love: How Culture Matters*, Chicago: University of Chicago Press.
Unger, L.S. (1995), 'Observations: a cross-cultural study on the affect-based model of humor in advertising', *Journal of Advertising Research*, **35** (Jan–Feb), 66–71.

Wacquant, L. (2004), *Body & Soul: Notebooks of an Apprentice Boxer*, New York: Oxford University Press USA.

Wagner L. and J.B. Banos (1973), 'A woman's place: a follow-up analysis of the role portrayed by women in magazine advertisements', *Journal of Marketing Research*, **10** (May), 213–14.

Watson, L. (1995), *Dark Nature: A Natural History of Evil*, New York: Harper Collins Publishers.

Weinberger, M.G. and C.S. Gulas (1992), 'The impact of humor in advertising: a review', *Journal of Advertising*, **21** (December), 35–59.

Weller, L., E. Amitsour and R. Pazzi (1976), 'Reactions to absurd humor by Jews of eastern and western descent', *Journal of Social Psychology*, **98** (April), 159–63.

Whipple, T.W. and A. Courtney (1980), 'Male and female differences in response to nonsensical humor in advertising', in J.E. Haefner (ed.), *Proceedings of the American Academy of Advertising*.

ZenithOptimedia (2007), Global Spending 2007.

Zhang, Y. (1996), 'The effect of humor in advertising: an individual difference perspective', *Psychology & Marketing*, **13** (September), 531–45.

Zhang, Y. and G.M. Zinkhan (1991), 'Humor in television advertising', in R.H. Holman and M.R. Solomon (eds), *Academy of Marketing Science Review*, **18**, Provo, UT: Association for Consumer Research: Advances in Consumer Research.

Zillmann, D. (1983), 'Disparagement humor', in P. McGhee and J. Goldstein (eds), *Handbook of Humor Research*, **1**, New York: Springer-Verlag.

Zillmann, D., J. Bryant and J.R. Cantor (1974), 'Brutality of assault in political cartoons affecting humor appreciation', *Journal of Research in Personality*, **7**, 334–345.

PART II

CONSUMERS IN CONTEXT

5 Retail and spatial consumer behaviour
Harry Timmermans

5.1 INTRODUCTION

Most attention in marketing and consumer studies has been devoted to the topic of product and store choice. The aim of most of this research has been to formulate and test hypotheses about various aspects of consumer choice behaviour in a retailing/shopping context. In general, these hypotheses relate to psychological concepts such as shopping value (Carpenter, 2008; Seo and Lee, 2008; Jackson et al., 2011), loyalty (Bridson et al., 2008; DeMoulin and Zidda, 2008; Helgeson et al., 2010), trust (MacIntosh, 2009), shopping experience (Borges et al., 2010), self-congruence (Ekinci and Riley, 2003), frugality (Lastovicka et al., 1999; Bove et al., 2009), shopping trip value (e.g., Diep and Sweeney, 2008), store shopping mode (Kim and Kim, 2008), and store and mall atmospherics (e.g., Chebat et al., 2009; Dennis et al., 2010; Massicotte et al., 2011) which are deemed important in better understanding principles and mechanisms underlying consumer choice behaviour.

In addition to this analytical research, there is a more limited tradition in marketing research of predicting consumer choice behaviour as a function of marketing measures. These studies go beyond the hypothesis-testing studies in that their focus is not only on testing whether an assumed difference or relationship is statistically significant but also on establishing (and testing) the strength and nature of the assumed relationship. It is especially this feature that makes these studies appropriate for assessing the consequences of marketing measures on choice probabilities and market shares.

While marketing studies have primarily focused at the product and store level, disciplines such as geography, regional science, transportation research and especially urban planning have been concerned with consumer choice of shopping centres (zones or districts). Often the choice of such locations is called spatial choice behaviour. The aim of these studies differs between disciplines and application contexts. The focus of attention in transportation research is typically to predict the traffic flow and transport demand implications of new retail development (e.g., Marker and Goulias, 2000). In contrast, urban planning studies are primarily conducted to assess the economic viability of new large scale retail development (e.g., Okuruwa et al., 1988, 1994; Gatzlaff et al., 1994; Porojan, 2001) and/or to predict the impact that such new development will likely have on the existing retail structure (e.g., Aberdeenshire Council, 2004). Results are input to the retail planning process in which municipal governments need to give permission to new retail development or withhold it. With an increasing laissez-faire policy in many countries, we can witness similar research rapidly emerging in real estate (e.g., Eppli and Benjamin, 1994; Mejia and Benjamin, 2002; Lee and Pace, 2005).

Due to these differences in purpose, orientation and objectives, the kind of variables included in these different studies tends to vary. Product choice is commonly predicted and analyzed as a function of brand image, product features and price, whereas store choice is often predicted as a function of store atmospherics, merchandise selection, price and some distance decay function. Studies on the choice of shopping centres tend to focus on variables such as size of the centres, range of shops, presence of anchor stores, parking facilities and relative location.

There is a scarcity of studies which have tried to figure out which attributes primarily trigger consumer choice behaviour: brand image or attributes, store attributes or shopping centre attributes. The answer to this question is likely situation and context-dependent. If consumers have strong preferences for a specific brand, it is most likely that there is no trade-off between brand and store/centre attributes and that they select the most convenient store which sells that brand. On the other hand, if they are relatively invariant across some subset of brands, differences between stores and centres more likely articulate the basis for their choice behaviour. Shopping centre attributes probably are relatively more important in the case of high uncertainty, comparative, multi-purpose shopping. If a consumer cannot be certain that she will be able to find the right dress in a particular store, she minimizes risk when she decides to visit a shopping centre with multiple clothing stores.

In this chapter, I will first discuss major progress in formulating models that have been used to predict the choice of shopping centre. The purpose is to show how increasingly complexity has been added to these models in an attempt to account for changes in society that have resulted in more complex and varied spatial choice behaviour. Next, I will focus on the typical variables that have been used to measure the attractiveness of space and argue that further improvements in application and relevance may be achieved by fusing approaches in marketing and the spatial disciplines.

5.2   TRADITIONAL MODELLING APPROACHES

5.2.1   Gravity or Spatial Interaction Models

The origins of the predictive models of consumer choice of store and shopping centre do not differ much between marketing and disciplines such as geography, urban planning and transportation. Many textbooks on retail marketing discuss the so-called Huff-model (Huff, 1963, 1964) which suggested that the probability of choosing a shopping centre is proportional to some function of its size and decreases with some function of distance. Working independently, Lakshmanan and Hansen (1965) modified a traffic model to arrive at a model of spatial shopping behaviour, which is very similar to the Huff model. Their model predicts that the flow of retail expenditure from residence zone i to shopping zone j equals:

$$S_{ij} = e_i P_i \frac{W_j f(d_{ij})}{\sum_{j'} W_{j'} f(d_{ij'})}$$

where,

S_{ij} is the flow of cash from residence zone i to shopping centre j;
e_i is the mean expenditure on shopping per person in zone i;
P_i is the population of zone i;
W_j is the size of the shopping centre in j;
d_{ij} is the distance between i and j;

Although the structure or specification of the models is the same, their theoretical foundations differ. Huff defended the model by referring to Luce's choice axiom (Luce, 1959), which states that when faced with several choice alternatives, the probability of an individual to choose a particular alternative is equal to the ratio of the utility of that alternative to the sum of the utilities across all choice alternatives in the individual's choice set. Applied to the choice of shopping centre problem, it implies that the probability of a consumer visiting a particular store or shopping centre is equal to the ratio of the utility of that store to the sum of utilities across all stores/centres considered by the consumer:

$$p_{ij} = \frac{F_j d_{ij}^{-\beta}}{\sum_{j'} F_{j'} d_{ij'}^{-\beta}}$$

where,

p_{ij} is the probability of a consumer at i visiting shopping centre j;
F_j is a measure of attractiveness of shopping centre j;
d_{ij} is the distance between i and j;
β is a distance decay parameter.

Examining the above equation shows that utility is conceptualized as a trade-off between the concepts attractiveness and distance decay. In principle, attractiveness may be measured by many different variables, at both the shopping centre and store level, including presence/absence of anchor stores, number of stores/assortment, parking space, parking fees, price level, quality of store, atmospherics, assortment, etc. The concept of distance decay indicates that, ceteris paribus, consumers are less willing to travel to shopping centres/stores with increasing distance/travel time.

To illustrate the model, assume a simple example of two shopping centres A and B. Furthermore, assume that the attractiveness of centre A is equal to 8 and the attractiveness of centre B is equal to 4. If we further assume that the distance decay effect of A for people in some selected residential area i is equal to 2, while the distance decay effect of B is equal to 4, then the probability of consumers living in this area (i) will choose centre A is equal to

$$p_{iA} = \frac{8/2}{8/2 + 4/4} = \frac{4}{5} = 80\%$$

Similarly, the probability that they will choose B, according to this model, is 20%. These numbers indicate that the attractiveness of A is twice that of B, while the willingness of consumers to travel to A (distance decay effect) is also double their willingness to travel to B. Thus, if we assume that utility is equal to the ratio of attractiveness and distance decay, consumers living in that area on average are four times as likely to choose A rather than B. Consequently, the choice probability for A is 80%.

Although in principle attractiveness can be measured in terms of a long list of variables, in Huff's model (and many that followed) it was measured as a function of size only. Size is assumed to be a good proxy variable for many other variables, potentially influencing the attractiveness of a shopping centre. Another reason in retail planning practice not to use a long list of especially marketing variables is that at the design stage of developing a shopping centre, when the viability and impact assessments need to be made, such detailed information is often not available. In addition to size, there may be information about the number of parking lots, but to the extent that such variables are proportional to size, the predictions will not be influenced (much).

In the above formulation, it is assumed that the choice probabilities are proportional to attractiveness/size. However, it may be that increasingly larger centres are extra attractive. An alternative hypothesis, however, may be that at some size, consumers start to less like the shopping centre because for example walking distances within the centre become cumbersome, or the centre may become too crowded. These alternative hypotheses may be tested by adding a parameter α to the model as follows:

$$p_{ij} = \frac{F_{jj}^{\alpha} d_{ij}^{-\beta}}{\sum_{j'} F_{j'j'}^{\alpha} d_{ij'}^{-\beta}}$$

If the estimated value of α exceeds 1.0, larger shopping centres attract consumers more than proportionally to their size; if it is smaller than one, larger centres attract a less than proportional number of consumers. This may indicate that consumers tend to avoid the congested, larger shopping centres.

While Huff referenced to the literature on utility and consumer behaviour, in contrast, the Lakshmanan and Hansen formulation was in line with the tradition of social physics that was dominant in disciplines such as transportation research and urban planning in those years. Their model was consistent with Reilly's Law of Retail Gravitation (Reilly, 1931). The gravity principle, which was used to delimit retail market areas, stated that two cities attract customers from an intermediate town in direct proportion to the populations of the two cities and in inverse proportion to the squares of the distances from these two cities to the intermediate town. Spatial-interaction models, of which the Lakshmanan-Hansen model is an example, underlie the analogous assumption that the share of customers that a shopping centre attracts from its environment is inversely proportional to distance and proportional to the attractiveness of the shopping centre.

These spatial interaction or gravity models have remained very popular at least until the 1980s, and in some academic networks they have never really been replaced by any other modelling approaches. In applied work, much effort was spent on the measurement and specification of the distance decay function, and the identification of factors contributing to the attractiveness of shopping centres. Should distance be measured in terms of straight-line distances or city-block distances, as true distance on the transportation network or in terms of travel time? It goes without saying that in terms of consumer behaviour, travel times are likely more valid.

However, one should realize that if the shopping model is used for forecasting, using travel times would imply that the planning agency should also apply a transport model to predict future travel times. Therefore, often distances along the transportation network have been used.

In addition, various functional forms such as inverse distance, negative exponential and even more complex, generalized functions have been used to represent distance decay or impedance effects. It is impossible to say which form is best. Their performance was found to differ in different study areas. In general, it is advisable to use generalized flexible forms of which specific distance decay functions are special cases. Similarly, the measurement of the concept of attractiveness has been the subject of discussion. It has been typically measured in terms of some size variable such as square footage of retail space, number of retail establishments, and number of anchor stores, etc. (e.g., Haines et al., 1972). Originally, single surrogate indicators were used, but later these have been replaced with multidimensional measures (e.g. Nevin and Houston, 1980; Stanley and Sewall, 1976). In addition to size, variables such as price level, number of parking lots and atmospherics have been added. Nevin and Houston (1980) argued that subjective, image variables are more relevant than objective measures. If their argument were to be accepted, the application of these models into planning practice would imply that the model should include an estimated relationship between the objective/physical measures and consumer's image (or whatever the psychological concept used). Because new shopping centres do not yet exist and practitioners tend to be reluctant to use the results of image studies concerned with other shopping centres, this added complexity has remained confined to academic research. As indicated in the introduction, urban planners have typically used size-related variables, distance decay and in some cases parking-related variables and type of retail development as explanatory variables in their model applications, whereas marketing researchers have been more inclined to include the full spectrum of marketing mix variables, albeit mostly at the level of store choice as opposed to shopping centre choice.

Spatial interaction models have not fundamentally changed since their inception if one examines current applications (e.g., González-Benito, 2005; Simmonds and Feldman, 2011). There has been one major generalization however. Fotheringham (1983) argued that choice probabilities do not only depend on the characteristics and distance decay to individual shopping centres, but that competition between destinations should also be taken into account. The relevance of this approach can be easily appreciated if we consider the following example. Suppose two shopping centres, a big and a small centre, make up the choices for residents living in a certain neighbourhood. Assume that planners intend to add another small shopping centre. The gravity model, and later on we will see that this property also applies to more modern modelling approaches, assumed that this new shopping centre will draw market shares proportional to the original shares of the two shopping centres. Is this property of the gravity model realistic? Wouldn't it be more realistic that, ceteris paribus, competition among the more similar, smaller centres is more intense than the competition between the large and the smaller centres? It led Fortheringham (1985), to formulate the competing destination model, which can be expressed as:

$$S_{ij} = e_i P_i \frac{W_j C_j^\lambda f(d_{ij})}{\sum_{j'} W_{j'} C_{j'}^\lambda f(d_{ij'})}$$

where,

$$C_j = \frac{1}{J-1} \sum_{j' \neq j} \frac{W_{j'}}{d_{jj'}}$$

Thus, the added term C_j measures the accessibility of shopping centre j to all other centres. Positive values of λ indicate agglomeration forces, implying that market demand is highest at locations in close proximity to other shopping centres. In contrast, negative values are indicative of spatial competition: compared to the standard gravity model, predictions of market shares are adjusted downward, due to competition between shopping centres in close proximity (Guy, 1987). Several other specifications to measure the similarity between competing destinations have been suggested (e.g., Borgers and Timmermans, 1987).

5.2.2 Discrete Choice Models

Input to the spatial interaction models are aggregated choice probabilities or interactions/trip frequencies between traffic zones and shopping centres or in more general terms between origins and destinations. Implicitly or explicitly, it is assumed that people living in the same residential zone exhibit the same behaviour. No attempt is made to differentiate between their characteristics, let alone between underlying choice and decision making strategies. One easy way of incorporating such observed heterogeneity would be to a priori segment the population, for example by age, race, income etc. and then develop and apply segment-specific models. However, even in planning practice, this more detailed approach has hardly been applied. Moreover, especially due to the strong, dominant foundation of spatial interaction models in social physics, shared by many disciplines such as transportation research, urban planning, regional science and geography until the 1980s, spatial interaction models were therefore criticized for their lack of theoretical foundation in terms of behavioural principles, although there have been several attempts to go beyond social physics and derive a behavioural foundation for these models. Ultimately, this criticism triggered a shift in major popularity from spatial interaction to discrete choice models (see McFadden, 1974, 1978, 1981; Ben Akiva and Lerman, 1985; Koppelman and Sethi, 2000; Train, 2003). This major breakthrough was made when developments in statistics allowed the estimation of disaggregate (i.e. data on individual choices) models. It led to many applications since the 1980s of the so-called multinomial logit model (MNL) which can be expressed as:

$$P_{ni} = \frac{e^{\mu V_{ni}}}{\sum_j e^{\mu V_{nj}}} = \frac{e^{\beta_1 X_{i1} + \beta_2 X_{i2} + \dots}}{\sum_j e^{\beta_1 X_{j1} + \beta_2 X_{j2} + \dots}}$$

where,

P_{ni} is the probability that individual n will choose shopping centre alternative i;

X_i is set of attributes of choice alternative i, one of which is distance or travel time.

This model can be derived from multiple theories, the most common of which is random utility theory. According to this theory, individuals derive a utility (U) from choosing a choice alternative (e.g., shopping centre). A consumer's utility for a choice alternative is assumed to consist of a deterministic or systematic utility plus a random or stochastic error term. That is

$$U_{ni} = V_{ni} + \varepsilon_{ni}$$

In practice, the deterministic part is measured in terms of a set of observed marketing or planning variables. Thus, this would be similar to the discussion of the Huff model. The utility of a shopping centre could be measured in terms of its size, parking, price, merchandising, store atmospherics etc. In fact, in applied research, the kinds of variables that have been used in the context of spatial interaction models were also used in these discrete choice models. Assuming that consumers are utility-maximizers, the probability that individual n will choose alternative i from it choice set C_n can then be expressed as:

$$p_{ni}|C_n = \Pr(U_{ni} > U_{nj}) \ \forall j \neq i \in C_n = \Pr[U_{ni} = \max_{j \in C_n} (U_{nj})]$$

In order to derive choice probabilities, a suitable assumption on the random error term has to be made. It enables the researcher to compute the probability that a choice alternative has the highest utility among all those available in the choice set. Because there are no strong theoretical reasons to choose a particular distribution, the quest was to search for a set of assumptions that would result in a so-called closed-form expression, i.e. an analytical solution. More specifically, the multinomial logit model was obtained by assuming that each error term is IID extreme value distributed (Gumbel distribution or a Type-I extreme value distribution). The density for each error term is:

$$f(\varepsilon) = \mu e^{-\mu(\varepsilon - \eta)} \exp[-e^{-\mu(\varepsilon - \eta)}]$$
$$\eta + \gamma/\mu, \ \gamma = 0.5772 \ (\text{Euler constant})$$

while the cumulative distribution is

$$F(\varepsilon) = \exp[-e^{-\mu(\varepsilon - \eta)}], \ \mu > 0$$

The variance of the distribution is $\pi^2/6\mu^2$

One should be aware of the fact that the very assumptions made with respect to the error terms to derive a closed-form expression resulted in a number of explicit or implicit features of the multinomial logit model. In turn, because these features were deemed restrictive, it gave rise to the formulation of more general discrete choice models. Progress in discrete choice modelling since the 1980s can be largely viewed as attempts to relax one or more of the limiting assumptions underlying the MNL model.

First, the assumption of independence implies the non-existence of any common unobserved factors affecting the utilities of the choice alternatives. This would be violated for example if shoppers assign a higher utility to all closed malls because of the protection from the weather. If such taste variation existed, it would not be measured by the deterministic part of the utility, and its effect (positive covariance between the enclosed malls) would not be captured by the error terms. Second, the assumption of identically distributed random utility terms (across alternatives) implies that the extent of variation in unobserved factors affecting the utility of an alternative is the same across all alternatives. This would be violated for example if crowdedness, which is typically unobserved, varies considerably for the big shopping malls but considerably less for the smaller centres.

Another critical assumption is the lack of any taste variation, also called response homogeneity. It states that all consumers with the same socio-demographic profile have the same responsiveness to the attributes of the choice alternatives. The model does not allow taste variations to an attribute due to unobserved individual characteristics (e.g. Ben-Akiva and Lerman, 1985). This assumption would be violated for example if consumers differ intrinsically in terms of environmental consciousness, reflected in their actual responsive behaviour and the utility they derive from the attributes of the choice alternatives. For example, environmentally conscious consumers may be more reluctant to use the car for shopping, implying that their willingness-to-travel (disutility of travel time by car) would differ from consumers less concerned about car use/the environment. Another assumption concerns error variance–covariance homogeneity, implying that the variance–covariance structure of the alternatives is identical across individuals. This would be violated if the extent of substitutability among alternatives differs across individuals. For example, some consumers may unfold their shopping behaviour in the choice between a local and a regional shopping centre, while other consumers may focus more strongly on two competing local centres. Consumers heavily involved in fashion may capture the substitutability of shopping centres primarily in terms of the number and kind of clothing stores, whereas consumers interested in other kinds of retailing will define substitutability in a different way. Error variance–covariance homogeneity implies the same competitive structure among alternatives (shopping centres) for *all* individuals, an assumption which is generally difficult to justify (e.g., Suarez et al., 2004).

A final property which perhaps has received most attention in the literature is the so-called independence from irrelevant alternatives (IIA). It states that the odds of choosing a particular alternative over another one are independent of the size and composition of the choice set. This is the same property that led to the competing destinations model, discussed above. The property can be easily shown by calculating the odds of choosing alternative A over alternative B.

$$\frac{p_A}{p_B} = \frac{\dfrac{\exp(V_A)}{\sum_j V_j}}{\dfrac{\exp(V_B)}{\sum_j V_j}} = \frac{\exp(V_A)}{\exp(V_B)}$$

This equation shows that these odds only depend on the deterministic utility of A and B. No other choice alternative or its attributes influence these odds. It implies that the introduction of a new choice alternative will detract market share from the existing choice alternatives in direct proportion to their current shares. Consider the following simple example. Let there be given shopping centres A and B. Assume that the utility of these centres are respectively $V_A = 3$ and $V_B = 2$. According to the MNL model, the probability that a consumer will choose centre A is then equal to exp(3)/[exp (3)+exp(2)] = 73%. Consequently, the probability that a consumer will choose B is equal to exp(2)/[exp (3)+exp(2)] = 27%. Now assume that another centre C is built and added to the choice set. Let C be an exact copy of B, located at the same distance or travel time. Consequently, $V_C = V_B = 2$. According to the MNL model, the predicted market shares in this new situation for centres A, B and C would respectively be equal to exp(3)/[exp (3)+exp(2)+exp(2)] = 58% and exp(2)/[exp (3)+exp(2)+exp(2)] = 21%. Note that the shift in market shares is equal to the original market shares. For A this shift is (0.731059−0.576117)=0.154942, whereas for B it is equal to 0.268941−0.211942=0.057. These changes in market share of 0.15942 and 0.057 for respectively shopping centres A and B are identical to their original market shares (73% and 27%).

Theoretically, this is an unrealistic property. One would expect that competition is stronger among more similar choice alternatives (B and C) and less among more distinct choice alternatives (A versus B/C). Moreover, an unrealistic implication of this property is that overall demand for a given alternative will rise if a perfect substitute for it is added to the choice set. For the shopping centre case, it is difficult to imagine a relevant example. However, imagine the choice between two cars of a different brand. If an identical brand (even car model) were added to the choice set, then the MNL would predict the market share of this brand (model) to increase. This may be an unrealistic assumption in many choice situations. To appreciate the next section, remember that when IIA is an inappropriate property, the model assumption that has actually been violated is that about the identically and independently distributed error terms (the stochastic portion of the utility is IID).

5.3   ADVANCED DISCRETE CHOICE MODELS

Over the years, several advanced models have been suggested to avoid or relax the IIA-property of the multinomial logit model. Two different approaches have been taken. First, several scholars have suggested including some measure of similarity directly into the utility function. The competing destination model is an example of this approach (when based on the exponential function) (Fortheringham, 1983). This approach has the advantage that variables that can be manipulated by policy are incorporated directly into the model. Consequently, the estimated model includes parameters that are directly related to these policy or marketing measures and the definition of similarity. Second, other scholars have suggested replacing the assumption of identically and independently distributed error terms by some other specification of the variance–covariance matrix of the error terms, allowing for variation in the variances and/or covariances. Remember that the IID assumption caused the IIA property of the MNL model. Examples include the Generalized Extreme Value (GEV) family of models, introduced by McFadden (1978), the generalized nested logit model (Wen and Koppelman, 2001; Koppelman and Wen, 1998, 2000), the cross-nested logit model (Vovsha, 1997), the paired combinatorial logit model (Chu, 1989), and the covariance nested logit model (Bhat, 1997) to name a few. It is beyond the purpose of this chapter to discuss these model alternatives in any detail. An important disadvantage of this approach is that similarity is captured in terms of a set of parameters. Estimated parameters reflect the variance–covariance among competing shopping centres derived from current observations of shopping behaviour. The development of new stores or centres will likely change the competition between centres. In forecasting, therefore, with the introduction of a new alternative/shopping centre, it seems realistic to assume that the estimated variance/covariance matrix should change. However, it is not readily evident how. If variance–covariance terms have not been expressed as some function of policy or marketing variables, there is no empirical basis to change these parameter values for the new competitive situation.

The model that has found widest application in a variety of disciplines is the mixed logit model. This model represents error components that create correlations among the utilities of the different choice alternatives. Consequently, it can be used to avoid the IIA property of the MNL model. Assume that the systematic part of the utility function can be defined as a linear function of attributes and that the stochastic part consists of a vector of random terms and random error. Thus,

$$U_{ni} = \alpha' x_{ni} + \mu_n' z_{ni} + \varepsilon_{ni}$$

where x_{ni} and z_{ni} are vectors of observed variables relating to choice alternative i, α is a vector of fixed coefficients, μ is a vector of random terms with zero mean, and ε_{ij} is IID extreme value. The unobserved (random) part of the utility function can be expressed as $\eta_{ni} = \mu_n' z_{ni} + \varepsilon_{ni}$. Different from the MNL model, the random or stochastic part of the utility function does not consist only of random error, but also of additional error components. It is important to note that with nonzero error components this part creates correlations across choice alternatives. Various correlation and hence substitution patterns can be obtained by appropriately specifying these error components. Details are provided in Ben-Akiva and Bolduc (1996) and Brownstone and Train (1999).

Equivalent to the random components structure is the random coefficients structure (Train, 2003; Hensher and Greene, 2005). Whereas the MNL model assumes that the utility function is identical for all individuals, mixed logit models assume that individuals share the same kind of utility function, but vary in terms of the weights (parameters estimates) they attach to the attributes. Such taste differentiation is captured by estimating a distribution for each of the parameters of the utility function. The MNL model has one parameter value for each variable included in the utility function. This parameter indicates the contribution of that variable to the overall utility. Because only one parameter is estimated for each variable, it is assumed that all individuals have the identical utility function and therefore that the contribution of each variable to the overall utility is exactly the same for all individuals. In the mixed logit model, however, these point estimates (single parameter values) are replaced by distributions. That is, for each attribute, a random component v_k with mean 0.0 and standard deviation σ_k is added:

$$U_i = \sum_k (\beta_k + v_k) X_{ik} + \varepsilon_i$$

Thus, rather than estimating a single parameter for each variable, common to all individuals, the mean and standard deviation of the distribution of parameter values are estimated. The standard deviation captures heterogeneity (differences in part-worth utilities across individuals).

The random component v_k can take on a number of distributional forms such as normal, lognormal or triangular. Often, a normal distribution is assumed. However, it may imply that part-worth utilities for some individuals may be positive, while they may be negative for others. The lognormal is appropriate if the sign of the parameter should be the same for all individuals. The probability that alternative i will be chosen, conditional on v_k can be described by the following multinomial logit form:

$$P(i|v_k) = \frac{\exp \sum_k (\beta_k + v_k) X_{ik}}{\sum_{j=1}^{J} \exp \sum_k (\beta_k + v_k) X_{jk}}$$

The unconditional probability is obtained by integrating the random terms out of the probability:

$$P_i = \int P(i|v_k) f(v_k) \, dv_k$$

where,

P_i is the probability that alternative *i* is chosen;
$P(i|\upsilon_k)$ is the logit probability that a person chooses alternative *i*, conditional on υ_k;
$f(\upsilon_k)$ is a density function for the distribution of the error terms regarding attribute *k* in the population.

Thus, using this specification, the mixed logit model can be used to capture taste variation.

The latent class (finite mixture) logit model accounts for taste variation in a different way. It assumes that individuals can be grouped into a set of latent classes or segments. Each class is characterized by its own utility function. Thus, rather than assuming some distribution for each parameter of the utility function, the actual utility functions for the different latent classes may differ. On the one hand, this increases the flexibility. On the other, one assumes that within each segment, the utility functions are still identical for all individuals. Membership is established based on socioeconomic variables. Thus, while the model accounts for different utility functions, the assumption of within-group homogeneity is rather restrictive. The latent class model states that the choice probability that an individual *n* of class *s* chooses alternative *i* from a particular set *J*, which is comprised of alternatives, is expressed as:

$$p_{ni|s} = \exp(\beta_s' X_{ni}) / \sum_j \exp(\beta_s' X_{nj}) \quad s = 1, 2, \ldots, S$$

where β_s' is the parameter vector associated with the vector of explanatory variables X_{ni}.

Then, the unconditional probability of choosing alternative *i* is given by:

$$p_{ni} = \sum_s p_{ni|s} P_{ns}$$

where P_{ns} the probability is that individual *n* belongs to latent class *s*.

While these modelling approaches have introduced further heterogeneity in the basic choice models, the nature of the underlying choice process by individual shoppers as reflected in the form of the utility function is still assumed to be the same across shoppers. The only difference between the latent classes concerns the parameters of the utility function, but the same standard choice model is assumed to reflect the choice behaviour within each class. A step forward would allow for the possibility that shoppers apply different behavioural processes: so called *behavioural mixing*. For example, well-informed shoppers with a lot of time may maximize their utility, which could be captured by the compensatory MNL or ML model. Other, time-constrained shoppers may exhibit satisficing behaviour, which could be captured in terms of a noncompensatory model. For this case, still a latent class structure can be used, with the main difference that the latent classes would in this case be based on different model specifications, representing different underlying behavioural processes (see e.g., Zhu and Timmermans, 2008, 2010; Hess et al., 2011).

5.4 COMPLEX BEHAVIOUR: MULTI-STOP, MULTI-PURPOSE SHOPPING AND ACTIVITY PATTERNS

In most applied retail research, shopping behaviour is differentiated between daily shopping, non-daily shopping and shopping for durable goods. Data on such behaviour are often collected by asking respondents how often they buy a long list of shopping items, where they buy these, the transport mode involved and sometimes how much they have spent on each item. Using these frequencies, these lists of items are then classified into daily shopping and non-daily shopping. Shopping for durable goods is often ignored due to their low purchase frequencies. Choice of transport mode is often not explicitly considered although the action space of consumers and therefore choice probabilities depend on the transport mode involved. It goes without saying that these are all simplifying, rigorous assumptions.

In reality, the process of stocking, depletion and new purchases is considerably more complicated. Households run out of stock for different goods at different times. The challenge then is when to go shopping and which items to buy. What is on the shopping list may also affect the choice of shopping centre. Consider the case that all items can be bought in the local shopping centre, except for one item which is not available in that centre. Will consumers then decide to make a separate trip to buy that item or will they buy all items on their shopping list in the other centre? If they visit both centres, will this involve two separate trips or will they visit both centres during one tour?

This is the problem of multi-stop, multi-purpose shopping behaviour. It is relevant because due to dynamics in their shopping lists, consumers may exhibit different shopping centre choice repertoires. Such variation may be further enhanced and stimulated by advertising campaigns of stores and centres. The consideration of multi-purpose shopping may improve viability and impact assessments because some stores may not be able to attract a sufficient number of consumers on their own, but depend on the presence of other stores and impulse or replacement shopping behaviour.

In principle, the modelling of multi-stop, multi-purpose shopping behaviour can be based on the same principles, discussed above. However, the complexity of the model specification will increase as the utility of a shopping trip in this case is a function of the utility of visiting a shopping centre for all items on the shopping list, and the disutility of travel also becomes more complicated. Arentze and Timmermans (2001) offer an example. They first predict choice probabilities for a particular purpose (i.e. a combination of goods to be bought) as a function of individual-specific and supply-dependent components using a nest logit model. Next, conditional on purpose, the probability of choosing a particular shopping centre is predicted. Shopping centre utility is assumed to depend on trip purpose as a function of the supply of the goods involved, shopping centre attributes and travel distance. In addition, the disutility of distance is made dependent on trip purpose. Further empirical work to support the latter decision was provided by Brooks et al. (2004, 2008).

While these and other models of multi-purpose shopping behaviour articulate the interrelationships between different shopping activities and the choice of shopping centre(s), implicitly or explicitly these models assume that shopping decisions are made only within the shopping context. However, a more realistic assumption seems to be that shopping activities should fit into daily schedules of individuals and households and thus compete with other mandatory and discretionary activities. This topic of activity analysis has recently received a lot of attention in especially transportation and time use research, but also in geography and urban planning. In transportation research, it has been realized that travel is rarely conducted for its own sake, but rather as a necessary consequence of the fact that people need or wish to be engaged in activities and that activity locations tend to be scattered in space. Hence, the goal of so-called activity-based models is to simultaneously predict which activities are conducted, where, with whom, when and for how long and the transport mode(s) involved.

Recently, several operational activity-based models have been completed and are now being applied in (transportation) planning practice. For example, Vovsha et al. (2004) report the development and application of discrete choice based models in the United States, mentioning Portland, New York City, San Francisco County and Columbus, Ohio. Similarly, CEMDEP (Bhat et al., 2004) has been applied in Texas, Famos (Pendyala et al., 2005) has found application in Japan and Florida, while Albatross (Arentze and Timmermans, 2000, 2005) is currently used by the Dutch Ministry of Transport in a series of scenario studies. Another example is

Tasha (Miller and Roorda, 2003; Roorda and Miller, 2005; Roorda et al., 2007). A more detailed discussion of the operational models is provided in Timmermans et al. (2002).

The majority of these models are further advanced and more complex (suites of) discrete choice models. These models are more complex in that they simulate the many interdependencies between the various choice facets (activity participation, timing, destination, multi-purpose/ trip chaining, etc.). On the other hand, Albatross and Tasha are rule-based systems. The fundamental claim of the activity-based approach is that a shopping trip is not an isolated event, but an event that is planned, scheduled and rescheduled as part of a daily or perhaps even weekly activity schedule (Arentze and Timmermans, 2005). The shopping activity decision is not only influenced by (opinions of) store or shopping centre attributes, but also by various temporal, spatial and institutional constraints (such as opening hours), the timing of other activities, the state of the transport system and task allocation mechanisms within households. Consequently, shopping preferences are context-dependent, subject to car availability, other elements in the schedule, travel party, time of day, week of day, etc. Arentze and Timmermans (2005) provide empirical evidence to that effect.

The discriminating feature of these activity-based models concerns their attempt to capture in a more coherent and integrated fashion the interrelated decisions of choice of activity, destination, transport mode, and timing and duration choices. Although "virtual travel" (teleworking, teleshopping, etc.) has been a research topic in this community, especially focused on the question whether teleshopping will decrease, be neutral to or increase physical travel, there have not been any attempts to systematically include teleshopping (e-commerce) in the modelling attempts. Recently, Liao et al. (2011) have however demonstrated how multi-state supernetworks can be used to represent in a single representation not only alternative transportation networks, but also activity engagement and Internet shopping. A specification of link costs (utilities) is used to measure the relative contribution of travel costs by different modes, shopping centre related attributes, activity characteristics, and Internet shopping/e-commerce. The identification of the optimal path in this super-network, subject to various space–time constraints, then represents the best choice. This best choice may involve multi-stop, multi-purpose shopping behaviour. It is shown how this approach can be used in large-scale agent or micro-simulations of daily activity-travel behaviour, in which (tele-) shopping is embedded, of the population of a city or region. It offers an alternative to other such recently proposed micro-simulations (e.g., Schenk et al., 2007; Hanaoka and Clarke, 2007).

5.5   INCORPORATING ATTITUDES AND OTHER PSYCHOLOGICAL CONSTRUCTS

The discussion about progress in choice modelling in disciplines such as urban and transportation planning indicates that the focus has primarily been on observed choice outcomes, which are assumed to reflect underlying preferences and utilities. Unlike in marketing research, there is not a very strong tradition of explicitly measuring psychological constructs such as attitudes and perceptions in explaining choice behaviour. Recently, however, there has been an attempt in the transportation research community to develop a framework in which psychometric indicators are combined with choice data to predict choice behaviour. More specifically, the hybrid choice model, proposed by Ben-Akiva et al. (2002a, 2002b), Morikawa et al. (2002), and Walker and Ben-Akiva (2002) is a framework including latent variables and latent classes, where psychometric indicators are combined with choice data to estimate the model. Their model combines a choice model with a latent variable model. The latent variable model is meant to model the formation of latent (unobserved) psychological constructs such as attitudes, perceptions, and plans. It is linked to the choice model to estimate the effect of these latent constructs on preferences.

Thus, this model is meant to deal with the case in which both observed (shopping) behavioural data are available (revealed preference) and stated preference data and/or psychometric measurements of attitudes, perceptions, etc. The model is not necessarily based on random utility theory as the above models in the sense that the utility function can be a paramorphic representation of any assumed behavioural process. Attitudes are usually measured using dedicated scales, and according to current practice a structural equation model is used to separate structure against measurement error. In that sense, hybrid choice models merge classical discrete choice models with the structural equation approach for latent constructs, well known in consumer behaviour research. In this field structural equations models have also been used to include behavioural intention, for example, based on the theory of planned behaviour and sometimes choice (e.g., Lunardo and Mbengue, 2009; Koo and Ju, 2010; Pookulangara et al., 2011). The difference between this approach and the hybrid choice model is primarily the more advanced treatment of the revealed preference component and in most cases the use of choice as opposed to behavioural intention.

The structural part of the hybrid choice model is given by the random utility function (ignoring subscripts):

$$U = V(X, Q, \beta) + \varepsilon$$

which can be decomposed into a deterministic part $V(\cdot)$ and a random part ε. What makes it different from the classical choice models is the inclusion of Q, the latent constructs (attitudes, perceptions, etc.). In turn, these latent constructs are specified as:

$$Q = f(X, \lambda) + \xi$$

where Q are latent constructs, $f(\cdot)$ is a function of explanatory variables X and unknown path coefficients λ, and ξ represents random error. Measurement equations of the form

$$I = g(Q, \alpha) + \tau$$

where α are factor loadings and τ measurement errors. A specific model can be obtained by making additional assumptions about the various functions and the distribution of all error terms. Usually, researchers assume that the functions are linear-in-parameters. The explanatory variables would thus include both attributes of the various choice alternatives (e.g., shopping centres) plus a set of socio-demographics.

One would expect that the inclusion of attitudes and other psychological constructs would improve our understanding of choice behaviour. Whether this advanced approach will lead to better forecasts remains an issue for further investigation. The problem is that not only the attributes of the choice alternatives need to be changed for some future point in time, but also the future attitudes need to be forecasted. In some cases, this is based on changing socio-demographics but it is doubtful that the attitudes of current age cohorts will be the same as those of the same cohorts in the future.

5.6   DISCUSSION: INTEGRATION?

The purpose of this chapter has been to discuss progress in consumer choice modelling in disciplines such as urban planning and transportation research, such as it has been applied for example to the modelling of spatial shopping centre choice. One might expect that these disciplines have paid a lot of attention to a wide spectrum of spatial/physical variables. Wind and other weather components may influence shoppers' outdoor comfort; design features such as size of the shopping environment and the configuration of stores may influence navigation/wayfinding and actual shopping behaviour; colours, window display and architecture may impact (impulse) shopping behaviour, etc. This overview has shown however that these spatial variables have hardly if at all been included in feasibility and assessment studies of shopping centres. It is understandable in the sense that at the early stage of development, often information about key characteristics such as size, anchor stores, location and parking is lacking and hence even if researchers feel that the variables do make a difference in predicting spatial shopping behaviour, it would be impossible to include them in the model building process.

This is not to say that no research at all exists about the impact of these variables. In fact, there is a scattered literature in building physics (e.g., Chun and Tamura, 1998), environmental psychology (e.g., Spiers and McGuire, 2008), urban design (e.g., Walford et al., 2011) and in store/mall atmospherics (Chebat et al., 2005) about these issues. However, the results have not been integrated in institutionalized applied research/modelling approaches. Thus, progress in spatial shopping behaviour research is not best summarized in terms of the inclusion of increasingly more variables and constructs over time, but rather progress can be best characterized as an attempt to improve behavioural realism in models of spatial shopping behaviour by allowing for different substitution patterns and heterogeneity in response patterns and by embedding single shopping trips include trip chaining/multi-stop, multi-purpose trips and even daily activity schedules.

Both former problems are reasons to account for IID violations in discrete choice models. The dominant approach has been to specify and estimate variance–covariance structures and random error components. Sometimes our only recourse is to account for IID violations in the stochastic part of the utility, in addition to estimation parameters distributions as opposed to parameter point estimates and to identify different classes. However, the effort in this direction has by no means been matched by attempts to identify the factors causing these violations. One would expect that the ultimate model would include a valid specification of the relationship between choice probabilities and the influencing factors/determinants and would account for substitution patterns, preference formation and other behavioural mechanisms, ideally reducing the remaining error term to random noise. For example, specifying what influences the degree of spatial substitution among shopping centres is preferable to picking up substitution through some arbitrary specification of the unobserved utility part.

Consistent with these developments, researchers developing and applying these choice models have not spent much effort on identifying and including a rich set of influential factors. To some extent, this might be explained by the fact that they focused only on those variables that could be manipulated from the perspective of their discipline. For example, urban planning authority does not go beyond site selection, size of retail developments and some basic features, including parking. It is not concerned with merchandising, pricing, marketing and the like, and in fact when their models are applied to assess the feasibility and impact of new retail development these variables are likely still unknown. Another partial explanation may be that researchers in urban planning and transportation often use existing data sets and collect original data less than marketing researchers. These data concentrate on aspects of actual behaviour, not on underlying motivations, perceptions and preferences.

The latest developments in choice modelling, however, offer some unique opportunities to blend these different worlds. Principles of behavioural mixing and the combined specification of choice mechanisms and underlying latent psychological constructs are potentially relevant to enrich traditional choice models with concepts of consumer choice behaviour developed in retailing. The notion of shopping orientation includes activities, interests and opinions about the shopping process (Moschis, 1992; Kuruvilla and Joshi, 2010). For example, Kemperman et al. (2009) found significant differences between hedonic and utilitarian shoppers. The latter group visited less (planned stores), spent less time on shopping, and evidenced shortest route behaviour. The former group explored more options, evidenced more impulse shopping, while their route choice behaviour was more erratic. In other words, a considerable amount of variation in observed shopping behaviour can be attributed to these differences in shopping orientation. Dellaert et al. (2008) argued and provided empirical evidence that shopping context influences consumer cognitive representation of the shopping task and results in context-dependent utilities and behaviour. Current choice models which capture consumer unobserved shopping heterogeneity only in terms of error structure and distributions for the coefficients in the utility function are unlikely to capture such underlying differences in spatial shopping behaviour. Explicit measurement of shopping orientations (e.g., Allard et al., 2009; Lunardo and Mbengue, 2009; Bäckström, 2011) and other related psychological concepts such as shopping attitudes (e.g., Shim and Eastlick, 1998), shopping value (e.g., Michon and Chebat, 2004; Jackson et al., 2011) and shopping motivation (e.g., Wagner and Rudolph, 2010) can serve as the basis for the specification of models allowing for behavioural mixing. Scales to measure these psychological concepts can be used in hybrid choice models. This blending offers fascinating new avenues of research on shopping behaviour and new ways to examine which combination of macro (centre), meso (stores) and micro (brand) factors influence consumer choice behaviour.

REFERENCES

Aberdeenshire Council (2004), *Assessing the Impact of Retail Developments in Aberdeenshire*, Abderdeen: Planning and Environmental Services.

Allard, Th., B.J. Babin and J.C. Chebat (2009), 'When income matters: customers' evaluation of shopping malls' hedonic and utilitarian orientations', *Journal of Retailing and Consumer Services*, **16**, 40–49.

Arentze, T.A. and H.J.P. Timmermans (2000), *Albatross: A Learning-Based Transportation Oriented Simulation System*, Eindhoven, The Netherlands: European Institute of Retailing and Services Studies.

Arentze, T.A. and H.J.P. Timmermans (2001), 'Deriving performance indicators from models of multipurpose shopping behavior', *Journal of Retailing and Consumer Services*, **8**, 325–334.

Arentze, T.A. and H.J.P. Timmermans (2005), *Albatross 2: A Learning-Based Transportation Oriented Simulation System*, Eindhoven, The Netherlands: European Institute of Retailing and Services Studies.

Bäckström, K. (2011), 'Shopping as leisure: an exploration of manifoldness and dynamics in consumers' shopping experiences', *Journal of Retailing and Consumer Services*, **18**, 200–209.

Ben-Akiva, M. and D. Bolduc (1996), 'Multinomial probit with a logit kernel and a general parametric specification of the covariance structure', Department of Civil Environmental Engineering, Massachusetts Institute of Technology, Cambridge, MA, and Départmente d'Economique, Université Laval, Sainte-Foy, QC, working paper.

Ben-Akiva, M. and S. Lerman (1985), *Discrete Choice Analysis*, Cambridge, MA, USA: MIT Press.

Ben-Akiva, M., D. McFadden, K. Train, J. Walker, C. Bhat, M. Bierlaire, D. Bolduc, A. Boersch-Supan, D. Brownstone, D.S. Bunch, A. Daly, A. De Palma, D. Gopinath, A. Karlstrom and M.A. Munizaga (2002a), 'Hybrid choice models: progress and challenges', *Marketing Letters*, **13**, 163–175.

Ben-Akiva, M., J. Walker, A. Bernardino, D. Gopinath, T. Morikawa and T. Polydoropoulou (2002b), 'Integration of choice and latent variable models', in H. Mahmassani (ed.), *In Perpetual Motion: Travel Behaviour Research Opportunities and Application Challenges*, Amsterdam: Elsevier, pp. 431–470.

Bhat, C.R. (1997), 'Covariance heterogeneity in nested logit models: economic structure and application to inter-city travel', *Transportation Research Part B*, **31**, 11–21.

Bhat, C.R., J.Y. Guo, S. Srinivasan and A. Sivakumar (2004), 'A comprehensive micro-simulator for daily activity-travel patterns', *Proceedings of the Conference on Progress in Activity-Based Models*, Maastricht, 28–31 May (CD-rom).

Borgers, A.W.J. and H.J.P. Timmermans (1987), 'Choice model specification, substitution and spatial structure effects: a simulation experiment', *Regional Science and Urban Economics*, **17**, 29–47.

Borges, A., J.-C. Chebat and B.J. Babin (2010), 'Does a companion always enhance the shopping experience?', *Journal of Retailing and Consumer Services*, **17**, 294–299.

Bove, L.L., A. Nagpal and A.D.S. Dorsett (2009), 'Exploring the determinants of the frugal shopper', *Journal of Retailing and Consumer Services*, **16**, 291–297.

Bridson, K., J. Evans and M. Hickman (2008), 'Assessing the relationship between loyalty program attributes, store satisfaction and store loyalty', *Journal of Retailing and Consumer Services*, **15**, 364–374.

Brooks, C.M., P.J. Kaufmann and D.R. Lichtenstein (2004), 'Travel configuration on consumer trip-chained store choice', *Journal of Consumer Research*, **31**, 241–248.

Brooks, C.M., P.J. Kaufmann and D.R. Lichtenstein (2008), 'Trip chaining behavior in multi-destination shopping trips: a field experiment and laboratory replication', *Journal of Retailing*, **84**, 29–38.

Brownstone, D. and K. Train (1999), 'Forecasting new product penetration with flexible substitution patterns', *Journal of Econometrics*, **89**, 109–129.

Carpenter, J. (2008), 'Consumer shopping value, satisfaction and loyalty in discount retailing', *Journal of Retailing and Consumer Services*, **15**, 358–363.

Chebat, J.-C., C. Gélinas-Chebat and K. Therrien (2005), 'Lost in a mall, the effects of gender, familiarity with the shopping mall and the shopping values on shoppers' wayfinding processes', *Journal of Business Research*, **58**, 1590–1598.

Chebat, J.-C., K. El Hedhli and M.J. Sirgy (2009), 'How does shopper-based mall equity generate mall loyalty? A conceptual model and empirical evidence', *Journal of Retailing and Consumer Services*, **16**, 50–60.

Chu, C.A. (1989), 'Paired combinatorial logit model for travel demand analysis', *Proceedings of the Fifth World Conference on Transportation Research*, Yokahama, Japan.

Chun, C.Y. and A. Tamura (1998), 'Thermal environment and human responses in underground shopping malls vs department stores in Japan', *Building and Environment*, **33**, 151–158.

Dellaert, B.G.C., T.A. Arentze and H.J.P. Timmermans (2008), 'Shopping context and consumers' mental representation of complex shopping trip decision problems', *Journal of Retailing*, **84**, 219–232.

DeMoulin, N.T.M. and P. Zidda (2008), 'On the impact of loyalty cards on store loyalty', *Journal of Retailing and Consumer Services*, **15**, 386–398.

Dennis, C., A. Newman, R. Michon, J.J. Brakus and L.T. Wright (2010), 'The mediating effects of perception and emotion: digital signage in mall atmospherics', *Journal of Retailing and Consumer Services*, **17**, 205–215.

Diep, V.C.S. and J.C. Sweeney (2008), 'Shopping trip value: do stores and products matter?', *Journal of Retailing and Consumer Services*, **15**, 399–409.

Ekinci, Y. and M. Riley (2003), 'An investigation of self-concept: actual and ideal self-congruence compared in the context of service evaluation', *Journal of Retailing and Consumer Services*, **10**, 201–214.

Eppli, M.J. and J.D. Benjamin (1994), 'The evolution of shopping center research: a review and analysis', *Journal of Real Estate Research*, **9**, 5–32.

Fotheringham, A.S. (1983), 'A new set of spatial interaction models: the theory of competing destinations', *Environment and Planning*, **15**, 15–36.

Fotheringham, A.S. (1985), 'Spatial competition and agglomeration in urban modelling', *Environment and Planning A*, **17**, 213–230.

Fotheringham, A.S. (1988), 'Market share analysis techniques: a review and illustration of current U.S. practice', *Store Location and Techniques of Market Analysis*, **5**, 120–159.

Gatzlaff, D.H., G.S. Sirmans and B.A. Diskin (1994), 'The effect of anchor tenant loss on shopping center rents', *Journal of Real Estate Research*, **9**, 99–110.

González-Benito, Ó. (2005), 'Spatial competitive interaction of retail store formats: modeling proposal and empirical results', *Journal of Business Research*, **58**, 457–466.

Guy, C.M. (1987), 'Recent advances in spatial interaction modelling: an application to the forecasting of shopping travel', *Environment and Planning A*, **19**, 173–186.

Haines, G.H., L. Simon and M. Alexis (1972), 'An analysis of central city neighborhood food trading areas', *Journal of Regional Science*, **12**, 95–105.

Hanaoka, K. and G.P. Clarke (2007), 'Spatial microsimulation modelling for retail market analysis at the small-area level', *Computers, Environment and Urban Systems*, **31**, 162–187.

Helgesen, O., J.I. Håvold and E. Nesset (2010), 'Impacts of store and chain images on the "quality–satisfaction–loyalty process" in petrol retailing', *Journal of Retailing and Consumer Services*, **17**, 109–118.

Hensher, D.A. and W.H. Greene (2003), 'The mixed logit model: the state of practice', *Transportation*, **30**, 133–176.

Hess, S., A. Stathopoulos and A. Daly (2011), 'Mixing of behavioural processes: a modelling framework and three case studies', *Proceedings of the Annual TRB Meeting*, Washington DC.

Huff, D.L. (1963), 'A probabilistic analysis of shopping center trade areas', *Land Economics*, **39**, 81–90.

Huff, D.L. (1964), 'Defining and estimating a trading area', *Journal of Marketing*, **28**, 34–38.

Jackson, V., L. Stoel and A. Brantley (2011), 'Mall attributes and shopping value: differences by gender and generational cohort', *Journal of Retailing and Consumer Services*, **18**, 1–9.

Kemperman, A.D.A.M., A.W.J. Borgers and H.J.P. Timmermans (2009), 'Tourist shopping behavior in a historic downtown area', *Tourism Management*, **30**, 208–218.

Kim, H.-Y. and Y.-K. Kim (2008), 'Shopping enjoyment and store shopping modes: the moderating influence of chronic time pressure', *Journal of Retailing and Consumer Services*, **15**, 410–419.

Koo, D.-M. and S.-H. Ju (2010), 'The interactional effects of atmospherics and perceptual curiosity on emotions and online shopping intention', *Computers in Human Behavior*, **26**, 377–388.

Koppelman, F.S. and V. Sethi (2000), 'Closed form discrete choice models', in *Handbook of Transport Modeling*, Oxford: Pergamon Press.

Koppelman, F.S. and C.-H. Wen (1998), 'Alternative nested logit models: structure, properties and estimation', *Transportation Research Part B*, **32**, 289–298.

Koppelman, F.S. and C.-H. Wen (2000), 'The paired combinatorial logit model: properties, estimation and application', *Transportation Research Part B*, **34**, 75–89.

Kuruvilla, S.J. and N. Joshi (2010), 'Influence of demographics, psychographics, shopping orientation, mall shopping attitude and purchase patterns on mall patronage in India', *Journal of Retailing and Consumer Services*, **17**, 259–269.

Lakshamanan, T.R. and W.G. Hansen (1965), 'A retail market potential model', *American Institute of Planners Journal*, **31**, 134–142.

Lastovicka, J.L., L.A. Bettencourt, R.S. Hughner and R.J. Kuntze (1999), 'Lifestyle of the tight and frugal: theory and measurement', *Journal of Consumer Research*, **26**, 85–98.

Lee, M.-L. and R.K. Pace (2005), 'Spatial distribution of retail sales', *Journal of Real Estate Finance and Economics*, **31**, 53–69.

Liao, F., T.A. Arentze and H.J.P. Timmermans (2011), 'Supernetwork representation and accessibility analysis: the case of multi-purpose, multi-stop shopping', *Proceedings EIRASS Conference*, San Diego.

Luce, R. (1959), *Individual Choice Behaviour*, New York: Wiley.

Lunardo, R. and A. Mbengue (2009), 'Perceived control and shopping behavior: the moderating role of the level of utilitarian motivational orientation', *Journal of Retailing and Consumer Services*, **16**, 434–441.

Macintosh, G. (2009), 'Examining the antecedents of trust and rapport in services: discovering new interrelationships', *Journal of Retailing and Consumer Services*, **16**, 298–305.

Marker, M.T. and K. Goulias (2000), 'Framework for the analysis of teleshopping', *Transportation Research Record*, **1725**, 1–8.

Massicotte, M., R. Michon, J.-C. Chebat, M.J. Sirgy and A. Borges (2011), 'Effects of mall atmosphere on mall evaluation: teenage versus adult shoppers', *Journal of Retailing and Consumer Services*, **18**, 74–80.

McFadden, D. (1974), 'Conditional logit analysis of qualitative choice behaviour', in P. Zarembka (ed.), *Frontiers in Econometrics*, New York: Academic Press, pp. 105–142.

McFadden, D. (1978), 'Modelling the choice of residential location', in A. Karlquist (ed.), *Spatial Interaction Theory and Planning Models*, Amsterdam: North Holland, Chapter 25, pp. 75–96.

McFadden, D. (1981), 'Econometric models of probabilistic choice', in C. Manski and D. McFadden (eds), *Structural Analysis of Discrete Data with Econometric Applications*, Cambridge, MA, USA: MIT Press, Chapter 5, pp. 198–272.

Mejia, L.C. and J.D. Benjamin (2002), 'What do we know about the determinants of shopping center sales? Spatial vs. non-spatial factors', *Journal of Real Estate Literature*, **10**, 3–26.

Michon, R. and J.-C. Chebat (2004), 'Cross-cultural mall shopping values and habitats: a comparison between English- and French-speaking Canadians', *Journal of Business Research*, **57**, 883–892.

Miller, E.J. and M.J. Roorda (2003), 'Prototype model of household activity/travel scheduling (TASHA)', *Transportation Research Record*, **1831**, 114–121.

Morikawa, T., M. Ben-Akiva and D.L. McFadden (2002), 'Discrete choice models incorporating revealed preferences and psychometric data', in P. Franses and A. Montgomery (eds), *Econometric Models in Marketing*, Vol. 16, Amsterdam: Elsevier, pp. 29–55.

Moschis, G.P. (1992), *Marketing to Older Consumers: A Handbook of Information for Strategy Development*, Westport, CT: Quorum Books.

Nevin, J.R. and M.J. Houston (1980), 'Image as a component of attractiveness to intra-urban shopping areas', *Journal of Retailing*, **56**, 77–93.

Okoruwa, A. Ason, Joseph V. Terza and Hugh O. Nourse (1988), 'Estimating patronization shares for urban retail centers: an extension of the Poisson gravity model', *Journal of Urban Economics*, **24**, 241–259.

Okoruwa, A. Ason, Hugh O. Nourse and Joseph V. Terza (1994), 'Estimating sales for retail centers: an application of the Poisson gravity model', *Journal of Real Estate Research*, **9**, 85–97.

Pendyala, R.M., R. Kitamura, A. Kikuchi, T. Yamamoto and S. Fujji (2005), 'FAMOS: Florida activity nobility simulator', Proceedings of the 84th Annual Meeting of the Transportation Research Board, Washington, DC.

Pookulangara, S., J. Hawley and G. Xiao (2011), 'Explaining consumers' channel-switching behavior using the theory of planned behavior', *Journal of Retailing and Consumer Services*, **18**, 311–321.

Porojan, A. (2001), 'Trade flows and spatial effects: the gravity model revisited', *Open Economic Review*, **12**, 265–280.

Reilly, W.J. (1931), *The Law of Retail Gravitation*, New York, NY: Pilsbury Publishers.

Roorda, M.J. and E.J. Miller (2005), 'Strategies for resolving activity scheduling conflicts: an empirical analysis', in H.J.P. Timmermans (ed.), *Progress in Activity Based Analysis*, Elsevier, Amsterdam: pp. 203–222.

Roorda, M., E.J. Miller and K. Nurul Habib (2007), 'Validation of TASHA: a 24-hour activity scheduling microsimulation model', *Proceedings of the 86th Annual Meeting of the Transportation Research Board*, Washington, DC (CD-rom).

Schenk, T.A., G. Löffler and J. Rauh (2007), 'Agent-based simulation of consumer behavior in grocery shopping on a regional level', *Journal of Business Research*, **60**, 894–903.

Seo, S. and Y. Lee (2008), 'Shopping values of clothing retailers perceived by consumers of different social classes', *Journal of Retailing and Consumer Services*, **15**, 491–499.

Shim, S. and M.A. Eastlick (1998), 'The hierarchical influence of personal values on mall shopping attitude and behavior', *Journal of Retailing*, **74**, 139–160.

Simmonds, D. and O. Feldman (2011), 'Alternative approaches to spatial modelling', *Research in Transportation Economics*, **31**, 2–11.

Spiers, H.J. and E.A. Maguire (2008), 'The dynamic nature of cognition during wayfinding', *Journal of Environmental Psychology*, **28**, 232–249.

Stanley, T.J. and Sewall, M.A. (1976), 'Image inputs to a probabilistic model: predicting retail potential', *Journal of Marketing*, **40**, 48–53.

Suárez, A., I. Rodríguez del Bosque, J.M. Rodríguez-Poo and I. Moral (2004), 'Accounting for heterogeneity in shopping centre choice models', *Journal of Retailing and Consumer Services*, **11**, 119–129.

Timmermans, H.J.P., T.A. Arentze and C.-H. Joh (2002), 'Analyzing space-time behavior: new approaches to old problems', *Progress in Human Geography*, **26**, 175–190.

Train, K.E. (2003), *Discrete Choice Methods with Simulation*, New York, NY, USA: Cambridge University Press.

Vovsha, P. (1997), 'Application of a cross-nested logit model to mode choice in Tel Aviv, Israel, Metropolitan Area', *Transportation Research Record*, **1607**, 6–15.

Vovsha, P., M. Bradley and J.L. Bowman (2004), 'Activity-based travel forecasting in the United States: progress since 1995 and prospects for the future', *Proceedings of the Conference on Progress in Activity-Based Models*, Maastricht, 28–31 May (CD-rom).

Wagner, T. and Th. Rudolph (2010), 'Towards a hierarchical theory of shopping motivation', *Journal of Retailing and Consumer Services*, **17**, 415–429.

Walford, N., E. Samarasundera, J. Phillips, A. Hockey and N. Foreman (2011), 'Older people's navigation of urban areas as pedestrians: measuring quality of the built environment using oral narratives and virtual routes', *Landscape and Urban Planning*, **100**, 163–168.

Walker, J. and M. Ben-Akiva (2002), 'Generalized random utility model', *Mathematical Social Sciences*, **43**, 303–343.

Wen, C.-H. and F.S. Koppelman (2001), 'The generalized nested logit model', *Transportation Research Part B*, **35**, 627–641.

Zhu, W. and H.J.P. Timmermans (2008), 'Bounded rationality cognitive process model of individual choice behavior incorporating heterogeneous choice heuristics, mental effort and risk attitude: illustration to pedestrian go-home decisions', *Proceedings of the 87th Annual Meeting of the Transportation Research Board*, Washington DC (CD-rom, 19 pp.).

Zhu, W. and H.J.P. Timmermans (2010), 'Cognitive process model of individual choice behavior incorporating principles of bounded rationality and heterogeneous decision heuristics', *Environment and Planning B*, **37**, 59–74.

6 Consumer behavior in a service context
Rodoula H. Tsiotsou and Jochen Wirtz

6.1 INTRODUCTION

In its early stages, the service literature focused on the unique characteristics of services (e.g., intangibility, heterogeneity, inseparability, and perishability, also referred to as "IHIP") and their impact on consumer behavior in this context (Shostack 1977; Zeithaml 1981; Wolak et al. 1998). Although there is much criticism about the uniqueness of these service characteristics, the process nature of services cannot be doubted. Grönroos (2000a) proposes that process is one of the main characteristics of services, in addition to simultaneous production and consumption and the customer's participation in the service production process. The consumption of services has been characterized as "process consumption" (Grönroos 1998) because the production process is considered to form an element of service consumption and is not simply seen as the outcome of a production process, as is the case in the traditional marketing of physical goods.

> Services are produced in a process wherein consumers interact with the production resources of the service firm . . . the crucial part of the service process takes place in interaction with customers and their presence. What the customer consumes in a service context is therefore fundamentally different from what traditionally has been the focus of consumption in the context of physical goods. (Grönroos 2000b, p. 15)

Thus, the research agenda gradually shifted from an output focus adapted from the goods literature to a focus on process. Several models incorporating various stages of the service consumption process have been proposed in the literature. This chapter adopts the three-stage perspective (comprising the pre-purchase, encounter and post-encounter stages) of consumer behavior (Lovelock and Wirtz 2011) and discusses relevant extant and emerging research on each stage.

The early service consumer behavior literature applied paradigms and approaches taken from the literature on goods. More recent research initiatives reflect an attempt to liberate services from the goods logic and develop new approaches more appropriate and relevant to services. In practice, the relationship marketing and service-dominant perspectives constitute recent theoretical developments that have enriched the research agenda and provided new lenses in explaining phenomena in services.

Originating in the B2B literature, the relationship-marketing paradigm prevails in contemporary marketing. According to Patterson and Ward (2000), relationship marketing "is the establishment of a long-term relationship between the service supplier and customer to their mutual benefit" (p. 320). Relationship marketing liberated current research from cognitive and attitudinal approaches in explaining consumer behavior in a service context. The relational perspective views traditional constructs such as trust and loyalty as qualitative elements of the relationship between consumers and service firms, and not as outcomes of transactions.

The service-dominant (S-D) or "service for service" logic has shifted the center of attention from a goods-dominant view, based on tangible outcomes, to one in which intangibility, relationships and service are central (Vargo and Lusch 2004). According to this notion, service is defined as a process (rather than a unit of output) and refers to the application of competencies (knowledge and skills) for the benefit of the consumer. Here, the primary goal of a business is value co-creation as "perceived and determined by the customer on the basis of value-in-use" (Vargo and Lusch 2004, p. 7).

The remainder of this chapter is organized as follows. First, the three-stage model of service consumption is presented along with key new research developments concerning each stage. This is followed by a discussion of the relational marketing perspective and the service-dominant logic. The chapter concludes by outlining emerging research topics and directions for future investigation.

6.2   THE THREE-STAGE MODEL OF SERVICE CONSUMPTION

The services marketing literature can be organized according to a multi-stage approach to analyzing consumer behavior and service performance. In particular, consumers go through three major stages when they consume services: the pre-purchase stage, the service encounter stage and the post-encounter stage (Lovelock and Wirtz 2011, pp. 36–37). This framework is helpful because it assists academics in forming a clear research focus and direction, and businesses in identifying the stages that need the most improvement and therefore need more resources allocated to them (Blackwell et al. 2003; Hensley and Sulek 2007). Research has been conducted on all three stages to examine their major determinants, influences (direct and indirect), processes and outcomes (Figure 6.1).

PRE-PURCHASE STAGE	
Consumer Behavior	**Key Concepts**
• **Need awareness** • **Information search** • **Evaluation of alternatives** • **Make decision on service purchase**	Need Arousal Information Sources Perceived Risk Multi-Attribute Model Search, Experience and Credence Attributes

SERVICE ENCOUNTER STAGE	
Consumer Behavior	**Key Concepts**
• **Request service from chosen supplier or initiation of self-service** • **Interaction with service personnel** • **Service delivery by personnel or self-service**	Theoretical Approaches: – Moments of Truth – Role Theory – Script Theory – The Servuction Model – The Servicescape/Environmental Perspective Frontline Employees-Consumer Interactions The Service Environment The Role of Other Consumers Low-Contact Service Encounters

POST-ENCOUNTER STAGE	
Consumer Behavior	**Key Concepts**

• **Evaluation of service performance**
 	
 • **Evaluation of service recovery**
 	
 • **Future intentions**
	The Expectancy/Disconfirmation Paradigm
	 The Attribute-Based Approach: Attribute
	   Satisfaction, Service Quality, Service Value
	 Service Failure & Dissatisfaction
	 – Complaining Behavior
	 – Dysfunctional Behavior
	 – Switching Behavior
	 Satisfaction and the "Service Recovery Paradox"
	 Repurchase Intentions, Trust, Engagement &
	   Loyalty

Figure 6.1   The three-stage model of service consumption

6.2.1   The Pre-Purchase Stage

According to Fisk (1981), the pre-purchase phase of the decision-making process for services is not linear, but is more complex in comparison with that for goods as it involves a composite set of factors and activities. Due to the participation of consumers in the service production process, the decision-making process takes more time and is more complicated than in the case of goods. Research supports the view that consumer expertise, knowledge (Byrne 2005) and perceived risk (Diacon and Ennew 2001) all play significant roles in this purchase decision process for services.

In the pre-purchase stage, consumers are triggered into action by arousing a need to start searching for information and evaluate alternatives before deciding whether or not to buy a particular service. Needs may be triggered by the unconscious mind (e.g., impulse buying), internal conditions (e.g., hunger) or external sources (e.g., marketing mix).

The information search process described in the next section assumes that consumer decision-making processes take place at a conscious level. However, it should be remembered that consumers can also engage in impulse buying or "unplanned behavior". Although impulse buying is an important phenomenon extensively studied in the goods context, it has been neglected in services research (Kacen and Lee 2002). Because services are generally associated with higher perceived risk and variability, it is suggested that impulse buying occurs less frequently in services than in goods (Murray and Schlacter 1990; Sharma et al. 2009).

According to the notion of "planned purchase behavior", once a need or problem has been recognized, consumers are motivated to search for solutions to satisfy that need or resolve that problem (Figure 6.2). It is well established in the marketing literature that a consumer's purchase decision is based on the information obtained in the pre-purchase stage (Alba and Hutchinson 2000; Mattila and Wirtz 2002; Konus et al. 2008).

6.2.1.1   Information search

The way in which consumers search for information on services differs from the way in which they search for information on goods in terms of the amount of information sought and the number and type of sources used for gathering information. Given that the uncertainty and perceived risk associated with a purchase decision are considered higher in services due to their intangible nature and variability (Murray and Schlacter 1990; Bansal and Voyer 2000) and because of the high degree of price uncertainty due to service firms' revenue management strategies (Kimes and Wirtz 2003; Wirtz and Kimes 2007), consumers engage in more extensive information search activities to reduce both (Alba and Hutchinson 2000; Mattila and Wirtz 2002).

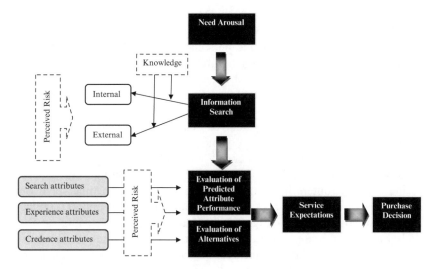

Figure 6.2   The pre-purchase process of consumers in services

Service consumers do not usually confine themselves to a single source of information, but employ multiple sources of information depending on their orientation (multichannel orientation), their tendency to innovate and the perceived pleasure of the shopping experience. They search for information from multiple sources to save money, to reduce risk, to develop performance expectations of service offers and to explore alternative service providers (Konus et al. 2008).

Consumers use a variety of methods to gather information: they seek information from trusted and respected personal sources such as family, friends and peers; they use the Internet to compare service offerings and search for independent reviews and ratings; they rely on firms with a good reputation; they look for guarantees and warranties; they visit service facilities or try aspects of the service before purchasing; they examine tangible cues and other physical evidence and ask knowledgeable employees about competing services (Boshoff 2002; Zeithaml and Bitner 2003; Lovelock and Wirtz 2011, pp. 41–42).

In the pre-purchase decision-making process for services, consumers not only exhibit a greater propensity to search for more information than they do in the goods context, but they also tend to explore more personal sources of information such as friends, family and co-workers (Murray and Schlacter 1990; Bansal and Voyer 2000; Mattila and Wirtz 2002; Xiao et al. 2011). Thus, word of mouth as a source of consumer information has become an important and influential concept within services due to their intangibility and higher perceived risk (Murray and Schlacter 1990; Bansal and Voyer 2000; Mattila and Wirtz 2002).

Consumers trust more specific personal sources of information. For example, it has been found that family is a predominantly trustworthy source of information considered more reliable than friends or professional advisors (e.g., accountants or financial planners) when buying retirement services (Rickwood and White 2009). Moreover, consumer expertise, perceived risk and perceived acquaintances' expertise contribute to the active search for word-of-mouth (Alba and Hutchinson 2000; Bansal and Voyer 2000; Mattila and Wirtz 2002).

Another source of information is the Internet, although consumers' online behavior differs in terms of the amount of search time spent on goods versus services websites. A study conducted in an online retailing context found that the average time consumers spent searching on the Web was 9.17 minutes on automotive sites, 9.26 minutes on telecom/Internet sites, 10.44 minutes on travel sites and 25.08 minutes on financial sites (Bhatnagar and Ghose 2004). Gender, education, age and Internet experience also influence the time consumers spend searching for information (Bhatnagar and Ghose 2004; Ratchford et al. 2003), while search patterns vary by product category in retail services (Bhatnagar and Ghose 2004). Moreover, the more time consumers devote to searching for information via the Internet and the more often they do so, the more the information gathered online influences the purchase decision (Bhatnagar and Ghose 2004).

One way in which online vendors help consumers make their choices is by providing electronic recommendation agents also known as "smart agents" as an element of their services (Aksoy et al. 2006; Diehl et al. 2003; Haubl and Murray 2003; Haubl and Trifts 2000). The use of recommendation agents and avatars as an entertainment and informational tool to fulfil consumers' desire for a more interpersonal shopping experience has recently attracted research attention (Holzwarth et al. 2006). Electronic recommendation agents assist consumers with their purchase decisions by providing information about products and their attributes after searching for a large amount of data using consumer-specified selection criteria (Aksoy et al. 2006; Diehl et al. 2003). Similarly, avatars or virtual salespeople acting as sales agents have been found to increase consumer satisfaction with the firm, enhance positive attitudes towards products, and increase purchase intentions (Holzwarth et al. 2006). Electronic recommendation agents can reduce the prices paid by consumers (Diehl et al. 2003) and improve the quality of their decisions (Ariely et al. 2004; Haubl and Trifts 2000). However, recommendation agents should have similarities with consumers in terms of either attribute weights or decision

	Current Dry Cleaner	Campus Dry Cleaner	New Dry Cleaner	Importance Weight
Quality of Dry Cleaning	9	10	10	30%
Convenience of Location	10	8	9	25%
Price	8	10	8	20%
Opening Hours	6	10	9	10%
Reliability of On-time Delivery	2	9	9	5%
Friendliness of Staff	2	8	8	5%
Design of Shop	2	7	8	5%
Mean Score	5.6	8.9	8.7	100%

Source: Wirtz, Chew and Lovelock, 2012.

Figure 6.3 *Application of the multi-attribute model in dry cleaning services*

strategies to achieve higher quality choices, reduced search time for consumers, and increased website loyalty and satisfaction (Aksoy et al. 2006).

6.2.1.2 Evaluation of alternative services

During the search process, consumers form their consideration set and learn about the service attributes they should consider, in addition to forming expectations of how firms in the consideration set perform on those attributes (Lovelock and Wirtz 2011, p. 42).

Once the consideration set and key attributes are understood, consumers typically proceed to making a purchase decision. Multi-attribute models have been widely used to simulate consumer decision making. According to these models, consumers use service attributes (e.g., quality, price and convenience) that are important to them to evaluate and compare alternative offerings of firms in their consideration set. Each attribute is weighted according to its importance. An example of a multi-attribute model applied to dry cleaning services is presented in Figure 6.3. To make a purchase decision, consumers might use either the very simple linear compensatory rule (in which case the consumer would choose "New Dry Cleaner" in the example in Figure 6.3) or the more complex but also more realistic conjunctive rule (e.g., if price should have a minimum rating of "9", then "Campus Dry Cleaner" would be chosen). Consumers using the same information can ultimately choose different alternatives if they use different decision rules.

Multi-attribute models assume that consumers can evaluate all important attributes before making a purchase. However, this is often not the case in the services arena, as some attributes are harder to evaluate than others. Attributes can be categorized into three types (Zeithaml 1981): search attributes, experience attributes and credence attributes. Search attributes refer to tangible characteristics consumers can evaluate before purchase (Wright and Lynch 1995; Paswan et al. 2004). These attributes (e.g., price, brand name, transaction costs) help consumers to better understand and evaluate a service before making a purchase and therefore reduce the sense of uncertainty or risk associated with a purchase decision (Paswan et al. 2004). Experience attributes, on the other hand, cannot be reliably evaluated before purchase (Galetzka et al. 2006). Consumers must "experience" the service before they can assess attributes such as reliability, ease of use and consumer support. Credence attributes are characteristics that consumers find hard to evaluate even after making a purchase and consuming the service (Darby and Karni 1973). This can be due to a lack of technical experience or means to make a reliable evaluation, or because a claim can be verified only a long time after consumption, if at all (Galetzka et al. 2006). Here, the consumer is forced to believe or trust that certain tasks have been performed at the promised level of quality. Because most services tend to be ranked highly on experience and credence attributes, consumers find them more difficult to evaluate before making a purchase (Zeithaml 1981; Mattila and Wirtz 2002).

After consumers have evaluated the possible alternatives, they are ready to make a decision and move on to the service encounter stage. This next step may take place immediately, or may involve an advance reservation or membership subscription.

6.2.2   The Service Encounter Stage

Consumers move on to the core service experience after making the decision to purchase. The service encounter stage is when the consumer interacts directly with the service firm, and is the means by which consumers co-create value and co-produce a service while evaluating the service experience.

Service encounters are complex processes where consumer interactions and surrounding environmental factors shape consumers' expectations (Coye 2004), satisfaction, loyalty, repurchase intentions and word-of-mouth behavior (Bitner et al. 2000). The service encounter is generally considered a service delivery process often involving a sequence of related events occurring at different points in time. When consumers visit the service delivery facility, they enter a service "factory" (e.g., a motel is a lodging factory and a hospital is a health treatment factory) (Noone and Mattila 2009). However, service providers focus on "processing" people rather than the inanimate objects found in traditional factories. Consumers are exposed to many physical clues about the firm during the service delivery process. These include the exterior and interior of its buildings, equipment and furnishings, as well as the appearance and behavior of service personnel and other customers. Even the pace of service encounters can affect consumer satisfaction (Noone et al. 2009). The average level of performance along these dimensions constitutes a significant predictor of consumer satisfaction (Verhoef et al. 2004).

6.2.2.1   Theoretical approaches to service encounters

A number of approaches have been proposed to provide a better understanding of consumer behavior and experiences during service encounters.

Moments of truth   Service encounters have been regarded as moments of truth (Normann 1991; Edvardsson et al. 2000). The concept of moments of truth underlines the importance of effectively managing touch-points. Richard Normann borrowed the moment of truth metaphor from bullfighting to show the importance of contact points with consumers. At the moment of truth, the relationship between the consumer and the firm is at stake (Normann 1991). The service encounter is a "moment of truth" because the consumer's experience of the encounter is the main factor contributing to their perception of overall service quality.

Role theory   Grove and Fisk (1983) define a role as "a set of behavior patterns learned through experience and communication, to be performed by an individual in a certain social interaction in order to attain maximum effectiveness in goal accomplishment" (p. 45). Roles have also been defined as expectations of society that guide behavior in a specific setting or context (Solomon et al. 1985). In service encounters, employees and consumers both have roles to play. If either party is uncomfortable in a role, or if they do not act according to their roles, it will affect the satisfaction and productivity of both parties.

According to this metaphor, service facilities constitute the stage and frontline personnel represent the members of the cast. The theater metaphor also includes the roles of the players on stage and the scripts they have to follow. The actors in a theater need to know what roles they are playing and be familiar with the script. Similarly, in service encounters, knowledge of role and script theories can help organizations to better understand, design and manage both employee and consumer behavior (Grove et al. 2000; Baron et al. 2003; Lovelock and Wirtz 2011).

Script theory   Just like a movie script, a service script specifies the behavioral sequences employees and consumers are expected to learn and follow during the service delivery process. Employees receive formal training (cf., Grandey et al. 2010), whereas consumers learn scripts through experience, observation, communication with others, and designed communications and education (Harris et al. 2003). The more experience a consumer has with a service company, the more familiar that particular script becomes. Any deviation from this known script may frustrate both consumers and employees and can lead to dissatisfaction. If a company decides to change a service script (e.g., by using technology to transform a high-contact service into a low-contact one), service personnel and consumers need to be educated about the new approach and the benefits it provides. In addition, unwillingness to learn a new script can give customers a reason not to switch to a competing service provider.

Many service dramas are tightly scripted (such as flight attendants' scripts for economy class), thus reducing variability and ensuring uniform quality. However, not all services involve tightly scripted performances. Scripts tend to be more flexible for providers of highly customized services—designers, educators, consultants—and may vary by situation and by consumer.

The theater is a good metaphor for understanding the creation of service experiences through the service production system, called the servuction system in short. This is because service delivery consists of a series of events that consumers experience *as a performance* (Grove et al. 2000; Baron et al. 2003). Role theory and script theory complement each other in how we understand both consumer and employee behavior during a service encounter. Together with the script and role theories, the theater metaphor gives us insights into how firms can look at "staging" service performances to create the desired experience.

The servuction model   The servuction model focuses on the various types of interactions that together create the consumer's service experience (Figure 6.4). The servuction system (combining the terms service and production) consists of a technical core *invisible* to the customer, and the service delivery system *visible* to and experienced by the consumer (Eiglier and Langeard 1977; Langeard et al. 1981). As in the theater, the visible components can be termed "front stage" or "front office", while the invisible components can be termed "back stage" or "back office" (Chase 1978; Grove et al. 2000).

The servuction system includes all the interactions that together make up a typical consumer experience in a high-contact service. Consumers

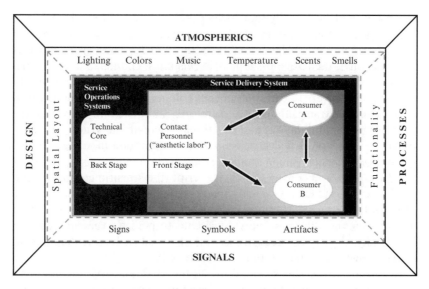

Figure 6.4   An integrative model of the servuction model and the servicescape environment

interact with the service environment, service employees, and even other consumers present during the service encounter. Each type of interaction can either create value (e.g., a pleasant environment, friendly and competent employees, and other consumers who are interesting to observe) or destroy value (e.g., another consumer blocking your view in a movie theater). Firms have to coordinate all interactions to ensure their consumers have the service experience they came for.

The servicescape/environmental perspective   This approach considers all the experiential elements consumers encounter in service delivery settings. The physical service environment consumers experience plays a key role in shaping the service experience and enhancing (or undermining) consumer satisfaction, especially in high-contact people-processing services (Figure 6.4).

Service environments, also called servicescapes, relate to the style and appearance of the physical surroundings and other experiential elements encountered by consumers at service delivery sites (Bitner 1992). Bitner (1992) identified several dimensions of service environments including ambient conditions, spatial layout/functionality, and signs, symbols and artifacts. Ambient conditions refer to environmental characteristics that pertain to the five senses. Ambient conditions are perceived both separately and holistically and include lighting and color schemes, size and shape perceptions, sounds such as noise and music, temperature, and scents or smells. Spatial layout refers to environmental design and includes the floor plan, the size and shape of furnishings, counters, and potential machinery and equipment, and the ways in which they are arranged. Functionality refers to the ability of such items to facilitate the performance of service transactions and, therefore, the process of delivering the core service. Spatial layout and functionality create the visual and functional servicescape in which delivery and consumption take place. Signs, symbols and artifacts communicate the firm's image, help consumers find their way, and convey the service script (the scenario consumers and employees should enact). Signals are aimed at guiding consumers clearly through the service delivery process and teaching the service script in an intuitive manner. Because individuals tend to perceive these dimensions holistically, the key to effective design is how well each individual dimension fits together with everything else (Bitner 1992).

According to Lovelock and Wirtz (2011, p. 255), servicescapes serve four purposes: (1) they engineer the consumer experience and shape consumer behavior; (2) they convey the planned image of the firm and support its positioning and differentiation strategy; (3) they are part of the value proposition; and (4) they facilitate the service encounter and enhance both service quality and productivity.

Inspired by Bitner's (1992) servicescape model and theoretical perspectives on behavioral settings, approach-avoidance models and social facilitation theory, Tombs and McColl-Kennedy (2003) propose the social-servicescape model to conceptualize human elements and provide an account of how they influence consumption experiences. The social-servicescape model recognizes three separate aspects of the overall service experience: elements of the social-servicescape (including the purchase occasion as context and social interaction aspects), consumers' affective responses, and consumers' cognitive responses. The social-servicescape model explains the influence of social interaction on consumer affect through social density, the displayed emotions of others, the susceptibility of the consumer to emotional contagion, and consumer awareness of the emotions of others (Tombs and McColl-Kennedy 2003).

The remainder of this section on the service encounter stage is arranged according to the key interactions that together make up the service encounter experience: the employee to consumer, consumer to environment, and consumer to consumer interactions. All these interactions are better used to explain high-contact service encounters than to illuminate low-contact or self-service encounters. The latter are discussed further at the end of this section.

6.2.2.2 Frontline employees and customer interactions

High-contact service encounters facilitate the development of high-quality relationships with consumers by encouraging consumer–employee bond-building (Heracleous and Wirtz 2010; Wirtz et al. 2008). Employees play an important role in service encounters because consumers' interactions with frontline personnel are a significant determinant of their satisfaction or dissatisfaction with the service firm. Customer interactions with courteous, knowledgeable and efficient frontline employees lead to an enhanced corporate image (Nguyen and Leblanc 2002) and to increased perceptions of service excellence, customer satisfaction (Swan et al. 1999) and repurchase intentions (Reynolds and Arnold 2000). In a similar vein, employee friendliness has been found to have a positive influence on unplanned purchasing behavior among consumers (Mattila and Wirtz 2008).

Recent empirical evidence also shows that consumer self–employee congruency directly influences consumer satisfaction with employee relationships and their loyalty towards employees, which in turn contribute to overall consumer satisfaction with the firm (Jamal and Adelowore 2008). Consumers' perceptions of their similarity to service employees allows them to identify with service personnel on a personal basis, which subsequently increases their comfort, reduces interpersonal barriers, enhances consumer satisfaction and trust (Coulter and Coulter 2002) and engenders positive word of mouth (WOM) (Gremler et al. 2001). Other reported sources of satisfaction in service encounters include consumer delight with unprompted and/or unsolicited employee actions, the ability of employees to accommodate consumer needs for customized services, and employee responses to difficulties related to core service delivery (Bitner et al. 1990).

However, employees do not always generate positive reactions from consumers. For example, the inability or unwillingness of employees to respond to service failures and to consumer needs for customized services have been found to be significant sources of consumer dissatisfaction (Bitner et al. 1990).

Furthermore, the appearance and behavior of both service personnel and consumers can reinforce or detract from the impression created by a service environment. Nickson et al. (2005) use the term "aesthetic labor" to capture the importance of the physical imagery of service personnel who serve consumers directly. Frontline personnel should play their roles effectively, including by ensuring their appearance, speech and movement are consistent with the servicescape in which they work.

6.2.2.3 Customer–service environment interactions

The service environment (i.e., "the stage" in the theater metaphor) refers to the physical surroundings of the servicescape (Pullman and Gross 2004) and can be used as an important proxy signaling the quality of the firm's services and its portrayal of its desired image.

Service environments are composed of hundreds of design elements and details that must work together if they are to create the desired service environment (Dunne et al. 2002). Even when not noted consciously, these elements may still affect emotional wellbeing, perceptions and even attitudes and behavior. The resulting atmosphere creates a mood that is perceived and interpreted by the consumer (Davies and Ward 2002). Recent research shows that the service environment is not only a cue for anticipated service quality, but also influences consumers' evaluations of the intangible elements of a service firm, especially for hedonic services (Reimer and Kuehn 2005). Moreover, the physical service environment influences consumers' perceptions of the experiential value of a service expressed in terms of aesthetics and playfulness, which in turn affect their purchase intentions (Keng et al. 2007).

Ambient conditions might also influence consumer behavior in a positive or negative way. For example, pleasant scents promote a favorable perception of the service environment (Morrin and Ratneshwar 2003) and have a positive effect on mood (Spangenberg et al. 1996), on the amount of time consumers spend in stores (Donovan et al. 1994; Spangenberg et al. 1996), and on overall expenditure and the number of brands purchased (Bone and Ellen 1999).

Contrary to the findings of early research endeavors on the topic, new developments support the conjecture that ambient conditions do not always affect consumer behavior or influence consumers in the same way. One precondition is that ambient conditions in the same service environment should be congruent with consumers' affective expectations (Wirtz et al. 2000, 2007b). Furthermore, Mattila and Wirtz (2001) report that when ambient scents and music are congruent with each other in relation to their arousing qualities, consumers make a significantly more positive evaluation of the service environment, exhibit a higher propensity for approach and impulse buying behavior, and are more satisfied than when these cues do not fit with each other.

Another precondition is that ambient conditions should be adapted to the service setting (e.g., a lavender aroma that is considered relaxing might not be the best choice for a dancing club, and loud music might not be appropriate for a hotel room). In the case of scents, evidence supports the proposition that not all scents affect consumer behavior. In an experiment conducted by Gueguen and Petr (2006), lemon and lavender aromas were diffused in a restaurant and compared to a no-aroma control condition. The study showed that the lavender aroma—but not the lemon aroma—increased the length of stay among consumers and the amount they purchased. Moreover, elements of the service environment should vary according to the setting—private (e.g., a guest room) versus public (e.g., a bar)—and be adjusted to consumer characteristics (e.g., arousal seeking tendency) (I. Lin 2010).

The importance of ambient conditions has also been recognized in online contexts. Companies have used technological advances to develop attractive online service environments equivalent to offline settings to enrich the experience of their consumers. Thus, companies like British Telewest Labs plug into PCs air fresheners that spray a scent related to a message to make the consumer's experience more effective. The U.S. Department of Defense cooperates with ScentAir, a company specializing in scent appliances, and uses air fresheners in simulators employed for its military education programs.

In an online context, scents have been found to enhance consumers' perceptions of interactivity (Ehrlichman and Bastone 1992) and vividness (Steuer 1992), as well as measures of approach behavior operationalized as time spent in the virtual store, number of brands examined, and money spent (Vinitzky and Mazursky 2011). However, new developments in the area suggest that environmental factors (e.g., scents) might not operate in the same way for all consumers, and might also have an interruption effect on their cognitive shopping processes depending on their cognitive thinking style (an intuitive style versus a systematic cognitive style). It has been found that consumers with a highly systematic cognitive thinking style are more affected by the presence of scents, which in turn reduces their ability to perform an effective search process (disruption of the consumer's focus and challenge). Thus, the use of scents to enrich the consumer experience might not always be desirable (Vinitzky and Mazursky 2011).

In line with the above reasoning, several environmental elements might have a negative impact on consumers' emotions, evaluations and behavior. Design elements such as a lack of mirrors in dressing rooms, inadequate directions, items being rearranged and small stores also irritate consumers (d'Astous et al. 1995). Social elements of the service environment might also affect consumers. For example, the sardine phenomenon—when too many consumers compete for space and service resources at the same time—can result in consumers experiencing discomfort (Chen et al. 2009). Crowding has a negative effect on (a) consumer satisfaction when the primary motive for the service experience is utilitarian; (b) the desire to spend more money; and (c) the time spent in a restaurant (Noone and Mattila 2009).

In addition to consumers, the service environment is a highly aesthetic element in the corporate image creation process and plays a significant role in employee experience and performance in the servicescape (Nguyen and Leblanc 2002). After all, employees spend much more time there than do consumers, and it is crucially important that the design of the service encounter environment enables frontline personnel to be productive and deliver quality services. Internal consumer and employee responses can be categorized into cognitive responses (e.g., quality perceptions and beliefs), emotional responses (e.g., feelings and moods), and psychological responses (e.g., pain and comfort) (Mattila and Wirtz 2008). These internal responses lead to overt behavioral responses such as avoiding a crowded department store or responding positively to a relaxing environment by remaining there longer and spending extra money on impulse purchases. It is important to understand that the behavioral responses of consumers and employees must be shaped in ways that facilitate production and the purchase of high-quality services (Mattila and Wirtz 2008).

6.2.2.4   Consumer-to-consumer interactions

In Grove and Fisk's (1983) theater metaphor, other consumers are identified as the service audience, whereas in Baker's (1987) framework, other consumers represent the social factor of the physical service environment. Other consumers have been found to play several roles: acting as help-seekers, reactive helpers, admirers, competitors, proactive helpers, observers, followers, judges, accused and spoilers (McGrath and Otnes 1995).

The presence of other consumers in the same service environment during an encounter can affect the service experience of a consumer in a negative or positive way (Grove and Fisk 1997). When consumers receive social support from other consumers, consumer-to-consumer interactions might enhance their service experience, build loyalty, and therefore increase the profits of the service firm (Rosenbaum et al. 2007). A study conducted in a gym setting revealed that consumers receiving social-emotional support (and not so much instrumental support) from other consumers exhibit more voluntary performance behavior toward the service firm and its other customers (Rosenbaum and Massiah 2007). In addition, Harris and Baron (2004) find that conversations between consumers in the same service environment stabilize their expectations and perceptions of the service experience, which in turn reduces their dissatisfaction.

Other factors proposed to affect satisfaction include consumers' compatibility and service settings. Consumers are more satisfied with the service experience when they perceive a high degree of compatibility with other consumers in the same service context (Martin and Pranter 1989; Grove and Fisk 1997). For example, non-smoking consumers in a restaurant will be more satisfied when the other consumers are non-smokers as well. However, it has been proposed that situational and service context variations are more important factors influencing consumer satisfaction.

For example, shouting might constitute acceptable behavior in a bowling center, but not in a restaurant (Martin 1996). A recent study reported that the degree of interaction with other consumers depends on the level of importance attached to other consumers according to the service setting (Zhang et al. 2010). For example, the presence of and interactions with other consumers are an essential element of the service experience of a sporting event, whereas this might not be the case in services such as hair salons or financial services. Moreover, Zhang et al. (2010) found that not only does the impact of other consumers differ across service settings, but certain settings are more strongly associated with negative incidents between consumers (e.g., movie theaters and skiing slopes) or positive incidents (e.g., retail stores, hair salons, and amusement parks), while others are related to both negative and positive incidents (e.g., restaurants and public transportation).

6.2.2.5   Low-contact services

Low-contact services involve little, if any, physical contact between consumers and service providers. Instead, contact takes place at arm's length through electronic or physical distribution channels. In practice, many high-contact and medium-contact services are becoming low-contact services as part of a fast-growing trend whereby convenience plays an increasingly important role in consumer choice (Lovelock and Wirtz 2011). Voice-to-voice and self-service encounters have become increasingly common and have recently attracted research interest.

Voice-to-voice encounters   have, until recently, been an under-investigated topic in the service literature. Service encounters with a telephone-based customer service representative are often moments of truth that influence consumers' perceptions of a firm. Voice-to-voice encounters can be important because the telephone is often the initial contact medium for the consumer (e.g., price checking) with a firm (Uzicker 1999), they can lead to purchase or non-purchase decisions, they are increasingly used as the platform through which transactions are conducted (e.g., placing an order), and are used as a channel for after-sales service and recovery processes (Whiting and Donthu 2006).

Voice-to-voice encounters play a significant role in developing, sustaining and managing consumer relationships (Anton 2000) and enhancing satisfaction (Feinberg et al. 2002). Voice-to-voice encounters often involve waiting time, music and information. Music and information have become two common tools firms use to keep consumers occupied while they wait and thereby reduce their perceptions of waiting time. However, recent research has shown that it is only when the customer likes the music that it reduces the perceived waiting time and increases satisfaction (Whiting and Donthu 2006).

Self-service encounters   Self-service technology-enabled encounters can benefit consumers because they allow for the production and consumption of services without relying on service personnel (e.g. automated teller machines, self-scanning checkouts and Internet banking). Self-service technologies (SSTs) allow consumers to "produce a service independent of direct service employee involvement" (Curran et al. 2003, p. 209). For consumers, SSTs often require the co-production of services, increased cognitive involvement, and new forms of service behavior, while they can offer greater customization and more satisfying experiences (Meuter et al. 2000; Prahalad and Ramaswamy 2004). However, self-service encounters not only benefit consumers, but also frequently benefit service providers by providing them with direct and immediate feedback from their consumers (Voorhees and Brady 2005), improving service design, developing consumer loyalty (Voss et al. 2004) and reducing costs. Research on the application of SSTs has focused on factors that either facilitate or inhibit their adoption and usage by customers. Perceived usefulness, ease of use, reliability and fun have been identified as key drivers of consumer attitudes toward SSTs (Weijters et al. 2007). Dabholkar et al. (2003) consider self-scanning checkouts in retail stores and find that control, reliability, ease of use and enjoyment are important usage determinants of this kind of SST. Consumer characteristics such as a lack of confidence, anxiety, technology-related attitudes, and self-efficacy might inhibit the use of SSTs and successful co-production, especially in complex services (Boyle et al. 2006; Dabholkar and Bagozzi 2002; Meuter et al. 2000).

Consumers are often dissatisfied with SSTs if they deliver poor service (Meuter et al. 2000) or the technology fails (Holloway and Beatty 2003; Meuter et al. 2000), and if they cause frustration they might engender poor service delivery and technological failure (Harris et al. 2006; Dabholkar et al. 2003). Due to these reasons and because SSTs might deter consumers from voicing their complaints (Forbes et al. 2005), consumers might avoid engaging in self-service technology-enabled encounters (Bitner et al. 2002) and even switch service providers (Forbes et al. 2005). Recent research shows that the ease with which complaints can be made in SST settings mediate the relationship between consumers' perceptions of the likelihood of voice success and their likelihood of complaining (Robertson and Shaw 2009). SST-enabled service encounters also reduce the opportunity for service providers to get in touch with consumers, determine their emotional state (Freidman and Currall 2003) and detect service failures (Pujari 2004).

6.2.3   The Post-Encounter Stage

Consumer satisfaction and perceived service quality have dominated the research agenda at this stage of the service consumption process due to their association with business performance (Brady and Robertson 2001). However, consumers who are satisfied and have high perceptions of service quality do not necessarily return to the same service provider or buy their services again (cf., Keiningham and Vavra 2001). As a result, there has recently been a shift in the consumer research agenda toward other important post-purchase outcomes such as perceived service value, consumer delight, consumer reactions to service failures (e.g., complaining and switching behavior), and consumer responses to service recovery.

6.2.3.1   Customer satisfaction with services
Several conceptual models such as the expectancy-disconfirmation paradigm (Oliver 1980) and the perceived performance model (Churchill and Surprenant 1982), as well as attribution models (Folkes 1984), affective models (Westbrook 1987; Wirtz and Bateson 1999; Mattila and Wirtz 2000) and equity models (Oliver and DeSarbo 1988) have been developed to explain consumer satisfaction with services.

The following section describes two prevailing approaches—the expectancy-disconfirmation paradigm and the attribution model of satisfaction—and reviews current research supporting these approaches.

6.2.3.2   The expectancy–disconfirmation paradigm
Most customer satisfaction research is based on the expectancy-disconfirmation model of satisfaction (Oliver 1980) where confirmation or disconfirmation of consumers' expectations is the key determinant of satisfaction (Oliver 1980; Wirtz and Mattila 2001). According to the expectancy–disconfirmation paradigm, consumers evaluate the service performance they have experienced and compare it to their prior expectations (Figure 6.5).

Consumers will be reasonably satisfied as long as perceived performance falls within the zone of tolerance, that is, above the adequate service level. When performance perceptions approach or exceed desired levels, consumers will be very pleased. Consumers with such perceptions are more likely to make repeat purchases, remain loyal to the service provider, and spread positive word of mouth (Wirtz and Chew 2002; Liang et al. 2009). Thus, satisfaction is related to important post-purchase attitudes and behavior such as consumer loyalty (Yang and Peterson 2004; Vazquez-Carrasco and Foxall 2006), frequency of service use (Bolton and Lemon 1999), repurchase intentions (Cronin et al. 2000), service

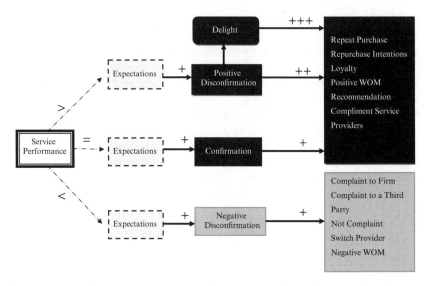

*Figure 6.5   Consumer satisfaction (expectancy–disconfirmation) and its
outcomes in services*

recommendations to acquaintances (Zeithaml et al. 1996), and compliments to service providers (Goetzinger et al. 2006).

When service performance is well above the expected level, consumers
might be delighted. Consumer delight is a function of three components:
(1) unexpectedly high levels of performance; (2) arousal (e.g., surprise,
excitement); and (3) positive affect (e.g., pleasure, joy or happiness) (Oliver
et al. 1997). It should be noted, however, that consumers' expectations
might be raised once they have been delighted (Santos and Boote 2003).
This can lead to consumers becoming dissatisfied if service levels return to
the previously lower levels, and it will probably take more effort to delight
them in the future (Rust and Oliver 2000).

The expectancy–disconfirmation framework generally works well when
consumers have sufficient information and experience to purposefully
choose a service from the consideration set expected to best meet their
needs and wants. However, this may not always be the case for services. For example, the expectancy–disconfirmation model seems to work
very well for search and experience attributes, but less so for credence
attributes. Consumers cannot assess the latter type of attributes directly
and rely on tangible cues and expectations to form their views on satisfaction. If no tangible evidence contradicts their expectations, customers tend
to evaluate credence attributes as meeting their expectations and will be
satisfied (Wirtz and Mattila 2001).

Probably the least investigated area of consumer behavior after a satisfying service experience is the giving of compliments. Service firms could use customer compliments as an opportunity to develop personal relationships with their customers (Goetzinger et al. 2006). Motives that stimulate complimenting behavior are a high level of satisfaction or delight, an improved relationship with a service employee, voting behavior to continue special services, being polite, dissonance reduction, the fun of providing compliments, reciprocity or social norms, a high degree of involvement with a service, softening complaints, and gaining a reward (Kraft and Martin 2001; Payne et al. 2002). In an online context, ease of use/ordering, consumer service, service delivery and pricing selection result in consumer compliments about a service provider via a third party (Goetzinger et al. 2006).

6.2.3.3 The attribute-based approach to satisfaction

Attribute-based perspectives have become a frequently used conceptual framework for explaining consumer satisfaction because they complement the expectancy–disconfirmation paradigm (Busacca and Padula 2005; Kano et al. 1984; Mittal and Kamakura 2001; Oliver 2000, p. 247). Based on the study of Weiner (2000), Oliver (2009, pp. 302–303) proposed that expectancy–disconfirmation precedes attribute evaluations, which in turn affect consumer satisfaction. Recent empirical evidence supports the significance of service attributes in influencing overall satisfaction (Mittal et al. 1999; Akhter 2010). The attribute-based approach argues that both cognitive (expectations) and affective (desires–motives associated with personal objectives) elements should be considered when examining the consumer satisfaction formation process (Bassi and Guido 2006; Oliver 2000, p. 250). Moreover, the affective component of satisfaction is expected to be greater in services than in goods due to the interactive and experiential nature of the former (Oliver 2000, p. 252).

Multi-attribute models provide several benefits to theory and practice in understanding the satisfaction formation process. Focusing on service attributes: (a) is useful for identifying the specific attributes which act as antecedents of customer satisfaction (Mittal et al. 1999); (b) facilitates the conceptualization of commonly observed phenomena such as mixed feelings toward a service (consumers are satisfied with certain attributes and dissatisfied with others) (Mittal et al. 1998); (c) allows customers to render evaluations of their post-purchase experiences at an attribute level rather than only at the product level (Gardial et al. 1994); (d) helps firms identify and manage attributes that have a strong impact on satisfaction and dissatisfaction (Mittal et al. 1998).

The attribute-based approach considers the evaluation of different attributes of a service as an antecedent of overall satisfaction (Oliver

1993). Singh (1991) stated there is sufficient and compelling evidence to suggest consumer satisfaction can be considered a collection of multiple satisfactions with various attributes of the service experience. Satisfaction with service attributes thus results from the observation of attribute-specific performance and strongly influences the overall satisfaction rating (Oliver 1993).

Although these satisfaction approaches offer a framework with which to examine and understand consumer behavior, they encourage the adoption of a "zero defects" service paradigm (Bowden 2009). In other words, in their effort to maximize satisfaction, these models treat all consumers within the consumer base as homogeneous. For example, they regard newly acquired consumers as the same as loyal consumers, although the two groups might differ in the importance they place on each attribute (Mittal and Kamakura 2001). Furthermore, service consumers cannot always freely choose the service that best fits their needs, wants and desires. Services are time- and location-specific, both of which restrict consumer choice, and consumers are frequently locked into a specific provider. For example, in situations where switching costs are high, needs congruency would be a better comparison standard for modeling satisfaction than would expectations (Wirtz and Mattila 2001). Consumers use multiple standards in the satisfaction process (e.g. expectations as well as needs), and because needs-congruence explains satisfaction better than do expectations, it should be incorporated into the modeling of satisfaction in reduced consumer choice situations.

Due to the above deficiencies in existing satisfaction modeling approaches, we propose an integrative model that combines the above-mentioned perspectives to provide a more comprehensive framework for explaining the formation of service satisfaction and its outcomes.

6.2.3.4   An integrative model of service satisfaction

When consumers use a service, they rate its transaction quality (e.g., the quality of food, the friendliness of the server and the ambiance of a restaurant), which when combined with the satisfaction derived from key attributes (i.e. attribute satisfaction) and the perceived value of the specific transaction then lead to a judgment of the level of overall satisfaction with a particular service experience. Over time and over many satisfaction judgments, customers then form a belief about the overall service quality a firm offers. This in turn influences behavioral intentions (e.g. purchase intentions, remaining loyal to the firm and positive word of mouth) (see Figure 6.6).

Using the general living systems theory, Mittal et al. (1999) propose that a consumption system consists of attribute-level evaluations, satisfaction

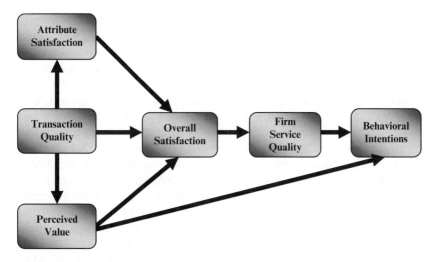

Figure 6.6   An integrative model of consumer satisfaction in services

and behavioral intentions and several subsystems. Their study shows that evaluations of a number of attributes lead to an overall level of satisfaction, which in turn influences customers' behavioral intentions. Akhter's (2010) recent study also supports the view that a service encounter is a multi-attribute experience comprising satisfaction with service attributes such as the provider, the offering, the location, information, and facilitation, which together form overall satisfaction. Overall satisfaction reflects the level of satisfaction with the overall service experience, and is a global evaluation of a specific service consumption experience.

The attribute-based model has also been used in an online context to explain the link between self-service technology (SST) attributes and quality satisfaction. In a recent study, Yen (2005) identified efficiency, ease of use, performance, perceived control and convenience as the main Internet-based self-service technology (ISST) attributes determining consumer satisfaction with service quality. The findings of the study indicate that consumer satisfaction with ISST is not only a function of the benefits associated with its usage (e.g., convenience) and the attributes related to reduced barriers to use (e.g., ease of use), but also of its ability to perform the expected functions properly.

However, the relationship between attribute-level performance and overall satisfaction is more complex than initially thought. Evidence has shown that there is a nonlinear and asymmetric relationship between service attribute importance and attribute-level performance evaluations, a relationship that can be unstable over time (Busacca and Padula 2005;

Kano et al. 1984; Mittal and Kamakura 2001). Research on consumer delight suggests that there is a nonlinear relationship in attribute-based judgments, probably due to the role affect plays in consumer satisfaction judgments as opposed to the weighting or importance consumers assign to a particular attribute only (Bowden 2009). Moreover, the phenomenon of "fundamental attribution error" has been observed in the literature (Oliver 2000, p. 252). According to this "error", negative attribute performance has a greater effect on overall satisfaction than does positive attribute performance (Mittal et al. 1998). Furthermore, research shows that attribute weights do not remain stable but change over time due to modified consumer goals (Mittal et al. 1999). One possible explanation for these findings might be found in the dimensions of attributions proposed by Weiner and adopted in the marketing field by Oliver (2010, pp. 295–296). The locus of causality (internal–self vs. external–others), the stability of service attribute performance (stable vs. variable) and the degree to which an attribute is under the control of the service provider might influence the relationship between attribute satisfaction and overall satisfaction.

However, factors other than attribute-level evaluations might also influence the formation of consumer satisfaction. Spreng et al. (1996, p. 17) stated that "attribute-specific satisfaction is not the only antecedent of overall satisfaction, which is based on the overall experience, not just the individual attributes". Lages and Fernandes (2005) suggest that any evaluation of a service provider is made at four abstract levels of a hierarchy comprising simple attributes of the service offering, transactional service quality, value, and more complex personal values. The present model proposes that in addition to attribute satisfaction, transaction quality and service values are further antecedents of overall satisfaction with services.

The role of service quality and service value   Before further proceeding to explain the model in Figure 6.5, it is necessary to distinguish between the transaction-specific and firm-related aspects of service quality. Transaction-specific quality refers to consumers' perceptions of a specific service encounter experience, whereas a firm's service quality reflects evaluations of quality based on cumulative experience that are developed over time. Inconsistencies in the literature regarding the role of service quality in relation to satisfaction and purchase intentions can be attributed to interchangeable use of the above types of service quality, which are often not distinguished from each other. We thus posit that transaction quality precedes overall consumer satisfaction, which in turn influences the formation of perceptions of a firm's overall service quality.

At a transaction level, it has been proposed that perceptions of the quality of service attributes are antecedents of satisfaction with the service experience (Otto and Ritchie 1995). Wilson et al. (2008, pp. 78–79) have proposed that satisfaction results from service quality evaluations (in addition to product quality and price) that mirror consumers' perceptions of its five dimensions: reliability, responsiveness, assurance, empathy and tangibles. It should be noted here that the early service literature considered these dimensions components of the perceived service quality of the firm (Boulding et al. 1993) and not as transaction-specific. Brady and Cronin (2001) proposed that service quality is a multifaceted concept comprising three dimensions and nine sub-dimensions (in parentheses): interaction quality (attitudes, behavior and expertise), physical environment quality (ambient conditions, design and social factors) and outcome quality (waiting time, tangibles and valence). Consumers evaluate service quality based on these three dimensions assessed via each of their three corresponding sub-dimensions. Additional empirical evidence has also demonstrated that the quality of the service delivery personnel (Johnson and Zinkham 1991) and physical environment (Bitner 1992) attributes have an impact on satisfaction with the service experience.

Another construct gaining increasing research attention is service value. Service value is the "utility of a product based on perceptions of what is received and what is given" (Zeithaml 1988, p. 14). Empirical evidence shows that transaction service quality is a significant determinant of service value (Cronin et al. 2000; Hu et al. 2009). Perceived service value is considered highly personal, idiosyncratic and variable among consumers (Holbrook 1994). It also seems reasonable to suggest that consumers evaluate transaction-specific attributes first before evaluating the service value of the service encounter experience. Transaction quality-related attributes may therefore represent most of the positive benefit drivers of consumer service value (Hu et al. 2009). Moreover, service value has been shown to have a direct effect on both consumer satisfaction with the service experience (Cronin et al. 2000; Hu et al. 2009; C.-H. Lin et al. 2005; Varki and Colgate 2001) and behavioral intentions (Cronin et al. 2000; Hu et al. 2009).

Service quality at the firm level has been linked to consumers' behavioral intentions. Boulding et al. (1993) conducted two studies in a service context and found that consumers' perceptions of a firm's overall service quality will influence their behavior intentions expressed as positive word of mouth and recommendation of the service. Perceptions of a firm's overall service quality are relatively stable but will change over time in the same direction as transaction satisfaction ratings (Boulding et al. 1993; Palmer and O'Neill 2003). Consumers' re-purchase intentions are influenced by their perceptions of overall service quality at the time of re-purchase (i.e. consumers try to predict how good the next service transaction will be), and not by the individual transaction satisfaction formed immediately after a consumption experience (Boulding et al. 1993; Palmer and O'Neill 2003). For example, consumers might return to a hair stylist if they think the stylist is generally fantastic, even if they were unhappy the last time they went there because they believe the poor haircut was an exception. However, a second or even third dissatisfaction evaluation will reduce the overall service quality perception of the firm more dramatically and jeopardize repeat purchases.

The strength of the relationship between satisfaction and consumers' behavioral intentions is often influenced, moderated or mediated by other factors. For example, consumers' adjusted expectations (Yi and La 2004) and characteristics such as personality traits (e.g., the need for social affiliation and relationship proneness) may act as mediators (Vazquez-Carrasco and Foxall 2006), whereas consumer demographics (e.g., age and income) may act as moderators (Homburg and Giering 2001) in the relationship between satisfaction and behavioral outcomes.

6.2.3.5   Service failure and behavior of dissatisfied customers

Service failures might result from various sources such as poor transaction quality due to long waits (Hensley and Sulek 2007), overbooking in excess of service capacity (Wangenheim and Bayon 2007) and other misbehavior among consumers (Huang 2010). Customers are less satisfied when the length of the service-entry wait increases, especially when they perceive that waiting time is under the control of the service provider (Diaz and Ruiz 2002). Dissatisfaction due to waiting time is also influenced by the physical comfort consumers experience during service delivery (e.g., temperature and noise) and the behavior of frontline employees (Gupta et al. 2004).

When the service experience does not meet customers' expectations and services fail, they may complain about poor service quality, suffer in silence, exhibit negative WOM, lose trust, complain to a third party, misbehave, or switch providers either immediately or in the future (Bitner et al. 2000; Chebat et al. 2005; Ganesh et al. 2000; Goetzinger et al. 2006; Mattila and Wirtz 2004; Reynolds and Harris 2009). Service failures result in negative disconfirmation of expectations and might induce negative emotional reactions such as cynicism toward the service provider (Chylinski and Chu 2010), which in turn could lead to complaints from consumers (Stauss and Siedel 2004; Mattila and Wirtz 2004).

Consumer complaining behavior   Depending on their level of seeking redress propensity (SRP), dissatisfied consumers might complain (high in SRP) or not complain (low in SRP) to service providers (Chebat et al.

2005). The range of purposes for which complaints are made include to change a criticized behavior, to inform a service provider of a harmful experience, to request compensation (Stauss and Siedel 2004, p. 95), and to reduce anger and frustration (Mattila and Wirtz 2004). Depending on their motives, consumers select different channels to make their complaints. Thus, when consumers intend to receive a tangible form of compensation due to a service failure, they prefer to relay their complaints by interactive means (e.g., face-to-face or by telephone), whereas when they aim to reduce their level of frustration, they tend to use remote channels (e.g., letters and e-mail) (Mattila and Wirtz 2004).

Complaining via third parties (e.g., agencies, the media, online social networks, user-generated content sites, blogs and forums) has probably received the least research attention (Goetzinger et al. 2006; Gregoire and Fisher 2008; Ward and Ostrom 2006), although the use of online third party intermediaries has become an increasingly common trend among consumers reacting to service failures, due to their convenience and accessibility (Ward and Ostrom 2006). After a poor service recovery, consumers might believe that they have been betrayed and that fundamental norms related to their relationship with the firm have been violated. They will often try to restore fairness by both retaliating against the firm and demanding reparation (Gregoire and Fisher 2008), or by misbehaving and engaging in acts such as vandalism, illegitimate complaining, and rage (Reynolds and Harris 2009).

Consumer dysfunctional behavior   Dysfunctional behavior among consumers of services—sometimes called the "dark side" of the consumer— has recently attracted a greater level of attention among researchers (Fisk et al. 2010). Such behavior includes illegitimate complaining, resistance and vandalism (Reynolds and Harris 2009), making opportunistic claims during service recovery (Wirtz and McColl-Kennedy 2010), and cheating on service guarantees (Wirtz and Kum 2004). Dysfunctional behavior takes place when "a customer deliberately behaves in a way that violates the norms and unwritten rules of an individual service setting in a negative fashion" (Reynolds and Harris 2009, p. 321). Due to the high frequency of incidents reported (Grandey et al. 2004; Bamfield 2006), consumer misbehavior is considered endemic within the service industry (Reynolds and Harris 2009).

The literature on dysfunctional behavior has focused on developing typologies of consumer misbehavior (Berry and Seiders 2008) and on examining the antecedents (Reynolds and Harris 2009) and consequences of such behavior (Harris and Reynolds 2003). Berry and Seiders (2008) have categorized consumers misbehaving into verbal abusers, blamers, rule breakers, opportunists and returnaholics. Reynolds and Harris (2009) recently found that disaffection with service (indicated by dissatisfaction and inequity), the servicescape and psychological obstructionism constitute significant factors related to dysfunctional behavior. Dysfunctional behavior has also been found to have a negative effect on other consumers, on the firm's employees and on the service firm (Harris and Reynolds 2003).

Consumer switching behavior   Dissatisfied customers are likely to switch service providers or consider doing so. Consumer switching behavior is considered serious for continuously delivered services (e.g., banking, insurance, public services, telecommunications, and medical insurance) and subscription-based services (Keaveney and Parthasarathy 2001). Dissatisfied switchers tend to be the most satisfied customers of their new service provider after the switch, and are the most likely to engage in active loyalty behavior (Ganesh et al. 2000).

Consumer switching behavior is complex. Several factors have been proposed as direct determinants of switching behavior. Poor service quality or changes in the firm's quality levels can lead to changes in consumers' attitudes and behavior toward the firm (Bansal et al. 2005), including the emergence of switching, especially when consumers are aware of alternative service providers (Anton et al. 2007). Moreover, switching intentions increase when consumers perceive they are not obtaining value for money or believe the price they paid for a service is unfair (Bansal et al. 2005; Homburg et al. 2005). Critical incidents that increase consumer anger and emotional reactions also significantly influence consumers' decisions to terminate a relationship with a firm and look for alternatives (Anton et al. 2007).

Researchers have proposed that consumer involvement, knowledge and expertise, the number of alternative service providers and the cost/risks associated with switching are factors that moderate switching behavior among consumers (Anton et al. 2007). Switching costs such as searching and learning costs, emotional cost, cognitive effort, and transaction cost, along with the associated risks (financial, social and psychological), may prevent consumers from changing service providers (Burnham et al. 2003).

Burnham et al. (2003) have categorized switching costs into three types: procedural (e.g., economic risk and expenditures in time and effort), financial (loss of benefits and financial resources) and relational (psychological and emotional discomfort due to termination of the relationship). When consumers are dissatisfied with a service provider and switching costs are high, then they may remain in the relationship and exhibit what has been called "false loyalty" (Burnham et al. 2003) or "spurious loyalty"

(Ganesh et al. 2000). However, consumers who switch providers can still harm the previous service provider by spreading negative word of mouth. Recent research shows that post-switching negative word of mouth is determined by product involvement, market mavenism, perceived risk, satisfaction with the new provider, and the reason for switching provider (Wangeneheim 2005).

6.2.3.6   Consumer responses to service recovery

To transform dissatisfied consumers into satisfied advocates of their services, firms respond to complaints by adopting service recovery tactics. Service recovery refers to all the "actions of a service provider to mitigate and/or repair the damage to a customer that results from the provider's failure to deliver the service as designed" (Johnston and Hewa 1997, p. 467). In relation to consumer behavior, the service recovery literature has focused on consumer attributions of service failures (Folkes 1984), consumer complaining behavior (Bell and Luddington 2006), consumers' expectations for service recovery (Kelley and Davis 1994), and recovery evaluations (Hoffman and Kelley 2000).

The handling of consumer complaints has become an increasingly important service research and management topic because of its value in pursuing long-term relationships with consumers (Bell and Luddington 2006). A new development in the service literature is satisfaction with service recovery and the "service recovery paradox". According to this paradox, consumers who perceive an excellent recovery after a service failure will be more satisfied than consumers who have never experienced a service failure (Andreassen 2001). Thus, when service recovery performance is high, consumers will be more satisfied with the service provider (McCollough et al. 2000; Smith and Bolton 1998), perceive higher service quality (Berry 1995), exhibit positive word of mouth (Berry 1995) and have stronger re-patronage intentions (Smith and Bolton 1998), increase their loyalty (Vazquez-Carrasco and Foxall 2006), trust and commitment to the service provider (Tax et al. 1998), and have a more positive image of the firm (Andreassen 2001; Zeithaml et al. 1996) (see Figure 6.7).

Recent studies, however, show that the service recovery paradox does not hold universally. Rather, it is a function of the frequency of service failure and of the severity and the "recoverability" of the failure. The paradox holds when consumers experience a service failure that is recovered and are satisfied with the recovery. However, the paradox no longer holds if a second service failure takes place. Consumers might forgive service providers once, but they become disappointed when failures recur. Moreover, when a service failure is considered serious and the service cannot be recovered (e.g., a ruined wedding video), then it might not be

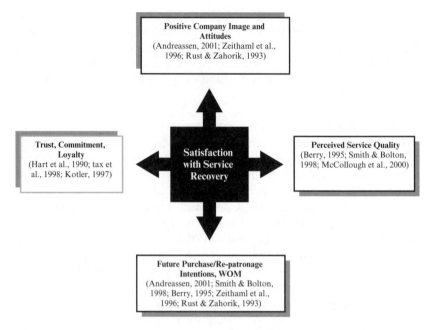

Figure 6.7   Consumer satisfaction outcomes from service recovery

possible to satisfy consumers with a service recovery. On the other hand, when a poor service is recovered by delivering a superior service, consumers are usually delighted and probably hope for another service failure in the future (e.g., a free upgrade on a flight due to a missed connection flight) (de Matos et al. 2007; Michel and Meuter 2008).

6.3   RELATIONSHIP MARKETING: DEVELOPING LONG-TERM RELATIONSHIPS WITH CUSTOMERS

As noted in the introduction to this chapter, the relationship marketing paradigm is the prevailing thesis in contemporary consumer behavior literature in the services field.

Adopting a relational approach to the marketing of services offers several advantages. A relational view revitalizes scientific research into major relationship constructs (Bolton 1998) such as consumer satisfaction, service quality, trust and loyalty, and introduces new ones such as attachment, commitment and engagement. These constructs can help distinguish relational services (e.g., high-contact services such as healthcare services) from transactional services (e.g., low-contact service encounters such as those in call centers) (Berry 1995) and identify appropriate strategies through which firms can build relationships with consumers who see value in such relationships. Moreover, relationship notions motivate cross-level research that links consumer- and firm-level domains, enabling us to examine how firms create, retain and profit from strong customer relationships (Sirdeshmukh et al. 2002).

In addition, service providers aim to develop stable customer–firm relationships because they can assist in many ways. Strong relationships can protect service providers from damage potentially caused by an occasional service failure or poor service performance (Berry 1995). Furthermore, a customer–firm relationship may act as a barrier to its termination because consumers gain several benefits through a long-term relationship (e.g., economic and psychological benefits, emotional and social bonds, customization and personalization of services) (Colgate et al. 2007). Strong consumer–firm relationships positively influence satisfaction with service recovery (Hess et al. 2003), mitigate the effect of poor service recovery on relational outcomes such as trust, commitment and loyalty (Mattila 2001), and reduce the propensity for consumer retaliatory behavior (Gregoire and Fisher 2006).

6.3.1 The Role of Trust and Loyalty in Developing Relationships

The desire among researchers and practitioners to move beyond consumer satisfaction to find other ways to build deeper and long-lasting relationships between customers and firms has led to the study of important relational constructs such as loyalty and trust (Morgan and Hunt 1994; Chaudhuri and Holbrook 2001; Singh and Sirdeshmukh 2000), and more recently social identity (Homburg et al. 2009), commitment (Ballester and Alemán 2001) and attachment (Esch et al. 2006; Tsiotsou 2011; Vlachos et al. 2010).

The link between trust and loyalty among consumers is well documented in the marketing literature (Morgan and Hunt 1994; Chaudhuri and Holbrook 2001; Singh and Sidershmukh 2000). Trust is considered an intrinsic feature of any valuable social relationship. Trust not only affects positive and favorable consumer attitudes, but also results in consumer commitment (Ballester and Alemán 2001) and loyalty (Morgan and Hunt 1994; Chaudhuri and Holbrook 2001), both of which are expressions of successful consumer–firm relationships (Morgan and Hunt 1994; Chaudhuri and Holbrook 2001; Park et al. 2006; Singh and Sirdeshmukh 2000). Consumer trust exists "when one party has confidence in the exchange partner's reliability and integrity" (Morgan and Hunt 1994,

p. 23). Consumers trust service providers to continue meeting their commitments and can be rewarded by remaining in a relationship with them (Doney and Cannon 1997). Furthermore, consumers' future expectations of using and benefiting from a service relationship can result in higher customer retention rates (Lemon et al. 2002). Based on commitment–trust theory, Morgan and Hunt (1994) consider trust a key variable in developing and maintaining enduring and highly valued relationships.

Trust affects consumer commitment even more than does overall satisfaction (Ballester and Alemán 2001), and is directly linked to purchase and attitudinal loyalty (Chaudhuri and Holbrook 2001). The association between trust and loyalty results from the conception that trust can create highly valued relational exchanges (Morgan and Hunt 1994). That is, consumers who trust a service firm will commit to a relationship with the firm and be willing to sustain the relationship over the long term.

However, recent findings indicate that the relation between trust and loyalty might not be equally strong across service types (Ball et al. 2004). In airlines and banks, trust determines consumer satisfaction but does not directly affect consumer loyalty, whereas in experiential services such as hotels, beauty salons and hospitals, trust is a direct determinant of intentional loyalty (Sirdeshmukh et al. 2002). Ball et al. (2004) study the trust–loyalty relationship in the banking sector where basic services are not well differentiated, and find that loyalty is explained less by trust and more by communication.

One explanation for the above findings might be the product context in which the trust–loyalty relationship is examined. Because much of our knowledge on the trust–loyalty and trust–commitment relationships comes from previous studies in goods, it seems that these models do not necessarily hold in the same manner in a services context, or in credence services. The relationship between trust and loyalty in services is more complex, thus indicating that the characteristics of services (e.g., credence and experiential attributes) might result in differences in the strength of the trust–loyalty relationship, while the process for developing loyal consumers is multifaceted and is carried out through avenues other than trust (e.g., communication, perceived value and attachment). Thus, building stable and long-term relationships with consumers in services is a more complicated process than in goods.

In addition, current empirical evidence indicates that the relationship between trust and loyalty might not be direct, but may be mediated by other affective factors such as consumer attachment to a service provider (Esch et al. 2006; Tsiotsou 2011; Vlachos et al. 2010) and consumer–firm affection (Yim et al. 2008). Recent research applies attachment theory in marketing (Thomson and Johnson 2006) and supports the conjecture that consumer attachment drives the strongest commercial relationships in services in areas such as the automotive sales (Paulssen and Fournier 2007). A recent study on a retail setting (Vlachos et al. 2010) indicates that firm trust and trust in employees act as antecedents of consumer–firm emotional attachment, which in turn is a strong predictor of behavioral loyalty and word of mouth. Moreover, attachment anxiety appears to multiply the effects of emotional attachment on behavioral loyalty and word of mouth. In a similar vein, Tsiotsou (2011) examines the direct and indirect effects of trust on loyalty in banking and insurance services. Although trust has a much weaker direct effect on loyalty than attachment in her structural model, it was found that consumer attachment to a service provider partially mediates the relationship between trust and loyalty.

6.3.1.1   Customer responses to firms' loyalty strategies

Service firms have been implementing various strategies and tools to build loyalty with their consumers. Consumer experience management (CEM) is considered an effective strategy for gaining loyal customers (Meyer and Schwager 2007). The purpose of consumer experience management is to ensure that every consumer's contact or interaction with the firm is positive so that it results in satisfaction (Goldsmith 2011). A consumer experience is considered successful when memorable and sustainable (Pine and Gilmore 1998). Service encounter stimuli such as tangible elements and process quality, brand relationships and interpersonal relationships have been proposed as the antecedents of consumer experience (Palmer 2010). Moreover, it has been suggested that facilitating the co-creation of value will affect consumer loyalty (Vargo and Lusch 2004).

Customer relationship management (CRM) is being touted as another key technique for creating loyal relationships with consumers. As important components of CRM, loyalty or reward programs have been used as tools for building consumer loyalty in services (Keh and Lee 2006; Uncles et al. 2003; Wirtz et al. 2007a). Rewards or incentives play a significant role in driving future consumer behavior, although they depend on the consumer's level of satisfaction and ties with a service provider. Reward programs might enhance consumer loyalty, but the timing of the reward functions differently between satisfied and dissatisfied consumers (Keh and Lee 2006). Satisfied consumers prefer a delayed redemption of rewards to immediate rewards when the former are of higher value, while dissatisfied consumers should be given immediate rewards to allay their dissatisfaction and secure their loyalty (Keh and Lee 2006).

In a development related to CRM programs, consumer concerns and responses regarding information privacy have been attracting increased attention in research showing key variables such as trust, information congruency and sensitivity explain consumer promotion and prevention-focused behavior (e.g. Lwin et al. 2007; Wirtz and Lwin 2009).

Because satisfied consumers do not always engage in positive word of mouth, rewards/incentives might increase the likelihood of generating positive word of mouth for a service provider (Xiao et al. 2011). Incentives targeted at satisfied customers and relatives and friends with whom they have strong ties are more likely to be effective than those targeted at customers to recommend to those with whom they have weak ties (Wirtz and Chew 2002). This is in line with the findings of Tsiotsou (2011), who indicates that in addition to rational/cognitive appeals (e.g., rewards and incentives), affective aspects of consumer–firm relationships should be considered when developing loyalty.

6.3.2   Service Brands as Relationship Builders

Human relationships have long inspired research on marketing relationships and, more recently, research on consumer–brand relationships (Fournier 1998). The consumer–brand relationship perspective suggests that there are relationship qualities between consumers and brands. Nowadays, marketers try to anchor brands not only in the minds of customers, but also in their hearts. Departing from the share-of-wallet notion, the share-of-heart approach is becoming increasingly important for marketing managers because it is related to post-consumption behavior and assists in developing long-term consumer–brand relationships.

Schultz et al. (2009, p. 12) defined brand relationships as "those bonds that bring the buyer and the seller of branded products or services together on a continuing basis". In services, consumers are inclined to consider all services offered by a firm as elements of a single brand. Riley and de Chernatony (2000) agree that in services, "relationships with consumers should be sought at the corporate brand level, rather than at the individual product level" (p. 145). Thus, the firm becomes the brand in services and consumers use the corporate brand name, size and reputation as indicators of brand quality when choosing between brands (Kotler and Bloom 1984). Although relationships based on functional and utilitarian benefits certainly exist, emotional relationships between consumers and firms tend to be more important. The desired relationship between firm and consumer is therefore based on the emotions evoked by the brand as it acquires meaning for the consumer (Allen et al. 2008).

As a result, an emerging aspect of consumer–brand relationships research is its focus on the emotional features of brand relationships expressed as consumer brand attachment (often referred to as affective commitment), brand engagement and brand love. Existing empirical investigations are, however, confined to goods (Albert et al. 2008; Carroll and Ahuvia 2006; Hemetsberger et al. 2009), and there are limited data on services. The following section briefly discusses these three qualities and their role in consumer–service brand relationship building and examines all the available research related to services.

Brand attachment   Fournier (1994) considers brand attachment one of the six dimensions relevant to a consumer–brand relationship. Brand attachment refers to "the strength of the cognitive and affective bond connecting the brand with the self" (Park et al. 2010, p. 2) in a symbolic manner (Wallendorf and Arnould 1988). The importance of brand attachment as a major determinant of consumption behavior is substantiated by several features endogenous to the concept. Attachment reflects emotional bonds that affect cognition, are characterized by persistence and resistance to change, and predict behavior (Krosnick and Petty 1995). Furthermore, brand attachment is critical because it should affect forms of behavior that boost brand profits and consumer lifetime value (Thomson et al. 2005; Tsiotsou 2011). A recent study by Park et al. (2010) in a retail banking setting shows that brand attachment is a direct determinant of consumers' purchase behavior (actual sales), brand purchase share and share-of-wallet. Moreover, Tsiotsou (2011) found that attachment to a service brand (e.g., in banking and insurance) is a direct determinant of trust and loyalty to these services. Park et al. (2010) went further by observing that brand attachment is more than an attitudinal construct and accounts for higher-order forms of consumer behavior associated with the commitment to a relationship.

Brand engagement   is the emotional tie that binds the consumer to the service provider (Goldsmith 2011). Brand engagement can be used as a proxy for the strength of a firm's consumer relationships based on both emotional and rational bonds consumers have developed with a brand (McEwen 2004). Bowden (2009) conceptualized brand engagement as "a psychological process that models the underlying mechanisms by which customer loyalty forms for new customers of a service brand as well as the mechanisms by which loyalty may be maintained for repeat purchase customers of a service brand" (p. 65). Bowden (2009) supported this concept in stating that engagement is a construct particularly applicable to services because they usually involve a certain degree of interactivity such as that seen between consumers and frontline personnel, and therefore imply a reciprocal relationship. Engagement might include feelings of confidence, integrity, pride and passion in a brand (McEwen 2004). In addition to these affective elements, consumer engagement with service brands has been considered a behavioral manifestation toward a brand or firm that goes beyond a purchase and includes positive word of mouth, recommendations, helping other consumers, blogging, writing reviews and even engaging in legal action (van Doom et al. 2010).

Brand love is considered a rich, deep and long-lasting feeling (Carroll and Ahuvia 2006) defined as "the degree of passionate emotional attachment that a person has for a particular trade name" (Carroll and Ahuvia 2006). It is conveyed as attachment and passion for the brand, assertions of love for the brand, and positive evaluations and emotions for the brand (Ahuvia 2005). Brand love plays a central role in post-consumption consumer behavior expressed either as positive word of mouth and brand loyalty (Carroll and Ahuvia 2006) or as willingness to forgive and pay a price premium (Heinrich et al. 2010). Although it plays a significant role in consumer–brand relationships, brand love has only recently attracted research attention in marketing (Albert et al. 2008). A recent study by Tsiotsou and Goldsmith (2011) examined the antecedents of brand love and compared its formation between goods (a coffee brand) and services (an insurance brand). It was found that brand attachment and brand trust acted as direct determinants of brand love and that their effects were stronger for the service brand than for the goods brand.

6.3.2.1   Brand communities

Developing online or offline clubs/brand communities for consumers has been employed as a means of creating loyalty (Roos et al. 2005). Brands not only foster links with consumers, but also connect consumers with each other through a set of common meanings (McAlexander et al. 2002). The consumer's relationship with the brand, the product and the firm is an influential antecedent to their integration into the brand group (McAlexander et al. 2002) and to their identification with the brand group (Algesheimer et al. 2005). The relationship of the consumer with the brand is described as a brand relationship, while the relationships consumers form with other consumers because of the brand are referred to as tribal behavior whereby consumers belong to a brand community or brand tribe (Tsiotsou and Veloutsou 2011).

The consumer's relationship with a brand precedes and contributes to their relationship with the brand tribe/community (Algesheimer et al. 2005). A recent study conducted by Veloutsou and Tsiotsou (2011b) in a service context supports the view that the perceived meaning of a service brand facilitates consumers' association with the brand, which in turn influences their intention to join groups of consumers sharing the same passion for the brand. Moreover, their findings indicate that consumers need to first develop close relationships with the brand before forming relationships with other consumers from the brand community. For example, sport fans first develop a relationship with a team before becoming members of a sport team community and actively engaging in the community. The degree to which consumers feel part of a brand community is a function of their perceived relationship with other members of the community (McAlexander et al. 2002) and the degree to which they want to interact with the other members of the brand community (Bagozzi and Dholakia 2006). Those who are actively engaged in the brand followers' group tend to stay in the group for a longer period (Algesheimer et al. 2005). A recent study among car-club communities' members in Europe showed that 67% of their brand loyalty intentions were explained by the quality of the relationship with the car brand and by membership continuance intentions (Algesheimer et al. 2005).

Social networking is being touted as another effective means to establish relationships with consumers (Li and Bernoff 2008) and promote word of mouth (Brown et al. 2007). Online social media environments provide new forms of consumer interaction in which the dyadic relationship seen in offline word of mouth no longer exists. Online communities and forums involve multiple participants at different stages, with some actively engaged and others simply observing interactions among their members (Libai et al. 2010). However, these communities might not be very effective without consumer engagement (Straczynski 2009). "Community engagement suggests that members are interested in helping other members, participating in joint activities, and otherwise acting volitionally in ways that the community endorses and that enhance its value for themselves and others" (Algesheimer et al. 2005, p. 21). Identification with a brand community results in higher community engagement, which in turn influences intentions for membership continuance, community recommendation and participation (Algesheimer et al. 2005).

6.4   THE SERVICE-DOMINANT LOGIC

The service-dominant (S-D) logic is an emerging paradigm in the marketing literature (Grönroos 1994, 2000b; Gummesson 1995; Rust 1998; Shostack 1977; Vargo and Lusch 2004) that provides "a new lexicon for marketing practices" linking transactional and relational approaches to marketing (Brodie et al. 2011, p. 79). According to this perspective, organizations, markets and society are basically involved in exchanges of service—the application of competencies (knowledge and skills) for the benefit of another party. Because services are exchanged for service, all firms should be considered service firms. The foundation of marketing theory and practice should thus come from service logic, principles and theories (Vargo and Lusch 2004, 2008). Due to the predominance of services, the S-D logic has been characterized as "the philosophical foundation of service science" (Maglio and Spohrer 2008, p. 18).

The S-D logic focuses on the concepts of value-in-use and co-creation of value rather than on the value-in-exchange and embedded value concepts of the goods perspective (G-D). Thus, firms market *with* consumers and other value-creation partners, called "actors", in their network, and do not market *to* consumers (Vargo and Lusch 2011). The service-centered approach is inherently consumer-centered and relational (Vargo and Lusch 2004).

The S-D perspective has its central focus on consumers. This means that firms not only are consumer-oriented, but also collaborate with and learn from their consumers to adapt and respond to their individual and continuously changing needs (Vargo and Lusch 2004). Vargo and Lusch (2004, 2008) have proposed several differences between the goods and service-centered dominant logics in relation to the primary unit of exchange, the role of goods, the role of the customer, the determination and meaning of value, firm-customer interaction and the source of economic growth. The goods perspective posits that consumers become involved in exchanges to acquire goods, whereas the service-centered view maintains that service is the fundamental basis of exchange. Goods are viewed as operand resources and end products in the G-D notion, whereas in the S-D logic they are considered transmitters of operant resources and intermediate "products" used by consumers in value-creation processes. In the G-D framework, value is determined by the producer and firms are limited to offering value propositions, whereas in the S-D perspective, value is perceived and determined by the consumer ("value in use"). Consumers are considered operand resources in the G-D notion, whereas they are seen as operant resources actively participating in relational exchanges and the co-creation of value in the S-D perspective.

Thus, the "service for service" approach has shifted the offering concept from one that views the offering as an output to one in which it is seen as a process of value creation where the role of the consumer changes. The consumer is no longer a receiver of business and is instead considered the source of business, a creator of firm value and a co-producer of value. In this sense, consumers play a fundamental joint role with the firm in creating value-in-use (Michel et al. 2008) through interactivity and collaboration (Grönroos 1994). Thus, the service perspective requires that consumer–firm relationships be developed for value to be created.

Because value creation is an interactive process, the interaction between a firm and a consumer should be viewed in a relational framework. "Value creation is always a collaborative and interactive process that takes place in the context of a unique set of multiple exchange relationships, though often somewhat tacitly and indirectly so" (Vargo 2009, p. 374). Moreover, to create value, these interactions should take place over extended periods in which new knowledge is combined with extant knowledge. The activities of consumers and service firms interactively and interdependently combine over time to create value. Therefore, relationships constitute a prerequisite to the creation of value, and are not optional. The S-D logic conceptualizes relationships through these joint, interactive, collaborative and reciprocal activities performed by all actors involved (i.e. consumers, service providers and stakeholders) to create value (Vargo 2009; Vargo and Lusch 2004; Chandler and Vargo 2011).

6.5 DISCUSSION

Consumer behavior in the services context has increasingly attracted research attention across all three stages of the consumption process. However, post-purchase behavior seems to dominate consumer behavior research in the services field, with the other two stages—the pre-purchase and service encounter stages—being under-investigated and requiring further research attention. Moreover, the consumer behavior literature in services has gradually become delinked from the goods perspective and has moved on from merely adapting models developed in the goods literature and trying to apply and contrast them to a service context. New models and approaches (e.g., the servuction model, the servicescape/environmental approach and relationship marketing) have increasingly been developed from a service perspective to explain consumer behavior related to service experiences.

The development of relationship marketing and the service-dominant logic have moved into the center of current thinking and research in the services arena. The service-dominant logic provides a promising consumer and marketing foundation and merits further development and empirical work. Furthermore, conceptual models integrating the service-dominant logic with existing consumer models and frameworks are needed to gain a better understanding of service consumer behavior. For example, this chapter illustrates that the service-dominant logic, relationship marketing and brand relationship frameworks could be integrated by using relationships as a common denominator of the three perspectives.

In addition to presenting new developments in the consumer behavior literature in services, this chapter also identifies several research gaps that warrant further attention. The first has emerged from the realization that the influence of the service environment on consumers' emotional reactions, evaluations and behavior is more complicated than initially thought. New research developments indicate that the effects of environmental elements depend on the service setting (e.g., private vs. public), the congruency between these elements, and consumers' individual characteristics. Research is needed to further clarify the complexities involved in the influence of the service environment not only on consumers, but also on employees and the social interactions taking place in a servicescape.

The application of new technologies and their impact throughout the three stages of service consumption is another important area for further research. The increasing growth of new technologies and their use in services is giving rise to questions about their acceptance in information kiosks, service delivery (self-service) and consumer service platforms by all kinds of consumers and in different situational contexts. The Internet has brought about several changes in consumer expectations, as well as true interactivity, consumer-specific, situational personalization, and the opportunity for real-time adjustments to a firm's offerings (Rust and Lemon 2001). One can expect the advent of smart phones and tablet computers (e.g., the iPhone and iPad) with their many applications being created by individual service firms (e.g., Singapore taxi firms have created applications to make booking taxis easier) to further revolutionize self-service applications.

Furthermore, the Internet has changed the role of consumers from being simply receivers of services to becoming actively involved in the production and delivery processes (Xue and Harker 2002). These new consumer roles and determinants of the co-creation of value in e-services need further examination. In an online context, e-service quality dominates the literature and is followed in importance by e-service value (Parasuraman et al. 2005; Santos 2003). However, all recent e-service quality and value models are based on traditional service models. For example, several e-service quality models are based on the SERVQUAL dimensions developed for traditional offline services (Parasuraman et al. 2005; Santos 2003). Using Grönroos' model, Heinonen (2006) initially proposes four dimensions of e-service value—technical, functional, temporal and spatial—but later also includes benefits and sacrifice components borrowed from the offline literature. Because consumer evaluations of e-services and mobile services differ from those of traditional offline services (Rust and Lemon 2001), there is a need to develop and test new models of e-service quality and value (Parasuraman et al. 2005).

The role of avatars in enhancing the consumer experience, increasing trust and loyalty and developing consumer relationships with service providers has not been investigated in much detail in the service literature. There is also limited research related to the use of recommendation agents and mobile services and their effect in improving the quality of consumer decisions (Haubl and Trifts 2000).

Consumers' responses to service failure and recovery continue to receive significant research attention. Several topics to have emerged in this area require further examination. Because the relative effectiveness of a service recovery might be situation-specific (Ruyter and Wetzels 2000), consumers' responses to service performance and process failures should be examined further, as should the role of other-consumer failure (Huang 2010). The role of other consumers in service failure has not been studied extensively in the service literature, although in several services (e.g., banks, gyms and restaurants), other consumers might be present and interact in a positive or negative way. The evolution of the employee–consumer relationship after a consumer complaint and service recovery constitutes another promising research direction.

Dysfunctional behavior among consumers is also an emerging topic in the service literature, as it seems this type of behavior might be endemic in the service industry (Fisk et al. 2010; Reynolds and Harris 2006). Understanding the motives, personality characteristics and situational contextual factors behind dysfunctional behavior among service consumers and how to prevent or control for such behavior are topics requiring further investigation.

Building longitudinal relationships with their consumers constitutes a significant challenge to contemporary service firms. Current empirical evidence questions the validity of traditional relationship models (e.g., satisfaction → trust → loyalty), highlights the complexity of consumers' post-purchase behavior, and shifts attention to the role of consumers' characteristics (e.g., relationship proneness) and affective reactions (e.g., attachment) to service firms and their employees as prerequisites for developing and maintaining longitudinal relationships.

Service brands are an under-researched area in which existing methods are largely confined to qualitative approaches (e.g., de Chernatony and Segal-Horn 2001). Consumers' responses to service brands and building consumer–service brand relationships are topics that demand more research attention. Recent calls argue for future research to develop comprehensive conceptual models of consumer engagement and test them empirically in services contexts (van Doom et al. 2010).

The role of consumer clubs (Roos et al. 2005) and consumer brand communities/e-communities/tribes (Veloutsou and Tsiotsou 2011) in building stable consumer relationships is another direction in which service research must be taken and developed further. Identifying the motives (e.g., utilitarian and affective) behind joining or remaining in a club/community and the antecedents (e.g., service provider image and personality) and outcomes of participating in such groups (e.g., behavioral intentions, commitment, loyalty, trust, positive word of mouth) are potential avenues for future research.

If the service-dominant logic prevails as a marketing paradigm in coming years, then consumer behavior models developed in the services field might be used as the foundation for the respective models for the marketing of other types of products (e.g., fast-moving consumer goods, durables and industrial goods). However, more research on consumer behavior in a service context is needed to shed light on various aspects of the purchase decision process and the development of relationships. This chapter provides an overview of key developments in the consumer behavior literature in the services field and highlights relevant issues warranting further research attention.

ACKNOWLEDGEMENT

The authors would like to thank Gary Daniel Futrell for his constructive comments on earlier versions of this chapter.

REFERENCES

Ahuvia, A.C. (2005), 'Beyond the extended self: loved objects and consumers' identity narratives', *Journal of Consumer Research*, **32**, 171–184.
Akhter, S.H. (2010), 'Service attributes satisfaction and actual repurchase behaviour: the mediating influence of overall satisfaction and intention', *Journal of Satisfaction and Dissatisfaction and Complaining Behaviour*, **23**, 52–64.
Aksoy, L., P.N. Bloom, N.H. Lurie and B. Cooil (2006), 'Should recommendation agents think like people?', *Journal of Service Research*, **8** (4), 297–315.
Alba, J.W. and J.W. Hutchinson (2000), 'Knowledge calibration: what consumers know and what they think they know', *Journal of Consumer Research*, **27** (2), 123–156.
Albert, N., D.R. Merunka and P. Florence-Valette (2008), 'Conceptualizing and measuring consumers' love towards their brands', *Society for Marketing Advances Proceedings*, 108–111.
Algesheimer, R., U.M. Dholakia and A. Herrmann (2005), 'The social influence of brand community: evidence from European car clubs', *Journal of Marketing*, **69** (3), 19–34.
Allen, Chris T., Susan Fournier and Felecia Miller (2008), 'Brands and their meaning makers', in Curtis P. Haugtvedt, Paul M. Herr and Frack R. Kardes (eds), *Handbook of Consumer Psychology*, New York: Psychology Press, pp. 781–821.
Andreassen, T.W. (2001), 'From disgust to delight: do customers hold a grudge?', *Journal of Service Research*, **4** (1), 39–49.
Anton, J. (2000), 'The past, present, and future of customer access centers', *International Journal of Service Industry Management*, **11** (2), 120–130.

Anton, C., C. Camarero and M. Carrero (2007), 'Analysing firm's failures as determinants of consumer switching intentions: the effect of moderating factors', *European Journal of Marketing*, **41** (1/2), 135–158.

Ariely, D., J.G. Lynch Jr. and M. Aparicio IV (2004), 'Learning by collaborative and individual-based recommendation agents', *Journal of Consumer Psychology*, **14** (1/2), 81–95.

Bagozzi, R.P. and U.M. Dholakia (2006), 'Antecedents and purchase consequences of customer participation in small group brand communities', *International Journal of Research in Marketing*, **23** (1), 45–61.

Baker, J. (1987), 'The role of the environment in marketing services: the consumer perspective', *The Services Challenge: Integrating for Competitive Advantage*, Chicago, IL: American Marketing Association, pp. 79–84.

Ball, D., P.S. Coelho and A. Machas (2004), 'The role of communication and trust in explaining customer loyalty: an extension to the ECSI model', *European Journal of Marketing*, **38** (9/10), 1272–1293.

Ballester, D.E. and M.J.L. Alemán (2001), 'Brand trust in the context of consumer loyalty', *European Journal of Marketing*, **35** (11/12), 1238–1258.

Bamfield, J. (2006), 'Sed quis custodiet? Employee theft in UK retailing', *International Journal of Retail & Distribution Management*, **34** (11), 845–859.

Bansal, H.S. and P.A. Voyer (2000), 'Word-of-mouth processes within a services purchase decision context', *Journal of Service Research*, **3** (2), 166–177.

Bansal, H.S., S.F. Taylor and Y. St. James (2005), '"Migrating" to new service providers: toward a unifying framework of consumers' switching behaviours', *Journal of the Academy of Marketing Science*, **33** (1), 96–115.

Baron, S., K. Harris and R. Harris (2003), 'Retail theater: the "intended effect" of the performance', *Journal of Service Research*, **4** (May), 316–332.

Bassi, F. and G. Guido (2006), 'Measuring customer satisfaction: from product performance to consumption experience', *Journal of Consumer Satisfaction, Dissatisfaction, and Complaining Behaviour*, **19**, 76–89.

Bell, S.J. and J.A. Luddington (2006), 'Coping with customer complaints', *Journal of Service Research*, **8** (3), 221–233.

Berry, L.L. (1995), 'Relationship marketing of services – growing interest, emerging perspectives', *Journal of the Academy of Marketing Science*, **23** (4), 236–245.

Berry, L.L. and K. Seiders (2008), 'Serving unfair customers', *Business Horizons*, **51** (1), 29–37.

Bhatnagar, A. and S. Ghose (2004), 'Online information search termination patterns across product categories and consumer demographics', *Journal of Retailing*, **80** (3), 221–228.

Bitner, M.J. (1992), 'Servicescapes: The impact of physical surroundings on customers and employees', *Journal of Marketing*, **56**, 57–71.

Bitner, M.J., B.H. Booms and M.S. Tetreault (1990), 'The service encounter: diagnosing favorable and unfavorable incidents', *Journal of Marketing*, **54** (January), 71–84.

Bitner, M.J., S.W. Brown and M.L. Meuter (2000), 'Technology infusion in service encounters', *Journal of the Academy of Marketing Science*, **28** (1), 138–149.

Bitner, M.J., A.L. Ostrom and M.L. Meuter (2002), 'Implementing successful self-service technologies', *Academy of Management Executive*, **16** (4), 96–109.

Blackwell, Roger D., Paul W. Miniard and James F. Engel (eds) (2003), *Consumer Behaviour*, Orlando, US: Harcourt College Publishers.

Bolton, R.N. (1998), 'A dynamic model of duration of the customer's relationship with a continuous service provider: the role of satisfaction', *Marketing Science*, **17** (1), 45–65.

Bolton, R.N. and K.N. Lemon (1999), 'A dynamic model of customers' sage of services: usage as an antecedent and consequence of satisfaction', *Journal of Marketing Research*, **36** (2), 171–186.

Bone, P. and P.S. Ellen (1999), 'Scents in the marketplace: explaining a fraction of olfaction', *Journal of Retailing*, **75** (2), 243–262.

Boshoff, C. (2002), 'Service advertising: an exploratory study of risk perceptions', *Journal of Service Research*, **4** (4), 290–298.

Boulding, W., A. Kalia, R. Staelin and V.A. Zeithaml (1993), 'A dynamic process model of service quality: from expectations to behavioural intentions', *Journal of Marketing Research*, **30** (1), 7–27.

Bowden, J.L.H. (2009), 'The process of customer engagement: a conceptual framework', *Journal of Marketing Theory and Practice*, **17** (1), 63–74.

Boyle, D., S. Clark and S. Burns (2006), *Hidden Work: Co-production by People Outside Paid Employment*, York: Joseph Rowntree Foundation.

Brady, M.K. and J.J. Cronin Jr. (2001), 'Some new thoughts on conceptualizing perceived service quality: a hierarchical approach', *Journal of Marketing*, **65** (3), 34–49.

Brady, M.K. and C.J. Robertson (2001), 'Searching for a consensus on the antecedent role of service quality and satisfaction: an exploratory cross-national study', *Journal of Business Research*, **51** (1), 53–60.

Brodie, R.J., M. Saren and J. Pels (2011), 'Theorizing about the service dominant logic: the bridging role of middle range', *Marketing Theory*, **11** (1), 75–91.

Brown, J., A.J. Broderick and N. Lee (2007), 'Extending social network theory to conceptualise on-line word-of-mouth communication', *Journal of Interactive Marketing*, **21** (3), 2–19.

Burnham, T.A., J.K. Frels and V. Mahajan (2003), 'Consumer switching costs: a typology, antecedents and consequences', *Journal of the Academy of Marketing Science*, **31** (2), 109–126.

Busacca, B. and G. Padula (2005), 'Understanding the relationship between attribute performance and overall satisfaction. Theory, measurement and implications', *Marketing Intelligence & Planning*, **23** (6), 543–561.

Byrne, K. (2005), 'How do consumers evaluate risk in financial products?', *Journal of Financial Services Marketing*, **10** (1), 21–36.

Carroll, B.A. and A.C. Ahuvia (2006), 'Some antecedents and outcomes of brand love', *Marketing Letters*, **17** (2), 79–89.

Chandler, J.D. and S.L. Vargo (2011), 'Contextualization and value-in-context: how context frames exchange', *Marketing Theory*, **11** (1), 35–49.

Chase, R.B. (1978), 'Where does the customer fit in a service organization?', *Harvard Business Review*, **56** (November/December), 137–142.

Chaudhuri, A. and M.B. Holbrook (2001), 'The chain of effects from brand trust and brand affect to brand performance: the role of brand loyalty', *Journal of Marketing*, **65** (April), 81–93.

Chebat, J.-C., M. Davidow and I. Codjovi (2005), 'Silent voices: why some dissatisfied consumers fail to complain', *Journal of Service Research*, **7** (4), 328–342.

Chen, R.R., E. Gerstner and Y. Yang (2009), 'Should captive sardines be compensated? Serving customers in a confined zone', *Marketing Science*, **28** (3), 599–608.

Churchill, G.A. Jr. and C. Surprenant (1982), 'An investigation into the determinants of customer satisfaction', *Journal of Marketing Research*, **19** (4), 491–504.

Chylinski, M. and A. Chu (2010), 'Consumer cynicism: antecedents and consequences', *European Journal of Marketing*, **44** (6), 796–837.

Colgate, M., V.T.-U. Tong, C.K.-C. Lee and J.U. Farley (2007), 'Back from the brink: why customers stay', *Journal of Service Research*, **9** (3), 211–228.

Coulter, K.S. and R.A. Coulter (2002), 'Determinants of trust in a service provider: the moderating role of length of relationship', *Journal of Services Marketing*, **16** (1), 35–50.

Coye, R.W. (2004), 'Managing customer expectations in the service encounter', *International Journal of Service Industry Management*, **15** (1), 54–71.

Cronin, J.J. Jr., M.K. Brady and G.T.M. Hult (2000), 'Assessing the effects of quality, value, and customer satisfaction on consumer behavioural intentions in service environments', *Journal of Retailing*, **76** (2), 193–217.

Curran, J.M., M.L. Meuter and C.F. Surprenant (2003), 'Intentions to use self-service technologies: a confluence of multiple attitudes', *Journal of Service Research*, **5** (3), 209–224.

d'Astous, A., N. Roy and H. Simard (1995), 'A study of consumer irritations during shopping', in Flemming Hansen (ed.), *European Advances in Consumer Research*, 2, Provo, UT: Association for Consumer Research, pp. 381–387.

Dabholkar, P.A. and R.P. Bagozzi (2002), 'An attitudinal model of technology-based self-service: moderating effects of consumer traits and situational factors', *Journal of the Academy of Marketing Science*, **30** (3), 184–201.

Dabholkar, P.A., L.M. Bobbit and E.-J. Lee (2003), 'Understanding consumer motivation and behaviour related to self-scanning in retailing: implications for strategy and research on technology-based self-service', *International Journal of Service Industry Management*, **14** (1), 59–95.

Darby, M.R. and E. Karni (1973), 'Free competition and the optimal amount of fraud', *Journal of Law and Economics*, **16** (1), 67–86.

Davies, B. and P. Ward (2002), *Managing Retail Consumption*, West Sussex, UK: John Wiley & Sons.

de Chernatony, L. and S. Segal-Horn (2001), 'Building on services' characteristics to develop successful services brands', *Journal of Marketing Management*, **17**, 645–669.

de Matos, C.A., J.L. Hernique and C.A.V. Rossi (2007), 'Service recovery paradox: a meta-analysis', *Journal of Service Research*, **10** (1), 60–77.

Diacon, S. and C. Ennew (2001), 'Consumer perceptions of financial risk', *Geneva Papers on Risk and Insurance: Issues and Practice*, **26** (3), 389–409.

Diaz, A.B.C. and F.J.M. Ruiz (2002), 'The consumer's reaction to delays in service', *International Journal of Service Industry Management*, **13** (2), 118–140.

Diehl, K., L.J. Kornish and J.G. Lynch Jr. (2003), 'Smart agents: when lower search costs for quality information increase price sensitivity', *Journal of Consumer Research*, **30** (1), 56–71.

Doney, P. and J.P. Cannon (1997), 'An examination of the nature of trust in buyer-seller relationships', *Journal of Marketing*, **61** (April), 35–51.

Donovan, R., J. Rossiter, G. Marcoolyn and A. Nesdale (1994), 'Store atmosphere and purchasing behaviour', *Journal of Retailing*, **70** (3), 283–294.

Doom, J. van, K.N. Lemon, V. Mittal, S. Nass, D. Pick, P. Pimer and P.C. Verhoef (2010), 'Customer engagement behaviour: theoretical foundations and research directions', *Journal of Service Research*, **13** (3), 253–266.

Dunne, Patrick M., Robert F. Lusch and David A. Griffith (2002), *Retailing*, 4th edn, Orlando, FL: Hartcourt.

Edvardsson, Bo, Anders Gustafsson, Michael D. Johnson and Bodil Sandén (2000), *New Service Development and Innovation in the New Economy*, Lund: Studentlitteratur.

Ehrlichman, Howard and Linda Bastone (1992), 'The use of odour in the study of emotion', in Steven van Toller and George H. Dodd (eds), *Fragrance: The Psychology and Biology of Perfume*, London: Elsevier, pp. 143–159.

Eiglier Pierre and Eric Langeard (1977), 'Services as systems: marketing implications', in Pierre Eiglier, Eric Langeard, Christopher H. Lovelock, John E.G. Bateson and Robert F. Young (eds), *Marketing Consumer Services: New Insights*, Report # 77–115 (November) Cambridge, MA: Marketing Science Institute, pp. 83–103.

Esch, F., T. Langner, B.H. Schmitt and P. Geus (2006), 'Are brands forever? How brand knowledge and relationships affect current and future purchases', *Journal of Product and Brand Management*, **15** (2), 98–105.

Feinberg, R., L. Hokama, R. Kadam and I. Kim (2002), 'Operational determinants of caller satisfaction in the banking/financial service call center', *International Journal of Bank Marketing*, **20**, 174–180.

Fisk, Raymond P. (1981), 'Toward a consumption/evaluation process model for services', in James H. Donnelly and William R. George (eds), *Marketing of Services*, Chicago, IL: American Marketing Association, pp. 191–195.

Fisk, R., S. Grove, L.C. Harris, D. Keeffe, K. Reynolds, R. Russell-Bennett and J. Wirtz (2010), 'Customers behaving badly: a state of the art review, research agenda and implications for practitioners', *Journal of Services Marketing*, **26** (6), 417–429.

Folkes, V.S. (1984), 'Consumer reactions to product failure: an attributional approach', *Journal of Consumer Research*, **10** (4), 398–409.

Forbes, L.P., S.W. Kelley and K.D. Hoffman (2005), 'Typologies of e-commerce retail failures and recovery strategies', *Journal of Service Marketing*, **19** (5), 280–292.

Fournier, S. (1994), 'A consumer–brand relationship framework for strategic brand management', Dissertation at the University of Florida.
Fournier, S. (1998), 'Consumers and their brands: developing relationship theory in consumer research', *Journal of Consumer Research*, **24**, 343–373.
Friedman, R.A. and S.C. Currall (2003), 'E-mail escalation: dispute exacerbating elements of e-mail communication', *Human Relations*, **56**, 1325–1348.
Galetzka, M., J.W.M. Verhoeven and T.H. Pruyn (2006), 'Service validity and service reliability of search, experience and credence services', *International Journal of Service Industry Management*, **17** (3), 271–283.
Ganesh, J., M.J. Arnold and K.E. Reynolds (2000), 'Understanding the customer base of service providers: an examination of the differences between switchers and stayers', *Journal of Marketing*, **64** (3), 65–87.
Gardial, S.F., S. Clemons, R.B. Woodruff, D.W. Schumann and M.J. Burns (1994), 'Comparing consumers' recall of prepurchase and postpurchase product evaluation experiences', *Journal of Consumer Research*, **20** (March), 548–560.
Goetzinger, L., J.K. Park and R. Widdows (2006), 'E-customers' third party complaining and complimenting behaviour', *International Journal of Service Industry Management*, **17** (2), 193–206.
Goldsmith, Ronald E. (2011), 'Brand engagement and brand loyalty', in Avinash Kapoor and Chinmaya Kulshrestha (eds), *Branding and Sustainable Competitive Advantage: Building Virtual Presence*, Hershey, PA: IGI Global, pp. 122–135.
Grandey, A., D. Dickter and H.-P. Sin (2004), 'The customer is not always right: customer verbal aggression towards service employees', *Journal of Organizational Behavior*, **25** (3), 397–418.
Grandey, A., A. Rafaeli, S. Ravid, J. Wirtz and D.D. Steiner (2010), 'Emotion display rules at work in the global service economy: the special case of the customer', *Journal of Service Management*, **21** (3), 388–412.
Gregoire, Y. and R.J. Fisher (2006), 'The effects of relationship quality on customer retaliation', *Marketing Letters*, **17** (1), 31–46.
Gregoire, Y. and R.J. Fisher (2008), 'Customer betrayal and retaliation: when your best customers become your worst enemies', *Journal of the Academy of Marketing Science*, **36** (2), 247–261.
Gremler, D.D., K.P. Gwinner and S.W. Brown (2001), 'Generating positive word-of-mouth communication through customer-employee relationships', *International Journal of Service Industry Management*, **12** (1), 44–69.
Grönroos, C. (1994), 'From marketing mix to relationship marketing: towards a paradigm shift in marketing', *Management Decision*, **32** (2), 4–20.
Grönroos, C. (1998), 'Marketing services: the case of a missing product', *Journal of Business and Industrial Marketing*, **13** (4/5), 322–338.
Grönroos, Christian (2000a), 'Service reflections: service marketing comes of age', in Teresa A. Swartz and Dawn Iacobucci (eds), *Handbook of Services Marketing & Management*, London, UK: Sage Publications, Inc., pp. 13–20.
Grönroos, Christian (2000b), 'Christian Grönroos: Hanken Swedish School of Economics, Finland', in Raymond P. Fisk, Stephen F. Grove and John Joby (eds), *Services Marketing Self-Portraits: Introspections, Reflections, and Glimpses from the Experts*, Chicago: American Marketing Association, pp. 71–108.
Grove, Stephen J. and Raymond P. Fisk (1983), 'The dramaturgy of services exchange: an analytical framework for services marketing', in Leonard L. Berry, G. Lynn Shostack and Gregory D. Upah (eds), *Emerging Perspectives on Services Marketing*, Chicago, IL: The American Marketing Association, pp. 45–49.
Grove, S.J. and R.P. Fisk (1997), 'The impact of other customers on service experiences: a critical incident examination of "getting along"', *Journal of Retailing*, **73** (1), 63–85.
Grove, Stephen J., Raymond P. Fisk and Joby John (2000), 'Services as theater: guidelines and implications', in Teresa A. Schwartz and Dawn Iacobucci (eds), *Handbook of Services Marketing and Management*, Thousand Oaks, CA: Sage, pp. 21–36.

Gueguen, N. and C. Petr (2006), 'Odors and consumer behaviour in a restaurant', *Hospitality Management*, **25**, 335–339.

Gummesson, Evert (1995), 'Relationship marketing: its role in the service economy', in William J. Glynn and James G. Barns (eds), *Understanding Services Management*, New York: John Wiley, pp. 224–268.

Gupta, S., D.R. Lehmann and J.A. Stuart (2004), 'Valuing customers', *Journal of Marketing Research*, **41** (1), 7–18.

Harris, K. and S. Baron (2004), 'Consumer-to-consumer conversations in service settings', *Journal of Service Research*, **6** (3), 287–303.

Harris, L. and K. Reynolds (2003), 'The consequences of dysfunctional customer behaviour', *Journal of Service Research*, **6**, 144–161.

Harris, R., K. Harris and S. Baron (2003), 'Theatrical service experiences: dramatic script development with employees', *International Journal of Service Industry Management*, **14** (2), 184–199.

Harris, K.E., D. Grewal, L.A. Mohr and K.L. Bernhardt (2006), 'Consumer responses to service recovery strategies: the moderating role of online versus offline environments', *Journal of Business Research*, **59** (4), 425–431.

Hart, C.W., J.L. Heskett and W.E. Sasser (1990), 'The profitable art of service recovery', *Harvard Business Review*, **68**, 148–156.

Haubl, G. and K.B. Murray (2003), 'Preference construction and persistence in digital marketplaces: the role of electronic recommendation agents', *Journal of Consumer Psychology*, **13** (1/2), 75–91.

Haubl, G. and V. Trifts (2000), 'Consumer decision making in online shopping environments: the effects of interactive decision aids', *Marketing Science*, **19** (1), 4–21.

Heinonen, K. (2006), 'Temporal and spatial e-service value', *International Journal of Service Industry Management*, **17** (4), 380–400.

Heinrich, D., C.-M. Albrecht and H.H. Bauer (2010), 'Love actually? Investigating consumers' brand love', *Proceedings of the 1st International Colloquium on the consumer–brand Relationship*, 22–24 April, Orlando, Florida.

Hemetsberger, A., C.M.T. Kittinger-Rosanelli and S. Friedmann (2009), '"Bye bye love". Why devoted consumers break up with their brands', *Advances in Consumer Research*, **36**, 430–437.

Hensley, R.L. and J. Sulek (2007), 'Customer satisfaction with waits in multi-stage services', *Managing Service Quality*, **17** (2), 152–173.

Heracleous, L. and J. Wirtz (2010), 'Singapore Airlines' balancing act – Asia's premier carrier successfully executes a dual strategy: it offers world-class service and is a cost leader', *Harvard Business Review*, **88** (7/8), 145–149.

Hess, R.L. Jr., S. Ganesan and N.M. Klein (2003), 'Service failure and recovery: the impact of relationship factors on customer satisfaction', *Journal of the Academy of Marketing Science*, **31** (2), 127–145.

Hoffman, K.D. and S.W. Kelley (2000), 'Perceived justice needs and recovery evaluation: a contingency approach', *European Journal of Marketing*, **34** (3/4), 418–432.

Holbrook, Morris (1994), 'The nature of customer value, an axiology of services in the consumption experience', in Ronald T. Rust and Richard L. Oliver (eds), *Service Quality. New Directions In Theory and Practice*, Thousand Oaks, CA: Sage Publications, pp. 21–71.

Holloway, B.B. and S.E. Beatty (2003), 'Service failure in online retailing: a recovery opportunity', *Journal of Service Research*, **6** (1), 92–106.

Homburg, C. and A. Giering (2001), 'Personal characteristics as moderators of the relationship between customer satisfaction and loyalty – an empirical analysis', *Psychology & Marketing*, **18** (1), 43–66.

Homburg, C., W.D. Hoyer and N. Koschate (2005), 'Customers' reactions to price increases: do customer satisfaction and perceived motive fairness matter?', *Journal of the Academy of Marketing Science*, **33** (1), 36–49.

Homburg, C., J. Wieseke and W.D. Hoyer (2009), 'Social identity and the service-profit chain', *Journal of Marketing*, **73** (2), 38–54.

Holzwarth, M., C. Janiszewski and M.M. Neumann (2006), 'The influence of avatars on online consumer shopping behaviour', *Journal of Marketing*, **70** (4), 19–36.

Hu, H., J. Kandampully and T. Juwaheer (2009), 'Relationships and impacts of service quality, perceived value, customer satisfaction, and image: an empirical study', *The Service Industries Journal*, **29** (2), 111–125.

Huang, W.-H. (2010), 'Other-customer failure: effects of perceived employee effort and compensation on complainer and non-complainer service evaluations', *Journal of Service Management*, **21** (2), 191–211.

Jamal, A. and A. Adelowore (2008), 'Customer-employee relationship: the role of self-employee congruence', *European Journal of Marketing*, **42** (11/12), 1316–1345.

Johnson, M. and G.M. Zinkham (1991), 'Emotional responses to a professional service encounter', *Journal of Services Marketing*, **5** (2), 5–16.

Johnston, T.C. and M.A. Hewa (1997), 'Fixing service failures', *Industrial Marketing Management*, **26** (5), 467–473.

Kacen, J.J. and J.A. Lee, (2002), 'The influence of culture on consumer impulsive buying behaviour', *Journal of Consumer Psychology*, **12** (2), 163–176.

Kano, N., N. Seraku, F. Takahashi and S. Tsuji (1984), 'Attractive quality and must-be quality, *Hinshitsu* (Quality, The Journal of the Japanese Society for Quality Control), **14** (2), 39–48.

Keaveney, S.M. and M. Parthasarathy (2001), 'Customer switching behaviour in online services: an exploratory study of the role of selected attitudinal, behavioural, and demographic factors', *Journal of Academy of Marketing Science*, **29** (4), 374–390.

Keh, H.T. and Y.H. Lee (2006), 'Do reward programs build loyalty for services?: the moderating effect of satisfaction on type and timing of rewards', *Journal of Retailing*, **82** (2), 127–136.

Keiningham, Timothy L. and Terry G. Vavra (eds) (2001), *The Customer Delight Principle: Exceeding Customers' Expectations for Bottom-Line Success*, New York: McGraw-Hill.

Kelley, S.W. and M.A. Davis (1994), 'Antecedents to customer expectations for service recovery', *Journal of the Academy of Marketing Science*, **22** (1), 52–61.

Keng, C.-J., T.-L. Huang, L.-J. Zheng and M.K. Hsu (2007), 'Modeling service encounters and customer experiential value in retailing: an empirical investigation of shopping mall customers in Taiwan', *International Journal of Service Industry Management*, **18** (40), 349–367.

Kimes, S.E. and J. Wirtz (2003), 'Has revenue management become acceptable? Findings from an international study on the perceived fairness of rate fences', *Journal of Service Research*, **6** (2), 125–135.

Konus, U., P.C. Verhoef and S.A. Neslin (2008), 'Multichannel shopper segments and their covariates', *Journal of Retailing*, **84** (4), 398–413.

Kotler, Philip (1997), *Marketing Management*, Prentice-Hall, Upper Saddle River, NJ.

Kotler, Philip and Paul N. Bloom (1984), *Marketing Professional Services*, New Jersey: Prentice-Hall.

Kraft, F.B. and C.L. Martin (2001), 'Customer compliments as more than complimentary feedback', *Journal of Consumer Satisfaction, Dissatisfaction and Complaining Behaviour*, **14**, 1–13.

Krosnick, Jon A. and Richard E. Petty (1995), 'Attitude strength: an overview', in Richard E. Petty and Jon A. Krosnick (eds), *Attitude Strength: Antecedents and Consequences*, Hillsdale, NJ: Erlbaum, pp. 1–24.

Lages, L.F. and J.C. Fernandes (2005), 'The SERPVAL scale: a multi-item measurement instrument for measuring service personal values', *Journal of Business Research*, **58** (11), 1562–1572.

Langeard, E., J.E. Bateson, C.H. Lovelock and P. Eiglier (1981), *Services Marketing: New Insights from Consumers and Managers*, Marketing Science Institute, Report # 81–104 (August).

Lemon, K.N., T.B. White and R.S. Winer (2002), 'Dynamic customer relationship management: incorporating future considerations into the service retention decision', *Journal of Marketing*, **66** (1), 1–14.

Li, Charlene and Josh Bernoff (2008), *Groundswell: Winning in a World Transformed by Social Technologies*, Boston, MA: Harvard Business Press.

Liang, C.-J., W.-H. Wang and J.D. Farquhar (2009), 'The influence of customer perceptions on financial performance in financial services', *International Journal of Bank Marketing*, **27** (2), 129–149.

Libai, B., R. Bolton, M.S. Bugel, K. de Ruyter, O. Gotz, H. Risselada and A.T. Stephen (2010), 'Customer-to-customer interactions: broadening the scope of word of mouth research', *Journal of Service Research*, **13** (3), 267–282.

Lin, C.-H., P.J. Sher and H.-Yu Shih (2005), 'Past progress and future directions in conceptualizing customer perceived value', *International Journal of Service Industry Management*, **16** (4), 318–336.

Lin, I.Y. (2010), 'The interactive effect of Gestalt situations and arousal seeking tendency on customers' emotional responses: matching color and music to specific servicescapes', *Journal of Services Marketing*, **24** (4), 294–304.

Lovelock, Christopher and Jochen Wirtz (2011), *Services Marketing: People, Technology, Strategy* (7th edn), Upper Saddle River, New Jersey: Prentice Hall.

Lwin, M.O., J. Wirtz and J.D. Williams (2007), 'Consumer online privacy concerns and responses: a power-responsibility equilibrium perspective', *Journal of the Academy of Marketing Science*, **35** (4), 572–585

Maglio, P.P. and Spohrer, J. (2008), 'Fundamentals of service science', *Journal of the Academy of Marketing Science*, **36**, 18–20.

Martin, C.L. (1996), 'Consumer-to-consumer relationships: satisfaction with other consumers' public behaviour', *Journal of Consumer Affairs*, **30** (1), 146–168.

Martin, C.L. and C.A. Pranter (1989), 'Compatibility management: customer-to-customer relationships in service environments', *Journal of Services Marketing*, **3**, 5–15.

Mattila, A.S. (2001), 'The impact on relationship type on customer loyalty in a context of service failures', *Journal of Service Research*, **4** (2), 91–101.

Mattila, A.S. and J. Wirtz (2000), 'The role of pre-consumption affect in post-purchase evaluation of services', *Psychology & Marketing*, **17** (7), 587–605.

Mattila, A.S. and J. Wirtz (2001), 'Congruency of scent and music as a driver of in-store evaluations and behaviour', *Journal of Retailing*, **77**, 273–289.

Mattila, A.S. and J. Wirtz (2002), 'The impact of knowledge types on the consumer search process: an investigation in the context of credence services', *International Journal of Service Industry Management*, **13** (3), 214–230.

Mattila, A.S. and J. Wirtz (2004), 'Consumer complaining to firms: the determinants of channel choice', *Journal of Services Marketing*, **18** (2), 147–155.

Mattila, A.S. and J. Wirtz (2008), 'The role of store environmental stimulation and social factors on impulse purchasing', *Journal of Services Marketing*, **22** (7), 562–567.

McAlexander, J.H., J.W. Schouten and H. Koenig (2002), 'Building brand community', *Journal of Marketing*, (January), 38–54.

McCollough, M.A., L.L. Berry and M.S. Yadav (2000), 'An empirical investigation of customer satisfaction after service failure and recovery', *Journal of Service Research*, **3** (2), 121–137.

McEwen, W. (2004), 'Why satisfaction isn't satisfying', *Gallup Management Journal Online*, November (1–4).

McGrath, M.A. and C. Otnes (1995), 'Unacquainted influences: when strangers interact in the retail setting', *Journal of Business Research*, **32** (3), 261–271.

Meuter, M.L., A.L. Ostrom, R.I. Roundtree and M.J. Bitner (2000), 'Self-service technologies: understanding customer satisfaction with technology-based service encounter', *Journal of Marketing*, **64** (3), 50–64.

Meyer, C. and A. Schwager (2007), 'Understanding customer experience', *Harvard Business Review*, **85** (February), 117–126.

Michel, S. and M.L. Meuter (2008), 'The service recovery paradox: true but overrated', *International Journal of Service Industry Management*, **19** (4), 441–457.

Michel, S., S.L. Vargo and R.F. Lusch (2008), 'Reconfiguration of the conceptual landscape: a tribute to the service logic', *Journal of the Academy of Marketing Science*, **36**, 152–155.

Mittal, V. and W.A. Kamakura (2001), 'Satisfaction and repurchase behaviour: the moderating influence of customer and market characteristics', *Journal of Marketing Research*, **38** (1), 131–142.

Mittal, V., W.T. Ross and P.M. Baldasare (1998), 'The asymmetric impact of negative and positive attribute-level performance on overall satisfaction and repurchase intentions', *Journal of Marketing*, **62** (1), 33–47.

Mittal, V., P. Kumar and M. Tsiros (1999), 'Attribute-level performance, satisfaction, and behavioural intentions over time: a consumption-system approach', *Journal of Marketing*, **63** (2), 88–101.

Morgan, R.M. and S. Hunt (1994), 'The commitment-trust theory of relationship marketing', *Journal of Marketing*, **58**, 20–38.

Morrin, M. and S. Ratneshwar (2003), 'Does it make sense to use scents to enhance brand memory?', *Journal of Marketing Research*, **40** (1), 10–25.

Murray, K.B. and J.L. Schlacter (1990), 'The impact of services versus goods on consumers' assessment of perceived risk and risk variability', *Journal of the Academy of Marketing Science*, **18** (1), 51–65.

Nguyen, N. and G. Leblanc (2002), 'Contact personnel, physical environment and the perceived corporate image of intangible services by new clients', *International Journal of Service Industry Management*, **13** (3), 242–262.

Nickson, D., C. Warhurst and E. Dutton (2005), 'The importance of attitude and appearance in the service encounter in retail and hospitality', *Managing Service Quality*, **2**, 195–208.

Noone, B.M. and A.S. Mattila (2009), 'Consumer reaction to crowding for extended service encounters', *Managing Service Quality*, **19** (1), 31–41.

Noone, B.M., S.E. Kimes, A.S. Mattila and J. Wirtz (2009), 'Perceived service encounter pace and customer satisfaction', *Journal of Service Management*, **20** (4), 380–403.

Normann, Richard (1991), *Service Management: Strategy and Leadership in Service Businesses*, 2nd edn, Chichester, UK: John Wiley & Sons.

Oliver, R.L. (1980), 'A cognitive model of the antecedence and consequences of customer satisfaction decisions', *Journal of Marketing Research*, **17** (September), 460–469.

Oliver, Richard L. (1993), 'A conceptual model of service quality and service satisfaction: compatible goals, different concepts', in Teresa A. Swartz, David E. Bowen and Stephen W. Brown (eds), *Advances in Services Marketing and Management*, Vol. 2, Greenwich, CT: JAI, pp. 65–85.

Oliver, R.L. (2000), 'Customer satisfaction with service', in Teresa A. Swartz and Dawn Iacobucci (eds), *Handbook of Services Marketing and Management*, Thousand Oaks, CA: Sage, pp. 247–254.

Oliver, Richard L. (2009), *Satisfaction: A Behavioral Perspective on the Consumer*, London: M.E. Sharpe.

Oliver, Richard L. (2010), *Satisfaction: A Behavioural Perspective on the Consumer* (2nd edn), New York, US: M.E. Sharpe Inc.

Oliver, R.L. and W.S. DeSarbo (1988), 'Response determinants in satisfaction judgments', *Journal of Consumer Research*, **14** (4), 495–507.

Oliver, R.L., R.T. Rust and S. Varki (1997), 'Customer delight: foundations, findings, and managerial insight', *Journal of Retailing*, **73** (3), 311–336.

Otto, J.E. and J.R.B. Ritchie (1995), 'Exploring the quality of the service experience: a theoretical and empirical analysis', *Advances in Services Marketing and Management*, **4**, 37–61.

Palmer, A. (2010), 'Customer experience management: a critical review of an emerging data', *Journal of Services Marketing*, **24** (3), 196–208.

Palmer, A. and M. O'Neill (2003), 'The effects of perceptual processes on the measurement of service quality', *Journal of Services Marketing*, **17** (3), 254–274.

Parasuraman, A., V.A. Zeithaml and A. Malhorta (2005), 'E-S-QUAL: a multiple-item scale for assessing electronic service quality', *Journal of Service Research*, **7** (3), 213–233.

Park, W.C., D.J. MacInnis and J. Priester (2006), 'Brand attachment: construct, consequences, and causes', *Foundation and Trends in Marketing*, **1** (3), 191–230.

Park, W.C., D.J. MacInnis, J. Priester, A.B. Eisingerich and D. Iacobucci (2010), 'Brand attachment and brand attitude strength: conceptual and empirical differentiation of two critical brand equity drivers', *Journal of Marketing*, **74** (4), 1–17.

Paswan, A.K., N. Spears, R. Hasty and G. Ganesh (2004), 'Search quality in the financial services industry: a contingency perspective', *Journal of Services Marketing*, **18** (5), 324–338.

Patterson, Paul G. and Tony Ward (2000), 'Relationship marketing and management', in Teresa A. Swartz and Dawn Iacobucci (eds), *Handbook of Services Marketing and Management*, Thousand Oaks, CA: Sage, pp. 317–342.

Paulssen, M. and S. Fournier (2007), 'Attachment security and the strength of commercial relationships: a longitudinal study', Discussion Paper No. 50, Department of Business and Economics, Humboldt University Berlin.

Payne, C.R., B.L. Parry, S.C. Huff, S.D. Otto and H.K. Hunt (2002), 'Consumer complimenting behaviour: exploration and elaboration', *Journal of Consumer Satisfaction, Dissatisfaction and Complaining Behaviour*, **15**, 128–147.

Pine, B.J. II and J.H. Gilmore (1998), 'Welcome to the experience economy', *Harvard Business Review*, **76** (4), 97–106.

Prahalad, C.K. and V. Ramaswamy (2004), 'Co-creation experiences: the next practice in value creation', *Journal of Interactive Marketing*, **18** (3), 5–14.

Pujari, D. (2004), 'Self-service with a smile? Self-service technology (STT) encounters among Canadian business-to-business', *International Journal of Service Industry Management*, **15** (2), 200–219.

Pullman, M.E. and M.A. Gross (2004), 'Ability of experience design elements to elicit emotions and loyalty behaviours', *Decision Sciences*, **35** (1), 551–578.

Ratchford, B.T., M.S. Lee and D. Talukdar (2003), 'The impact of the Internet on information search for automobiles', *Journal of Marketing Research*, **40** (2), 193–209.

Reimer, A. and R. Kuehn (2005), 'The impact of servicescape on quality perceptions', *European Journal of Marketing*, **39** (7/8), 785–808.

Reynolds, K.E. and M.J. Arnold (2000), 'Customer loyalty to the salesperson and the store: examining relationship customers in an upscale retail context', *Journal of Personal Selling and Sales Management*, **20** (2), 89–98.

Reynolds, K.L. and L.C. Harris (2006), 'Deviant customer behavior: an exploration of frontline employee tactics', *Journal of Marketing Theory and Practice*, **14** (2), 95–111.

Reynolds, K.L. and L.C. Harris (2009), 'Dysfunctional customer behaviour severity: an empirical examination', *Journal of Retailing*, **85**, 321–335.

Rickwood, C. and L. White (2009), 'Pre-purchase decision-making for a complex service: retirement planning', *Journal of Services Marketing*, **23** (3), 145–153.

Riley, F.D.O. and L. de Chernatony (2000), 'The service brand as relationships builder', *British Journal of Management*, **11**, 137–150.

Robertson, N. and R.N. Shaw (2009), 'Predicting the likelihood of voiced complaints in the self-service technology context', *Journal of Service Research*, **12** (1), 100–116.

Roos, I., A. Gustafsson and B. Edvardsson (2005), 'The role of customer clubs in recent telecom relationships', *International Journal of Service Industry Management*, **16** (5), 436–454.

Rosenbaum, M.S. and C. Massiah (2007), 'When customers receive support from other customers: exploring the influence of intercustomer social support on customer voluntary performance', *Journal of Service Research*, **9** (3), 257–270.

Rosenbaum, M.S., J. Ward, B.A. Walker and A.L. Ostrom (2007), 'A cup of coffee with a dash of love', *Journal of Service Research*, **10** (1), 43–59.

Rust, R. (1998), 'What is the domain of service research?', *Journal of Service Research*, **1** (2), 107.

Rust, R.T. and K.N. Lemon (2001), 'E-service and the consumer', *International Journal of Electronic Commerce*, **5** (3), 85.

Rust, R.T. and R.L. Oliver (2000), 'Should we delight the customer?', *Journal of the Academy of Marketing Science*, **28** (1), 86–94.

Rust, R.T. and A.J. Zahorik (1993), 'Customer satisfaction, customer retention and market share', *Journal of Retailing*, **69** (Summer), 193–215.

Ruyter, K. and M. Wetzels (2000), 'Customer equity considerations in service recovery: a cross-industry perspective', *International Journal of Service Industry Management*, **11** (1), 91–108.

Santos, J. (2003), 'E-service quality: a model of virtual service quality dimensions', *Managing Service Quality*, **13** (3), 233–246.

Santos, J. and J. Boote (2003), 'A theoretical exploration and model of consumer expectations, post-purchase affective states and affective behaviour', *Journal of Consumer Behaviour*, **3** (2), 142–156.

Schultz, Don E., Beth E. Barnes, Heidi F. Schultz and Marian Azzaro (2009), *Building Customer-Brand Relationships*, Armonk, NY: M.E. Sharpe, Inc.

Sharma, P., B. Sivakumaran and R. Marshall (2009), 'Exploring impulse buying in services vs. products – towards a common conceptual framework', *Advances in Consumer Research – Asia-Pacific Conference Proceedings*, **8**, 195–196.

Shostack, G.L. (1977), 'Breaking free from product marketing', *Journal of Marketing*, **41** (2), 73–80.

Singh, J. (1991), 'Understanding the structure of consumer satisfaction evaluation of service delivery', *Journal of the Academy of Marketing Science*, **19** (3), 223–224.

Singh, J. and D. Sirdeshmukh (2000), 'Agency and trust mechanisms in consumer satisfaction and loyalty judgments', *Journal of the Academy of Marketing Science*, **28** (1), 150–167.

Sirdeshmukh, D., J. Singh and B. Sabol (2002), 'Consumer trust, value, and loyalty in relational exchanges', *Journal of Marketing*, **66** (1), 15–37.

Smith, A.K. and R.N. Bolton (1998), 'An experimental investigation of customer reactions to service failure and recovery encounters: paradox or peril?', *Journal of Service Research*, **1** (1), 65–81.

Solomon, M.R., C. Suprenant, J.A. Czepiel and E.G. Gutman (1985), 'A role theory perspective on dyadic interactions: the service encounter', *Journal of Marketing*, **49** (Winter), 99–111.

Spangenberg, E.R., A.E. Crowley and P.W. Henderson (1996), 'Improving the store environment: do olfactory cues affect evaluations and behaviours?', *Journal of Marketing*, **60**, 67–80.

Spreng, R.A., S.B. MacKenzie and R.W. Olshavsky (1996), 'A reexamination of the determinants of consumer satisfaction', *Journal of Marketing*, **60** (July), 15–32.

Stauss, Bernd and Wolfgang Seidel (2004), *Complaint Management: The Heart of CRM*, Mason, Ohio: Thomson Business and Professional Publishing.

Steuer, J. (1992), 'Defining virtual reality: dimensions determining telepresence', *Journal of Communication*, **42** (4), 73–93.

Straczynski, S. (2009), 'Social network branding fails to sway female purchasing', http://www.salesandmarketing.com/article/social-network-branding-fails-sway-female-purchasing, accessed 24 November 2010.

Swan, J.E., M.R. Bowers and L.D. Richardson (1999), 'Customer trust in the salesperson: an integrative review and meta-analysis of the empirical literature', *Journal of Business Research*, **44** (2), 93–107.

Tax, S.S., S.W. Brown and M. Chandrashekaran (1998), 'Customer evaluations of service complaint experiences: implications for relationship marketing', *Journal of Marketing*, **62** (April), 60–76.

Thomson, M. and A. Johnson (2006), 'Marketplace and personal space: investigating the differential effects of attachment style across relationship contexts', *Psychology & Marketing*, **23** (8), 711–726.

Thomson, M., D.J. MacInnis and C.W. Park (2005), 'The ties that bind: measuring the strength of consumers' emotional attachments to brands', *Journal of Consumer Psychology*, **15** (1), 77–91.

Tombs, A. and J.R. McColl-Kennedy (2003), 'Social-servicescape conceptual model', *Marketing Theory*, **3** (4), 37–65.

Tsiotsou, R.H. (2011), 'Developing brand loyalty in services: a hierarchy of effects model', *Proceedings of the 2011 Summer Marketing Educators' Conference*, American Marketing Association, San Francisco, USA, 5–7 August 2011, pp. 391–398.

Tsiotsou, R.H. and R.E. Goldsmith (2011), 'Exploring the formation process of brand love: a comparison between goods and services', *2011 Academy of Marketing Science World Marketing Congress* (19–23 July), Reims, France, pp. 557–561.

Tsiotsou, R.H. and C. Veloutsou (2011), 'The role of brand personality on brand relationships and tribal behaviour: an integrative model', 40th European Marketing Academy Conference (24–27 May 2011), Slovenia, pp. 1–8.

Uncles, M.D., G.R. Dowling and K. Hammond (2003), 'Customer loyalty and customer loyalty programs', *Journal of Consumer Marketing*, **20** (4), 294–316.

Uzicker, D. (1999), 'The psychology of being put on hold: an explanatory study of service quality', *Psychology and Marketing*, **16** (4), 327–350.

Vargo, S.L. (2009), 'Toward a transcending conceptualization of relationship: a service-dominant logic perspective', *Journal of Business and Industrial Marketing*, **24** (5/6), 373–379.

Vargo, S.L. and R.F. Lusch (2004), 'Evolving to a new dominant logic for marketing', *Journal of Marketing*, **68** (January), 1–17.

Vargo, S.L. and R.F. Lusch (2008), 'Service-dominant logic: continuing the evolution', *Journal of the Academy of Marketing Science*, **36** (Spring), 1–10.

Vargo, S.L. and R.F. Lusch (2011), 'It's all B2B and beyond . . .: toward a systems perspective of the market', *Industrial Marketing Management*, **40** (2), 181–187.

Varki, S. and M. Colgate (2001), 'The role of price perceptions in an integrated model of behavioural intentions', *Journal of Service Research*, **3** (3), 232–240.

Vazquez-Carrasco, R. and G.R. Foxall (2006), 'Influence of personality traits on satisfaction, perception of relational benefits, and loyalty in a personal service context', *Journal of Retailing and Consumer Services*, **13**, 205–219.

Veloutsou, C. and R. Tsiotsou (2011), 'Examining the link between brand relationships and tribal behaviour: a structural model', *Proceedings of the 2011 7th Thought Leaders International Conference in Brand Management*, Lugano, Switzerland, 10–12 March 2011, pp. 1–7.

Veloutsou, C. and R.H. Tsiotsou (2011b), 'Examining the link between brand relationships and tribal behaviour: a structural model', Proceedings of the 2011 7th Thought Leaders International Conference in Brand Management, Lugano, Switzerland, 10–12 March 2011, pp. 1–7.

Verhoef, P.C., G. Antonides and A.N. de Hoog (2004), 'Service encounters as a sequence of events: the importance of peak experience', *Journal of Service Research*, **7** (1), 53–64.

Vinitzky, G. and D. Mazursky (2011), 'The effects of cognitive thinking style and ambient scent on online consumer approach behaviour, experience approach behaviour and search motivation', *Psychology & Marketing*, **28** (5), 496–519.

Vlachos, P.A., A. Theotokis, K. Pramatari and A. Vrechopoulos (2010), 'Consumer-retailer emotional attachment: some antecedents and the moderating role of attachment anxiety', *European Journal of Marketing*, **44** (9/10), 1478–1499.

Voorhees, C.M. and M.K. Brady (2005), 'A service perspective on the drivers of complaint intentions', *Journal of Service Research*, **8** (2), 192–204.

Voss, C.A., A.V. Roth, E.D. Rosenzweig, K. Blackmon and R.B. Chase (2004), 'A tale of two countries' conservatism, service quality and feedback on customer satisfaction', *Journal of Service Research*, **6** (3), 212–230.

Wallendorf, M. and E.J. Arnould (1988), '"My favorite things": a cross-cultural inquiry into object attachment', *Journal of Consumer Research*, **14** (March), 531–547.

Wangenheim, F. (2005), 'Postswitching negative word of mouth', *Journal of Service Research*, **8** (1), 67–78.

Wangenheim, F. and T. Bayon (2007), 'Behavioural consequences of overbooking service capacity', *Journal of Marketing*, **71** (October), 36–47.

Ward, J.C. and A.L. Ostrom (2006), 'Complaining to the masses: the role of protest framing in customer-created complaint web sites', *Journal of Consumer Research*, **33** (2), 220–230.

Weijters, B., D. Rangarajan, T. Falk and N. Schillewaert (2007), 'Determinants and outcomes of customers' use of self-service technology in a retail setting', *Journal of Service Research*, **10** (1), 3–21.

Weiner, B. (2000), 'Attributional thoughts about consumer behaviour', *Journal of Consumer Research*, University of Chicogo Press, **27** (3), 382–387.

Westbrook, R.A. (1987), 'Product/consumption-based affective responses and postpurchase processes', *Journal of Marketing Research*, **24** (3), 258–270.

Whiting, A. and N. Donthu (2006), 'Managing voice-to-voice encounters: reducing the agony of being put on hold', *Journal of Service Research*, **8** (3), 234–244.

Wilson, Alan, V.A. Zeithaml, Mary-Jo Bitner and Dwayne Gremler (2008), *Service Marketing – Integrating Customer Focus Across the Firm*, Berkshire: McGraw-Hill.

Wirtz, J. and J.E.G. Bateson (1999), 'Consumer satisfaction with services: integrating the environmental perspective in services marketing into the traditional disconfirmation paradigm', *Journal of Business Research*, **44** (1), 55–66.

Wirtz, J. and P. Chew (2002), 'The effects of incentives, deal proneness, satisfaction and tie strength on word-of-mouth behaviour', *International Journal of Service Industry Management*, **13** (2), 141–162.

Wirtz, J., L. Heracleous and N. Pangarkar (2008), 'Managing human resources for service excellence and cost effectiveness at Singapore Airlines', *Managing Service Quality*, **18** (1), 4–19.

Wirtz, J. and S.E. Kimes (2007), 'The moderating effects of familiarity on the perceived fairness of revenue management pricing', *Journal of Service Research*, **9** (3), 229–240.

Wirtz, J. and D. Kum (2004), 'Consumer cheating on service guarantees', *Journal of the Academy of Marketing Science*, **32** (2), 159–175.

Wirtz, J. and M.O. Lwin (2009), 'Regulatory focus theory, trust and privacy concern', *Journal of Service Research*, **12** (2), 190–207.

Wirtz, J. and A.S. Mattila (2001), 'Exploring the role of alternative perceived performance measures and needs-congruency in the consumer satisfaction process', *Journal of Consumer Psychology*, **11** (3), 181–192.

Wirtz, J. and J.R. McColl-Kennedy (2010), 'Opportunistic customer claiming during service recovery', *Journal of the Academy of Marketing Science*, **38** (5), 654–675.

Wirtz, J., A.S. Mattila and R.L.P. Tan (2000), 'The moderating role of target-arousal state on the impact of affect on satisfaction – an examination in the context of service experiences', *Journal of Retailing*, **76** (3), 347–365.

Wirtz, J., A.S. Mattila and M.O. Lwin (2007a), 'How effective are loyalty reward programs in driving share of wallet?', *Journal of Service Research*, **9** (4), 327–334.

Wirtz, J., A.S. Mattila and R.L.P. Tan (2007b), 'The role of desired arousal in influencing consumers' satisfaction evaluations and in-store behaviours', *International Journal of Service Industry Management*, **18** (2), 6–24.

Wirtz, J., P. Chew and C. Lovelock (2012), *Essentials of Services Marketing*, 2nd edn, Singapore: Prentice Hall.

Wolak, R., S. Kalafatis and P. Harris (1998), 'An investigation into four characteristics of services', *Journal of Empirical Generalisations in Marketing Science*, **3** (2), 22–41.

Wright, A.A. and J.G. Lynch Jr. (1995), 'Communication effects of advertising versus direct experience when both search and experience attributes are present', *Journal of Consumer Research*, **21** (4), 708–718.

Xiao, P., C. Tang and J. Wirtz (2011), 'Optimizing referral reward programs under impression management consideration', *European Journal of Operational Research*, **215**, 730–739.

Xue, M. and P.T. Harker (2002), 'Customer efficiency: concept and its impact on e-business management', *Journal of Service Research*, **4** (4), 253–267.

Yang, Z. and R.T. Peterson (2004), 'Customer perceived value, satisfaction, and loyalty: the role of switching costs', *Psychology & Marketing*, **21** (10), 799–822.

Yen, H.R. (2005), 'An attribute-based model of quality satisfaction for Internet self service technology', *Service Industries Journal*, **25** (5), 641–659.

Yi, Y. and S. La (2004), 'What influences the relationship between customer satisfaction and repurchase intentions?', *Psychology & Marketing*, **21** (5), 351–373.

Yim, C.K., D.K. Tse and K.W. Chan (2008), 'Strengthening customer loyalty through intimacy and passion: roles of customer-firm affection and customer-staff relations in services', *Journal of Marketing Research*, **45** (6), 741–756.

Zeithaml, Valerie A. (1981), 'How consumer evaluation processes differ between goods and services', in James A. Donnelly and William R. George (eds), *Marketing of Services*, Chicago: American Marketing Association, pp. 186–190.

Zeithaml, V.A. (1988), 'Consumer perceptions of price, quality and value: a means-end model and synthesis of evidence', *Journal of Marketing*, **52** (3), 2–22.

Zeithaml, Valerie A. and Mary Jo Bitner (eds) (2003), *Services Marketing: Integrating Customer Focus across the Firm*, New York, NY: McGraw-Hill.

Zeithaml, V.A., L.L. Berry and A. Parasuraman (1996), 'The behavioural consequences of service quality', *Journal of Marketing*, **60** (2), 31–46.

Zhang, J., S.E. Beatty and D. Mothersbaugh (2010), 'A CIT investigation of other customers' influence in services', *Journal of Services Marketing*, **24** (5), 389–399.

7. Researching the unselfish consumer
Ken Peattie

7.1 INTRODUCTION: REAL WORLD CONSUMER BEHAVIOUR

The marketing of the late twentieth and early twenty-first centuries has been notable for the growing attention paid to consumption behaviours and practices that are, to some extent, motivated by social, ethical and environmental concerns. Consumers increasingly express an interest in socio-environmental issues, and an expectation that trusted brands and companies should respond to them. Policy makers have sought to harness growing consumer interest to promote market-based solutions to difficult socio-environmental challenges, in preference to employing the less popular policy levers of taxation and regulation (Hobson, 2004). Marketers have perceived opportunities to generate differentiation and competitive advantage by demonstrating the ethical credentials of their products and companies. No less a figure in the marketing and strategy academy than Michael Porter argued that proactive and innovative environmental strategies were likely to be beneficial to companies through reduced costs and increased opportunities, partly because customers would respond positively (Porter and van der Linde, 1995). More broadly, in recent years, the social, ethical and environmental dimensions of consumer behaviour have become an increasing focus of research activity amongst marketing scholars and market research practitioners (Harrison et al., 2005). A wide range of studies have sought to understand what type of consumers respond to which socio-environmental issues, and to explore the nature of that response in terms of its extent, motivations, consistency and predictability.

The difficulty in researching this agenda for the marketing academy, and consumer behaviourists in particular, is that it exists beyond their normal comfort zone. The natural habitat for the marketing academic is a territory close to the confluence of the streams of knowledge derived from economics and psychology. Each of these is essentially a selfish discipline. When economics is not being called "dismal" it is often labelled the "Selfish Science" for giving us Homo economicus (or oeconomicus), the individual dedicated to the rational pursuit of personal gain (Hirschman, 1982). Psychology balances this by illuminating all those irrational individual tendencies that explain why there is more to marketing than finding the optimal point on the value curve, but psychology is also a somewhat literally "self obsessed" discipline. Over the years marketing alchemists have blended the elements of economics and psychology in a quest to explain and better manage the central relationship between a company and its customers. This relationship however has conventionally been portrayed as a rather introspective, exclusive and selfish affair, with other stakeholders deemed important only to the extent that they might influence the company–customer relationship.

Until relatively recently the process of satisfying consumer wants and needs was widely accepted as essentially amoral within both the conventional marketing management mainstream and the wider culture within consumer societies. If a customer desired a product, could afford it, and a company could legally supply it, there was little appetite for debating the rights and wrongs of the process of consumption, or the production systems that exist to meet consumer needs. Where production and consumption systems produced negative social and environmental consequences, these have tended to be addressed practically, politically or economically rather than ethically. The ultimate consumer good, the car, provides a simple illustration of this. Production and use of private cars is annually responsible for 1.2 million deaths and 50 million injuries from accidents; hundreds of thousands of deaths related to air pollution; 17% of energy-related greenhouse gas emissions; the use of half the world's rubber and a quarter of its steel resources; and for contributing to problems such as obesity and the erosion of social capital within communities (Woodcock and Aldred, 2008). This has led to many technologies aimed at reducing the harm that cars do, and policies to encourage people to choose alternative means of transport. It has not led to any serious mainstream debate about the ethics of the societal and environmental costs attached to satisfying consumer demand for car travel. The consumer is assumed to have a right to drive irrespective of the social and environmental costs. Conventionally, such socio-environmental costs were dealt with either through regulation that forced companies to address them and pass the costs onto customers, or by treating them as externalities that are not factored into the prices consumers pay and are left for policy makers to address (theoretically by spending the taxes that they have levied on producers and consumers).

In practice many environmental and social consequences of consumption and production systems are becoming increasingly severe, and the resulting costs are neither being factored into market transactions nor adequately addressed by governments. This has led to increasing concern across society, in the media and amongst consumers, leaving the argument that marketing is amoral increasingly untenable. Other stakeholders and other issues clearly matter, ethically as well as strategically. As they become significant to consumers, so we can identify elements of consumption behaviours that are at least partly unselfish in going beyond simply addressing the consumer's own needs. Since the turn of the millennium such behaviours have become the focus of an increasing volume of research, leading to research monographs (e.g. Jackson, 2005a), edited collections (e.g. Harrison et al., 2005), journal special issues and conference themes and streams. This chapter seeks to explore this expanding field of research and considers how the wider world is impinging on the relationship between companies and consumers and how concerns about the socio-environmental consequences of consumption are leading to new notions of the consumer and their responsibilities.

7.2   THE EVOLVING NOTION OF THE "UNSELFISH" CONSUMER

Unselfish consumption is not new, and elements of it can be traced back over decades, centuries and even millennia. Ethically motivated consumption has been a focus of social science research since at least the early 1960s, and in relation to consumer behaviour since at least the early 1970s (Anderson and Cunningham, 1972). There is however a school of marketing thought which argues that apparently socially or environmentally motivated consumption behaviours are still essentially selfish because consumers indulge in them to generate moral gratification or some other form of self-interested payoff through better health, improved taste or the prestige that conspicuously socially-responsible consumption may generate (Miller, 2001). This type of hyper-rationalist position has been criticised for effectively commodifying every aspect of human interaction (Agnew, 2003), and it also appears slightly strange for two reasons. Firstly it denies the existence of altruism, which seems an unnecessarily dismal view to take of humanity. Witnessing the outpouring of generosity that occurred in response to *LiveAid*, it seems extraordinary to explain it on the basis that each of the millions of donors could find no more personally pleasurable or rewarding thing to do with the money involved. Research evidence, historical anecdote and day-to-day experiences of the small courtesies that still exist within society clearly demonstrate altruism in people (and indeed there is evidence of it in some other species). It therefore seems reasonable to assume that altruism can be found within consumption behaviours, and it seems odd to insist on assuming or arguing otherwise.

Secondly, it represents a curious form of neo-puritanism in which the altruistic elements of consumption behaviour become somehow disqualified if one takes any pleasure from, or satisfaction in, acting unselfishly. This is despite the fact that the maxim of taking pleasure from unselfishness is embedded within the world's major systems of religious belief and philosophy. Overall it seems more reasonable to argue that no consumption behaviours are entirely selfless and unrewarding, but this is a very different proposition to viewing all aspects of consumer behaviour as entirely selfish.

What might represent "good" consumption, that at least partly reflects unselfish ethical motives, and is not simply focused on the satisfaction of the wants and needs of the purchaser (and those who a product or service is purchased for), is not a straightforward question to address. Partly this is because it involves people's motivations, and motives are notoriously difficult to research. People are often not entirely honest about their motives to researchers, their friends or even to themselves, and disentangling motives and attaching them to particular actions is fraught with difficulties. Partly it reflects two "disconnects" that can emerge, between an individual's motives and intentions and their eventual actions; and between the motivations for, and consequences of, any given consumption decision or behaviour.

Among those things that it is safe to say about consumption with some element of ethical motivation, is that notions of ethical or unselfish consumption behaviour have evolved over time. It is also safe to state that throughout this evolution a number of different conceptions of such consumption have emerged, each with a different basis and outlook. A roughly chronological exploration of these different, but sometimes overlapping, conceptions would be as follows:

7.2.1 The Pious Consumer

Consumption behaviours that are not simply dictated by one's desires and discretionary spending power have existed for thousands of years. Most major religions proscribe particular behaviours, such as the consumption of alcohol, pork, shellfish, or of meat on a Friday. Whether such behaviours are inspired by ethics or indoctrination is something that individuals will perceive according to their views on organised religion, but the "pious consumer" has undoubtedly been around for millennia. In increasingly secular Western European consumer economies pious consumption may seem like an anachronism in the twenty-first century. However, in much of Asia and Africa, some American communities and throughout countries where Islam is the principal religion, it is both prevalent and conspicuous, as a book title like *Proper Islamic Consumption* (Fischer, 2008) or the emergence of specific Islamic banking products demonstrates.

Although religious principles may only influence certain forms of consumption, pious consumption is worth dwelling on momentarily because of two peculiarities. Firstly it is unlike other forms of ethical consumption that are inspired by their perceived external social and/or environmental consequences. Eating a prawn will neither particularly damage the environment nor harm other people (although in pre-refrigeration society it may have represented a relatively high risk food choice). Religious observance in consumption is inspired by a desire to adhere to a principle or, one could argue, to avoid the personal consequences that would accrue from any lapse (such as distress caused by guilt or the disapproval of others). The second is that religious observance in consumption is typically so deeply ingrained in the devout that it over-rides consumer decision making processes as we generally understand them. For a devout believer consuming a proscribed food might be unthinkable, even if it became a matter of life and death. Pious consumption therefore represents one form of ethically motivated consumption, but it is a rather atypical one that sits uncomfortably with other notions of consumer ethics and responsibility.

7.2.2   The Patriotic Consumer

Consumption reflecting patriotic sentiments is both centuries old and a modern phenomenon, and marketing activity that encourages and exploits it is often visible at times of national crisis, such as wars or natural disasters. Since the American Civil War the purchase of war bonds has represented a patriotic consumption choice, with the patriotic appeal compensating for the below-market-rate yields on offer. Appeals to patronise national producers were commonplace between the two World Wars as policy makers struggled to prevent the expansion of their trade deficits. The British Empire Marketing Board of the 1920s and 1930s for example sought to promote trade amongst Commonwealth countries, and similar organisations with a national basis were established in countries like Austria and Switzerland. Nationally based organisations to promote the consumption of domestic products from foodstuffs to tourism destinations are still a feature within many countries and still frequently appeal explicitly or implicitly to consumers' sense of patriotism.

Curiously patriotic appeals can focus on both consumption reduction and expansion. Consumption reduction tends to focus on reducing resource use during times of national stress, for example conserving water during a drought, or power when there are supply problems. Patriotic pleas to Japanese consumers to conserve energy and water in the wake of the tragic March 2011 tsunami is one recent example. Expanding consumption as a form of patriotic duty has also been promoted in a bid to reflate a struggling economy in several countries including Japan and the USA (Princen, 1999). During late 2008 a London shop display featuring the iconic image of Lord Kitchener's recruiting poster with the legend "Shop dammit shop – its your patriotic duty" became the focus of considerable online and media attention, particularly from the environmentally concerned.

At one level patriotic appeals to discriminate against foreign imports represents a form of collective selfishness because it aims to protect the prosperity of the society the individual belongs to. Patriotic marketing appeals also risk becoming unethical once they begin to imply that a particular form of consumption is, of itself, a patriotic act (Stearns et al., 2003). More recently there was an upsurge in marketing activity intended to capitalise on the upsurge in American patriotic sentiment that arose in the wake of the 9/11 attacks. The extent to which patriotism represents an ethical basis for consumption and marketing is debatable, but patriotic appeals from commercial marketers or policy makers are clearly asking individuals to think beyond their personal needs.

7.2.3 The Frugal Consumer

Frugality is an explicit core virtue in Roman, Jewish and Muslim tradition, is strongly implied in the Hindu values of restraint and moderation, is still a core (if eroding) social value and virtue in Japanese culture, and was an item on Benjamin Franklin's checklist for "Moral Perfection". It has typically been promoted during times of crisis and resource shortage, particularly during wars or post-war eras of austerity (often involving patriotic appeals). Although frugality in design has periodically been promoted as a modern aesthetic virtue through the minimalist movement, as a social value frugality can appear somewhat old-fashioned in the context of contemporary consumer culture. However given increasing levels of personal debt, concerns about diminishing natural resources and climate change, and major issues surrounding the disposal of waste, frugality appears more relevant than ever (Bove et al., 2009).

Despite its newfound relevance, frugality as an aspect of consumer behaviour has been largely overlooked by researchers (Lastovicka et al., 1999). Within marketing scholarship frugal consumption was integral to Fisk's (1974) notion of the "responsible consumer". Fisk's vision of a consumer who constrained their own consumption for reasons of environmental responsibility was many years ahead of its time. It lay dormant until revived in the 1980s and 1990s amidst renewed concerns about environmental resources and the viability and stability of environmental systems. Since then it has most often been referenced in relation to "downshifting" and lifestyles of voluntary simplicity (Leonard-Barton, 1981; Jackson, 2005b; McDonald et al., 2006).

7.2.4   The Green Consumer

Fisk's "responsible consumer" was concerned about the limits of environmental resources following the early 1970s oil shocks and the impact of the Club of Rome's "Limits to Growth" report (Meadows et al., 1972). The growth in ecological concerns during the 1970s was also reflected in the emergence of the "ecologically concerned consumer" (Ahmed et al., 1974; Kardash, 1976) as the focus of a new concept of "ecological marketing" (Henion and Kinnear, 1976). Early ecological concern was focused relatively narrowly on resource conservation, energy use behaviours and pollution concerns linked to particular industries, including automobiles, oil, and chemicals. Consumer research therefore focused mostly on recycling and energy saving behaviours, as well as on consumer responses to advertising and labelling information (Kilbourne and Beckmann, 1998).

During the 1980s, environmental concern became increasingly widespread in response to high-profile incidents, such as the *Exxon Valdez* oil spill and Chernobyl nuclear disaster, and to mounting scientific evidence and media coverage concerning environmental degradation. Environmental concern became increasingly mainstream and visible as a societal value, a public policy issue and an aspect of commercial marketing strategies as part of a "green" agenda that engulfed a far wider range of industries and companies. It was also reflected in the growth of "green consumption" in which purchase and non-purchase decisions were reportedly influenced by socio-environmental criteria, and often informed by the emergence of numerous green consumer guides. New brands, products and technologies emerged to exploit market niches comprising green consumers, who gradually became a focus for research attention amongst marketing academics (for a review of the evolution of distinctly "green" forms of consumer behaviour, see Peattie, 2010).

7.2.5   The Socially Conscious/Ethical Consumer

Research in marketing began to focus on the "socially conscious consumer" in the early to mid 1970s (Anderson and Cunningham, 1972; Webster, 1975; Brooker, 1976), although the term "ethical consumer" has become more prevalent over time. Ethical consumption is most commonly associated with behaviours influenced by concerns for other people impacted by our production and consumption systems. Ethical consumption is rooted in boycotts organised in support of social causes going back at least as far as the anti-slavery movement of the early nineteenth century. Over time the range of socio-environmental causes to which ethical consumption is linked has broadened to include concerns about child labour, forced or sweatshop labour, discrimination, political corruption and excessive market power, to name a few.

Although boycotts remain commonplace, during the late twentieth century the emphasis in ethical consumption shifted from boycotts to more positive purchasing, particularly through the development of the Fair Trade movement. Fair Trade began with social solidarity marketing campaigns organised by NGOs and churches in the 1940s and 1950s, and formalised into a movement with the establishment of Oxfam's Fair Trade operation in the mid 1960s. The core principle is "Trade not Aid", a belief that the development challenges of poorer countries are best addressed, not by charitable donations, but by paying a fair living wage for the commodity crops and goods that they produce. Fair Trade began with the marketing of products with limited intrinsic value (as in the case of some handicrafts) or questionable product quality that demanded some sacrifice on consumers' part. More recently Fair Trade marketing has become increasingly sophisticated with improved product quality and strong branding, to the point that fairly traded coffee has become strongly mainstreamed (Golding and Peattie, 2005). Fair Trade was once the province of alternative niche brands, but by 2010 Cafédirect represented the third largest UK coffee brand, and global brand Starbucks represented the worlds largest purchaser of Fair Trade coffee.

7.2.6 The Responsible Consumer

Fisk's (1974) vision of consumers as "responsible" was significantly ahead of its time in an era of marketing thought based on a doctrine of consumer rights and sovereignty. As interest in the social and environmental impacts and responsibilities of companies has grown, so interest in the responsibilities of consumers has remerged. That a consumer may choose whether or not to patronise a company on account of the socio-environmental implications of that company's behaviour is well established within consumer research. Less well developed and explored is the principle that there are ethical dimensions to the behaviour of the consumers themselves. When ethical consumer behaviour is examined it is usually in relation to criminal, or at least ethically questionable behaviour, such as shoplifting, illegal downloads of digital content or owning up to being undercharged (Harrison et al., 2005). The majority of that research applies Vitell and

Hunt's (1990) scale of the ethics of consumer behaviour. It is a curious paradox that in the company–consumer market relationship the company is widely acknowledged to have corporate social responsibilities (i.e. responsibilities for its behaviour that go beyond regulatory compliance), whilst the consumer is frequently assumed to have rights but no responsibilities (beyond respecting the law). A notion of consumer social responsibility as a corollary to CSR is a relatively new and under-researched concept (Brinkmann and Peattie, 2008). There are however studies emerging in which consumers do expressly recognise a share of the responsibility for both causing and tackling key socio-environmental challenges such as climate change (Pepper et al., 2009; Barr et al., 2010; Wells et al., 2011).

7.2.7   The Citizen Consumer

As expressions of unselfish and ethically motivated consumer behaviour, both green and ethical consumerism have largely been researched from the perspective of the behaviour of the individual consumer. However, the ultimate social or environmental significance of those behaviours generally depends upon the consumption behaviours of others. On its own one act of unselfish consumption is no more than a gesture. Particular forms of ethical consumption have frequently emerged from a campaign or collective response to a social or environmental issue. This has led to an emphasis on the ability of the consumer to wield a positive collective influence and to the concept of political consumption or consumer citizenship. These concepts both seek to integrate the inward-looking and personally orientated perspective of the consumer, with the outward-looking, publicly orientated perspective of the concerned citizen, which have traditionally been viewed as separate (Korthals, 2001).

Gabriel and Lang (1995) define a consumer citizen as "a responsible consumer, a socially-aware consumer, a consumer who thinks ahead and tempers his or her desires by social awareness, a consumer whose actions must be morally defensible and who must occasionally be prepared to sacrifice . . .". However, this definition does not necessarily capture any difference from an ethical or green consumer. The difference perhaps lies in the notion of a motivation linked to social solidarity rather than simply principle-based individualism. The citizen consumer will not simply reject products they view as unethical, they will actively join together to boycott them in an effort to drive them from the market. As Andersen and Tobiasen (2004) argue, it is the intention to influence and promote social change, coupled with a belief in the collective power of individual consumption choices, that differentiates political from simple ethical consumption.

Solidaric behaviour (to revive a sadly neglected term) can take other forms that go beyond reflecting ethical principles. Local purchasing can, in part, be an expression of local loyalty, akin to patriotic purchasing. A tourist visiting a particular destination may go out of their way to spend money to support the local economy or protect an element of its cultural heritage. A music fan may buy music that they can access legally for free online in order to deliberately reward and encourage an artist in an act of solidarity. A consumer may choose to patronise a social enterprise with a work integration mission to bring those at the margins of society into productive employment. Such actions involve the consumer consciously seeking to benefit others through the social and economic benefits associated with their patronage, rather than simply seeking to accrue benefits and value for themselves.

7.2.8   The Mindful Consumer

Sheth et al. (2011) seek to provide an integrating framework for the conventional and unselfish, social and environmental dimensions of consumption that includes both consumption behaviours and the mindset behind them, through their vision of "mindful consumption". This involves having a mindset that values (and therefore cares for) the self, the community and nature, and these values are then expressed by tempering consumption behaviours which are repetitive, acquisitive and aspirational. Such mindful consumption is premised on consciousness and caring in thought and behaviour about the consequences and implications of one's consumption. The authors frame mindfulness of action rather narrowly as the temperance of over-consumption, since in practice caring for oneself, the community or the environment can have a variety of other expressions. It is however a rather elegant term compared to describing consumers that are ethically, socially or environmentally concerned. The fact that the notion of the mindful consumer was presented (within a special issue on sustainable marketing) in the *Journal of the Academy of Marketing Science*, a bastion of conventional marketing scholarship, is in itself noteworthy. It suggests that the unselfish consumer had completed a journey that began at the very fringes of the marketing discipline to become at last recognised at its very core.

7.3   INTEGRATING ETHICS AND ENVIRONMENT

Researching and understanding unselfish consumption behaviour creates a range of challenges for researchers. The problem of accurately diagnosing motivations is one; the variety of labels and different types of unselfish motivation that abound is another; and a third is the complex relationship between socially motivated (often referred to as "ethical"), and environmentally motivated (often referred to as "green") consumption.

A common assumption within the marketing literature is that the environmentally concerned and socially conscious consumer will be one and the same, since both express ethical concerns through consumption behaviours. Although there is evidence that social and environmental concerns are correlated, confounding examples clearly exist, such as the misanthropic animal lover, or those people who object to public spending on environmental protection because it could be used to build hospitals or relieve poverty. Roberts (1995) conducted a cluster analysis contrasting socially responsible and environmentally conscious consumer behaviours, resulting in four statistically significant segments. Three of these balanced their levels of social and environmental responsiveness relatively evenly, but a small segment of "Greens" (accounting for 6% of the adult population), combined a high degree of environmentally conscious consumption behaviour with a low level of socially responsible consumption behaviour.

The reality is that the relationship between environmental protection and social welfare is not straightforward, and attempts to categorise issues as either social or environmental lead to falsely over-simplified dichotomies and choices. Fair Trade coffee provides a simple example. It is perceived as an archetypal socially motivated ethical purchase, yet Fair Trade certification standards include provisions relating to the protection of environmental biodiversity in cultivation (Golding and Peattie, 2005). Similarly, most people would consider climate change to be an inherently environmental issue, but as the analysis of the eminent economist Sir Nicholas Stern (2006) highlighted, climate change will have profound economic and social consequences, and will impact the already poor and vulnerable worst of all.

The complex interrelationship between social welfare, economic prosperity and environmental quality became widely acknowledged within business and policy circles following the publication of the Brundtland Report *Our Common Future* (WCED, 1987). This brought into mainstream debate "Sustainable Development", encapsulated as development that "meets the needs of the present without compromising the ability of future generations to meet their own needs". It is based on the principles of equity and fairness, addressing global social needs (and particularly the needs of the global poor rather than the wants of the already prosperous), inter-generational futurity and treating the world holistically as a global environmental system. These principles took marketing practice and research into previously unexplored territories involving the needs of future generations of consumers and stakeholders; the social and environmental implications of production and consumption (which have traditionally been ignored by treating them as "externalities"); and the basic needs of the poor majority of the world's citizens instead of the richer minority within consumer societies (Peattie, 2001a). These issues had conventionally been the concern of researchers operating in the field of macromarketing, but as the pursuit of sustainability became adopted by an increasing number of companies as a core element of their strategy and part of the basis on which they appealed to consumers, sustainability became relevant to the wider marketing academy including consumer behaviourists.

Sustainability has proved a controversial concept, subject to fierce debate about its meaning (or lack it), definition, measurement and operationalisation (Gladwin et al., 1995). If you ask an ecologist, a botanist, an economist, a sociologist, an ethicist and a systems modeller to define "sustainability" you will get a variety of answers. If you ask a geologist or a physicist they will tell you there is no such thing because nothing lasts forever. Gladwin et al. (2005) argue that the failure to develop a simple and widely agreed notion of sustainability is not surprising since it is a relatively new idea, and that it is like other broadly based but important concepts such as health, freedom or democracy in being open to varying and contested interpretations and difficult to encapsulate in a "soundbite" definition.

One helpful way to understand the different types of initiatives which have been put forward as contributing to sustainable development comes from Hopwood et al. (2005). They map sustainable development initiatives (which could include organisations, policies, products or research paradigms) against two axes. The first represents the extent to which something is more or less progressive in contributing to greater social equity and justice. The second represents the extent to which something promotes the protection of environmental quality. This simple model is helpful because it accommodates initiatives with a very different mix of social and environmental orientation, and it can accommodate both initiatives that are essentially defensive in seeking to maintain the status quo (sometimes referred to as "soft" sustainability), and those which proactively seek to radically transform our production and consumption systems to become substantially more sustainable ("hard sustainability").

What sustainability (the end state which sustainable development aims to reach) brings to the debate is a unifying concept of quality of life that encompasses economic prosperity, social welfare and environmental protection. It can also be supported as an ethical position, or through rational objective analysis of the social and environmental costs that accrue from unsustainable consumption and production systems. It allows us to envisage the most important aspects of socially, ethically or environmentally motivated unselfish consumer behaviour as some form of "pro-sustainability behaviour" (PSB). The pursuit of sustainability as both a public policy goal and a commercial strategy, will depend heavily on the ability and willingness of people to consume more mindfully and less selfishly, and to adopt a range of PSBs.

7.4   DECOUPLING INTENTIONS AND IMPACTS

Marketing tends to consider the various forms of unselfish consumption according to their underlying motivations. Therefore "pro-environmental" behaviours are considered as those motivated by environmental concern, rather than those that necessarily benefit the environment. This creates the potential for perverse outcomes linked to behaviours adopted for good environmental or social motivations. For example Speirs and Tucker (2001) argue that the action of some consumers in driving to recycling "bring sites" expends energy that outweighs the energy and material savings benefits of the recycling behaviour. Similarly, although local food is assumed to be more sustainable than food with a high number of embedded "food miles", in practice the environmental impact comparisons can be complex and dependent on factors including production methods, soil types, and energy inputs, as well as distance travelled to market (Edwards-Jones et al., 2008).

Conversely, a behaviour without environmental or ethical motivations can still represent a more sustainable option through lower socio-environmental impacts. Frugality for example could be motivated by religious principle, concern for the environment or a personal preference for hoarding wealth over spending it. One of the most pro-sustainability behaviours that could be embraced by consumers is the adoption of a vegetarian diet. This is because of the comparatively large amounts of embedded CO_2 emissions in meat and its poor performance in terms of the ratio of energy and water needed to produce a given calorific value (Carlsson-Kanyama and González, 2009). Adopting a vegetarian diet might reflect climate change concerns, but it could equally well be motivated by religious conviction, concern for animal welfare or concerns about personal health or economic savings. Whatever the intention, it will have benefits linked to the environment and to climate change in particular (de Boer et al., 2006).

The potential asymmetries and disconnection between the motivations for, and environmental impacts of, green consumption behaviours is considerable (Whitmarsh, 2009), but the research literature rarely recognises this. This was highlighted by Barr et al. (2010) who found that relatively affluent middle class consumers who expressed strong environmental values and concern about climate change were also the group accumulating the most air miles and were strongly wedded to the idea of foreign travel as an essential part of their lifestyle.

Conventional approaches to consumer research tend to focus on specific consumption behaviours linked to a particular type of product. From a sustainability perspective such research is not particularly meaningful. Instead it is the overall lifestyle and the collective impacts of all the consumption activities of a household that determines the overall sustainability of its occupants. A growth in the consumption of organic foods, greater uptake of green energy tariffs or increased sales of Fair Trade products are typically taken as evidence of more sustainable consumption. However, if these behaviours are undertaken by affluent middle-class consumers with a lifestyle based around heavy car use, frequent international trips for business or pleasure and a household full of energy-using devices, they will be making less of a contribution to a more sustainable economy than a consumer with no interest in social or environmental interests but insufficient disposable income to do much real damage.

The importance of differentiating between impacts and intentions when discussing sustainable consumption behaviour becomes particularly clear in relation to so-called "rebound effects". Sustainable consumption is frequently promoted by highlighting the economic savings that can accrue from behaviours that save energy and other resources. The overall sustainability benefits of such behaviours however depend strongly on what the money saved through energy efficiency is spent on (Herring, 1999). If the consumer uses the energy savings to reward themselves for their frugality and eco-awareness with a cheap flight overseas, the overall environmental impact of the apparently PSB may well be negative.

Moving the discussion of sustainable consumption beyond individual purchase decisions to consider the overall socio-environmental impacts of consumer lifestyles shifts it into the sphere of policy making and the interests of governments at local and national levels of influencing consumer behaviour towards sustainability. On the whole both consumption policy, and consumer research, have tended to focus on the goal of consuming "differently" in terms of choices between technologies, products, and brands and the adoption of particular household management practices, rather than the goal of consuming less (Mont and Pleyps, 2008). This reflects the perceived incompatibility of consumption reduction and established public policy priorities of maintaining economic growth and a culture that prioritises consumer sovereignty, and the uninhibited acquisition of material possessions (Cohen, 2005). Therefore much of the debate and research into sustainable consumption concerns relatively uncontroversial behaviours such as energy saving, waste reduction, organic food or discrimination in favour of green brands. Although these are all worthy, they are unlikely to either generate significant progress towards a more sustainable society, or to impact the affluence and lifestyles of the populace (Connolly and Prothero, 2003). Critics of green consumerism argue that such superficial changes may both fail to generate real progress towards sustainability, whilst also creating an illusion of progress for consumers, businesses and government that works to perpetuate overconsumption (Princen et al., 2002).

The more one examines mindfulness and PSB amongst consumers, the more potentially complicated it becomes to define, examine and research. The traditional view of consumption behaviour as expressing rational preferences in pursuit of self-satisfaction is seductively simple by comparison. It is little wonder that some have argued that even apparently unselfish behaviour amongst consumers may be rooted in selfish motives concerned with how we feel about ourselves or are perceived by others (Brooker, 1976; Miller, 2001).

There is also an argument that PSB can reflect a different type of rationality, since consumers who understand the social and economic threats posed by phenomena such as climate change and the resulting degradation of ecosystem services, may respond with highly rational enlightened self-interest in seeking to mitigate them. Ultimately the unselfishness of a consumer's behaviour is impossible to diagnose without an ability to peer directly into their heart. Those who are sceptical about unselfish consumer behaviour will remain unconvinced by research findings derived by asking consumers about their behaviour and the motivations behind it. Ultimately, although it is interesting to ponder the motivations for unselfish behaviour, from a socio-environmental perspective it is what consumers actually do, and the resulting collective impacts, that really matters.

7.5   FORMS OF PSB

The majority of consumer behaviour research is dedicated to a single type of behaviour: purchasing. What motivates purchases, what influences them, how, when and where they are made, and what can be done to encourage us to repeat them, are the dominant research questions of the discipline. However, this represents the marketer's perspective on consumer behaviour rather than that of the consumer or the interested policy maker. For marketers the purchase is naturally the focus because it is the moment of ultimate success or failure, when the money changes hands, and the ownership of, and therefore responsibility for, the product passes from producer to consumer. From the consumer's perspective, the consumption behaviour story linked to that product may be only just beginning. In the case of durable purchases such as homes, cars, music, furniture or jewellery that story may unfold over decades. The marketing literature is dominated by studies linked to purchase as an activity, but consumption is a process involving many activities and behaviours. It also goes through a number of stages which may include pre-purchase information gathering and choice, and post-purchase product use, maintenance and disposal.

From a sustainability perspective, a significant portion of a product's socio-environmental impacts will effectively be "embedded" at the point of purchase, reflecting the socio-environmental costs of resource extraction and product manufacture down the supply chain. Other impacts will depend upon post-purchase use and disposal, particularly for some of the most environmentally significant purchases. The European Environmental Impact of Products (EIPRO) project rigorously analyzed the research base on the environmental impacts of 255 domestic consumer product types against a range of impacts including pollution, human and environmental health risks, and greenhouse gas emissions (Tukker, 2006). It concluded that around 70–80% of total impacts from domestic consumption relate to the food and drink we consume, the homes we live in (including their construction and maintenance, and domestic energy use); and transport (including commuting, leisure and holiday travel). The remaining impacts were dominated by domestic water use, domestic equipment (appliances, computers, and home entertainment), furniture, clothing, and shoes. PSB can therefore takes a number of forms, but most fall within six broad types (Gulyás, 2008):

Type 1:   Non-consumption
Consumer behaviour research naturally focuses on consumption behaviours and decisions, and on purchasing in particular. Not purchasing and consuming are therefore rarely recognised or addressed as a form of behaviour. The consumer who is mindful of environmental issues may try to find alternative ways of meeting their needs beyond conventional consumption. Deciding to eschew a particular product (like a car or foreign travel), repairing consumer durables to extend their lives, making a product themselves, delaying a purchase or borrowing a product from friends or family all represent PSB responses to a particular need. The situation is analogous to the concept of the informal economy in which people work without necessarily being employed. However, whilst there

is a relatively established body of research addressing the informal work economy, the informal consumption economy is comparative under-researched, particularly by marketing scholars.

Recently there has been an upsurge in research interest in "anti-consumption" behaviours, with special issues on the topic of the *Journal of Consumer Behaviour* (2010, Vol. 9/6), *Journal of Business Research* (2009, Vol. 62/2), *Consumption, Culture and Markets* (2010, Vol. 13/1) and *European Marketing Journal* (forthcoming). Although it may be going too far to construct an "Anti-Consumer" to add to our list of unselfish consumers, anti-consumption is an interesting research field because of its focus, not on brands or behaviours that consumers are adopting in response to their concerns, but on consumers actively rejecting over-consumption, the consumer lifestyle or aspects of it.

Type 2:   Value-based regular shopping
The most widely recognised and researched type of PSB involves consumers choosing particular products or brands on the basis of social or environmental criteria. This is something that many commercial marketers, social marketers in the public sector and campaigning organisations have all sought to promote. A significant influence on shopping behaviour is social and environmental labelling schemes that inform consumers about ingredients, production methods, trading practices or in-use resource efficiency. Such labels have been a key focus for research and they have been shown to help in addressing lack of environmental literacy among consumers, information asymmetry between producers and consumers, and the erosion of consumer trust that can result from media coverage of business "greenwashing" (Rex and Baumann, 2007). Labels can contain both visual cues and textual information, and consumers appear to respond to both (Tang et al., 2004). However, there is evidence suggesting that the presence of eco-labels can also stimulate additional consumption, which may negate any environmental benefits from greener choices (Bougherara et al., 2005).

Mindful pro-sustainability responses during regular shopping can go beyond choices between product types and brands. Shopping destination choice can reflect sustainability concerns, with consumers either seeking to shop locally to support the local economy and reduce the carbon emissions associated with shopping behaviours, or patronising particular outlets on the basis of their socio-environmental performance. The reuse of shopping bags has become something of an iconic mindful shopping behaviour encouraged by both regulatory measures and levies and voluntary retailer strategies and charges to encourage consumers to use fewer disposable bags (Sharp et al., 2010).

Type 3: Boycotts
One of the most visible and well-researched expressions of value-based consumer behaviour and consumer citizenship is involvement in protests and boycotts (Kozinets and Handelman, 2004). Boycotts can be linked to social or environmental values and applied to specific products or companies, whole industries or the products of an entire country with a corrupt or repressive regime. Such consumer actions are frequently influenced by the media and campaigning organisations, and by using online social media and campaign or anti-brand websites as a focal point, these activities can be organised and internationalised at great speed (Krishnamurthy and Kucuk, 2009).

Type 4: Buycotts (positive boycotts)
An alternative form of consumer citizenship is through the positive response of a "buycott" (Friedman, 1996) in which consumers intentionally seek out and reward producers they view as particularly ethical. An internet age variation on the buycott is the "carrotmob" a movement that emerged out of San Fransisco, which uses a variation on the "flashmob" phenomenon to mobilise a group of consumers to collectively descend upon a business with good social and environmental credentials to patronise and thank them personally (the businesses at the receiving end of a carrotmob must be pleased with the ensuing publicity, but presented with an unexpected stock management problem).

Type 5: Responsible usage
How a product is consumed can strongly influence both the environmental impact and social responsibility of its usage. This is usually considered in relation to environmental impacts since how food is prepared, how and how far a car is driven, or what temperature a garment is washed at will all significantly influence their ultimate ecological footprint. There can also be a need for responsible usage behaviour in terms of the social impacts of consumption. How a car is driven will have implications for the safety and mental wellbeing of others as well as for the environment. How travellers behave when on holiday will significantly effect the socio-environmental costs that the residents of a tourist destination experience in return for the economic prosperity that tourism may bring. The post-purchase nature of usage behaviour means that it is a comparatively under-researched set of behaviours within marketing.

Type 6: Post-use placement or disposal
Although disposal is the final consumption behaviour linked to most tangible products, consumer behaviourists have shown far less interest in this end

of the consumption process than the purchase end (Albinsson and Perrera, 2009). The *Journal of Marketing* had been in circulation for 40 years before Jacoby et al. (1977) posed the question 'what about disposition?'. Product disposal in an era of growing material consumption and shrinking landfill resources presents a considerable challenge to policy makers. It also represents a significant field of research, even if most of it is published outside of marketing and consumer behaviour journals. The ultimate environmental impacts of tangible products will depend on behaviours linked to consumers' willingness to resell rather than discard used durables, often using online resources such as eBay (Denegri-Knott and Molesworth, 2008); recycle packaging materials (van Birgelen et al., 2008); and consume or compost rather than discard food leftovers (Cappellini, 2009).

These six types reflect everyday consumption behaviours that are commonplace within a consumer economy. They are not exhaustive and there are other forms of PSB behaviour that some consumers engage in, including the consumer activist practice of discarding excessive packaging within stores; "relationship purchasing" in which consumers seek to directly educate and persuade retailers to adopt more ethical practices (Harrison et al., 2005); or co-operative bulk purchasing of goods to reduce costs, packaging and ecological impacts (Bekin et al., 2007). It is also important to note that although the type of value-based regular shopping behaviours involving product or brand choices is where consumer behaviourists are going to be happiest researching, it is not necessarily where the most important behaviours are occurring. What we buy in stores will determine part of the socio-environmental impacts of our consumer lifestyles, but how we manage energy, water and waste within our households, how we maintain our homes, and how and where we travel for work, leisure or shopping will be more important than any individual purchase.

7.6   INFLUENCES ON PSB

Although we may think of PSB as being motivated by social, environmental or ethical concerns, there are a range of potential influences that will determine the forms of PSB (if any) that a consumer will engage in, including:

7.6.1   Economic Rationality

PSB goes beyond simple economic rationality as a driver of behaviour, but across the entire body of consumer research examining PSB, perceived costs and benefits remain one of the most frequently cited influences. Both governments and businesses may seek to provide economic incentives in the form of direct financial rewards or penalties for specific PSB, or subsidies to encourage the consumption of particular products or services. A levy on plastic bags in supermarkets, whether through government regulation as in Ireland, or voluntary action by retailers such as Marks and Spencer, is one simple example (Sharp et al., 2010). Economic incentives can influence end-of-life/use consumption behaviours as well, for example through government incentive schemes for scrapping old cars or boilers, or "pay-as-you-throw" waste charging schemes. However, the inconsistency that tends to be exhibited in responses to financial incentives suggests that models and theories that rely heavily on rational choice have limited explanatory power (Sorrell et al., 2000).

One significant area of consumer research into PSB that is highly orientated towards economic rationality concerns the extent to which consumers are willing to pay a premium for ethical or environmental products in principle and in practice (McGoldrick and Freestone, 2008). Such research is notable for the extent to which conventional assumptions about consumers, products and markets are embedded within research designs and communicated to consumers. Asking consumers whether they are willing to pay a premium for such products communicates to them that conventional product prices are "normal" and greener products are abnormally expensive, and therefore a luxury for which sacrifices must be made. The reality is that conventional products are unrealistically inexpensive because many of the socio-environmental costs relating to their production and consumption are not being met. In effect normal consumption is subsidized by the environment or the poverty of others, but these are not the terms on which research questions are framed for consumers.

7.6.2 Demographics

Between the early 1970s and mid 1990s, research into PSB was dominated by attempts to profile green or ethical consumers and develop actionable market segmentations using a variety of criteria (Kilbourne and Beckmann, 1998; Straughan and Roberts, 1999). Much of the early research focused on socio-demographic variables including sex, age, presence and number of children, educational level, and socio-economic class (Laroche et al., 2001; Casimir and Dutilh, 2003). The most consistent finding within this research was inconsistency, with the conclusions of one study simply being contradicted by another (Kilbourne and Beckman, 1998). Diamontopoulos et al. (2003) in reviewing this literature concluded that, although socio-demographics cannot be ignored, of themselves they are of only limited value when trying to understand PSB and profile consumers.

7.6.3   Knowledge

Linked to the view of consumers as rational actors, knowledge about environmental and social issues is frequently assumed to drive PSB, and both marketers and policy makers have used consumer education and information provision strategies in an attempt to promote it. Again, however, the research evidence is equivocal. Some researchers have found that both self-reported and objectively measured environmental knowledge correlates positively with PSB (e.g. Bartkus et al., 1999). Others have reported that providing more consumer information has little impact (Jackson, 2005a), or can even become counterproductive by leaving consumers feeling confused or overwhelmed (Moisander, 2007; Horne, 2009).

Such inconsistencies have yet to be fully explored or explained by research, but we can speculate about why the apparently obvious relationship between greater knowledge and "better" behaviour fails to work in practice. Partly it may reflect the relatively low levels of environmental literacy within the population, so that widespread knowledge about an issue in terms of awareness is not matched by any depth of understanding that allows consistent links to be forged between socio-environmental issues and one's lifestyle or consumption (Ellen, 1994). For consumers who do become genuinely knowledgeable, that expertise may alert them to the environmentally unsustainable nature of existing systems of consumption and production and the absolute shortcomings in sustainability terms of product offerings (Peattie, 2001b). For future research, important distinctions may need to be drawn between knowledge and understanding about environmental issues, about the environmental consequences of consumption behaviour, and about the relationship between them.

7.6.4   Emotions, Attitudes, Beliefs, Norms and Values

The failure of much early research emphasising objective factors related to knowledge and economic rationality to adequately explain PSB led to a greater interest in research looking at the influence of intuitive and emotional factors on behaviour (Carrus et al., 2008). Emotional responses (such as fear, anger, guilt, shame, or pride) are a potentially significant influence on behaviour (Han et al., 2007), but they remain little-researched beyond a few studies on responses to advertising appeals (for example, Obermiller, 1995).

More fully researched is the influence of attitudes, beliefs, and values in influencing PSB (Jackson, 2005a; Kilbourne and Beckmann, 1998). In several studies pro-environmental attitudes have, perhaps not surprisingly, been shown to be good predictors of PSB, including a willingness to pay premium prices for products such as organic food or green electricity tariffs (Laroche et al., 2001; Diamontopoulos et al., 2003; Krystallis and Chryssohoidis, 2005); or to engage in recycling of electronic waste (Nixon et al., 2009). Although we can conclude from the research literature that values are influential, it is also clear that the same values do not influence all types of PSB (Corraliza and Berenguer, 2000). Barr (2007) found that product reuse and waste-minimisation intentions and behaviours were strongly related to values concerning environmental protection and the importance of nature, but this was not the case for recycling, where practicalities and more normative social influences were more influential.

Another focus for research is social norms, exploring the extent to which consumers engage in particular types of behaviour that reflect social norms in terms of what people believe to be ethically proper behaviour (injunctive norms) and what we consider to be common practice or "normal" (descriptive norms). Both types of norm have been shown to have an influence on PSB (Zukin and McGuire, 2004; Jackson, 2005a), but most research has focused on descriptive norms and the extent to which particular behaviours are perceived as "normal" or "alternative". The positioning of sustainability orientated products, behaviours and lifestyles as "alternative" via commercial marketing strategies and media coverage may tend to contain PSB to a segment of the market who wish to be perceived as "alternative" whilst deterring uptake within the broader market. Barr (2007) found that whilst engaging in recycling behaviours was perceived as "normal" by consumers, consumption reduction strategies were perceived as "alternative" and adopted by a small minority of consumers.

7.6.5   Responsibility, Control, and Personal Effectiveness

Although Fisk's (1974) responsible consumer is an important departure point for the evolution of research on PSB, there has been remarkably little research into consumer attitudes, values and beliefs ascribing responsibilities for both causing and solving socio-environmental problems. This scarcity of research into consumers' sense of personal responsibility for environmental damage perhaps reflects the dominant business culture based on consumer sovereignty, which emphasises the consumer's right to engage in any (legal) form of consumer behaviour. How consumers ascribe responsibilities for environmental problems, whether they feel a sense of control over their consumption behaviours, and whether they believe they have the ability to make a significant contribution to solving them all have the potential to influence behaviour (Wells et al., 2011). Perceived consumer effectiveness (PCE), the extent to which consumers believe that any action they take can have a meaningful impact on a particular issue, has been shown to be a significant influence on consumer response and is one of the most frequently cited factors in the research literature (De Young, 2000; Barr, 2007; Gupta and Ogden, 2009).

7.6.6   Lifestyles and Habits

One of the shortcomings of research into PSB has been a tendency to develop models and theories that assume a high degree of consumer involvement and conscious decision making. An alternative perspective is that much of our environmental impact as consumers relates to those everyday activities, which are influenced more by habit than conscious thought, including household management, everyday grocery shopping, and travel between homes and workplaces (Shove, 2003; Carrus et al., 2008). This has led to a distinct research stream that seeks to understand consumption through sociological theories of practice (Warde, 2005), emphasising routine and habit, and the influence of shared understandings, social conventions, technical know-how and infrastructure, and competing values (Shove, 2003). Knussen et al. (2004) argue that household behaviours cannot easily be separated out into the deliberate and the habitual, since their research revealed relatively complex domestic routines that involved semi-automatic patterns of behaviour.

Another shortcoming has been to focus on individual behaviours, and particularly purchases, one at a time. From a sustainability perspective, individual purchases and other behaviours have little meaning: it is the collective impact of all a consumer's behaviours that is more significant (as the previously mentioned issue of "rebound effects" demonstrates). Addressing consumption behaviours as part of more sustainable lifestyles will be important in making progress towards a more sustainable society and economy, and will require research and practical interventions that seek to understand a range of consumption behaviours and how they interrelate. For example, the EcoTeam program addresses a suite of 38 household behaviours (Leiserowitz et al., 2010). Behaviour as an expression of lifestyle is an important avenue for research because it can help explain some of the inconsistencies and compromises embedded in consumers' behaviours when examined as a whole (Empacher and Götz, 2004).

Other research has sought to integrate lifestyle perspectives with theories of practice and habitual behaviours. Barr et al.'s (2005) analysis of household behaviours revealed three significant clusters: (a) purchase decisions (shopping, composting, and reuse), (b) habits (domestic water and energy use and conservation) and (c) recycling behaviours. These varied between several distinct lifestyle types as defined by socio-demographic characteristics and values (NB although from a consumer behaviour perspective it may seem odd to include composting as a type of "purchase decision", and this may represent a poor choice of label for that particular cluster, the reality is more likely that those three behaviours were all perceived by consumers as higher effort/involvement behaviours).

Another important aspect about a lifestyles and habits perspective is that it goes beyond the static snapshot view of a particular behavioural intention or behaviour (such as a purchase) at a point in time. The significance of PSBs such as consumption reduction, product boycotts, choice of greener alternatives, frugal household management, or engagement in recycling depends on whether or not those behaviours persist over time (Staats et al., 2004). Tucker and Speirs' (2003) study of household waste management behaviours found that the factors that influenced a decision to initially engage in home composting were different to those that then helped to later maintain that behaviour. They concluded that attitudes towards composting were shaped by the consumers' experience of composting. Many of the models of green consumption behaviours work on the principle that attitudes shape behaviour, but it is also important to acknowledge that experience of a behaviour can also shape underlying attitudes.

7.6.7   Identities and Personalities

A comparatively under-researched topic derived from psychology concerns the extent to which a consumer's sense of self-identity can influence the nature and extent of their PSB (Fekadu and Kraft, 2001). For example, whether or not you view yourself as a recycler strongly predicts whether or not you will recycle (Mannetti et al., 2004), and those seeing themselves as green consumers are more likely to purchase organic foods (Sparks and Shepherd, 1992). Broad consumer identification with a green or alternative lifestyle was found to be reflected in a range of PSBs (Connolly and Prothero, 2003). Particular personality types may also be more or less prone to engaging in PSB, with Fraj and Martinez (2006) finding that personality factors, such as extroversion, agreeableness, and conscientiousness, were positively related to PSB.

7.7   UNDERSTANDING PSB

Consumer behaviour research exploring PSB generally seeks to make connections between the different types of consumer behaviour and the various potential influences on any given type of behaviour. Tim Jackson's (2005a) research monograph *Motivating Sustainable Consumption* provides a comprehensive synthesis of the different research streams, theories, models and factors that help to explain and therefore potentially motivate more sustainable consumer lifestyles and behaviours. It is a recommended starting point for anyone seeking to understand PSB. However, there are several observations that can usefully be made here about the extent to which consumer behaviour research has helped us to understand PSB.

7.7.1   Modelling PSB

Consumer behaviour research is strongly orientated towards developing and testing behavioural models involving brand choice, retailer choice, repeat purchase behaviour, consumer information gathering, use of e-commerce websites and a host of other specific behaviours. PSB is no exception to this and there is a wide range of available papers that model consumers' selection of green brands, energy supply choices, willingness to purchase carbon offsets when travelling or household management behaviours. The challenge in modelling PSB is that sustainability considerations impose an additional layer of complexity onto already complex behaviours.

The range of different models that have been applied to, adapted for, or developed to explore, consumption are reviewed by Jackson (2005a) from a sustainability perspective. In general the variables emphasised by the different models applied to PSB are indicated by their names, and examples include the Value-Belief-Norm model (P. Stern et al., 1999); Attitude-Behaviour-Context (ABC) model (P. Stern, 2000); or the Motivation-Opportunity-Ability model (Gatersleben et al., 2002). The most popular modelling approach involves applied or adapting models based on the Theory of Planned Behaviour (Ajzen and Madden, 1986) which emphasises the importance of behavioural intention on eventual behaviour and the role of attitudes, norms and perceived behavioural control in shaping intention and behaviour. The attractions of this model lie in the fact that it is relatively simple, widely used (and therefore validated) within the consumer behaviour literature, and can easily be adapted by adding in social or environmental values and norms. It has however been subject to considerable criticism, particularly for failing to reflect the importance of context and the strongly habitual nature of many consumption behaviours (Davies et al., 2002).

Despite the popularity of model building and testing, such research has tended to produce results that are inconsistent at best and meaningless at worse. Such models tend to emphasise a very narrow selection of the potentially significant influences on a PSB, and also to treat highly heterogeneous PSBs as though they were alike. Jackson (2005a) points out the paradoxical situation that as models become comprehensive enough

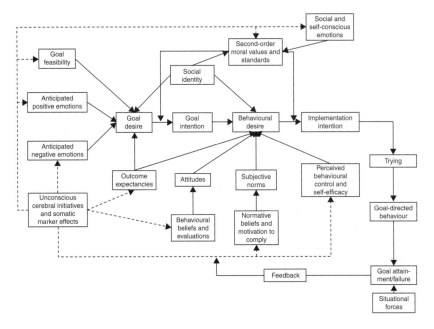

Source: Bagozzi et al., 2002.

Figure 7.1 Bagozzi's Comprehensive Model of Consumer Action

to be representative, so they become untestably complex. By contrast as models are simplified and abstracted enough to be testable, they soon become unrepresentative of complex realities. As Jackson notes, the most ambitious attempt to incorporate the full range of influences on any form of consumer behaviour is Bagozzi's Comprehensive Model of Consumer Action, reproduced as Figure 7.1 (Bagozzi et al., 2002).

This model has not been testable for even straightforward conventional consumption behaviours as a whole, although individual linkages within it have been modelled and tested. For PSBs the value of such a model does not lie in attempts to test it, but in helping us to understand the overall complexity of behaviour and why the results of any study based on quantitative modelling need to be treated cautiously.

There have been some successful attempts to develop and test models that combine insights from a variety of disciplines, such as by Barr (2007) who tested a model of post-use behaviours (including waste minimization, product reuse, and recycling) that integrates values, psychological factors, and situational factors. The results confirmed the complexity of reality, showing that pro-environmental values were significant in waste minimisation and reuse (but not recycling) behaviours, and that all the key behaviours were significantly influenced by a range of variables including:

- perception of the environmental problem,
- global environmental knowledge,
- active concern and sense of obligation,
- ascription of responsibility to act,
- outcome beliefs of behaviour,
- subjective norms,
- citizenship beliefs, and intrinsic motivation and perceived response efficacy,
- practical logistics of behaviour,
- available service provision,
- socio-demographics,
- behavioural experience,
- policy interventions/instruments and knowledge about them,
- waste knowledge, and
- knowing where/how to recycle.

7.7.2   Segmenting Green/Ethical Markets

The quest for a meaningful and consistent segmentation of markets in relation to socio-environmental issues has been a recurrent theme within marketing research for both scholars and practitioners. The emphasis has been on identifying the most ethically motivated consumers as a particular market niche in order to market to them (Kilbourne and Beckman, 1998; Shaw and Clarke, 1999). One of the earliest and best-known examples, the "Green Gauge Segmentation", produced by the Roper Organisation, acted as something of a template for future efforts by stratifying the population into layers of enthusiasm and involvement. This stretched from the active and committed "True Blue Greens", down to the disinterested and inactive "Apathetics". Straughan and Roberts (1999) reviewed many of the segmentations developed during the 1980s and 1990s and conclude broadly that socio-demographic factors, which dominated many early efforts, are less effective than psychographics as a basis for segmentation, but that PCE is also important.

The emphasis on segmentation-based research is interesting to reflect on for two reasons. Firstly it illustrates the difficulties caused by the disconnection between intentions and impacts when discussing PSB. Those occupying the segment with the strongest pro-environmental attitudes, and most likely to engage in specific PSBs such as purchasing Fair Trade goods, supporting local food, adopting a green energy tariff and actively recycling are also entirely likely to be those engaged in relatively damaging behaviours such as foreign air travel and substantial private car use (Barr et al., 2005). Secondly, segmentation studies tend to assume a degree of consistency whereby people will remain within a particular segment across a range of behaviours because it reflects their socio-demographic status, values or knowledge which all tend to be relatively static. The reality is that such consistency is generally missing in actual behaviour, and that it is perhaps more fruitful to focus on categorising types of purchase or other behaviour according to their sustainability instead of trying to categorise the consumer (Peattie, 2001b).

7.7.3   Behaviour catalysts and spillovers

One research stream looking to introduce some consistency into PSB concerns the notion of behavioural "spillover", in which involvement in one form of PSB acts as a catalyst to engage in others (Thøgersen and Ölander, 2002; Whitmarsh, 2009). Thøgersen and Ölander's (2002) research on Danish consumers showed that individuals were fairly consistent within similar categories of behaviour. There were significant correlations amongst the behaviours of buying organic food, recycling and using alternative transport. These connections were all accounted for by common motivational causes linked to general environmental values and concern. Such connections may come about because as a consumer engages in one form of PSB, they begin to construct an identity for themselves, which increases the propensity to engage in others. Alternatively involvement in one behaviour may lead to a greater awareness of environmental issues or social norms linked to other behaviours.

7.7.4   Tokenism

A contrary view is that there is a risk of negative spillovers (or perhaps more accurately behavioural containment) in which consumers trade one form of PSB off against another with engagement in one type of behaviour providing reluctant consumers with a reason not to adopt others (Chatzidakis et al., 2007). This can allow consumers to adopt behaviours with a relatively low set of transaction costs, such as buying Fair Trade coffee or recycling more, and use those as a reason not to engage with more challenging behaviours such as reducing energy consumption or private car use (Barr et al., 2010).

   One criticism of efforts to research, understand and promote more sustainable consumption behaviours by researchers, companies and policy makers is a tendency to focus on behaviours that are relatively insignificant in terms of their sustainability impacts. Any behavioural change is worthwhile if it generates positive socio-environmental benefits from an "every little helps" perspective. However, there is a danger that a focus on relatively easy behavioural changes that are essentially tokenistic will deflect attention and consumer motivation away from more significant changes. For example, not leaving mobile phone chargers on overnight is frequently promoted as an "environmental tip", but as Mackay (2008) points out, the environmental impacts of doing so are roughly equivalent to driving a car for one additional second. Similarly the plastic shopping bag has become an iconic product in the debate about marketing and sustainability and a focus for NGO campaigning, government bans and taxes and voluntary manufacturer levies (Sharp et al., 2010). This is often justified on the basis of the oil resources conserved by reducing plastic bag use, entirely overlooking the fact that such bags are mostly made from ethylene, a waste by-product of oil refining.

7.7.5   Attitude-behaviour Gap

One of the most remarked upon phenomena within the research literature on PSB is the so called "attitude-behaviour gap". This reflects the common finding that socio-environmental knowledge and strongly held values, attitudes, and intentions frequently fail to translate into purchases or other forms of PSB in practice (Pickett-Baker and Ozaki, 2008; Fraj and Martinez, 2006). This is frequently ascribed to studies over-reporting the strength of socio-environmental attitudes or intentions owing to a bias caused by interview respondents providing socially acceptable responses (Follows and Jobber, 2000). Although this undoubtedly explains part of the gap, there are other potential causes. In some cases the gap may reflect the limitations of consumers' ability to respond since habits, service infrastructure, disposable income, or lifestyles may act as a constraint; in others it may reflect purchase types in which old brand loyalties, uncertainties, or perceived trade-offs between different socio-environmental factors provide disincentives to PSB (Peattie, 2001b; Chatzidakis et al., 2007; Biel and Dahlstrand, 2005). There is also evidence that although consumers may state a preference for more ethical products, they will assume (rightly or wrongly) that improved social or environmental attributes will inevitably lead to compromises in primary performance (Luchs et al., 2010).

7.7.6   Scepticism and Consumer Resistance

An alternative explanation for the attitude-behaviour gap is that although consumers are interested in more sustainable purchasing and consumption, they may be sceptical about the offerings and motives of companies (Mohr et al., 1998). More sustainable goods and services are often priced at a premium. Sometimes this is unnecessary since resource efficiency and the removal of environmental costs and risks can reduce costs. In such cases the premium price may reflect a demand-based pricing strategy of a company seeking to serve the most socially or environmentally concerned consumers. In other cases premium pricing is necessary since it reflects the internalising of socio-environmental costs previously treated as externalities. However, the impact of increased prices can raise suspicions amongst consumers that manufacturers and retailers are using ethical marketing strategies unethically as a means of generating greater profits. There is an irony that companies are often interested in segmenting markets in order to identify and market to relatively green and/or ethical consumers, but these are the very consumers who are likely to be most resistant to being targeted by conventional marketing strategies.

7.7.7 Qualitative Methodologies

Quantitative research based on survey instruments and the building and testing of models is the dominant methodology within consumer behaviour, but it has a number of limitations when it comes to understanding PSB. As well as the risk of socially motivated over-reporting of behaviours, such research suffers from a tendency to measure behavioural intentions as a proxy for behaviour or to measure self-reported rather than actual behaviours (Follows and Jobber, 2000). Given that there tends to be a significant gap between expressed intentions and actual behaviour, and that respondents frequently over-estimate the extent to which they engage in PSB in practice, the explanatory power of such research has limitations. This has led to an increasing trend towards practical social experiments that seek to measure actual behaviour (particularly amongst environmental psychologists) and to more qualitative methodologies as a means to explore and understand PSB. The edited collection by Harrison, Newholm and Shaw (2005), for example, includes chapters on the use of case studies, focus groups and existential-phenomenological interviewing techniques as well as conventional modelling and quantitative survey based studies.

7.7.8 Sociological Perspectives

Unselfish and mindful consumer behaviour is also notable for the extent to which the research illuminating it originates from, or is at least informed by, sociology (and to a lesser extent anthropology). Consumption in general is a key way in which individuals relate to the society in which they live, and consumption can express our self-identity, values, social connections, worldview and those things we stand for or against (Schaefer and Crane, 2005; Gulyás, 2008). The sociology of consumption is a well-established research field, but it is particularly significant for understanding PSB for several reasons. Firstly, as already mentioned, social practices and habits linked to lifestyle are more significant to some aspects of PSB than conscious decision making processes linked to purchasing or other consumption behaviours. Secondly, the key goods and services from an environmental impacts and sustainability perspective come heavily laden with social and symbolic meaning. The private car and its use is one obvious example, but the form and management of our homes are also both socially and ecologically significant, as is our consumption and preparation of food. Finally, the barriers to promoting consumption reduction and other PSB may lie more in the social and symbolic role and value of key aspects of consumption than in relation to any real sense of personal fulfilment or wellbeing they generate. The annual foreign holiday as a reward for a year's hard work; over-consumption at Christmas to brighten the gloom of a European mid-winter; the "fashionisation" of products like furniture or electrical goods that were once seen as durables; the cultural equation of material consumption with wellbeing at an individual level (and between economic growth and progress at a collective level) – the full list of social and cultural challenges we need to overcome to successfully promote PSB would be considerable. Schaefer and Crane (2005) highlight that there has generally been a failure to integrate the understanding of PSB derived from conventional consumer behaviour research that has emphasised rational choice, information processing and hedonism with the sociological and anthropological research which emphasises practices, social roles, symbolism, identity and social relationships. Jackson's (2005a) review of sustainable consumption also highlights the importance of such integration and provides an in-depth review of the different research traditions into PSB and attempts to develop more integrative theories and models to understand it.

7.8   THE IMPORTANCE OF CONTEXT

Much consumer behaviour research into PSB has involved a search for consistency, by identifying either particular segments of the market that consistently exhibit consumption behaviours, or consistent patterns of behaviour that can be explained by particular models, consumer attributes or other factors. The most consistent finding across this field of research is inconsistency, with most consumers showing little regard for consistency across time, space, circumstance and type of purchase. Although we could put this down to capriciousness on the part of the consumer, or to flaws in the research conducted about them, it more probably reflects the fact that when it comes to consumer behaviour, context matters. Where we are, exactly what we are doing or purchasing, the reasons behind it and who else is involved, all appear to influence the extent to which we are willing to integrate social and environmental considerations into our behaviours.

The innocuous box marked "situational forces" in Bagozzi's Comprehensive Model of Consumer Action masks a powerful array of potential influences on aspects of consumer behaviour that reflect our circumstances rather than our nature, values or motivations as individuals. Whether or not we engage in home composting and whether or not we cycle will be influenced by the nature of our homes and the storage opportunities they provide. Travel choices will depend upon where we live, the infrastructure available and may be influenced by factors including weather, time of day and traffic conditions.

The context for consumption behaviours can vary in ways that significantly impact the likelihood of a consumer engaging in PSB. For example, purchasing behaviour may differ across types of purchase (McDonald et al., 2009). We may vary our behaviour according to whether it is products or services being purchased, necessities or luxuries, durables or consumables, inexpensive everyday items or an infrequent high value purchase. Behaviour may also vary according to the type of shopping trip. Megicks et al. (2008) found that consumers were more likely to purchase ethically during their "main" shopping trip of a week than during smaller local "top up" shops to buy specific items. One simple illustration of the importance of context is the finding that consumers typically do not maintain the PSB that they usually adopt in their domestic lifestyle when they are on holiday at another location (Dolnicar and Grün, 2009; Barr et al., 2010).

One particular context that represents an interesting arena for PSB is the online environment. Conventional wisdom is that online environments may provide opportunities for new forms of environmentally orientated and less materially intensive consumption, for example through the download of music instead of the purchase of a tangible CD. However in practice the comparative consumption impacts between a downloaded MP3 and store-bought CD would depend upon the number of listenings and the comparative energy efficiency of the equipment used (Weber et al., 2009). Online environments also provide new opportunities for consumers to gather and share relevant socio-environmental information linked to products and companies and to organise consumer boycotts or buycotts. It is also a sphere in which unselfish consumer behaviour is commonplace from uploading digital content for others to freely enjoy, or freely sharing expertise to solve posted problems (Belk, 2010). Online environments also provide opportunities for new forms of unethical behaviour, particularly in relation to the illegal downloading of music and films. Consumers who would not consider stealing a tangible product can find ways of persuading themselves that pirating digital content is acceptable. However, as Chatzidakis and Mitussis (2007) observe there is curiously little research considering the ethical implications of the growth in online consumption given the growth in research in interest in ethical consumption and online consumption separately.

7.9   IMPLICATIONS OF UNSELFISH CONSUMPTION

Consumer behaviour that is in some way partially unselfish and ethically motivated has a number of implications for the study of consumer behaviour and marketing because it challenges us to rethink some of these fields' standard assumptions and boundaries. Some of the implications are relatively obvious from the foregoing discussion, for example that unselfish consumption shifts the focus beyond purchasing to consider consumption as a process encompassing a range of stages, activities and behaviours that can be influenced by ethical criteria. Some of the other noteworthy implications of unselfish consumption are as follows.

7.9.1   Beyond Individualism

Consumer behaviour theories and models of choice are frequently criticised for an over-emphasis on the individual as the unit of choice and behaviour (Jackson, 2005a). Many of the most significant consumption behaviours from an environmental perspective (food consumption, private travel and household energy management) typically reflect the structure, nature and lifestyle of an entire family or household. However, family influences and negotiation processes are frequently overlooked in consumer research, particularly in relation to ethical consumption (Grønhøj and Olander, 2007).

An important aspect of unselfish consumption behaviour which is commonplace in practice, particularly in the context of families and households, is sharing. Belk (2010) explores sharing and the relative lack of consumer research concerning it, and concludes that, as with other forms of unselfish consumption, it suffers from neglect because it happens within the home rather than at the supermarket checkout and that it does not fit comfortably with the stereotype of the rational and selfish consumer.

Within families, communities and friendship groups, goods and services are frequently shared, sometimes for self-interested reasons of lowering unit prices, reciprocity or building social cohesion, but often sharing is simply part of the way people live or is about ensuring that everyone's needs are met.

Collective consumption behaviours have become a focus of research in relation to "alternative consumption communities" which people join with the explicit aim of adopting a lower-consumption lifestyle, usually through processes of voluntary simplicity (McDonald et al., 2006). Such communities are typically founded on shared environmental values or religious beliefs, and evolve a set of norms, which influence the consumption behaviours of members. PSB includes an emphasis on frugality, and responsible consumption through ethical choices, such as reduced levels of meat consumption. Other PSBs include communal bulk purchasing to reduce packaging and transport impacts, purchasing second-hand products, and extending product life spans through repairs (Bekin et al., 2007).

In some cases significantly changing consumption practices depends upon collective efforts. Some waste reducing strategies for post-use product disposition would be impossible for individual consumers to implement, and depend upon collective solutions (Bekin et al., 2007). Community schemes for the provision of more sustainable energy, food, and transport are emerging as part of the sustainable communities movement, yet the consumer behaviour implications of such collective efforts remain under-researched. Anecdotal evidence suggests that community-based approaches to promoting PSB, such as Global Action Plan's Action at Home initiative or the EcoTeam program are particularly effective (Burgess, 2003). A better understanding of group norms and consumption processes in community settings could help develop other effective community schemes for the future.

Opportunities for consumers to collaborate can extend well beyond the communities to which they belong through the use of social networking technology. This increasingly allows consumers to meet their needs through sharing, bartering, lending, trading, renting, donating or swapping. Such unconventional consumption behaviours were one focus of the book on collaborative consumption *What's Mine is Yours: The Rise of Collaborative Consumption* by Botsman and Rogers (2010). The best-known channels for such behaviours are global networks like Freecycle and eBay, but there are many emerging online channels for "swap trading" like Zwaggle, Swaptree, Swap.com and Zunafish. Collaborative consumption through social networking technology connects and empowers consumers to redistribute and recycle existing products and value in ways that circumvent conventional markets and commercial marketing. Such collaborative consumption may be only partly motivated by concerns about frugality and resource effectiveness, but it is both under-researched and growing in importance. In 2011 *Time Magazine* named collaborative consumption as one of the '10 Ideas That Will Change the World'.

7.9.2   Blurring the Boundaries of Consumption

Another distinctive feature of PSB is that it can blur the conventional boundaries between production and consumption issues and roles. For example, alternative consumption communities are typified by a desire to be more self-reliant by producing some of their own food and certain other products like clothes, as well as changing their more conventional shopping behaviours (McDonald et al., 2006). Home composting is on one level a household waste behaviour, but it also represents the production of a useful soil conditioner that can be consumed instead of peat-based products.

Extended producer responsibility regulations in markets such as cars, electronic goods or packaging can also require producers to reclaim end-of-life/use products to allow for remanufacture, recycling or responsible disposal. Such supply loops turn consumers into resuppliers of value to producers, and introduce a new sphere of consumer behaviours which remains largely under-researched. Lebel and Lorek (2008) propose that ultimately the design of sustainable consumption and production systems will require more co-operative value creation processes involving co-design effforts between producers and consumers. Crane (2000) suggests that such collaborations between consumers and producers may represent a lower risk approach to marketing to mindful consumers after the difficulties that many first generation green products encountered. Such a collaborative approach has been documented in certain markets, such as Heiskanen and Lovio (2010) in interactions between producers and users in the adoption of low-energy housing developments in Finland. They found that user involvement in the innovation process and good communication and knowledge sharing between the two can aid the process of innovation and the adoption of innovations.

7.10   CONCLUSIONS: LET'S DO THE PARADIGM SHIFT

Research aiming to understand unselfish consumption and PSB has grown over the last 40 years, but it still remains something of a "minority sport" within consumer behaviour and mainstream marketing research. The best available scientific evidence shows that the global economy is already engaged in unsustainable levels of over-consumption that are degrading ecosystem services and the prospects for future prosperity (Princen, 1999; Jackson, 2009). It therefore seems extraordinary that sustainability-based approaches to marketing and consumer behaviour still tend to get labelled as "alternative" and relegated to the disciplinary fringes. Although PSB has become an increasing focus of consumer research, this has concentrated on a relatively narrow range of behaviours and market sectors relating to organic and fairly traded products, green energy tariffs, ethical investments, low-energy lighting, reduced car use and domestic recycling.

The overall impression is that sustainability issues within consumer behaviour research are subject to "ghettoisation" (to use the original Venetian meaning of the word "ghetto" as an area kept separate for communal safety, relating to when the city's foundry was placed on a separate island away from the mass of inflammable wooden buildings, rather than its more modern racially linked connotations). Sustainability seems to be suitable for special editions of journals, particular conference streams or lectures within a course. It is viewed as a topic, an influence on marketing strategy or one potential source of competitive advantage for some players within certain markets to appeal to the most ethically concerned consumers. This misses the point of sustainability, which ultimately does not represent a topic in marketing (or in policy making, business strategy or education); rather, it represents an alternative approach to marketing and to our entire systems of production, consumption and governance. As Schaefer and Crane (2005) argue, if we over-emphasise a techno-rationalist approach and treat green and ethical issues as no more than a discriminating purchase factor alongside price, quality and convenience, the opportunity to develop a more valuable discourse about consumption and sustainability has been missed. Sustainability is not something that needs to be grappled with in order to accommodate it within the conventional consumer behaviour research paradigm. Instead, we need to reconfigure consumer behaviour practices and research to become compatible with sustainability.

This need for a paradigm shift is one that goes beyond the study of consumer behaviour to its practice, and to the broader social paradigm within which both take place. In both research and policy making, the focus on harnessing consumer choice to promote sustainable development, on reforming rather than reducing consumption, on individual consumptions and decisions instead of the overall impact of our lifestyle, and on consumption behaviours that are relatively trivial (either of themselves or in the context of overall impacts) such as plastic shopping bags or mobile phone charging are all symptomatic of a dominant social paradigm that is based around the acceptance, pursuit and promotion of over-consumption (Kilbourne et al., 2002; Connolly and Prothero, 2003).

Part of the problem for marketers in embracing sustainability as a paradigm shift may be that the treatment of social and environmental issues in marketing is less well developed compared to its parent disciplines of economics and psychology. Both ecological economics and environmental psychology are well-established sub-disciplines with their own dedicated journals, conferences and schemes of study. Macromarketing has evolved as a marketing sub-discipline, but its emphasis on the implications of marketing and consumption as a whole is not ideal for combining conventional consumer behaviour research with socio-environmental issues. Sustainability marketing has yet to emerge as a fully fledged sub-discipline of marketing, but recent developments in new courses and teaching texts suggest that, at the time of writing, it may be relatively imminent. The challenge for those who wish to promote more sustainable marketing and consumption is to take this emerging "proto-sub-discipline" and use it as the basis on which to build a new sustainability orientated mainstream (Belz and Peattie, 2009).

Consumer behaviour is well established as a sub-discipline of marketing, and conceiving it as such is useful in giving the field focus and manageable boundaries (Macinnis and Folkes, 2009). It may however make consumer behaviour myopic by over-emphasising those aspects of behaviour that marketers find most interesting. As this chapter has explored, although what consumers buy is economically significant, it is how consumers live that is often more important in determining the ultimate socio-environmental implications of their consumption. Therefore it is perhaps not surprising that much of the progress regarding unselfish, mindful and pro-sustainability consumption comes, not from conventional marketing or consumer behaviour researchers, but from sociologists, ecological economists, social geographers and social or environmental psychologists. It is notable how much of the research utilised for this chapter does not come from consumer behaviour journals or from consumer behaviourists (despite the author's efforts to focus on such sources). Macinnis and Folkes (2009) suggest that consumer behaviour has a tradition that is essentially multi-disciplinary rather than inter-disciplinary, and perhaps sustainability is the issue that will encourage the development of more inter-disciplinary research.

Improving our understanding of PSB by integrating the knowledge of other disciplines will depend upon shifting the emphasis of PSB research beyond consumption as purchasing, to consumption as a total process involving a range of relationships we have with businesses, public services and each other. This chimes with the broader shift in the research paradigm of marketing observed by Vargo and Lusch (2004), moving gradually away from a focus on tangible products and marketing as transactions to a focus on marketing as relationships based on intangible resources and the co-creation of value. A more sustainable approach to marketing and consumer behaviour will depend upon integrating this shift towards relationship marketing with the field of macromarketing, and both the green and ethical micromarketing traditions (Belz and Peattie, 2009).

Our understanding of consumer behaviour that is in some way unselfish (if not selfless), and inspired by ethical, social or environmental motives has grown rapidly over the last twenty years or so partly through an expanding volume of research, but also because of the evolving nature of the research being conducted. What began as a largely quantitative investigation informed by economics and psychology into what we actively do and do not buy for ethical reasons, has evolved into a multi-disciplinary and mixed-methods exploration of how we live, and the implications of our consumer lifestyles for other people and the future of the planet. It may not yet be a primary focus for the efforts of mainstream consumer behaviour researchers, but there is a compelling argument that no aspect of consumer behaviour is more important to understand and promote in the decades ahead.

REFERENCES

Agnew, Jean-Christophe (2003), 'The give-and-take of consumer culture', in S. Strasser (ed.), *Commodifying Everything*, London: Routledge, pp. 11–42.

Ahmed, S., T.C. Kinnear and J.R. Taylor (1974), 'Ecologically concerned consumers: who are they?', *Journal of Marketing*, **38** (2), 20–24.

Ajzen, I. and T. Madden (1986), 'Predictions of goal-directed behaviour: attitudes, intentions and perceived behavioral control', *Journal of Experimental Social Psychology*, **22** (5), 453–474.

Albinsson, P.A. and B.Y. Perera (2009), 'From trash to treasure and beyond: the meaning of voluntary disposition', *Journal of Consumer Behaviour*, **8** (6), pp. 340–353.

Andersen, J. Goul and Mette Tobiasen (2004), 'Who are these political consumers anyway? Survey evidence from Denmark', in Michele Micheletti, Andreas Follesdal and Dietlind Stolle (eds), *Politics, Products and Markets – Exploring Political Consumerism Past and Present*, New Jersey: Transaction Publishers, pp. 203–221.

Anderson, W.T. and W.H. Cunningham (1972), 'The socially conscious consumer', *Journal of Marketing*, **36** (3), 23–31.

Bagozzi, Richard P., Zeynep Gürnao-Canli and Joseph R. Priester (2002), *The Social Psychology of Consumer Behaviour*, Buckingham: Open University Press.

Barr, S. (2007), 'Factors influencing environmental attitudes and behaviors: a U.K. case study of household waste management', *Environment and Behaviour*, **39** (4), 435–473.

Barr, S., A.W. Gil and N. Ford (2005), 'The household energy gap: examining the divide between habitual and purchase-related conservation behaviours', *Energy Policy*, **33** (1), 1425–1444.

Barr, S.W., G. Shaw, T. Coles and J. Prillwitz (2010), '"A holiday is a holiday": practicing sustainability, home and away', *Journal of Transport Geography*, **18** (3), 474–481.

Bartkus, K.R., C.L. Hartman and R.D. Howell (1999), 'The measurement of consumer environmental knowledge: revisions and extensions', *Journal of Social Behavior & Personality*, **44** (1), 129–146.

Bekin, C., M. Carrigan and I. Szmigin (2007), 'Beyond recycling: "commons-friendly" waste reduction at new consumption communities', *Journal of Consumer Behavior*, **6** (5), 271–286.

Belk, R. (2010), 'Sharing', *Journal of Consumer Research*, **36** (5), 715–733.

Belz, Frank-Martin and Ken Peattie (2009), *Sustainability Marketing: A Global Perspective*, Chichester, UK: Wiley.

Biel, A. and U. Dahlstrand (2005), 'Values and habits: a dual process model', in S. Krarup and C.S. Russell (eds), *Environment, Information and Consumer Behavior*, Cheltenham, UK and Northampton, MA, USA: Edward Elgar, pp. 33–50.

Botsman, R. and R. Rogers (2010), *What's Mine is Yours: the Rise of Collaborative Consumption*, New York: Harper Collins.

Bougherara, D., G. Grolleau and L. Thiebaut (2005), 'Can labelling policies do more harm than good? An analysis applied to environmental labelling schemes', *European Journal of Law and Economics*, **19** (1), 5–16.

Bove, L.L., A. Nagpal and A.D.S. Dorsett (2009), 'Exploring the determinants of the frugal shopper', *Journal of Retailing and Consumer Services*, **16** (4), 291–297.

Brinkmann, J. and K. Peattie (2008), 'Consumer ethics research: reframing the debate about consumption for good', *Electronic Journal of Business Ethics and Organization Studies*, **13** (1).

Brooker, G. (1976), 'The self-actualizing socially conscious consumer', *Journal of Consumer Research*, **3** (2), 107–112.

Burgess, J. (2003), 'Sustainable consumption: is it really achievable?', *Consumer Policy Review*, **13** (3), 78–84.

Cappellini, B. (2009), 'The sacrifice of re-use: the travels of leftovers and family relations', *Journal of Consumer Behaviour*, **8** (6), 365–375.

Carlsson-Kanyama, A. and A.D. González (2009), 'Potential contributions of food consumption patterns to climate change', *American Journal of Clinical Nutrition*, **89** (Suppl.), 1704–1709.

Carrus, G., P. Passafaro and M. Bonnes (2008), 'Emotions, habits and rational choices in ecological behaviors: the case of recycling and use of public transportation', *Journal of Environmental Psychology*, **28** (1), 51–62.

Casimir, G. and C. Dutilh (2003), 'Sustainability: a gender studies perspective'. *International Journal of Consumer Studies*, **27** (4), 316–325.

Chatzidakis, A. and D. Mitussis (2007), 'Computer ethics and consumer ethics: the impact of the internet on consumers' ethical decision-making process', *Journal of Consumer Behavior*, **6** (5), 305–320.

Chatzidakis, A., S. Hibbert and A.P. Smith (2007), 'Why people don't take their concerns about Fair Trade to the supermarket: the role of neutralization', *Journal of Business Ethics*, **74** (1), 89–100.

Cohen, M.J. (2005), 'Sustainable consumption American style: nutrition education, active living and financial literacy', *International Journal of Sustainable Development and World Ecology*, **12** (4), 407–418.

Connolly, J. and A. Prothero (2003), 'Sustainable consumption: consumption, consumers and the commodity discourse', *Consumer Marketing Cultures*, **6** (4), 275–291.

Corraliza, J.A. and J. Berenguer (2000), 'Environmental values, beliefs and actions: a situational approach', *Environment and Behavior*, **32** (6), 832–848.

Crane, A. (2000), 'Facing the backlash: green marketing and strategic reorientation in the 1990s', *Journal of Strategic Marketing*, **8** (3), 227–296.

Davies, J., G.R. Foxall and J. Pallister (2002), 'Beyond the intention–behaviour mythology: an integrated model of recycling', *Marketing Theory*, **2** (1), 29–113.

de Boer, J., M. Helms and H. Aiking (2006), 'Protein consumption and sustainability: diet diversity in EU-15', *Ecological Economics*, **59** (3), 267–274.

De Young, R. (2000), 'Expanding and evaluating motives for environmentally responsible behavior', *Journal of Social Issues*, **56** (3), 509–526.

Denegri-Knott, J. and M. Molesworth (2008), 'The playfulness of eBay and the implications for business as a game-makes', *Journal of Macromarketing*, **28** (4), 369–380.

Diamantopoulos, A., B.B. Schlegelmilch, R.R. Sinkovics and G.M. Bohlen (2003), 'Can socio-demographics still play a role in profiling green consumers? A review of the evidence and an empirical investigation', *Journal of Business Research*, **56** (6), 465–480.

Dolnicar, S. and B. Grün (2009), 'Environmentally friendly behavior: can heterogeneity among individuals and contexts/environments be harvested for improved sustainable management?', *Environment and Behavior*, **41** (5), 693–714.

Edwards-Jones, G., L.M. Canals, N. Hounsome, M. Truninger and G. Koerber (2008), 'Testing the assertion that "local food is best": the challenges of an evidence-based approach', *Trends in Food Science and Technology*, **19**, 265–274.

Ellen, P.S. (1994), 'Do we know what we need to know? Objective and subjective knowledge effects on pro-ecological behaviours', *Journal of Business Research*, **30** (1), 43–52.

Empacher, Claudia and Konrad Götz (2004), 'Lifestyle approaches as a sustainable consumption policy – a German example', in Lucia A. Reisch and Inga Røpke (eds), *The Ecological Economics of Consumption*, Cheltenham, UK and Northampton, MA, USA: Elgar, pp. 190–206.

Fekadu, Z. and P. Kraft (2001), 'Self-identity in planned behavior perspective: past behavior and its moderating effects on self-identity-intention relations', *Social Behavior and Personality*, **29** (7), 671–686.

Fischer, Johan (2008), *Proper Islamic Consumption: Shopping Among the Malays in Modern Malaysia*, Nordic Institute of Asian Studies Monograph No. 113, Copenhagen.

Fisk, George (1974), *Marketing and the Ecological Crisis*, New York: Harper & Row.

Follows, S.B. and D. Jobber (2000), 'Environmentally responsible purchase behaviour: a test of a consumer model', *European Journal of Marketing*, **34** (5/6), 723–746.

Fraj, E. and E. Martinez (2006), 'Influence of personality on ecological consumer behavior', *Journal of Consumer Behavior*, **5** (3), 167–181.

Friedman, M. (1996), 'A positive approach to organized consumer action: the "boycott" as an alternative to the boycott', *Journal of Consumer Policy*, **19** (4), 439–451.

Gabriel, Yiannis and Tim Lang (1995), *The Unmanageable Consumer: Contemporary Consumption and Its Fragmentations*, London: Sage.

Gatersleben, B., L. Steg and C. Vlek (2002), 'Measurement and determinants of environmentally significant consumer behavior', *Environment and Behavior*, **34** (3), 335–362.

Gladwin, T.N., J.J. Kennelly and T.S. Krause (1995), 'Shifting paradigms for sustainable development: implications for management theory and research', *Academy of Management Review*, **20** (4), 874–907.

Golding, K. and K. Peattie (2005), 'In search of a golden blend: perspectives on the marketing of fair trade coffee', *Sustainable Development*, **13** (3), 154–165.

Grønhøj, A. and F. Olander (2007), 'A gender perspective on environmentally related family consumption', *Journal of Consumer Behavior*, **6** (4), 218–235.

Gulyás, E. (2008), 'Interpretations of ethical consumption', *Review of Sociology*, **14** (1), 25–44.

Gupta, S. and D.T. Ogden (2009), 'To buy or not to buy? A social dilemma perspective on green buying', *Journal of Consumer Marketing*, **26** (6), 376–91.

Han, S., J.S. Lerner and D. Keltner (2007), 'Feelings and consumer decision making: the appraisal-tendency framework', *Journal of Consumer Psychology*, **17** (3), 156–168.

Harrison, Robert, Terry Newholm and Deirdre Shaw (2005), *The Ethical Consumer*, Sage: London.

Heiskanen, E. and R. Lovio (2010), 'User-producer interaction in housing energy innovations: energy innovation as a communication challenge', *Journal of Industrial Ecology*, **14** (1), 91–102.

Henion, Karl E. and Thomas C. Kinnear (1976), *Ecological Marketing*, Chicago, IL: American Marketing Association.

Herring, H. (1999), 'Does energy efficiency save energy? The debate and its consequences', *Applied Energy*, **63** (3), 209–226.

Hirschman, A.O. (1982), 'Rival interpretations of market society: civilizing, destructive or feeble?', *Journal of Economic Literature*, **20** (4), 1463–1484.

Hobson, K. (2004), 'Sustainable consumption in the United Kingdom: the "responsible" consumer and government at "arm's length"', *Journal of Environment & Development*, **13** (2), 121–139.

Hopwood, B., M. Mellor and G. O'Brien (2005), 'Sustainable development: mapping different approaches', *Sustainable Development*, **13** (1), 38–52.

Horne, R.E. (2009), 'Limits to labels: the role of eco-labels in the assessment of product sustainability and routes to sustainable consumption', *International Journal of Consumer Studies*, **33** (2), 175–182.

Jackson, Tim (2005a), *Motivating Sustainable Consumption: A Review of Evidence on Consumer Behaviour and Behavioural Change*, London: Policy Studies Institute.

Jackson, T. (2005b), 'Live better by consuming less? Is there a "double dividend" in sustainable consumption?', *Journal of Industrial Ecology*, **9** (1/2), 19–36.

Jackson, Tim (2009), *Prosperity without Growth*, London: Sustainable Development Commission.

Jacoby, J., C.K. Berning and T.F. Dietvorst (1977), 'What about disposition?', *Journal of Marketing*, **41** (2), 22–28.

Kardash, W.J. (1976), 'Corporate responsibility and the quality of life: developing the ecologically concerned consumer', in Karl E. Henion and Thomas C. Kinnear (eds), *Ecological Marketing*, Chicago: American Marketing Association.

Kilbourne, W.E. and S.C. Beckmann (1998), 'Review and critical assessment of research on marketing and the environment', *Journal of Marketing Management*, **14** (6), 513–532.

Kilbourne, W.E., S.C. Beckmann and E. Thelen (2002), 'The role of the dominant social paradigm in environmental attitudes: a multinational examination', *Journal of Business Research*, **55** (3), 193–204.

Knussen, C., F. Yule, J. Mackenzie and M. Wells (2004), 'An analysis of intentions to recycle household waste: the roles of past behavior, perceived habit, and perceived lack of facilities', *Journal of Environmental Psychology*, **24** (2), 237–46.

Korthals, M. (2001), 'Taking consumers seriously: two concepts of consumer sovereignty', *Journal of Agricultural and Environmental Ethics*, **14** (2), 201–217.

Kozinets, R.V. and J. Handelman (2004), 'Adversaries of consumption: consumer movements, activism, and ideology', *Journal of Consumer Research*, **31** (3), 691–704.

Krishnamurthy, S. and S.U. Kucuk (2009), 'Anti-branding on the internet', *Journal of Business Research*, **62** (11), 1119–1126.

Krystallis, A. and G. Chryssohoidis (2005), 'Consumers' willingness to pay for organic food: factors that affect it and variation per organic product type', *British Food Journal*, **107** (5), 320–343.

Laroche, M., J. Bergeron and G. Barbaro-Forleo (2001), 'Targeting consumers who are willing to pay more for environmentally friendly products', *Journal of Consumer Marketing*, **18** (6), 503–520.

Lastovicka, J.L., L.A. Bettencourt, R.S. Hughner and R.J. Kuntze (1999), 'Lifestyle of the tight and frugal: theory and measurement', *Journal of Consumer Research*, **26** (1), 85–98.

Lebel, L. and S. Lorek (2008), 'Enabling sustainable production-consumption systems', *Annual Review of Environment and Resources*, **33**, 241–275.

Leiserowitz, A., E. Maibach and C. Roser-Renouf (2010), *Americans' Actions to Conserve Energy, Reduce Waste, and Limit Global Warming: January 2010*, New Haven, CT: Yale Project Climate Change, Yale University and George Mason University.

Leonard-Barton, D. (1981), 'Voluntary simplicity lifestyles and energy conservation', *Journal of Consumer Research*, **15** (13), 374–378.

Luchs, M.G., R. Walker-Naylor, J.R. Irwin and R. Raghunathan (2010), 'The sustainability liability: potential negative effects of ethicality on product preference', *Journal of Marketing*, **74** (5), 18–31.

Macinnis, D.J. and V.S. Folkes (2009), 'The disciplinary status of consumer behavior: a sociology of science perspective on key controversies', *Journal of Consumer Research*, **36** (6), 899–914.

Mackay, David (2008), *Sustainable Energy: Without the Hot Air*, Cambridge: UIT.

Mannetti, L., A. Piero and S. Livi (2004), 'Recycling: planned and self-expressive behavior', *Journal of Environmental Psychology*, **24** (2), 227–236.

McDonald S., C.J. Oates, C.W. Young and K. Hwang (2006), 'Toward sustainable consumption: researching voluntary simplifiers', *Psychology and Marketing*, **23** (6), 515–534.

McDonald, S., C. Oates, M. Thyne, P. Alevizou and L. McMorland (2009), 'Comparing sustainable consumption patterns across product sectors', *International Journal of Consumer Studies*, **33** (2), 137–145.

McGoldrick, P.J. and O.M. Freestone (2008), 'Ethical product premiums: antecedents and extent of consumers' willingness to pay', *International Review of Retail, Distribution and Consumer Research*, **18** (2), 185–201.

Meadows, Donella H., Dennis L. Meadows, Jorgen Randers and William W. Behrens III (1972), *The Limits to Growth*, New York: Universe Books.

Megicks, P., J. Memery and J. Williams (2008), 'Influences on ethical and socially responsible shopping: evidence from the UK grocery sector', *Journal of Marketing Management*, **24** (5/6), 637–659.

Miller, Daniel (2001), *The Dialectics of Shopping*, Chicago: The University of Chicago Press.

Mohr, L.A., D. Eroglu and P.S. Ellen (1998), 'The development and testing of a measure of skepticism toward environmental claims in marketers' communication', *Journal of Consumer Affairs*, **32** (1), 30–55.

Moisander, J. (2007), 'Motivational complexity of green consumerism', *International Journal of Consumer Studies*, **30** (4), 404–409.

Mont, O. and A. Plepys (2008), 'Sustainable consumption progress: should we be proud or alarmed?', *Journal of Cleaner Production*, **16** (4), 531–537.

Nixon, H., J.-D.M. Saphores, O.A. Ogunseitan and A.A. Shapiro (2009), 'Understanding preferences for recycling electronic waste in California: the influence of environmental attitudes and beliefs on willingness to pay', *Environment and Behaviour*, **41** (1), 101–124.

Obermiller, C. (1995), 'The baby is sick/the baby is well. A test of environmental communications appeals', *Journal of Advertising*, **24** (2), 55–70.

Peattie, K. (2001a), 'Towards sustainability: the third age of green marketing', *Marketing Review*, **2** (2), 129–146.

Peattie, K. (2001b), 'Golden goose or wild goose? The hunt for the green consumer', *Business Strategy and the Environment*, **10**, 187–199.

Peattie, K. (2010), 'Green consumption: behavior and norms', *Annual Review of Environment and Resources*, **35**, 195–228.

Pepper, M., T. Jackson and D. Uzzell (2009), 'An examination of the values that motivate socially conscious and frugal consumer behaviours', *International Journal of Consumer Studies*, **33** (2), 126–136.

Pickett-Baker, J. and R. Ozaki (2008), 'Pro-environmental products: marketing influence on consumer purchase decision', *Journal of Consumer Marketing*, **25** (5), 281–293.

Porter, M. and C. van der Linde (1995), 'Green and competitive – ending the stalemate', *Harvard Business Review*, **73** (3/4), 120–134.

Princen, T. (1999), 'Consumption and environment: some conceptual issues', *Ecological Economics*, **31** (3), 347–363.

Princen, Thomas, Michael Maniates and Ken Conca (2002), 'Confronting consumption', in Thomas Princen, Michael Maniates and Ken Conca (eds), *Confronting Consumption*, Cambridge, MA: MIT Press, pp. 1–20.

Rex, E. and H. Baumann (2007), 'Beyond ecolabels: what green marketing can learn from conventional marketing', *Journal of Cleaner Production*, **15** (6), 567–576.

Roberts, J.A. (1995), 'Profiling levels of socially responsible consumer behaviour: a cluster analytic approach and its implications for marketing', *Journal of Marketing Theory and Practice*, **3** (4), 97–117.

Schaefer, A. and A. Crane (2005), 'Addressing sustainability and consumption', *Journal of Macromarketing*, **25** (1), 76–92.

Sharp, A., S. Høj and M. Wheeler (2010), 'Proscription and its impact on anti-consumption behaviour and attitudes: the case of plastic bags', *Journal of Consumer Behavior*, **9** (6), 470–484.

Shaw, D. and I. Clarke (1999), 'Belief formation in ethical consumer groups: an exploratory study', *Marketing Intelligence & Planning*, **17** (2), 109–119.

Sheth, J., N. Sethia and S. Srinivas (2011), 'Mindful consumption: a customer-centric approach to sustainability', *Journal of the Academy of Marketing Science*, **39** (1), 21–39.

Shove, E. (2003), 'Converging conventions of comfort, cleanliness and convenience', *Journal of Consumer Policy*, **26** (4), 395–418.

Sorrell, S., J. Schleich, S. Scott, E. O'Malley, F. Trace, U. Boede, K. Ostertag and P. Radgen (2000), *Barriers to Energy Efficiency in Public and Private Organisations: Final Report*, Brussels: European Commission.

Sparks, P. and R. Shepherd (1992), 'Self-identity and the theory of planned behavior: assessing the role of identification with green consumerism', *Social Psychology Quarterly*, **55** (4), 388–399.

Speirs, D. and P. Tucker (2001), 'A profile of recyclers making special trips to recycle', *Journal of Environmental Management*, **62** (2), 201–220.

Staats, H., P. Harland and H.A.M. Wilke (2004), 'Effecting durable change: a team approach to improve environmental behaviour in the household', *Environment and Behavior*, **36** (3), 341–367.

Stearns, J.M., S. Borna and G. Oakenfull (2003), 'Buying for love of country: assessing the ethics of patriotic appeals in advertising', *Business and Society Review*, **8** (4), 509–521.

Stern, N. (2006), *The Stern Review Report: The Economics of Climate Change*, London: HM Treasury.

Stern, P.C. (1999), 'Information, incentives and pro-environmental consumer behavior', *Journal of Consumer Policy*, **22** (4), 461–478.

Stern, P.C., T. Dietz, T. Abel, G.A. Guagnano and L. Kalof (1999), 'A value-belief-norm theory of support for social movements: the case of environmental concern', *Human Ecology Review*, **6** (2), 81–97.

Straughan, R.D. and J.A. Roberts (1999), 'Environmental segmentation alternatives: a look at green consumer behaviour in the new millennium', *Journal of Consumer Marketing*, **16** (6), 558–575.

Tang, E., G. Fryxell and C.S.F. Chow (2004), 'Visual and verbal communication in the design of eco-label for green consumer products', *Journal of International Consumer Marketing*, **16** (4), 85–105.

Thøgersen, J. and F. Ölander (2002), 'Human values and the emergence of a sustainable consumption pattern: a panel study', *Journal of Economic Psychology*, **23** (5), 605–630.

Tucker, P. and D. Speirs (2003), 'Attitudes and behavioral change in household waste management behaviors', *Journal of Environmental Planning and Management*, **46** (2), 289–307.

Tukker, A. (2006), 'Environmental impacts of products: a detailed review of studies', *Journal of Industrial Ecology*, **10** (3), 159–182.

van Birgelen, M., J. Semeijn and M. Keicher (2008), 'Packaging and proenvironmental consumption behavior: investigating purchase and disposal decisions for beverages', *Environment & Behavior*, **41** (1), 125–146.

Vargo, S.L. and R.F. Lusch (2004), 'Evolving to a new dominant logic for marketing', *Journal of Marketing*, **68** (1), 1–17.

Vitell, S.J. and S.D. Hunt (1990), 'The general theory of marketing ethics: a partial test of the model', *Research in Marketing*, **10**, 237–265.

Warde, A. (2005), 'Consumption and theories of practice', *Journal of Consumer Culture*, **5** (2), 131–153.

WCED (1987), *Our Common Future (The Brundtland Report)*, World Commission on Environment and Development, Oxford: Oxford University Press.

Weber, C.L., J.G. Koomey and H.S. Matthews (2009), *The Energy and Climate Change Impacts of Different Music Delivery Methods*, Final report to Microsoft Corporation and Intel Corporation, Stanford, CA: Stanford University, http://download.intel.com/pressroom/pdf/CDsvsdownloadsrelease.pdf accessed 19 July 2011.

Webster, F.E. (1975), 'Developing the characteristics of the socially conscious consumer', *Journal of Consumer Research*, **2** (12), 185–196.

Wells, V.K., C. Ponting and K. Peattie (2011), 'Behaviour and climate change: consumer perceptions of responsibility', *Journal of Marketing Management*, **27** (7–8), 808–833.

Whitmarsh, L. (2009), 'Behavioural responses to climate change: asymmetry of intentions and impacts', *Journal of Environmental Psychology*, **29** (3), 13–23.

Woodcock, J. and R. Aldred (2008), 'Cars, corporations and commodities: consequences for the social determinants of health', *Emerging Themes in Epidemiology*, **5** (4), www.ete-online.com/content/5/1/4 accessed 19 July 2011.

Zukin, S. and J.S. Maguire (2004), 'Consumers and consumption', *Annual Review of Sociology*, **30**, 173–197.

8 New developments in the diffusion of innovations

Ronald E. Goldsmith

8.1 INTRODUCTION

The theory of innovation diffusion has many different aspects and has been applied in a variety of contexts. Although its origins lie in anthropology, the practical implications of diffusion theory quickly became apparent to researchers in many fields, leading to vibrant research streams in the diffusion of new educational practices, the diffusion of new farming practices (rural sociology, the study of social life in non-metropolitan areas), the diffusion of medical advances by medical sociologists, international development, marketing, and others. The field of marketing and consumer behavior made diffusion theory a central topic from its earliest days. The first books to introduce and define the domain of consumer behavior as an academic study included the topics of innovation adoption and innovation diffusion (Engel et al. 1968; Zaltman 1965). This makes perfect sense. After all, the decision to adopt or reject a new product is an important application of models of consumer decision theory. Moreover, the growth imperative faced by all companies entails the active creation of new products, the success of which shapes their futures. That is: 'innovation, the process of bringing new products and services to market, is one of the most important issues in business research today' (Hauser et al. 2006, p. 687). New product failure rates, however, are notoriously high, and companies are eager to learn what they can about consumer reaction to new products so they can improve their new product introduction success rate (McDonald and Alpert 2007). Researchers in marketing and consumer behavior have responded to this need by studying consumer innovativeness, new product adoption decision making, and new product diffusion extensively. The purpose of the present chapter is to review some of this recent literature and to discuss and evaluate some of its important new findings.

However, one challenge faced by anyone confronting the large recent literature on diffusion theory is the diversity of topics studied across various fields. Many papers that appear on diffusion topics describe the diffusion of specific products or categories in specific countries or among specific groups of adopters (or combinations thereof). These papers represent efforts to extend and to apply diffusion theory and make a significant contribution to our understanding of this phenomenon, but often they do not make substantial contributions to the theory itself. The present chapter is limited to recent contributions that add substantial new information to the core theory of diffusion that researchers can apply across a variety of products, categories, populations, and interests. The chapter begins with a brief review of the elements of diffusion theory and its related topics. The subsequent sections describe some of what researchers have done recently that contributes to the theory itself, focusing on three topic areas: conceptualizing and measuring innovativeness, resistance to innovations, and modeling the adoption and diffusion process. The chapter concludes with speculation about what the future holds in store for this topic.

8.2   THE BASICS OF DIFFUSION THEORY

Although the roots of diffusion theory date back to early thinkers in diverse fields such as anthropology and sociology (see Rogers 1983), the basic elements of the modern research tradition were set forth by Rogers (1962), who reinforced and expanded the field in subsequent editions of his work. Rogers is thus responsible for the most widely accepted definitions of the key concepts in diffusion theory. For example, an innovation is 'an idea, practice, or object perceived as new by an individual' (Rogers and Shoemaker 1971, p. 19). Adoption is the behavior that describes how an individual reacts to the innovation and is a 'micro-process' that takes place at the individual level; as the individual adoption decisions are made they aggregate into the macro-process of diffusion. Thus, diffusion can be thought of as a social process by which (1) an innovation (2) is communicated through certain channels (3) over time (4) among the members of a social system (Rogers 1983, p. 10). Rogers is also the source of the famous normal distribution of time-of-adoption and its accompanying five adopter categories (innovators, early adopters, early majority, late majority, and laggards), as well as the S-shaped curve of cumulative adoption. Over the years, marketing scholars have debated the precise definitions of 'new product' as an innovation and of 'innovativeness' or what it means to be an innovator (e.g., Rogers 1962; Midgley and Dowling 1978; Gatignon and Robinson 1991). A great deal of scholarly attention has been devoted to answering the questions, 'who buys first' and 'how did they come to do this.' Nevertheless, Rogers's definitions set the parameters of this field of study and remain influential to the present day. However, scholars continue to expand the application of the theory, to refine it, and adapt it to new technologies and new contexts. Thus, much of the summary below consists of accounts of their work in modifying the original theory.

Figure 8.1 presents a summary of many of the major topics in adoption research.[1] The figure is organized firstly to depict the antecedent conditions or influences on new product adoption and diffusion. These antecedent conditions include the influence of the macro environment, third parties, competitors, the diffusing agency itself, and situational factors. At the heart of this model are the individuals or consumers who make adoption decisions. Researchers have proposed a wide variety of individual characteristics that influence adoption, they have elucidated several (objective and perceived) features of the new product itself that play a role (the major ones are due to Rogers 1962, 1983), and they have discussed the important impact that perceived risk has when consumers make new product adoption decisions. Different researchers have modeled the adoption decision itself, so several models compete as the best explanation of how decision makers make this decision (most recently, Venkatesh et al. 2003). Because theorists often develop these models within the contexts of specific fields of study, there are several of them, but only a few of the most recent are discussed within the chapter. Finally, we should not view adoption as a simple yes/no decisional outcome. The complexity of the consequences of the adoption process includes behavioral outcomes, psychological changes in consumers, and various social outcomes. No review could do justice to the complexity of this topic in less than book-length form, so this chapter is a highly selective review of a few examples of the new thinking and research that enliven this topic.

8.3   NEW DEVELOPMENTS IN DIFFUSION THEORY

The present review focuses on three major areas in which particularly exciting new work has been done. First, several scholars have proposed new and different ways to conceptualize and to measure the concept of innovativeness (Midgley and Dowling 1978; Steenkamp et al. 1999; Tellis et al. 2009), providing new tools for understanding innovation adoption and the diffusion process. Second, recent years have witnessed a new interest in resistance to innovations and the development of several new scales to measure the opposite of innovativeness. Finally, long-held models of how adopters make their decisions have been supplemented by new models; and the Internet and the growth of online networks and other forms of social interactions have stimulated several new approaches to the study of diffusion networks.

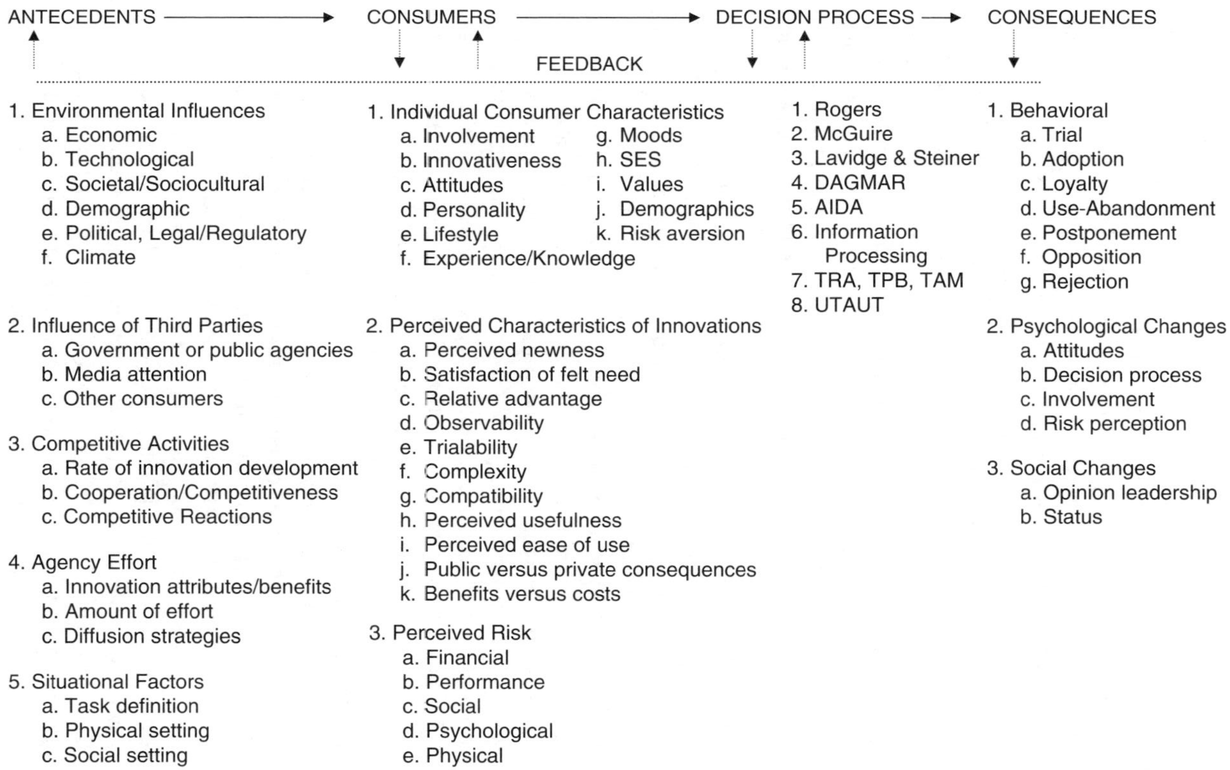
ANTECEDENTS
CONSUMERS
DECISION PROCESS
CONSEQUENCES
FEEDBACK
1. Environmental Influences
a. Economic
b. Technological
c. Societal/Sociocultural
d. Demographic
e. Political, Legal/Regulatory
f. Climate
2. Influence of Third Parties
a. Government or public agencies
b. Media attention
c. Other consumers
3. Competitive Activities
a. Rate of innovation development
b. Cooperation/Competitiveness
c. Competitive Reactions
4. Agency Effort
a. Innovation attributes/benefits
b. Amount of effort
c. Diffusion strategies
5. Situational Factors
a. Task definition
b. Physical setting
c. Social setting
1. Individual Consumer Characteristics
a. Involvement
b. Innovativeness
c. Attitudes
d. Personality
e. Lifestyle
f. Experience/Knowledge
g. Moods
h. SES
i. Values
j. Demographics
k. Risk aversion
2. Perceived Characteristics of Innovations
a. Perceived newness
b. Satisfaction of felt need
c. Relative advantage
d. Observability
e. Trialability
f. Complexity
g. Compatibility
h. Perceived usefulness
i. Perceived ease of use
j. Public versus private consequences
k. Benefits versus costs
3. Perceived Risk
a. Financial
b. Performance
c. Social
d. Psychological
e. Physical
1. Rogers
2. McGuire
3. Lavidge & Steiner
4. DAGMAR
5. AIDA
6. Information Processing
7. TRA, TPB, TAM
8. UTAUT
1. Behavioral
a. Trial
b. Adoption
c. Loyalty
d. Use-Abandonment
e. Postponement
f. Opposition
g. Rejection
2. Psychological Changes
a. Attitudes
b. Decision process
c. Involvement
d. Risk perception
3. Social Changes
a. Opinion leadership
b. Status

Source: Adapted from Goldsmith, 2002.

Figure 8.1 A framework of the adoption process

8.3.1   Conceptualizing and Measuring Innovativeness

Because innovativeness plays such an influential role in the diffusion paradigm, before researchers can study innovation diffusion, especially the adoption process, they must define and operationalize the concept of innovativeness, described by Hauser et al. (2006, p. 689) as 'the propensity of consumers to adopt new products'. Researchers have done a great deal of work on the problem of measuring innovativeness. They have also continued to refine theoretical descriptions of innovativeness as an individual difference concept where the focus is on describing 'the mental, behavioral, and demographic characteristics associated with consumer willingness to adopt innovations' (Hauser et al. 2006, p. 689). Note that discussions of innovativeness such as that below often refer to 'innovators', 'early adopters', or 'laggards' as a convenience. The concept is of course a normally distributed individual difference with near infinite gradations, so that what is meant is that consumers toward one end of the distribution are more innovative than those at the other end, but the discrete groups are arbitrary divisions (see for example Goldenberg and Oreg 2007) used to simplify the discussion.

If diffusion is about change, innovativeness is about how people react to change. To study innovativeness, it must be measured. But how is innovativeness measured? Measurement depends on conceptualization. Different scholars have proposed different methods to operationalize the concept of innovativeness because they have conceptualized innovativeness in different ways (Goldsmith and Foxall 2003). Figure 8.2 presents a summary of the four important conceptualizations of innovativeness prominent in the literature, in descending order from the most general or abstract conceptualization to its most specific, concrete manifestation.

8.3.1.1   Global innovativeness
At the most abstract or global conceptual level, innovativeness refers to a dispositional individual difference in how people react to the new and different, approaching or avoiding it. The most prominent systems contain a dimension that refers to an eagerness to experience the new and different. For instance, Jackson's (1994) personality theory and inventory contains a trait labeled 'innovation'. This trait describes a person who is creative and inventive, capable of originality and motivated to develop novel solutions to problems. The innovation subscale is positively related to the other Jackson scales, Breadth of Interest (intellectual curiosity), Complexity ('seeks intricate solutions to problems'), Tolerance, and Risk Taking, but negatively to Conformity (Jackson 1976). Paunonen and Jackson (1996) report that Jackson's Innovation,

Descending level of generality	Conceptualization	Operationalization
Global Personality Trait Inventory	Openness to experience Willingness to try new things	Personality scale
Consumer Innovativeness	Marketplace innovativeness Market Maven	Global consumer innovativeness scale EBBT Market Maven scale
Domain specific innovativeness	e.g., Fashion innovator	Domain specific innovativeness scale
Adoption Behavior	Overt behavior	Behavioral intent Time of adoption Number of new items adopted

Figure 8.2   The concept of innovativeness

Breadth of Experience, Complexity, Innovation and Tolerance form a second-order factor that correlates highly (r = .73) with the Openness to Experience dimension of the Big Five personality theory (Costa and McCrae 1992). The Innovation scale alone correlates .5 with the Big Five Openness to Experience dimension. The Big Five Model proposed by Costa and McCrae (1992) is the most influential recent trait theory of personality. They argue that along with Conscientiousness, Agreeableness, Neuroticism, and Extraversion, Openness to Experience is one of the most important individual differences that characterize human behavior.

Also at the global level of conceptualization, Hurt et al. (1977; see also Pallister and Foxall 1998) attempted to operationalize innovativeness as an independent concept detached from any broader theoretical framework as a 'willingness to try new things'. Their scale consists of 20 items, one of which reads: 'I enjoy trying out new ideas'. Goldsmith (1990) showed that this scale actually operationalized the concepts of creativity and global opinion leadership as well as an eagerness to try the new and different and proposed a shorter version of the scale to focus on the latter. His data showed that this unidimensional measure is correlated in theoretically hypothesized ways with other concepts relevant to innovative behavior such as risk taking, arousal seeking, and sensation seeking. Pallister and

Foxall (1998), who also examine Hurt et al.'s scale, confirm that it is multidimensional, but that the willingness to try dimension was related to purchase of novel financial products.

Kirton (1976, 1989) worked within the context of organizational behavior, trying to determine why individuals and businesses react differently to the need for change when it calls for problem solving, creativity, and decision making. He proposed a broad personality trait distinction of adaption-innovation as a cognitive style of problem solving and decision making. At one extreme, Adaptors solve problems by preserving as much of the problem context as possible, improving and changing existing systems without transforming them, while Innovators see original solutions that upset the status quo and profoundly transform the context of the problem as it is solved. The Kirton Adaption-Innovation Inventory, a 32-item self-report scale, operationalizes this version of innovativeness as differences in cognitive style of decision making and problem solving consisting of three subcomponents: originality, efficiency, and conformity. Goldsmith (1986) shows that three scales purporting to measure global innovativeness, the Hurt et al. scale, Kirton's AI scale, and Jackson's Innovation scale, tend to converge, indicating that they measure similar concepts.

Steenkamp and Baumgartner (1995) describe the development of a short self-report scale to measure change seeking. Based on Garlington and Shimota's (1964) instrument, the Change Seeker Index (CSI) consists of seven items derived from the 95 items in the original scale. The theoretical background for the scale lies in the idea that people engage in exploratory behavior derived from their global desire to seek variety and change in their lives. People differ in how much change they find desirable; they have preferred levels of stimulation and adjust their behaviour to reach an optimal level of stimulation. One item from this scale reads: 'I am continually seeking new ideas and experiences.' This disposition manifests itself in the marketplace as an eagerness to try new products and brands and is thus a version of dispositional innovativeness. They argue that the CSI can be used to study consumer behaviors that involve '(1) exploratory information seeking, variety seeking, risk taking and innovativeness, (2) responses to stimulus characteristics such as novelty, ambiguity and complexity, and (3) the effects of stimulus (e.g., advertising) repetition' (p. 98).

Like Kirton, Kleysen and Street (2001) worked within an organizational behavior context to argue that innovativeness is a multidimensional construct and thus should be operationalized by a scale that represents its different facets. They propose that innovative behavior should be defined as 'all individual actions directed at the generation, introduction and or application of beneficial novelty at any organizational level' (p.

285). They derived a five-factor model of dispositional innovativeness consisting of opportunity exploration ('traveling extensively through innovation opportunities in order to learn or discover more about them'), generativity ('behaviors directed at generating beneficial change for the purpose of "growing" organizations, their people, products, processes, and services'), formative investigation ('giving form to and fleshing out ideas, solutions, and opinions and trying them out through investigation'), championing ('the socio-political behaviors involved in processes of innovation'), and application ('working at making innovations a regular part of business as usual'). Their empirical results, however, did not support this five-factor model and instead yielded a unidimensional scale of 14 items, which seems to represent a broadly conceived disposition to behave in an innovative fashion within an organization context. One item, for example, reads: 'In your current job, how often do you take the risk to support new ideas?'

Although operationalizing global innovativeness reliably and validly is necessary for the study of this concept, in reality, the global conceptualization of innovativeness as openness to experience has limited value as a way to explain and predict behavior at more specific levels of generality. It is best suited for exploring relationships between innovativeness and other concepts at the same level of generality. For example, Jackson (1976) shows that innovativeness in this regard is related positively to propensity to take risks, which suggests important insights into the nature of openness. In order to explain and predict diffusion within specific fields of activity, such as organization behavior, consumer behavior, education, and so forth, operationalizations of innovativeness need to be developed that are suitable for those specific domains. Our focus is chiefly on consumer behavior, so we next turn to recent studies of innovativeness within the marketplace.

8.3.1.2   Marketplace innovativeness

Broad trait concepts of personality such as those described by the Big Five theory or Kirton's adaption-innovation theory are very useful in explaining a variety of attitudinal and behavioral outcomes (Ozer and Benet-Martinez 2006). This is true as well in marketing and consumer behavior research. For example Wang et al. (2010) show that Kirton's adaption-innovation distinction can be combined with the concept of consumer involvement with a product category to explain consumer intention to remain loyal to online reputation systems. Despite this usefulness, researchers find they must trade off the important insights broad concepts provide with regard to the antecedents (such as motivations and predispositions) of behavior against the weakness with which they predict and explain variation in concrete or specific behaviors. To gain greater explanatory power and precision within the consumer behavior field we must conceptualize innovativeness at a specific level of generality such as a product domain or field (e.g., clothing), or even at a more specific level such as type of product (e.g., Internet banking). In the fields of marketing and consumer behavior, where diffusion of innovation theory is so widely used, innovativeness is often conceptualized as a description of general consumer innovativeness, or marketplace innovativeness. That is, innovativeness is seen as a predisposition to adopt new products across a variety of product fields or domains. It is accompanied by the notion that there are 'consumer innovators and early adopters' who form the earliest group of buyers.

Much resent research has been devoted to conceptualizing consumer innovativeness and developing accompanying operationalizations at the marketplace level. These concepts and their measures provide more precise estimates of the relationships between dispositional innovativeness and a variety of other constructs than do the global concepts because they operationalize both innovativeness and the other constructs at the same level of abstraction. The variety of these measures, however, yields a body of findings that resists summary because we lack evidence that they measure the same construct.

For instance, Feick and Price (1987) conceptualized a pattern of consumer behavior they termed market mavenism, and they proposed a self-report scale to measure this individual difference. Consumers who score high on this scale are termed Market Mavens and are described as those consumers who are involved in the marketplace in general. They find the marketplace intrinsically interesting so that they actively learn about product and stores. They are also eager to share their knowledge with other consumers and try to influence where they shop and what they buy. Thus, mavenism describes a type of marketplace opinion leader (an individual whom others seek out for advice and information; see Goldsmith 2011), who is attuned to the latest developments across a variety of product categories, and consequently should know about new products soon after they are introduced. Goldsmith et al. (2003) showed that indeed, mavenism is positively associated with both opinion leadership and innovativeness, but that it is a concept distinct from them. Although mavenism is interesting and potentially useful in its own right, it seems to be more of a manifestation of involvement than of dispositional innovativeness. That is, the involvement motivation, through which consumers find the marketplace interesting and exciting, leads them to be both innovators and opinion leaders, but it is not itself a good way to conceptualize and measure dispositional consumer innovativeness at the level of the marketplace because its construct validity focused on mavenism and not on consumer innovativeness per se.

Trying to focus more precisely on dispositional innovativeness at the marketplace level, Baumgartner and Steenkamp (1996) argue that innovative behavior is a variety of exploratory consumer buying behavior. By this they mean that consumers sometimes behave in ways that reflect a desire for novelty, to satisfy curiosity, and variety seeking. They state that 'there is now general agreement that such activities as risk taking and innovative behaviour in product purchase, variety seeking and brand switching, recreational shopping and information search, and interpersonal communication about purchases may be regarded as manifestations of exploratory tendencies in the consumer buying process' (p. 122). Thus, they see exploratory tendencies as a more global or abstract motivating force that influences more specific marketplace activities such as innovative behavior. Baumgartner and Steenkamp (1996) propose that Exploratory Buying Behavior Tendencies (EBBT) can be measured by a self-report scale as a trait measure assessing individual differences in people's disposition to engage in two forms of exploratory buying behavior: exploratory acquisition of products and exploratory information seeking. Their 20-item scale contains 10 items to measure exploratory acquisition of products (e.g., 'When I see a new brand on the shelf, I'm not afraid of giving it a try') and 10 items to measure exploratory information seeking (e.g., 'I like to shop around and look at displays'). Unfortunately, this scale contains a mixture of items that refer to specific product fields (food, fast-moving consumer goods, etc.) so that exactly what it is measuring is difficult to assess. Thus, it might be an acceptable operationalization of an exploratory buying concept, but that remains to be determined. Instead, it is likely comprised of subcomponents that measure exploratory buying in specific product areas instead of a marketplace level measure of innovativeness.

Steenkamp et al. (1999) used a five-item, modified version of the Exploratory Acquisition of Products scale developed by Baumgartner and Steenkamp (1996) to measure a consumer-level manifestation of dispositional innovativeness. They surveyed consumers in 11 countries and concluded that there were consistent relationships between their proposed antecedents of consumer innovativeness in all countries. Namely, they found a negative relationship between innovativeness and age, but not with education and income. They found that the more importance consumers attach to conservation, corresponding to less openness to change, the less innovative consumers were. They also showed a negative relationship of consumer innovativeness with ethnocentrism and with a favorable attitude toward the past. They also investigated cultural differences and reported that consumers in societies that tended to increased individualism and higher levels of masculinity were more innovative than their corresponding collectivist and feminine counterparts. Finally, they found that innovativeness was lower in cultures that expressed uncertainty avoidance than in cultures characterized by risk taking.

Steenkamp and Gielens (2003) used a revised, eight-item scale, similar in some respects to the scale used by Steenkamp et al. (1999) to operationalize general consumer innovativeness. For instance, two items read: 'When I see a new product on the shelf, I'm reluctant to give it a try' and 'I am usually among the first to try new brands.' They combined their measure of consumer innovativeness with measures of 'market factors' such as number of brands in a category and differences in advertising intensity to predict the occurrence and timing of first purchases for 239 new consumer packaged goods over a 52-week period determined by scanner data. They found that dispositional innovativeness did have a positive influence on the purchase of these new products, suggesting that consumers can accurately self-identify themselves as innovators and that this individual difference variable does account for some of the variation in at least trial of new products. In addition to showing that income (but not age) was also positively related to trial of new products, they confirmed that 'usage intensity' or amount of use of a product also has a positive relationship with innovative purchasing, consistent with Goldsmith (2000).

Hartman et al. (2004) focus on young consumers and technology-oriented products for their study of consumer innovativeness and its measurement. They adopt the position that consumer innovativeness is a multidimensional construct oriented around the basic idea that it is the desire and preference for new and different consumption experiences. They develop a scale to reflect this conceptualization containing three dimensions and subscales: adoptive innovativeness, vicarious innovativeness, and use innovativeness. They define adoptive innovativeness as acquisition of a product; vicarious innovativeness as active search for information about new or unfamiliar products or imagining the adoption of a new product; and use innovativeness as variety seeking in product use such as using an existing product in new ways. Data from their survey of U.S. middle-school students yielded a three-dimensional, 20-item scale reflecting their conceptualization. Although they provide no evidence for the validity of the scale, the item content suggests that it yields results similar to other studies of consumer innovativeness at the marketplace level of generality-specificity. Example items include: 'When I see new name brands, I want to try them out' (vicarious innovativeness); 'I like to try different things when using products' (use innovativeness); and 'I usually buy high-tech products before my friends do' (adoptive innovativeness). The absence of further evidence for the construct and predictive validity of this scale, as well as its limited focus, however, suggest that much further research needs to be done with it before researchers can use it with confidence.

Combining the consumer characteristic of dispositional innovativeness with product factors and competitive conduct, Gielens and Steenkamp (2007) used data from a consumer panel consisting of households in four European countries to model first-year purchase level and first-year trend in purchases of new products. Their results showed that consumer innovativeness, measured by the eight-item scale developed by Steenkamp and Gielens (2003), was consistently related in a positive way to first-year purchase level and negatively to first-year purchase trend, indicating that innovative consumers like to buy the latest new products, but are likely to switch away from them when even newer products are introduced. In their study, larger household size was also positively related to new product purchase, but age was, as in some other studies, negatively related.

Another international study (Tellis et al. 2009) provides additional valuable information about consumer innovativeness. These authors studied consumer 'relative eagerness to buy' new products in six distinct product categories (major home appliances, automobiles, cosmetics, food and grocery products, sporting goods, and financial services, as well as high tech products as a base category) across 12 countries. They operationalized consumer innovativeness with a 10-item self-report scale consisting of three conceptual dimensions of the construct: openness to new things, enthusiasm for new products, and reluctance to adopt new products). Their analysis yielded an interesting conclusion:

> These results suggest that openness and enthusiasm are poor, and perhaps seriously biased, measures of innovativeness. It may be that some consumers overrate their level of innovativeness on openness and enthusiasm but not on reluctance. Intuitively, it seems that respondents (more so in some countries) understand that high scores on the positively valenced measures reflect socially desirable traits and rate themselves high on these. However, they fail to see that high scores on the negatively valenced items reflect socially undesirable traits and so reveal their true positions on the latter items. Accordingly, reluctance is a less biased (more honest) representation of consumers' actual innovativeness than openness and enthusiasm. (pp. 11–12)

Consequently, Tellis et al. (2009) used four negatively valenced items representing reluctance to adopt new products as their operationalization of consumer innovativeness and tested for its relationships with individual consumers, country characteristics, and eagerness to purchase new products. Their findings using their Global Consumer Innovativeness scale show that a global consumer innovator across countries is more likely than a non-adopter to be wealthy, young, mobile, educated, and male. After comparing their findings with those of other transnational studies, however, they conclude that there is little consistent evidence for general relationships between demographics and consumer innovativeness. Most likely, the relationships between demographics and desire to purchase new products do vary so much across product categories that there is little likelihood that any worthwhile generalizations can be made. They report a variety of country differences in both consumer innovativeness and eagerness to buy in specific categories as well as interactions between demographics and countries. Thus, the more closely we examine consumer innovativeness for specific product categories, the more likely we are to discover a unique set of relationships with other variables, suggesting that conceptualizing and studying consumer innovativeness at the marketplace level will yield only modest and weak conclusions. Two avenues for additional research can be suggested. First, instead of focusing on the positive concept of openness to new things, a better approach might be to focus on its obverse, reluctance to buy new products, as a less biased way to operationalize the construct of consumer innovativeness (as suggested by Tellis et al. 2009). Scholars have begun to pursue this interest, as is discussed below in the section on Innovation Resistance. Second, if we are willing to abandon the search for marketplace generalities, perhaps the best approach to studying consumer innovativeness is to focus on the product category or domain as the better locale for understanding consumer innovativeness. That is, given the unique influence of other variables such as demographics across product domains, the best way to get valuable information about consumer innovativeness is to study it at the domain specific level. In addition, since managers work within highly product specific domains, this approach might be the most useful one for their needs as well.

Both the concepts of market mavenism and exploratory buying behavior touch upon dispositional innovativeness as a component or consequence, but neither describes precisely the innovativeness concept itself, and so additional ideas and measures are needed to bring this concept into focus. To address this limitation in existing measures, Vandecasteele and Geuens (2010) developed a scale to measure the motivations people have for adopting innovations. Stressing the relationships and interactions that consumers have with products, Vandecasteele and Geuens propose that consumers have a variety of underlying goals and motivations for acquiring innovations. Their multi-motivational consumer innovativeness construct and scale are based on general motivation and value taxonomies. The first motive they describe as a functional motive category, emphasizing mastery, improvement, performance, and efficiency. In short, people acquire new products because they accomplish the useful, utilitarian goals of the product better than older versions. An example of their scale item reads: 'If an innovation is more functional, then I usually buy it.' Their second motive category is hedonic. These motives are described as largely affective and sensory, and include happiness, excitement, and satisfaction derived from the new product. An example of this questionnaire item reads: 'Innovations make my life exciting and stimulating.' The third set of motives is termed social. These motives are associated with how people relate to others, specifically how they differentiate themselves from others and feel unique, especially in terms of status and success. An example of a scale item representing this dimension of innovativeness reads: 'I love to use innovations that impress others.' Finally, the fourth dimension of innovativeness is cognitive. That is, innovations can be adopted because they fulfill a cognitive need for mental stimulation. A consumer highly motivated by this need has a great desire to know and to understand, and delights in satisfying it. An example of an item used to operationalize this dimension reads: 'I find innovations that need a lot of thinking intellectually challenging and therefore I buy them instantly.'

Vandecasteele and Geuens (2010) show that their Motivated Consumer Innovativeness scale explains small but significant amounts of variance in attitude toward and intention to purchase a variety of fictional new products. In this regard, it seems to do a better job of accounting for variation in these dependent variables than does the Global Consumer Innovativeness scale developed by Tellis et al. (2009; see above). Moreover, they further use their scale to assess the common finding that age is negatively related to consumer innovativeness. They report that the dimensions for which older consumers are less innovative than younger consumers are the hedonic, social, and cognitive dimensions. They report that for functional innovativeness, older people are as innovative as younger people. Like many of the other researchers in this field, they find no evidence for differences or relationships between innovativeness and the socio-economic characteristics of education, income, or family situation.

8.3.1.3 Domain specific innovativeness

As with the global personality approach, conceptualizing and operationalizing innovativeness at the marketplace level yields estimates of relationships that are stronger with concepts and behaviors at the same level of generality, but are less effective when trying to explain and predict attitudes and behaviors at more specific conceptual levels, especially at the level of actualized behavior (buying the new thing). In an attempt to improve this situation, Goldsmith and Hofacker (1991) proposed that consumer innovativeness could be described and measured at the domain specific level, that is, for a specific product category or field. To this end, they developed the Domain Specific Innovativeness Scale or DSI, a short, valid, reliable self-report measure adaptable to a wide variety of product domains (e.g., clothing, wine, mobile services) so that innovativeness for a specific category of product could be assessed. In addition, the scale has been adapted to operationalize specific aspects of personal innovativeness for specific categories. Cardoso et al. (2010) use the DSI to reveal an innovative segment of apparel consumers among Portuguese buyers. Pagani (2007) showed that the DSI could be adapted to measure 'vicarious innovativeness' for third generation mobile services and integrated with other psychological and cognitive measures to segment the market for this product category and provide insights into the motivations and attitudes of the important early adopter segment. Wang et al. (2006a, 2006b, 2006c) show in a series of studies of online buying behavior that consumer choice is shaped by a combination of consumer dispositional innovativeness measured by the DSI plus involvement in a product category. Wang et al. (2010) further confirm the powerful influence involvement in a product category has on innovative behavior in that category. Combining involvement and innovativeness seems to be the best way to explain and predict the extent of adoption behavior (see Foxall and James 2009).

8.3.1.4   Adoption behavior

The least abstract level at which innovativeness is conceptualized is not in fact dispositional innovativeness, but can be described as actualized innovativeness, or the result of the dispositional construct that leads some consumers to be the earliest to learn about and purchase new products. Thus, adoption is the dependent variable the theories, models, and measures are designed to predict and explain. Rogers and Shoemaker (1971) originally conceptualized adoption as a yes/no dichotomous outcome and proposed that time of adoption since new product introduction was the desired way to operationalize this construct. Another operationalization is the number of new products adopted from a list of new products. Hoffmann and Soyez (2010) use the latter method to operationalize domain specific innovativeness for new automobile interiors. They showed that consumers who are involved with this product category (evidenced by their heavy use of media sources of automotive interior information, their frequent use of automobiles, and their activity as automotive opinion leaders) owned more of the automotive interior products than less involved consumers, verifying this well-established relationship. Finally, a variable that is often used in diffusion studies to represent adoption behavior is actually the intention to adopt or the intention to behave in an innovative manner (Vandecasteele and Geuens 2010; Venkatesh et al. 2003; Yi et al. 2006). Conceptually, intention to behave is a hypothetical construct that might be described as the plans consumers form or the predictions they make about their future behavior. It intervenes between the dispositions thought of as innovativeness and the overt behaviors thought of as adoption. Because intention to behave is a good but not perfect predictor of actual behavior, it serves as a reasonable dependent variable in diffusion studies.

At the lowest level of abstraction, innovativeness is sometimes misidentified as the behavior that diffusion theory is trying to predict and explain. Thinking of innovativeness as a behavior is problematical for two reasons. First, not all innovators adopt a new product, and new products are not all adopted by innovators. At any point in time, some of the adopters (buyers, users) of an innovation might be innovators seeking the new and different, but some might be laggards who adopt for reasons not connected with their inherent level of innovativeness (see Goldenberg and Oreg 2007). Moreover, focusing simply on dispositional constructs to explain and predict adoption behavior ignores important social and situational influences on this behavior. The second reason we should not identify innovativeness as the behavior we are trying to explain is that behavioral variables cannot be operationalized prior to the behavior, thus they cannot be used to test predictive hypotheses. Moreover, time of adoption and number of products adopted from a list of new products are very imprecise measures themselves (see Midgley and Dowling 1978), and measures of behavioral intent are not perfect predictors of actual behavior (Ovans 1998). Thus, we must keep in mind that time of adoption, number of new products purchased, and buying intentions are the (behavioral) dependent variables diffusion theory is meant to explain and not operationalizations of the (dispositional) innovativeness concept itself. As Hartman et al. (2004, p. 354) state, 'there is a need to measure innovativeness in a manner that transcends acquisition'.

Thus, researchers must conceptualize and measure innovativeness at the level of specificity appropriate for the requirements of a given research objective in order to be most effective. Moreover, when researchers fail to make clear the level at which they are operating their findings and conclusions are likely to blur the larger picture instead of clarifying it. Finally, global innovativeness is a poor predictor of actual adoption behavior unless one operationalizes adoption behavior across time, across types of adoption behavior, and across a variety of domains. Marketplace innovativeness is limited to predicting and explaining innovativeness for specific product domains, which in turn can explain and predict more specific adoption behaviors *within their relevant domains*. Using concepts and measures of innovativeness at unspecified and inappropriate levels of specificity reduces their practical value. Proper attention to this issue will help the field of innovation research to create more comprehensive and useful generalizations about diffusion and adoption.

8.3.2   Innovation Resistance

Much new theorizing has focused on the extreme right side of the model shown in Figure 8.1. These efforts have attempted to specify and to explain a variety of behavioral outcomes in the adoption process. As the model shows, a simple dichotomous adoption/non-adoption conceptualization of how innovations fare in the marketplace is not sufficient to capture the rich diversity of how consumers respond to new things. Until recently, most research has focused only on adoption and on understanding why consumers adopt new products, with the assumption that adoption meant permanent commitment. The overwhelming content of this innovativeness research is with identifying and understanding innovators, their characteristics and behaviors, and assessing why and how they decided to adopt (Kleijnen et al. 2009). Other outcomes, however, can be visualized, not all of which have been studied extensively by researchers. Product trial is one outcome. As products range from the durable, expensive, high-risk, and complex (e.g., technology, appliances, and products with high switching costs) end of a continuum to the disposable, inexpensive, low-risk, and simple end (e.g., fast-moving consumer goods, new services), product trial represents a more and more important result of the innovation introduction strategy. Thus, simply getting consumers to try a new product might be the proximal goal and more or less permanent adoption the distal goal. Thus, when faced with a new product, especially one like a FMCG, some consumers will try it. Innovators are likely to be among the first to try such products and diffuse word-of-mouth about them (Steenkamp and Gielens 2003). Whether they will permanently adopt the new product and become loyal users, however, is a different question. Creating long-term brand loyalty and relationships with consumers after trial (see Goldsmith 2010) becomes a topic more correctly described as 'relationship building' and passes from the diffusion topic. New triers might decide not to continue to consume the product for a variety of reasons, including dissatisfaction with the product, failure to see a compelling reason to switch from their current brand, and a need to move on to the next new version. This means that one outcome of the adoption process can be described as trial followed by abandonment rather than by loyalty. Libai et al. (2009) explore the neglected topic of the diffusion of new services by highlighting the problem of attrition whereby many service customers leave the service, so that these industries are especially characterized by efforts to follow up successful new service introduction with intensive retention strategies.

The flip side of adoption is failure-to-adopt and can be termed resistance to innovations (Szmigin and Foxall 1998). Innovation can be resisted by both innovators and non-innovators, and they may resist the innovation for both shared reasons and for reasons uniquely related to their individual levels of innovativeness. For example, Laukkanen et al. (2007) found that older consumers both shared concerns about perceived performance-to-price value of mobile banking that predisposed them to resist this innovation with younger consumers, and differed from younger consumers in certain key ways. Compared to younger consumers, the more mature consumers saw more risk in adopting, and they were more influenced by tradition and the image of mobile banking. Thus, when we examine innovation non-adoption we confront a complex set of elements that have yet to be successfully modeled by researchers or studied empirically, although several piecemeal suggestions have been made.

Szmigin and Foxall (1998) argue that resistance to innovation or non-adoption takes three forms: postponement, opposition, and rejection. Postponement represents a decision not to adopt at this point in time, but simply delays adoption until 'circumstances are more suitable' (Kleijnen et al. 2009, p. 346). Innovators and non-innovators might postpone adoption both for shared reasons and because of unique circumstances. Shared reasons for delay might stem from lack of product availability, inadequate current resources, need to exhaust current supplies. Situations might contribute to consumers not adopting a new product soon after it is introduced. Network externalities can delay adoption of new technologies that depend on a sizable number of other users adopting before they become attractive, or the availability of additional applications that enhance their value. New technology especially might diffuse slowly due to postponement as users wait until doubts about its soundness can be assuaged. Postponement can be thought of as a temporary situation that will ultimately lead to adoption.

Opposition is a stronger resistance to the innovation. In contrast to postponement, opposition will ultimately lead to rejection. Postponers can be persuaded and encouraged to adopt; opponents will likely not adopt even in the face of marketing efforts. Situational factors may account for part of this opposition. Dispositional factors also play a role. Innovation resistors are motivated by habit, satisfaction with the status quo, psychological barriers, and risk perceptions (Kleijnen et al. 2009; Laukkanen et al. 2008; Szmigin and Foxall 1998). Although the dividing line is ill defined, between who is a postponer and likely to adopt and who is an opponent who is not likely to adopt, arbitrary designations can make this concept empirically useful (e.g., Laukkanen et al. 2008).

The most extreme form of resistance is rejection, which occurs when consumers outright reject the new product ('send it back to the kitchen'). Kleijnen et al. (2009, p. 346) argue that resistance stems from two basic sources: (1) innovations 'might require a change in consumer's established behavioral patterns, norms, habits, and traditions', and (2) innovations 'which in some way cause a psychological conflict or problem for consumers'. Non-innovators might reject the new product simply because they do not embrace new product offerings; they are satisfied with the status quo, avoid risk, or lack interest in the new and different. Innovators might reject the new product because it fails to provide novel benefits. Companies can learn from these product failures and take steps to avoid repeating them. Perhaps modifications can be made to the product so that it can be reintroduced.

A specific characteristic of new technology adoption illustrates the complexity of this phenomenon and the fact that not all new products are adopted by innovators. This situation is called the leapfrogging effect. It can be seen when new products are adopted by laggards in the product category who wait for their existing goods to fail or wear out before they buy the newest version (Goldenberg and Oreg 2007). In effect, some of the adopters of a new product, typically a technological product, skip generations of products because they hold on to their older versions, but when they need to purchase a replacement or an upgrade, opt for the latest version. These buyers of the newest version of the technology are dispositional laggards: that is, they do not seek out the latest technology, but find themselves buyers of a new technology anyway. This phenomenon highlights the important distinction between abstract conceptualizations of innovativeness as a predisposition to learn about and buy the newest products, and the actual time of adoption of new products.

As noted above, innovation resistance can come from two sources. The first is the non-adoption by innovators in a product category. For a variety of reasons, most likely linked to the perceived characteristics of the innovation itself (see Figure 8.1), innovators may decide that they do not like a new product and refuse to buy it and/or spread negative word-of-mouth about it. The second source of resistance comes from the consumers who occupy the opposite tail of the innovativeness distribution, the later adopters and laggards. These are consumers for whom innovations may not be welcome. They are the resistors of change. Deslandes and Flynn (2000) describe a self-report scale that can be used to measure degree of laggardism within a specific product category. It reflects a resistance to new things and perceived risk in purchasing them. Like innovators (innovativeness), laggardism can be conceptualized as a global resistance to all new things

(Oreg 2003) as well as resistance to new things in specific product categories (Deslandes and Flynn 2000), so that we may have the seemingly paradoxical consumer who likes new things in general, but hates change in a
favored category, or the general resistor of new things, who unexpectedly
craves some new thing in a single category or who must adopt to replace
an outmoded or non-working older version.

One explanation of this paradox is that involvement or interest, enthusiasm, and excitement regarding a product category seems to be a major
driver of innovative behavior (Goldsmith 2000). Thus, a consumer who in
general resists the new and different might avidly seek the latest version of
a product in a category in which he or she is highly involved (Foxall and
James 2009). A few scholars have recently examined this aspect of diffusion to provide a different perspective on adoption behavior. Another
side of the paradox is that consumers most committed to the brand may
be those who resist changes in the brand, while less committed consumers
might be more tolerant of these changes (Walsh and Lipinski 2008). Thus,
the study of resistance needs to be conducted following the same lines
as the study of innovativeness, and not as an afterthought. Fortunately,
several scholars have tried to do this.

From the global perspective, for example, Oreg (2003) developed a
general self-report measure of resistance to change, 'an individual's tendency to resist or avoid making changes, to devalue change generally,
and to find change aversive across diverse contexts and types of change'
(p. 280). Consisting of four dimensions, a preference for routine seeking, a
negative emotional reaction, a short-term focus, and cognitive rigidity, the
Resistance to Change Scale possesses good psychometric characteristics
and might prove useful in understanding consumer rejection of innovative
products.

At the marketplace level of abstractness, Saaksjarvi and Morel (2010)
propose that innovations may fail partially because consumers may doubt
that the new product will fulfill its promises. This concept is focused on
specific aspects of the perceived characteristics of new products: relative
advantage, risk, compatibility, and complexity/simplicity. Thus, consumers' doubts about new products increase the more they perceive them to
possess fewer advantages, to be riskier than existing product, to be less
compatible with existing contexts, and to be too complex. Saaksjarvi and
Morel (2010) developed a self-report scale reflecting three dimensions,
performance risk, compatibility, and relative advantage to operationalize their concept of doubt and show that higher levels of doubt lead to
increased information search and lowered purchase intent by consumers
facing new products. Items in their scale reflect doubts that the product is
simple, easy to use, worth its money, or really needed.

Walsh and Lipinski (2008) studied consumer resistance to change in a vacation destination among tourists. Resistance to change in their study seemed to stem from two main sources: firstly the perception that change threatened their experience and the satisfaction they derived from the locale, and secondly lack of understanding for the rationale motivating the change. In addition, they expressed feelings of ownership of the destination and resented changes being thrust upon them without consideration of their feelings or opinions. Their findings indicate that when consumers encounter changes to product attributes and characteristics, such as those making up a tourism destination, resistance to change is likely to be higher among the more committed, loyal visitors than among newer ones. Thus, we again see the important role that product involvement (appearing in Walsh and Lipinski's study as 'brand commitment', or emotional attachment to the brand) plays in diffusion. Just as Foxall's studies (e.g., Wang et al. 2006a, 2006b, 2006c) show that involvement with the product category interacts with a willingness to try new things to shape adoption behavior, involvement can stimulate resistance to a new product or a product change. Finally, Laukkanen et al. (2008) studied resistance to Internet banking among Finnish consumers. They divided non-adopters into three groups, postponers, opponents, and rejecters, and compared their perceptions of Internet banking across a variety of concerns. They found significant differences among these groups.

The study of non-adoption provides important new insights into adoption and diffusion. The studies suggest that consumers can be divided into four groups as the product (successfully) moves through the diffusion curve. After introduction, the group of adopters increases. The group of non-adopters decreases as some consumers move through the successive stages of postponement to become adopters. Moreover, even some opponents can ultimately adopt, as the leapfrogging phenomenon attests. Two conclusions are unavoidable: adoption depends greatly on the type of product being examined, and laggardism is not as simple as Rogers implied. Consumer adoption behavior (including trial, adoption or rejection, postponement, and resistance) varies across product types, suggesting that a comprehensive theory and model of this aspect of diffusion remains to be developed. Understanding innovation resistance is not only an important theoretical supplement to understanding innovation adoption. The study of innovation resistance has practical implications as well. As noted by Szymanski et al. (2007, p. 38):

> With regard to negative consumer-based factors, firms might find that members of the target audience are risk averse to new product, especially when they are new-to-the-market products, because of a heightened potential of social, performance, or financial risks that could accompany the purchase of such

offerings. Consumers also may resist learning about innovative offerings that are new-to-the-firm or the market to the detriment of new product sales if consumers are cognitive misers and learning is considered arduous.. . . The need to purchase compatible items even if the innovation is just new-to-the-firm, the resulting obsolescence of current possessions, or the necessity to adopt new behavior when using new offerings are other factors that can impede the marketplace success of highly innovative goods . . . Finally, members of the target audience may be reluctant customers when maintaining or storing the innovative offering is difficult or loyalty to competitors' offerings is high.

Thus, one of the major recent developments in the study of innovation adoption has been the focus by some scholars (e.g., Foxall and James 2009; Oreg 2003) on understanding resistance to innovations as a topic in its own right and not simply as the residual results of studying adoption. Both factors, 'willingness to adopt new things' and 'resistance to new things' are independent constructs that each play a role in explaining how individuals react to the new and different.

8.3.3 Network Models and Adoption Models Diffusion

Diffusion is about change and how change happens. One principal element in the traditional definition of innovation diffusion is the notion that innovations spread through social systems or networks and change something about the members such as an attitude, intention, or behavior. The impetus for the innovation comes from some outside agency or arises organically from certain members of the social system. In either case, much of the 'spreading' takes place from individual to individual. Consequently, the study of innovativeness has always gone hand in hand with the study of social influence. The early research of this sort focused on interpersonal networks and personal influence (e.g., Coleman et al. 1966; Katz and Lazarsfeld 1955; Ryan and Gross 1943) and this tradition continues today (e.g., Gladwell 2000; Keller and Berry 2003). The relationship between innovation adoption and social influence is evidenced by the strong association between being an innovator for new products and being an opinion leader for them as well (e.g., Goldsmith et al. 2003). Moreover, the spread of word-of-mouth about innovations is argued by some to be the driving force for diffusion itself (Bass 1969). This is why the topic of innovation diffusion contains the topics of opinion leadership, word-of-mouth, and change agents (power users, influencers) and why researchers have invested quite a lot of energy into modeling diffusion. The development of diffusion models has a long and distinguished history pioneered by Bass (1969). Mahajan et al. (2000) provide a detailed review of developments in this field, but recent studies extend the precision and complexity of such new product growth models in addition to adapting them to the social networks that have become so important in many people's lives (see Goldenberg et al. 2009; Meade and Islam 2006).

8.3.3.1   Network diffusion models

A recent examination of innovation and new product growth models (Peres et al. 2010) presents an updated review of the major changes occurring in this field of diffusion studies. Noting that the type and complexity of innovations has grown in the 21st century, they propose a new definition of diffusion of innovation:

> Innovation diffusion is the process of the market penetration of new products and services, which is driven by social influences. Such influences include all of the interdependencies among consumers that affect various market players with or without their explicit knowledge. (p. 92)

They go on to describe several of the most important features of diffusion relevant to this definition. With regard to diffusion of innovations within markets and technologies, researchers have modified earlier models' reliance on interpersonal communication such as word-of-mouth as the chief driver of diffusion. Peres et al. (2010) show that this concept has been extended to include additional social interdependencies of all kinds, such as network externalities (the attractiveness of a new product increases as more consumers adopt it) and social signals (the social information potential adopters infer from the adoption of an innovation by others). Second, they note that many diffusion life cycles depart from the traditional smooth sigmoid curve to exhibit unique features, turning points that they term 'takeoffs' and 'saddles'. A takeoff is the transition from introduction of the new product into its growth phase, characterized by a dramatic increase in sales, seemingly stimulated not by social interdependencies but by price and risk reductions. Saddles are fall-offs in sales during early growth followed by recovery. These sudden dips or troughs can occur when changes in technology or negative macroeconomic events are magnified by consumer interactions, or are due to differences in adoption groups who adopt at different rates and who do not communicate with each other. The third feature of the diffusion process they describe is termed 'technology generations'. As innovations saturate the market, leaving few potential adopters, marketers introduce newer generations of the technology, thus stimulating a new round of adoption. Thus a remarkable similarity between the field of technology adoption and that of fashion adoption is that each field is characterized by avid groups of innovators eagerly awaiting the newest version of the product, which is equally eagerly supplied by the manufacturer.

The final new field of study in diffusion models that Peres et al. (2010) discuss encompasses the ever prevalent social networks interpenetrating modern life (c.f., Wejnert 2002). As these new forms of social life use technology to greatly facilitate interpersonal communication or social interactions, researchers have focused on understanding their structure and function and the important roles central individuals play in influencing diffusion. These individuals can be thought of in traditional terms as opinion leaders or influentials, but the common term used to depict them in social networks is hubs, people with a large number of social ties (Goldenberg et al. 2009). Researchers and theorists see hub behavior in modern online social networks to be different from its offline counterpart. Modeling diffusion in online social networks is often done using agent-based models such as neural networks, cellular automata, and small-world models, in which individual behavior is prescribed to the 'agents' as decision rules, the parameters are set, and the model describes their activities over time (Barabasi 2002; Centola 2010; Goldenberg et al. 2009). These approaches thus link individual adoption behaviour to the final diffusion pattern by aggregating numerous individual decisions over the network. These programs can mimic online behavior and help explain the patterns observed there. Much of the cutting edge research on diffusion takes place using these modeling approaches.

For example, most traditional studies of diffusion networks are based largely on the normal distribution and the S-shaped curve description of diffusion pioneered by Rogers. They are derived from epidemiological models of disease and assume a random distribution of innovators and influencers. In diffusion models, the innovators, the first individuals to adopt the innovation, influence the opinion leaders (influencers), who are the hubs of social networks (Barabasi 2002), and these highly connected individuals pass along the news of the innovation to the many social contacts to whom they are linked. These diffusion models are characterized by a 'spreading rate', representing the likelihood that the innovation will be adopted by a person introduced to it and by a 'critical threshold', a property of the network reflecting the point at which the innovation will dominate or die out depending on whether the spreading rate exceeds the critical threshold. Gladwell (2000) was referring to the critical threshold, which he termed the 'tipping point', and Alkemade and Castaldi (2005) describe it as a 'cascade', the point at which the innovation reaches the majority of the network.

Such modeling efforts often share similar elements or concerns. These include focusing on either the role of an external source or agent (mass media, marketing agency) seeking to introduce the innovation into a social network, or how the members of the network (opinion leaders, opinion followers) themselves influence the spread of the innovation (Strang and Soule

1998). For example, Van den Bulte and Lilien (2001) show that *Medical Innovation*, the influential study by Coleman et al. (1966), incorrectly identified social contagion (word-of-mouth among physicians) as the driver of the decision to adopt tetracycline. Instead, they argue, aggressive marketing efforts may have played an important role. Other papers combine the external influence of change agents with the internal activities of the social network members to model diffusion. Alkemade and Castaldi (2005) describe the spread of a new product in a social network as a manifestation of an epidemic or herd behavior. Their approach is to simulate the behavior of members of a social system with a genetic algorithm in a study of network economics. They model the network to consist of consumers who must decide to buy or not buy a new product. The consumers decide based on their own preferences and the decisions of their neighbors. For instance, Kozinets et al. (2010) examine the effects of word-of-mouth marketing or WOMM, the strategy some marketers use when they intentionally influence consumer-to-consumer communications in social media by seeding the network with paid bloggers who promote the product. This interaction between the external change agent and the members of the network produces different narrative forms of word-of-mouth in online communities. This strategy takes advantage of the change in marketer/consumer relationship described by 'coproduction' of the brand and its promotion by consumers who actively change and shape what the marketers give them into unique, creative productions. Kozinets et al. (2010) discovered that the marketing messages are not merely amplified and diffused; they are altered and transformed into new narratives that appeal to different audiences.

Other attempts to model the social process of diffusion emphasize the importance of psychological factors characterizing consumers as important influences. For example, Janssen and Jager (2001) created a multi-agent simulation of a social network to reflect consumer interactions and social influence. The social network was structured to reflect the small-world effect (people are connected to each other by a minimal number of links) and the clustering effect (people's acquaintances tend to overlap). By systematically varying the innovation preferences of consumers, social and marketplace influences, and size of social system, they showed how important psychological variables such as social networks, preferences, and the need for identity influence diffusion of an innovation.

Although such models have served well in marketing to predict new product success, recent developments in network science have supplemented them with new models of networks that might be a more accurate description of both the physical and social worlds. Some of the newer research into modeling diffusion challenges the assumptions of the traditional models. The growth of the Internet and the many social networks that it has spawned have produced entirely new views of networks. Scholars in a variety of fields study the spread of new things or new behavior through online social networks by modeling social network structure and the behavior of individuals within it. The key difference in the new modeling approach is abandoning the assumption that the innovators and opinion leaders are randomly distributed in the network (Barabasi 2009). Instead, the newer models propose that instead of being randomly wired together, networks are 'scale-free', that is, instead of being randomly related, the elements of the network are more clustered. Instead of following a Poisson distribution predicted by random network theory, these networks follow power law distributions in which certain individuals have many more links with others so they act as 'hubs' of social influence. This occurs because as new nodes or individuals are added to the network, they are attracted to the more connected nodes by a process Barabasi (2009) terms 'preferential attachment'. Thus, by making different assumptions about the typology of the network, researchers are better able to construct models of social influence, especially on the Internet where so much of the interest in social network theory has recently focused.

The benefit of adopting this new perspective is illustrated by Alkemade and Castaldi (2005), who show that firms can learn from the behavior of these networks how to improve their advertising. They contrast the spread of an innovation introduced by an agency into randomly connected networks, 'star' networks that have a key opinion leader who influences many other members of the network, and regular networks, which lack such opinion leaders. They find that agencies can achieve advertising efficiencies through directed advertising even when limited information about consumers is available. In another study, Centola (2010) modeled the influence of the social network itself on the spread of behavior in an experiment. Centola created artificially structured online health communities. Participants were recruited from health-interest web sites and assigned randomly to one of two experimental conditions defined by the topological structure of their network. One consisted of a random network, the other condition consisted of a 'clustered-lattice' network in which there was a high level of clustering of the members. The latter is a version of the scale-free type of network described by Barabasi (2002, 2009). Findings such as these show that diffusion is a pervasive characteristic of online environments and that social influence is a powerful driver of the spread of new things online.

8.3.3.2 Adoption models

While the diffusion models discussed above describe the spread of new things in social systems, many scholars strive to model the adoption decision process at the individual level by detailing the antecedents of the adoption decision. Although not formally a model, Wejnert (2002) presents a conceptual framework that integrates several of the commonly studied variables in sociology that impact innovation adoption. Much like the diagram in Figure 8.1, this framework consists of three categories of influences: characteristics of the innovation itself, characteristics of the decision makers (especially the innovators), and characteristics of the environmental context in which the adoption decision is made as potential moderators.

In Wejnert's (2002) framework, the two most important characteristics of the innovation itself are the public versus private consequences of the innovation's adoption on entities other than the actor (public consequences) versus the actor itself (private consequences) and the perceived benefits versus costs of the innovation. Examples of innovations that result in public consequences are those that involve collective actors (e.g., countries, states within countries, and social movements) that are concerned with policy and legal innovations related to societal well being. Innovations with private consequences are those that concern smaller social collectives such as organizations or peer groups. These innovations improve the quality of individual lives (e.g., new fertility-control methods, regulation of hypertension, or dieting). The distinction is important because the means of directing information about the innovation differs in each situation. 'Innovations with public consequences are mainly adopted when information and imitative models are uniformly distributed around the world. This process is most effective when norms, values, or expectations about certain forms or practices become deeply ingrained in society – institutionalized – and reflect widespread and shared understanding of social reality' (p. 300). Wejnert (2002) proposes mass education and social security systems as exemplars of these types of innovations that spread from country to country. In this light, we might interpret the 2011 uprisings against long-standing governments in the Middle East as manifestations of this type of diffusion; as these countries gradually modernized and became more integrated, it became easier for people to communicate with each other and to organize resistance to their regimes. The role of social communication via the Internet and mobile phones in spreading information is of course a good example of how diffusion through a social system influences the nature of the system. In particular, Wejnert (2002) proposes that the media also play a role in promoting these types of innovations, although we would supplement this explanation with reference to the importance of social networking via the Internet to these profound events. The second important characteristic of the innovation is the assessment of the benefits versus the costs of the innovation. Costs are broadly conceptualized to include both monetary and non-monetary direct and indirect costs (in this conceptualization, risk is counted as a cost). Indirect costs could include upgrading technology and retraining needs. Social costs could be innovation-induced social conflict, societal opposition, or stigmatization of innovation adopters.

Wejnert (2002) reviews many studies showing that innovator characteristics can influence diffusion and adoption. These include such factors as the status of the potential adopter, his or her position in the societal context, and how knowledgeable they are about the innovation. In particular, Wejnert emphasizes the many studies that show how flows of information in social networks significantly influence the spread of innovations through them.

The third component in Wejnert's (2002) framework consists of the environmental context of the innovation's introduction: factors such as the geographical settings in which it diffuses, the societal culture, political conditions, and how globally oriented the potential adopter is, referring to degrees of institutionalization and standardization, compatibility with new technologies, and exposure to media that give access to globally current ideas. Innovations unsuited to an actor's ecological conditions are unlikely to be adopted (e.g., Jansen et al. 1990). Social culture includes belief systems and societal values that influence rates of adoption (e.g., Straub 1994). Political conditions such as stability can retard or promote diffusion (Berry and Berry 1992). Wejnert (2002) cites numerous studies showing that as the world becomes more uniform and integrated politically, economically, and technologically, diffusion of new things can spread more easily than in the past.

Much of the work in modeling individual-level adoption has been done in the area of new technology adoption, perhaps because marketplace acceptance of innovations is so crucial to success in technological fields, and so the models tend to reflect the specific concerns of this field. We discuss some of these adoption models to illustrate new developments in the field.

For example, MacVaugh and Schiavone (2010) review much of the literature on non-adoption of new technology to format a model categorizing innovation diffusion as affected by technological, social structure, and learning 'conditions' as well as how these operate within the context of individual, community or market/industry 'domains'. Their conclusions are highly relevant to the study of innovation adoption across other categories as well. They emphasize that technology adoption is a multidimensional process in which individual behavior is influenced by a wide set of interactions between the conditions and the domains. At the micro level we find differences in learning conditions (individual characteristics of the user). At the meso level variation in social conditions and the community (relationships among individual users) exert their influence. And at the macro level, technological conditions and market/industry (the comparative utility, complementarity, and complexity of the innovation) reflect the general features of the economic context of adoption. In addition, differences in the domains of diffusion affect outcomes. The micro domain level is the behavior of the individual consumer, the meso level is the community of users and their mutual interactions, and the macro level is the market/industry. The interaction of these conditions and domains can explain an innovation's success or outright failure, and the paradox whereby older technologies survive and are not completely supplanted by newer ones.

One of the most influential and widely used models of individual level technological innovation adoption is Davis's (1989) Technology Adoption Model or TAM. Based on the theory of reasoned action originally proposed by Fishbein and Ajzen (1975) and the theory of planned behavior or TPB (Ajzen 1985), the TAM proposed that end user acceptance of a new technology could be explained and predicted quite well based on two factors: the perceived usefulness of the technology and the perceived ease with which the technology could be used. The TAM has over the years been used multiple times to study technological innovation adoption either in a 'pure' form or in combination with other variables. For instance, Swilley and Goldsmith (2007) used the TAM in conjunction with measures of prior e-commerce experience and perceived involvement with m-commerce to explain and predict intention to use this new technology. Yi et al. (2006) developed an original measure of domain specific innovativeness in information technology termed the Adopter Category Description (ACD) to operationalize and compared its performance with an older measure, the Personal Innovativeness in the domain of Information Technology (PIIT). The ACD consists of four short descriptions of adoption behavior corresponding to four of the adoption categories: Innovative Adopters, Early Majority, Late Majority, and Laggards. Their results showed that the two methods of operationalizing innate innovativeness for IT were quite comparable, but suggested some advantages for the newer method. They found that individual innate innovativeness had both direct and indirect effects on intention to adopt an IT innovation and that innovativeness had consistent positive relationships with perceived usefulness, ease of use, and compatibility of the innovation. They also tested two models of the influence of domain specific innovativeness combined with the TAM, a direct effects model (with mediators) and a moderator model. They rejected the role of innovativeness as a moderator of the influence of user perceptions and intended use in favor of the mediating effects model.

As influential as the TAM has been, accumulated evidence from its use has led scholars to modify and expand it. These efforts seem to have culminated in a sweeping proposal for a new model proposed by Venkatesh et al. (2003). These researchers compared the explanatory power of eight existing models of information technology acceptance, including the TAM. Based on these results, the researchers identified seven constructs contained in one or more of these models that significantly explained variance in behavioral intention and use behavior of new information technologies. The new model they propose is termed the User Acceptance of Information Technology or UTAUT. This model contains four primary independent variables representing the most important direct influences on behavioural intention and use behaviour. They are, in order of size of influence, performance expectancy, effort expectancy, social influence, and facilitating conditions. Performance expectancy is defined as 'the degree to which an individual believes that using the system will help him or her to attain gains in job performance' (p. 447). Effort expectancy is 'the degree of ease associated with the use of the system' (p. 450). Social influence is 'the degree to which an individual perceives that important others believe he or she should use the new system' (p. 451). Facilitating conditions are defined as 'the degree to which an individual believes that an organizational and technical infrastructure exists to support use of the system' (p. 453). In the UTAUT model, performance expectancy, effort expectancy, and social influence directly impact behavioral intention, which in turn influences use behavior, while facilitating conditions directly impact use behavior. These relationships are significantly moderated by gender, age, experience with technology, and voluntariness of use. Although the UTAUT represents a significant improvement over the TAM, it is not without its critics, for example Bagozzi (2007), who wishes to replace such deterministic models of adoption with general models of goal-directed decision making that incorporate self-regulation as an influence on the decision.

8.4   CONCLUSION

The theory of innovation diffusion is a large and influential stream of research that has provided considerable knowledge to scientists, marketers, and other decision makers. Its success, however, has brought with it a knowledge base that is becoming increasingly fragmented. This fragmentation will continue because of three prominent features of current diffusion and adoption research. These fragmenting activities, however, do suggest the lines that integration should follow.

First, researchers continue to apply diffusion theories to new products, to new consumers, and in new contexts. For example, technological change, especially new information technologies such as mobile devices and social networks, creates a flood of new things that offer opportunities to study how these new things spread. The adoption of new eco-friendly products and practices (e.g., Jansson et al. 2011) is an important application of diffusion theory that benefits not only consumers and policy makers, but traditional marketing oriented research as well. Each new good or service offers a topic for diffusion study, which can be applied to phenomena rarely studied in the past, but each new application seems to entail modifications to the theory or measures that make such studies less than comparable and thus contribute to a fragmented knowledge base. In addition, studies of adoption in cultures other than the West is becoming more common as the process of globalization increases the affluence of the world's population and its exposure to modern products and services, thereby inviting the application of the theories of adoption and diffusion to more cross-cultural and inter-cultural situations (Tellis et al. 2009). Collating and integrating this variety of findings is an important challenge to researchers.

Second, researchers concern themselves increasingly with the psychological mechanisms lying at the heart of adoption and diffusion to gain an understanding of what is happening in the decision process individuals use when they try, adopt, reject, postpone, and so forth. A recent example of this concern can be found in Castano et al. (2008), who found that initial consumer reaction to really new product concepts, which entail adopting new behaviors or discontinuing past behaviors, may be more positive than actual adoption of them because initial reaction to near future adoption emphasizes benefit-related uncertainties (performance and symbolic uncertainties) while the shift to distant future adoption leads to more consideration of cost-related uncertainties (switching-cost and affective uncertainties).

An important goal for adoption research is to integrate adoption into a larger framework of understanding human decision making such as that proposed by Bagozzi (2007) 'to form a general, parsimonious motivational mechanism most proximal to actual decision making' (p. 246) or the behavioral approach described by Foxall (2010). The latter combines the insights from evolutionary psychology with a behavioral perspective and proposes that consumer behavior can best be described as a continuum from routine everyday purchases to compulsive and addictive consumption. Foxall emphasizes that consumer behavior needs a theory that integrates social, psychological, economic, and neurophysiological mechanisms into a unified causal explanation. Foxall (2010) focuses on the phenomenon of temporal discounting (valuing present rewards over future ones even though they are worth less) as a key component of consumer choice. Foxall and James (2009) explain that a simple reliance on the concept of consumer innovativeness is insufficient to account for adoption behavior and that the important role of involvement in the product category must also be incorporated. As Bagozzi (2007) and Foxall (2010) show, quite different and broad approaches to understanding decision making might be adapted to include innovation adoption as a special case of decision making.

Third, new answers will be forthcoming when researchers bring to bear new technologies and frameworks to studying adoption and diffusion. For example, researchers will apply the new techniques of neuroscience to innovation adoption and to network analysis, perhaps revealing the biological substrate of the activity other researchers have been studying since the field's inception. As more and more consumer behavior comes to be seen from a Darwinian perspective following the path of evolutionary psychology, fundamental insights about the characteristics of innovators and the adoption process will be found (Gill and Saad 2010). However these findings will have to be reconciled with what we already know about adoption and diffusion.

Finally, some effort should be made to more closely integrate the study of adoption operating at the individual, group, or organizational level with the study of diffusion, which concerns itself with the macro topic of the spread of new things through social systems. The former results in the latter. A better integration of these separate theories would benefit especially the users of the theories, namely the innovating agencies who seek to promote the success of their innovations.

A first step that researchers could make in this direction would be to agree on a standard definition of what they mean by 'innovativeness'. As Tellis and Yin (2011) point out, at least three different definitions are prominent in the literature: innovativeness as a 'predisposition or propensity to buy or adopt new products', innovativeness as 'a willingness to change', and innovativeness as 'a preference of new and different experiences'. Because these refer to distinct concepts and are confounded by their differences in level of conceptualization (global, marketplace, product domain) consolidating and compiling research findings will be difficult until researchers become clear which concept and level they are using. The logical second step would be to standardize the measures used to operationalize the concepts in the theory, especially consumer innovativeness itself (Hauser et al. 2006). The key to success in this regard is to standardize and explicitly describe the level of conceptualization at which the measurement is taking place: global, marketplace, or product domain. As noted above, several researchers have developed self-report scales for this purpose, but there is little comparative study of their respective advantages and disadvantages. A systematic effort to develop a standard measure of innovativeness would greatly facilitate work in this area. Ideally, such a measure will be adaptable to and comparable across the different levels at which innovativeness is conceptualized (globally, marketplace, specific domain). The domain specific nature of innovation adoption especially requires that the measure be adaptable and equivalent to the huge variety of fields in which it would be applied. It will need to be short, reliable, and valid and flexible enough to use in different survey modes (interview, self-administered, telephone, online). It will need to be equivalent across cultures and languages. This instrument would be a very powerful tool for researchers to use in studying innovation adoption and permit easier comparisons of findings across studies. This is a lot to ask of an instrument, but other fields in science, not to mention psychology, benefit greatly in the power and scope of their theories by having standardized measuring instruments.

The study of innovation adoption and diffusion has a long history and a bright future. Interest is increasing in several related fields such as marketing, consumer behavior, and network analysis. Increasingly sophisticated methods are being developed for and adapted to its study. As progress is made in understanding this aspect of human consumer behaviour, application of this research to the world of decision makers will undoubtedly benefit the innovative agencies, consumers, and society at large.

NOTE

1. Because the research seems to focus on either the adoption of innovations as a decision process for individuals and diffusion describes the study of the aggregate spread of new things in social systems, these two research streams are mutually reinforcing but clearly distinct in the models, data, and analysis methods they use. The focus in this chapter is largely on the adoption side of the picture to the neglect of the diffusion side, which would require at least an entire separate chapter to review. Thus, only a brief scan of some recent studies of diffusion is presented, with apologies to the scholars in this field.

REFERENCES

Ajzen, I. (1985), 'From intentions to actions: a theory of planned behaviour', in J. Kuhi and J. Beckmann (eds), *Action-control: From Cognition to Behaviour*, Heidelberg: Springer, pp. 11–39.
Alkemade, F. and C. Castaldi (2005), 'Strategies for the diffusion of innovations on social networks', *Computational Economics*, **25** (1–2), 3–23.
Bagozzi, R.P. (2007), 'The legacy of the technology acceptance model and a proposal for a paradigm shift', *Journal of the Association for Information Systems*, **8** (4), 244–254.

Barabasi, A.-L. (2002), *Linked*, New York: Penguin.

Barabasi, A.-L. (2009), 'Scale-free networks: a decade and beyond', *Science*, **325** (5939), 412–413.

Bass, F.M. (1969), 'A new product growth model for consumer durables', *Management Science*, **15** (January), 215–227.

Baumgartner, H. and J.-B.E.M. Steenkamp (1996), 'Exploratory consumer buying behaviour: conceptualization and measurement', *International Journal of Research in Marketing*, **13** (2), 121–137.

Berry, F.S. and W.D. Berry (1992), 'Tax innovation in the states: capitalizing on political opportunity', *American Journal of Political Science*, **36** (3), 715–742.

Cardoso, P.R., H.S. Costa and L.A. Novais (2010), 'Fashion consumer profiles in the Portuguese market: involvement, innovativeness, self-expression and impulsiveness as segmentation criteria', *International Journal of Consumer Studies*, **34** (6), 638–647.

Castano, R., M. Sujan, M. Kacker and H. Sujan (2008), 'Managing consumer uncertainty in the adoption of new products: temporal distance and mental simulation', *Journal of Marketing Research*, **45** (3), 320–336.

Centola, D. (2010), 'The spread of behaviour in an online social network experiment', *Science*, **329**, 1194–1197.

Coleman, J.S., E. Katz and H. Menzel (1966), *Medical Innovation: A Diffusion Study*, New York: Bobbs-Merrill.

Costa, P.T. and R.R. McCrae (1992), *Revised NEO Personality Inventory and NEO Five-factor Inventory Professional Manual*, Odessa, FL: Psychological Assessment Resources.

Davis, F.D. (1989), 'Perceived usefulness, perceived ease of use, and user acceptance of information technology', *MIS Quarterly*, **13** (3), 319–340.

Deslandes, D. and L.R. Flynn (2000), 'Towards a measure of domain specific laggard behaviour', in Dawn Deeter-Schmelz and Timothy P. Hartman (eds), *Society for Marketing Advances Proceedings*, pp. 55–59.

Engel, J.E., D.T. Kollat and R.D. Blackwell (1968), *Consumer Behaviour*, New York: Holt, Rinehart and Winston, Inc.

Feick, L.F. and L.L. Price (1987), 'The market maven: a diffuser of marketplace information', *Journal of Marketing*, **51** (January), 83–97.

Fishbein, M. and I. Ajzen (1975), *Belief, Attitude, Intention and Behaviour: An Introduction to Theory and Research*, Reading, MA: Addison-Wesley.

Foxall, G.R. (2010), 'Accounting for consumer choice: inter-temporal decision making in behavioural perspective', *Marketing Theory*, **10** (4), 315–345.

Foxall, G. and V.K. James (2009), 'The style/involvement model of consumer innovation', in *The Routledge Companion to Creativity*, T. Richards and M.A. Runco and S. Moyer (eds), Oxford, UK: Routledge, pp. 71–87.

Garlington, W.K. and H. Shimota (1964), 'The change seeker index: a measure of the need for variable stimulus input', *Psychological Reports*, **14**, 919–924.

Gatignon, H. and T.S. Robertson (1991), 'Innovative decision processes', in Thomas S. Robertson and Harold H. Kassarjian (eds), *Handbook of Consumer Behaviour*, Englewood Cliffs, NJ: Prentice-Hall, pp. 316–348.

Gielens, K. and J.-B.E.M. Steenkamp (2007), 'Drivers of consumer acceptance of new packaged goods: an investigation across products and countries', *International Journal of Research in Marketing*, **24** (2), 97–111.

Gill, T. and G. Saad (2010), 'Consumer behaviour in the realm of technology', in Hossein Bigdoli (ed.), *The Handbook of Technology Management*, Vol. 2, New York: Wiley, pp. 277–289.

Gladwell, M. (2000), *The Tipping Point*, Boston: Little, Brown and Co.

Goldenberg, J. and S. Oreg (2007), 'Laggards in disguise: resistance to adopt and the leapfrogging effect', *Technological Forecasting and Social Change*, **74** (8), 1272–1281.

Goldenberg, J., S. Han, D.R. Lehmann and J.W. Hong (2009), 'The role of hubs in the adoption process', *Journal of Marketing*, **73** (2), 1–13.

Goldsmith, R.E. (1986), 'Convergent validity of four innovativeness scales', *Educational and Psychological Measurement*, **46** (1), 81–87.

Goldsmith, R.E. (1990), 'The validity of a scale to measure global innovativeness', *Journal of Applied Business Research*, **7** (2), 89–97.

Goldsmith, R.E. (2000), 'Characteristics of the heavy user of fashionable clothing', *Journal of Marketing Theory and Practice*, **8** (4), 1–9.

Goldsmith, R.E. (2002), 'A model of the diffusion process', in Brenda Ponsford (ed.), *Proceedings of the Association of Marketing Theory and Practice*, Vol. 11, Savannah, GA.

Goldsmith, R.E. (2010), 'The goals of customer relationship to management', *International Journal of Customer Marketing and Management*, **1** (1), 16–27.

Goldsmith, R.E. (2011), 'Opinion leadership and market mavens', in Richard P. Bagozzi and Ayalla A. Ruvio (eds), *Wiley International Encyclopedia of Marketing*, Vol. 3., Chichester, UK: John Wiley & Sons, pp. 208–209.

Goldsmith, R.E. and G.R. Foxall (2003), 'The measurement of innovativeness', in *International Handbook on Innovation*, L.V. Shavinina (ed.), Oxford, UK: Elsevier Science, pp. 321–330.

Goldsmith, R.E. and C.F. Hofacker (1991), 'Measuring consumer innovativeness', *Journal of the Academy of Marketing Science*, **19** (3), 209–221.

Goldsmith, R.E., L.R. Flynn and E.B. Goldsmith (2003), 'Innovative consumers and market mavens', *Journal of Marketing Theory and Practice*, **11** (4), 54–65.

Hartman, J.B., K.C. Gehrt and K. Watchravesringkan (2004), 'Re-examination of the concept of innovativeness in the context of the adolescent segment: development of a measurement scale', *Journal of Targeting, Measurement & Analysis for Marketing*, **12** (4), 353–365.

Hauser, J., G.J. Tellis and A. Griffin (2006), 'Research on innovation: a review and agenda for marketing science', *Marketing Science*, **25** (6), 687–717.

Hoffmann, S. and K. Soyez (2010), 'A cognitive model to predict domain-specific consumer innovativeness', *Journal of Business Research*, **63** (7), 778–785.

Hurt, H.T., K. Joseph and C.D. Cook (1977), 'Scales for the measurement of innovativeness', *Human Communications Research*, **4** (1), 58–65.

Jackson, D.N. (1976), *Jackson Personality Inventory Manual*, Goshen, NY: Research Psychologists Press.

Jackson, D.N. (1994), *Jackson Personality Inventory-Revised Manual*, Port Huron, MI: Sigma Assessment Systems.

Jansen, H.G.P., T.S. Walker and R. Barker (1990), 'Adoption ceilings and modern coarse cereal cultivars in India', *American Journal of Agricultural Economics*, **72** (3), 653–663.

Janssen, M.A. and W. Jager (2001), 'Fashions, habits, and changing preferences: simulation of psychological factors affecting market dynamics', *Journal of Economic Psychology*, **22**, 745–772.

Jansson, J., A. Marell and A. Nordlund (2011), 'Exploring consumer adoption of a high involvement eco-innovation using value-belief-norm theory', *Journal of Consumer Behaviour*, **10** (1), 51–60.

Katz, E. and P.F. Lazarsfeld (1955), *Personal Influence: The Part Played by People in the Flow of Mass Communication*, New York: The Free Press.

Keller, E.B. and J.L. Berry (2003), *The Influentials: One American in Ten Tells the Other Nine How to Vote, Where to Eat, and What to Buy*, New York: Free Press.

Kirton, M.J. (1976), 'Adaptors and innovators: a description and measure', *Journal of Applied Psychology*, **61**, 622–629.

Kirton, M.J. (1989), *Adapters and Innovators: Styles of Creativity and Problem-Solving*, London: Routledge.

Kleijnen, M., N. Lee and M. Wetzels (2009), 'An exploration of consumer resistance to innovation and its antecedents', *Journal of Economic Psychology*, **30** (3), 344–357.

Kleysen, R.F. and C.T. Street (2001), 'Toward a multi-dimensional measure of individual innovative behaviour', *Journal of Intellectual Capital*, **2** (3), 284–296.

Kozinets, R.V., K. de Valck, A.C. Wojnicki and S.J.S. Wilner (2010), 'Networked narratives: understanding word-of-mouth marketing in online communities', *Journal of Marketing*, **74** (2), 71–89.

Laukkanen, T., S. Sinkkonen, M. Kivijarvi and P. Laukkanen (2007), 'Innovation resistance among mature consumers', *Journal of Consumer Marketing*, **24** (7), 419–427.

Laukkanen, P., S. Sinkkonen and T. Laukkanen (2008), 'Consumer resistance to internet banking: postponers, opponents and rejectors', *International Journal of Bank Marketing*, **26** (6), 440–455.

Libai, B., E. Muller and R. Peres (2009), 'The diffusion of services', *Journal of Marketing Research*, **46** (2), 163–175.

MacVaugh, J. and F. Schiavone (2010), 'Limits to the diffusion of innovation: a literature review and integrative model', *European Journal of Innovation Management*, **13** (2), 197–221.

Mahajan, Vijay, Eitan Muller and Yoram Wind (2000), *New-Product Diffusion Models*, Boston: Kluwer Academic Publishers.

McDonald, H. and F. Alpert (2007), 'Who are "innovators" and do they matter?' *Marketing Intelligence & Planning*, **25** (5), 421–435.

Meade, N. and T. Islam (2006), 'Modelling and forecasting the diffusion of innovation: a 25-year review', *International Journal of Forecasting*, **22** (3), 519–545.

Midgley, D.F. and G.R. Dowling (1978), 'Innovativeness: the concept and its measurement', *Journal of Consumer Research*, **4** (March), 229–242.

Oreg, S. (2003), 'Resistance to change: developing an individual differences measure', *Journal of Applied Psychology*, **88** (4), 680–693.

Ovans, A. (1998), 'Market research – the customer doesn't always know best', *Harvard Business Review*, **76** (May–June), 12–13.

Ozer, D.J. and V. Benet-Martinez (2006), 'Personality and the prediction of consequential outcomes', *Annual Review of Psychology*, **57**, 401–421.

Pagani, M. (2007), 'A vicarious innovativeness scale for 3G mobile services: integrating the domain specific innovativeness scale with psychological and rational indicators', *Technology Analysis & Strategic Management*, **19** (6), 709–728.

Pallister, J.G. and G.R. Foxall (1998), 'Psychometric properties of the Hurt-Joseph-Cook scales for the measurement of innovativeness', *Technovation*, **18** (11), 663–675.

Paunonen, S.V. and D.N. Jackson (1996), 'The Jackson personality inventory and the five-factor model of personality', *Journal of Research in Personality*, **30** (1), 42–59.

Peres, R., E. Muller and V. Mahajan (2010), 'Innovation diffusion and new product growth models: a critical review and research directions', *International Journal of Research in Marketing*, **27** (2), 91–106.

Rogers, E.M. (1962), *Diffusion of Innovations* (1st edn), New York: The Free Press.

Rogers, E.M. (1983), *Diffusion of Innovations* (3rd edn), New York: The Free Press.

Rogers, E.M. and F.F. Shoemaker (1971), *Communications of Innovations*, New York: The Free Press.

Ryan, B. and N.C. Gross (1943), 'The diffusion of hybrid seed corn in two Iowa communities', *Rural Sociology*, **8** (March), 15–24.

Saaksjarvi, M. and K.P.N. Morel (2010), 'The development of a scale to measure consumer doubt toward new products', *European Journal of Innovation Management*, **13** (3), 272–293.

Steenkamp, J.-B.E.M. and H. Baumgartner (1995), 'Development and cross-cultural validation of a short form of csi as a measure of optimum stimulation level', *International Journal of Research in Marketing*, **12** (2), 97–104.

Steenkamp, J.-B.E.M. and K. Gielens (2003), 'Consumer and market drivers of the trial probability of new consumer packaged goods', *Journal of Consumer Research*, **30** (3), 368–384.

Steenkamp, J.-B.E.M., F. ter Hofstede and M. Wedel (1999), 'A cross-national investigation into the individual and national cultural antecedents of consumer innovativeness', *Journal of Marketing*, **63** (2), 55–69.

Strang, D. and S.A. Soule (1998), 'Diffusion in organizations and social movements: from hybrid corn to poison pills', *Annual Review of Sociology*, **24**, 265–290.

Straub, D.W. (1994), 'The effect of culture on IT diffusion: e-mail and FAX in Japan and the U.S.', *Information Systems Research*, **5** (1), 23–47.

Swilley, E. and R.E. Goldsmith (2007), 'The role of involvement and experience with electronic commerce in shaping attitudes and intentions toward mobile commerce', *International Journal of Electronic Marketing and Retailing*, **1** (4), 370–384.

Szmigin, I. and G. Foxall (1998), 'Three forms of innovation resistance: the case of retail payment methods', *Technovation*, **18** (6/7), 459–468.

Szymanski, D.M., M.W. Kroff and L.C. Troy (2007), 'Innovativeness and new product success: insights from the cumulative evidence', *Journal of the Academy of Marketing Science*, **35** (1), 35–52.

Tellis, G.J. and E. Yin (2011), 'Consumer innovativeness', in Richard P. Bagozzi (ed.), *Wiley International Encyclopedia of Marketing*, Vol. 3, Chichester, UK: John Wiley & Sons, pp. 107–108.

Tellis, G.J., E. Yin and S. Bell (2009), 'Global consumer innovativeness: cross-country differences and demographic commonalities', *Journal of International Marketing*, **17** (2), 1–22.

Van Den Bulte, C. and G.L. Lilien (2001), 'Medical innovation revisited: social contagion versus marketing effort', *American Journal of Sociology*, **106** (5), 1409–1435.

Vandecasteele, B. and M. Geuens(2010), 'Motivated consumer innovativeness: concept, measurement, and validation', *International Journal of Research in Marketing*, **27** (4), 308–318.

Venkatesh, V., M.G. Morris, G.B. Davis and F.D. Davis (2003), 'User acceptance of information technology: toward a unified view', *MIS Quarterly*, **27** (3), 425–478.

Walsh, M.F. and J. Lipinski (2008), 'Unhappy campers: exploring consumer resistance to change', *Journal of Travel & Tourism Marketing*, **25** (1), 13–24.

Wang, H.-C., H.-S. Doong and G.R. Foxall (2010), 'Consumers' intentions to remain loyal to online reputation systems', *Psychology & Marketing*, **27** (9), 887–897.

Wang, H.-C., J.G. Pallister and G.R. Foxall (2006a), 'Innovativeness and involvement as determinants of website loyalty: I. A test of the style/involvement model in the context of internet buying', *Technovation*, **26** (12), 1357–1365.

Wang, H.-C., J.G. Pallister and G.R. Foxall (2006b), 'Innovativeness and involvement as determinants of website loyalty: II. Determinants of consumer loyalty in B2C e-commerce', *Technovation*, **26** (12), 1366–1373.

Wang, H.-C., J.G. Pallister and G.R. Foxall (2006c), 'Innovativeness and involvement as determinants of website loyalty: III. Theoretical and managerial contributions', *Technovation*, **26** (12), 1374–1383.

Wejnert, B. (2002), 'Integrating models of diffusion of innovations: a conceptual framework', *Annual Review of Sociology*, **28** (1), 297–326.

Yi, M.Y., K.D. Fiedler and J.S. Park (2006), 'Understanding the role of individual innovativeness in the acceptance of IT-based innovations: comparative analyses of models and measures', *Decision Sciences*, **37** (3), 393–426.

Zaltman, G. (1965), *Marketing: Contributions from the Behavioural Sciences*, New York: Harcourt, Brace & World, Inc.

PART III

CONSUMER IMPULSIVITY, COMPULSIVENESS AND BEYOND

9 Discounting and impulsivity: overview and relevance to consumer choice

Luís L. Oliveira and Leonard Green

Choice and decision-making are ubiquitous and incessant processes in our lives. Our daily choices range from the most ordinary decisions, such as what to wear and what to have for breakfast, to life-defining ones, such as which college to attend and which job offer to accept. We make decisions that range from the relatively insignificant, as the movie we will watch tonight, to ones as grave as those concerning our health. In many choice situations, we are faced with options that differ in their short-term and long-term consequences. Some of us may be more influenced by the more immediate consequences whereas others may be more influenced by the long-term consequences of the choice options. For example, do we purchase cheaper incandescent light bulbs that are relatively short-lived and energy inefficient, and appliances with a lower initial cost but poor energy efficiency levels, or do we make a larger initial investment in energy efficient light bulbs and appliances in order to save money in the long run? Similarly, many choice situations involve options that differ in the probabilities associated with the outcomes. In these cases, some of us may feel compelled to avoid sources of risk, whereas others may be more prone to taking chances. For example, do we keep our money in an interest-bearing savings account and invest in certificates of deposit that pay a low rate of interest and involve little risk, or do we invest in high-risk but potentially high-return venture capital funds?

The present chapter explores processes of choice and decision-making within a reward discounting framework (i.e., how reward value changes with delay to or probability of receipt of a reward). An understanding of the role of discounting may provide insight into many everyday choice behaviors that are viewed as instances of impulsivity, self-control, and risk-taking.

Over the last two centuries, attempts to understand and model choice behavior have differentially emphasized the role of impulsivity, self-control, and other psychological variables. Following an historical overview of the importance placed on psychological variables throughout different stages of development of choice and decision theories (what Loewenstein (1992) has referred to as the 'fall and rise of psychological explanations'), we show how current models of hyperbolic discounting recognize the influence of such variables. We also explore some of the visceral factors (e.g., hunger, thirst, pain avoidance) that exacerbate the tendency towards choosing immediate temptations, and then discuss how different types of commitment strategies lead to an increase in choice of long-term outcomes.

In the final sections of the chapter, we explore some of the implications of discounting, impulsivity, and self-control for consumer choice behavior, focusing on food consumption and credit card usage, as well as some of the ways in which commitment strategies may help consumers avoid the negative effects of steep discounting and impulsive choice.

9.1   CHOICE AND DISCOUNTING

For research and modeling purposes, many of the choices we make can be conceptualized as being between two different amounts of reward to be received at some point in the future. Naturally, individuals will most likely choose the larger reward if both rewards are to become available at the same time. For example, a child will prefer to receive three candy bars tomorrow rather than just one candy bar tomorrow. Similarly, when facing a choice between two equally sized rewards, individuals will most likely choose the one that will become available sooner – that same child would prefer a candy bar tomorrow to a candy bar next week.

Choices are less easy to make or predict, however, when the options are a smaller reward that one can receive sooner and a larger reward for which one must wait longer. The child from our example might prefer a candy bar right now rather than wait a day for three candy bars. In understanding why the smaller reward might be chosen, psychologists and economists invoke the concept of discounting. It is proposed that the subjective value of the delayed reward (i.e., the three candy bars) is reduced as a function of the time until its availability such that its present value is less than that of the single candy bar that is available right now.

The process of evaluating the present, subjective value of a delayed reward is termed delay or temporal discounting. The typical delay discounting experiment has participants choosing between different hypothetical amounts of money, the larger of which is associated with a longer delay. Depending on the participant's choice, one of the variables (i.e., amount or delay) is adjusted, and the participant is offered another choice, following which the amount or delay again is adjusted. This procedure is repeated until the participant is indifferent between the smaller-sooner and the larger-later reward, providing an estimate of the subjective value of the delayed reward.

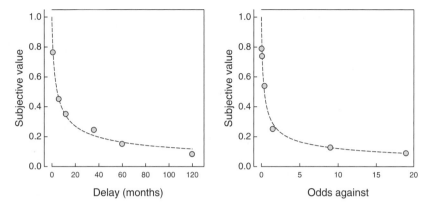

Note: On the left graph, the present subjective value of a $200 delayed reward decreases as the delay to the reward increases; on the right graph, the certain subjective value of a $200 probabilistic reward decreases as the odds against its receipt increases. The curved lines represent the best-fitting hyperboloid discounting functions (Equation 9.3).

Source: Green and Myerson, 2004. Adapted with permission from the American Psychological Association.

Figure 9.1 Examples of delay and probability discounting

For example, in an *adjusting-amount procedure* (Rachlin et al. 1991), an initial choice might be between receiving $100 immediately or $200 in six months. If the participant were to choose to wait the six months, then the amount of the immediate reward would be increased and the participant then would be presented with a choice between receiving $150 immediately or $200 in six months. If the participant now were to choose the immediate amount, then the amount of the immediate reward would be decreased, and the next choice would be between $125 immediately and $200 in six months. This procedure converges on an estimate of the indifference point – that is, the point at which the participant shows no preference for one or the other reward. This procedure is repeated at a number of delays in order to obtain a discounting function that describes the change in subjective value of the $200 reward as the time to its receipt increases (see Figure 9.1, left graph). A similar procedure, the *adjusting-delay procedure* (Mazur, 1987), would present the participant with a choice between $100 immediately and $200 after a specified delay (e.g., six months), but in this procedure the delay to the larger amount is adjusted based on the participant's choices while the amounts are held constant (for a review on different methods used to obtain discounting functions, see Madden and Johnson, 2010).

Steep discounting of delayed rewards may denote impulsivity and impatience, whereas being willing to wait for a larger reward is assumed to reflect self-control (Green and Myerson, 2010). More impulsive or impatient individuals are more prone to accepting smaller, more immediate rewards, as shown by their higher degree of discounting, whereas individuals with greater self-control would, presumably, show a lesser degree of discounting, being more prone to wait for the larger, delayed rewards.

Many choice situations involve uncertainty rather than delay. In such situations, one must decide between a smaller reward that is to be received for sure or is associated with a given degree of certainty and a larger reward that is less certain. For example, one might choose to invest in certificates of deposit, guaranteeing a small return, or choose to make a riskier, but potentially very profitable investment such as venture capital. The process of evaluating the certain subjective value of a probabilistic reward is termed probability discounting.

Probability discounting studies also may use an adjusting-amount procedure similar to that used for delay discounting. To use a similar example, suppose a participant was presented with a choice between $100 to be received for certain and $200 with a 40 per cent chance of receipt. If the participant were to choose the certain reward, then its amount would be decreased on the next choice trial, and the participant would be offered the choice of receiving $50 for certain or $200 with a 40 per cent chance. As is the case with delay discounting, the amount of the smaller reward is decreased or increased in successive trials according with the participant's choices until a point of indifference between the two outcomes is achieved. This procedure is repeated at several probabilities associated with the larger reward to produce a discounting function that plots the subjective value of a $200 reward as the odds against its receipt increases (see Figure 9.1, right graph). (In order to provide a direct comparison with the delay discounting function, the probability, p, is converted into odds against, Θ, such that $\Theta = [1-p]/p$. For both delay and probability discounting functions, then, subjective value decreases as a function of the dependent variable, time to or odds against the larger amount.)

It is important to note that for both delay and probability discounting, subjective values are usually different from their objective or expected values. An individual's decisions are influenced by factors in addition to the amount, delays, and probabilities of the rewards. Such factors include, for example, the individual's current assets, personal tastes, and biases (Kahneman and Tversky, 1979). Similarly to what occurs with delay discounting, differences in degree of probability discounting between individuals may represent differences in underlying psychological processes or traits. In the case of probability discounting, an individual who shows very steep discounting may have greater aversion to risk and thus be less prone to risky behavior in general, whereas an individual who shows shallow discounting may be more willing to take risks. Notice that in probability discounting choosing the larger amount is the more impulsive (i.e., risky) choice whereas in delay discounting choosing the smaller amount is the more impulsive, impatient choice (for a review of both delay and probability discounting, see Green and Myerson, 2004).

Choices often involve delayed or probabilistic losses rather than gains. For example, in a delayed losses situation, an individual chooses between making a smaller payment sooner (e.g., liquidating a debt) or a larger payment later (e.g., due to accumulated interest on the debt). In a probabilistic losses situation, the choice would be between a smaller but certain loss and a larger, probabilistic loss. As with the discounting of gains, the way individuals discount losses also may depend on behavioral tendencies toward impulsivity and risk-taking. In the case of delay discounting, an individual might be averse to making a smaller, immediate payment, thereby paying more in the longer term. In the case of probability discounting, a risk-prone individual might be more likely to choose a larger, probabilistic payment, rather than a smaller, but certain payment.

9.2   IMPULSIVITY IN ECONOMIC THEORIES OF CHOICE: AN HISTORICAL ACCOUNT

The role of impulsivity and other psychological variables that influence how patient or risk-averse people are when faced with choices was recognized in early models of decision-making put forward by economists. However, the dominant models in the field of economics are rooted in the assumption that human decisions are based on the individuals' or markets' rationality.

Loewenstein (1992) identified four stages in the history of intertemporal choice. Early accounts of temporal discounting acknowledged the role of motivation and emotion in an individual's willingness to delay gratification, thus affecting the decision-making process. Specifically, Senior (1836) stated that the existence of interest was fundamental in promoting abstinence from immediate consumption, thereby encouraging investment. In contrast, Jevons (1871) attributed an individual's willingness to delay gratification to the capacity to predict future hedonistic outcomes, thereby allowing the individual to derive pleasure in the present (the 'pleasure of expectation') for which one would thus forego immediate consumption.

In the second stage identified by Loewenstein (1992), a more cognitive approach to the analysis of delay of gratification was developed by Böhm-Bawerk (1889). He denied Jevons' idea that the pleasure associated with future rewards can actually be experienced in the present, and favored the view that the rewards to be received presently or in the future are compared at a cognitive level. According to this view, discounting would occur in part because of the individual's incapacity to accurately imagine future rewards, resulting in the underestimation of how much those rewards will be wanted. Fisher (1930) attempted to formalize Böhm-Bawerk's views on intertemporal choice in mathematical terms by resorting to the use of indifference curves that show how subjective equality between present and future consumption varies with the willingness to wait for future rewards (see Loewenstein, 1992, for details). Furthermore, Fisher tried to advance the psychological account of choice behavior by reiterating the role that some factors have in discounting, as suggested by some of his predecessors. Such factors include self-control, habit, and life expectancy. Fisher broke from Böhm-Bawerk's account by defending the view that steep discounting is more likely to be the product of poverty rather than its cause, and also argued that cultural influences ('fashion') have a major role in determining degree of discounting.

According to Loewenstein (1992), Fisher was unable to integrate his mathematical formalizations with the psychological accounts of discounting. This inability facilitated the abandoning of psychological factors in the third stage of the history of intertemporal choice theories, most notably championed by Samuelson's Discounted Utility (DU) model. In the fourth and last stage, research conducted by both economists and psychologists revealed serious flaws in the assumptions and predictions made by the DU model. Consequently, we have witnessed a return to the inclusion of psychological variables in the explanations and models of intertemporal choice.

9.3   DISCOUNTED UTILITY MODEL

Samuelson (1937) developed the DU model with the purpose of creating an alternative to the measurement of marginal utility. To accomplish this, Samuelson made certain assumptions. One assumption was that individuals will behave at all times in a way that will maximize utility. Another assumption was that all future utilities are discounted in a lawful fashion that could be described by the equation:

$$V = Ae^{-kD}, \tag{9.1}$$

where V is the present value of a future reward of amount A, D is the delay to its receipt, and k is a parameter that represents the discounting rate. The larger the value of k, the steeper the discounting, and the more value the delayed reward loses with time. This exponential decay function is grounded on the notion that the longer one has to wait to receive a reward, the higher the risk that one will end up not receiving it. Furthermore, the function implies that the degree of discounting is the same for any given time interval, irrespective of when in the future that time interval occurs. In other words, it is assumed that the degree of discounting that occurs between tomorrow and the day after is the same as the degree of discounting that occurs between a month from now and a month and a day from now (Green and Myerson, 1996; Prelec and Loewenstein, 1991). This assumption is termed the stationarity axiom, which holds that if an individual is indifferent between two outcomes that are to be received at different delays, then adding a constant delay to both outcomes will not change this indifference (Koopmans, 1960).

Within this framework of normative models of utility maximization, the process of probability discounting occurs in an identical fashion to that of temporal discounting and shares similar assumptions. The expected utility model describes how individuals ought to decide under conditions of risk or uncertainty (Kahneman and Tversky, 1979). Specifically, it is assumed that individuals calculate the expected utility of probabilistic outcomes by multiplying the subjective utility of each of the outcomes by the probability of their occurrence. The outcome yielding the highest expected utility is the preferred alternative (see von Neumann and Morgenstern, 1944).

The assumptions made by these normative models do not take into account factors that have been shown to affect individuals' decisions, such as one's accumulated wealth, individual tastes, behavioral tendencies, and other psychological factors that have long been described as influencing the processes of choice and decision-making (see Loewenstein, 1992, for a review). Samuelson (1937), for his part, was aware of the limitations inherent in the assumptions made by the DU model, and he explicitly enunciated them:

> Our task now is to indicate briefly the serious limitations of the previous kind of analysis, which almost certainly vitiate it even from a theoretical point of view. In the first place, it is completely arbitrary to assume that the individual behaves so as to maximise an integral of the form envisaged in [equation 9.1]. This involves the assumption that at every instant of time the individual's satisfaction depends only upon the consumption at that time, and that, furthermore, the individual tries to maximise the sum of instantaneous satisfactions reduced to some comparable base by time discount. (1937, p. 159)

Consistent with this analysis, Samuelson strongly advised against the application of the DU model to policy-making strategies, stating that 'the idea that the results of such a statistical investigation could have any influence upon ethical judgments of policy is one which deserves the impatience of modern economists' (1937, p. 161).

In spite of this caveat, attraction toward the DU model grew swiftly. The model has been applied to several distinct areas that involve intertemporal choice, from savings behavior to different types of addiction (Loewenstein, 1992; Prelec and Loewenstein, 1991). In fact, the DU model remains the dominant and most widely accepted normative model of rational choice in the field of economics (Ainslie and Haslam, 1992a). Nonetheless, the empirical evidence against the model's assumptions has grown considerably in the last several decades, and alternative models have been proposed.

9.4   EARLY CRITIQUES OF UTILITY MAXIMIZATION MODELS

One of the earliest developments addressing the shortcomings of Samuelson's model was put forward by Simon (1955). Simon criticized the near-omniscient rationality necessarily attributed by the model to *Homo economicus* and argued that a more accurate model needs to assume that individuals behave rationally, although under the limitations of both their access to information from the environment and their computational ability. To account for these limitations on an individual's behavior, Simon introduced the idea of 'bounded rationality'. He considered it necessary to simplify the assumptions made by the classical concept of rationality used in game-theory-based models, in light of the 'complete lack of evidence that [. . .] these computations can be, or are in fact, performed' (p. 104). To this effect, he suggested that when confronted with a choice between different options, individuals would use simplified decision rules, such as the consideration of pairs or triplets of possible options and their respective payoffs, as opposed to evaluating every possible course of action in search of the 'highest attainable point on his preference scale' (p. 99).

Strotz (1955) went further and questioned the intertemporal consistency assumption of utility maximization models, that is, the assumption that individuals decide in an optimal fashion (given their budget constraints) and will always stick to their decision in the future. According to Strotz, individuals' future behavior will typically be inconsistent – or myopic – with their original plan or decision. Such 'dynamic inconsistency' would be in direct contradistinction to the DU model assumption of a constant rate of discounting. Depending on whether the individual realizes this inconsistency, different types of behavior may emerge. If the individual does not realize the existence of this conflict between past decision and present behavior, or between current decision and future behavior, then his behavior will be 'spendthrifty', that is, characterized by cycles of high consumption followed by thriftiness imposed by budgetary constraints. If the individual does realize the conflict, then his behavior will be 'thrifty'. The individual 'may try to precommit his future activities either irrevocably or by contriving a penalty for his future self if he should misbehave' (p. 173). Alternatively, if the individual does realize the conflict but believes he will not be able to stay committed to his decision, he may choose a present course of action 'which will be best in the light of future disobedience' (p. 173). Because of the dynamic inconsistency apparent in choice and decision-making, Strotz defended the adoption of a discounting function that reflects the greater relative value attributed to proximate rewards than to distant ones. More recently, O'Donoghue and Rabin (2001) proposed a model in many ways similar to that of Strotz. In this model, besides 'naïve' (equivalent to Strotz's 'spendthrifty') and 'sophisticated' (equivalent to Strotz's 'thrifty'), O'Donoghue and Rabin introduce the concept of 'partial naïvete'. An individual who is partially naïve shows a more realistic, intermediate level of self-awareness about his own future choice behavior, which is characterized by the underestimation of future behavioral inconsistency. In other words, a partially naïve individual is aware that his future choice behavior will tend to be sub-optimal, but he underestimates the influence of this tendency and does not fully compensate for it when making his present choices.

9.5   ANOMALIES

Concepts such as 'bounded rationality' (Simon, 1955) and 'dynamic inconsistency' (Strotz, 1955) spawned different lines of research that highlighted several anomalies of the DU model. These anomalies question the usefulness of the exponential function for describing discounting phenomena (for reviews on the DU anomalies, see Frederick et al., 2002; Loewenstein and Thaler, 1989; for a parallel between delay and probability discounting anomalies, see Prelec and Loewenstein, 1991).

9.5.1   Exponential vs. hyperbolic discounting

The utility maximization model presented above is described mathematically by an exponential function (equation 9.1), which defines that each additional unit of time before receipt of a reward (in the case of temporal discounting) or each additional unit of risk associated with a reward (in the case of probability discounting) is weighted equally in terms of the discounting of those rewards (Prelec and Loewenstein, 1991). Simply put, the rate of discounting, described by the b parameter,[1] is constant and does not differ across amounts or time or probability. The parameter reflects how steeply an individual or group discounts an outcome. Larger values of b are associated with steeper discounting, and smaller values are associated with shallower discounting, and individuals and groups differ in their degree of discounting. There are two possible implications for the variation in b. In cases involving delay discounting, a large b value could mean that an individual is relatively impulsive or unable to delay gratification in a given situation, or it could mean that the situation at hand carries a high level of risk – for example, waiting for a monetary reward is less risky than waiting for perishable goods and so individuals will show steeper discounting of perishable goods (Estle et al., 2007). In the case of probability discounting, variations in the discounting parameter have the opposite interpretation because the discounting function represents the subjective value of a reward as the odds against its receipt increases (see Figure 9.1). In this circumstance, a steep discounting curve (i.e., large b value) means that the individual is highly averse to risk, preferring a smaller reward for sure; a shallow discounting function is typical of an individual who is more willing to take risks.

In order to provide a more accurate account of the empirical data on discounting phenomena, Mazur (1987) proposed a hyperbolic function of the form

$$V = A/(1 + bX), \tag{9.2}$$

where V and A have the same meaning as that for (9.1). The parameter X represents either delay (for delay discounting) or odds against (for probability discounting), and b represents the rate of delayed or probabilistic discounting. The main difference between equations (9.1) and (9.2) is that, whereas with the exponential function (equation (9.1) the risk rate associated with increasing delays or odds against remains constant, in the hyperbolic function the risk is initially much higher and becomes proportionately lower with each unit of time added to the delay or with increases in the odds against receiving the outcome (Green and Myerson, 1996). In other words, compared with the exponential discounting function, the hyperbolic discounting function predicts that the subjective value of a delayed or probabilistic reward will initially decrease at a higher rate, but will then decrease at a lower rate as the time to or the odds against the receipt of the reward increases (see Figure 9.2 for a comparison between the models).

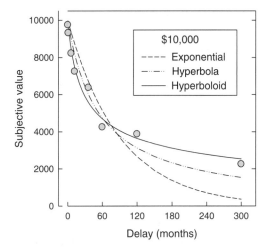

Note: For the exponential function, rate of discounting is constant; for the hyperboloid functions, rate of discounting is higher at shorter delays. The fits provided by the hyperboloid models are significantly better than the fit provided by the exponential model.

Source: Green and Myerson, 2004. Reprinted with permission from the American Psychological Association.

Figure 9.2   *Comparison among the shapes and fits of the exponential (Equation 9.1), simple hyperbola (Equation 9.2), and hyperboloid (Equation 9.3) discounting functions*

The differences between the two proposed forms of the discounting function may be understood as being due to the different strategies followed by economists and psychologists when developing mathematical descriptions of the decision-making process. Economists attempt to derive what individuals ought to do from a rational standpoint based on the DU model; psychologists attempt to derive a mathematical conceptualization based on empirically supported behavioral considerations. Rachlin et al. (1991) showed that the hyperbolic function provides a better fit to group data as compared to the exponential function, and Myerson and Green (1995) then did the same comparison for individual data and concluded that the hyperbola provided significantly better fits at the individual level as well.

One reason why psychologists favor the hyperbolic model is that it is consistent with the Weber-Fechner law, which states that stimulus comparison and discrimination depend not on the absolute difference between the stimuli, but on the ratio between the measures of the stimuli being compared. Accordingly, the perceived difference between tomorrow and the day after tomorrow, for example, would be 30 times larger than the perceived difference between a month and a month and one day – this would explain why the rate of discounting decreases as the delay to or odds against the receipt of a reward increases.

More recently, a more general hyperbolic discounting function has been proposed in which the denominator of the hyperbola is raised to a power (Green et al., 1994b; Loewenstein and Prelec, 1992; Myerson and Green, 1995):

$$V = A/(1 + bX)^s, \qquad\qquad (9.3)$$

where s is a non-linear scaling parameter that reflects the form of psychophysical scaling of amount and/or time (Stevens, 1957; for details on the psychological justification for the s parameter, see Green et al., 1994a). Notice that the hyperboloid (equation 9.3) reduces to a simple hyperbola (equation 9.2) when $s = 1.0$ (see Figure 9.2 for a comparison between the fits).

Myerson and Green (1995) showed that the hyperboloid discounting model provides significantly better fits than an exponential model of similar complexity, that is, an exponential function that also has an extra parameter to account for the fact that individual discounting functions decrease less steeply at longer delays than predicted by equation 9.1. Furthermore, when compared to the exponential model (equation 9.1) and the simple hyperbola (equation 9.2), the hyperboloid also significantly improves the fit to individual data (e.g., Myerson and Green, 1995; Simpson and Vuchinich, 2000). According to Green and Myerson (2004), this ability to account for the data of 'all individual participants is theoretically significant because it suggests that individual differences in discounting are primarily quantitative and may reflect variations on fundamentally similar choice processes' (p. 774). This may also be the case regarding systematic differences in discounting between different groups. For example, data from children indicate that they generally have larger discount parameters and smaller exponents than adults (Green et al., 1994b).

9.5.2   Magnitude Effect

It was previously noted that the parameter b reflects the steepness by which delayed and probabilistic rewards are discounted. More impulsive individuals would display higher b values representing their steeper delay discounting, whereas more self-controlled individuals would show the opposite pattern. Utility maximization theory assumes that, for any given individual, the discounting rate parameter should be the same regardless of the amount of reward being discounted. A large body of

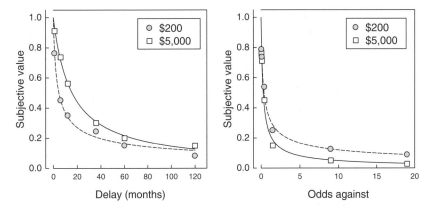

Note: The subjective value of $200 and $5000 rewards (expressed as a proportion of their nominal amounts) is plotted as a function of the time until their receipt (delay discounting) or odds against their receipt (probability discounting). The curved lines represent the best-fitting hyperboloid discounting functions (Equation 9.3). Notice that the effect of amount on the discounting of delayed rewards is opposite that on the discounting of probabilistic rewards.

Source: Green and Myerson, 2004. Reprinted with permission from the American Psychological Association.

Figure 9.3   *Magnitude effect in delay (left graph) and probability (right graph) discounting*

evidence, however, clearly demonstrates that smaller delayed rewards are discounted more steeply than larger delayed rewards. This can be seen in Figure 9.3 (left graph) which shows that the discounting function for the $200 delayed reward is steeper than the function for the $5000 delayed reward. This phenomenon is referred to as the *magnitude effect*, and has been obtained in numerous delay discounting studies using monetary and directly consumable rewards, both real and hypothetical (e.g., Estle et al., 2007; Jimura et al., 2009; Kirby, 1997; Kirby and Maraković, 1996), and a number of other commodities from medical treatments (Chapman, 1996) to vacation time (Raineri and Rachlin, 1993) to job choices (Schoenfelder and Hantula, 2003).

A magnitude effect also is observed in probability discounting studies (e.g., Green et al., 1999a), but the effect of amount on degree of discounting is in the direction opposite that of delay discounting – that is, the larger the probabilistic amount being discounted, the steeper the discounting function. Figure 9.3 (right graph) shows that, opposite to that observed with delay discounting (left graph), the $200 probabilistic reward is discounted less steeply than the $5000 probabilistic reward. Of interest, no systematic effect of amount on degree of discounting has been observed when individuals are discounting monetary losses (e.g., Estle et al., 2006; Mitchell and Wilson, 2010; cf. Ostaszewski and Karzel, 2002).

It is not yet clear why the magnitude effect occurs. Loewenstein and Thaler (1989) offered a 'mental account' explanation for the magnitude effect with delayed rewards. They proposed that individuals treat smaller amounts as spending money ('mental checking account') and larger amounts as savings ('mental savings account'). Longer delays to smaller amounts may be viewed by the individual as a lost opportunity for the immediate consumption of goods, whereas longer delays to larger amounts may be viewed simply as a lost opportunity to accrue interest. Thus, individuals would be more willing to wait for larger than for smaller rewards. The lack of a magnitude effect with losses runs contrary to this hypothesis, provided we assume that small payments and large payments also would be associated with distinct mental accounts (Green and Myerson, 2010). The fact that the magnitude effect has been obtained using a variety of commodities such as duration of good health (Chapman, 1996) and real and hypothetical consumable rewards (Estle et al., 2007; Jimura et al., 2009) presents further problems to this account of the magnitude effect.

Other hypotheses have been advanced to account for a magnitude effect (e.g., see Green and Myerson, 2004; Raineri and Rachlin, 1993). However, the exceptions to the main effect (e.g., lack of a magnitude effect with hypothetical monetary losses) render these tentative explanations incomplete. Whatever the real cause behind the magnitude effect might be, its occurrence in situations involving delayed and probabilistic gains is a robust and general phenomenon, one which cannot be accounted for by the DU model.

9.5.3   Preference Reversals

One of the assumptions made by the DU model is that the discounting rate is constant. This assumption is best captured by the stationarity axiom (Koopmans, 1960). Stationarity means that an individual's preference between a set of rewards should remain unaltered if a common delay is added to the time until those rewards are to be received. In other words, the point of indifference between two alternatives should depend only on the time difference between the smaller-sooner and the larger-later rewards, and not on the absolute delay to the alternatives. For example, if an individual is indifferent between receiving $100 in a month and $200 in two months, then that individual also should be indifferent between $100 in one year and $200 in one year and one month. In practice, however,

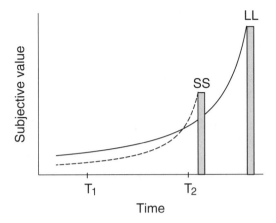

Note: The curved lines show how subjective value changes as a function of time to receiving the rewards according to the hyperbolic model of discounting. The cross-over indicates the point of preference reversal. The heights of the bars represent the nominal amount of reward.

Figure 9.4   *Choice between a smaller-sooner (SS) reward and a larger-later (LL) reward*

the stationarity axiom typically is not observed. People generally will prefer the larger-later reward when both rewards are distant enough in the future, but as time to the rewards approaches, people oftentimes will reverse their preference and now choose the smaller-sooner reward. The preference reversal findings are clearly at odds with the stationarity axiom, a core principle of the DU model, but consistent with the hyperboloid model of discounting (equations 9.2 and 9.3) which assumes that rate of discounting is not constant throughout time.

Figure 9.4 depicts the preference reversal phenomenon. The heights of the bars represent the actual (undiscounted) value of two rewards and the curved lines depict their subjective (i.e., discounted) values as predicted by equation 9.2. The likelihood of choosing a particular alternative at any point in time depends on the relative subjective values of the two rewards. As may be seen, choice of the larger reward is more likely if the decision is made at an earlier point in time (e.g., at T_1), whereas choice of the smaller reward is more likely if the decision is made later (e.g., at T_2). Indeed, both humans and non-human animals show the preference reversals predicted by Figure 9.4 (e.g., Ainslie and Herrnstein, 1981; Green et al., 1981; Green et al., 1994a; for a review of preference reversals, see Rachlin and Raineri, 1992).

For example, Green et al. (1981) described a procedure in which pigeons had to choose between a smaller-sooner reward and a larger-later reward.

When the smaller reward was available after 28 seconds and the larger after 32 seconds, all the pigeons strongly preferred the larger reward. However, when the smaller reward was available after 2 seconds and the larger after 6 seconds, all the pigeons overwhelmingly preferred the smaller reward. These two conditions are analogous to the time points T_1 and T_2 in Figure 9.4, thus illustrating the preference reversal with the passage of time. Using a similar procedure, Green et al. (1994a) observed preference reversals in human participants. For example, the majority of participants in Green et al. preferred receiving $50 in one year and six months to $20 in one year. When the choice was offered much closer in time to reward availability, however, the percentage of participants who now preferred the $50 decreased. This preference reversal was replicated using several delays to the smaller reward, inter-reward delays, and pairs of amounts.

Preference reversals also have been reported with losses. For example, a study on delay discounting of hypothetical monetary losses (Holt et al., 2008) showed that when smaller-sooner and larger-later payments were to be made in the distant future, participants preferred the smaller-sooner payment option. However, as the delay to when these payments were to be made was reduced, preferences reversed and participants now preferred the larger-later payment option. Note that choice of the larger-later option is the more impulsive choice, given that the outcomes are losses.

The phenomenon of preference reversals is not only empirically reliable, but also consistent with our intuition about human choice and decision-making processes. In fact, preference reversals are an almost daily affair; succumbing to a hamburger or a slice of cake when on a diet is a common example. Samuelson, too, was fully aware of this shortcoming of the DU model:

> Contemplation of our particular equations will reveal that the results are unchanged even if the individual always discounts from the existing point of time rather than from the beginning of the period. He will still make at each instant the same decision with respect to expenditure as he would have, if at the beginning of the period he were to decide on his expenditure for the whole period. But the fact that this is so is in itself, a presumption that individuals do not behave in terms of our functions. (1937, p. 160)

Other DU model anomalies have been described that are related in one way or another to those of the magnitude effect and preference reversals (for reviews, see Frederick et al., 2002; Prelec and Loewenstein, 1991). Taken together, the consistent occurrence of such anomalies has weakened the accounts of choice behavior provided by normative models such as the DU model. It is important to note, however, that these anomalies are not to be regarded as mistakes on the part of the individual. Rather, they are 'anomalies' only with reference to 'a model that was constructed without regard to its descriptive validity, and which has no compelling normative basis' (Frederick et al., 2002, p. 365). These anomalies are, then, constancies in the mechanisms underlying our decision-making skills and our choices. In order to properly explain their existence and accommodate their occurrence in models of choice, it is necessary to recognize the role of psychological factors, such as patience, risk-aversion, impulsivity, and self-control. The pervasiveness of these psychological variables in choice behavior is evident in the literature on discounting, which has proven to be a very reliable and far-reaching phenomenon.

9.6   IMPULSIVITY: TRAIT OR TRAITS?

Discounting is a ubiquitous finding (Rachlin, 2006). Individuals discount all types of outcomes, including money, food and drinks, drugs, health, among many others (for reviews, see Green and Myerson, 2004; Odum and Baumann, 2010). Similar findings have been obtained with both real and hypothetical rewards (e.g., Jimura et al., 2009, 2011; Johnson and Bickel, 2002; Kirby, 1997; Kirby and Maraković, 1995), and the hyperboloid discounting function describes the results across age groups (Green et al., 1999b), cultures (e.g., Du et al., 2002; Weber and Hsee, 1998), and species (e.g., Green et al., 2004; Mazur, 2000; Richards et al., 1997; Woolverton et al., 2007).

In view of these findings, it is adequate to consider the possibility that our ability to exert self-control over our own behavior, or, in other words, the extent to which we are unable to control our impulsivity, is a reflection of a personality trait – by which is meant a persistent tendency to behave in a certain manner over a wide array of different environments or situations. To view impulsivity as a personality trait, at least two conditions must be met. First, a clear working definition of the concept of impulsivity is needed. Second, there must be a general tendency for impulsive and/ or risky behavior to be prevalent throughout an individual's lifespan and across a number of behaviors (Green and Myerson, 2010).

Although most researchers likely agree on the classification of a number of behaviors or decisions as reflecting a higher or lesser degree of impulsivity, agreement on a definition of impulsivity is less apparent. Evenden (1999) noted that 'researchers interested in the personality trait of impulsivity, in the experimental analysis of impulsive behavior, in psychiatric studies of impulsivity or in the neurobiology of impulsivity form largely independent schools, who rarely cite one another's work' (pp. 348–349). Considering that, even within psychology, different areas approach the topic of impulsivity from distinctly different research traditions and theoretical approaches, such division seems unavoidable. Within personality psychology alone, the construct of impulsivity receives several different classifications, some of which have become more and more multifaceted over the years (e.g., Barratt and Patton, 1983; Barratt and Stanford, 1995; Dickman, 1990, 1993; Eysenck, 1993).

In the field of behavioral economics, the concept of impulsivity may be defined by the degree of discounting observed. In the case of delay discounting, impulsivity could be equated with impatience or the inability to delay gratification. Impulsive individuals would tend to choose smaller, more immediate rewards over larger, more delayed rewards or, in the case of losses, choose larger, more delayed losses over smaller, more immediate losses. In the case of probability discounting, impulsivity could be defined as a tendency toward risky behavior. Risk-seeking individuals would tend to choose larger, more uncertain rewards over smaller, surer rewards or, in the case of losses, choose larger, more uncertain losses over smaller but certain losses (Green and Myerson, 2010). One way of measuring degree of discounting in a quantitative, directly comparable fashion (across different amounts and different types of discounting) is by using the area-under-the-curve (AuC) method. The AuC measure represents the area under the observed subjective values, and provides a single, theoretically neutral measure of the degree of discounting. Both subjective value and delay or odds against are normalized for purposes of calculating the AuC measure which, as a result, ranges between 0.0 (maximally steep discounting) and 1.0 (no discounting) (for more details, see Myerson et al., 2001).

The first condition required by Green and Myerson (2010) to consider impulsivity a personality trait, namely that of a working definition, is, then, at least partially met by operationally defining impulsivity through its measurement in terms of discounting, such as the AuC measure. The second condition requires that impulsivity be manifested in a reliable and stable fashion. Certain individuals or groups should discount various types of outcomes more steeply than do other individuals or groups, and these differences in discounting should be stable over time and observed across a variety of situations (e.g., with both real and hypothetical rewards).

The results from several studies support the view that impulsivity or the ability to delay gratification is consistent across time and situations. Mischel et al. (1989) placed 4- and 5-year-olds in a choice situation where they could have a smaller reward (e.g., one marshmallow) whenever they wanted, or a larger reward (e.g., two marshmallows) for which they would have to wait 15 minutes. The amount of time they would wait before eating the smaller reward was associated, in follow-up studies conducted about a decade later, with parental reports of greater academic and social competence (Mischel et al., 1988) and with higher SAT (Scholastic Aptitude Test) scores (Shoda et al., 1990).

The findings from studies using delay discounting procedures also are consistent with the conclusion that certain groups of individuals show steeper discounting across a variety of rewards. For example, individuals with opioid dependence discount hypothetical monetary rewards more steeply than controls (Kirby and Petry, 2004; Madden et al., 1997). Similar results were obtained with cigarette smokers (e.g., Bickel et al., 1999), pathological gamblers (Petry and Casarella, 1999), and obese women with binge eating disorder (Manwaring et al., in press), among others.

Given these results, it is plausible to consider impulsivity a single personality trait. If this were the case, then one would expect to find a consistent association between the inability to wait for delayed rewards (steep delay discounting) and the tendency toward risky behaviors (shallow probability discounting). Specifically, delay and probability discounting should be negatively correlated. In contrast, if delay and probability discounting are each associated with different personality traits, then the degree of discounting delayed rewards should not be correlated with the degree of discounting probabilistic rewards. In other words, both types of discounting should be relatively independent, and the correlation between them should be close to zero.

Myerson et al. (2003) assessed the relation between delay and probability discounting. Each participant was studied under both delay and probability discounting tasks, each of which included two amounts of reward. Results showed that the correlation between the areas under the delay and probability discounting curves was near zero or slightly positive. Other studies where both types of discounting were directly compared also obtained positive correlations (Estle et al., 2007; Mitchell, 1999; Reynolds et al., 2004; Richards et al., 1999). These findings suggest that the inability to delay gratification and the tendency to engage in risky behaviors are relatively independent, a result inconsistent with a single-trait account of impulsivity as measured by degree of discounting. These results do not mean, however, that there are not individuals or groups (e.g., drug addicts) who are consistently more impulsive than average and for whom the degree of delay and probability discounting are negatively correlated.

9.7 VISCERAL INFLUENCES IN IMPULSIVITY

Regardless of whether impulsivity is reflected by a single trait, or whether there are separate traits of impatience and risk-taking, among others, the fact remains that some people or groups are more impulsive than others in certain situations involving probability discounting-type and/or delay discounting-type decisions. These individuals are more likely to suffer the adverse effects that often are associated with impulsive behaviors, such as overspending, overeating, and other types of compulsive or addictive behaviors. Understanding some of the factors that increase the likelihood of behaving impulsively could shed insight into the sort of procedures that might be implemented to help avoid engaging in these behaviors. Moreover, identifying those factors and explaining how they affect one's decisions and choices may provide a better understanding of consumer behavior, broadly defined so as to encompass not only the day-to-day purchasing of commodities, but also the making of decisions that relate to health, financial stability, the environment, and certain types of compulsive and/or addictive behaviors (e.g., gambling, substance abuse). By extension, this knowledge could be used by consumers to reduce impulsive consumption or by marketers to explore these impulsive tendencies.

We noted earlier that the hyperbolic discounting model predicts preference reversals – that is, preference shifts from a larger-later reward to a smaller-sooner reward as the latter becomes imminently available. Loewenstein (1996) proposed that a number of visceral factors – hunger, thirst, sexual desire, drug addiction, and pain avoidance – exacerbate the tendency to forego our choice of a larger-later reward in favor of a smaller, more immediate one. The experience of craving associated with visceral factors would cause a disproportionate increase in the desirability of the relevant reward. For example, food would have an increased value for the hungry individual, whereas other types of commodities would have lesser value. Loewenstein explored the effects that timing, intensity, and proximity have when associated with visceral factors.

Loewenstein (1996) noted that people have a hard time imagining the precise consequences of events that are distant in time. For example, people tend to underestimate the level of pain they felt in past situations. Underestimation also occurs when considering future events. For example, one of the causes of substance abuse relapse is that, after a period of abstinence, many addicts believe they are capable of consuming small amounts of their substance of choice without relapsing (e.g., Stewart and Wise, 1992). Individuals often assume that future visceral factors will have little or no influence on the decisions they are making in the present. Such discounting of the effect of future visceral factors could help explain why many pregnant women express the desire to abstain from having an epidural analgesia but change their decision after going into labor (Christensen-Szalanski, 1984).

Another variable that affects how strongly visceral factors affect choice is their intensity. Whereas mild visceral influences might easily be ignored, intense visceral influences may completely override an individual's rational deliberations. Loewenstein (1996) proposed that higher levels of deprivation of, say, food or drugs, would intensify the preference for immediate rewards, thus increasing the discounting rate of the relevant commodity and increasing the likelihood of choosing the smaller-sooner outcome. The effect of deprivation on discounting has been studied in both human and non-human animals, but the results are not always consistent with this assumption, particularly with food and water rewards (e.g., Logue and King, 1991; Richards et al., 1997). More consistent results have been obtained with drug addicts, whose degree of discounting of monetary rewards and their substance of abuse is greater when they are experiencing withdrawal (e.g., Giordano et al., 2002; Odum and Baumann, 2007).

Finally, one's proximity to commodities relevant to each of the visceral factors also plays a role in the degree to which the commodity's value is discounted. One well-known example refers to the finding that children are more likely to wait longer for food snacks if the snacks are present but covered as compared to when the snacks are present and visible. Similar results are obtained when comparing waiting times in the presence of photographs of rewards versus in the presence of the rewards themselves, and also if the children are told to engage in distracting thoughts versus thoughts about the rewards themselves (for a review, see Mischel et al., 1989).

The mere thought or visual representation of a snack can elicit craving, but the sight and smell of, as well as the physical proximity to, the snack will elicit an even stronger appetitive response. Virtually any environmental cue associated with the reward can elicit a visceral appetitive response, but when the reward is not available or when there is no expectation of reward availability, the visceral response tends to be diminished. For example, in a study with heroin addicts and alcoholics, periods of drug availability were alternated with periods of non-availability of the respective drug, and a strong correlation between drug availability and reported feelings of craving was observed (Meyer, 1988).

Visceral factors and the variables that influence their effectiveness have significant effects on choice and may provide an important addition to the hyperbolic model of discounting in understanding why individuals who prefer the larger-later reward may come to reverse their preference and select the smaller-sooner reward. Sensorial cues, proximity, and availability elicit visceral responses (possibly via classical conditioning; Ainslie, 2010) that can increase appetite for the relevant reward, thereby exacerbating the likelihood of making the more impulsive choice.

9.8   COMMITMENT AND OTHER FORMS OF SELF-CONTROL

The degree to which visceral factors and temporal proximity to rewards affect the choices people make is significant. When long-term preferences or plans become threatened by short-term influences, it is as if individuals are divided between two forces, one more impulsive, the other more considered. This sort of psychological conflict, not unlike the one postulated by Freud between id and ego, has received a lot of attention in the decision-making literature. One of the ways in which this sort of decision conflict has been approached relates to the different self-control methods available and the extent to which each of them successfully keeps people's long-term choices from dissolving in the face of more immediate persuasions.

Rachlin (1995) proposed that an individual's likelihood of engaging in self-control can be increased through the use of different forms of external commitment, by which he means 'the self-imposition of behavioral constraints' (p. 111). There are three main forms of external commitment: strict commitment, commitment with punishment, and soft commitment. Strict commitment involves making choices that preclude future opportunities of choosing the smaller-sooner rewards; in other words, the commitment response prevents the occurrence of preference reversals. This form of commitment can be achieved, for instance, through the use of physical restraints. One recurrently used example is that of Ulysses trying to prevent himself from succumbing to the sirens' song and thus wrecking his ship on the rocks. Following Circe's advice, Ulysses filled his men's ears with beeswax and ordered them to tie him against the mast so that he could not escape and they would be unable to hear his future orders to untie him or turn the ship toward the sirens' wail.

Rachlin and Green (1972) developed an animal procedure that illustrates strict commitment. It first is to be noted that when pigeons are presented with a choice between a red and a green key, and choice of the red key leads to 2-sec of food immediately, whereas choice of the green key leads to 4-sec of food but only after a 4-sec period of delay, pigeons overwhelmingly choose the red key (the smaller-sooner reward option). However, if a common delay is added to both alternatives, then the pigeons overwhelmingly choose the green key (the larger-later reward) (see Green et al., 1981). In the Rachlin and Green experiment proper (depicted in Figure 9.5, panel A), pigeons could initially choose between two white (W) keys (Choice 1). After this choice, there was a T-sec long delay, common to both alternatives, the duration of which varied across conditions of the experiment. If pigeons chose the top white key at

A. Strict Commitment

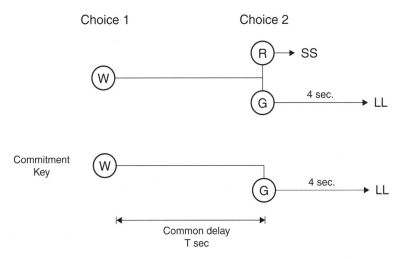

B. Commitment with Punishment

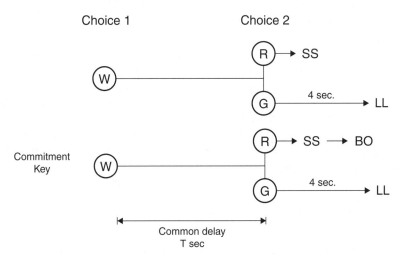

Note: In the strict commitment procedure (top panel), pecking the commitment key (Choice 1) precludes the possibility of a preference reversal (adapted from Rachlin and Green, 1972). In the commitment using punishment procedure (bottom panel), pecking the commitment key does not preclude a preference reversal, but choosing the smaller-sooner reward at Choice 2 is punished with a blackout (BO) period (adapted from Green and Rachlin, 1996). W, R, and G represent the color of the response keys (i.e., white, red, and green).

Figure 9.5   Schematic illustrations of commitment procedures

Choice 1, they would wait for, say, 10 seconds before being confronted with a second choice (Choice 2), this time involving the red (R) and green (G) keys associated with the smaller-sooner and larger-later rewards described above. When then offered the choice between the red and green keys (the SS and LL outcomes, respectively), all the pigeons chose the red key. However, if pigeons chose the bottom white key at Choice 1 (the 'Commitment Key'), only the green key would be presented after the initial 10-sec wait. To put it another way, the initial choice between the two white keys represents an opportunity to make a strict commitment; by choosing the bottom white key, pigeons avoid the future temptation of pecking the red key. Results showed that as the common delay (time T between Choices 1 and Choice 2) increased, preference for the white commitment key also increased. Similar results have been obtained with humans (e.g., Solnick et al., 1980).

The strict commitment exemplified in Figure 9.5 may not be very common in practice, mostly because it is not always desirable or even possible to eliminate any chance of reversing one's decision in the future, especially given that future conditions could change. A more flexible alternative is available and, possibly, preferable, namely commitment with punishment. Green and Rachlin (1996) conducted an experiment similar to the one described above except that if the pigeons chose the white commitment key, Choice 2 still included both the red and green keys (Figure 9.5, panel B). However, if at Choice 2 the pigeon chose the red key, the smaller-sooner reward would be followed by a prolonged period of darkness (a punitive outcome for pigeons). Results again indicated that as the common delay (T) increased, preference for the white commitment key increased. In this case, even though pigeons are given the opportunity to reverse their preference for the larger-later reward, the punishment contingency in effect prevented them from doing it most of the time, although, interestingly, not all the time.

Depending on the form and severity of the punishment contingencies used, this type of commitment can be as strong as that of strict commitment. Schelling (1992) offers one such example:

> In a cocaine addiction center in Denver, patients are offered an opportunity to submit to extortion. They may write a self-incriminating letter, preferably a letter confessing their drug addiction, deposit the letter with the clinic, and submit to a randomized schedule of laboratory tests. If the laboratory finds evidence of cocaine use, the clinic sends the letter to the addressee. An example is a physician who addresses the letter to the State Board of Medical Examiners confessing that he has administered cocaine to himself in violation of the laws of Colorado and requests that his license to practice be revoked. Faced with the prospect of losing career, livelihood, and social standing, the physician has a powerful incentive to stay clean. (p. 167)

Of course, very few commitment situations actually involve such restrictive levels of punishment. More commonly, an individual might pledge to donate a significant amount of money to a hated cause or institution. Publicly announcing resolutions may also provide additional motivation to see them through in order to avoid being embarrassed or seen as weak-willed.

The third type of external commitment, 'soft commitment', is identical in nature to the punishment commitment in that it is possible to reverse one's choices but doing so involves a cost. However, whereas punishment is contingent upon the receipt of the smaller-sooner reward, the cost associated with soft commitment is incurred before or during the impulsive behavior. For example, Siegel and Rachlin (1995) describe a procedure in which pigeons chose between a red and a green key, each of which is associated with an outcome similar to the ones used in the two experiments described above. In the experiment, the pigeons had to make a total of 31 responses, distributed in any way across the two response keys, and the key on which the last peck occurred determined whether the smaller-sooner or larger-later reward would be delivered. The time to complete the first 30 keypeck responses is analogous to the common delay between Choices 1 and 2 in the previous experiments. Because making 30 responses takes a considerable amount of time, the pigeons would often begin pecking the green key (which led to the larger-later reward). Although they could change over to the red key as time to food delivery approached, the pigeons were much less likely to switch if they initially began pecking the green than if they were pecking the red key. Pecking the green key is, then, a form of commitment that can reduce the likelihood of changing over to the red key as time to the reward approaches. (For a detailed description of the different types of commitment and some examples, see Rachlin, 2000.)

Some theorists have offered a broader view of commitment, one which includes internal mechanisms of commitment. For example, Hoch and Loewenstein (1991) describe the choice between impulsive and non-impulsive alternatives as a struggle between the individual's desires and willpower. Self-control methods then fall into one of two general categories: reduction of the desire for the impulsive choice, and enhancement of one's willpower. Some of these methods can be analyzed in terms of environmental constraints and contingencies associated with the individual's choice. For instance, 'avoidance' is a type of desire-reduction method that consists of staying away from the environment in which the tempting choices are presented – a person who is trying to stop smoking might be better off avoiding social situations associated with tobacco consumption altogether (a form of commitment).

Other methods are of a more cognitive and/or emotional nature. For example, 'postponement' is another desire-reduction method that entails the use of self-enforced rules to avoid making purchases on impulse. To enhance willpower, an individual would think about the negative consequences that are associated with immediate consumption ('economic cost assessment') or consider the positive aspects of waiting for the larger-later reward ('time binding') (Hoch and Loewenstein, 1991). Some authors claim that our capacity for self-control improves with age, in part because we learn to successfully devalue the impulsive alternatives by associating negative emotions such as guilt, fear, and disgust with the smaller-sooner rewards (e.g., Frank, 1992). In different circumstances, self-control can be best achieved by inhibiting certain emotions (Ainslie, 1992). Rachlin (1995) includes most of these processes under the 'internal commitment' category, and states that this concept 'fails on both theoretical and empirical grounds' (p. 113), in part because these processes (i.e., thoughts and emotions) are not directly observable and can be inferred or speculated upon only based on verbal reports or physiological measurements.

In order to explain individual choices that are not under the influence of commitment strategies without resorting to such a wide array of hypothetical constructs, Ainslie (1975; see also Ainslie and Haslam, 1992b; Rachlin, 1995) proposed that individuals develop 'personal rules' that bundle a foreseeable series of similar choices. For example, someone on a weight-loss diet knows that they will face an almost countless number of opportunities to eat calorie-dense snacks. Single instances of indulgence may have a negligible effect on the diet, but they may change the individual's perception about her ability to resist future urges to eat snacks. Thus, exerting self-control in single choice situations may help maintain the expectation of long-term success. Some studies support the idea that bundling a series of similar individual choices may increase self-control (e.g., Ainslie and Monterosso, 2003; Kirby and Guastello, 2001).

9.9   APPLICATIONS

We showed how the form of the discounting function is hyperbolic and how the hyperbolic model of discounting explains the occurrence of preference reversals. We then noted how some of the causes of impulsive behavior relate to visceral factors such as hunger, sexual drive, and pain avoidance. Finally, we discussed various types of commitment strategies that provide ways for people to deal with impulsivity and increase the likelihood of their engaging in self-control behavior. In the final section of the chapter, we illustrate how the hyperbolic model and our understanding of impulsivity and self-control methods can be applied to select areas of real-life problems and, to some extent, ameliorate them.

9.9.1   Food Consumption and Obesity

Many of the decisions we make on a daily basis relate in one way or another to caloric intake: what foods to purchase, what to eat, when or where to eat. Evolutionarily, humans are hardwired to find sweet and fatty flavors reinforcing, presumably due to the fact that these flavors tend to occur in foods that are high in calories (high-energy-dense food items) and that such food items were relatively hard to come by (e.g., Saad, 2006). This may be a reason why the visceral cravings for food described in Loewenstein (1996) are so pervasive and hard to control. In present society, it is clear, however, that such adaptive tendencies may lead to maladaptive behavior due to the abundance and accessibility of food items that are high in sugar and fat content. In particular, people with a stronger tendency to ingest high-calorie foods will be at higher risk of becoming overweight or obese because of the imbalance between the amounts of calories consumed and spent. The health consequences of obesity are grave and well known. Obesity is the leading cause of death in the world, particularly in Western societies; it plays a crucial role in the development of cardiovascular diseases, stroke, diabetes, musculoskeletal disorders, and certain types of cancers (WHO, 2011).

From a behavioral economics point of view, there are several important factors that relate to the causes of obesity, the understanding of which then might suggest possible solutions. We can consider factors that influence which of several different food items to choose, or whether to consume food or engage in other activities, and how to balance our current food consumption with future health outcomes.

Obesity has been linked to an inability to delay gratification or to self-regulate caloric intake. For example, Bonato and Boland (1983) showed that obese children show steeper discounting than do normal weight children, but only when the reward is edible. This difference may be because the reinforcing value of food is greater for obese individuals than for non-obese individuals (e.g., Saelens and Epstein, 1996). However, other studies seem to indicate that individuals who are less capable of self-regulation also are more likely to become obese in the future (Francis and Susman, 2009; Seeyave et al., 2009). In addition, the ability to delay gratification for edible rewards is associated with long-term positive social outcomes such as academic achievement (Mischel et al., 1989). In other words, perhaps it is not only the case that obesity leads to more impulsive food-related behaviors, so much as the fact that more impulsive individuals are more likely to prefer smaller-sooner to larger-later rewards.

Other causes of obesity are related to the process of food purchasing. Notably, monetary resources influence which foods a household purchases. Higher income households purchase larger amounts of more healthy as well as less healthy food items, and lower income families consume fewer fruit, vegetables, and fiber, and obtain a higher proportion of their caloric intake from fat (French et al., 2010). This differential purchasing pattern could help explain the high correlation between socio-economic status and obesity (Drewnowski and Specter, 2004). Another study reported that individuals from lower income households purchase their food mostly based on taste and cost (Glanz et al., 1998). This finding is important because several studies have shown that healthier diets (those lower in fat and which include more fruits and vegetables) tend to be more expensive (e.g., Cade et al., 1999) and that energy-density shows a negative correlation with price (e.g., Drewnowski and Darmon, 2005, but see Lipsky, 2009).

Results from behavioral interventions aimed at increasing consumption of fruit and vegetables and decreasing consumption of fat and sugar in children show that providing information and the tools necessary to make better food choices to parents may be an effective way to reduce child obesity (Epstein et al., 2001). Goldfield and Epstein (2002) also have shown that by increasing the behavioral cost (i.e., required effort) associated with consumption of snack foods, children are more likely to substitute these with fruit and vegetables – in other words, increased effort to obtain the smaller-sooner reward reduces its value, which makes choice of the healthier food outcome more likely.

One's level of food deprivation also has been associated with what appears to be curious food purchasing patterns. Nisbett and Kanouse (1969) reported that normal weight individuals tend to purchase greater amounts of food at the supermarket when hungry; however, obese individuals show the opposite pattern, actually buying more food when shopping just after a meal. If indeed these differences are significant and reliable, then individuals who are trying to lose weight should either eat or fast just prior to a visit to the supermarket depending on their current weight level.

As mentioned above, the occurrence of obesity depends only in part on caloric intake. The amount of calories expended also is of obvious importance, and the balance between caloric intake and expenditure must be understood. Sedentary behavior is increasing in both developed and developing countries and in both adult and young individuals (e.g., Bernstein et al., 1999; Durant et al., 1994). Furthermore, certain sedentary behaviors, such as television watching, seem to be complementary to eating, in both children (Epstein et al., 2005a) and adults (Gerbner et al., 1982). Limitations in time resources necessitate that increases in certain types of activities produce decreases in the amount of time devoted to other activities. That is, increases in activities such as television watching or playing video games are associated with decreases in the amount of physical activity. Likewise, if one could increase the number of hours of physical activity, the amount of sedentary behavior and the complementary food intake behavior would necessarily decrease (Epstein et al., 2005a, 2005b).

In summary, there are a number of factors associated with food purchasing, food consumption, and exercise that ultimately change the balance between caloric intake and expenditure. By understanding how these variables affect the discounting of food rewards, and the visceral influences associated with hunger, we may be in a better position to devise personal strategies to control our impulses for consumption of unhealthy foods. This knowledge may also inform possible plans of action at the government level, both to reduce its healthcare spending and to increase the health of individuals.

9.9.2 Credit Cards and Other Consumer Contracts

The introduction of credit cards allowed the middle class to significantly improve their quality of life by empowering individuals as consumers (Bernthal et al., 2005). This facilitation of the consumption process comes with a price, however. Several studies indicate that, when in possession of a credit card, people are more likely to make purchases (e.g., Hirschman, 1979; Feinberg, 1986) and more willing to pay more for identical goods (e.g., Prelec and Simester, 2001). As consequence, credit card debt has become a serious problem for a large percentage of credit card holders in the United States (Bernthal et al., 2005), and there is growing concern about this problem in several Asian countries (Wang et al., 2011).

The use – and particularly the misuse – of credit cards may be associated with the individual's level of impulsivity (Ottaviani and Vandone, in press; Wang et al., 2011). Few studies have investigated behavioral economic aspects of credit card use, but discounting and the influence of visceral factors on choice behavior would appear to be significant factors in the phenomena of over-purchasing and high levels of debt.

An individual is more likely to purchase a product on credit that he or she cannot afford because the loss associated with the purchase (in terms of available financial resources) is delayed, and so the costs are discounted. From a discounting perspective, because larger delayed losses may come to be preferred to immediate smaller losses, individuals may over-indulge in impulsive and even more deliberative purchases. Importantly, the discounting of losses may also help explain the increasing debt problem. As mentioned previously, preference reversals occur in the discounting of losses (Holt et al., 2008). As a consequence, an individual who may plan to pay off much of his credit card debt when the bill arrives, may then change his preference and choose to pay the minimum amount, thereby incurring the delayed but greater monetary loss.

It is to the credit card companies' advantage to exacerbate or facilitate this preference reversal 'trap'. For example, 'credit card statements that prominently highlight low minimum monthly payments as opposed to the total debt invite users to discount the total economic cost of their purchases' (Bernthal et al., 2005, p. 140). Other marketing strategies allow consumers to delay the negative consequences of their debt. For instance, 'card shuffling' consists of using several credit cards with different features that allow the consumer to transfer debt from card to card and prioritize different debts. Converting credit card debt into different forms of revolving credit also allows debtors to continue using their credit cards (Bernthal et al., 2005).

Shui and Ausubel (2004) describe other time inconsistencies in individuals' choice of credit cards. For example, significantly more customers prefer credit cards with lower introductory interest rates to those with higher introductory interest rates, even when, in the long run, the latter is the better choice (i.e., lower effective interest rates), a phenomenon they termed 'rank reversal'. Moreover, the customers who choose the lower initial rates fail to switch again to a different credit card at the expiration of the introductory offer, despite receiving several new solicitations to do so. This tendency to choose more attractive short-term offers is comparable to a choice of a smaller-sooner reward. Furthermore, the tendency to stick with one's initial choice (in spite of it eventually becoming disadvantageous) is reminiscent of soft commitment (see Rachlin, 2000).

Another reason why so many individuals make poor choices of credit cards is that they have overly optimistic expectations about their credit card usage, specifically about the possibility of becoming indebted (Ausubel, 1991; Yang et al., 2007). According to Yang et al. (2007), 'the more prone consumers are to unrealistic optimism, regarding their future borrowing behavior, the more likely they are to prefer credit cards with features that are sub-optimal in light of their actual borrowing behavior' (p. 170). Consistent with this result, several authors have indicated that it is mostly the naïve or partially naïve (O'Donoghue and Rabin, 2001) consumers who tend to choose inadequately in face of their financial profile (e.g., DellaVigna and Malmendier, 2004; for a review, see Heidhues and Kőszegi, 2010).

D'Astous and Miquelon (1991) argue that consumers can be educated so as to facilitate a realistic assessment of their borrowing behavior and to adequately compare the different credit card plans available. This information could be provided by governmental agencies, but 'such intervention will have an impact only if the information programs conceived allow consumers to improve the quality of their decisions' (p. 293).

Educating the consumer to make optimal decisions regarding which credit card to choose may be particularly difficult, however, because the credit card market purposefully targets naïve consumers and their systematic decision-making mistakes (DellaVigna and Malmendier, 2004). Additionally, if a common misperception becomes salient and consumers correct for it, the market adjusts accordingly (see Ausubel, 1991). For example, Bar-Gill (2008) noted that '[w]hen consumers focused on annual fees, issuers charged high interest rates. When interest rates became salient, issuers began adding late fees and other less relevant prices' (p. 772).

Credit card plans are not the only type of consumer contract in which the market exploits customers' time inconsistency and unrealistic optimism toward their future behavior. Bar-Gill (2008) describes how rebates are a good example of a 'misperception-based pricing' (p. 769). Suppose a number of sellers offer a product for a competitive price of $100. One of the sellers may try to explore consumers' naïveté by introducing a price of $110 and offer a $20 rebate, hoping to attract customers from other sellers by advertising the post-rebate price. In order for this seller not to lose money, at least half of the customers must not redeem their rebates, which, it appears, is usually the case (see Sovern, 2006). In order for this offer to be advantageous, the post-rebate offer ($90) must attract more customers than would have the fixed price of $100. This will occur so long as a number of naïve consumers overestimate the likelihood of redeeming their rebate.

Health club enrollment practices provide another example of how customer naïveté may produce sub-optimal choices. DellaVigna and Malmendier (2006) describe how members with a $70 monthly contract which permits unlimited access, actually attend the gym 4.8 times per month, on average, when the pay-as-you-go contract charges $10 per visit. Members with a monthly contract pay an average of 70 per cent more than members who pay per visit, and as many as 80 per cent would save money with a pay-as-you-go contract.

There are commitment strategies one can implement so as to avoid behaviors such as the ones described in the examples above. Prelec and Simester (2001) describe how willingness-to-pay dramatically increases (with premiums reaching over 100 per cent for goods of uncertain market value) when participants are instructed to use their credit card rather than paying in cash (see also Feinberg, 1986). It is plausible to assume that committing to not using the credit card by simply leaving it at home and carrying cash instead (strict commitment) would lead to a decrease in spending behavior. Likewise, committing to redeem rebates by setting up undesirable contingencies in case one does not follow through (commitment using punishment) may also increase the likelihood of redeeming one's rebate offers. Alternatively, one could commit to spending the rebate money on a desired good.

There are numerous other examples that illustrate how the market designs consumer contracts that target the unrealistic optimism that consumers have about their own future behavior. These consumers' naïveté may lead them to display sub-optimal choices with respect to life insurance, mail order purchases, and mobile phone contracts, among others (DellaVigna and Malmendier, 2004). The processes of impulsivity and discounting also may provide a valuable framework for increasing our understanding of other behaviors that may be less directly related to consumer behavior. Some examples include environmentally friendly behaviors, health-related behavior, gambling and other compulsive behaviors, addictive behaviors, and impulsive buying (for reviews of the role of visceral processes and discounting on these behaviors, see, e.g., Loewenstein, 1996; Odum and Baumann, 2010).

The pervasiveness of discounting and visceral factors in choice and decision-making processes are a strong indicator of their importance in almost all areas of consumer behavior. Future research should try and further our understanding of how consumers' choices are affected by their impulsivity and how the market exploits their naïveté. Research on how different commitment strategies extend to different areas of consumer behavior can aid in the development of programs aimed at informing the population about these commitment strategies, thereby helping consumers make better use of their financial resources and better control their impulsivity or develop more efficient self-control behaviors.

ACKNOWLEDGEMENTS

Preparation of this chapter was supported by a fellowship from the Foundation for Science and Technology (FCT, Portugal) to Luís Oliveira and by a grant from the National Institutes of Health (Grant Number MH055308) to Leonard Green. We thank Mark Povich for comments on an early version of the chapter.

NOTE

1. Henceforth, we will denote the discounting rate parameter as b. This b parameter is comparable to the k parameter (equation 9.1) used in formulas representing delay discounting, and to the h parameter used in formulas representing probability discounting.

REFERENCES

Ainslie, G. (1975), 'Specious reward: a behavioral theory of impulsiveness and impulse control', *Psychological Bulletin*, **82** (4), 463–496.

Ainslie, George (1992), *Picoeconomics: The Strategic Interaction of Successive Motivational States Within the Person*, Cambridge, UK: Cambridge University Press.

Ainslie, George (2010), 'Recursive self-prediction as a proximate cause of impulsivity: the value of a bottom-up model', in Gregory J. Madden and Warren K. Bickel (eds), *Impulsivity: The Behavioral and Neurological Science of Discounting*, Washington, DC: American Psychological Association, pp. 67–92.

Ainslie, George and Nick Haslam (1992a), 'Hyperbolic discounting', in George Loewenstein and Jon Elster (eds), *Choice Over Time*, New York: Russell Sage Foundation, pp. 57–92.

Ainslie, George and Nick Haslam (1992b), 'Self-control', in George Loewenstein and Jon Elster (eds), *Choice Over Time*, New York: Russell Sage Foundation, pp. 177–209.

Ainslie, G. and R.J. Herrnstein (1981), 'Preference reversal and delayed reinforcement', *Learning and Behavior*, **9** (4), 476–482.

Ainslie, G. and J.R. Monterosso (2003), 'Building blocks of self-control: increased tolerance for delay with bundled rewards', *Journal of the Experimental Analysis of Behavior*, **79** (1), 37–64.

Ausubel, L.M. (1991), 'The failure of competition in the credit card market', *American Economic Review*, **81** (1), 50–81.

Bar-Gill, O. (2008), 'The behavioral economics of consumer contracts', *Minnesota Law Review*, **92** (3), 749–802.

Barratt, Ernest S. and Jim H. Patton (1983), 'Impulsivity: cognitive, behavioral and psychophysiological correlates', in Marvin Zuckerman (ed.), *Biological Bases of Sensation Seeking, Impulsivity, and Anxiety*, Hillsdale, NJ: Lawrence Erlbaum Associates, pp. 77–122.

Barratt, Ernest S. and Matthew S. Stanford (1995), 'Impulsiveness', in Charles G. Costello (ed.), *Personality Characteristics of the Personality Disordered*, New York: John Wiley & Sons, pp. 91–119.

Bernstein, M.S., A. Morabia and D. Sloutskis (1999), 'Definition and prevalence of sedentarism in an urban population', *American Journal of Public Health*, **89** (6), 862–867.

Bernthal, M.J., D. Crockett and R.L. Rose (2005), 'Credit cards as lifestyle facilitators', *Journal of Consumer Research*, **32** (1), 130–145.

Bickel, W.K., A.L. Odum and G.J. Madden (1999), 'Impulsivity and cigarette smoking: delay discounting in current, never, and ex-smokers', *Psychopharmacology*, **146** (4), 447–454.

Böhm-Bawerk, Eugen v. (1889), *Capital and Interest: A Critical History of Economical Theory*, London, New York: Macmillan.

Bonato, D.P. and F.J. Boland (1983), 'Delay of gratification in obese children', *Addictive Behaviors*, **8** (1), 71–74.

Cade, J., H. Upmeier, C. Calvert and D. Greenwood (1999), 'Costs of a healthy diet: analysis from the UK Women's Cohort Study', *Public Health Nutrition*, **2** (4), 505–512.

Chapman, G.B. (1996), 'Temporal discounting and utility for health and money', *Journal of Experimental Psychology: Learning, Memory, and Cognition*, **22** (3), 771–791.

Christensen-Szalanski, J.J.J. (1984), 'Discount functions and the measurement of patients' values: women's decisions during childbirth', *Medical Decision Making*, **4** (1), 47–58.

D'Astous, A. and D. Miquelon (1991), 'Helping consumers choose a credit card', *Journal of Consumer Affairs*, **25** (2), 278–294.

DellaVigna, S. and U. Malmendier (2004), 'Contract design and self-control: theory and evidence', *Quarterly Journal of Economics*, **119** (2), 353–402.

DellaVigna, S. and U. Malmendier (2006), 'Paying not to go to the gym', *American Economic Review*, **96** (3), 694–719.

Dickman, S.J. (1990), 'Functional and dysfunctional impulsivity: personality and cognitive correlates', *Journal of Personality and Social Psychology*, **58** (1), 95–102.

Dickman, Scott J. (1993), 'Impulsivity and information processing', in William G. McCown,

Judith L. Johnson and Myrna B. Shure (eds), *The Impulsive Client: Theory, Research and Treatment*, Washington, DC: American Psychological Association, pp. 151–184.

Drewnowski, A. and N. Darmon (2005), 'Food choices and diet costs: an economic analysis', *Journal of Nutrition*, **135** (4), 900–904.

Drewnowski, A. and S.E. Specter (2004), 'Poverty and obesity: the role of energy density and energy cost', *American Journal of Clinical Nutrition*, **79** (1), 6–16.

Du, W., L. Green and J. Myerson (2002), 'Cross-cultural comparisons of discounting delayed and probabilistic rewards', *Psychological Record*, **52** (4), 479–492.

Durant, R.H., T. Baranowski, M. Johnson and W.O. Thompson (1994), 'The relationship among television watching, physical activity, and body composition of young children', *Pediatrics*, **94** (4), 449–455.

Epstein, L.H., C.C. Gordy, H.A. Raynor, M. Beddome, C.K. Kilanowski and R.A. Paluch (2001), 'Increasing fruit and vegetable intake and decreasing fat and sugar intake in families at risk for childhood obesity', *Obesity Research*, **9** (3), 171–178.

Epstein, L.H., J.N. Roemmich, R.A. Paluch and H.A. Raynor (2005a), 'The influence of changes in sedentary behavior on energy and macronutrient intake in youth', *American Journal of Clinical Nutrition*, **81** (2), 361–366.

Epstein, L.H., J.N. Roemmich, R.A. Paluch and H.A. Raynor (2005b), 'Physical activity as a substitute for sedentary behavior in youth', *Annals of Behavioral Medicine*, **29** (3), 200–209.

Estle, S.J., L. Green, J. Myerson and D.D. Holt (2006), 'Differential effects of amount on temporal and probability discounting of gains and losses', *Memory & Cognition*, **34** (4), 914–928.

Estle, S.J., L. Green, J. Myerson and D.D. Holt (2007), 'Discounting of monetary and directly consumable rewards', *Psychological Science*, **18** (1), 58–63.

Evenden, J.L. (1999), 'Varieties of impulsivity', *Psychopharmacology (Berlin)*, **146** (4), 348–361.

Eysenck, Hans J. (1993), 'The nature of impulsivity', in William G. McCown, Judith L. Johnson and Myrna B. Shure (eds), *The Impulsive Client: Theory, Research and Treatment*, Washington, DC: American Psychological Association, pp. 57–69.

Feinberg, R.A. (1986), 'Credit cards as spending facilitating stimuli: a conditioning interpretation', *Journal of Consumer Research*, **13** (3), 348–356.

Fisher, Irving (1930), *The Theory of Interest as Determined by Impatience to Spend Income and Opportunity to Invest it*, New York: Macmillan.

Francis, L.A. and E.J. Susman (2009), 'Self-regulation and rapid weight gain in children from age 3 to 12 years', *Archives of Pediatrics & Adolescent Medicine*, **163** (4), 297–302.

Frank, Robert H. (1992), 'The role of moral sentiments in the theory of intertemporal choice', in George Loewenstein and Jon Elster (eds), *Choice Over Time*, New York: Russell Sage Foundation, pp. 265–284.

Frederick, S., G. Loewenstein and T. O'Donoghue (2002), 'Time discounting and time preference: a critical review', *Journal of Economic Literature*, **40** (2), 351–401.

French, S.A., M. Wall and N.R. Mitchell (2010), 'Household income differences in food sources and food items purchased', *International Journal of Behavioral Nutrition and Physical Activity*, **7** (77), 1–8.

Gerbner, George, Michael Morgan and Nancy Signorielli (1982), 'Programming health portrayals: what viewers see, say, and do', in David Pearl, Lorraine Boutherilet and Joyce Lazar (eds), *Television and Behavior: Ten Years of Scientific Progress and Implications for the Eighties, Volume II*, Washington, DC: National Institute of Mental Health, pp. 291–307.

Giordano, L.A., W.K. Bickel, G. Loewenstein, E.A. Jacobs, L. Marsch and G.J. Badger (2002), 'Mild opioid deprivation increases the degree that opioid-dependent outpatients discount delayed heroin and money', *Psychopharmacology*, **163** (2), 174–182.

Glanz, K., M. Basil, E. Maibach, J. Goldberg and D. Snyder (1998), 'Why Americans eat what they do: taste, nutrition, cost, convenience, and weight control concerns as influences on food consumption', *Journal of the American Dietetic Association*, **98** (10), 1118–1126.

Goldfield, G.S. and L.H. Epstein (2002), 'Can fruits and vegetables and activities substitute for snack foods?', *Health Psychology*, **21** (3), 299–303.

Green, L. and J. Myerson (1996), 'Exponential versus hyperbolic discounting of delayed outcomes: risk and waiting time', *American Zoologist*, **36** (4), 496–505.

Green, L. and J. Myerson (2004), 'A discounting framework for choice with delayed and probabilistic rewards', *Psychological Bulletin*, **130** (5), 769–792.

Green, Leonard and Joel Myerson (2010), 'Experimental and correlational analyses of delay and probability discounting', in Gregory J. Madden and Warren K. Bickel (eds), *Impulsivity: The Behavioural and Neurological Science of Discounting*, Washington, DC: American Psychological Association, pp. 67–92.

Green, L. and H. Rachlin (1996), 'Commitment using punishment', *Journal of the Experimental Analysis of Behavior*, **65** (3), 593–601.

Green, L., E.B. Fisher Jr., S. Perlow and L. Sherman (1981), 'Preference reversal and self-control: choice as a function of reward amount and delay', *Behaviour Analysis Letters*, **1** (1), 43–51.

Green, L., N. Fristoe and J. Myerson (1994a), 'Temporal discounting and preference reversals in choice between delayed outcomes', *Psychonomic Bulletin & Review*, **1** (3), 383–389.

Green, L., A.F. Fry and J. Myerson (1994b), 'Discounting of delayed rewards: a life-span comparison', *Psychological Science*, **5** (1), 33–36.

Green, L., J. Myerson and P. Ostaszewski (1999a), 'Amount of reward has opposite effects on the discounting of delayed and probabilistic outcomes', *Journal of Experimental Psychology: Learning, Memory, and Cognition*, **25** (2), 418–427.

Green, L., J. Myerson and P. Ostaszewski (1999b), 'Discounting of delayed rewards across the life span: age differences in individual discounting functions', *Behavioural Processes*, **46** (1), 89–96.

Green, L., J. Myerson, D.D. Holt, J.R. Slevin and S.J. Estle (2004), 'Discounting of delayed food rewards in pigeons and rats: is there a magnitude effect?', *Journal of the Experimental Analysis of Behavior*, **81** (1), 39–50.

Heidhues, P. and B. Kőszegi (2010), 'Exploiting naïvete about self-control in the credit market', *American Economic Review*, **100** (5), 2279–2303.

Hirschman, E. (1979), 'Differences in consumer purchase behavior by credit card payment system', *Journal of Consumer Research*, **6** (1), 58–66.

Hoch, S.J. and G.F. Loewenstein (1991), 'Time-inconsistent preferences and consumer self-control', *Journal of Consumer Research*, **17** (4), 492–507.

Holt, D.D., L. Green, J. Myerson and S.J. Estle (2008), 'Preference reversals with losses', *Psychonomic Bulletin & Review*, **15** (1), 89–95.

Jevons, William S. (1871), *The Theory of Political Economy*, London: Macmillan.

Jimura, K., J. Myerson, J. Hilgard, T.S. Braver and L. Green (2009), 'Are people really more patient than other animals? Evidence from human discounting of real liquid rewards', *Psychonomic Bulletin & Review*, **16** (6), 1071–1075.

Jimura, K., J. Myerson, J. Hilgard, J. Keighley, T.S. Braver and L. Green (2011), 'Domain independence and stability in young and older adults' discounting of delayed rewards', *Behavioural Processes*, **87** (3), 253–259.

Johnson, M.W. and W.R. Bickel (2002), 'Within-subject comparison of real and hypothetical money rewards in delay discounting', *Journal of the Experimental Analysis of Behavior*, **77** (2), 129–146.

Kahneman, D. and A. Tversky (1979), 'Prospect theory: an analysis of decision under risk', *Econometrica*, **47** (2), 263–292.

Kirby, K.N. (1997), 'Bidding on the future: evidence against normative discounting of delayed rewards', *Journal of Experimental Psychology: General*, **126** (1), 54–70.

Kirby, K.N. and B. Guastello (2001), 'Making choices in anticipation of similar future choices can increase self-control', *Journal of Experimental Psychology: Applied*, **7** (2), 154–164.

Kirby, K.N. and N.N. Maraković (1995), 'Modeling myopic decisions: evidence for hyperbolic delay-discounting within subjects and amounts', *Organization Behavior and Human Decision Processes*, **64** (1), 22–30.

Kirby, K.N. and N.N. Maraković (1996), 'Delay-discounting probabilistic rewards: rates decrease as amounts increase', *Psychonomic Bulletin & Review*, **3** (1), 100–104.

Kirby, K.N. and N.M. Petry (2004), 'Heroin and cocaine abusers have higher discount rates for delayed rewards than alcoholics or non-drug-using controls', *Addiction*, **99** (4), 461–471.

Koopmans, T.C. (1960), 'Stationary ordinal utility and impatience', *Econometrica*, **28** (2), 287–309.

Lipsky, L.M. (2009), 'Are energy-dense foods really cheaper? Reexamining the relation between food price and energy density', *American Journal of Clinical Nutrition*, **90** (5), 1397–1401.

Loewenstein, George (1992), 'The fall and rise of psychological explanations in the economics of intertemporal choice', in George Loewenstein and Jon Elster (eds), *Choice Over Time*, New York: Russell Sage Foundation, pp. 3–34.

Loewenstein, G. (1996), 'Out of control: visceral influences on behavior', *Organizational Behavior and Human Decision Processes*, **65** (3), 272–292.

Loewenstein, G. and D. Prelec (1992), 'Anomalies in intertemporal choice: evidence and an interpretation', *Quarterly Journal of Economics*, **107** (2), 573–597.

Loewenstein, G. and R.H. Thaler (1989), 'Anomalies: intertemporal choice', *Journal of Economic Perspectives*, **3** (4), 181–193.

Logue, A.W. and G.R. King (1991), 'Self-control and impulsiveness in adult humans when food is the reinforcer', *Appetite*, **17** (2), 105–120.

Madden, Gregory J. and Patrick S. Johnson (2010), 'A delay-discounting primer', in Gregory J. Madden and Warren K. Bickel (eds), *Impulsivity: The Behavioral and Neurological Science of Discounting*, Washington, DC: American Psychological Association, pp. 11–37.

Madden, G.J., N.M. Petry, G.J. Badger and W.K. Bickel (1997), 'Impulsive and self-control choices in opioid-dependent patients and non-drug-using control participants: drug and monetary rewards', *Experimental and Clinical Psychopharmacology*, **5** (3), 256–262.

Manwaring, J.L., L. Green, J. Myerson, M.J. Strube and D.E. Wilfley (in press), 'Discounting of various types of rewards by women with and without binge eating disorder: evidence for general rather than specific differences', *Psychological Record*.

Mazur, James E. (1987), 'An adjusting procedure for studying delayed reinforcement', in Michael L. Commons, James E. Mazur, John A. Nevin and Howard H. Rachlin (eds), *Quantitative Analyses of Behavior: Vol. 5. The Effect of Delay and of Intervening Events on Reinforcement Value*, Hillsdale, NJ: Erlbaum, pp. 55–73.

Mazur, J.E. (2000), 'Tradeoffs among delay, rate, and amount of reinforcement', *Behavioural Processes*, **49** (1), 1–10.

Meyer, Roger E. (1988), 'Conditioning phenomena and the problem of relapse in opioid addicts and alcoholics', in Barbara A. Ray (ed.), *Learning Factors in Substance Abuse (NIDA Research Monograph 84)*, Rockville, MD: National Institute on Drug Abuse, pp. 161–179.

Mischel, W., Y. Shoda and P.K. Peake (1988), 'The nature of adolescent competencies predicted by preschool delay of gratification', *Journal of Personality and Social Psychology*, **54** (4), 687–696.

Mischel, W., Y. Shoda and M.L. Rodriguez (1989), 'Delay of gratification in children', *Science*, **244** (4907), 933–938.

Mitchell, S.H. (1999), 'Measures of impulsivity in cigarette smokers and non-smokers', *Psychopharmacology*, **146** (4), 455–464.

Mitchell, S.H. and V.B. Wilson (2010), 'The subjective value of delayed and probabilistic outcomes: outcome size matters for gains but not for losses', *Behavioural Processes*, **83** (1), 36–40.

Myerson, J. and L. Green (1995), 'Discounting of delayed rewards: models of individual choice', *Journal of the Experimental Analysis of Behavior*, **64** (3), 263–276.

Myerson, J., L. Green and M. Warusawitharana (2001), 'Area under the curve as a measure of discounting', *Journal of the Experimental Analysis of Behavior*, **76** (2), 235–243.

Myerson, J., L. Green, J.S. Hanson, D.D. Holt and S.J. Estle (2003), 'Discounting delayed and probabilistic rewards: processes and traits', *Journal of Economic Psychology*, **24** (5), 619–635.

Nisbett, R.E. and D.E. Kanouse (1969), 'Obesity, food deprivation, and supermarket shopping behavior', *Journal of Personality and Social Psychology*, **12** (4), 289–294.

O'Donoghue, T. and M. Rabin (2001), 'Choice and procrastination', *Quarterly Journal of Economics*, **116** (1), 121–160.

Odum, A.L. and A.A.L. Baumann (2007), 'Cigarette smokers show steeper discounting of both food and cigarettes than money', *Drug and Alcohol Dependence*, **91** (2–3), 293–296.

Odum, Amy L. and Ana A.L. Baumann (2010), 'Delay discounting: state and trait variable', in Gregory J. Madden and Warren K. Bickel (eds), *Impulsivity: The Behavioral and Neurological Science of Discounting*, Washington, DC: American Psychological Association, pp. 39–66.

Ostaszewski, P. and K. Karzel (2002), 'Discounting of delayed and probabilistic losses of different amounts', *European Psychologist*, **7** (4), 295–301.

Ottaviani, C. and D. Vandone (in press), 'Impulsivity and household indebtedness: evidence from real life', *Journal of Economic Psychology*, doi:10.1016/j.joep.2011.05.002.

Petry, N.M. and T. Casarella (1999), 'Excessive discounting of delayed rewards in substance abusers with gambling problems', *Drug and Alcohol Dependence*, **56** (1), 25–32.

Prelec, D. and G. Loewenstein (1991), 'Decision making over time and under uncertainty: a common approach', *Management Science*, **37** (7), 770–786.

Prelec, D. and D. Simester (2001), 'Always leave home without it: a further investigation of the credit-card effect on willingness to pay', *Marketing Letters*, **12** (1), 5–12.

Rachlin, H. (1995), 'Self-control: beyond commitment', *Behavioral and Brain Sciences*, **18** (1), 109–121.

Rachlin, Howard (2000), *The Science of Self-control*, Cambridge, MA: Harvard University Press, pp. 108–129.

Rachlin, H. (2006), 'Notes on discounting', *Journal of the Experimental Analysis of Behavior*, **85** (3), 425–435.

Rachlin, H. and L. Green (1972), 'Commitment, choice and self-control', *Journal of the Experimental Analysis of Behavior*, **17** (1), 15–22.

Rachlin, Howard and Andres Raineri (1992), 'Irrationality, impulsiveness, and selfishness as discount reversal effects', in George Loewenstein and Jon Elster (eds), *Choice Over Time*, New York: Russell Sage Foundation, pp. 93–118.

Rachlin, H., A. Raineri and D. Cross (1991), 'Subjective probability and delay', *Journal of the Experimental Analysis of Behavior*, **55** (2), 233–244.

Raineri, A. and H. Rachlin (1993), 'The effect of temporal constraints on the value of money and other commodities', *Journal of Behavioral Decision Making*, **6** (2), 77–94.

Reynolds, B., J.B. Richards, K. Horn and K. Karraker (2004), 'Delay discounting and probability discounting as related to cigarette smoking status in adults', *Behavioural Processes*, **65** (1), 35–42.

Richards, J.B., S.H. Mitchell, H. de Wit and L.S. Seiden (1997), 'Determination of discount functions in rats with an adjusting-amount procedure', *Journal of the Experimental Analysis of Behavior*, **67** (3), 353–366.

Richards, J.B., L. Zhang, S.H. Mitchell and H. de Wit (1999), 'Delay or probability discounting in a model of impulsive behavior: effect of alcohol', *Journal of the Experimental Analysis of Behavior*, **71** (2), 121–143.

Saad, G. (2006), 'Blame our evolved gustatory preferences', *Young Consumers: Insight and Ideas for Responsible Marketers*, **7** (4), 72–75.

Saelens, B.E. and L.H. Epstein (1996), 'The reinforcing value of food in obese and non-obese women', *Appetite*, **27** (1), 41–50.

Samuelson, P.A. (1937), 'A note on measurement of utility', *Review of Economic Studies*, **4** (2), 155–161.

Schelling, Thomas C. (1992), 'Self-command: a new discipline', in George Loewenstein and Jon Elster (eds), *Choice Over Time*, New York: Russell Sage Foundation, pp. 167–176.

Schoenfelder, T.E. and D.A. Hantula (2003), 'A job with a future? Delay discounting, magnitude effects, and domain independence of utility for career decisions', *Journal of Vocational Behavior*, **62** (1), 43–55.
Seeyave, D.M., S. Coleman, D. Appugliese, R.F. Corwyn, R.H. Bradley, N.S. Davidson, N. Kaciroti and J.C. Lumeng (2009), 'Ability to delay gratification at age 4 years and risk of overweight at age 11 years', *Archives of Pediatrics & Adolescent Medicine*, **163** (4), 303–308.
Senior, Nassau W. (1836), *An Outline of the Science of Political Economy*, London: W. Clowes and Sons.
Shoda, Y., W. Mischel and P.K. Peake (1990), 'Predicting adolescent cognitive and self-regulatory competencies from preschool delay of gratification: identifying diagnostic conditions', *Developmental Psychology*, **26** (6), 978–986.
Shui, H. and L.M. Ausubel (2004), 'Time inconsistency in the credit card market', 14th Annual Utah Winter Finance Conference. Available at SSRN: http://ssrn.com/abstract=586622
Siegel, E. and H. Rachlin (1995), 'Soft commitment: self-control achieved by response persistence', *Journal of the Experimental Analysis of Behavior*, **64** (2), 117–128.
Simon, H.A. (1955), 'A behavioral model of rational choice', *Quarterly Journal of Economics*, **69** (1), 99–118.
Simpson, C.A. and R.E. Vuchinich (2000), 'Reliability of a measure of temporal discounting', *Psychological Record*, **50** (1), 3–16.
Solnick, J.W., C. Kannenberg, D.A. Eckerman and M.B. Waller (1980), 'An experimental analysis of impulsivity and impulse control in humans', *Learning and Motivation*, **11** (1), 61–77.
Sovern, J. (2006), 'Toward a new model of consumer protection: the problem of inflated transaction cost', *William and Mary Law Review*, **47** (5), 1635–1709.
Stevens, S.S. (1957), 'On the psychophysical law', *Psychological Review*, **64** (3), 153–181.
Stewart, J. and R.A. Wise (1992), 'Reinstatement of heroin self-administration habits: morphine prompts and naltrexone discourages renewed responding after extinction', *Psychopharmacology*, **108** (1–2), 779–784.
Strotz, R.H. (1955), 'Myopia and inconsistency in dynamic utility maximization', *Review of Economic Studies*, **23** (3), 165–180.
von Neumann, John and Oskar Morgenstern (1944), *Theory of Games and Economic Behavior*, Princeton, NJ: Princeton University Press, pp. 15–31.
Wang, N., W. Lu and N.K. Malhotra (2011), 'Demographics, attitude, personality and credit card features correlate with credit card debt: a view from China', *Journal of Economic Psychology*, **32** (1), 179–193.
Weber, E.U. and C. Hsee (1998), 'Cross-cultural differences in risk perception, but cross-cultural similarities in attitudes toward perceived risk', *Management Science*, **44** (9), 1205–1217.
Woolverton, W.L., J. Myerson and L. Green (2007), 'Delay discounting of cocaine by rhesus monkeys', *Experimental and Clinical Psychopharmacology*, **15** (3), 238–244.
World Health Organization (2011), 'Obesity and overweight – Fact sheet N°311', March, http://www.who.int/mediacentre/factsheets/fs311/en/index.html, accessed 25 April 2011.
Yang, S., L. Markoczy and M. Qi (2007), 'Unrealistic optimism in consumer credit card adoption', *Journal of Economic Psychology*, **28** (2), 170–185.

10 Addictive, impulsive and other counter-normative consumption

Don Ross

10.1 INTRODUCTION

Popular discussion of consumption behaviour is rich with normative associations around patterns taken to be reckless and/or pathological. A partial list of such putative pathologies includes addictive consumption, extremely risky consumption, immoral consumption, hoarding, and compulsive/obsessive consumption. In this chapter, I will organize these normative ideas according to the conceptual framework of standard (meaning neoclassical and Austrian) economics. (For an accessible, historically structured, survey see Backhouse 2002.) This framework differs in various respects from alternatives that might be favoured by psychologists, psychiatrists or philosophers. I choose the economic conceptualization here not because I insist that it is necessarily best for all purposes, but because it has the advantage of forcing us to discipline accounts of consumption that is taken to be normatively deviant by reference to the logic of consumption in general. That is, one begins from a broad but precise idea of consumption, and then addresses special features of some consumption patterns that are normatively controversial and often discouraged by public policy. Contrary to widespread caricatures (e.g., Ormerod 1997, Keen 2002) the logical framework of standard economics is extremely flexible and empirically open, and so allows psychological, neuroscientific and philosophical themes to be visited without restriction.

The chapter is structured as follows. In the second section I present and explain the technical idea of 'consumption' as used in economics. The point of this is to allow us to talk precisely about counter-normative consumption as a particular kind of consumption in general. And the point of *that*, in turn, is to allow us to compare what is unusual about counter-normative consumption as consumption with what might be counter-normative about it in everyday moral or prudential terms. This is essential lest an attempt to address the topic turns into either an exercise in pure philosophy, or a dressing of conventional prejudices in academic language. Following this rather abstract discussion, beginning in the third section the focus is on specific examples. We start with drug addiction, which of all forms of counter-normative consumption is at once the most costly in terms of social welfare, the most profitable for suppliers, and the most universally acknowledged as something that public policy should actively discourage. The fourth section builds on this platform to show how addiction applies to behavioural patterns that don't involve exogenous substances. Only one such pattern, pathological gambling, is currently recognized by psychiatrists as a clear case of addiction in the strict sense, so the discussion here concentrates on that case. But then we explain how future evidence is expected to lead to the careful extension of the model of addictive consumption to other behavioural phenomena, while avoiding the question-begging association of addiction with every kind of consumption that casual popular moral judgment intuitively regards as excessive. Finally, in the concluding section, we discuss the logic by which policies to regulate counter-normative consumption can be economically evaluated in ways that do not depend on arbitrary ethical assumptions— including arbitrary assumptions of the economist. It is sometimes thought that avoidance of such assumptions necessarily leads to a laissez-faire attitude to counter-normative consumption. The chapter ends by explaining why such a conclusion is hasty, which in turn explains why sound regulatory policy on counter-normative consumption should be evidence-based.

10.2   THE MICROECONOMICS OF CONSUMPTION

Consumption interests economists insofar as it involves *choice*. Thus the economist's concept of consumption is parasitic upon that of an *agent*. The ideas of choice and agency in economics are thin and non-psychological in character;[1] specifically, they make no necessary allusion to any sort of explicit deliberation, let alone conscious reasoning. A consumption pattern is chosen just in case there are specifiable shifts in incentivizing conditions, that is, in relative real or expected costs and benefits, that would be expected to alter the pattern. This conception of course includes deliberate comparative evaluations of scarce alternatives, but it also includes conditioned responses of which the subject need not be explicitly aware. To borrow an example of the latter due to Gene Heyman (2009), between the early 1970s and the early 1990s most male business executives in Western economies stopped winking at their female colleagues on the job. It seems likely that few of them made a deliberate or conscious decision to change their behaviour; rising probabilities of being frowned at or sensing adverse body language signaled rising costs and declining benefits associated with the behaviour, and so altered its frequency in the population. In calling it 'chosen' we simply draw attention to this contingency, which distinguishes it from physically similar but unchosen blinking behaviour: if someone wanted to change the incidence of blinking they would need to use eye-drops or goggles rather than social sanctions or rewards.

Anything that behaviourally responds to incentives is an agent in economic terms. Thus individual people, but also groups of brain cells, non-human organisms, clubs, firms, countries and even, on evolutionary timescales, species can be modeled as agents whenever there is motivation to do so on the part of an analyst. Choice implies that information about changes in costs and benefits must be processed somewhere, but the processing in question need not be 'internal' to the agent. For example, a person may choose to consume sweeter bread by moving from Europe to a city in the American South, even if she never entertains thought of the fact that her move shifts the price of unsweetened bread upward—because she would have to travel a long distance to get it—to the point where she will stop consuming it. This disassociation of choice from internal processing is why it is harmless, if we are engaged in economics rather than natural history, to speak of (for example) whales' ancestors 'choosing' to live in the sea (Dennett 1987). On the other hand, rocks do not consume, in the economic sense, chemical elements when they undergo transformative reactions, because no part of the process is a response to incentives.

I have been explicit about the ontology that underlies standard economic consumer theory in order to subsequently make clear why economists often understand normatively awkward consumption in terms of inconsistency. Economists impose few restrictions on agency, but treat the few that they do maintain as axiomatic. We can understand an agent's possible circumstances as involving costs and benefits (for that agent) only insofar as we attribute relatively consistent preferences to the agent. Put more technically, economic agents are reference points for utility functions. Utility functions are formal representations of actual and hypothetical behavioural patterns—not psychological states—constructed from preference functions or relations. Following the formulation of Rubinstein (2006), a preference function or relation generalizes the answers to a series of evaluative questions about elements $x, y, \ldots, n$ of a set X, with one answer per question of the form 'x is preferred to y' $(x > y)$, 'y is preferred to x' $(y > x)$, or 'x and y are interchangeable in preference ranking' (I). Two forms of generalization are equivalent:

1. Preferences on a set X are a function f that assigns to any pair (x, y) of distinct elements in X exactly one of $x > y, y > x$, or I, restricted by two properties: (i) *no order effect*: $f(x, y) = f(y, x)$; and (ii) *transitivity*: if $f(x, y) = x > y$ and $f(y, z) = y > z$ then $f(x, z) = x > z$ and if $f(x, y) = I$ and $f(y, z) = I$ then $f(x, z) = I$.

2. A preference on a set X is a binary relation $\geq$ on X satisfying (i) *completeness*: for any $x, y \in X, x \geq y$ or $y \geq x$; and (ii) *transitivity*: for any $x, y, z \in X$ if $x \geq y$ and $y \geq z$ then $x \geq z$

A utility function is a representation of a preference relation according to: $U: X \rightarrow \Re$ represents $\geq$ if all $x, y \in X, x \geq y$ if and only if $U(x) \geq U(y)$.

An economic agent distributes his or her investments in alternative feasible states of the world in accordance with the weak axiom of revealed preference, which can be glossed as follows: for two complete states of the world x, y: $x \neq y$, if the agent pays opportunity cost $c + y$ in exchange for x, then the agent will never pay opportunity cost $c + x$ in exchange for y. This implies that the agent's behaviour will be consistent with the hypothesis that he or she maximizes a utility function according to which $U(x) \geq U(y)$.

When agents are located in markets where they encounter consumption problems, the economist generally assumes a bit more. In particular, when agents are faced with alternative investments in quantitatively measurable combinations of elements (bundles) from their utility functions, their preferences satisfy monotonicity (for any element $x \in X, x + \varepsilon > x$), continuity, and convexity (consumption behaviour is consistent with representation by neoclassical indifference curves). Stronger assumptions, particularly that utility functions are differentiable, are typically added if we are concerned to show that a particular model of a consumer's optimization of consumption given a budget is explained by reference to his or her preferences. In most applications this is taken for granted.

When the economist applies this framework to the choices of real human individuals or populations, his or her justifiable reason for taking monotonicity, continuity and convexity for granted is *not* empirically derived confidence that people arrive at their choices by computing the optima implied by their utility functions given their opportunity and budget sets. Being himself or herself human, the economist knows that most human agents never do this at all and only a few do it generally. Rather, the economist takes these properties for granted in order to maintain a concept of consumption to which he or she can apply differential analysis. This is not the only useful way in which to understand individual consumption, but it is (by far) the best way to explain and predict changes in *aggregate* consumption. Since this is the level at which public policy aims to discourage patterns of consumption that are considered harmful, and since policy generally aims at this by manipulating costs and benefits, I will assume the economist's conceptual restrictions in this chapter. Maintaining the standard economic modeling framework for the sake of mathematical tractability attracts considerable rhetorical abuse from 'anti-establishment' populists. In a context such as the present one, this is best ignored.

Emphasizing these foundational issues in advance enables us, when addressing the topic of counter-normative consumption, to avoid becoming entangled in muddled issues around normative interpretations of 'rationality'. It is often asserted that addiction, reckless spending, hoarding and so on are 'irrational'. Many people are persuaded by rhetoric that assumes rationality to be a desirable state and irrationality to be an undesirable one. However, this leads directly to circularity if, as often, the mark of rationality is taken to be the living of a life that mainstream opinion finds intuitively endorsable. The circle consists in the fact that everything normatively forceful about 'rationality' in the context of practical reasoning is inherited from more basic norms of 'good living'. Philosophers struggle incessantly to break out of the circle. Some try to do so directly by following Aristotle, while others think they should resort to Kantian principles that restrict the set of good lives to those derived from principles that all could endorse being followed by everyone at once. The first approach inevitably ends in question begging and the second in analyses that game theory shows to be incoherent (Binmore 1994, 1998). Thus despite their efforts philosophers have not added enlightenment on the subject of pathological consumption. One need not deny Aristotle's dictum that the best life should be a life of balance, which sounds very sensible; but as a guide to policy it is no more practically helpful than the advice to try to buy enough things that you could sell with mark-ups to cover the costs of those that depreciate with use.

Economists have not been immune to thinking that they can recover normative differences among consumption patterns in terms of what is and isn't 'rational'. A substantial literature exists that aims to isolate consumption patterns that imply vulnerability to 'Dutch books' (implied willingness to buy sequences of lotteries with long-run negative expected utility) or 'money pumps' (sequences of exchanges that end in the agent being stripped of all wealth). Preference structures that are open to Dutch books or money pumps are often taken to be irrational; and so this work by economists has attracted much attention from formally minded philosophers (see Hájek 2005, 2008). Cubitt and Sugden (2001) show that conditions under which literal money pumps could be practically significant are impossible in a real market. On the other hand, the counter-normative status of gambling in many cultural traditions may be related to the fact that commercial games with house advantages strike people as analogous to money pumps, with gamblers then regarded as irrational for feeding them. Drug addicts whose resources (including resources for financing continued drug use) are predictably and steadily run down are often regarded as irrational in the same way.

Running against this popular attitude, Becker and Murphy (1988) have promoted a famous model of 'rational addiction', which shows how an agent might optimize their welfare from each point of choice between consuming another unit of (e.g.) alcohol and a non-addictive alternative, despite the fact that repeating such choices lowers the welfare they could have had ex ante had they never consumed the addictive substance in the first place. Such consumption patterns might imply social disaster if too widely adopted, as a Kantian would stress, and they directly violate Aristotle's counsel; but unless we are prepared to have recourse to the moral opinions of these philosophers after all, there is no obviously persuasive normative force to reminding the addict that he or she manifests a strong preference for present consumption over future consumption. Why shouldn't the agent have such a preference? Perhaps he or she is merely too risk averse to trust much in the future.

Economists have an alternative basis for introducing normativity that is related to the Kantian philosopher's point immediately above, but differs from it in putting no weight on fantastic principles that declare it to be 'rational' for everyone to identify their own utility function with the utility function of society as a collective agent. We can rely instead on the foundational insight of welfare economics, directly refined and expanded in practical power by game theory, that wherever individual choices interact, we may encounter negative externalities that enter into the vector of incentives. I might have a happy, though shorter, life as one of a small group of perpetually drunken partiers in the social context of a sober majority who fund our revels out of their productivity. However, we merry-makers impose costs on that majority—the welfare transfers themselves, plus all our loud singing and brawling and neglected children and run-over pedestrians, etc.—that they might avoid by making public policy to change our incentives (through, for example, high taxes on alcohol). While it is hard to identify what is compellingly normatively wrong with irrationality per se, there is no corresponding mystery around what is *negative* about negative externalities: agents have incentives to limit, where they can efficiently do so, the power of others to choose in ways that unilaterally reduce their welfare.

It will not be immediately evident that this brings us any closer to the special characteristics of the classic pathological consumption patterns. After all, many typically 'normal' consumption patterns give rise to negative externalities; indeed, one need not be a green activist to agree that the point applies to all consumption of non-renewable commodities and manufactured goods. But now let us remind ourselves of the point made above that no whole human being behaviourally conforms to the axioms of microeconomic consumer theory. In every human life that lasts for more than a few years, tastes naturally change over time. One can formally cope with this by indexing preferences to life-stages, so that, for example, a person maximizes a single lifetime utility function by consuming in accordance with a preference for 'candy floss at age eight and whiskey at age forty-five' over 'whiskey at age eight and candy floss at age forty-five'. However, the only motivation for introducing such complex and perfectly far-sighted preferences is to preserve commitment to associating the micr-oeconomic agent with a single, whole biological person (Ross 2011). The best motivation for that association is that older people hold the assets and liabilities acquired by their younger selves. However, a bad motivation for modeling whole human biographies as single agents is the urge to rational-ize the fact that people obviously and naturally change their minds. This should be avoided as an application of a more general rule against invok-ing the purely constructed concept of utility to 'justify' biological or psy-chological patterns that call for no justification in the first place (Binmore 2009). An alternative modeling convention invites less cross-disciplinary confusion: insofar as a person's behaviour responds coherently to incen-tives over a period of time, assign a locally stable utility function to him or her; but recognize that a typical natural person implements a *sequence* of microeconomic agents. This opens space in which negative externalities can be said to arise even when we consider the choices of a single person, with one temporary agent's choices imposing costs on other agents in the sequence that those agents would not choose. It is helpful to (sometimes) model things this way because it reflects real normative practice, for example, our forcing children to go to school when they'd rather not.

There is a rich tradition of 'multiple self' models in economics. It is no coincidence that these have been especially popular in work on putatively pathological consumption patterns such as addiction. The economic psy-chiatrist George Ainslie (1992, 2001) has reflected carefully for decades on the complex dynamics by which people try to regulate grants and withdrawals of permission to themselves to consume addictive substances. For example, most people have rules about when it is acceptable to drink alcohol: not before lunchtime, or not before sundown, or not when they get up in the middle of the night. People typically complicate these rules with special option clauses; champagne is alright on a leisure flight even if it leaves in the morning; two glasses of wine with lunch is allowed if it's Saturday; outright drunkenness is forgivable at weddings; and so on. Such option clauses raise risks of anarchy if their boundaries are too easy to fudge: 'I can drink whenever I have something to celebrate' is likely to lead to many minor self-congratulatory episodes and to too much alcohol. As

Ainslie (2011) points out, these regulatory legalisms make no sense except insofar as people understand themselves as composed out of communities of entities with conflicting interests. It is incoherent to 'forbid' oneself to smoke cigarettes while 'allowing' oneself to smoke cigars after nice meals unless there is, in some real sense, an agent on the scene that wants to smoke, but is a target for regulation because of the negative externalities his or her choice would impose on some other agent—in this instance, another frame of the same person.

Ainslie's multiple selves, bargaining with one another over the distribution of externalities, are diachronic: one succeeds another in time, with each having control of the full cognitive and other resources of the person. Formal versions of such models have proliferated in recent economic literature; Bénabou and Tirole (2004) and Fudenberg and Levine (2006) are examples. Other contributions posit synchronic sub-personal agents, which jostle for control of personal behaviour at a time. Such models have become especially popular with behavioural economists who are influenced by the suggestion of McClure et al. (2004) that different brain regions directly implement conflicting preference structures (that is, different agents). The evidence for this hypothesis is found unpersuasive by a number of commentators (Ross et al. 2008), including some leading neuroeconomists who have experimentally tested it (Glimcher et al. 2007, Pine et al. 2009). However, rejection of models that reduce synchronic sub-personal agents to anatomical or functional brain regions does not necessarily rule out models in which more abstract, virtual conflicting interests—perhaps consisting mainly in rival dispositions to behaviourally respond to environmental cues that trigger alternative consumption patterns—vie for influence (Ross 2011).

It may seem undeniable on the basis of phenomenology that people are sites of intrapersonal bargaining over the relative values of actions and consumption bundles, whether this is modeled diachronically or synchronically. After all, the experience of conflicting internal pushes and pulls in the face of incompatible options is universal. However, an alternative modeling philosophy is available. This involves treating the person's 'true' agency as logically prior to all neural processing, that is, regarding parts of their brain as generating exogenous impacts on their choice and budget sets, just like features of the environment outside their skulls. Allowing for important variations in details, this modeling approach is shared by Loewenstein (1996, 1999), Read (2001, 2003), and Gul and Pesendorfer (2001). These models all explain personal-scale consumption inconsistencies as resulting from physiologically caused temptations to immediately consume so-called visceral rewards, where such temptations sometimes physically overwhelm agents' higher valuation of non-visceral alternatives. Consider an analogy: I might fail to avoid being hit by a lorry simply because it's moving faster than I can; this shouldn't be regarded as a basis for assigning to me a preference for being run over. In the models under discussion, temptations similarly sideswipe preferences from time to time. (In cases where temptations of a certain type always win, we do have good reason to attribute a preference for the tempting consumption path, even where the agent explicitly disavows the preference in question.) In these models, resisting temptation is expensive for agents (paid for in short-range suffering), but so is succumbing (paid for in lower longer-range utility). Thus the appearance of a temptation constitutes a negative shock along the agent's optimizing path, just like any other price increase.

These different families of models encourage somewhat different normative interpretations. If people's brains are understood as aspects of their exogenous circumstances, then it seems natural to think that other people, and public policy, should side with the true agents and their true preferences when neurochemical storms impede their paths to their own—or others'—welfare optimization. This attitude finds direct expression in so-called nudge paternalism (Camerer et al. 2003; Sunstein and Thaler 2003a, 2003b), which has been successfully popularized by Thaler and Sunstein (2008), and mentioned approvingly as a basis for policy choice by both UK Prime Minister David Cameron and US President Barack Obama. Nudge paternalism potentially greatly widens the class of counter-normative consumption patterns. For example, if most people would truly prefer not to be or become obese, but have brains that frequently fail to resist the temptation to eat fatty or sweet food, then other people, including regulators and law-makers, can argue that it is both in the public interest and in the person's own interest to raise the cost of such food through higher taxes or, in the limit, bans on production or distribution. Potentially sinister applications of this sort of reasoning are self-evident. However, the 'nudge' in 'nudge paternalism' refers to the normative thesis that the state should not *force* behaviour to conform to the long-range optimizing course, but should merely make such conformity easier for people than the opposite. Nevertheless, by hypothesizing true latent preferences that authorities can identify and favour unilaterally, nudge paternalism abandons the bulwark against subversions of consumer sovereignty that standard economics imposes as a matter of definition when it identifies preferences with (patterns of) actual choices. According to revealed preference theory (Samuelson 1938, 1947), the best possible evidence that a person actually prefers a cheeseburger and chips to fruit salad is that, controlling for relative prices and budget constraints, they buy the former rather than the latter. Of course, if brain properties are taken to be exogenous contributors to relative prices then this methodological blockade against paternalism begs the question, since preferences should then be associated only with choices made when anti-temptation resources are at full strength—perhaps because authorities have intervened to pump them up.[2]

Normative considerations raised by sub-personal bargaining models are yet more complicated. If a person is a community of agents, some of which impose negative externalities on others, then other people face the issue of which sub-personal agents they should side with after public negative externalities have been taken into account. Even if one thinks that the state should avoid taking sides in such conflicts, for a person to refuse to do so with his or her intimates would be interpreted as tantamount to declining to participate in the whole institution of friendship. There is a widespread disposition, perhaps universal or perhaps an essential assumption of all successful cultures, to think that longer-range interests are normatively superior to shorter-range ones. Though this disposition no doubt often favours sound policies, it can also work against wisdom. For example, as of current writing in 2011, many Americans insist that the government should not assist people who bought houses with mortgages they cannot support, regardless of whether doing so is in the public interest for macro-economic reasons, because this implicitly rewards indulgent short-range interests that wickedly triumphed over prudent long-range ones. Such positions are sometimes based on concerns about the public negative externalities associated with moral hazard: if imprudent home-owners are partially bailed out, the bargaining power of longer-range interests will be weakened in general. However, some prevalent rhetoric seems insensitive to public cost–benefit considerations, and simply asserts brute normative partiality to longer-range interests.

In the review of some specific consumption patterns typically regarded as counter-normative that follows, I will not be directly concerned, at least in the first place, with patterns that are often deemed immoral simply on the basis of intuitive ethical judgments, including sectarian religious indictments. A common view among liberals is that such 'bossy' other-regarding preferences, however common they might be, are not defensible by appeal to public reason. Nor will I have much directly to say about con-sumption patterns that public policy opposes simply because it is more or less obvious that their public negative externalities overwhelm the possible private gains they yield. For example, it is not controversial that people are prohibited from using very rare ancient human artifacts for making jewelery. The reason for my passing over these cases is that they have less to do with any specific aspects of consumption behaviour—the topic of the present Handbook—than with principles of public policy justification more broadly. My review will be confined to types of consumption that are widely thought to represent pathological or disordered behaviour in and of themselves, regardless of the relationship between the costs they impose on society and the costs of incentives to discourage them. At the end of the chapter, however, I will indicate why these common distinctions among consumption patterns are less clear-cut than they are often taken to be.

To begin with, I will illustrate the distinctions just drawn by means of a non-contrived example. Consider private consumption of pornography. Many people find this viscerally disgusting, even when they merely know about it abstractly and do not observe it. Liberalism may lead us to refuse to acknowledge this as in itself a basis for classifying the consumption as counter-normative. Other criticisms of pornography consumption focus on possible harms—that is, public negative externalities—that have been associated with it either in documented and statistically tested fact or in allegation. For example, consumption of pornography may reinforce sexual discrimination, or, because it cannot be perfectly or even very well hidden, may pollute the environment in which children and adolescents learn norms of sexual taste and conduct. I take these issues as matters for objective cost–benefit analysis of a kind that potentially applies to the consumption of *any* good. But now suppose that many consumers of pornography are ambivalent about their behaviour, for any of a number of reasons: because it seems to them to involve surrender to temptations they resent in themselves, or because they think it interferes with their appreciation of their sexual partners, or because they find it crowding out other activities with which they associate higher longer-range value. Then we would expect to observe all of the following phenomena as economically, psychologically, sociologically and perhaps neuroscientifically interesting characteristics of this specific form of consumption:

(i)   many people would simultaneously pay for pornography and pay for mechanisms—so-called 'commitment devices'—they could use to limit or block their own access to more pornography;

(ii) the demand for commitment devices would call forth some supply of them; this would most often take the form of norms for signaling disapproval of pornography consumption, of laws and regulations restricting pornography production, product features or conditions under which consumption was permitted, and of special consumption taxes on pornography; and these devices would all be produced at higher rates than standard cost–benefit analysis would imply;

(iii) there would be controversy about the extent to which pornography consumption, especially at very high rates, involved culpable choice, versus the extent to which attraction to it revealed an exogenous disability.

All of (i)–(iii) are in fact observed in most societies; so patterns of pornography consumption, along with patterns of recreational drug consumption, gambling, junk food consumption, household or personal accumulation of debt to fund discretionary purchases, hiring of prostitutes, medically and socially risky sex, and obsessional consumption of abnormally large proportions of any single good or service, all fall within the ambit of the review.

I will begin by focusing on the limiting case of true addiction, starting with the form in which application of this concept is least in doubt: recreational drug dependence. Then I will consider the more controversial class of putative addictions to some other behavioural patterns. I will explain why, at present, only one such form of addiction, to gambling, is clinically recognized. This will leave a wide class of consumption patterns to which characteristics indicated in (i)–(iii) above apply, but to which policy arguments based on the properties of addiction are usually taken to be not relevant. The chapter will conclude by addressing reasons for regarding the normative issues that arise most clearly for addictive consumption as, in fact, generalizing much more broadly.

10.3   DRUG ADDICTION

Drug addiction is often regarded as the classic form of pathological consumption. The justification for this is not, per se, that drug addicts may destroy their health, gravely harm their families, ruin their opportunities for wealth, and massively damage their social and career prospects. If someone happens to have a dominant taste for a short life of self-oriented extreme stimulation, then regarding their choice to consume addictive drugs as normatively disordered after negative externalities to other parties had been accounted for would simply amount to morally persecuting them with bossy preferences. What is prima facie peculiar about addictive consumption is extreme manifestation of characteristic (i) above: the typical addict spends financially substantial resources on his or her addictive substance, and simultaneously spends psychic resources that he or she values at least as highly trying to develop and maintain barriers against access to these same substances. The point intended by reference to 'substantial resources' is that, for most drug addicts except nicotine addicts—and for some nicotine addicts too—their struggle with their own addiction is the central consumption-related pattern in their lives.

A common folk understanding of addiction, implicit in the very etymology of the word,[3] denies that it involves pathological choice beyond an initial one made in ignorance. On this understanding, the future addict underestimates the hedonic cost of withdrawal from physical dependence, or does not know that he or she will face any such cost. By the time the addict discovers this, he or she has crossed a physiological threshold and it is too late. The person's state of addiction can then be regarded as a physical disability or disease.

This essential identification of addiction with dependence leads immediately to a puzzling confrontation with facts about the courses of most actual addictions, which involve repeated successful withdrawals and relapses into regular consumption (Heyman 2009). Even heroin addicts are not generally so averse to the miseries of withdrawal that they feel compelled to stick with their drug; most suffer through full cold-turkey experiences all the way to temporary success several times in their lives. It is of course implausible to attribute relapse by experienced addicts to ignorance of the risk of dependence. This pattern puts irrecoverable strain on the Becker-Murphy (1988) model of 'rational' addiction mentioned above, at least as a specific model of addiction rather than a model of habit-forming consumption in a much more abstract and general sense. One could try to save the model by hypothesizing that addicts go through repeated withdrawal not in hopes of quitting for good, but to lower their tolerance so as to make their future drug consumption less expensive; but there is no empirical evidence at all for such an hypothesis.

The disease model of addiction is better able to adapt to the common pattern of withdrawal and relapse. Discovery of a strong genetic and inherited basis of vulnerability to addiction (MacKillop et al. 2010) leads naturally to the idea that the underlying disease is the vulnerability itself. The idea that drug addicts are helpless in the face of their dependence has been vigorously promoted by the ideology of so-called '12 steps' recovery groups such as Alcoholics Anonymous, which regards addicts who are currently abstaining as in 'remission', but denies that any addict can be regarded as 'cured' or 'recovered'.

Heyman (2009) vigorously criticizes the disease model on the grounds that addicts' consumption patterns are manifestly sensitive to incentives, most notably price changes (Chaloupka 1991; DeGrandpre et al. 1992; Leung and Phelps 1993; Carroll 1996; Bickel et al. 1998; Chaloupka et al. 1999; Higgins et al. 2004) and changes in career and life prospects (Heyman 2009, pp. 65–88). Indeed the evidence that addictive consumption is *chosen* in the economist's sense as described in the previous section is overwhelming. All this shows, however, is that disease models and choice models are not the incompatible alternatives they are often taken to be. Genetic and other physiological factors make it more likely that some people will choose addictive consumption, controlling for environmental triggers such as availability and social and legal sanctions, than others.

Logically, there is no difference here from allowing that the following pair of uncontroversial statements imply no mutual contradiction: in consequence of an inherited condition, lactose tolerant people are more likely to quench their thirst with milk than are lactose-intolerant people; and everyone who drinks milk chooses to do so.

The special tendency of addicts to relapse most likely goes beyond their initial genetic vulnerability. A good deal of evidence, both behavioral and based on neuroimaging, indicates that addictive drugs work by exploiting the reward valuation learning systems of the brain (Koob et al. 1998; Koob and Le Moal 2000; Berke and Hyman 2000; Wise 2000; Martin-Soelch et al. 2001; Everitt et al. 2001; Robinson et al. 2001; Goldstein and Volkow 2002; Ahmed 2004; Redish 2004; Everitt and Robbins 2005; Kalivas et al. 2005; Koob 2006). The brain of a mobile animal that actively seeks nourishment and mating opportunities must be able to learn cross-modal changes in comparative values. The vertebrate system that implements this learning, based mainly in a dopaminergic circuit that projects from ventral tegmental area through ventral striatum to orbitofrontal cortex, produces dopamine spikes when rewards turn out to be better than expected, and learns by transferring such spikes to cues that regularly precede reward delivery. The system thus learns by classical conditioning. Since the point of learning comparative reward values is to be primed to exploit optimal consumption opportunities that arise unpredictably, the dopamine system tightly integrates valuation, attention and motor preparation.

Addictive drugs influence the brain by multiple and varying pathways from one to another, but all ultimately disrupt the stability of reward timing signals in ventral striatum. Thus the reward system of the person enjoying an addictive drug experiences continuous surprise regardless of what actually happens, and is repeatedly hyper-stimulated with dopamine. This suggests to the mechanism that the organism has come across an unusually reward-rich environment. The brain 'sensibly' (from an evolutionary perspective) responds to this by reducing inhibitory GABA and serotonin signals in prefrontal areas that prevent the reward circuit from directly controlling behavior. In consequence, the addict's brain learns to respond to cues that have been associated with consumption of the drug—for example, drinking buddies' faces or a cigarette package or the route home from work—by directly priming the motor actions involved in the consumption routine. When consumption does not or cannot occur, this priming is experienced as craving. A typical addict has learned to associate a broad range of perceptions and thoughts with his or her drug, and so may experience cravings almost continuously when not indulging, unless his or her attention is distracted by a very powerful alternative stimulus. Thus the addict tends to be preoccupied with thoughts of his or her drug, and to have difficulty attending to work, other leisure activities, or, except when he or she is high, other people.

The most statistically common life course of drug addiction begins with escalating frequency of use and dosage sizes over periods of months or years beginning in adolescence or early adulthood. The majority of drug addicts either become abstinent or develop controlled use—which, common to popular stereotype, is not rare—in middle age (Heyman 2009). Threats of marriage breakup or job loss are frequent triggers for successful control of addictive consumption. Self-engineered recovery is significantly less frequent in addicts who suffer from co-occurring psychiatric disorders such as major depression. As this group of addicts is over-represented in clinical samples, Heyman (2009) argues convincingly that the image of addiction as an intractable, chronic condition is based on the salience of convenient clinical populations in prevalence and treatment research. At the same time, the fact that relapses among recovered addicts lead to faster escalation of use frequency and dosage, controlling for age, than is observed in the early stages of dependency among people without addiction histories, suggests that the reward circuits of addicts do not entirely forget their training. This hypothesis is consistent with general theory and observation of conditioned learning mechanisms in animals. It is plausibly the element of truth in the popular dogma that addiction is a lifelong condition that goes into remission but is not cured.

Over and above its genetic basis, drug addiction appears to have numerous environmental triggering and maintenance conditions, many of which are self-reinforcing and which also interact to reinforce one another. West (2006) provides an outstanding comprehensive review of these factors. Addicts are more likely than non-addicts to be impulsive, relatively intolerant of delays to rewards, motivated by external rather than internal loci of behavioral control, and prone to anxiety and depression. Addiction is more likely to arise and to persist in social and economic conditions of uncertainty than in circumstances characterized by secure expectations. The more advanced the age at which addictive consumption is first manifest in a person's life, the more likely it is to be associated with a major stressful life event such as divorce or job loss.

There is no accepted best treatment for addiction, let alone a style of clinical intervention that can be applied with high confidence. This fact also contributes to addiction's false popular image as intractable. Support of family members is a frequently cited contributor to successful recovery, but addicts' behavior often alienates such support irrevocably. In light of the importance of cue-driven cravings in the maintenance of addiction, theory predicts what much clinical lore confirms: addicts seeking recovery are well advised to take themselves into unfamiliar environments where learned associative triggers are less likely to be encountered. In a famous series of studies, Lee Robins and her colleagues (Robins et al. 1975; Robins et al. 1980; Robins 1993) examined several hundred US Vietnam War veterans, recently returned home, who had been diagnosed as opiate addicts prior to the conclusion of their tours of duty. 88% ceased regular use of opiates after they withdrew from the surroundings they associated with drug-taking. Only 14% sought professional help for their addictions, and the relapse rate for this group was over five times that of the cohort that chose to manage their condition on their own.

In consequence of recent advances in knowledge of the neural dynamics of addictive learning, research on neuropharmaceutical agents that block phasic dopamine signals to cues for addictive substances, and on other agents that reduce tonic dopamine levels in ventral striatum, is highly active. See Ross et al. (2008, pp. 181–192) for a review. Although no evidence of a breakthrough drug has yet been reported from any large randomized clinical trial, the complexity of the interacting causal factors for addiction as identified by West (2006) should not necessarily undermine confidence in the eventual discovery of such an agent, if the paths through the various causal networks all ultimately converge on a common syndrome in the midbrain and orbitofrontal area. This is the sense in which the disease model that Heyman (2009) unequivocally rejects could be vindicated as the appropriate guide to clinical intervention even though, as Heyman stresses, all addictive consumption is chosen behavior.

So far as consumer theory is concerned, addictive consumption is not unusual except with respect to the intensity of the addict's internal struggle between maintenance and change. Addicted consumers buy fewer drugs when prices rise and increase their consumption when prices fall. They may be enticed by the aura created around a particular drug or (in the case of legal drugs, such as alcohol and tobacco) advertised brand. Product innovation tends to stimulate increased consumption; the introduction of a new illicit drug into a market often produces a short-term epidemic of addiction.

Prevailing normative attitudes to addictive consumption, and to non-addictive consumption of substances associated with addiction, are highly complex. Most addictive drugs produce impaired judgment that interferes with ability to work, supervise children, or operate potentially dangerous equipment such as motor vehicles. Many addictive drugs encourage impulsive social behavior, including violence. It is of course not surprising that societies use laws and regulations to try to limit the magnitude of the resulting negative externalities to bystanders, co-workers and family members. All existing national jurisdictions ban some addictive substances outright. This implies a normative ideal of zero consumption; however, no society pays for levels of monitoring consistent with zero consumption as a genuine policy objective. The one major addictive drug that does not cause impairment, tobacco, leads to negative externalities wherever medical risk is partly pooled, because tobacco is highly toxic and contributes to a wide range of severe morbidities.

If the only counter-normative aspect of addictive drugs arose through their generation of negative externalities for non-consumers and non-addicts, then it would be most efficient policy to simply aim to recover these costs through consumption taxes. This would avoid deadweight losses through costs of enforcement of consumption restrictions, and deny rents to black-market providers who typically use their returns to undermine the rule of law in other ways. Libertarians, who implicitly argue that the state should be neutral in intrapersonal bargaining among sub-personal interests, tend to favour deregulation of addictive drugs, combined with use of tax policy to offset interpersonal negative externalities. However, libertarian attitudes seldom if ever generally prevail in driving public policy, probably because libertarian philosophical views are not maintained by a majority of any national population. Among the majority of people who think the state should intervene against short-range sub-personal interests in consuming addictive drugs, views as to the appropriate level of force this intervention should take vary widely. Possession and use of *some* addictive drugs is criminal behavior in all countries; but use of tobacco by adults under some circumstances is permitted in all countries. In general, public policy with respect to addictive drug consumption reflects the general fact that no body of law and regulation reflects philosophical consistency as between rights-based liberalism, utilitarianism, and paternalistic conservatism. Like most of their citizens, countries' policies and statutes embody historically path-dependent and opportunistic blends of these three basic moral stances.

Within this pragmatic framework, two special aspects of the economics of addictive drug consumption management stand out for technical attention.

First, to the extent that addiction is perceived as a condition that is beyond the effective control of the addict, policy must acknowledge trade-offs between (1) the general motivation to provide fair social insurance to actual and potential sufferers of disabilities; and (2) the moral hazard that arises from the fact that most people find at least moderate levels of intoxication pleasant and entertaining. (By contrast, for most expensive medical conditions people strongly prefer never to experience the symptoms, so public and private incentives are aligned.) Heyman (2009, p. 90) suggests that emphasis on the moral hazard problem is among his motivations for favouring rhetoric that treats disease models as false, as opposed to promoting the more nuanced conclusion that disease models and choice models are not mutually exclusive, for reasons emphasized earlier. In defense of Heyman's approach, it must be recognized that aggregate social welfare might indeed be elevated by denying all publicly subsidized social insurance to addicts; this is an open empirical question, but it is not difficult to construct models in which it is true. However, such a policy, if exercised entirely consistently, would lead to practices that majorities would almost certainly consider unacceptably inhumane and unfair, such as denying all medical attention to alcoholics with liver disease or smokers with cardiac complaints in cases where the sufferers lack resources to privately purchase care. It is morally very demanding, to an extent that unreasonably undermines desirable moral sentiment, to refuse help to a presently suffering person for the sake of reducing moral hazard arising from the incentives of abstract third parties.

Second, the standard practice of disincentivizing consumption of addictive drugs through special taxes requires careful economic analysis if it is to have optimal effects. An obvious point is that such taxes can be set too high, in the sense that they can promote black market activity, or sourcing from alternative jurisdictions, that is more socially costly than the addictive consumption they eliminate. For example, in 1994 the Canadian federal government and the Province of Quebec combined to reduce cigarette taxes by approximately 50% of the retail price in response to a massive upsurge of consumer travel to native reservations that straddle the Canada–US border and could sell tax-exempt cigarettes (Poddar and English 1995). One might therefore suppose that it is prudent to err on the side of setting taxes lower than the optimum. However, this can have ambiguous consequences where addictive drugs are concerned that do not arise for other types of consumption goods. Van Walbeek (2006) finds that tobacco companies in South Africa have a history of not absorbing tax increases through reductions in their profit margins per unit, as one might expect, but of adding mark-ups of their own to retail prices. A possible explanation of this is as follows. Price increases deter less addicted smokers first. Thus, demand elasticity falls with increased prices, and tobacco companies maximize profits by following tax increases with complementary price increases of their own, rather than by partly counteracting the increases or simply transferring them to consumers. The tax increases thereby cause a welfare transfer from present or more chronic addicts to potential or less chronic addicts. This finding ironically suggests that, at least in this instance, industry policy has been alert to the addictive character of tobacco consumption while public policy has disregarded it. Van Walbeek shows that the hypothesis that the industry takes addiction into account in setting prices while the South African Treasury does not take addiction into account in calculating tax increases explains the fact that Treasury has consistently fallen short of its declared target of 50% of the retail price of cigarettes being captured as public revenue.

The South African example illustrates a more general point, that structurally modeling addictive consumption using parameters that represent its addictive character is important for public policy and demand forecasting. It has not been uncommon for public health economists to use the Becker-Murphy (1988) model of rational addiction in their demand analyses for addictive drugs. However, as noted earlier, Becker and Murphy's model is in fact a model of habit-formation generally—applying as well to goods such as breakfast cereal brands—rather than of addiction specifically, and so may often overestimate demand elasticities. Unfortunately, no structural alternative has yet been tested against large data sets and become established as a gold standard.

It has sometimes been suggested, following Ainslie (1975, 1992) that hyperbolic discounting models could provide the basis for such a standard. Ross et al. (2008) discuss this in detail as a framework for modeling addictive consumption.

The Becker-Murphy model of rational addiction incorporates the standard exponential model of the decline in the value of a reward as its consumption is postponed. The case for the rationality of temporal discounting rests on the idea that risk increases with delays to consumption and with the length of intervals between investments and returns. Risk factors arise with respect to two general issues: accuracy in estimating magnitudes and signs of future returns, and questions about which agents will still be around to enjoy benefits. Assuming an intertemporally consistent utility function and rational expectations, an agent will discount delay to returns and consumption as a linear function of the passage of time. In the simple linear case, the discount formula is given by

$$v_i = A_i e^{-kD_i} \tag{10.1}$$

where v_i, A_i, and D_i represent, respectively, the present value of a delayed reward, the amount of a delayed reward, and the delay of the reward; e is the base of the natural logarithms; and the parameter $0 > k > 1$ is a constant that represents the influence of uncertainty and the agent's idiosyncratic attitude to risk.

Based on experimental work with animals, Ainslie (1975, 1992) argued that the default intertemporal discount function for animals, including people, is given not by the exponential function (10.1) but by a hyperbolic function. The most common such function in the current literature is Mazur's (1987) formula (10.2):

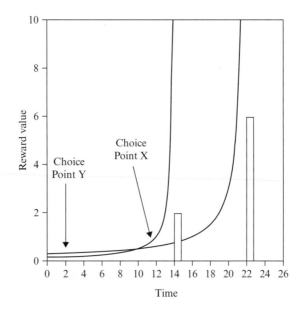

Figure 10.1   Preference reversal as crossing hyperbolae

$$v_i = \frac{A_i}{1 + kD_i} \tag{10.2}$$

Hyperbolic intertemporal discounting allows for (though it does not entail) intertemporal preference reversals when agents choose between smaller, sooner rewards (SSRs) and larger, later ones (LLRs). It has often been suggested that this characterizes the drug addict's choice between getting high now—sacrificing some future utility to hangover, uncompleted work, health problems and damaged relationships—and more prudent consumption alternatives. A pair of temporally spaced rewards a [t_1], b [t_2] for which the person's utility function gives $b > a$ at a point well out into the future from the current reference point, where the slope of the hyperbolic discount function is relatively gentle, may swivel into the relation $a > b$ as the time of a's possible consumption comes closer to the reference point, where hyperbolic discounting is steeper. Thus the hyperbolically discounting drug addict at t_1 might prefer to stay sober at t_2, but reverse this preference in favour of getting high—or, particularly in the case of the tobacco addict, in favour of accommodating cravings—when t_2 becomes imminent.

Figure 10.1 shows a diagram of the kind Ainslie favours for illustrating preference reversal associated with hyperbolic discounting. The short bar shows the value of an SSR, perhaps a line of cocaine. The long bar gives the value to be realized if this indulgence is resisted. The crossing of the two hyperbolae illustrates preference reversal: at choice point Y perception of relative values is such that the person chooses sobriety; at choice point X temptation looms large, and the person parties with his or her drug. At the point where the curves cross, we would expect a probe of the person to find them wavering.

Ainslie refers to graphs such as Figure 10.1 as "discount curves", but this usage, along with the labeling of the x-axis as "time", are somewhat misleading, and for the same reason. In microeconomic theory temporal discounting is purely a function of time, and a discount function should be estimated only after controlling for all other influences, such as attitude to risk and the curvature of the utility function (Andersen et al. 2008). By contrast, as Ainslie emphasizes, the dynamic valuation of reward over time that is the object of his modeling is a function of sub-personal bargaining. When the curves cross, as in Figure 10.1, this represents not only the passage of time, but a victory for a sub-personal interest in consuming the SSR. For this reason, it is helpful that Ainslie's graphs are drawn with the opposite orientation to economists' discount curves, since this reminds us that they describe different kinds of relationships.

To the non-economist reader, this point may seem to be so much quibbling. However, it implicates substantive issues. Ainslie's model is not an application of the microeconomic framework described earlier because it violates the weak axiom of revealed preference. A consequence of that is that we cannot necessarily solve for the optimization of a hyperbolic discounter's utility function by applying limit theorems. A defender of Ainslie's model should not be discouraged by this problem, because it reiterates one of Ainslie's central conceptual points, that to make sense of the kind of apparent reversal in the consumption preference pattern characteristic of addicts, we must posit multiple sub-personal agents. Since these different agents have different preferences, there is no reason why we should expect to be able to aggregate them into those of a single, consistent consumer except where bargaining equilibria have stabilized around successful personal rules. (Where such stabilization has occurred, discounting should not appear to be hyperbolic in the first place.)

A consequence of this technical constraint is that we cannot replace the Becker-Murphy model of rational addiction with Ainslie's model when we seek to solve at the population level for tax rates that will minimize the cost of negative externalities from drug addiction. Hyperbolic functions can be approximated by so-called 'quasi-hyperbolic' functions that represent agents as discounting SSRs at one exponential rate and LLRs at another, shallower, rate (Phelps and Pollack 1968; Laibson 1997). However, data and analysis due to Andersen et al. (2008, 2011) indicate that only small minorities of real populations choose according to patterns that are best described by either hyperbolic or quasi-hyperbolic functions. Andersen et al. use so-called 'mixture models' that allow them to estimate actual proportions of applications of different functional forms of discounting to choices in populations. Methodological questions about how to use this technology to derive welfare maximizing policies remain a subject of early and tentative exploration. Thus the reader should expect to find that, for the moment, economic studies of addictive drug consumption that are intended for practical application still primarily employ the Becker-Murphy framework. But the limitations of this framework for capturing all the relevant empirical regularities should be acknowledged in all applications.

Ainslie does not view the drug addict as unusual in being driven by the dynamics of a sub-personal marketplace of competing interests. According to him, this characterizes people in general. The drug addict, rather, is someone who has failed to find effective personal rules that constitute equilibria in his or her sub-personal bargaining games, and so does not successfully regulate consumption where his or her drug of addiction is concerned. Ainslie's model is open to a wide range of possible explanations of such failures. Typical proximate causes could be absence of reliable social support for prudent interests, and the attenuation of prefrontal circuits that normally inhibit direct dopaminergic control of motor responses; while a common more distal cause might be genetic vulnerability. Such explanations, operating at different scales of abstraction in identifying causal factors, are complementary rather than competing (Ross et al. 2008, Chapter 6). As West (2006) emphasizes, a comprehensive theory of addiction should be expected to include reference to all of them.

The counter-normative status of addictive consumption of drugs, even after factoring for public negative externalities, seems compelling in light of the facts as reviewed. Almost all drug addicts find their conflicted state aversive in itself, so their friends and relatives—and indeed the state—can readily justify taking sides in their internal bargaining. Then, to take the side of the sub-personal interest in drug consumption will typically be regarded by the addicted person as outright evil. (No such point applies to *non*-conflicted drug-dependent people. But in their case, if public negative externalities are indeed fully paid for, then there is no basis for applying the concept of addiction in the first place, other than the traditional identification of addiction with biochemical dependence that, for reasons discussed above, has been rejected by clinicians.)

10.4 'BEHAVIORAL ADDICTIONS' AND PATHOLOGICAL GAMBLING

The preceding section focused on drug addiction in order to defer controversies over necessary conditions for addiction. Restriction to drug addiction achieves this purpose because there is, though only recently and following years of controversy, an approximate consensus among psychologists and psychiatrists that some drugs produce distinctive neuroadaptations that tend to sustain preoccupation and acute cravings as an equilibrium. This majority agreement is the basis for the expected return of addiction as a recognized class of pathologies in the forthcoming 5th edition of the *Diagnostic and Statistical Manual of Mental Disorders* (DSM-V) (American Psychiatric Association 2004).

It is also expected that the new DSM-V addiction entry will include one, but only one, so-called behavioral addiction: to gambling. This may strike readers familiar only with the popular use of the concept of addiction as peculiar. Casual references in popular discourse to numerous non-drug 'addictions'—to sex, shopping, video games, Internet surfing, work, god (!), etc.—are commonplace. Users of such locutions seem to be divided over whether they think of this as mere metaphorical extension, or believe instead that literal clinical addiction is ubiquitous. The anticipated DSM-V policy is consistent with neither of these assumptions: on the one hand, it acknowledges that literal addiction is not necessarily focused on drugs; but on the other hand, in allowing (for now) only one behavioral addiction, it implies that the paradigm built on drug addiction does not extend liberally on the mere basis of unusually dedicated or concentrated consumption patterns.

No psychologist or psychiatrist, to my knowledge, has defended the hypothesis that gambling addiction is the only behavioral addiction that will ultimately be clinically recognized. Indeed, there is some support in the DSM client community for immediate additional inclusion of Internet surfing addiction. The conservative policy of recognizing, for the present, only gambling addiction simply reflects the severely incomplete current state of rigorously scrutinized empirical evidence. Putative sex addiction is a special case because, in light of the widespread enthusiasm for this idea in the popular media and in church-sponsored behavioral counseling programmes in the US (see Ross et al. 2008, pp. 212–216), researchers have looked for evidence of biological and stable clinical correlates—and failed to find them.

Thus the conception of addiction that is to be cautiously extended to some but not most non-drug reward types, beginning with gambling, is not simply a loose open file folder waiting to be populated as empirical studies roll in. There is at present a widely accepted, clearly incomplete but nevertheless conditionally demanding, *theory* of addiction that some reward-seeking behavioral patterns may plausibly satisfy but most will probably not.

As indicated above, West (2006) emphasizes that addictions are highly complex, and heterogeneous, networks of causal pathways and mutually reinforcing processes, some neural, some behavioral, and still others social. This point is not seriously open to dispute, and West's is the outstanding short, comprehensive overview of the main elements that feature in this complex (see also Redish et al. 2008). However, the fact that addiction has a wide set of necessary and sufficient conditions is compatible with the suggestion that it has a quite restricted set of merely necessary conditions, and that these are, indeed, all based in the brain.

All addictive drugs, along with severe pathological gambling, involve preoccupation, cravings, and increasing tolerance (i.e., the need, up to some physically restricted plateau, for progressively larger doses to achieve elimination of cravings over a fixed post-consumption interval). Despite many unresolved issues around specific details, the neuropsychological account of the way in which the striatal reward circuit comes to be captured by a dominant network of attention-arresting cues converging on one or two targets (e.g., alcohol, cocaine, gambling, tobacco, or two or more rarely three of these), and then comes to gain increasingly direct control of motor response, as outlined in the previous section, identifies the necessary (but not sufficient) conditions for the distinctive patterns characteristic of addiction.

We can use these conditions to reflect on patterns of consumption that are more and less likely to trigger the kind of learning that draws the dopamine circuit into the attractor space of addiction. The signature pattern is one in which a small set of easily performed and routinized actions—for examples: removing a cigarette from the box and the lighter from one's pocket and igniting; assembling glass, ice cubes and bottle; inserting tokens in the slot machine and pushing the button—reliably produce rewards that are surprising either in magnitude or in exact timing, thus producing dopamine spikes to support learning. Because the simple routine is under the person's control but involves little effort, the addict can readily produce his or her own cues for reward learning, and thereby enjoys a self-manipulable dopamine pump. Addictive drugs may support this learning pattern by disrupting internal clocks used by the brain to measure intervals between cues and reward receipt, which would have the effect of making familiar types of events in the intoxicated person's environment seem fresh and interesting. Gambling does this directly: the entire point of the activity is setting in motion a short time-course over which an interesting and unpredictable outcome awaits resolution. Money must be at stake to make the outcome worthy of attention in the first place, but pathological gamblers are not mainly motivated by the desire to increase their incomes; in general, people find simple repeated actions they take for the sake of a paycheque boring and aversive. What is stimulating about gambling and makes it potentially addictive is uncertainty providing scope for continuous, though specious, neural learning.[4]

Because of this unusually direct relationship between gambling and basic triggering conditions for addictive learning, Ross et al. (2008) argue that gambling addiction is the purest specific form of the general addictive syndrome. Different classes of addictive drugs, by contrast, influence the dopamine circuit through neural pathways that vary from class to class, and have diffuse and distinctive ranges of effects on the nervous system over and above the core addiction-establishing influences.

Thinking of gambling as the paradigm of a consumption pattern that invites addiction allows us to speculatively pre-assess other behavioral patterns for their potentially addictive character by reference to the extent to which they resemble gambling in the relevant respects. Even some forms of gambling do not fit the pattern: standard 'national' lotteries impose too long a waiting time until resolution, while poker played with a table of other people (as opposed to one-on-one poker against a machine or dealer) involves too much cognitive strategy for prefrontal inhibition of striatal signals to 'switch off'. There is, as this model predicts, no evidence of lottery addicts,[5] nor is addiction risk a general concern among people who play even high-stakes poker in the traditional format. Ross et al. (2008) argue that interpersonal sex is also a poor behavioral arena for addictive learning because the range of initiating actions is complex, situationally various, and subject to adjustment based on feedback from an autonomous partner. On the other hand, viewing of pornography to stimulate masturbation, especially when the consumer has apparatus—a mouse and an Internet connection—for quickly generating novel images is a strong candidate for addictive learning. Indeed, Internet surfing in general has the key addictive properties, as noted above. Shopping may well be addictive, as may fatty foods if their neurochemical effects include disruption of reward interval measurement. Literal 'workaholism', on the other hand, is extremely unlikely.

Pathological gambling is a particularly interesting form of counter-normative consumption for other reasons besides its direct exemplification of the general addictive learning pattern. First, it implicates other aspects of consumption against which social norms arise, beginning with expenditures that, when interpreted as investments, imply negative expected utility unless the investor is highly risk-loving. In addition, Collins (2003,

2010) discusses the presumption in almost all societies that income earned in exchange for productive labour is morally superior to income secured by chance; this presumption explains both widespread religious discouragement or prohibition against gambling, and general public ambivalence that results in tight regulation of gambling availability where it is legal. It seems likely that the conditions obtaining in rich countries before the 1970s, in which commercial gambling was illegal in the majority of jurisdictions, would have persisted but for the lure of the flow of public revenues available from taxing it.

Opponents of liberal commercial gambling policy tend to emphasize higher levels of pathological gambling as its leading negative consequence. The need to resolve the resulting policy choice controversies has occasioned numerous prevalence studies of gambling behavior generally, and pathological gambling specifically, over the past decade. Resulting estimates vary widely, which is thought mainly to derive from differences in the screening instruments used for measurement. Most researchers rely on screens intended for clinical use which, in the interests of not missing people who could benefit from help, are designed to favour type-1 over type-2 errors. Thus screens tend to over-estimate the prevalence of pathological gambling. Because the research community has sought to correct this, there has been a recent trend toward decreasing over-estimation.

Table 10.1 shows a sample range of some prevalence studies of pathological gambling reported since 2004, indicating the screens used. During the first generation of prevalence studies, up to about 2000 (Dickerson and Baron 2000), the dominant instrument was the South Oaks Gambling Screen (SOGS) introduced in 1987 (Lesieur and Blume 1987) and closely based on the DSM-III-R criteria for pathological gambling. (Changes subsequently introduced with DSM-IV were not reflected in any updates to the SOGS.) The current most popular instrument is the Problem Gambling Severity Index (PGSI), the scored module of the Canadian Problem Gambling Index (CGI) (Ferris and Wynne 2001), which facilitates distinguishing amongst levels of severity of risky behaviors. Other screens used in studies included in Table 10.1 are direct applications of DSM-IV and DSM-IV-R criteria, along with the National Opinion Research Center DSM Screen for Problem Gambling (NODS) (Gerstein et al 1999).

Notwithstanding the high variance shown in Table 10.1, as screening accuracy improves it is becoming increasingly evident that pathological gambling, of which addictive gambling is expected to be a subset, is a statistically relatively minor public health problem, afflicting significantly less than 1% of most populations at any given time point in rich countries. Preliminary analysis of one very restricted data set (Kincaid et al. 2011)

Table 10.1 A comparative sample of pathological gambling prevalence reports

Country	Year	Screen	Life time	Past year	Reference
Australia	2008	CPGI		0.47 to 1.20%[1]	*Problem Gambling in Australia* Australasian Gaming Council (2008)
South Australia	2001	SOGS		2.0%	*Gambling Prevalence in South Australia 2005*
	2005	CPGI		1.6%	Department for Families and Communities, Government of South Australia (2005)
Belgium	2006	DSM-IV	0.4%		Druine, C. (2009)
Brazil		DSM-IVR	1%		Tavares et al. (2010)
Canada	2002	PGSI		0.5%	Canadian Community Health Survey (CCHS 1.2) Marshall & Wynne (2003)
Denmark	2005	NODS	0.26%	0.13%	Danish gambling survey Bonke & Borregaard (2006)
Estonia	2006	SOGS	3.4%		*Gambling Prevalence in Estonia* Turu-uuringud (2006) Laansoo & Niit (2009)
Finland	2007	SOGS	1.6%		*Gambling in Finland 2007* Aho & Turja (2007)
Germany	2007	SOGS	0.19%		Gambling behavior and problem gambling in Germany in 2007 Meyer & Hayer (2008)
Hong Kong	2005	DSM-IV	2.2%		*Study on Hong Kong People's Participation in Gambling Activities* Home Affairs Bureau (2005)
Korea	2006	DSM-IV and DIS	0.8%		Korean Epidemiologic Catchment Area Study Park et al. (2010)
Northern Ireland	2010	PGSI		2.2%	*Northern Ireland Gambling Prevalence Survey 2010 – statistical first release* Department for Social Development [Northern Ireland] (2010)

Table 10.1 (continued)

Country	Year	Screen	Life time	Past year	Reference
Norway	2007	NODS (DSM-IV)		0.7%	'Gambling behavior and gambling problems in Norway 2007' Bakken et al. (2009)
Singapore	2008	DSM IV		1.2%	*Report of Survey on Participation in Gambling Activities Among Singapore residents, 2008* Ministry of Community Development, Youth and Sports [Singapore] (2008)
Sweden	2000	SOGS-R	2.0%	3.9%	'Prevalence and risks of pathological gambling in Sweden' Volberg et al. (2001)
	2008	CPGI		0.3%	*Swedish Longitudinal Gambling Study* SWELOGS [Swedish National Institute for Public Health] (2008)
Switzerland	2005	SOGS		0.5%	'Prevalence of pathological gambling in Switzerland after the opening of casinos and the introduction of new preventive legislation' Bondolfi et al. (2008)
UK	2007	DSM-IV PGSI	0.6% 0.5%		*British Gambling Prevalence Survey 2007* National Centre for Social Research (2007)
	2010	DSM-IV PGSI	0.9% 0.7%		*British Gambling Prevalence Survey 2010* National Centre for Social Research (2010)
US	2004	DSM-IV	0.3%	0.6%	'The prevalence and correlates of DSM-IV Pathological gambling in the national comorbidity Survey Replication' Kessler et al. (2008)

Note: [1] This aggregates figures that vary across states.

350

suggests that severe pathological gamblers—the set of which is expected to be strongly coextensive with the set of gambling addicts—are statistically distinctive across a range of behavioral indicators, rather than forming one end of the distribution of a continuous range of dimensions. Observed similarity in prevalence of severe pathological gambling across jurisdictions, which appears to be independent of the accessibility of commercial gambling venues, raises the possibility that gambling addiction is relatively resistant to changes in variables that are typically under policy control or market influence.

Much higher proportions of people—but still not more than 3% when efforts are made to exclude false positives—encounter episodes of gambling beyond their budgets. This pattern resembles that of occasional problem drinking and non-chronic depression. Growing but still inconclusive evidence links these issues to high-stress life events such as divorce, bereavement and involuntary unemployment.

The impression that liberalized casino access can lead to 'epidemics' of pathological or addictive gambling is attributable to the following, not necessarily exclusive, factors: (1) the existence of anti-gambling lobby groups with incentives to report high estimates; (2) the fact that, at least until the recent rise of Internet gambling, addictive gambling has been an unusually publicly visible form of addiction, with addicts closely concentrated on casino floors; (3) the fact that public authorities typically require gaming industry associations to fund public awareness campaigns around problem gambling, lending it disproportionate salience relative to more prevalent disorders. Jacques et al. (2000) report the first of several subsequent observations that the opening of new gambling venues in an area produces a temporary spike in rates of problem gambling, but that populations tend to learn strategies for managing the dangers of this new form of entertainment on timescales of months. Resulting cautionary anecdotes about bad consequences of casino liberalization for some households may, however, contribute to popular perceptions of risk that are biased upwards.

Thus the primary interest of pathological gambling, beyond what it reveals about the basic or core properties of addictive consumption, lies in its illustration of the theme that risk, as an attractive source of psychological attention, has ambiguous effects on the value of consumption streams: on the one hand it reduces the expected value of assets, but on the other hand can add entertainment value to their acquisition. Some limited evidence links gambling problems to impatience with respect to reward timing, but not—at least yet—to generalized love of risk in reward choice. This may be less surprising than it seems: one way to indulge a taste for entertainment from risk without unduly compromising expected personal or household wealth may be to compartmentalize the disposition. For some people, controlled high-risk gambling might thus be the expression of a personal rule that stabilizes sub-personal bargaining dynamics. The first law of the human consumer is that his or her motivational structure is not simple. Contrary to widespread myth, economic modeling technology does not impede recognition of this complexity, or ingenuity in coping with it (Wilcox 2008).

To the extent that prizes, rather than entertainment from surprise, are treated as the consumption rewards from gambling, this form of consumption differs from the standard case in offering no scope for genuine learning. I emphasize 'genuine' because it may be that the dopamine reward system, which is largely impenetrable to flexible general cognition, cannot avoid responding to gambles as learning opportunities (Chase and Clark 2010). This may be one respect in which all gamblers, including addicts, are ranged along a continuum. It leads to the interesting question of whether investors in asset markets that follow random or near-random walks should expect to struggle to behave rationally unless they remove their biological biasing tendencies from the picture by relying on machine-implemented algorithms. Influences on the general accuracy of consumer reward learning at the neural level are a major frontier for future study. Results of such studies can be expected to be associated with strong normative weight, since efforts to protect consumers from common vulnerabilities to manipulation of learning are a primary focus of consumer protection practice.

10.5   INTERNALIZED NORMS AND PATERNALISM

All normative judgment of consumption implies an element of paternalism: if I judge that your consumption patterns are in some way wrong, I implicitly convey a judgment that either my epistemic or moral sensitivities, or both, are superior to yours. If I go as far as promoting regulation or legislation to reform or prevent your consumption preferences from being realized, then I make a claim to political authority over you based on my claimed superiority in judgment. The first sort of paternalism is generally unavoidable: almost everyone except addicts believes that their main consumption habits are better choices, conditional on their budget constraints, than available alternatives, including alternatives actually chosen by some other people. However, some people—libertarians—maintain an explicit stance in opposition to bossy paternalism, that is, against efforts to regulate counter-normative consumption on the basis of premises other than dominance of private benefits by interpersonal negative externalities.

Consistent libertarians about consumption usually advocate interpersonal neutrality with respect to intrapersonal allocations of costs and benefits among sub-personal interests.

A long tradition in economics, inherited from the liberal political philosophy of Locke and Hume, stacks the deck in favour of libertarianism about consumption by supplementing strict, formal microeconomic consumer theory, as outlined at the beginning of this chapter, with a view of personal preferences as exogenous to social and economic interactions. According to this tradition, people's preferences are formed individually—whether by intrapersonal bargaining or some other process—and can then be assessed with respect to social and economic efficiency independently of their origins. If this were true, there is a straightforward (though still not uncontroversial) normative logic leading to the conclusion that the only justifiably counter-normative consumption patterns are those that impose negative externalities on others for which the primary consumer cannot or will not provide compensation.

This reasoning path is at least greatly complicated by attention to a more realistic model of both primary preference formation and secondary normative judgments of preferences. In modern urban societies, consumption preferences are a fundamental element of an individual's distinctive self. Such selves are not given exogenously or genetically (even if the core dimensions of personality are heavily genetically influenced). Rather, they are narratively constructed over time, under strong pressure and guidance from parents and, to an even greater extent in the development of the relatively stable adult self, influential peers in adolescence and early adulthood (Harris 2007; Ross 2004, 2005, 2006, 2007). The classical normative atomist might regard such receptiveness to social influence as a form of regrettable vulnerability and infirmity of conviction. This attitude rests on ignoring the fact that the promotion of human welfare through exchange of goods and services, which in turn both depends on and amplifies specialization of labour, requires coordinated expectations. These in turn depend on mutual normative understanding, and at least background elements of normative agreement (Smith 1759).

On the other hand, traditional individualist doctrine is highly alert to the equally fundamental fact that specialization of labour, the basis of humans' material dominance of global ecology (Ofek 2001), depends on exploitation of individual differences in tastes, capacities and inclinations to innovate.

Modern humans resolve this tension by requiring one another to create distinctive *selves* that are re-identifiable across social and economic interactions, entailing simultaneous demands for both uniqueness and consistency (Ross 2012b). Members of a person's social network regulate his or her biographical construction by showing disapproval of inexplicable departures from coherence, while also strongly reinforcing personal innovations they can understand. As pointed out by various authors (Bruner 1992; Dennett 1991; Ross 2005), this process is mirrored in and explicitly exemplified by the creation of fictional characters by authors. Such characters must be both comprehensible by readers (for example, Tarzan must not suddenly be overcome by enervating panic in the face of a physical threat) and sufficiently idiosyncratic to be interesting. The maintenance of an effective fictional character over the course of a novel is a significant achievement (even if my example, Tarzan, was a relatively undemanding one compared with, say, Madame Bovary). Exactly the same sources of difficulty apply to the development and management of a self that is attractive as an exchange partner to other people. Thus it is rational for people to tenaciously defend the integrity of the selves they have created, treating them as assets that embody irreversible investment histories. This is the sound economic basis of normative individualism, which libertarianism amplifies into a dominant moral principle.

Ironically, then, the best defense of the libertarian's normative individualism rests on denying the descriptive individualism of classical liberal atomism (Ross 2012b). It is because consistent personal preferences are socially mandated structures that are constructed only with difficulty that they are so valuable. This deeply complicates any attempt to draw a simple line between bossy paternalism and regulation of consumption that is deemed counter-normative due to public negative externalities. The preferences of a self that is narratively constructed to adapt to social expectations dynamically incorporate a history of interventions by others in the individual's intrapersonal bargaining; these are the processes to which the common locution of 'norm internalization' makes reference. Communities of people are interconnected as normative models for one another—indeed, this statement comes close to identifying the very meaning of the idea of 'community'. Thus whenever a person normatively turns against some aspect of their own consumption history, he or she gives others motivation to effect similar switches in attitudes, regardless of whether he or she explicitly endorses bossy paternalism. In consequence, any consumption pattern that attracts widespread disapproval within a person's normative reference groups—typically, his or her political, religious, ethnic or professional communities—will tend to produce the kind of internal ambivalence and effortful self-control that is manifest in its most extreme form in addicts and chronic procrastinators.

The majority of consumers are not addicted to anything. However, the point of the reflections offered in this closing section is that the complexities involved in the addict's management of his or her consumption profile generalize to a surprising degree across all consumption behavior that is normatively controversial, at least within groups who share joint social, economic and political projects. Marketers who promote products that attract non-trivial levels of disapproval thus cannot avoid taking implicit sides in conflicts of normative judgment that arise not only between people, but within them. Many marketing strategies, and not only those promoting obviously self-destructive goods such as cigarettes or crack cocaine, are aimed at influencing such conflicts, regardless of whether this is generally acknowledged. For reasons indicated, recognition of this fact, which communitarians tend to celebrate, is also forced by the libertarian's assumptions. Thus it is independent of the main ideologies that contend for influence over consumer policy and corporate ethics.[6]

ACKNOWLEDGMENT

Thanks to Harold Kincaid for contributing research.

NOTES

1. Behavioural economics is the offshoot of economics in which choice *is* understood in psychological terms. I argue elsewhere (Ross 2012a) that, in consequence of this, behavioral economics ultimately reduces to the psychology and neuroscience of valuation and is not economics in any substantive sense.
2. Regardless of this logic, one might anyway prefer for other reasons that authorities be strongly restrained where such intervention is concerned. See note 6.
3. Historically, 'addiction' is related to slavery.
4. I call the learning 'specious' because in a true game of chance there is of course no real pattern to be learned.
5. This point does not apply to 'instant' lotteries based on scratch cards, where the very point of the design is to shrink the resolution period on the gamble into the 'dopamine-pump' timescale.
6. These remarks should not be interpreted as endorsement of nudge paternalism. I am uneasy about any generalization of paternalism beyond specific cases, because of my interest in protecting the precious and historically unusual English social virtue of outright approval of eccentricity for its own sake.

REFERENCES

Ahmed, S. (2004), 'Addiction as compulsive reward prediction', *Science*, **306**, 1901–1902.
Aho, P. and T. Turja (2007), *Gambling in Finland 2007*, Helsinki: Ministry of Social Affairs and Health.
Ainslie, G. (1975), 'Specious reward: a behavioral theory of impulsiveness and impulse control', *Psychological Bulletin*, **82**, 463–496.
Ainslie, G. (1992), *Picoeconomics*, Cambridge: Cambridge University Press.

Ainslie, G. (2001), *Breakdown of Will*, Cambridge: Cambridge University Press.
Ainslie, G. (2011), 'Pure hyperbolic discount curves predict "eyes-open" self control', *Theory and Decision*, forthcoming.
American Psychiatric Association (2004), *Diagnostic and Statistical Manual of Mental Disorders, Fourth Edition, Text Revision*, Washington DC: American Psychiatric Publishers.
Andersen, S., G. Harrison, M. Lau and E. Rutström (2008), 'Eliciting risk and time preferences', *Econometrica*, **76**, 583–619.
Andersen, S., G. Harrison, M. Lau and E. Rutström (2011), 'Discounting behavior: a reconsideration', Working Paper 2011-03, Center for the Economic Analysis of Risk, Robinson College of Business, Georgia State University, http://cear.gsu.edu/papers/index.html.
Australasian Gaming Council (2008), *Problem Gambling in Australia*, AGC FS 18/08. http://austgamingcouncil.org.au/images/pdf/Fact_Sheets/agc_fs18pginaust.pdf
Backhouse, R. (2002), *The Ordinary Business of Life*, Princeton: Princeton University Press.
Bakken, I., K. Götestam, R. Gråwe, H. Wenzel and A. Øren (2009), 'Gambling behavior and gambling problems in Norway 2007', *Scandinavian Journal of Psychology*, **50**, 333–339.
Becker, G. and K. Murphy (1988), 'A theory of rational addiction', *Journal of Political Economy*, **96**, 675–700.
Bénabou, R. and J. Tirole (2004), 'Willpower and personal rules', *Journal of Political Economy*, **112**, 848–886.
Berke, J. and S. Hyman (2000), 'Addiction, dopamine and the molecular mechanisms of memory', *Neuron*, **25**, 515–532.
Bickel, W., G. Madden and N. Petry (1998), 'The price of change: the behavioral economics of drug dependence', *Behavior Therapy*, **29**, 545–565.
Binmore, K. (1994), *Game Theory and the Social Contract, Volume One: Playing for Real*, Cambridge, MA: MIT Press.
Binmore, K. (1998), *Game Theory and the Social Contract, Volume Two: Just Playing*, Cambridge, MA: MIT Press.
Binmore, K. (2009), *Rational Decisions*, Princeton: Princeton University Press.
Bondolfi, G., F. Jermann, F. Ferrero, D. Zullino and C. Osiek (2008), 'Prevalence of pathological gambling in Switzerland after the opening of casinos and the introduction of new preventive legislation', *Acta Psychiatrica Scandinavica*, **117**, 236–239.
Bonke, J. and K. Borregaard (2006), *The Prevalence and Heterogeneity of At-Risk and Pathological Gamblers—The Danish case* [Working Paper 15: 2006], Copenhagen: Danish National Institute of Social Research.
Bruner, J. (1992), *Acts of Meaning*, Cambridge, MA: Harvard University Press.
Camerer, C., S. Issacaroff, G. Loewenstein, T. O'Donaghue and M. Rabin (2003), 'Regulation for conservatives: behavioral economics and the case for asymmetric paternalism', *University of Pennsylvania Law Review*, **151**, 1211–1254.
Carroll, M. (1996), 'Reducing drug abuse by enriching the environment with alternative non-drug reinforcers', in L. Green and J. Kagel (eds), *Advances in Behavioral Economics: Vol. 3. Substance Use and Abuse*, Norwood, NJ: Ablex, pp. 37–68.
Chaloupka, F. (1991), 'Rational addictive behavior and cigarette smoking', *Journal of Political Economy*, **99**, 722–742.
Chaloupka, F., M. Grossman and J. Tauras (1999), 'The demand for cocaine and marijuana by youth', in F. Chaloupka, W. Bickel, M. Grossman, and H. Saffer (eds), *The Economic Analysis of Substance Use and Abuse: An Integration of Econometric and Behavioral Economic Perspectives*, Chicago: University of Chicago Press, pp. 133–156.
Chase, H. and L. Clark (2010), 'Gambling severity predicts midbrain response to near-miss outcomes', *Journal of Neuroscience*, **30**, 6180–6187.
Collins, P. (2003), *Gambling and the Public Interest*, Westport CT: Praeger.
Collins, P. (2010), 'Defining addiction and identifying the public interest in democracies', in D. Ross, H. Kincaid, D. Spurrett and P. Collins (eds), *What Is Addiction?*, Cambridge, MA: MIT Press, pp. 409–433.

Cubitt, R. and R. Sugden (2001), 'On money pumps', *Games and Economic Behavior*, **37**, 121–160.
DeGrandpre, R., W. Bickel, J. Hughes and S. Higgins (1992), 'Behavioral economics of drug self-administration: III. A reanalysis of the nicotine regulation hypothesis', *Psychopharmacology*, **108**, 1–10.
Dennett, D. (1987), *The Intentional Stance*, Cambridge, MA: MIT Press.
Dennett, D. (1991), *Consciousness Explained*, Boston: Little Brown.
Department for Families and Communities, Government of South Australia (2005), *Gambling Prevalence in South Australia: October–December 2005*, Government of South Australia.
Department for Social Development [Northern Ireland] (2010), Northern Ireland Gambling Prevalence Survey 2010, http://www.dsdni.gov.uk/gambling_summary_bulletin_first_release.doc.
Dickerson, E. and E. Baron (2000), 'Contemporary issues and future directions for research into pathological gambling', *Addiction*, **95**, 1145–1159.
Druine, C. (2009), 'Belgium', in G. Meyer, T. Hayer and M. Griffiths (eds), *Problem Gambling in Europe: Challenges, Prevention, and Interventions*, New York: Springer, pp. 3–16.
Everitt, B. and T. Robbins (2005), 'Neural systems of reinforcement for drug addiction: from actions to habit to compulsion', *Nature Neuroscience*, **8**, 1481–1489.
Everitt, B., A. Dickinson and T. Robbins (2001), 'The neuropsychological basis of addictive behavior', *Brain Research Reviews*, **36**, 129–138.
Ferris, J. and H. Wynne (2001), 'The Canadian Problem Gambling Index draft user manual', www.ccsa.ca/pdf/ccsa-009381-2001.pdf.
Fudenberg, D. and J. Levine (2006), 'A dual-self model of impulse control', *American Economic Review*, **96**, 1449–1476.
Gerstein, D., R. Volberg, M. Toce, H. Harwoord, R. Johnson and T. Buie (1999), *Gambling Impact and Behavior Study: Report to the National Gambling Impact Study Commission*, Chicago: National Opinion Research Center.
Glimcher, P., J. Kable and K. Louie (2007), 'Neuroeconomic studies of impulsivity: now or just as soon as possible?', *American Economic Review*, **97**, 142–147.
Goldstein, R. and N. Volkow (2002), 'Drug addiction and its underlying neurobiological basis: neuroimaging evidence for the involvement of the prefrontal cortex', *American Journal of Psychiatry*, **159**, 1642–1652.
Gul, F. and W. Pesendorfer (2001), 'Temptation and self control', *Econometrica*, **69**, 1403–1436.
Hájek, A. (2005), 'Scotching Dutch books', *Philosophical Perspectives*, **19**, 139–151.
Hájek, A. (2008), 'Dutch book arguments', in P. Anand, P. Pattanaik and C. Puppe (eds), *The Oxford Handbook of Rational and Social Choice*, Oxford: Oxford University Press, pp. 173–195.
Harris, J. (2007), *No Two Alike*, New York: Norton.
Heyman, G. (2009), *Addiction: A Disorder of Choice*, Cambridge, MA: Harvard University Press.
Higgins, S., S. Heil and J. Lussier (2004), 'Clinical implications of reinforcement as a determinant of substance use disorders', *Annual Reviews of Psychology*, **55**, 431–461.
Home Affairs Bureau [Hong Kong], (2005), *Study on Hong Kong People's Participation in Gambling Activities Key Statistics*, http://www.hab.gov.hk/file_manager/en/documents/whats_new/gambling/KeyStat_200514_e.pdf
Jacques, C., R. Ladouceur and F. Ferland (2000), 'Impact of availability on gambling: a longitudinal study', *Canadian Journal of Psychiatry*, **45**, 810–815.
Kalivas, P., N. Volkow and J. Seamans (2005), 'Unmanageable motivation in addiction: a pathology in prefrontal-accumbens glutamate transmission', *Neuron*, **45**, 647–650.
Keen, S. (2002), *De-bunking Economics*, New York: Zed Books.
Kessler, R., I. Hwang, R. LaBrie, M. Petukhova, N. Sampson, K. Winters and H. Shaffer (2008), 'The prevalence and correlates of DSM-IV Pathological Gambling in the National Comorbidity Survey Replication', *Psychological Medicine*, **38**, 1351–1360.

Kincaid, H., R. Daniels, A. Dellis, A. Hofmeyr, R. Rousseau, C. Sharp and D. Ross (2011), 'A taxometric analysis of the performance of the Problem Gambling Severity Index in a South African national urban sample', University of Cape Town, under review; available at http://www.academia.edu/dronross

Koob, G. (2006), 'The neurobiology of addiction: a neuroadaptational view relevant for diagnosis', *Addiction*, **101** (Supplement 1), 23–30.

Koob, G. and M. Le Moal (2000), 'Drug addiction, dysregulation of reward and allostasis', *Neuropsychopharmacology*, **24**, 1–129.

Koob, G., P. Paolo Sanna and F. Bloom (1998), 'Neuroscience of addiction', *Neuron*, 21, 467–476.

Laansoo, S. and T. Niit (2009), 'Estonia', in G. Meyer, T. Hayer and M. Griffiths (eds), *Problem Gambling in Europe: Challenges, Prevention, and Interventions*, New York: Springer, pp. 37–52.

Laibson, D. (1997), 'Golden eggs and hyperbolic discounting', *Quarterly Journal of Economics*, **112**, 443–477.

Lesieur, H. and S. Blume (1987), 'The South Oaks Gambling Screen (The SOGS): A new instrument for the identification of problem gamblers', *American Journal of Psychiatry*, **144**, 1184–1188.

Leung, S.-F. and C. Phelps (1993), '"My kingdom for a drink . . . ?" A review of the estimates of the price sensitivity of demand for alcoholic beverages', in M. Hilton and G. Bloss (eds), *Economics and the Prevention of Alcohol-Related Problems*, Rockville, MD: National Institute on Alcohol Abuse and Alcoholism Research Monograph No. 25, NIH Pub. No. 93-3513, pp. 1–31.

Loewenstein, G. (1996), 'Out of control: visceral influences on behavior', *Organizational Behavior and Human Decision Processes*, **65**, 272–292.

Loewenstein, G. (1999), 'A visceral account of addiction', in J. Elster and O.-J. Skog (eds), *Getting Hooked: Rationality and Addiction*, Cambridge, MA: Cambridge University Press, pp. 235–264.

MacKillop, J., J. McGeary and L. Ray (2010), 'Genetic influences on addiction: alcoholism as an exemplar', in D. Ross, H. Kincaid, D. Spurrett and P. Collins (eds), *What is Addiction?*, Cambridge, MA: MIT Press, pp. 53–98.

Marshall, K. and H. Wynne (2003), 'Fighting the odds', *Perspectives on Labour and Income*, **4**, 5–13.

Martin-Soelch, C., K. Leenders, A. Chevally, J. Missimer, G. Künig, S. Magyar, A. Milno and W. Schultz (2001), 'Reward mechanisms in the brain and their role in dependence: evidence from neurophysiological and neuroimaging studies', *Brain Research Reviews*, **36**, 139–149.

Mazur, J. (1987), 'An adjusting procedure for studying delayed reinforcement', in M. Commons, J. Mazur, J. Nevin and H. Rachlin (eds), *Quantitative Analysis of Behavior Vol. 5: The Effect of Delay and of Intervening Events on Reinforcement Value*, Hillsdale, NJ: Lawrence Erlbaum Associates, pp. 55–73.

McClure, S., D. Laibson, G. Loewenstein and J. Cohen (2004), 'Separate neural systems value immediate and delayed monetary rewards', *Science*, **306**, 503–507.

Meyer, G., and T. Hayer (2008), 'Germany', in G. Meyer, T. Hayer and M. Griffiths (eds), *Problem Gambling in Europe: Challenges, Prevention, and Interventions*, New York: Springer, pp. 85–101.

Ministry of Community Development, Youth and Sports [Singapore] (2008), *Report of Survey on Participation in Gambling Activities Among Singapore Residents, 2008*, http://www.mcys.gov.sg/MCDSFiles/Resource/Materials/GamblingSurveyReport2008.pdf

National Centre for Social Research (2007), *British Gambling Prevalence Survey 2007*, http://www.gamblingcommission.gov.uk/research__consultations/research/bgps/bgps_2007.aspx

National Centre for Social Research (2010), *British Gambling Prevalence Survey 2010*, http://www.natcen.ac.uk/study/british-gambling-prevalence-survey-2010

Ofek, H. (2001), *Second Nature*, Cambridge: Cambridge University Press.

Ormerod, P. (1997), *The Death of Economics*, New York: Wiley.

Park, S., M.J. Cho, H.J. Jeon, H.W. Lee, J.N. Bae, J.I. Park, J.H. Sohn, Y.R. Lee, J.Y. Lee and J.P. Hong (2010), 'Prevalence, clinical correlations, comorbidities, and suicidal tendencies in pathological Korean gamblers: results from the Korean Epidemiologic Catchment Area Study', *Social Psychiatry and Psychiatric Epidemiology*, http://www.ncbi. nlm.nih.gov/pubmed/20724004

Phelps, E. and R. Pollack (1968), 'On second-best national saving and game equilibrium growth', *Review of Economic Studies*, **35**, 201–208.

Pine A., B. Seymour, J. Roiser, P. Bossaerts, K. Friston, H. Curran and R. Dolan (2009), 'Encoding of marginal utility across time in the human brain', *Journal of Neuroscience*, **29**, 9575–9581.

Poddar, S. and M. English (1995), 'Fifty years of Canadian commodity taxation: key events and lessons for the future', *Canadian Tax Journal / Revue fiscale Canadienne*, **43**, 1096–1119.

Read, D. (2001), 'Is time-discounting hyperbolic or subadditive?', *Journal of Risk and Uncertainty*, **23**, 5–32.

Read, D. (2003), 'Subadditive intertemporal choice', in G. Loewenstein, D. Read and R. Baumeister (eds), *Time and Decision: Economic and Psychological Perspectives on Intertemporal Choice*, New York: Russell Sage Foundation, pp. 301–322.

Redish, A.D. (2004), 'Addiction as a computational process gone awry', *Science*, **306**, 1944–1947.

Redish, A.D., S. Jensen and A. Johnson (2008), 'A unified framework for addiction: vulner-abilities in the decision process', *Behavioral and Brain Sciences*, **31**, 415–437.

Robins, L. (1993), 'Vietnam veterans' rapid recovery from heroin addiction: a fluke or normal expectation?', *Addiction*, **88**, 1041–1054.

Robins, L., J. Helzer and D. Davis (1975), 'Narcotic use in Southeast Asia and afterward: an interview study of 898 Vietnam returnees', *Archives of General Psychiatry*, **32**, 955–961.

Robins, L., J. Helzer, M. Hasselbrock and E. Wish (1980), 'Vietnam veterans three years after Vietnam: how our study changed our view of heroin', in L. Brill and C. Winick (eds), *The Yearbook of Substance and Abuse*, New York: Human Sciences Press, pp. 214–230.

Robinson, I., G. Gorny, E. Milton and B. Kolb (2001), 'Cocaine self-administration alters the morphology dendrites and dendritic spines in the nucleus accumbens and neurocortex', *Synapse*, **39**, 257–266.

Ross, D. (2004), 'Meta-linguistic signalling for coordination amongst social agents', *Language Sciences*, **26**, 621–642.

Ross, D. (2005), *Economic Theory and Cognitive Science: Microexplanation*, Cambridge, MA: MIT Press.

Ross, D. (2006), 'The economics and evolution of selves', *Cognitive Systems Research*, **7**, 246–258.

Ross, D. (2007), '*H sapiens* as ecologically special: what does language contribute?', *Language Sciences*, **29**, 710–731.

Ross, D. (2011), 'The economic agent: not human, but important', in U. Mäki (ed.), *Handbook of the Philosophy of Science, v. 13: Economics*, London: Elsevier.

Ross, D. (2012a), 'Estranged parents and a schizophrenic child: concepts of choice in econom-ics, psychology and neuroeconomics', *Journal of Economic Methodology*, forthcoming.

Ross, D. (2012b), 'The evolution of individualistic norms', in R. Joyce, K. Sterelny and B. Calcott (eds), *Evolution, Cooperation and Complexity*, Cambridge, MA: MIT Press.

Ross, D., C. Sharp, R. Vuchinich and D. Spurrett (2008), *Midbrain Mutiny: The Picoeconomics and Neuroeconomics of Disordered Gambling*, Cambridge, MA: MIT Press.

Rubinstein, A. (2006), *Lecture Notes in Microeconomic Theory: The Economic Agent*, Princeton: Princeton University Press.

Samuelson, P. (1938), 'A note on the pure theory of consumer's behavior', *Economica*, **5**, 61–72.

Samuelson, P. (1947), *Foundations of Economic Analysis*, Enlarged edition (1983), Cambridge, MA: Harvard University Press.

Smith, A. (1759), *The Theory of Moral Sentiments*, reprinted 1976, Indianapolis: Liberty Classics.

Sunstein, C. and R. Thaler (2003a), 'Libertarian paternalism', *American Economic Review, Papers and Proceedings*, **93**, 175–179.

Sunstein, C. and R. Thaler (2003b), 'Libertarian paternalism is not an oxymoron', *University of Chicago Law Review*, **70**, 1159–1202.

SWELOGS [Swedish National Institute of Public Health], (2008), *Swedish Longitudinal Gambling Study*, http://www.fhi.se/PageFiles/10850/SWELOGS-studie-om-spel-o-halsa.pdf

Tavares, H., E. Carneiro, M. Sanches, I. Pinsky, R. Caetano, M. Zaleski and R. Laranjeira (2010), 'Gambling in Brazil: lifetime prevalences and socio-demographic correlates', *Psychiatry Research*, **180**, 35–41.

Thaler, R. and C. Sunstein (2008), *Nudge*, London: Penguin.

Turu-uuringud (2006), *Elanikkonna kokkupuude hasart- ja õnnemängudega (Gambling Prevalence in Estonia)*, Tallinn: Turu-uuringud.

van Walbeek, C. (2006), 'Industry responses to the tobacco excise tax increases in South Africa', *South African Journal of Economics*, **74**, 110–122.

Volberg, A., M. Abbott, S. Rönnberg and I. Munck (2001), 'Prevalence and risks of pathological gambling in Sweden', *Acta Psychiatrica Scandinavica*, **104**, 250–256.

West, R. (2006), *Theory of Addiction*, Oxford: Blackwell.

Wilcox, N. (2008), 'Stochastic models for binary discrete choice under risk: a critical primer and econometric comparison', in J. Cox and G. Harrison (eds), *Risk Aversion in Experiments*, Bingley, UK: Emerald, pp. 197–292.

Wise, R. (2000), 'Addiction becomes a brain disease', *Neuron*, **26**, 27–33.

11 A template matching technique of personality classification for the study of consumer behavior: case study of Lois the compulsive buyer

Paul J. Albanese

11.1 INTRODUCTION

The results are presented for a template matching technique of personality classification based on the California Adult Q Set that can be used for the study of consumer behavior, and an application is made to a case study of the personality organization of a compulsive buyer. Quantitative approaches to personality have been mired in individual difference or trait measures that treat people as parts and present a limited view of the person. The big five factor model of personality is an improvement in that it provides scores on an aggregation of five traits, but it does not identify the person's personality in the terms meaningful to a clinician, and therefore does not connect to the vast clinical literature rich with detailed observations of consumer behavior.

The development of the California Adult Q Set was led by Jack Block between 1952 and 1957 (Block 1961). Block (1961) described the California Q Set as a language instrument which permits the comprehensive description of an individual's personality in a form suitable for quantitative comparison and analysis. The California Q Set consists of 100 cards containing descriptive statements that are sorted into 9 categories from extremely characteristic (9) to extremely uncharacteristic (1) with a fixed number of cards in each category forming a forced symmetric distribution with a mean of 5 and a standard deviation of 2.089 (Block 1961). When a sort is done on a person, 'the subject is described as he appears and is understood by the observer at the time of observation' (Block 1961, p. 5). Using family members as sorters automatically controls for many factors such as social class, culture and ethnicity, race, religion, and to some extent, genetic endowment.

'Q technique and its methodology, invented and advanced primarily by William Stephenson, was designed to assist in the orderly examination of human subjectivity' (Brown 1980, p. 5). According to Stephenson (1954,

p. 106), 'Q-technique operates by synthesis, not further reductionism,' thereby providing a holistic technique that captures the person's entire personality. The specific adaptation of the California Q Set, the template matching technique, was developed by Bem and Funder (1978). The California Q Set was modified by Bem and Funder (1978) by adding simplifying paraphrases in parentheses below the original statements so that nonprofessionals could use it, a process Block completed in 1990.

A set of eight personality templates created from the California Q Set were examined. A personality template is a prototype or ideal conception of a personality disorder constructed from the 100 statements of the California Q Set. A comparison is made between a subject sort and a personality template by calculating a Pearson product-moment correlation coefficient across all 100 items, thereby expressing directly and quantitatively the degree of similarity between the two sorts (Bem and Funder 1978).

A person's particular personality represents the predominant predisposition of the individual, and classification is based on the highest and most significant positive correlation with one of the eight personality templates. A person is likely to have more than one diagnostic label on his or her personality, however, and that configuration or pattern would represent the person's entire personality or personality organization. The classification of a person's entire personality organization is based on the pattern of correlations across all eight personality templates. While the classification of a person's particular personality is based on the highest and most significant positive correlation with a personality template, this decision rule should not be applied too stringently, because in most cases only minimal interpretation of the pattern of correlations across all of the personality templates is required to arrive at an accurate description of a person's entire personality organization.

The person is also classified by the level of personality development. The classification at the level of personality development is provided by the Personality Continuum, an integrative framework for the interdisciplinary study of consumer behavior (see Albanese 2002, 2006). The Personality Continuum is divided into four qualitatively different levels of personality development that are hierarchically arranged in descending order from highest to lowest level: normal, neurotic, primitive, and psychotic (Albanese 2002). The classification of a person into a range of the Personality Continuum connects that person to a general pattern of human behavior, an overall pattern of consumer behavior, a specific pattern of consumption behavior, and a qualitatively different pattern of shopping behavior amongst others (Albanese 2002). The template matching technique of personality classification was developed to classify a person along the Personality Continuum. The Personality Continuum provides a theoretical framework that adds a useful level of analysis for interpreting the results of the template matching technique of personality classification.

The information useful for the study of personality and consumer behavior begins with the classification of a person's level of personality development and particular personality organization along the Personality Continuum. The entire subject sort is used for the purposes of personality classification with the template matching technique. The California Adult Q Set can be used in three different ways to establish the relationship between personality and consumer behavior: the entire sort, an aggregation of items to form a behavioral template, and a single item. The entire sort can be used to study the relationship between personality and consumer behavior by acquiring sorts on subjects who manifest the pattern of consumer behavior under investigation to identify the particular personality organization that is prone to this pattern of consumer behavior. The aggregation of items to form behavioral templates is based on the selection of a subset of the 100 items of the California Adult Q Set that are descriptive of a particular pattern of consumer behavior. This was the original application of the template matching technique to study the delay of gratification by Bem and Funder (1978). A single item can be used to identify a particular pattern of consumer behavior. Item 53 of the California Adult Q Set is descriptive of a compulsive and more extreme addictive pattern of consumer behavior characteristic of the personality organizations arrested at the primitive level of personality development: 'Needs and impulses tend toward relatively direct and uncontrolled expression; unable to delay gratification (is impulsive, has little self-control; unable to postpone pleasure).' For personality organizations arrested at the primitive level of personality development item 53 should be rated as extremely characteristic (9), quite characteristic (8), or fairly characteristic (7).

A case study of a typical compulsive buyer will be presented to explore the relationship between personality and consumer behavior. The detailed analysis presented in the case study of Lois the compulsive buyer illustrates the strength of Q methodology in investigating in depth the case study of one person. In Q methodology, the sort of one person can provide a specimen who can be used to research valid conclusions in relation to a theory (Stephenson 1953, p. 3).

The results for the eight personality templates are each presented in a separate section organized into four parts: (1) the pattern of correlations of the subjects with the eight personality templates; (2) the correlations among the subjects; (3) the factor analysis; (4) discussion. The overall success rate of the template matching technique of personality classification in identifying the level of personality development and the particular personality organization and a factor analysis of the 36 subjects is then presented. The template matching technique of personality classification is then applied to the case study of Lois the compulsive buyer.

11.2   METHODOLOGY

Eight personality templates acquired from a variety of sources were eventually deemed useful for this project: Optimally Adjusted, representing the normal range of the Personality Continuum; Obsessive, Histrionic, and Paranoid, representing the neurotic range of the Personality Continuum; and Borderline, Narcissistic, Antisocial, and Schizoid, representing the primitive range of the Personality Continuum. There are as yet no templates for the psychotic range of the Personality Continuum and no sorts of psychotic subjects were sought. The optimally adjusted and male paranoid personality templates were provided in Block (1961). These personality templates were created by nine experienced clinical psychologists. The average inter-correlation among the nine sorters for the optimally adjusted personality template was r = .78 and for the male paranoid personality template r = .55. The Stanford Histrionic, Stanford Borderline, and Stanford Antisocial were provided to me by Jack Block. The Wink Narcissism Prototype is based on the ratings of nine judges and has an alpha reliability of .91 (Wink 1991). The Obsessive Personality Template was provided by Dr. Polly Young-Eisendrath on 17 February 2005. I created the Schizoid Personality Template based primarily on the clinical studies of Fairbairn (1952), Sullivan (1956), and Kernberg (1985) and it was completed on 3 March 1989.

The personality diagnoses of experienced clinicians were required to compare with the classification of the template matching technique of personality classification to explore the validity of the eight personality templates. It was necessary to work with experienced clinicians because it is their personality diagnoses that are compared with the classification of the template matching technique. Once the validity of the eight personality templates has been explored, the best sorters for research purposes are family members and friends who know the subject well.

Five subjects were sought from experienced clinicians—psychologists, psychiatrists, and counselors—for each personality template. Q methodology operates with a relatively small number of subjects because the statements are the sample and the persons are the variables. The ideal subject to sort is a chronologically adult person, at least 18 years of age, who has been in therapy long enough for an experienced clinician to have made a clear diagnosis of his or her personality organization under ordinary functioning. The clinicians were instructed to sort the actual subject rather than the theoretical conception of any particular personality organization. The typical sort takes less than an hour and does not involve the subject in any direct way. The statement numbers are recorded on a Sorting Guide and a Personality Diagnosis Information Form was completed by the clinician, which included the diagnostic codes for personality disorders from the *Diagnostic and Statistical Manual of Mental Disorders* (DSM-IV-TR) (2000). The clinicians were offered full compensation for the time spent sorting the subject and completing the two forms. Only four clinicians requested payment.

Thirty six useable subjects were acquired gradually over a two year period of intensive effort: Optimally Adjusted (4); Obsessive (5); Histrionic (5); Paranoid (4); Borderline (5); Narcissistic (5); Schizoid (5); Antisocial (3). Despite the persistence and determination of some very capable research assistants, we were unable to acquire five subjects for each personality template that met the criteria for selection for both clinician and the subject. Only four subjects were acquired for the Optimally Adjusted and Paranoid Personality Templates, and only three subjects were acquired with great difficulty for the Antisocial Personality Template.

Each subject sort is designated by the name of the person doing the sort and the particular personality of the subject being sorted. This naming convention was chosen over a more simplified approach to maintain as much connection between the sorter and subject as possible. Q methodology is about human subjectivity and that connection is critical to the analysis.

11.3   RESULTS FOR THE BLOCK OPTIMALLY ADJUSTED PERSONALITY TEMPLATE

The results of the correlation analysis of the four optimally adjusted subjects with the eight personality templates are presented in Table 11.1a. All four optimally adjusted subjects are correctly classified with the highest positive significant correlation with the Optimally Adjusted Personality Template at the normal level of personality development: Cort/Optimally Adjusted ($r = .683$, $p < .000$); Rosenbaum/Optimally Adjusted/MRS S ($r = .588$, $p < .000$); McKenzie/Optimally Adjusted ($r = .699$, $p < .000$); Rosenbaum/Optimally Adjusted/DR D ($r = .685$, $p < .000$). All four normal subjects are negatively and significantly correlated with the four personality templates at the primitive level of personality development, with the exception of the Rosenbaum/Optimally Adjusted/DR D with the

Table 11.1a   Correlations of the four optimally adjusted subjects with personality templates

	Cort/ Optimally Adjusted	Rosenbaum/ Optimally Adjusted/MRS S	McKenzie/ Optimally Adjusted	Rosenbaum/ Optimally Adjusted/DR D
Block Optimally Adjusted Personality Template	**.683** .000	**.588** .000	**.699** .000	**.685** .000
Young-Eisendrath Obsessive Personality Template	-.009 .927	-.113 .261	.199 .047	.000 1.000
Stanford Histrionic Prototype	-.097 .336	.012 .909	-.234 .019	-.051 .615
Block Paranoid Personality Template	**-.312** .002	**-.394** .000	-.220 .028	**-.333** .001
Stanford Borderline Prototype	**-.500** .000	**-.447** .000	**-.606** .000	**-.602** .000
Wink Narcissism Prototype	**-.350** .000	**-.229** .022	**-.299** .003	**-.264** .008
Stanford Antisocial Prototype	**-.250** .014	-.187 .062	**-.262** .009	-.134 .183
Albanese Schizoid Personality Template	**-.421** .000	**-.396** .000	**-.225** .025	**-.539** .000

Table 11.1b   Correlations of the four optimally adjusted subjects

	Cort/ Optimally Adjusted	Rosenbaum/ Optimally Adjusted/ MRS S	McKenzie/ Optimally Adjusted	Rosenbaum/ Optimally Adjusted/ DR D
Cort/Optimally	1.000	.468	.565	.671
Adjusted	.	.000	.000	.000
Rosenbaum/MRS S	.468	1.000	.521	.546
	.000	.	.000	.000
McKenzie/	.565	.521	1.000	.627
Optimally Adjusted	.000	.000	.	.000
Rosenbaum/	.671	.546	.627	1.000
Optimally Adjusted	.000	.000	.000	.

Table 11.1c   Rotated component matrix: four normal subjects

	Component
	1
Cort/Optimally Adjusted	.826
Rosenbaum/Optimally Adjusted/MRS S	.759
McKenzie/Optimally Adjusted	.827
Rosenbaum/Optimally Adjusted/DR D	.873

Stanford Antisocial prototype (r = −.134, p = .183), and in each case, the highest negative correlation is with the Stanford Borderline Prototype: Cort/Optimally Adjusted (r = −.500, p < .000); Rosenbaum/Optimally Adjusted/MRS S (r = −.447, p < .000); McKenzie/Optimally Adjusted (r = −.606, p < 000); and Rosenbaum/Optimally Adjusted/DR D (r = −.602, p < .000). At the neurotic level of personality development, the correlations are consistently negative and significant only with the Paranoid Personality Template: Cort/Optimally Adjusted (r = −.312, p < .002); Rosenbaum/Optimally Adjusted/MRS S (r = −.394, p < .000); McKenzie/Optimally Adjusted (r = −.220, p < .028); and Rosenbaum/Optimally Adjusted/DR D (r = −.333, p < .001). Table 11.1b shows that the four optimally adjusted subjects are highly and significantly correlated with one another. Table 11.1c presents the factor analysis of the four optimally adjusted subjects. Only one factor emerges explaining 67.61% of the total variance.

The validity of the Optimally Adjusted Personality Template is clear cut as the pattern of correlations and factor analysis demonstrate. The Optimally Adjusted Personality Template was created by nine experienced clinical psychologists with an average inter-correlation of .78 (Block 1961). The acquisition of the four optimally adjusted subjects was particularly difficult because a normal person is not the type of client that a clinician is likely to see in the clinical situation. In one case, the subject was the spouse of a client who was working with the clinician.

11.4   RESULTS FOR THE YOUNG-EISENDRATH OBSESSIVE PERSONALITY TEMPLATE

The results of the correlation analysis of the five obsessive subjects with the eight personality templates are presented in Table 11.2a. Three subjects were correctly classified as having a predominantly obsessive personality organization at the neurotic level of personality development: Young-Eisendrath/Obsessive ($r = .484$, $p < .000$), Rosenbaum/Obsessive/ MS B ($r = .322$, $p < .001$), and Rosenbaum/Obsessive/MRS G ($r = .197$, $p < .05$). The Grzegorek/Obsessive subject is significantly correlated with the Young-Eisendrath Obsessive Personality Template ($r = .310$, $p < .01$), but has a higher and more significant correlation with the Paranoid Personality Template ($r = .426$, $p < .000$), therefore, this subject is correctly classified at the neurotic level of personality development but not with a predominantly obsessive personality organization. The Wilde/ Obsessive subject is not significantly correlated with the Young-Eisendrath Obsessive Personality Template. The highest positive correlation is with the Schizoid Personality Template ($r = .252$, $p < .01$), and there are significant negative correlations with the Stanford Histrionic Prototype ($r = -.331$, $p < .001$) and the Wink Narcissism Prototype ($r = -.215$, $p < .05$). None of the correlations with the Stanford Antisocial prototype are significant. The Wilde/Obsessive subject was not correctly classified at the level of personality development or particular personality organization by the template matching technique. Four of the five obsessive subjects were correctly classified at the neurotic level of personality development and three as having an obsessive personality organization.

Table 11.2b shows that the three obsessive subjects who were correctly classified by personality organization, Young-Eisendrath/ Obsessive, Rosenbaum/Obsessive/MRS G, Rosenbaum/Obsessive/MS B, are all significantly correlated. The two subjects that were not correctly classified by personality organization, Grzegorek/Obsessive and Wilde/Obsessive, are significantly correlated ($r = .308$, $p < .01$).

In Table 11.2c two rotated factors emerge explaining 61.60% of total variance with Factor 1 explaining 32.28% and Factor 2 29.31%. Factor 1 contains the three obsessive subjects who were correctly classified by

Table 11.2a Correlations of five obsessive subjects with personality templates

	Grzegorek/ Obsessive	Young-Eisendrath/ Obsessive Subject	Wilde/ Obsessive	Rosenbaum/ Obsessive/ MS B	Rosenbaum/ Obsessive/ MRS G
Block Optimally Adjusted Personality Template	-.181 .072	.123 .224	-.025 .801	.222 .026	.025 .801
Young-Eisendrath/Obsessive Personality Template	.310 .002	.484 .000	.181 .072	.322 .001	.197 .050
Stanford Histrionic Prototype	-.400 .000	.065 .522	-.331 .001	-.225 .025	-.009 .927
Block Paranoid Personality Template	.426 .000	.081 .423	.067 .507	.137 .175	.093 .360
Stanford Borderline Prototype	-.111 .271	-.028 .784	-.192 .055	-.292 .003	-.093 .360
Wink Narcissism Prototype	.072 .478	.104 .302	-.215 .031	-.067 .507	-.127 .207
Stanford Antisocial Prototype	.111 .271	.062 .537	-.174 .084	-.028 .784	-.042 .681
Albanese Schizoid Personality Template	.243 .015	.005 .964	.252 .011	-.002 .982	.116 .251

Table 11.2b Correlations among the five obsessive subjects

	Grzegorek/ Obsessive	Young-Eisendrath/ Obsessive Subject	Wilde/ Obsessive	Rosenbaum/ Obsessive/MS B	Rosenbaum/ Obsessive/ MRS G
Grzegorek/Obsessive	1.000 .	-.028 .784	.308 .002	.183 .069	.144 .154
Young-Eisendrath/Obsessive Subject	-.028 .784	1.000 .	.079 .436	.326 .001	.208 .038
Wilde/ Obsessive	.308 .002	.079 .436	1.000 .	.370 .000	.347 .000
Rosenbaum/Obsessive/MS B	.183 .069	.326 .001	.370 .000	1.000 .	.345 .000
Rosenbaum/Obsessive/ MRS G	.144 .154	.208 .038	.347 .000	.345 .000	1.000 .

Table 11.2c   Rotated component matrix: five obsessive subjects

	Component	
	1	2
Young-Eisendrath/Obsessive Subject	.804	−.262
Rosenbaum/Obsessive/MS B	.711	.328
Rosenbaum/Obsessive/MRS G	.588	.372
Grzegorek/Obsessive		.798
Wilde/Obsessive	.334	.718

personality organization: Young-Eisendrath Obsessive (.80), Rosenbaum/ Obsessive/MS B (.71), and Rosenbaum/Obsessive/MRS G (.59). The latter two subjects are mixed with loadings on Factor 2 for Rosenbaum/ Obsessive/MS B (.33) and Rosenbaum/Obsessive/MRS G (.37). Factor 2 contains the Grzegorek/Obsessive subject (.80), correctly classified at the neurotic level of personality development and significantly correlated with the Young-Eisendrath Obsessive Personality Template (r = .31, p < .002), and the Wilde/Obsessive subject (.72), misclassified at the level of personality development and particular personality organization, and a mixed subject also loading on Factor 1 (.33).

The ultimate outcome of the analysis of Q methodology is a factor array, an idealized sort representing each rotated factor. The factor array is derived from the normalized factor scores for each statement, ranked in descending order, and converted into the original rating from 1 to 9 used in the forced symmetric distribution of the California Q Set. The factor score for each statement is calculated by weighting the original ratings from 1 to 9 by the subject's factor loading summed across the subjects that load on that factor. The factor scores are then normalized to remove the effect of differences in the number of subjects loaded on each factor (Brown 1980, p. 243).

For each personality organization there is a spectrum of variation. Two different conceptions on the spectrum of variation of the obsessive personality organization are clearly represented, one a more conventional clinical conception and the other more favorable or *high functioning* conception. In the California Q Set five items receive a rating of 9, extremely characteristic or salient. The five statements with the highest normalized factor scores on Factor 2 capture more of the conventional diagnostic criteria for Obsessive-Compulsive Personality Disorder (DSM-IV-TR 2000, p. 729): 'A pervasive pattern of preoccupation with orderliness, perfectionism, and mental and interpersonal control.' (The normalized factor scores appear in parentheses following the statements.)

Table 11.2d   Rotated component matrix with personality template

	Component	
	1	2
Young-Eisendrath/Obsessive Subject	.895	
Young-Eisendrath/Obsessive Template	.741	.227
Rosenbaum/Obsessive/MS B	.527	.495
Wilde/Obsessive		.798
Grzegorek/Obsessive		.693
Rosenbaum/Obsessive/MRS G	.316	.547

6.   Is fastidious; meticulous, careful and precise (2.67)
47. Tends to fantasize, engage in fictional speculation (2.14)
26. Is productive, gets things done (2.01)
25. Over-controls impulses; delays gratification unnecessarily (1.96)
70. Sensitive to demands or requests for favors (1.63)

On Factor 1, the five statements that received the highest normalized factor scores represent a more favorable variation of the obsessive personality organization:

8.   Appears to have a high degree of intellectual capacity (2.23)
72. High aspiration level for self; sets high personal goals (1.81)
16. Introspective; thinks about self; examines own thoughts (1.71)
79. Ruminates and has persistent, preoccupying thoughts (1.69)
89. Is personally charming (1.68)

When the five obsessive subjects are factor analyzed with the Young-Eisendrath Obsessive Personality Template, the two factors become somewhat clearer (Table 11.2d). The Young-Eisendrath/Obsessive subject (.90) defines Factor 1, and the Wilde/Obsessive (.80) and Grzegorek/Obsessive (.69) subjects define Factor 2. Rosenbaum/Obsessive/MS B is a mixed subject loading more on Factor 1 (.53) than Factor 2 (.50). Rosenbaum/Obsessive/MRS G is also a mixed subject with MRS G loading more on Factor 2 (.55) than Factor 1 (.32). Total explained variance is 57.63% with each factor almost exactly equal. Factor 2 contains the Wilde/Obsessive (.80) subject, misclassified at the level of personality development and personality organization, and the Grzegorek/Obsessive subject (.69), correctly classified at the level of personality development but not the particular personality organization. The two factor structure remained when the Wilde/Obsessive subject was eliminated. When the Grzegorek/Obsessive subject is also eliminated only one factor emerges. The Young-Eisendrath Obsessive Personality Template loads on Factor 1 (.74) and Factor 2 (.23); thus it is capable of capturing both variations on the spectrum of the obsessive personality organization.

11.5 RESULTS FOR THE STANFORD HISTRIONIC PROTOTYPE

The results of the correlation analysis of the five histrionic subjects with the personality templates are presented in Table 11.3a. Three of the five histrionic subjects were correctly classified as having a predominantly histrionic personality organization at the neurotic level of personality development: Gilbertson/Hysteric (r = .558, p < .000), Friedman/Hysteric (r = .336, p < .001), and Kanake/Histrionic (r = .583, p < .000). The Martin/Hysteric subject is not significantly correlated with the Stanford Histrionic Prototype (r = .146, p = .148), but is significantly correlated with the Optimally Adjusted Personality Template (r = .359, p < .000). The Sharp/Histrionic subject is significantly correlated with the Stanford Histrionic Prototype (r = .359, p < .000), but has a slightly higher correlation with the Optimally Adjusted Personality Template (r = .484, p < .000), and there are strong negative correlations with the Paranoid (r = −.289, p < .01) and Schizoid (r = −.509, p < .000) Personality Templates. The Martin/Hysteric and Sharp/Histrionic subjects are misclassified at the level of personality development and particular personality organization.

The Gilbertson/Hysteric and Kanake/Histrionic subjects have strong positive and significant correlations with personality templates at the primitive level of personality development. The Gilbertson/Hysteric subject is positively correlated with the Stanford Borderline Prototype (r = .507, p < .000), Wink Narcissism Prototype (r = .396, p < .000), and Stanford Antisocial Prototype (r = .359, p < .000) at the primitive level and the Paranoid Personality Template (r = .231, p < .05) at the neurotic level of personality development. The Kanake/Histrionic subject is positively correlated with the Stanford Borderline Prototype (r = .315, p < .001), Wink Narcissism Prototype (r = .405, p < .000), and the Stanford Antisocial Prototype (r = .435, p < .000). The Friedman/Hysteric and Martin/Hysteric subjects were negatively and significantly correlated with the primitive personality templates. The Friedman/Hysteric subject is negatively correlated with the Wink Narcissism Prototype (r = −.296, p < .003), the Stanford Antisocial Prototype (r = −.199, p < .05), and the Schizoid Personality Template (r = −.289, p = .004) at the primitive level and the Paranoid Personality Template (r = −.368, p = .000) at the

Table 11.3a   Correlations of five histrionic subjects with personality templates

	Gilbertson/ Hysteric	Friedman/ Hysteric	Martin/ Hysteric	Sharp/ Histrionic	Kanake Histrionic
Block Optimally Adjusted Personality Template	**-.282** **.004**	.137 .175	**.359** **.000**	**.484** **.000**	-.019 .855
Young-Eisendrath/Obsessive Personality Template	.083 .410	-.079 .436	.086 .397	-.144 .154	-.139 .168
Stanford Histrionic Prototype	**.558** **.000**	**.336** **.001**	.146 .148	**.359** **.000**	**.583** **.000**
Block Paranoid Personality Template	**.231** **.020**	**-.368** **.000**	**-.204** **.042**	**-.289** **.004**	-.028 .784
Stanford Borderline Prototype	**.507** **.000**	-.132 .191	**-.206** **.040**	-.160 .112	**.315** **.001**
Wink Narcissism Prototype	**.396** **.000**	**-.296** **.003**	**-.208** **.038**	.039 .697	**.405** **.000**
Stanford Antisocial Prototype	**.359** **.000**	**-.199** **.047**	-.125 .215	.162 .107	**.435** **.000**
Albanese Schizoid Personality Template	.174 .084	**-.289** **.004**	**-.225** **.025**	**-.509** **.000**	-.169 .093

Table 11.3b   Correlations of the five histrionic subjects

	Gilbertson/ Hysteric	Friedman/ Hysteric	Martin/ Hysteric	Sharp/ Histrionic	Kanake/ Histrionic
Gilbertson/	1.000	.225	.090	.093	.340
Hysteric	.	.025	.372	.360	.001
Friedman/	.225	1.000	.433	.380	.155
Hysteric	.025	.	.000	.000	.123
Martin/	.090	.433	1.000	.438	.148
Hysteric	.372	.000	.	.000	.141
Sharp/	.093	.380	.438	1.000	.470
Histrionic	.360	.000	.000	.	.000
Kanake/	.340	.155	.148	.470	1.000
Histrionic	.001	.123	.141	.000	.

neurotic level of personality development. The Martin/Hysteric subject is negatively correlated with the Stanford Borderline Prototype ($r = -.206$, $p < .05$), the Wink Narcissism Prototype ($r = -.208$, $p < .05$), and the Schizoid Personality Template ($r = -.225$, $p < .05$) at the primitive level and the Paranoid Personality Template ($r = -.204$, $p < .05$) at the neurotic level. The Sharp/Histrionic subject is strongly negatively correlated with the Schizoid Personality Template ($r = -.509$, $p = .000$) and negatively correlated with the Paranoid Personality Template ($r = -.289$, $p = .004$).

In Table 11.3b the three histrionic subjects who were correctly classified by the particular personality organization are significantly correlated. The correlation of the Gilbertson/Hysteric and Friedman/Hysteric ($r = .225$, $p < .05$) subjects is lower than with the Gilbertson/Hysteric and Kanake/ Histrionic ($r = .340$, $p < .001$) subjects, as would be expected given the borderline and narcissistic features shared by the latter two subjects. The Martin/Hysteric and Sharp/Histrionic, classified at the normal level of personality development, are significantly correlated ($r = .438$, $p < .000$). The highest correlation is between the Sharp/Histrionic and Kanake/ Histrionic subjects ($r = .470$, $p < .000$).

In Table 11.3c two rotated factors emerged explaining 64.69% of the total variance, with Factor 1 explaining 36.64% and Factor 2 28.05%. The Martin/Hysteric (.84), Friedman/Hysteric (.74), and Sharp Histrionic (.73) subjects load on Factor 1, and the Gilbertson/Hysteric (.80) and Kanake/Hysteric (.80) subjects load on Factor 2. Factor 2 makes sense because of the similarities between the Gilbertson/Hysteric and Kanake/ Hysteric subjects with high, positive, and significant correlations with the Stanford Histrionic Prototype, and the strong borderline, narcissistic,

Table 11.3c   Rotated component matrix: five histrionic subjects

	Component	
	1	2
Martin/Hysteric	.836	
Friedman/Hysteric	.740	
Sharp/Histrionic	.728	.318
Gilbertson/Hysteric		.803
Kanake/Histrionic	.238	.799

and antisocial features at the primitive level of personality development. Factor 1 represents the subjects who are more clearly neurotic without the strong borderline, narcissistic, and antisocial features.

Two different conceptions on the spectrum of variation of the histrionic personality disorder are represented here, one a more conventional clinical conception, and the other a more favorable or high functioning variation. This is similar to the finding on the spectrum of variation of the obsessive personality disorder. A comparison of the five statements that received the highest factor scores for Factors 1 and 2 reveal clear differences in the conception of the histrionic personality disorder among the clinicians doing the subject sorts. Factor 1 represents a high functioning histrionic personality organization:

81. Is physically attractive; is good looking (1.73)
 8. Appears to have a high degree of intellectual capacity (1.75)
26. Is productive, gets things done (1.68)
17. Behaves in a sympathetic and considerate manner (1.65)
11. Protective of those close to him/her (1.51)

Factor 2 represents a more conventional conception of the histrionic personality disorder which accords quite closely with the diagnostic criteria for this disorder in the DSM-IV-TR (2000, p. 714).

99. Is self-dramatizing; histrionic (2.022)
31. Regards self as physically attractive (1.850)
43. Is facially and/or gesturally expressive (1.822)
50. Unpredictable and changeable in attitudes and behavior (1.553)
67. Is self-indulgent; tends to pamper himself or herself (1.522)

PQMETHODS 2.11 is a specialized program for doing Q methodology that provides detailed statement-by-statement comparisons of all

Table 11.3d Rotated component matrix with Stanford Histrionic Prototype

	Component	
	1	2
Stanford Histrionic Prototype	.861	.217
Gilbertson/Hysteric	.785	
Friedman/Hysteric		.720
Martin/Hysteric		.838
Sharp/Histrionic	.286	.736
Kanake/Histrionic	.744	.241

100 items of the California Q Set. The top five statements alone have been very useful and much additional information is contained in the remaining 95 statements. To calculate the factor score for each statement, the original ratings from 1 to 9 for each of the subjects that load on a factor are weighted by the subject's factor loading and then summed. The factor weight is $f \div (1 - f^2)$, where f is the factor loading. The factor score for that statement is then normalized. To create the factor arrays in PQMETHODS, factors are flagged so that only the subjects who load significantly on one factor are chosen as defining variables. The normalized factor scores in PQMETHODS and SPSS, therefore, will be different because the weighting is different, and because only subjects that have been flagged on each factor are used in PQMETHODS. The rankings of normalized factor scores, although not exactly the same, are quite close; thus the factor arrays may be slightly different. The advantages of using a specialized program like PQMETHODS, however, far outweigh any discrepancies with SPSS. For reporting factor scores and creating factor arrays SPSS is preferable, but for detailed statement-by-statement comparisons of difference, consensus and disagreement, and distinguishing statements, PQMETHODS is preferable.

The following are top three distinguishing statements from PQMETHODS, significant at $p < .01$, out of a total of 48 distinguishing statements that were significant at the $p < .05$:

8. Appears to have a high degree of intellectual capacity (1.75)
26. Is productive, gets things done (1.59)
81. Is physically attractive; is good looking (1.52)

Similar to the analysis of the obsessive personality organization, a more conventional conception of the histrionic personality organization emerged on Factor 2 and a high functioning conception on Factor 1. The distinguishing statements for Factor 1 emphasize a high degree of intellectual capacity and productivity. Factor 2 is self-dramatizing, expressive, unpredictable, changeable in attitudes and behavior, and self-indulgent. It is quite interesting to note that on Factor 1, physically attractive and good looking represents the judgment of the sorter, while on Factor 2, regards self as physically attractive is the judgment of the subject. The statement 'Is physically attractive; is good looking' is the third strongest distinguishing statement between the two factors.

What we are seeing is a conception of a person on the spectrum of variation of the histrionic personality organization who is better off (Factor 1), relatively speaking, than another person with an histrionic personality organization who is worse off (Factor 2). The more favorable conception of the histrionic personality organization represented by Factor 1 clearly indicates a person who has achieved the higher neurotic level of personality development, while Factor 2 represents an individual arrested at the lower primitive level of personality development. A person arrested at the neurotic level of personality development has many higher level human capacities that make him or her basically a good person, including the human capacity for concern for another person and oneself (Albanese 2002). The human capacity for concern is captured by item 17, 'Behaves in a sympathetic and considerate manner,' received a 9, extremely characteristic, on the original rating scale, and ranked fourth with a factor score of 1.66 on Factor 1. On Factor 2, item 17 received a factor score of −1.68, ranked 95th, and received a rating of 2, quite uncharacteristic or negatively salient.

A success rate for classification of three out of five, or 60%, undervalues the usefulness of the Stanford Histrionic Prototype. The psychiatrist who sorted the Martin/Hysteric subject indicated that this person was a 'high-functioning' hysteric on the Personality Diagnosis Information Form. To be high functioning as a neurotic personality organization would mean to behave at the higher normal level of personality development. That is precisely what the pattern of correlations of the template matching technique of personality classification is indicating so clearly. As further evidence, in Table 11.3a, the correlations are negative and significant with the Paranoid ($r = −.204$, $p < .05$), Stanford Borderline ($r = −.206$, $p < .05$), Wink Narcissism ($r = −.208$, $p < .05$), and Schizoid ($r = −.225$, $p < .05$) Personality Templates. Nonetheless, given the stringent criterion that defines a correct classification of the particular personality organization, this subject must be regarded as a misclassification. In a similar way, the Sharp/Histrionic subject could be described as a high functioning histrionic personality organization—significantly correlated with the Stanford

Histrionic Prototype (r = .359, p < .000), but with a higher correlation on the Optimally Adjusted Personality Template (r = .484, p < .000). Thus, with only minimal interpretation of the pattern of correlations with all of the personality templates, the Martin/Hysteric and Sharp/Histrionic subjects can be accurately described by the template matching technique. The success rate for classification of the Stanford Histrionic Prototype can be improved, perhaps, to as high as five out of five.

The Personality Continuum offers some useful insights into the interpretation of the pattern of correlations with the personality templates. The Friedman/Hysteric subject (r = .336, p < .001), correctly classified by the level of personality development and particular personality organization, but with the lowest correlation of the four subjects significantly correlated with the Stanford Histrionic Prototype, has a pattern of negative and significant correlations with personality templates that are ranked lower within the neurotic range (Paranoid Personality Template r = −.368, p < .000), and with personality disorders in the lower primitive range of the Personality Continuum: Wink Narcissism Prototype (r = −.296, p < .01), Stanford/Antisocial Prototype (r = −.199, p < .05), and Schizoid Personality Template (r = −.289, p < .01). This pattern of correlations is similar to the Martin/ Hysteric and Sharp/Histrionic subjects. In contrast to these three similar histrionic subjects, the Gilbertson/Hysteric and Kanake/Histrionic subjects have in common strong, positive, and significant correlations with the Stanford Borderline Prototype, the Wink Narcissism Prototype, and the Stanford Antisocial Prototype, but not the Schizoid Personality Template (Table 11.3a). For the Gilbertson/Hysteric subject, the correlations with the Stanford Borderline Prototype (r = .507, p < .000), the Wink Narcissism Prototype (r = .396, p < .000), and Stanford Antisocial Prototype (r = .359, p < .000), and for the Kanake/Histrionic subject the correlations with the Stanford Borderline Prototype (r = .315, p < .001), the Wink Narcissism Prototype (r = .405, p < .000), and the Stanford Antisocial Prototype (r = .435, p < .000). The Gilbertson/ Hysteric subject in particular has a strong, positive and significant correlation with the Stanford Borderline Prototype (r = .507, p < .000), a significant positive correlation with the Paranoid Personality Template (r = .231, p < .05), and a negative and significant correlation with the Optimally Adjusted Personality Template (r = −.282, p < .01).

These histrionic subjects illustrate the difficulties of differentiating between an individual with a personality organization arrested at the neurotic level of personality development under ordinary functioning from a person arrested at the primitive level under high functioning. To some extent, both subjects represent a manifestation of the hypothesis advanced by W.R.D. Fairbairn (1952) that a person with a personality organization arrested at the primitive level of personality development under high functioning can use a range of neurotic defenses to deal with severe anxiety in interpersonal relations. The pattern of correlations provided by the template matching technique contributes to a clarification of this difficult delineation along the Personality Continuum. This critical issue will be explored further in the discussion of the case study of a compulsive buyer.

11.6   RESULTS FOR THE BLOCK PARANOID PERSONALITY TEMPLATE

The correlation analysis of the four paranoid subjects is presented in Table 11.4a. Three of the four paranoid subjects are correctly classified as having a predominantly paranoid personality organization at the neurotic level of personality development: Myerscough/Paranoid (r = .366, p < .000); Koricke/Paranoid (r = .722, p < .000); Kanake/Paranoid (r = .748, p < .000). The Crawford/Paranoid subject is highly and significantly correlated with the Paranoid Personality Template (r = .563, p < .000), but has a slightly higher correlation with the Stanford Borderline Prototype (r = .590, p < .000), along with significant positive correlations with the Wink Narcissism Prototype (r = .551, r = .000), the Stanford Antisocial Prototype (r = .484, p = .000), and the Schizoid Personality Template (r = .368, p = .000). Using the stringent criterion that the highest and most significant positive correlation be used for classification of the particular personality organization, this subject must be regarded as a misclassification; however, with only minimal interpretation of the overall pattern of correlations with the personality templates, the Crawford/Paranoid subject can be accurately described.

When compared to the Kanake/Paranoid and Koricke/Paranoid subjects, the similarity in the pattern of positive and significant correlations with all of the personality organizations at the primitive level of personality development and the strong negative and significant correlations with the Optimally Adjusted Personality Template is unmistakable. The Myerscough/Paranoid subject is more clearly neurotic and is significantly correlated with the Young-Eisendrath Obsessive Personality Template (r = .354, p < .000), as is the Koricke/Paranoid subject (r = .363, p < .000) and the Kanake/Paranoid subject (r = .3945, p < .000), but lacking the positive correlations with the personality organizations arrested at the primitive level of personality development. All four paranoid subjects are significantly correlated (Table 11.4b), and the results of the factor analysis

Table 11.4a   Correlations of four paranoid subjects with personality templates

	Myerscough/ Paranoid	Koricke/ Paranoid	Crawford/ Paranoid	Kanake/ Paranoid
Block Optimally Adjusted Personality Template	-.005	-.458	-.394	-.623
	.964	.000	.000	.000
Young-Eisendrath/Obsessive Personality Template	.354	.363	.125	.394
	.000	.000	.215	.000
Stanford Histrionic Prototype	.012	-.299	.074	-.160
	.909	.003	.464	.112
Block Paranoid Personality Template	.366	.722	.563	.748
	.000	.000	.000	.000
Stanford Borderline Prototype	.060	.340	.590	.502
	.552	.001	.000	.000
Wink Narcissism Prototype	.016	.382	.551	.396
	.873	.000	.000	.000
Stanford Antisocial Prototype	.053	.338	.484	.329
	.599	.001	.000	.001
Albanese Schizoid Personality Template	.171	.549	.368	.627
	.088	.000	.000	.000

Table 11.4b   Correlations among four paranoid subjects

	Myerscough/ Paranoid	Koricke/ Paranoid	Crawford/ Paranoid	Kanake Paranoid
Myerscough/	1.000	.299	.292	.262
Paranoid	.	.003	.003	.009
Koricke/	.299	1.000	.569	.697
Paranoid	.003	.	.000	.000
Crawford/	.292	.569	1.000	.495
Paranoid	.003	.000	.	.000
Kanake/	.262	.697	.495	1.000
Paranoid	.009	.000	.000	.

Table 11.4c   Rotated component matrix: four paranoid subjects

	Component
	1
Myerscough/Paranoid	.523
Koricke/Paranoid	.875
Crawford/Paranoid	.785
Kanake/Paranoid	.837

show that only one factor emerges explaining 58.91% of total variance (Table 11.4c). The Myerscough/Paranoid subject has the lowest factor loading (.42).

Although only one paranoid factor forms, there is at least a semblance of two variations on the spectrum of the paranoid personality organization, one clearly more neurotic, exemplified by the Myerscough/Paranoid subject, and the other more clearly primitive, especially schizoid, represented by the Koricke/Paranoid, Crawford/Paranoid, and Kanake/Paranoid subjects. To some extent, the latter three subjects may represent Fairbairn's hypothesis, as high functioning primitive personality organization using a variety of neurotic defenses, such as histrionic, paranoid and obsessive. The correlations with the Schizoid Personality Template are strong and significant for the Koricke/Paranoid ($r = .549$, $p < .000$), Crawford/Paranoid ($r = .368$, $p < .000$), and Kanake/Paranoid ($r = .627$, $p < .000$). The paranoid-schizoid and depressive positions occupy a central place in Fairbairn's (1952) conception of personality. The Myerscough/Paranoid subject would represent the depressive position, a person at the higher neurotic level of personality development with human capacity for concern and the capacity for guilt.

11.7 RESULTS FOR THE STANFORD BORDERLINE PROTOTYPE

The correlation analysis of the five borderline subjects is presented in Table 11.5a. Three out of the five borderline subjects were correctly classified as having a predominantly borderline personality organization at the primitive level of personality development: Hirt/Borderline (r = .785, p < .000), Sharp/Borderline (r = .539, p < .000), and Kanake/Borderline (r = .715, p < .000). The Irwin/Borderline subject has a significant positive correlation with the Stanford Borderline Prototype (r = .366, p < .000), but a higher correlation with the Schizoid Personality Template (r = .463, p < .000), and a strong negative and significant correlation with the Optimally Adjusted Personality Template (r = −.438, p < .000). The Irwin/Borderline subject is correctly classified at the primitive level of personality development, but not the particular personality organization. The Smith/Borderline subject is not significantly correlated with the Stanford Borderline Prototype (r = .185, p = .065), and the strongest positive significant correlations are with the Paranoid Personality Template (r = .451, p < .000) and the Schizoid Personality Template (r = .403, p < .000), and strong negative correlations with the Optimally Adjusted Personality Template (r = −.516, p < .000) and the Stanford Histrionic Personality Template (r = −.363, p < .000). The Smith/Borderline subject is misclassified with regard to the particular personality organization and the level of personality development if the highest positive correlation with the Paranoid Personality Template (r = .451, p < .000) is used to classify this subject at the neurotic level of personality development. The strong positive and significant correlation with the Schizoid Personality Template (r = .403, p < .000), and the negative and significant correlation with the Stanford Histrionic Prototype (r = −.363, p < .000), would argue against the classification at the neurotic level in favor of the primitive level of personality development. The Smith/Borderline subject would then be correctly classified at the primitive level of personality. In Table 11.5b the Kanake/Borderline subject is significantly correlated with all of the borderline subjects, and is the only subject significantly correlated with the Smith/Borderline subject. The Hirt Borderline subject is significantly correlated with all but the Smith/Borderline subject.

In Table 11.5c two factors emerge that explain 70.66% of total variance. The dominant Factor 1 explains 41.50% of total variance and contains the Hirt/Borderline (.84), Sharp/Borderline (.85), Irwin/Borderline (.55) subjects, and the Kanake/Borderline (.58) subject as a mixed subject. Factor 2 explains 24.15% of total variance, and contains mainly the Smith/

Table 11.5a   Correlations of the five borderline subjects with personality templates

	Hirt/ Borderline	Irwin/ Borderline	Smith/ Borderline	Sharp/ Borderline	Kanake/ Borderline
Block Optimally Adjusted Personality Template	-.519	-.438	-.516	-.329	-.708
	.000	.000	.000	.001	.000
Young-Eisendrath/Obsessive Personality Template	.042	.215	.116	.009	.282
	.681	.031	.251	.927	.004
Stanford Histrionic Prototype	.435	.083	-.363	.363	.090
	.000	.410	.000	.000	.372
Block Paranoid Personality Template	.338	.308	.451	.125	.667
	.001	.002	.000	.215	.000
Stanford Borderline Prototype	.785	.366	.185	.539	.715
	.000	.000	.065	.000	.000
Wink Narcissism Prototype	.451	.069	.178	.306	.560
	.000	.507	.271	.007	.000
Stanford Antisocial Prototype	.382	.067	.111	.269	.431
	.000	.507	.271	.007	.000
Albanese Schizoid Personality Template	.280	.463	.403	.192	.576
	.005	.000	.000	.055	.000

Table 11.5b Correlations among the five borderline subjects

	Hirt/ Borderline	Irwin/ Borderline	Smith/ Borderline	Sharp/ Borderline	Kanake/ Borderline
Hirt/Borderline	1.000	.294	.060	.567	.532
	.	.003	.552	.000	.000
Irwin/Borderline	.294	1.000	.079	.269	.338
	.003	.	.436	.007	.001
Smith/Borderline	.060	.079	1.000	−.139	.505
	.552	.436	.	.168	.000
Sharp/Borderline	.567	.269	−.139	1.000	.356
	.000	.007	.168	.	.000
Kanake/Borderline	.532	.338	.505	.356	1.000
	.000	.001	.000	.000	.

Table 11.5c Rotated component matrix: five borderline subjects

	Component	
	1	2
Hirt/Borderline	.838	
Irwin/Borderline	.551	
Smith/Borderline		.942
Sharp/Borderline	.849	
Kanake/Borderline	.584	.696

Borderline subject (.94) and part of mixed Kanake/Borderline subject (.70). The Smith/Borderline subject was classified by the template matching Q technique as strongly paranoid (r = .451, p < .000) and schizoid (r = .403, p < .000), without a significant correlation with the Stanford Borderline Prototype. The Kanake/Borderline subject was classified correctly as to particular personality organization with a strong correlation with the Stanford Borderline Prototype (r = .715, p < .000), and strong correlations with the Paranoid Personality Template (r = .667, p < .000) and the Schizoid Personality Template (r = .576, p < .000), similar to the Smith/Borderline subject. Thus it makes some sense that these two subjects would load on the same factor.

On Factor 1 the five statements that were rated 9, extremely characteristic, clearly represent a borderline personality organization and compare closely to the diagnostic criteria of the borderline personality disorder (DSM-IV-TR 2000, p. 710):

Table 11.5d   Rotated component matrix without smith/borderline subject

	Component
	1
Hirt/Borderline	.839
Irwin/Borderline	.589
Sharp/Borderline	.754
Kanake/Borderline	.762

55. Self-defeating; undermines own chances (2.43)
45. Brittle ego defense system; small reserve of integration (2.35)
72. Doubts about own adequacy as a person (2.24)
50. Unpredictable and changeable in attitudes and behavior (1.79)
82. Has fluctuating moods; moods go up and down (1.70)

On Factor 2, however, the five statements that were rated 9, extremely characteristic or salient, are more clearly representative of a schizoid personality organization:

49. Distrustful of people in general; questions motivations (1.98)
97. Unemotional person; emotionally bland; no strong emotions (1.91)
25. Over-controls impulses; delays gratification unnecessarily (1.86)
36. Is subtly negativistic; tends to undermine, obstruct, or sabotage other people (1.80)
86. Handles anxiety/conflicts by refusing to recognize their presence, repressive or dissociative tendencies (1.79)

When the Smith/Borderline subject is removed from the factor analysis, only one clarified factor forms explaining 55% of the total variance with the same five statements rated 9, extremely characteristic, as on Factor 1 (Table 11.5d). The Smith/Borderline subject represents a manifestation of Fairbairn's paranoid-schizoid position (Fairbairn 1952).

11.8   RESULTS FOR THE WINK NARCISSISM PROTOTYPE

The results of the correlation analysis of the five narcissistic subjects with the eight personality templates are presented in Table 11.6a. All five narcissistic subjects are significantly correlated with the Wink Narcissism Prototype. Three of the narcissistic subjects were correctly classified

Table 11.6a   Correlations of five narcissistic subjects with personality templates

	Wilde/ Narcissistic	Weikel/ Narcissistic	Friedman/ Narcissistic	Dowling/ Narcissistic	Sharp/ Narcissistic
Block Optimally Adjusted Personality Template	-.076 .450	.123 .224	.079 .436	**-.396** **.000**	.039 .697
Young-Eisendrath/Obsessive Personality Template	-.083 .410	.021 .837	.106 .292	.035 .732	.076 .450
Stanford Histrionic Prototype	**.495** **.000**	**.201** **.045**	-.127 .207	**.213** **.033**	-.012 .909
Block Paranoid Personality Template	.032 .749	**.231** **.020**	**.391** **.000**	**.366** **.000**	**.405** **.000**
Stanford Borderline Prototype	**.333** **.001**	.176 .080	.102 .313	**.560** **.000**	**.271** **.006**
Wink Narcissism Prototype	**.227** **.023**	**.558** **.000**	**.502** **.000**	**.442** **.000**	**.484** **.000**
Stanford Antisocial Prototype	**.271** **.006**	**.597** **.000**	**.444** **.000**	**.463** **.000**	**.410** **.000**
Albanese Schizoid Personality Template	-.100 .324	-.113 .261	.023 .819	.271 .006	.046 .647

Table 11.6b   Correlations of five narcissistic subjects

	Wilde/ Narcissistic	Weikel/ Narcissistic	Friedman/ Narcissistic	Dowling/ Narcissistic	Sharp/ Narcissistic
Wilde/	1.000	.201	−.009	.187	.007
Narcissistic	.	.045	.927	.062	.945
Weikel/	.201	1.000	.567	.220	.368
Narcissistic	.045	.	.000	.028	.000
Friedman/	−.009	.567	1.000	.206	.581
Narcissistic	.927	.000	.	.040	.000
Dowling/	.187	.220	.206	1.000	.275
Narcissistic	.062	.028	.040	.	.006
Sharp/	.007	.368	.581	.275	1.000
Narcissistic					

as having a predominantly narcissistic personality organization at the primitive level of personality development: Weikel/Narcissistic (r = .558, p < .000), Friedman/Narcissistic (r = .502, p < .000), and Sharp/ Narcissistic (r = .484, p < .000). The Dowling/Narcissistic subject is significantly correlated with the Wink Narcissism Prototype (r = .442, p < .000), but has a higher correlation with the Stanford Borderline Prototype (r = .560, p < .000). This subject is correctly classified at the primitive level of personality development, but not as having a predominantly borderline personality organization using the stringent criterion. The Wilde/Narcissistic subject is significantly correlated with the Wink Narcissism Prototype (r = .227, p < .05), but it is most highly and significantly correlated with the Stanford Histrionic Prototype (r = .495, p < .000) at the neurotic level of personality development. This subject is not correctly classified at either the level of personality development or particular personality organization. In common with the Wilde/ Narcissistic subject, the Dowling/Narcissistic subject is significantly correlated with the Stanford Histrionic Prototype (r = .213, p < .05), and the Wilde/Narcissistic subject is significantly correlated with the Stanford Borderline Prototype (r = .333, p < .001). The four narcissistic subjects who were correctly classified at the primitive level of personality development are all significantly correlated (Table 11.6b). The Wilde/ Narcissistic subject is only significantly correlated with the Weikel/ Narcissistic subject (r = .201, p < .05).

In Table 11.6c two factors emerge explaining 65.75% of the total variance, with Factor 1 explaining 43.67% and Factor 2 23.15%. The three narcissistic subjects who were correctly classified by particular personality organization loaded onto the dominant Factor 1: Weikel/Narcissistic (.70),

Table 11.6c   Rotated component matrix: five narcissistic subjects

	Component	
	1	2
Wilde/Narcissistic		.894
Weikel/Narcissistic	.703	.322
Friedman/Narcissistic	.887	
Dowling/Narcissistic	.326	.574
Sharp/Narcissistic	.810	

Tables 11.6d   Rotated component matrix without Wilde/Narcissistic subject

	Component
	1
Weikel/Narcissistic	.760
Friedman/Narcissistic	.853
Dowling/Narcissistic	.484
Sharp/Narcissistic	.786

Friedman/Narcissistic (.89), and Sharp/Narcissistic (.81). The Dowling/Narcissistic subject is mixed loading on Factor 2 (.57) and Factor 1 (.33). The misclassified Wilde/Narcissistic subject loads on Factor 2 (.894). When the Wilde/Narcissistic subject is removed, only one factor forms explaining 53.92% of total variance (Table 11.6d).

The top five statements that are extremely characteristic of the narcissistic personality organization are virtually identical to the dominant Factor 1:

91. Is power oriented; values power in self and others (2.45)
52. Assertive; not afraid to express opinions (1.84)
12. Defensive; unable to acknowledge shortcomings or failures (1.80)
38. Has hostility towards others (1.79)
27. Is condescending toward others; acts superior to others (1.70)

The removal of the Wilde/Narcissistic subject has clarified the conception of the narcissistic personality organization. This is not the case encountered with the histrionic and obsessive personality organizations, with two variations on the spectrum of the personality organization, one more conventional and the other high functioning.

11.9   RESULTS FOR THE STANFORD ANTISOCIAL PROTOTYPE

The results of the correlation analysis of the three antisocial subjects with the personality templates are presented in Table 11.7a. Although the three antisocial subjects are significantly correlated with the Stanford Antisocial Prototype (McKenzie/Antisocial r = .255, p < .01, Koricke/Antisocial r = .201, p < .05, and Crawford/Antisocial r = .275, p < .01), none of the correlations are the highest and most significant for any of these subjects. The correlations of the three antisocial subjects with the Wink Narcissism Prototype are all significant and two are higher and more significant than the correlations with the Stanford Antisocial Prototype: McKenzie/Antisocial (r = .329, p < .001) and Crawford/Antisocial (r = .368, p < .000). In Table 11.7b only the McKenzie/Antisocial and Crawford Antisocial subjects are correlated (r = .262, p < .01). The factor analysis of the three antisocial subjects forms just one factor explaining 42.499% of the variance. In Table 11.7c the factor analysis of the three antisocial and five narcissistic subjects constrained to two factors explained 61.998% of the variance, with factor 1 clearly more narcissistic and factor 2 clearly more antisocial, but with some subjects loading more strongly on the opposite factor.

Table 11.7a   Correlations of three antisocial subjects with personality templates

	McKenzie/ Antisocial	Koricke/ Antisocial	Crawford/ Antisocial
Block Optimally Adjusted	−.375	.046	−.593
Personality Template	.000	.647	.000
Young-Eisendrath/Obsessive	.287	−.391	.002
Personality Template	.004	.000	.982
Stanford Histrionic Prototype	.123	.213	.319
	.224	.033	.001
Block Paranoid	.414	−.199	.194
Personality Template	.000	.047	.053
Stanford Borderline Prototype	.414	.076	.671
	.000	.450	.000
Wink Narcissism Prototype	.329	.197	.368
	.001	.050	.000
Stanford Antisocial Prototype	.255	.201	.275
	.011	.045	.006
Albanese Schizoid	.377	−.201	.359
Personality Template	.000	.045	.000

Table 11.7b   Correlations of three antisocial subjects

	McKenzie/ Antisocial	Koricke/ Antisocial	Crawford/ Antisocial
McKenzie/Antisocial	1.000	−.060	**.262**
		.552	.009
Koricke/Antisocial	−.060	1.000	−.025
	.552		.810
Crawford/Antisocial	.262	−.025	1.000
	.009	.801	

Table 11.7c   Rotated component matrix: three antisocial and five narcissistic subjects

	Component	
	1	2
Friedman/Narcissistic	**.867**	−.053
Weikel/Narcissistic	**.777**	.077
Sharp/Narcissistic	**.766**	.112
Koricke/Antisocial	−.275	.057
Crawford/Antisocial	−.200	**.836**
Dowling/Narcissistic	.332	**.614**
Wilde/Narcissistic	.056	**.593**
McKenzie/Antisocial	.087	**.425**

It is difficult to discriminate between the narcissistic and antisocial personality organizations. The correlations of the five narcissistic subjects with the Stanford Antisocial Prototype are all significant, and four out of the five are higher than the correlations with the Wink Narcissism Prototype (see Table 11.6a). Of the four narcissistic subjects that were classified into the right range of the Personality Continuum by the Wink Narcissism Prototype, two are more highly correlated with the Stanford Antisocial Prototype (Weikel/Narcissistic r = .597, p < .000 and Dowling/Narcissistic r = .463, p < .000), but it is only the highest and most significant correlation for the Weikel/Narcissistic subject. The Wink Narcissism Prototype and the Stanford Antisocial Prototype are highly correlated (r = .89, p < .001). Factor analysis of the Wink Narcissism Prototype and Stanford Antisocial Prototype yields one factor that explains 94.56% of total variance. Three statements rise to the top of the list based on factor scores:

13.   Thin-skinned; sensitive to criticism; takes offense easily (1.97)
71.   High aspiration level for self; sets high personal goals (1.97)
72.   Doubts about own adequacy as a person (1.97)

Statement 13 matches with diagnostic criteria 4A for the Antisocial Personality Disorder: irritability and aggressiveness, as indicated by repeated physical fights or assaults (DSM-IV-TR 2000, p. 706). Statements 71 and 72 capture the contradictory character of a person with a narcissistic personality organization with a grandiose sense of self-importance but requiring excessive admiration.

The Stanford Antisocial Prototype may be capturing the antisocial features of a narcissistic personality organization, and that is indicative of the lowest level of functioning on the spectrum of variation of the narcissistic personality organization: a narcissistic personality organization operating at an overt borderline level (Kernberg 1985). A similar result for the Wink Narcissism Prototype was found by Reise and Oliver (1994, p. 141) in validating the Psychopathy Prototype constructed from the California Adult Q Set, where psychopathy is seen as a severe type, or manifestation of, the narcissistic character. The factor analysis of the three antisocial subjects and five narcissistic subjects yielded separate antisocial and narcissistic factors, but not with all of the subjects clearly loading on the appropriate factor based on the clinicians' diagnoses. Westen and Shedler (1999B) developed distinct SWAP-200 prototypes for both the antisocial and narcissistic personality disorders. From the perspective of the entire person organization, all eight subjects were significantly correlated with both the narcissistic and antisocial personality templates, therefore the subjects have both narcissistic and antisocial features in varying degrees. Clearly more antisocial subjects are necessary to clarify the complex relationship between the narcissistic and antisocial personality disorders.

11.10   RESULTS FOR THE ALBANESE SCHIZOID PERSONALITY TEMPLATE

The results of the correlation analysis of the five schizoid subjects with the eight personality templates are presented in Table 11.8a. All five schizoid subjects were correctly classified with a predominantly schizoid personality organization arrested at the primitive level of personality development: Byrnes/Schizoid ($r = .433$, $p < .000$), Silverberg/Schizoid ($r = .356$, $p < .000$), Aronson/Schizoid ($r = .472$, $p < .000$), Grzegorek/ Schizoid ($r = .690$, $p < .000$), and Goldstein/Schizoid ($r = .567$, $p < .000$). All five schizoid subjects are negatively and significantly correlated with

Table 11.8a   Correlations of five schizoid subjects with personality templates

	Grzegorek/ Schizoid	Goldstein/ Schizoid	Aronson/ Schizoid	Byrnes/ Schizoid	Silverberg/ Schizoid
Block Optimally Adjusted Personality Template	**-.454**	**-.303**	**-.315**	**-.197**	**-.231**
	.000	**.002**	**.001**	**.050**	**.020**
Young-Eisendrath Obsessive Personality Template	**.440**	**.502**	.176	**.271**	.188
	.000	**.000**	.080	**.006**	.062
Stanford Histrionic Prototype	**-.352**	**-.347**	.028	-.113	.060
	.000	**.000**	.784	.261	.552
Block Paranoid Personality Template	**.565**	**.417**	**.338**	**.269**	.176
	.000	**.000**	**.001**	**.007**	.080
Stanford Borderline Prototype	**.255**	.072	**.382**	.153	.208
	.011	.478	**.000**	.129	.038
Wink Narcissism Prototype	.125	.016	.148	-.032	-.090
	.215	.873	.141	.749	.372
Stanford Antisocial Prototype	-.012	-.062	.116	.060	.019
	.909	.537	.251	.552	.855
Albanese Schizoid Personality Template	**.690**	**.567**	**.472**	**.433**	**.356**
	.000	**.000**	**.000**	**.000**	**.000**

Table 11.8b   Correlations of five schizoid subjects

	Grzegorek/ Schizoid	Goldstein/ Schizoid	Aronson/ Schizoid	Byrnes/ Schizoid	Silverberg/ Schizoid
Grzegorek/	1.000	.623	.370	.407	.243
Schizoid	.	.000	.000	.000	.015
Goldstein/	.623	1.000	.461	.424	.417
Schizoid	.000	.	.000	.000	.000
Aronson/	.370	.461	1.000	.470	.507
Schizoid	.000	.000	.	.000	.000
Byrnes/	.407	.424	.470	1.000	.539
Schizoid	.000	.000	.000	.	.000
Silverberg/	.243	.417	.507	.539	1.000
Schizoid	.015	.000	.000	.000	.

Tables 11.8c   Rotated component matrix: five schizoid subjects

	Component
	1
Silverberg/Schizoid	.723
Byrnes/Schizoid	.763
Aronson/Schizoid	.754
Grzegorek/Schizoid	.703
Goldstein/Schizoid	.788

the Optimally Adjusted Personality Template. All but the Silverberg/ Schizoid subject are significantly correlated with the Paranoid Personality Template. Three of the schizoid subjects are significantly correlated with the Young-Eisendrath Obsessive Personality Template: Byrnes/Schizoid ($r = .271$, $p < .006$), Grzegorek/Schizoid ($r = .440$, $p < .000$), and Goldstein/ Schizoid ($r = .502$, $p < .000$). Table 11.8b shows that all five schizoid subjects are significantly correlated at the $p < .000$. The correlation between the Grzegorek/Schizoid and the Goldstein/Schizoid subject is the highest ($r = .623$, $p > .000$), and the similarity between these two subjects is apparent from Table 11.8a showing in common significant correlations with the Optimally Adjusted (negative), Obsessive, Histrionic (negative), and Paranoid Personality Templates. The factor analysis is presented in Table 11.8c. All five schizoid subjects are significantly loaded on one factor explaining 55.77 % of the variance.

With the five-for-five correct classification and single factor, the Albanese Schizoid Personality Template should be considered validated.

It may be that the relatively simple structure of the schizoid personality organization made the classification straightforward. Fairbairn's (1952) explorations of the schizoid personality organization are at the foundation of British Object Relations Theory; what we are seeing here clearly is the fundamental schizoid-paranoid position.

11.11 SUCCESS RATE OF PERSONALITY CLASSIFICATION

Table 11.9 presents the results of the classification of the eight personality templates for all 36 subjects: 66.67% were correctly classified by their predominant personality using the stringent criterion of the highest and most significant positive correlation. If the three antisocial subjects are excluded, 72.7% of the subjects were correctly classified by their predominant personality. 86.11% of the subjects were correctly classified at the appropriate level of personality development along the Personality Continuum. With only minimal interpretation of the overall pattern of correlations with the eight personality templates 91.67% of the subjects were accurately described in terms of their entire personality organization. With minimal interpretation the Grzegorek/Obsessive, Martin/ Hysteric, Sharp/Histrionic, Crawford/Paranoid, Irwin/Borderline, Smith/ Borderline, and Dowling/Narcissistic subjects were correctly classified. The Martin/Hysteric subject, for example, was described by the clinician (a psychiatrist) as a 'high-functioning hysteric' and this is reflected in the

Table 11.9 *Classification by Personality Organization, Level of Personality Development, and Interpretation of Pattern of Correlations*

Personality Template	Personality Organization	Level of Personality Development	Interpretation of Pattern of Correlations
Optimally Adjusted	4/4	4/4	4/4
Obsessive	3/5	4/5	4/5
Histrionic	3/5	3/5	5/5
Paranoid	3/4	3/4	4/4
Borderline	3/5	5/5	4/5
Narcissistic	3/5	4/5	4/5
Antisocial	0/3	3/3	3/3
Schizoid	5/5	5/5	5/5
Total	24/36 (66.67%)	28/33 (86.11)	30/33 (91.67%)

significant correlation with the Optimally Adjusted Personality Template ($r = .359$, $p < .000$); however, with the stringent criteria for classification, this subject was regarded as incorrectly classified at the level of personality development and the particular personality.

The results for the Optimally Adjusted and Schizoid Personality Templates are clearly spectacular. The validity of the Optimally Adjusted Personality Template may reflect the stable and consistent pattern of behavior descriptive of a person at the normal level of personality development (Albanese 2002). For the Albanese Schizoid Personality Template, it may be the relatively simple structure of the schizoid personality organization that made the classification straightforward. Overall, the results for the 36 subjects—real persons—are quite remarkable.

11.12   RESULTS OF THE FACTOR ANALYSIS OF THE 36 SUBJECTS

The results of the factor analysis of the 36 subjects are presented in Table 11.10. Five orthogonal factors explaining 59.865% of total variance were extracted based on the Scree plot using a principal components analysis and a Varimax rotation. Factor 1 clearly represents a normal or high functioning factor containing the four optimally adjusted subjects plus the high functioning histrionic and high functioning obsessive subjects (19.358%). Factor 2 is predominantly schizoid with paranoid and obsessive features (12.976%). Factor 3 is predominantly borderline, histrionic, narcissistic, and antisocial (10.987%). Factor 4 is predominantly narcissistic with paranoid features (10.2283%). Factor 5 is an emerging neurotic factor with the histrionic, paranoid, the obsessive subjects who are more clearly neurotic, and without the primitive borderline and narcissistic features (6.317%). The factor analysis of the 36 subjects yielded seven factors with an eigenvalue > 1 and the Scree plot revealed five factors. Both the seven and five factor solutions can be easily interpreted; however, the seven factor solution did not represent a separate factor for each of the seven personality templates, nor did the factors clearly represent the normal, neurotic, and primitive ranges of the Personality Continuum.

The factor analysis reflects the comorbidity of the real subjects: a person may have more than one personality disorder. Factor 3 represents the well-documented high comorbidity between the histrionic and borderline personality disorders (Westen and Shedler 1999b, 2004). The Gilbertson/Hysteric and Kanake/Hysteric subjects with high positive and significant correlations with the Stanford Histrionic Prototype, the Stanford Borderline Prototype, and the Wink Narcissism Prototype

Table 11.10 Rotated component matrix for 36 useable subjects

	Component				
	1	2	3	4	5
Cort/Optimally Adjusted	**.769**				
Rosenbaum/Optimally Adjusted/MRS S	**.719**				
McKenzie/Optimally Adjusted	**.729**	.211	−.279		
Rosenbaum/Optimally Adjusted/DR D	**.879**				
Grzegorek/Obsessive		.291	−.396	.383	**.470**
Young-Eisendrath/Obsessive Subject	**.333**	**.325**			
Wilde/Obsessive		**.640**	−.256		
Rosenbaum/Obsessive/MS B	**.425**	**.593**			−.201
Rosenbaum/Obsessive/MRS G	.236	**.587**			
Gilbertson/Hysteric			**.589**		**.398**
Friedman/Hysteric	**.395**		.319	−.525	**.336**
Martin/Hysteric	**.556**				**.398**
Sharp/Histrionic	**.734**		.380		
Kanake/Histrionic			**.634**		
Myerscough/Paranoid		.207			**.665**
Koricke/Paranoid	−.426	.262		**.617**	.294
Crawford/Paranoid	−.419		.320	**.498**	.251
Kanake/Paranoid	−.514	**.439**		**.428**	.271
Hirt/Borderline	−.494		**.631**		
Irwin/Borderline	−.294	**.687**			
Smith/Borderline	−.653		−.411	.270	
Sharp/Borderline	−.210	.300	**.704**		−.226
Kanake/Borderline	−.742			**.435**	
Wilde/Narcissistic			**.713**		
Weikel/Narcissistic	.218	−.290	.267	**.628**	
Friedman/Narcissistic		−.198		**.770**	
Dowling/Narcissistic	−.344		.335	**.392**	
Sharp/Narcissistic				**.781**	.406
McKenzie/Antisocial	−.367				−.527
Koricke/Antisocial		−.289	**.232**		
Crawford/Antisocial	−.622		**.510**		
Byrnes/Schizoid		**.766**			
Silverberg/Schizoid		**.736**	−.214	−.214	.224
Aronson/Schizoid	−.325	**.581**			.202
Grzegorek/Schizoid	−.519	**.462**	−.248	.243	
Goldstein/Schizoid	−.212	**.604**	−.270	.261	.328

loaded predominantly on Factor 3, while the high functioning histrionic subjects (Sharp/Histrionic and Martin/Hysteric) loaded mainly on Factor 1. The more clearly neurotic histrionic subjects loaded on Factor 5.

The issue of comorbidity is critical to an understanding of the relationship between personality and consumer behavior. An observable pattern of behavior alone may not lead uniquely to a particular personality organization or level of personality development because a pattern of behavior may be shared by different personality organizations and those personality organizations can be at different levels of personality development. This is the same critical issue that economists had to come to grips with in the transformation from cardinal to ordinal utility theory, when the consumer's scale of preferences became the last vestige of a consumer left in economics. Knowing the consumer's scale of preferences does "not enable us to proceed from the scale of preferences to a particular utility function" (Hicks 1934, p. 52).

The factor analysis reflects the difficulty in differentiating between personality organizations at the neurotic and primitive levels of personality development. This difficulty can be attributed, at least in part, to Fairbairn's hypothesis (Albanese 2002). Fairbairn (1952) observed that what may appear to be obsessional, hysterical, paranoid, or phobic neuroses may actually be neurotic defenses against severe anxiety in interpersonal relations. Fairbairn (1952) was referring to a person arrested at the primitive level of personality development functioning at the higher neurotic level; i.e. high functioning. The Gilbertson/Hysteric and Kanake/Hysteric subjects may represent high-functioning borderline personality organizations using a neurotic histrionic defense against severe anxiety in interpersonal relationships. The Friedman/Hysteric and Sharp/Histrionic subjects are clearly at the neurotic level of personality development, and the Sharp/Histrionic subject, with the high correlation with the Optimally Adjusted Personality Template, is a high functioning neurotic personality organization. The clinician's diagnosis of the Martin/Hysteric subject was a high functioning histrionic personality organization, but the only significant positive correlation was with the Optimally Adjusted Personality Template; for a neurotic person, high functioning means functioning at the normal level of personality development. The template matching technique for personality classification can detect high functioning primitive personality organizations using neurotic defenses; therefore, it can differentiate between the neurotic and primitive levels of personality development. This is an important contribution to personality classification.

The subject sorts should be of real people and the classification of a person's entire personality organization should be based on the interpretation of the pattern of correlations across all of the personality templates.

The template matching technique of personality classification is capable of capturing the stable and consistent pattern of behavior at the normal level, the *complicated* personality organizations at the neurotic level, and the *complexity* of personality organizations at the primitive level, but perhaps not the *changing and capricious* behavior of personality organizations at the psychotic level, of personality development along the Personality Continuum.

11.13   CASE STUDY OF LOIS THE COMPULSIVE BUYER

The case study of Lois the compulsive buyer will be presented to identify the personality organization of a compulsive buyer. There are four qualitatively different patterns of shopping behavior along the Personality Continuum: the prudent shopper at the normal level; the neurotic shopper at the neurotic level; the compulsive buyer at the primitive level; and the manic spender at the psychotic level of personality development. Prudent Shoppers carefully plan their shopping activities, spend less than they earn, and save for future purchases they cannot afford in the present. Neurotic Shoppers spend an excessive amount of time shopping for the perfect purchase, exhausting anyone who shops with them, often not buying anything, and when a purchase is made it is sometimes returned. They typically spend money they have and do not impair family and social relationships. Compulsive Buyers are driven by severe anxiety to spend money they do not have on things they do not need in repetitive buying binges and then hide their purchases away, often in the original packaging with the price tags left on. The shopping behavior seriously impairs family, social and professional relationships and results in serious financial problems. Manic Spenders engage in episodic spectacular spending sprees that severely impair family, social, and professional relationships and result in severe financial and legal problems that can lead to hospitalization or incarceration.

Lois is a classic compulsive buyer. She is driven by severe anxiety to spend money she does not have on things she does not need in repetitive buying binges and then hide her purchases away, often in the original packaging with the price tags left on. The shopping behavior seriously impairs family, social and professional relationships, and results in serious financial problems (O'Guinn and Faber 1989; Faber and O'Guinn 1992; McElroy et al. 1991, 1994; Lejoyeux et al. 1996). I first became aware of Lois when one of the sorters asked me for advice on acquiring items for a silent auction for an AIDS benefit. I suggested identifying compulsive buyers because they tended to hide purchases away that they did not need. A van was required to remove the items that Lois donated to the AIDS benefit.

The original sort of Lois with the California Adult Q Set was done on 22 September 2004, by a good friend of Lois's, a 'bud' of 40 years, in collaboration with a mutual friend and fellow co-worker at a local supermarket who had known the subject for over 30 years. For comparison purposes, the same two sorters, plus a third person who had also worked with Lois and knew her well, came together on 9 March 2008 to sort Lois using the Shedler-Westen Assessment Procedure (SWAP-200), a newer 200-item personality assessment instrument also using a template matching Q technique (Shedler and Westen 1998; Westen and Shedler 1999a, 1999b, 2000). At the time of the original sort, Lois, who was born in 1936, was 68, and she was 71 at the time of the SWAP-200 sort. Information for this case is taken from the Consumer Behavior Information Form completed by the principal sorter after the original sort, and from the verbatim notes of a debriefing I conducted with the three sorters after the sort with the SWAP-200. This information was woven into a narrative without interpretation. The written case was then reviewed by the sorters and changes were made.

Lois is a bubbly, talkative, outgoing, funny person, who does not look her age even at 71. Short at five feet tall, she is a cute, very pretty, blonde with impeccable hair always dyed. She is very stylish, always wears high heels and looks classy. She never wears the same thing twice. She loves jewelry and had a 3.5 carat diamond. She loves to eat and drink. She loves to cook and was an impeccable chef. She learned to fly.

Lois was born in a log cabin in West Virginia without electric power. Her mother deserted her and she was left with her father's family. She was sexually abused by her paternal grandfather. When her grandmother found out, it was Lois who was sent away. Lois's brother was also sexually abused and had died of AIDS. A person who owned a boarding house took her in and made her work, cooking, cleaning, etc. Then an aunt took her in for several years during high school and they were good years for her. She married at 19 and had three children and then divorced. She had a fourth child between her two marriages who was given up for adoption. She lived for a time with an alcoholic man who beat her before she married her second husband.

Her second husband was a successful business owner. Lois married her second husband for his money and she told him so. He had three children of his own. Lois had worked as a cashier at a local grocery store for a long time but quit soon after marrying her second husband to take care of his kids. With more money, Lois shopped more. Her 5,000 sq ft house was exquisite, like a show room, everything matched, everything in its place, with custom built cabinetry throughout and a full finished basement. She liked to display things she collected—dolls, dishes, clothes. She is a perfectionist and was never satisfied. She was always redoing rooms, and when they were all done, she would do them over again. When the house had to be sold as a result of bankruptcy, they could not get their money out of the house because it was so overvalued compared to surrounding properties.

Lois's shopping was compulsive. She felt like she had to have the items that she bought. She needed to buy things to make herself feel better. Lois said she felt high. She always looked good and surrounded herself with beautiful things, but at the expense of her family and herself. She likes to spend lots of time out and about. She developed close relationships with sales people—people who waited on her, took care of her, were kind to her. She went to an upscale spa weekly. Saks sales people would call her on the phone to tell her about outfits, new lines, etc. She would find something beautiful which she liked but could not afford and would put it on hold until she could figure out how to buy it; e.g., putting it on several charge cards. After the bankruptcy Saks would not let her buy anything else.

She gave great parties that were catered and extravagant. Her house was clean. She had two cleaning ladies, but she cleaned with them. At Christmas, she would have an upscale nursery come in to decorate, inside and out. She was generous, overly generous, at Christmas giving extravagant gifts (e.g. a $200 purse). She had expensive clothes with the price tags left on: $400 shoes, $1900 dresses. She let friends borrow things. She was very generous.

She could not live without deception and was always trying to get out of trouble. She had many boyfriends and numerous affairs, and charged her trysts to her husband's charge cards. She met a man on a flight once and had an affair with him that night. She knew she was in financial trouble, but still continued to shop. She would hide the costs from her boyfriend or husband. She would hock[1] things to buy more things. She hocked her 3.5 carat diamond. Her husband knew what was going on and allowed it. Her shopping resulted in the bankruptcy of her second husband's business.

The couple eventually bought a house and moved to Florida to declare bankruptcy, because in Florida they don't take your house. She was depressed before leaving and began to take antidepressants. In Florida, her husband got a job parking cars at a car dealership and she worked as a salesperson for a furniture store. Her husband died of cancer a year and a half ago. She is still working there. Lois is a hard worker and a resilient person. She had ten years of a lot of wealth before the bankruptcy. Sad that she started out poor and ended up poor.

11.14   THE PERSONALITY ORGANIZATION OF A COMPULSIVE BUYER

The results of the correlation analysis for Lois with the eight personality templates are presented in Table 11.11. There are four significant correlations in descending order: Stanford Histrionic Prototype (r = .562, p < .000), the Stanford Borderline Prototype (r = .421, p < .000), the Wink Narcissism Prototype (r = .259, p = .01), and Stanford Antisocial Prototype (r = .220, p < .05). While the highest and most significant positive correlation is with the Stanford Histrionic Prototype at the neurotic level of personality development, I would argue that the strong positive correlations with the borderline, narcissistic, and antisocial personality templates anchor Lois's personality organization at the primitive level of development. I would interpret the pattern of correlations of Lois's personality organization as a *high functioning borderline personality organization with narcissistic and antisocial features and strong histrionic tendencies*. Lois would not be compulsive without the predominantly borderline personality organization arrested at the primitive level of personality development, and the strong borderline features would not be present in a predominantly histrionic personality organization at the higher neurotic level of personality development. Lois's strong histrionic tendencies, therefore, must be regarded as a neurotic defense against severe anxiety in interpersonal relationships, and the use of a neurotic defense by a person

Table 11.11   Lois: correlations with eight CAQ personality templates

Block Optimally Adjusted Personality Template	−.079
	.436
Young-Eisendrath/Obsessive Personality Template	−.150
	.135
Stanford Histrionic Prototype	**.562**
	.000
Block Paranoid Personality Template	−.051
	.615
Stanford Borderline Prototype	**.421**
	.000
Wink Narcissism Prototype	**.259**
	.009
Stanford Antisocial Prototype	**.220**
	.028
Albanese Schizoid Personality Template	−.074
	.464

arrested at the primitive level of personality development represents high functioning (Fairbairn 1952; Albanese 2002).

The first diagnostic criteria for the borderline personality disorder, 'frantic efforts to avoid real or imagined abandonment,' clearly fits Lois's past interpersonal history, having been abandoned first by her own mother and then by her paternal grandmother (DSM-IV-TR 2000, p. 710). The purpose of the compulsive behavior is to reduce focusing on her painful inner experience and to escape from severe anxiety (Kernberg 1985; Albanese 2002). The panoply of compulsive behaviors indulged in by Lois support the classification of a predominantly borderline personality organization at the primitive level of personality development. Compulsive buying behavior, as the specific pattern of shopping behavior, is one part of an overall compulsive, and in the more extreme case, addictive pattern of consumer behavior that characterizes the personality organizations arrested at the primitive level of personality development along the Personality Continuum (Albanese 2002).

The second diagnostic criteria for the borderline personality disorder, 'a pattern of unstable and intense interpersonal relationships,' is clearly characteristic of Lois's interpersonal history of having had multiple marriages, many boyfriends and numerous affairs (DSM-IV-TR 2000, p. 710). The second diagnostic criteria for the borderline personality disorder also includes 'alternating between extremes of idealization and devaluation' (DSM-IV-TR 2000, p. 710). At the primitive level of personality development the general pattern of human behavior is characterized by a chaotic pattern of alternating and contradictory behavior (Albanese 2002, 2006). The borderline personality organization is characterized by the use of the primitive defense of splitting as the predominant defense against severe anxiety in interpersonal relationships (Kernberg 1985). Splitting involves actively holding apart the good and bad aspects of oneself and others; it is regarded as a primitive defense because it occurs within consciousness. When the defense of splitting is in place, the person is free from severe anxiety. But the defense of splitting is easily overloaded by additional anxiety resulting in the breakdown of splitting and the proliferation of severe anxiety that becomes intolerable (Albanese 1982, 1988, 1990, 1991, 2002, 2006). It is the severe anxiety that has become intolerable that drives the person to engage in a compulsive, and in the more extreme case, addictive pattern of consumer behavior as a way to restore the defense of splitting. Lois felt high when she went on a buying binge. When the primitive defense of splitting is restored, the person is free from severe anxiety once again, until the next breakdown. The breakdown and restoration of splitting results in the chronic pattern of repetitive buying binges over time characteristic of the true compulsive buyer (Albanese 2002, 2006).

The compulsive pattern of behavior, characteristic of the borderline personality disorder, is captured in diagnostic criterion 4: 'Impulsivity in at least two areas that are potentially self-damaging (e.g. spending, sex, substance abuse, reckless driving, binge eating)' (DSM-IV-TR 2000, p. 710). Lois was rated 9, extremely characteristic, on item 53 of the California Adult Q Set: 'Needs and impulses tend toward relatively direct and uncontrolled expression; unable to delay gratification (is impulsive, has little self-control; unable to postpone pleasure).' This single item can be used to identify a pattern of compulsive consumer behavior. Although this is a single item, it is descriptive of a trait, because the repetitive buying binges of the true compulsive buyer are rigidly patterned over time. Lois was also rated 9, extremely characteristic, on item 67, 'Is self-indulgent; tends to pamper himself or herself,' and she was rated 1, extremely uncharacteristic, on item 25, 'Over-controls needs and impulses; binds tension excessively; delays gratification unnecessarily (has excessive self-control; keeps a tight rein on feelings; postpones pleasures unnecessarily).'

The narcissistic features of Lois's personality organization add the element of grandiosity to her compulsive consumption behavior, represented in diagnostic criterion 1, 'has a grandiose sense of self-importance,' and diagnostic criterion 2, 'is preoccupied with fantasies of unlimited success, power, brilliance, beauty, or ideal love' (DSM-IV-TR 2000, p. 717). It is with the narcissistic features of Lois's personality organization that the expression in conspicuous consumption behavior is most direct, because envy is a motivation for materialism (Albanese 2002; Belk 1985). This is captured in diagnostic criterion 8, 'is envious of others or believes that others are envious of him or her,' and criterion 5, 'has a sense of entitlement, i.e., unreasonable expectations of especially favorable treatment or automatic compliance with his or her expectations' (DSM-IV-TR 2000, p. 717).

Narcissistic individuals tend to be perfectionists and are never satisfied, and Lois is described in just these terms in the case. For Lois, item 6 was rated 8, quite characteristic, 'Is fastidious; meticulous; careful and precise,' and item 74 was rated 2, quite uncharacteristic, 'Feels satisfied with self; is consciously happy with person s/he believes self to be; is unaware of self-concern.' Lois's treatment of her second husband certainly speaks to diagnostic criterion 6, 'is interpersonally exploitative, i.e., takes advantage of others to achieve his or her own ends,' and criterion 7, 'lacks empathy: is unwilling to recognize or identify with the feelings and needs of others' (DSM-IV-TR 2000, p. 717). Lois was rated 7, fairly characteristic, on item 88, 'Is personally charming,' typical of narcissistic individuals.

The antisocial features of Lois's personality organization exacerbate the severity of the narcissistic features by adding extreme impulsivity, consistent irresponsibility, deceitfulness, as indicated by repeated lying, and lack of remorse, as indicated by being indifferent to or rationalizing having hurt, mistreated, or stolen from another (DSM-TR IV 2000, p. 706). Lois was rated 9, extremely characteristic, on item 65 of the California Adult Q Set: 'Characteristically pushes and tries to stretch limits and rules; sees what s/he can get away with.' Lois could not live without deception and was always trying to get out of trouble.

The manifestations of the neurotic histrionic defense as indicated by diagnostic criterion (2) of the histrionic personality disorder, 'interaction with others is often characterized by inappropriate sexually seductive or provocative behavior,' and diagnostic criterion (4), 'consistently uses physical appearance to draw attention to self' (DSM-IV-TR 2000, p. 714), are clearly represented in the items of the California Adult Q Set. Lois was rated 9, extremely characteristic, on item 93, 'Behaves in a feminine style or manner,' and 8, quite characteristic, on item 81, 'Is physically attractive; is good looking (as defined by our culture),' item 31, 'Regards self as physically attractive,' item 80, 'Interested in members of the opposite sex,' item 73, 'Tends to see sexual overtones in many situations; erotizes situations (high placement implies that person reads sexual meanings into situations where none exist; low placement implies inability to recognize sexual signals),' and item 66, 'Enjoys aesthetic impressions; is aesthetically sensitive,' and she was rated 7, fairly characteristic, on item 58 'Appears to enjoy sensuous experiences (such as touch, taste, smell, bodily contact).'

The histrionic tendencies expressed sexually are given a driven character that makes them compulsive by the predominantly borderline personality organization, and the histrionic tendencies give direction to the compulsive drive to buy. Individuals with a histrionic personality disorder 'are overly concerned with impressing others by their appearance and expend an excessive amount of time, energy, and money on clothes and grooming' (DSM-IV-TR 2000, p. 711).

Lois can serve as a specimen of the personality organization of a compulsive buyer. The personality organization of a compulsive buyer can be described succinctly as a high functioning borderline personality organization with narcissistic and antisocial features and strong histrionic tendencies used as a neurotic defense against severe anxiety in interpersonal relationships. Lois's personality organization is like that of the Gilbertson/Hysteric ($r = .424$, $p < .000$) and Kanake/Histrionic ($r = .417$, $p < .000$) subjects, with strong borderline and narcissistic features, and the Hirt/Borderline ($r = .444$, $p < .000$) and Sharp/Borderline ($r = .417$, $p < .000$) subjects, with narcissistic and antisocial features and strong histrionic tendencies. These four subjects load significantly on Factor 3: Gilbertson/Hysteric (.622), Kanake/Histrionic (.634), Hirt/Borderline (.659), and

Sharp/Borderline (.696). Lois is not correlated with the more clearly neurotic Friedman/Hysteric (r = .187, p < .062) or the high functioning Martin/Hysteric (r = .007, p < .945) subjects or the Kanake/Borderline (r = .146, p < .148) and Irwin/Borderline (r = .095, p < .348) subjects with strong schizoid features and without the histrionic tendencies. Factor 3 may represent a high functioning borderline personality organization with narcissistic features and histrionic tendencies, and therefore, constitute a compulsive buyer factor. Shedler and Westen (2004) found a similar factor made up of the borderline, histrionic, narcissistic, and antisocial personality disorders and referred to it as the *dramatic cluster*.

Helga Dittmar (2004), a leading authority on compulsive buying behavior, created a Compulsive Buyer Template from the California Adult Q Set at my request. Lois is significantly correlated with the Dittmar Compulsive Buyer Template (r = .356, p < .000), and the Dittmar Compulsive Buyer Template is significantly correlated with the Gilbertson/Hysteric (r = .417, p < .000), Kanake/Histrionic (r = .414, p < .000), Hirt/Borderline (r = .396, p < .000), and Sharp/Borderline (r = .407, p < .000) subjects.

I requested a subject sort of a compulsive buyer from April Lane Benson (2000), a clinician specializing in treating problematic shopping behavior. The subject is significantly correlated with Lois (r = .319, p < .001) and significantly correlated with the Dittmar Compulsive Buyer Template (r = .259, p = .009). The subject is bipolar suggesting perhaps that Lois may have some bipolar features. In a manic episode a person with bipolar disorder can engage in a spectacular spending spree that results in severe financial and legal problems. The 'expansiveness, unwarranted optimism, grandiosity, and poor judgment often lead to an imprudent involvement in pleasurable activities such as buying sprees, reckless driving, foolish business investments, and sexual behavior unusual for the person, even though these activities are likely to have painful consequences' (DSM-IV-TR 2000, p. 358). This pattern of behavior is exacerbated when a person with bipolar disorder has psychotic features. The manic spender is a qualitatively different pattern of shopping behavior at the psychotic level of personality development; the true compulsive buyer is arrested at the higher primitive level of personality development.

The Shedler-Westen Assessment Procedure (SWAP-200) is a 200-item personality assessment instrument using a template matching Q technique (Shedler and Westen 1998; Westen and Shedler 1999a, 1999b, 2000). The comparison of the classification of Lois's personality organization by the Shedler-Westen Assessment Procedure (SWAP-200) provides direct evidence of the validity of the adaptation of the California Adult Q Set advocated here for the study of personality and consumer behavior along the Personality Continuum. On 9 March 2008 the same two sorters who

Table 11.12   Lois: correlations with 11 SWAP-200 prototypes

Hi-Functioning Prototype	.053
	.458
Dependent Prototype	−.044
	.539
Avoidant Prototype	**−.284**
	.000
Obsessive Prototype	**−.227**
	.001
Histrionic Prototype	**.433**
	.000
Paranoid Prototype	.116
	.102
Borderline Prototype	**.134**
	.058
Narcissistic Prototype	**.339**
	.000
Antisocial Prototype	**.377**
	.000
Schizoid Prototype	**−.374**
	.000
Schizotypal Prototype	**−.238**
	.001

had sorted Lois on the California Adult Q Set (CAQ), along with a third related person who also knew Lois well, sorted Lois using the SWAP-200. Table 11.12 presents the correlation results for Lois on the eleven SWAP-200 Personality Prototypes. The significant positive correlations in descending order are with the Histrionic Prototype (r = .433, p < .000), Antisocial Prototype (r = .377, p < .000), Narcissistic Prototype (r = .339, p < .000), and a weakly significant Borderline Prototype (r = .134, p = .058). The significant negative correlations in descending order are with the Schizoid Prototype (r = −.374, p < .000), Avoidant Prototype (r = −.284, p < .000), Schizotypal Prototype (r = −.238, p = .001), and Obsessive Prototype (r = −.227, p <.000).

The correlation with the Histrionic Prototype is the strongest and most significant positive correlation; however, the strong and positive correlations with the Antisocial and Narcissistic Prototypes, and the barely significant Borderline Prototype, clearly anchor Lois's personality organization at the primitive level of personality development. The significant negative correlations with the Schizoid and Schizotypal Personality Prototypes mean that Lois is not detached from social relationships and does not have a restricted range of expression of emotions in social settings characteristic of the schizoid personality disorder (DSM-IV-TR 2000, p. 697), nor is her behavior odd, eccentric, or peculiar as is characteristic of the schizotypal personality disorder (DSM-IV-TR 2000, p. 701). The significant negative correlations with the Avoidant and Obsessive Prototypes support the interpretation that Lois's personality organization is not at the neurotic level of personality development, and that the histrionic tendencies represent a neurotic defense of a high functioning personality organization anchored at the primitive level of personality development. This pattern of correlations parallels closely the results of the California Adult Q Set presented in Table 11.11 and provides strong support for the classification of Lois's personality organization by the California Adult Q Set.

With the SWAP-200, the sorter rates 100 items from 1 to 7, where 7 is extremely characteristic and 1 is somewhat characteristic, and 100 items are rated 0 as uncharacteristic, statements that are clearly not true, and do not describe, or are irrelevant to a description of the patient (Shedler and Westen 1998). On items of the SWAP-200 with consumer behavior content, Lois was rated 7, extremely characteristic, on item 134, 'Tends to act impulsively, without regard for consequences,' and she was rated 5 on item 66, 'Tends to oscillate between undercontrol and overcontrol of needs and impulses (i.e., needs and wishes are expressed impulsively and with little regard for consequences, or else disavowed and permitted virtually no expression),' and on item 62, 'Tends to be preoccupied with food, diet, or eating,' and 4 on item 147, 'Tends to abuse alcohol,' and item 161, 'Tends to abuse illicit drugs.'

The SWAP-200 contains one bipolar item and Lois was rated 2 on item 64, 'Mood tends to cycle over intervals of weeks or months between excited and depressed states (high placement implies bipolar mood disorder),' providing additional evidence indicating that Lois may have some bipolar tendencies, and that would contribute directly to the more extreme nature of Lois's buying behavior. Further, Lois was rated 3 on item 157, 'Tends to become irrational when strong emotions are stirred up; may show a noticeable decline from customary functioning.' Bipolar disorder with transient psychotic episodes would be manifested in the spectacular spending sprees more characteristic of a manic spender. Bipolar disorder has been integral to the description of the phenomenon of compulsive buying behavior from the beginning (McElroy et al. 1991, 1994); in many ways, the episodic spectacular spending sprees of the manic spender appear to epitomize the blind buying binges characteristic of the compulsive buyer and can be easily mistaken for one another. It is important to understand the psychotic level of personality development to delineate the boundary between the primitive and psychotic levels of personality development. The true compulsive buyer is arrested at the primitive level of personality development.

Although the weak correlation with the Borderline Prototype appears somewhat troubling, this prototype occupies a precarious position in the development of the SWAP-200: 'The empirically derived portrait of actual patients with borderline personality disorder is substantially different from its DSM-IV (1994) description' (Westen and Shedler 1999a, p. 267). The differentiation between the borderline and histrionic personality disorders becomes blurred with the 'histrionic diagnostic category that included many items currently in the DSM description of histrionic personality disorder with several items associated with the borderline personality disorder—a category that shows high comorbidity with histrionic personality disorder in all studies of which we are aware' (Westen and Shedler 1999b, p. 282). An alternative thirteen prototype version of the SWAP-200 that goes well beyond the personality disorders described in the DSM-IV-TR (2000) does not even differentiate the histrionic from the borderline personality organization and does not have a separate Borderline Prototype.

The factor structure is also comparable between the California Adult Q Set and the SWAP-200, providing additional support, including factor 3, which Shedler and Westen (2004) refer to as the dramatic cluster, which also includes the histrionic, borderline, narcissistic, antisocial personality disorders. Factor 2 is similar to their 'odd cluster', which includes the paranoid, schizoid, and schizotypal personality disorders and represents the lower bound of the primitive range of the Personality Continuum (Shedler and Westen 2004). Factor 5 is similar to their anxious cluster, which includes the avoidant, dependent, and obsessive-compulsive personality disorders and clearly represents the neurotic level of personality development (Shedler and Westen 2004).

The Personality Continuum clarifies the confusion resulting from the failure to differentiate between a personality organization arrested at the primitive level of personality development using a neurotic defense and a true neurotic personality organization. The consistently positive and significant correlations with the personality templates at the primitive level of personality development anchor Lois's personality organization at that level. The clearest portrait of Lois's personality organization is provided by the pattern of correlations with eight personality templates of the California Q Set (Table 11.11). The pattern of correlations of Lois's personality organization with the eleven prototype SWAP-200 (Table 11.12) closely parallels and supports the classification of the California Q Set, but with a weaker correlation with the Borderline Prototype (r = .134, p = .058), a clearer delineations of Lois's personality organization as not being at the neurotic level of personality development—the negative correlations with the Avoidant Prototype ($r = -.284$, p < .00) and the Obsessive Prototype ($r = -.227$, p < .000)—and delimiting the lower bound of her personality organization within the primitive range as not being Schizoid ($r = -.374$, p < .000) or Schizotypal ($r = -.238$, p < .001).

This rather spare and analytical portrait of Lois's personality organization has been focused on the classification along the Personality Continuum and the manifestation of her personality organization in an overall pattern of consumer behavior. Once the personality classification is made by interpreting the pattern of correlations across all of the personality templates, the person's personality organization can be elaborated in a richly detailed portrait; and greater depth can be achieved in the analysis through the developmental approach of investigating the interpersonal origins of the person's personality organization.

11.15   METHODOLOGICAL ISSUES WITH THE SWAP-200

The SWAP-200 takes the California Adult Q Set to its logical conclusion. In Q methodology, the statements constitute the sample, and the sample is drawn from the universe of all possible statements, called the concourse, that could be used to describe a phenomenon (Brown 1980). Q methodologists believe any number of different Q samples can be drawn from the concourse that would adequately describe the underlying phenomena. Westen and Shedler (1999a, p. 271) described themselves as 'a task force of two.'

The SWAP-200 distribution is not symmetrical. The 8 items that describe the patient especially well are rated 7, extremely characteristic, the next 10 items are rated 6, the next 12 are rated 5, the next 14 are rated 4, the next 16 are rated 3, the next 8 are rated 2, and 22 are rated 1, somewhat characteristic, and the remaining 100 items are rated 0, and listed as uncharacteristic on the score sheet used to record SWAP-200 data. Although the distribution is not symmetrical, a distribution is being imposed, and the forced choice aspect of the Q technique is maintained. In Q methodology, it is the ranking, not the distribution, that matters (Brown 1980). The 100 items that are rated zero are somewhat troubling. When does a zero rating mean extremely *un*characteristic, irrelevant, or that the sorter does not know that about the person being sorted? Direct item-by-item comparisons between subjects may not be as meaningful. It may be easier to toss a card into the zero pile rather than to make a tough decision. The CAQ Set requires that all 100 statements be sorted for each subject, and the forced symmetrical distribution with positive or characteristic items and negative or uncharacteristic items is critical to the deliberations that must be made by the sorter to rank each statement in relation to all the other statements. Block (2008) was quite critical of the 100 items that are rated zero because they possess appreciable psychometric weight and create a built-in correlational artifact that heightens intercorrelations among items. With 100 items of the SWAP-200 rated = 0, the ranking of items is called into question.

The SWAP-200 is primarily designed for use by professional clinicians, requires specialized training, and may require detailed knowledge about a person that a clinician may be more likely to have than a family member, friend, or acquaintance. Block (2008, p. 112) described the SWAP-200 'as a descriptive procedure applicable by mental health practitioners for describing patients.' With the SWAP-200 a clinician may do a sort with as little as five to six hours of exposure to the subject. Block (2008, p. 117) was critical that 'most busy mental health practitioners are likely to find this recommendation difficult to implement.' From the clinical perspective, the template matching technique of personality classification offers a relatively easy to use instrument for diagnostic purposes. At the time of the intake interview, sorts by family members, friends, and by the subject, could provide a wealth of information to the clinician for diagnostic purposes. The California Adult Q Set was designed by clinicians but was made more useable for nonprofessionals with the addition of clarifying statements. The SWAP-200 may be a superior personality classification instrument for professional clinicians, but the California Adult Q Set is more appropriate for use by family members and friends and for the study of personality and consumer behavior by researchers who are not clinicians.

The SWAP-200 is a remarkable achievement and the development of the SWAP-200 is unprecedented. 'A national sample of experienced psychiatrists and psychologists used the SWAP-200 to describe either their conceptions (prototypes) of personality disorders (N = 267) or current patients with personality disorder diagnoses (N = 530)' (Shedler and Westen 2004, p. 1350). The sample is described as random and the instrument as validated (Westen and Shedler 1999A). I intend to use the eleven prototype SWAP-200 in future research on personality and consumer behavior, but, on the whole, I prefer the template matching technique of personality classification based on the California Adult Q Set.

11.16   LIMITATIONS OF THE STUDY

The two principal limitations of this study of the Template Matching Technique of Personality Classification based on the California Adult Q

Set are the missing avoidant, dependent, and bipolar disorders personality templates and the need for more subjects. The addition of dependent and avoidant personality templates would fill out the personality organizations in the neurotic range of the Personality Continuum. Neurotic consumers are notoriously indecisive and that makes them fascinating but frustrating subjects for study (Albanese 2002, 2006). Factor 5 is an emerging neurotic factor that explained only 6.317% of total variance, but that would be improved by the addition of the two neurotic personality templates and additional neurotic subjects. Shedler and Westen (2004) found an anxious cluster made up of the avoidant, dependent, and obsessive-compulsive personality disorders. Factor 5 and the anxious cluster represent the neurotic factor that is necessary for the investigation of the neurotic pattern of consumer behavior. A bipolar disorder personality template would add a template to the psychotic range of the Personality Continuum that would capture the manic spender.

More subjects in general would clarify the spectrum of variation of each personality organization and contribute to the delineation of the ranges along the Personality Continuum. More subjects with a specific pattern of consumer behavior like compulsive buying behavior would further the exploration of the personality organization prone to that pattern of behavior. The advantage of having a national random sample of subject sorts is that it would permit the estimation of the prevalence of each personality organization in the population and the proportion of the American population in each range of the Personality Continuum.

ACKNOWLEDGEMENTS

Many people contributed to this research project over more than twenty years. The original set of personality templates was assembled in the spring of 1989 while I was at the University of Michigan, Ann Arbor. I would like to thank Richard P. Bagozzi for his early support and encouragement of my research on personality and consumer behavior while I was making my career change into marketing at the University of Michigan. I began to solicit subject sorts for the validation of a template matching technique of personality classification based on the California Adult Q Set in the fall of 1991 at Kent State University. A subject sort is a sort of the 100 descriptive statements printed on cards of the California Adult Q Set to represent a particular person. The first two subject sorts were done by Dr. Robert L. Byrnes and analyzed on October 2, 1991 by Professor Steven Brown, Kent State University (with an autographed photograph of William Stephenson staring down at us). A description of this adaptation of the template matching technique was published in Albanese (1990) and the early results were published in Albanese (1993). Due to the difficulty encountered with the acquisition of subject sorts, the project was suspended until funding could be obtained to compensate the clinicians for their time under the belief that this would increase the number of sorts. The project was resumed in the fall of 2004 and the remaining subject sorts were acquired. Professor John Akamatsu, Kent State University, was instrumental in the revival of the project by providing me with a list of clinical psychologists. Professor Donald L. Bubenzer, Kent State University, provided a list of counselors after I had exhausted local psychologists with this project. I had to acquire subject sorts from experienced clinical psychologists who had worked with the subject long enough to have made a clear diagnosis of his or her personality organization, and for which I had a personality template, and that required cultivating a wide range of contacts that eventually included psychiatrists and counselors.

I would like to thank all of the clinical psychologists, psychiatrists, and counselors over the years who contributed subject sorts or assisted in the acquisition of subjects: David Aronson, Robert L. Byrnes, Gina M. Crawford, Janet Dix, A. Scott Dowling, Karen Fleming, Greg Friedman, Al Gilbertson, David M. Goldstein, Alfred E. Grzegorek, Michael Hirt, Sharon Irwin, Walter Kanake, Deborah A. Koricke, Shelley J. Korshak, Robert J. Lipgar, Patricia Martin, Rodney Myerscough, Kay Q. McKenzie, Arthur L. Rosenbaum, Richard Rynearson, Janet L. Sharp, Robert T. Silverberg, Carole P. Smith, Charles A. Waehler, Kim Weikel, Catherine Wilde, and Polly Young-Eisendrath. I would especially like to thank Polly Young-Eisendrath for creating the Obsessive Personality Template and Shelley J. Korshak for a Dependent Personality Template. I would like to thank Helga Dittmar for creating the Compulsive Buyer Template and April Lane Benson for providing me with a subject sort of a compulsive buyer from her clinical practice. I would like to thank Valerie and Joe Czerwien, Anne M. Albanese, and Cathy Cort for providing additional subject sorts. I would like to thank my colleague Robert D. Jewell for his assistance with the data analysis and Michael Hu for his clarification of the significance of a single item. Part of the data analysis was supported by a 2006 Summer Research and Creative Award from Kent State University.

I would like to gratefully acknowledge the research assistance of Vanessa Ledbetter from 2004–2005 for her diligence and patience in making the professional decks of Block's 1990 version of the California Adult Q Set and for professionalizing the subject acquisition process. I would like to thank Andrea Reynolds for the management of the acquisition of subjects during the second year of the project from 2005–2006, especially for her drive to complete the process and her determination to acquire the remaining antisocial subjects. From 2005–2006 Sarah Roach assisted with the acquisition of subjects and with providing sorts on two subjects used to compare the CAQ and SWAP-200.

I would like to thank Morris B. Holbrook for his continued support of my research on personality and consumer behavior from the beginning of my career in marketing and for reviewing an earlier version of this chapter. I would also like to thank Michael Bosnjak for reviewing an earlier version of this chapter and for giving me the opportunity to present the preliminary results of the template matching technique of personality classification at the 2005 Consumer Personality and Research Conference in Dubrovnik, Croatia.

I would like to thank Gordon Foxall for his steadfast support of my research on personality and consumer behavior, starting with a presentation at the 1992 European Association for Consumer Research conference in Amsterdam and the subsequent publication of an article in the *European Journal of Marketing* (1993), and culminating in the opportunity to publish this research in the *Handbook of Developments in Consumer Behavior*.

Finally, I would like to thank Jack Block for providing me with a treasure trove of prototypes to work with that he had worked on over a lifetime of research with the California Adult Q Set and for his permission to create CAQ decks for the 1990 version of the instrument. Jack was reviewing the manuscript for this chapter when he passed away. The California Adult Q Set and the California Way he pioneered have made a lasting contribution to personality assessment. The debate that has raged on endlessly between Q technique and Q methodology purists should not dampen the enthusiasm for his enduring legacy.

NOTE

1. To pawn in the UK.

REFERENCES

Albanese, Paul J. (1982), 'Toward a methodology for investigating the formation of preferences', Doctoral Dissertation, Harvard University, Cambridge, MA.
Albanese, Paul J. (1988), 'The intimate relations of the consistent consumer: psychoanalytic object relations theory applied to economics', in Paul J. Albanese (ed.), *Psychological Foundations of Economic Behavior*, New York: Praeges, pp. 59–80.

Albanese, Paul J. (1990), 'Personality, consumer behavior, and marketing research: a new theoretical and empirical approach', in Elizabeth C. Hirschman (ed.), *Research in Consumer Behavior*, vol. 4, Greenwich, CT: JAI Press, pp. 1–50.

Albanese, Paul J. (1991), 'Behavioral economics, psychological economics, and socioeconomics: object relations theory at the crossroads', in Roger Frantz, (ed.), *Handbook on Behavioral Economics*, vol. 2A, Greenwich, CT: JAI Press, pp. 19–34.

Albanese, Paul J. (1993), 'Personality and consumer behavior: an operational approach', *European Journal of Marketing*, **27** (8), 28–37.

Albanese, Paul J. (2002), *The Personality Continuum and Consumer Behavior*, Westport, CT: Quorum Books.

Albanese, Paul J. (2006), 'Inside economic man: behavioral economics and consumer behavior', in Morris Altman (ed.), *Handbook of Contemporary Behavioral Economics: Foundations and Developments*, Armonk, NY: M.E. Sharpe, pp. 3–23.

Belk, Russell (1985), 'Materialism: trait aspects of living in the material world', *Journal of Consumer Research*, **12** (3) (December), 265–280.

Bem, Daryl J. and David C. Funder (1978), 'Predicting more of the people more of the time: assessing the personality of situations', *Psychological Review*, **85** (6) (November), 485–501.

Benson, April Lane (ed.) (2000), *I Shop, Therefore I Am: Compulsive Buying and the Search for Self*, Northvale, NJ: Jason Aronson.

Block, Jack (1961), *The Q-Sort Method in Personality Assessment and Psychiatric Research*, Springfield, IL: Charles C. Thomas Publisher, reprinted in 1978 by Consulting Psychologists Press, Palo Alto, CA.

Block, Jack (2008), *The Q-Sort in Character Appraisal: Encoding Subjective Impressions of Persons Quantitatively*, Washington, DC: American Psychological Association.

Brown, Steven (1980), *Political Subjectivity: Applications of Q Methodology in Political Science*, New Haven and London: Yale University Press.

Diagnostic and Statistical Manual of Mental Disorders, Fourth Edition (1994) (DSM-IV), Washington, DC: American Psychiatric Association.

Diagnostic and Statistical Manual of Mental Disorders, Fourth Edition, Text Revision (2000) (DSM-IV-TR), Washington, DC: American Psychiatric Association.

Dittmar, Helga (2004), 'Understanding and diagnosing compulsive buying,' in R.H. Coombs (ed.), *Handbook of Addictive Disorders: A Practical Guide to Diagnosis and Treatment*, John Wiley and Sons: New York, pp. 411–450.

Faber, Ronald J. and Thomas C. O'Guinn (1992), 'A clinical screener for compulsive buying', *Journal of Consumer Research*, **19**, 459–469.

Fairbairn, W.R.D. (1952), *Psychoanalytic Studies of the Personality*, London: Routledge & Kegan Paul.

Hicks, J.R. (1934), 'A reconsideration of the theory of value', *Economica*, n. s., 1 (February), 52–76.

Kernberg, Otto F. (1985), *Borderline Conditions and Pathology Narcissism*, New York: Jason Aronson.

Lejoyeux, Michel, Jean Ades and Jacquelyn Solomon (1996), 'Phenomenology and psychopathology of uncontrolled buying', *American Journal of Psychiatry*, **154** (10), 1477–1478.

McElroy, Susan L., Andrew Satlin, Harrison G. Pope, Jr., Paul E. Keck, Jr. and James Hudson (1991), 'Treatment of compulsive shopping with antidepressants: a report of three cases', *Annals of Clinical Psychiatry*, **3**, 199–204.

McElroy, Susan L., Paul E. Keck, Jr., M.D., Harrison G. Pope, Jr., M.D., Jacqueline M.R. Smith and Stephen M. Strakowski, M.D. (1994), 'Compulsive buying: a report of 20 Cases', *Journal of Clinical Psychiatry*, **55** (6), 242–248.

O'Guinn, Thomas C. and Ronald J. Faber (1989), 'Compulsive buying: a phenomenological exploration', *Journal of Consumer Research*, **16** (2) (September), 147–157.

Reise, Steven P. and Craig J. Oliver (1994), 'Development of a California Q-Set indicator of primary psychopathy', *Journal of Personality Assessment*, **62** (1), 130–144.

Shedler, Jonathan and Drew Westen (1998), 'Refining the measurement of Axis II: a Q-sort procedure for assessing personality pathology', *Assessment*, **5** (4), 335–355.

Shedler, Jonathan and Drew Westen (2004), 'Refining personality disorder diagnosis: integrating science and practice', *American Journal of Psychiatry*, **161** (8) (August), 1350–1365.

Stephenson, William (1953), *The Study of Behavior: Q-Technique and its Methodology*, Chicago: University of Chicago Press.

Stephenson, William (1954), *Psychoanalysis and Q-Methodology: A Scientific Model for Psychoanalytic Doctrine*, unpublished manuscript.

Sullivan, Harry Stack (1956), *Clinical Studies in Psychiatry*, New York: W.W. Norton.

Westen, Drew and Jonathan Shedler (1999a), 'Revising and assessing Axis II, Part I: developing a clinically and empirically valid assessment method,' *American Journal of Psychiatry*, **156** (2) (February), 258–272.

Westen, Drew and Jonathan Shedler (1999b), 'Revising and assessing Axis II, Part II: toward an empirically based and clinically useful classification of personality disorders', *American Journal of Psychiatry*, **156** (2) (February), 273–285.

Westen, Drew and Jonathan Shedler (2000), 'A prototype matching approach to personality disorders: Toward DSM-V', *Journal of Personality Disorders*, **14** (2), 104–126.

Wink, Paul (1991), 'Self- and object-directedness in adult women', *Journal of Personality*, **59** (4) (December), 769–791.

PART IV

NEUROSCIENCE AND CONSUMER CHOICE

12 Consumer neuroscience
Peter Kenning, Mirja Hubert and Marc Linzmajer

12.1 INTRODUCTION

Recent years have seen enormous progress in academic research at the intersection of neuroscience, psychology and economics (Foxall et al. 1998). The outcome of this progress is summarized by the introduction of new and transdisciplinary fields like neuroeconomics or decision neuroscience (Shiv et al. 2005). Their joint aim is to integrate and apply neuroscientific theories, concepts, findings and methods to develop a sound idea of how humans make decisions (Kenning and Plassmann 2005).

The aim of this chapter is to give a detailed overview of the research area of consumer neuroscience. This transdisciplinary field can be viewed as a sub-discipline of neuroeconomics, in which consumer psychologists and business economists are dedicated to investigating consumer research and marketing questions with methodological and conceptual approaches from neuroscience (Fugate 2007; Lee et al. 2007). In addition they aim to add a new theoretical perspective to consumer research. Therefore, the academic research in consumer neuroscience takes place at the nexus of neuroscience, psychology, and marketing. Classical research in consumer behaviour and marketing necessarily looked at the human organism as being a "black box" and consequently used mainly theoretical constructs to interpret bodily processes and resulting behaviour (Howard and Sheth 1969). Today, modern techniques and methods from neuroscience enable researchers to get a more direct look into the "black box" of the human organism and provide the basis for the emergent field of consumer neuroscience (Kenning et al. 2007). On the whole the use of neurobiological methods such as electroencephalography is not entirely new to marketing research (Kroeber-Riel 1979). Nevertheless the direct observation of brain processes through methods such as functional magnetic resonance imaging (fMRI) provides a completely new and different perspective (Plassmann et al. 2007a; Riedl et al. 2010b). To get an introduction to the field of consumer neuroscience, this chapter is organized as follows. After the introduction, section 12.2 elucidates major academic cornerstones that led to the emergence of the transdisciplinary field of consumer neuroscience and provides a clear-cut definition of the discipline in the end. Section 12.3 briefly presents basic knowledge about brain physiology and relevant anatomical terms and areas for consumer neuroscience. Section 12.4 provides an overview of recent methods in neuroscience used by consumer researchers. After a brief insight into selected theories and concepts from neuroscience that consumer researchers can benefit from (section 12.5), a variety of preliminary findings is detailed in section 12.6 and structured alongside the traditional marketing-mix elements and brand research. Section 12.7 concludes with a look at the future of consumer neuroscience research.

12.2   CONSUMER NEUROSCIENCE – HISTORY AND DEFINITION

12.2.1   The Emergence of Consumer Neuroscience

In order to provide a deeper understanding of the emerging branch – consumer neuroscience – it is necessary to take a look at its historical roots.

At the beginning of the 19th century economists recognized that demand can not only be explained with simple purchase power. Rather it is a complex construct that is also influenced by psychological aspects of the consumer. Since its emergence in the 1920s, marketing and consumer research has therefore always been influenced by other scientific disciplines such as anthropology, sociology, decision theory and above all psychology.

During its "foundation phase" (1900–1920) marketing research mainly focussed on economic theories and the distribution sector (Wilkie and Moore 2003). During this time, researchers tried to explain consumer behaviour with an important approach from psychology – behaviourism. Behaviourism investigates the coherence between environment (stimulus) and observable behaviour (reaction) with the help of clearly defined experiments (Plomin et al. 1990). The aim of behaviourism is to scientifically describe behaviour by applying exclusively natural scientific methods. The organism is thereby regarded as a "black box", because it is not possible to directly observe internal psychological or physiological processes. Instead, behaviour can be regarded as a function of a given stimulus (stimulus-response model: S-R model). These early models of consumer behaviour included various assumptions that proved to be untenable. One important assumption that was also central to classical and neoclassical economic theory was for example that consumers or economic actors were seen to be completely rational (Homo economicus) and always react in the same way to a given stimulus (Jacoby 2002).

Influenced by findings in psychology, for example neobehaviourism,

Input (Stimuli)	Organism (Black Box)	Output (Reactions)
S_i	I_j	R_k

• Demographic (e.g., age, gender) and socioeconomic (e.g., education, income) characteristics of a person
• Social environment of a person (e.g., reference groups, opinion leader)
• Economic environment of a person (e.g., price demand of vendors)
	Decision making process dependent on:
	
	• *Cognitive components*
	  Perception
	  Thinking
	  Learning
	
	• *Activating components*
	  Emotions
	  Motivation
	  Attitudes
		Choice of product
		Choice of brand
		Choice of retailer
		Time of purchase
		Amount of purchase

observable	unobservable	observable

Source: Kotler and Armstrong, 2009.

Figure 12.1   The SOR model

the S-R model was further advanced in the mid-1960s (Jacoby 2002). The S-R Model was enhanced through a greater emphasis on internal processes and the implementation of intervening variables (Woodworth 1921). Processes inside the organism that have not been accessible within the S-R Model were now described in a fictive way. The decision-making process is initiated by an observable stimulus (e.g., price) that influences the person. Phase 2 consists of the non-observable processes inside the organism ("black box") that can only be explained by theoretical constructs (intervening variables). The theoretical constructs can be distinguished by cognitive processes, where the individual acts deliberately and considerately, and activating processes, which are associated with inner arousal or emotions. The third phase consists of the observable reaction of a consumer (e.g., the purchase) (Kotler and Armstrong 2009, see Figure 12.1).

At the beginning of the 1960s and in the 1970s, Jerome McCarthy and Philip Kotler constituted "modern marketing" with the development of the "marketing-mix instruments" (Kotler 1976; McCarthy 1960). They put forward the consequent orientation of all activities of a company on the needs and demands of the consumers. This claim led to a strong concentration of marketing research on consumer behaviour. In 1969 the Association for Consumer Research (ACR) was founded and the first consumer behaviour textbooks and courses appeared in the late 1960s (Engel et al. 1968; Kassarjian and Robertson 1968). In these early days of consumer research the most important frameworks were comprehensive

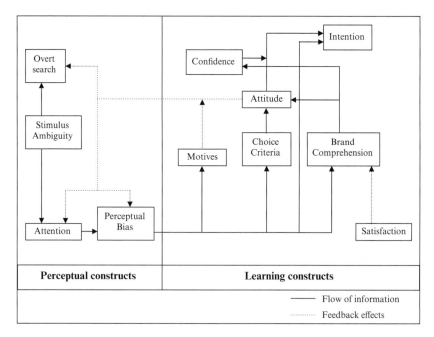

Source: Howard and Sheth, 1969.

Figure 12.2   Simplified description of the Howard-Sheth model

models of consumer behaviour (Engel et al. 1968; Howard and Sheth 1969; Nicosia 1966). These models primarily focussed on activities associated with satisfying consumer needs and were based on the theoretical construction of processes inside the "black box". Distinction can be made between parietal models of consumer behaviour that only concentrate on single psychological factors that influence the decision-making process (e.g., activating components, involvement etc.) and total models that try to explain all of the non-observable processes inside the consumer.

A very important total model of consumer behaviour is the model put forward by Howard and Sheth (1969), which explains cognitive, controlled decisions in a purchase-situation by arranging different variables in certain ways. The model distinguishes between observable input (S) and output (R) variables and the non-observable hypothetical constructs (I) which reflect the buyer's internal state. The hypothetical constructs can be divided into perceptual constructs that are involved in information processing and learning constructs that are associated with concept formation. Figure 12.2 depicts the intervening variables inside the organism. Beside the input and the output variables there are exogenous variables that construct the frame of the purchase process, but are not directly included in the model.

Another relevant total model of buying behaviour is the approach of Engel et al. (1978, 1995). They distinguish between extensive, limited, impulsive and habituated buying decisions that differ with regard to the degree of involvement and risk perception of the consumer. The decision-making process can be classified in consecutive phases. The starting point is the need recognition defined as the differences between the target state and the actual condition. If the consumer recognized the problem, the next phase – the search for information – begins. The decision-making process is completed with the last phase – the evaluation of different alternatives.

A further approach to model consumer decision-making and to illuminate the intervening variables is the decision-net approach of Bettman (1974). This model constructs networks that graphically depict consumer behaviour. An interviewer accompanies the purchase process of a customer in order to create networks that reflect purchase behaviour with the help of protocols (observations and questions). The aim of this approach is to develop a theoretical structure of the black box by directly collecting empirical data.

From these exemplary models that attempt to theoretically construct the processes inside the organism we can deduce that it is essential for consumer research to know more about physiological and psychological processes in order to understand their influence on consumer decision-making. However, in contrast to market shares, unemployment rates and economic growth, theoretical constructs are neither observable nor objectively measurable. The only way to solve this dilemma was to use tools or methods that enable researchers to investigate behaviour in a more objective way (Kenning and Plassmann 2005).

Efforts to include biological components are not new in consumer research (Kroeber-Riel 1979). Physiological processes have been detected with different traditional measurement methods. For example, the first studies that applied EEG to marketing relevant subjects appeared in the 1970s (Krugman 1971). However, generally consumer research has paid only scant attention to biological processes that determine consumer behaviour over a long time. Saad (2008) even talks about a "collective amnesia of marketing scholars regarding consumers' biological and evolutionary roots". He claims that marketing and consumer research should seek law-like generalizations as in the natural sciences, by concentrating on the evolutionary and biological roots of the consumer.

Groundbreaking developments of neuroscientific techniques (e.g., fMRI) and the insight that biological processes influence economic actions to a high degree led to the emergence of neuroeconomics (Camerer et al.

2005). This research area integrates neuroscientific methods and findings into the investigation of economic problems. But also marketing research discovered neuroscience for a better understanding of consumer behaviour. In the late 1990s imaging techniques were starting to be used for marketing research processes and in 2002 the term "neuromarketing" was coined (Lewis and Bridger 2005).

12.2.2   Definition and Relevance

The emergence of neuroeconomics showed that economics and neuroscience can learn a lot from each other. Both disciplines try to understand and predict human behaviour, but they have used quite different methods in the past. Whereas economic research has tried to explain behaviour through observational data and theoretical constructs such as utility or preferences, neurology contemplates the physiological elements and somatic variables that influence behaviour. Neuroeconomics, which evolved from the combination of both disciplines, proposes an interdisciplinary approach and specifically examines the neural correlates of decision-making (Sanfey et al. 2006). It can be defined as the application of neuroscientific theories, findings and methods to economic problems. Within empirical neuroeconomic studies subjects are confronted with intrapersonal or interpersonal decision situations, while their brain activity is measured with neuroscientific methods such as fMRI. Hence, neuroeconomics can be classified as part of behavioural economics and experimental economics. However, the neuroeconomic scope of interest reaches beyond experimental economic studies. Neuroeconomics does not only investigate economic decision behaviour, but this research stream also examines the motivation and neural correlates of economic behaviour. Compared to the classical economic model of the Homo economicus it implies a totally different idea of man. From a neuroscientific perspective the counterpart of the Homo economicus is the Homo neurobiologicus, whose behaviour and social and economic nature are the result of biology (Kenning and Plassmann 2005). Biological factors largely determine his thinking and feeling, deciding and acting, as well as his buying and selling, i.e. his economic life (Kenning and Plassmann 2005). In this regard neuroeconomics can contribute to create models of economy that are based on a realistic description of human behaviour and the comprehension of the biological driving forces of behaviour. With the help of these more realistic models it may be possible not only to explain, but also to better predict how people make decisions (Glimcher and Rustichini 2004). Thereby neuroeconomics not only seeks to identify brain regions associated with specific behaviour, but is also interested in examining neural circuits or systems that are associated with, for example, choice, preference, and judgement (Camerer et al. 2005; Foxall 2008).

Overall, Glimcher and Rustichini (2004) argue that psychology, economics, and marketing are converging under the umbrella of the neuroscience literature to provide a unified theory of human behaviour. Therefore, we expect neurophysiological studies to increasingly inform inter-disciplinary phenomena in the social sciences that span across these core disciplines.

Consumer neuroscience is a sub-area of neuroeconomics that addresses marketing and consumer behaviour relevant problems with methods and insights from brain research (Fugate 2007; Grosenick et al. 2008; Lee et al. 2007). The term "neuromarketing" is often used to identify this development as well, but the label may be a misnomer. "Marketing" describes the idea of market-orientated corporate management (see Kotler 1976; section 12.2.1.). Accordingly, the term "retail marketing" denotes the concept of market-orientated management of retailers. Furthermore, the branch of "service marketing" is concerned with the market-orientated management of service companies (e.g., Evanschitzky et al. 2006). Given these exemplary uses for the term "marketing", the notion of "neuromarketing" poses an impractical ambiguity. We therefore distinguish between "consumer neuroscience" as the scientific proceeding of this research approach, and "neuromarketing" as the application of the findings from consumer neuroscience within the scope of managerial practice (Hubert and Kenning 2008). With better comprehension and steadily improving methods, it may be possible to derive new theories for marketing research and to arrive at a higher level of explained variance (Grosenick et al. 2008; Kenning and Plassmann 2008; Knutson et al. 2007). This may in turn help to improve companies' actions, for example, marketing responses that are based on a better satisfaction of unconscious emotional consumer needs. However, consumer neuroscience is still in its infancy (Reimann et al. 2011) and should not be seen as a challenge to traditional consumer research. Rather, it constitutes a complementing advancement for further investigation of specific decision-making behaviour.

The increasing relevance of this area of research is indicated by the growing interest of science and practice (Fugate 2007; Hubert and Kenning 2008; Lee et al. 2007; Plassmann et al. 2007a). For example, numerous conferences, calls for papers from prominent scientific journals, and calls for research by institutes such as the Marketing Science Institute, the Institute for the Study of Business Markets (Lee et al. 2007), and the World Advertising Research Centre focus on this subject. The

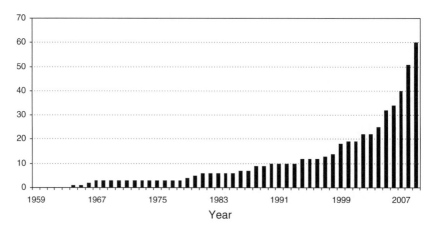

Note: * Included are the following journals: *Journal of Consumer Psychology, Journal of Consumer Research, Journal of Marketing, Journal of Marketing Research, Management Science, Marketing Letters,* and *Marketing Science.*

Source: Hilke Plassmann, INSEAD, 2010.

Figure 12.3   Contributions related to neuroscientific research in the seven most canonical marketing journals* from 1959 to 2009

Association of Consumer Research even implemented a new content area code for neuroscience. Established conferences that are exclusively concerned with neuroeconomics are for example the NeuroPsychoEconomics Conference and the Annual Neuroeconomics Conference of the Society for Neuroeconomics. Furthermore, the absolute number of papers in international renowned marketing journals tripled within a decade up until 2009, which establishes the field's move into the mainstream of research.

12.3   THE BRAIN – FOCUS OF NEUROECONOMIC AND CONSUMER NEUROSCIENCE RESEARCH

Neuroeconomic research is interested in the neurobiological correlates of human behaviour and focuses on the brain as the organ of (buying) decision-making. Therefore, a necessary prerequisite to understand neuroeconomic research is a detailed knowledge of the structure and function of the human brain. Generally, neuroeconomic publications use precise specifications of different brain areas and require a deep understanding of anatomical structures. In order to explain neuroeconomic results we first want to provide an anatomical overview of important brain structures. The description of the human central nervous system starts with a macro-biological view of the brain. For an overview of the different functions and a microbiological perspective of the nerve cells we recommend further readings as given in the citations of the next sections. The depiction here is intended to help the reader to better understand selected studies and discussions in the field of consumer neuroscience. Therefore the following offers a relatively broad anatomical overview and does not claim to be medically exhaustive.

12.3.1 The Central Nervous System

The central nervous system (CNS) serves as a higher-ranking head-quarter that coordinates and controls all conscious and unconscious processes inside and outside the organism and is responsible for the collection and processing of information within the body (Kandel et al. 1995). It comprises a very complex entity where many reactions coop-erate, overlap and counteract in such a way that a clear distinction of single operation sequences is usually not possible. For neuroeconomic research the interaction of these extensive processes is of great interest, because it investigates how different components interact and influence human behaviour. Depending on location and morphology the CNS can be distinguished between the central and peripheral nervous system. The central nervous system comprises a functional entity of brain (Encephalon, gr. enképhalos = brain) and spinal cord (Medulla spinalis, lat. medulla = marrow, spina = spine). The peripheral nervous system (PNS) consists of nerves that emerge from the brain and spinal cord and branch out in the entire organism in order to connect the central nervous system to the limbs and organs (Kandel et al. 1995). Another approach divides the peripheral nervous system additionally accord-ing to its function, but due to the great conjunction density inside the body many processes can be assigned to both the PNS and the CNS. The somatic (animal, cerebro-spinal) nervous system is mainly actu-ated deliberately and controls the sense organs, the skeletal muscles and the conscious perception of the body periphery (Kandel et al. 1995). The autonomic (vegetative, visceral) nervous system coordinates the viscera and mainly works unconsciously. The autonomic nervous system can be further distinguished in two anatomical separate sections that work antagonistically. The subunit that controls all activities associ-ated with physical effort, energy consumption, stress and excitement and that helps the body to be ready for action (fight or flight) is called

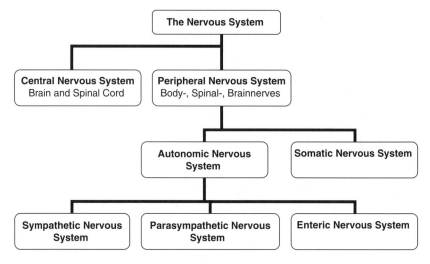

Figure 12.4   Schematic diagram of the nervous system

sympathetic nervous system. The parasympathetic nervous system fulfils the function to allay the body (rest and digest) (Carlson 2004; Kandel et al. 1995). The enteric nervous system is located inside the intestine and controls the gastrointestinal system.

12.3.2   Orientation in the Body: Axes, Planes and Terms of Location

Because of the tridimensionality of the body it is very important to be able to appoint directions correctly. In medical sciences the use of Latin names is well established so that detailed location information can be provided with the help of orientation lines (Tortora and Derrickson 2006). Table 12.1 outlines the most important anatomical terms of location in order to provide a better understanding of the technical terms that are used in the further course of the chapter (Carlson 2004; Purves et al. 2001; Zak 2004)

Diagrams of anatomical planes and the corresponding slices in the human brain often appear in neuroeconomic studies, because the different imaging techniques map and evaluate activations within the various brain slices (Carlson 2004; Zak 2004).

In order to define single brain areas their localization is of crucial importance. Due to individual shapes of the human head this exercise can be very difficult. After the data collection it is important to find a consistent norm for the different brain structures in order to better compare the individual brains. In this coherence the Talairach and

Table 12.1   Axes, planes and terms of location

Axis	
Vertical (longitudinal)	The upright position
Transversal (horizontal)	Across the body from right to left (and the other way round)
Sagittal (ventrodorsal)	Following the arrow from the front to the back (and the other way round)

Planes	
Median	Midsagittal, divides the body into right and left halves
Transversal	Plane running across the body parallel to the ground (horizontal). It divides the body into upper and lower portions, also called cross sectional plane
Sagittal (lateral)	Lengthwise vertical plane that divides the body into left and right structures
Frontal	Vertical plane that divides into anterior and posterior portions, also called coronal plane

Terms of Location	
Superior, cranial	Running upwards to the top of the head
Inferior, caudal	Running downwards to the sacrum
Anterior, ventral	Pointing towards the front
Posterior, dorsal	Pointing towards the back
Lateral	Pointing towards the side
Medial, median	Pointing towards the center – near the middle plane
Central-periphery	Central-peripheral pointing inwards and pointing outwards

Tournoux-coordinate system is used, which localizes specific brain areas relatively to anatomical landmarks (Talairach and Tournoux 1888). Another important approach to localize brain regions is the use of Brodmann areas. This method divides the human cerebrum in 52 fields that bear similarities in their cell and lamellae structure (Brodmann 1909). Even though they lack a consistent systematic, they are still in common use.

12.3.3   The Brain (Encephalon)

The human brain is a very sensitive organ that is protected by the bony skull, the meningeals and the cerebrospinal fluid (CSF, Liquor cerebrospinalis) against internal or external pressure alterations (Kandel et al. 1995). The cerebrospinal fluid circulates in four cavities – the so called ventricles

Table 12.2   The anatomical subdivisions of the brain

Major division	Ventricle	Subdivision	Principal structures
Forebrain (Prosencephalon)	Lateral	Cerebrum (Telencephalon)	Cerebral cortex Basal ganglia Limbic system
	Third	Interbrain (Diencephalon)	Thalamus Hypothalamus
Midbrain (Mesencephalon)	Cerebral aqueduct	Midbrain (Mesencephalon)	Midbrain tectum Tegmentum
Hindbrain (Rhombencephalon)	Fourth	Afterbrain (Metencephalon) Myelencephalon	Cerebellum Pons Medulla oblongata

Source: Carlson, 2004; Kandel et al., 1995.

(lat. ventriculus = little venter). The division in the fore-, middle- and afterbrain is based on the development of the human brain during the embryogenesis. These structures emerge from subdivisions of the neural tube that develop into distinct directions of the nervous system (Carlson 2004). The brain consists of a closely connected network of billions of neurons, a somatic centre that coordinates all life functions of the organism, mental and psychological activities and the processing of incoming information (Kandel et al. 1995).

The dimension of the complex neural nexus in the brain is particularly impressive. It is estimated that the cerebral cortex alone consists of approximately 10^{10} neurons each with connections to approximately 10 000 other nerve cells. The brain's greatest crosslinking is with itself. The adjustment of the processes is relatively decentralized. Visual, auditory or motor processes in the organism take place simultaneously and are assembled by the brain to provide an overall picture of perception. In order to coordinate all the different processes, the major subdivisions of the brain are constructed to interact (Table 12.2). In this context neuroeconomics attempts to investigate on the one hand the function of the human brain and on the other hand tries to explain economic behaviour with the help of neurobiological findings.

When it comes to the concrete identification of brain areas, it is important to use appropriate measurement tools. Here it is pivotal to have a high resolution as well as the ability to measure activity in sub-cortical brain structures such as the nucleus accumbens which are often the focus of neuroeconomic studies.

12.4 OVERVIEW OF CURRENT NEUROSCIENCE TOOLS FOR CONSUMER RESEARCH

Using neuroimaging tools in consumer research is a new and exciting development (Ariely and Berns 2010), but a general lack of in-depth knowledge creates the need to provide some explanation of these methods. On the basis of already existing overviews (Camerer et al. 2005; Kenning and Plassmann 2005; Kenning et al. 2007; Lee et al. 2007; Shiv et al. 2005), the purpose here is to present selected neuroscience tools available to consumer research, rather than to discuss each tool extensively. (For an additional overview of costs and benefits, see, for example, Ariely and Berns 2010; Dimoka et al. 2011; Perrachione and Perrachione 2008; Riedl et al. 2010a; Riedl et al. 2010b).

For a long time in consumer research, examinations of the processes inside the human organism were based on established indirect measurement methods such as electrodermal response (EDR) measurement, pupillography, and, most commonly, self-assessment methods (Bagozzi 1991; Groeppel-Klein 2005). A more direct view into the black box of the organism should be feasible with the help of advanced techniques and methods of brain research that are applied in the field of consumer neuroscience (Kenning et al. 2007). Even though the application of neurobiological methods such as electroencephalography (EEG) is not new in marketing research, the direct observation of brain reactions that is available through the use of steadily improving methods of imaging techniques, is providing a completely different perspective (Plassmann et al. 2007a).

The determination of cortical areas that are stimulated during consumer decision processes by applying neurological methods offers various advantages over conventional procedures:

1. The approach of consumer neuroscience enables the researcher to reassess existing theories that theoretically assume different brain mechanisms (e.g., hemisphere theory (Hansen 1976, 1981)) by investigating the actual brain activations.
2. The observation of the total brain has the potential to yield new, unpredictable results, and enhances the explorative character of consumer neuroscience. This contrasts measuring the brain activity by recording only one signal, as is used, for example, in EDR or eye tracking, which can be compared to an effort to capture the musical sounds of an orchestra by measuring only the noise level (Kenning et al. 2007).
3. Concerning the empirical data ascertainment, the observation of brain activity can offer another, and more objective, perspective:

self-assessment methods that rely totally on the ability of the respondent to describe and reconstruct feelings and thoughts are very subjective. Many effects in the human organism that influence behaviour are not perceived consciously; hence, the cognitive filter of the test taker may bias the results. For example, a person who has a temperature may determine that his body feels cold, even though the objective measurement of a clinical thermometer indicates that it is not.

4.   Strategic behaviour and social desirability, which can confound findings of self-assessment methods, can be eliminated, given that the participating subjects have little to no influence on the measurement of their brain activity (Camerer et al. 2005).

5.   A last, but very important, advantage of determining the cortical stimulation is the simultaneousness of measurement and experiment. Some processes might not be stable over time, making it very difficult for researcher and participant to reconstruct them after the experiment (Lee et al. 2007).

Table 12.3 provides a brief overview of current neuroimaging techniques and other neurological methods that are applied increasingly in marketing research. These can be organized into two categories: the first considers the electrical activity of the brain and the second measures neural metabolism processes (Dimoka et al. 2011; Huesing et al. 2006; Kenning et al. 2007; Riedl et al. 2010b). Novel procedures do not observe the working brain but are able to have a direct influence on the neural activity.

In the preceding discussion, all neuroimaging techniques currently available have been shown to have both advantages and disadvantages. While the *where* of brain activity is more easily assessed by fMRI or PET, the question of *when* – such as the discrimination between parallel and sequential processing – can be answered more precisely by EEG or MEG. Therefore, a better understanding of the haemodynamic processes and a multimodal approach is necessary that combines the different methods in order to achieve better insights in the human brain (Logothetis 2008). In this context, it is important that market and consumer researchers keep in mind, that various research issues are still in their infancy and basic research is necessary to facilitate an application of these techniques to marketing. Although taking into account that approximately 50 percent of all neuroimaging studies are conducted with the use of fMRI (Huesing et al. 2006), this specific method may also provide an appropriate instrument for market and consumer researchers (Plassmann et al. 2007a).

Table 12.3 Simplified overview of relevant neurophysiological measurement techniques

Classification	Method	Description
Imaging methods		
Electrical activity	Electro-encephalography (EEG)	Measurement of voltage fluctuation at the surface of the brain + good temporal resolution + relative equipment costs + relatively straightforward data analysis − very limited potential for locating brain areas which are responsible for voltage fluctuations
	Magneto-encephalography (MEG)	Registration of changes in magnetic streams induced by voltage fluctuations + good temporal resolution − limited spatial resolution (but better than EEG) − relatively high measurement costs − relatively complex data analysis
Metabolic activity	Positron-emission-tomography (PET)	Nuclear medicine technique for analyzing metabolic procedures in neurons: + good spatial resolution − very poor temporal resolution − application of radioactive contrast (invasive) − relatively high measurement costs − relatively complex data analysis

Table 12.3 (continued)

Classification	Method	Description
Imaging methods		
Metabolic activity	Functional magnetic resonance imaging (fMRI)	Measurement of metabolic activity using the magnetic properties of blood + good spatial resolution – lower temporal resolution than EEG and MEG – relatively high measurement costs – relatively complex data analysis
Psychophysiological methods		
Activity of the periphery nervous system	Electrodermal response (EDR), galvanic skin response	Measures activation changes via the electrical resistance of the skin + relatively easy application and data analysis + relatively low measurement costs – no assumptions can be made about the valence of the activation – many confounders that are difficult to eliminate
Activity of the cardiovascular system	Heart and pulse rate measurement	Measures activation changes via variances of the heart and pulse rate + relatively simple equipment + relatively low measurement costs – no assumptions can be made about the valence of the activation – many confounders that are difficult to eliminate

Activity of the facial muscles	Facial electromyography	Measurement of the mien by assigning the movement of single facial areas to certain facial expressions, "Facial Acting Coding System"
		+ relatively simple equipment
		+ relatively low measurement costs
		− many confounders that are difficult to eliminate
		− complex data analysis
Activity of the eyes	Eye-tracking measurement	The movement of the pupil is used as indicator of stimulus perception
		+ relatively simple equipment
		+ relatively low measurement costs
		− many confounders that are difficult to eliminate

Note: + and − indicate positive and negative features within a row respectively; this table is simplified but provides an overview for non-technical readers.

Source: Kenning et al., 2007.

435

12.4.1   Transcranial Magnetic Stimulation (TMS)

Another neuroscientific method that uses magnetic fields to stimulate nerve cells in the brain is transcranial magnetic stimulation (TMS). This method stimulates the brain by sending electromagnetic impulses through the skull. This requires placing an electromagnetic coil directly over a specified location of the head and introducing a transient high intensity current. The generated magnetic field induces additional currents in the concerned neurons, activating nerve cells that temporarily disrupt brain function in this area (Camerer et al. 2005; Lee et al. 2007; Shiv et al. 2005). The differences in cognitive and behavioural functioning that result from such disruptions allow determination of whether the region is, in fact, critical for a certain function. Theoretically, TMS adds external validity and permits a more causal testing of brain function than do correlative measures such as fMRI and EEG (Camerer et al. 2005). However, TMS also has several disadvantages. First, the use of TMS is currently limited to the cortical areas close to the skull. Second, due to the interconnectedness of brain areas, the effects of TMS are not limited to the stimulated region, making causal interpretations difficult. Third, there is some evidence that TMS may have longer-lasting effects on neural tissue (Jones 2007). Though TMS is not physically invasive in the way that a surgical procedure is invasive, the radiation produced by TMS affects the body, and headaches and, rarely, seizures have been reported (Heckman and Happel 2006).

Notwithstanding potential concerns related to TMS, it has the potential to better explain the occurrence of phenomena in consumer research: an example of a TMS study that is relevant for consumer research is an experiment conducted by Basso et al. (2006). They used repetitive TMS to investigate the role of the prefrontal cortex in visuospatial planning. The results indicate that, in a visuospatial problem-solving task, the prefrontal cortex is involved in switching between heuristics during the execution of a plan. Given the importance of the use of heuristics in decision-making tasks (Brandstätter et al. 2006; Gigerenzer 1991; Goldstein and Gigerenzer 2002), these findings are likely to have implications for consumer research. Another repetitive TMS study was conducted by Plassmann et al. (2008). They addressed the question of what role the dorsolateral prefrontal cortex plays in decoding so called decision values (DV). Decision values are subjective value computations of how much resources (e.g., money) one is willing to give up in order to obtain a reward (e.g., having candy) or avoid experiencing a punishment (e.g., staying hungry). From their results, Plassmann et al. (2008) conclude that repetitive TMS designed to suppress the function of the right dorsolateral prefrontal cortex downmodulates the computation of DVs during a simple economic decision-making task. This might be a first step to a better understanding of the brain structures responsible for the computation of value in simple everyday choices of consumers.

12.4.2 Combination of Neuroscience Tools and Responsible Conduct of Research

Each individual neuroscience tool has its strengths and weaknesses (for overviews see Ariely and Berns 2010; Dimoka et al. 2011; Perrachione and Perrachione 2008; Riedl et al. 2010a; Riedl et al. 2010b). Therefore, combining two or even more methods may improve the validity of research findings. Like filling in rows and lines in sudoku games, clues from one tool help fill in what is learned from other tools. For example, fMRI and EEG can be used in combination. Using fMRI-compatible electrodes, EEG can be measured within an fMRI scanner, combining the high temporal resolution of EEG with the high spatial resolution of fMRI. An advantage of fMRI is that it allows identification of the neural generators or underlying neural substrates of different components of an EEG signal (Debener et al. 2006). Moreover, recent studies using TMS in combination with brain imaging techniques have found that TMS does affect the activation in several interconnected brain areas (Ruff et al. 2008), which indicates that there is often no simple causal relationship between activation in one specific brain area and behavioural performance (Huettel et al. 2009a). This complexity of causal relationship advocates the use of TMS with other imaging methods (Riedl et al. 2010a).

With respect to responsible research conduct when applying neuroscience-based technologies, Shamoo and Resnik (2009) set up the principles honesty, objectivity and respect for research subjects (Newland et al. 2003; Shamoo 2010). Together with other guidelines (e.g., World Medical Association Declaration of Helsinki) these principles should always be adhered to when using neuroscience tools in consumer research. Furthermore, Shamoo (2010) defines eight sub-guidelines, especially referring to the research with human subjects, which should be an essential basis for every researcher using neuroscience tools. Oversight by independent institutional review boards to ensure subject and consumer protection is critical for responsible research in consumer neuroscience. Their responsibility is to embrace and monitor issues of ethical research conduct as identified in discussions from the fields of neuroethics (Farah and Wolpe 2004; Farah 2002, 2007; Murphy et al. 2008; Shamoo 2010; Shamoo and Resnik 2009; Shamoo and Schwartz 2008) and, especially, neuromarketing (Ariely and Berns 2010; Foxall 2008; Murphy et al. 2008; Perrachione and Perrachione 2008; Wilson et al. 2008).

12.5   NEUROSCIENTIFIC THEORIES AND CONCEPTS RELEVANT FOR CONSUMER RESEARCH

Consumer researchers can refer to a number of higher-order theories from cognitive neuroscience that might help explain how human processes guide behaviour. To understand phenomena of potential relevance to consumer behaviour, it is useful to review and integrate the neuroscience literature on particular research topics that consumer researchers are interested in.

12.5.1   The Somatic Marker Hypothesis

Economic theory has neglected the importance of emotions for the generation of behaviour for a very long time (Hansen 2005, 2007; Hansen et al. 2007). A possible explanation is that they are not directly measurable, have no "intelligence" and can therefore influence rational decision-making only in a negative way (Camerer et al. 2005; Bechara and Damasio 2005; Bettman et al. 1998). Sometimes they are even mistakenly considered as cognition, because they are involved in information processing (LeDoux 1995). Consumer research differentiates between emotions and cognition and investigates their role for the buying process. In this context emotions are often seen as activating and propulsive components that give cognitive actions – through the concept of involvement – a certain direction. Consumer neuroscience recesses the idea of traditional consumer research and tries to get a deeper understanding of emotions, by the use of changed terminologies, the enlargement of their functions, neural localization and the investigation of different somatic reaction patterns. Emotions, feelings and intuitions are classified as affective processes that are only perceived consciously if a certain intensity level is reached (Camerer et al. 2005). On the one hand emotions are defined as "a collection of changes in body and brain states triggered by a dedicated brain system that responds to specific contents of one's perceptions, actual or recalled, relative to a particular object or event" (Bechara and Damasio 2005, p. 339). Thus, they lead to a change in the somatic state – for example through physiological modifications of heart beat or muscle tonus. Analogous, different processes are induced in the brain, which influence further mental processes (Bechara and Damasio 2005). On the other hand, emotions are seen as direct answers to reward, punishment, and changes in the anticipation of both, such as frustration after a loss (Rolls 1999). In contrast, feelings are defined as the mental representation – the conscious experience of physiological states induced by emotions (Damasio 2001). Consumer neuroscience emphasizes the role of emotions – beyond the activating function

– as one of the most important components of the cognitive (economic) decision-making process.

Against this background the somatic marker hypothesis (Bechara and Damasio 2005) constitutes a close relationship between emotions and decision-making. The starting point of this theory was investigations of patients with lesions in certain brain structures such as the ventromedial prefrontal cortex, who showed problems in social and economic decision-making. Although their intellectual capacities stayed the same, it was very difficult for them to make advantageous decisions. Instead of a fast decision-making mechanism, these persons used a logical thinking process, by applying a kind of cost-utility analysis. Due to the great number of possibilities, this procedure was very difficult and time consuming. In the end they often came to an unfavourable result (Bechara et al. 2000b). Damasio and his team concluded that for normal decision-making an automatic, emotional process is applied that helps subconsciously to make the right choice (Bechara and Damasio 2005). In this context, somatic markers are defined as the physiological component of an emotion that is "marked" or associated with a certain event, an idea or individual memories (primary or secondary inducer). Somatic markers can previously facilitate the decision-making process. An important aspect of these considerations is that emotional decision-making should not be seen as a replacement of cognitive thought processes, but rather fulfils a supporting and complementary function. Thus, somatic markers do not relieve us of rational thinking; instead they previously sort out disadvantageous alternatives and help to reach faster and beneficial decisions (Bechara and Damasio 2005).

12.5.2 Theory of Mind

The theory of mind is another prominent theory that explains how people infer how others will behave (Fletcher et al. 1995; Singer 2009). The study of our capacity to reason about other people's minds has become the focus of cognitive neuroscience research as modern image techniques emerged. In these imaging studies, stories are typically told on the basis of certain stimuli – like texts or videos – to subjects in the scanner. Participants are then asked to understand beliefs, desires or intentions of the protagonist in the respective stories (for an overview, see Gallagher and Frith 2003). Therefore, the theory of mind investigates which neural structures underlie our capacity to reason about other people's non-observable internal states. Cognitive neuroscience literature links areas like the posterior superior temporal sulcus, the medial prefrontal cortex and sometimes also the temporal poles as the brain areas associated with predicting of other's behaviour (McCabe et al. 2001; Singer 2009; Singer and Lamm 2009). It is important to note though, that the medial prefrontal cortex (mPFC) is not only involved when people think about other people's thoughts, but also when people are reflecting on their own states of mind (Mitchell et al. 2005). For consumer neuroscience it is particularly interesting to explore whether brain data can predict what decisions are made during social exchanges (e.g., interaction with sales people at the POS) and whether it makes a difference if we perceive for example sales people as being similar or dissimilar to ourselves.

12.5.3   Mirror Neurons

Mirror neuron research focuses not on complex inferences about abstract mental states (like theory of mind), but on the ability to understand other people's goals and intentions by merely observing their actions, or imitating their behaviour (Iacoboni et al. 1999). Originally discovered in brains of macaque monkeys (Rizzolatti et al. 1996), mirror neurons were the first evidence of a brain mechanism that not only represents a subject's own world, but also the world of another person. Naturally it was suggested that mirror neurons may represent the basis for imitation. There should be a translation mechanism in the primate brain that allows us to transform actions that we see in our own motor programs. By now several studies on mirror neurons have shown a similar coding of the perception and generation of motor actions in the human brain (for an overview see Grezes and Decety 2001). The study design followed a similar structure: participants were scanned while they watched short motor actions. The observed brain activation was then compared to that observed when scanned participants performed the same motor action themselves. Similar to the studies on monkeys, results revealed that the same brain areas were recruited when participants merely observed another person performing an action and when they performed the same action themselves. These shared activated brain areas include supplementary motor area (SMA), pre-SMA, premotor cortex, the supramarginal gyrus, intraparietal sulcus and superior parietal lobe (e.g., Singer 2009; Singer and Lamm 2009). In which ways the idea of mirror neurons can be applied to broader concepts in social cognition – for example not only understanding motor action but also emotions of others – is subject to a lot of discussion in the field (Iacoboni and Dapretto 2006; Saxe 2005). Nevertheless consumer neuroscience can benefit from the idea of mirror neurons and might integrate results from cognitive neuroscience to better explain adoption behaviours by consumers. Moreover, it could explain why marketing companies often use rewarding elements in their brand communication. It helps to tie positive emotions to certain brands.

12.5.4 Decision-making and Cognitive Processing

The cognitive neuroscience literature also focused on inferring the brain bases of decision-making. The aim of this research is to provide accurate models of decision-making (Sanfey et al. 2006). Different aspects of decision-making can be calculative and/or emotional under different conditions (Sanfey et al. 2006), such as balancing rewards and risks (e.g., Foxall 2008; McClure et al. 2004a), managing uncertainty, risk, and ambiguity (e.g., Huettel et al. 2005; Krain et al. 2006), and assessing various utility trade-offs (e.g., Camerer 2003). The literature has identified the prefrontal cortex (primarily the orbitofrontal and dorsolateral prefrontal cortex) and the limbic system (mostly the anterior cingulate cortex and amygdala) as the major decision-making areas (e.g., Ernst and Paulus 2005). Moreover, the prefrontal cortex is responsible primarily for the calculative or cognitive aspects of decision-making and the limbic system for the emotional aspects (Bechara et al. 2000a; Sharot et al. 2004). Cognitive and emotional aspects of decision-making are examined with imaging techniques in which participants are asked to engage in decision-making activities. Bechara et al. (1994) showed, for example, by means of the Iowa gambling task, that the orbifrontal cortex is responsible for decision-making associated with calculating reward and punishment. In their task healthy subjects learned to choose only the "good" decks, whereas patients with lesions in the orbifrontal cortex continued to choose the "bad" decks. In this line of research Hsu et al. (2005) showed that the level of effort required in decision-making correlates with activation in the orbifrontal cortex and the amygdala. Recognizing that decision-making has a cognitive and an emotional component, Bhatt and Camerer (2005) showed that participants whose brain activations exhibited good cooperation between the limbic system and the prefrontal cortex were most successful in experimental games of decision-making.

Being closely connected to the cognitive aspects of decision-making, cognitive processing is an area that also received much attention in the neuroscience literature. Cognitive processing focuses on how the brain manages information. As with decision-making processes, the brain distinguishes between cognitive and emotional information (Ferstl et al. 2005). Following Ferstl et al. (2005), cognitive information is processed in the lateral prefrontal cortex while emotional information processing is associated with the dorsal frontomedial cortex. Cognitive effort and working memory for short-term information storage and real-time information processing are linked to the dorsolateral prefrontal cortex (e.g., Braver et al. 1997; Linden et al. 2003; Owen et al. 2005; Rypma and

D'Esposito 1999). As information processing and decision-making is at the heart of consumer research, these concepts and brain circuits identified by cognitive neuroscience might help consumer researchers to expand their theoretical models of marketing stimuli processing and decision-making in various buying situations.

To sum up, consumer researchers can benefit from higher-order theories and concepts from cognitive neuroscience. As the above examples show, neuroscience literature has also focused on the localization of mental activity in the brain or body, usually termed neural correlates. Neuroscientists have created virtual maps of the human brain and body by indicating where activity occurs when people engage in various activities. Dimoka et al. (2010) offer an extensive summary of many human brain processes that are likely to be of interest for consumer research, especially as they are categorized under (1) decision-making, (2) cognitive, (3) emotional, and (4) social processes. It is noteworthy though that besides these specific neural correlates there are numerous other processes whose neural correlates have been examined in the vast neuroscience literature. To get an idea of the potential of what consumer researchers can learn from neuroscience and how knowledge and methods from this discipline can help derive testable hypotheses about consumer behaviour, the next section presents selected studies that have already been executed in the field of consumer neuroscience.

12.6   OVERVIEW OF FINDINGS RELATED TO MARKETING AND CONSUMER BEHAVIOUR

In order to show the close alliance between consumer neuroscience and established market research, we present specific results and implications of selected studies from this recent field of research (for an overview see Hubert and Kenning 2008). The subjective selection takes into account whether or not the study was related to marketing and/or consumer issues. Regarding content, the overview is structured according to the traditional marketing-mix instruments, product, price, communication, and distribution policy, as well as brand research. These fields represent predominant and essential elements of marketing theory, consumer behaviour and operational marketing management (Constantinides 2006; Foxall 1981; Foxall 1983; Foxall 2005; Foxall 2007; Winer 1986). In this connection, neural activation patterns evoked by stimuli of each mix instrument, as well as by stimuli of brand research are identified. Finally, we point out some limitations of consumer neuroscience regarding theory building and methodological application.

12.6.1 Product Policy and Consumer Behaviour

Product policy includes all decisions that a company makes regarding the market-driven composition of its offered services (Kotler and Armstrong 2009) and is, therefore, often labelled as "the heart of marketing". Corporate policy depends on this fundamental element, because a product range that satisfies the needs, demands, and problems of the consumer is the key to sustainable corporate success (Bailetti and Litva 1995; Cooper 1979; Ernst et al. 2011; Selnes 1993). Problems for researchers in the field of product policy arise with the application of conventional market research methods such as self-reports, which often do not yield the desired information about consumers' real opinions of a product. As subjects are not always able to reconstruct and interpret their thoughts and feelings retrospectively, self-reports are sometimes in contrast to their actual inner states (Bagozzi 1991). With this understanding, there is some reason to believe that consumer neuroscience is able to yield a more complete and objective understanding of the inner states of consumers in this area, and may, consequently, assist consumers in better reproducing their own decisions. For instance, one central aspect of product policy is the optimal design of a product according to the real preferences of consumers (Bloch 1995). In this regard, product packaging can be seen as one of the most important marketing instruments to influence the preferences of consumers at the point of sale (Silayoi and Speece 2007). Stoll et al. (2008) conducted an fMRI study to investigate how the brain processes attractive packages compared to unattractive packages. They found that attractive packages led to activity changes in regions linked to processing of visual stimuli and attention. In contrast, unattractive packages led to enhanced activity changes in prefrontal areas and the insula. These regions are generally associated with cognitive control, inhibition and negative affect (Bechara 2005; McClure et al. 2004a; Sanfey et al. 2003). Another interesting study that provided first insights into how the brain responds to differently designed goods (e.g., small cars, sports cars, and limousines) was conducted by Erk et al. (2002). The fMRI results of their investigations showed that reward-related brain areas are activated by objects that have gained a reputation as status symbols through cultural conditioning. In relation to the perceived attractiveness of the products, pictures of the cars in their study led to activation in the ventral striatum, the orbitofrontal cortex as well as in the anterior cingulate cortex. According to present knowledge, these regions are associated with motivation, the encoding of rewarding stimuli, the prediction of rewards, and decision-making (Bechara et al. 2000b; Glimcher et al. 2008; O'Doherty 2004). Erk et al. (2002) concluded that the relative activation in the ventral striatum can be seen as an indicator for how attractive a visual stimulus (i.e., product design or shape) is evaluated to be. The activity changes in the reward system of the brain induced by an attractive product design can be used in order to predict purchasing behaviour, assuming a relation between product design and purchase decision. Knutson et al. (2007) found evidence for such a relation: results from their study showed that activation of the nucleus accumbens, which is located in the ventral striatum, correlates with individual product preferences, and that activation in this area during product presentation may predict, to a high degree, subsequent purchasing decisions (Grosenick et al. 2008).

Besides the package and design of a product, the way a product is presented can also significantly influence the decision-making of the consumer (Hedgcock and Rao 2009). For example, a consistent finding in the marketing and psychological literature is the so called attraction effect. If consumers are faced with trade-off type options where they have to decide between two products that are equally attractive, but for different reasons, the introduction of a third (normatively irrelevant) alternative can influence their behaviour. For example, a consumer has to decide between two types of cookie, where the first alternative is very tasty, but also has a very high fat content, and the second alternative is not as appetizing as the first, but has a low fat content. If now a third type of cookie is introduced in the choice process, that is fairly tasty but also has a high fat content, alternative number 1 (tasty, but high fat content) will be more attractive to the consumer. Hedgcock and Rao (2009) investigated this effect with functional magnetic resonance imaging. They found that the introduction of the third alternative evoked less negative emotions than the presentation of the trade-off alternatives. Thus, the way products are presented to the consumers significantly influences the choice process of consumers.

12.6.2   Price Policy and Consumer Behaviour

As a central concept in marketing, price policy constitutes a fundamental factor of a company's sales and profits (Lichtenstein et al. 1993; Pasternack 2008; Rao 1984). A quite interesting phenomenon often observed in price policy is that a similar price level can be perceived by consumers in two different ways, relative to the product category. On the one hand, increased price levels can have a negative influence on demand and deter consumers from buying a product, because they create a perception of loss. On the other hand, high prices can be seen as an indicator of high quality, enhancing the product value and the probability that consumers will buy the goods due to the complementary rewarding function of a higher price (Lichtenstein et al. 1993; Völckner 2008; Völckner and Hofmann 2007).

For researchers, however, problems arise with asking consumers about pricing issues. For instance, consumers are often unable to recall prices (Evanschitzky et al. 2004; Ofir et al. 2008; Vanhuele and Drèze 2002), and it is also very difficult for them to specify abstract economic concepts such as willingness to pay, experienced utility, or price fairness. Against this background, Knutson et al. (2007) examined the neural correlates of the negative price effect. While lying in the fMRI scanner, subjects were first shown the image of a product, and then the same image with the price information. From this, they had to decide whether or not to buy the product. The results matched with those studies examining the neural correlates of anticipation and the receipt of gains (Breiter et al. 2001; Knutson and Peterson 2005) and losses (Samanez-Larkin et al. 2007; Sanfey et al. 2003). The activation of the nucleus accumbens (activated by the anticipation of gains) correlates with product preferences, the activation of the insula (activated by the anticipation of losses) corresponds to excessive prices, and the activation of the medial prefrontal cortex (activated by the processing of gains and losses) correlates with reduced prices. This result supports the hypothesis that activity changes in the insula might reflect the neural representation of a negative price effect. Looking forward, this information could be an important element for identification of price limits and/or thresholds. In this respect, Plassmann et al. (2008) examined the contrasting positive-skewing impact of price setting on the evaluation of a specific product. In their fMRI study, subjects consumed wine and were presented with explicit price information. Among other things, results demonstrated that the participants not only evaluated the more expensive wine as being better, but also that the neural activation – in the medial orbitofrontal cortex – indicated significant activation differences in relation to higher price information. Based on these results, Plassmann et al. (2008) carefully assumed that the experienced utility of a product is not only dependent on intrinsic aspects such as the taste of the wine or thirst, but is also impacted by adjustable factors within the frame of marketing-mix instruments, such as price setting. It is possible, therefore, to conclude that under certain circumstances the product's price is positively correlated with the product's utility. Another central concept for price policy is the willingness to pay – defined as the maximum price that a consumer is willing to pay for a certain product. In an fMRI study conducted by Plassmann et al. (2007d), hungry participants engaged in an auction task, where they bid on different snacks for the right to eat the food after the scanning session. In the free bid trial subjects were free to choose the price of their bids, thus they computed their individual willingness to pay. In the forced bid trials, participants were instructed how much to bid on the different food items. The data analysis showed that the computation of the willingness to pay particularly involves the medial orbitofrontal cortex and the dorsolateral prefrontal cortex.

12.6.3   Communications Policy and Consumer Behaviour

Besides product and price policy, communications policy is a cornerstone in the marketing-mix. For instance, in order to inform consumers, the budget of US companies spent on advertising grew about 40.9 per cent from $115878m in 1998 to $163260m in 2007 (*International Journal of Advertising* 2010; www.internationaljournalofadvertising.com). Against this background one future challenge crucial for the increasingly impor-tant marketing-mix instrument of communication is the psychological differentiation of brands (Meenaghan 1995; Milgrom and Roberts 1986) and consumer specific advertising in a global marketplace (Backhaus et al. 2001). We expect that, especially within communication policy, con-sumer neuroscience can help to overcome the existing lack of theory (Pitt et al. 2005), with only few specific attempts to study the role of theory in advertising research (Plassmann et al. 2007a). In this regard, the question of how the brain processes, learns, and stores advertising stimuli may have essential importance. Considering the short-term processing of advertise-ments, two studies by Kenning et al. (2009) and Plassmann et al. (2007c) examined the neural correlates of attractive advertisements. In order to measure brain activity, subjects lying in the fMRI scanner were asked to rate different advertisements according to their attractiveness. The primary results showed that advertisements perceived to be attractive led to higher activation in brain areas associated with the integration of emotions in the decision-making process (ventromedial prefrontal cortex) and the percep-tion of rewards (ventral striatum/ nucleus accumbens), relative to those advertisements perceived to be unattractive (see Kenning et al. 2009).

Kenning et al. (2009) concluded from these results that attractive ads resemble a rewarding stimulus. In addition, the studies revealed that highly attractive and unattractive advertisements led to increased ad recall compared to neutral ads, and that positive facial expressions are an essen-tial component of attractive advertisements. A possible explanation of the role of facial perceptions can be found in the experiment of Aharon et al. (2001), who showed that a female face that was perceived to be beautiful led to the activation of reward-related areas in the brains of heterosexual males. Future studies may provide further information about the effects of conventional advertising stimuli such as the devices of using childlike characteristics, puppies, or even rather new forms such as computer-ized humans (avatars) in advertisements. Riedl et al. (2010b) conducted another fMRI study, which investigated how marketing communication influences neural responses and trustworthiness ratings in an online setting. During the scan sessions subjects had to evaluate eBay offers with regard to their trustworthiness. The offers differed only in the description of the product. Results show that there are gender specific trust regions and that women activate more brain regions compared to men. Moreover, Riedl et al. (2010b) showed that just small variations in the product description can alter brain activation and trustworthiness ratings of products. It follows that marketing communication can have a strong influence on the perception of the consumer. Furthermore, online shop managers and marketers should differentiate their offers between men and women in order to induce higher trust levels.

12.6.4   Distribution Policy and Consumer Behaviour

Distribution policy is concerned with all decisions leading to the optimal distribution of goods between manufacturer and retailer (Yoo et al. 2000). The optimal distribution of products can have a sustainable and prominent influence on the buying decisions of consumers (Ailawadi and Keller 2004; Kotler and Keller 2005). Therefore, in order to set the optimal frame for the presentation of a brand, a central aspect of this important marketing-mix instrument is the choice of product marketing channels and appropriate marketing channels for specific brands (Choi 1991; Eliashberg and Steinberg 1987; Lee and Staelin 1997; Pasternack 2008). In two similarly constructed experiments, Deppe et al. (2005a and 2007) examined the neural correlates of this "framing effect." A primary finding of their investigations was that, in particular, the medial prefrontal cortex and the anterior cingulate cortex play a central role for the integration of implicit framing information. This implicit framing information can consist of, for example, the importance of emotions and unconscious memories in the decision-making process. Another study that provided insights for distribution policy was conducted by Hubert et al. (2009). They examined the neural correlates associated with different retail brand frames and addressed the question of whether participants' product evaluation is biased by the framing information (logos of retail brands) in comparison to an unframed decision task. Besides individual judgement biases during the choice tasks, Hubert et al. (2009) found corresponding positive cortical activation changes within regions of the medial prefrontal cortex, an area associated with emotions, memories and decision-making. In a similar vein, Plassmann et al. (2007b) identified the neural correlates of retail brand loyalty. In their fMRI study, subjects had to choose between retail brands for the purchase of an identical garment, selecting the brand which they would prefer. With the results of that fMRI session and previously collected information about subjects' buying behaviour, the researchers were able to identify the favourite retail brand of the participants. Next, subjects were divided into two groups, according to their average buying behaviour. The group of "A" customers spent a minimum of 250€ on five or more shopping days per month at a certain retailer, and constituted the group of so-called "loyal customers". The group of "C" customers spent a maximum of 50€ and had only one shopping day per month at the same retailer, resulting in the group label "disloyal customers". Data analysis showed that loyal customers integrate emotions into the decision-making process in a more intense way, through the activation in the ventromedial prefrontal cortex, and that the favourite retail brand can act as a relevant rewarding stimulus on a behavioural level. In contrast, a comparable activation in these regions was not measurable for disloyal participants. Plassmann et al. (2007b) developed an interesting conclusion from their results: the use of emotional reinforcers in marketing and within the distribution policy can constitute the base for sustainable, long-term customer retention. In this way, a learning process can be triggered, in which a customer's positive experiences are combined with the retail brand, then stored in the memory and recalled for future buying decisions (Kenning and Plassmann 2009).

12.6.5   Brand Research and Consumer Behaviour

Brand research examines the influence of brand information on decision-making (Ailawadi and Keller 2004). One central topic of brand research is whether or not consumer decisions are influenced by brand information. Deppe et al. (2005b) addressed this question in a study designed to determine which neural processes in the brain are involved during the processing of brand information. In their fMRI experiment, subjects had to make fictitious buying decisions, choosing between two very similar products that were differentiated only by brand information. The data analysis showed a significant difference in subjects' brain activity when a brand used in the fMRI experiment had been designated as their preferred brand. This group was labelled as the first choice brand (FCB) group. A closer look into the brain activities of the FCB group showed reduced activity in the dorsolateral prefrontal cortex, left premotor area, posterior parietal and occipital cortices – areas that are associated with working memory, planning, and logic decisions. Deppe et al. (2005b) assumed that for decisions comprising the favourite brand of the consumer, strategic processes are no longer as relevant as they are in comparison to diverse brands, so that the responsible brain region is deactivated and a "cortical release" occurs (Kenning et al. 2002). In contrast, Deppe et al. (2005b) measured increased activity in the ventromedial prefrontal cortex, the inferior precuneus, and the posterior cingulate cortex. These areas operate as association cortices and have important functions in combining incoming information with background knowledge, in the recall of episodic memories, and in self-reflection. The increased activation in the ventromedial prefrontal cortex during decisions for the FCB group could be interpreted as integration of emotions into the decision-making process (Bechara and Damasio 2005). Thus, the results revealed a so-called "winner-takes-all" effect: only the favourite brand of the subject is able to emotionalize the decision-making process. This finding is crucial for marketing research because it contradicts the well-established consideration-set concept. The consideration-set concept assumes that there is a set of goal-satisfying alternatives (Shocker et al. 1991), yet the results of Deppe et al. (2005b) provide evidence that only the favourite brand is able to trigger significant cortical activation patterns. These findings are in line with the neural activation patterns determined by McClure et al. (2004b), providing evidence that consumer product brands employed as emotionalized stimuli can specifically modulate cortical activation in the ventromedial prefrontal cortex and, thus, can influence buying behaviour. Accordingly, and analogous to the "Coca-Cola" test, McClure et al. (2004b) described a consistent neural response in the ventromedial prefrontal cortex correlating with the subjects' behavioural preferences for different beverages (Coca-Cola® and Pepsi®). Intriguingly, a lesion study conducted by Koenigs and Tranel (2008) confirmed the suggestions of Deppe et al. (2005b) and McClure et al. (2004b). Congruent to their results, persons with damage within the ventromedial prefrontal cortex who exhibited irregularities in emotional processing did not show the normal preference biases when exposed to brand information. One potential reason for this might be that emotions could provide additional conscious or unconscious information to consumers' decision-making. Another concept in the framework of brand research that is often applied in advertising is "brand personality" (Aaker 1997). For example, companies often assign humanlike traits to brands in order to differentiate against their competitors (e.g., Henkel "a brand like a friend"). In an fMRI study, Yoon et al. (2006) investigated whether the brain processes these semantic judgements about persons and brands in the same way. Their results provide evidence that the concept of brand personality needs to be revised. Whereas the characterization of persons leads to higher activity changes in the medial prefrontal cortex, the attributes of products activated different, object-related brain areas. Yoon et al. (2006) concluded that human-like attributes can not always be transferred to brands. Future studies might show whether consumers can use these insights to better understand and finally improve their buying decisions.

12.6.6   Limitations

As with any new approach, consumer neuroscience faces the challenge posed by limitations. For example, studies are very cost- and time-intensive (for an overview see Ariely and Berns 2010 or Riedl et al. 2010b). In addition, the outcomes of experiments carried out to date need to be further validated and expanded (Vul et al. 2009) because of the complex data analysis required, the relatively small number of existing studies, and the relatively simple setting necessary for conducting brain imaging studies, which leads to a oversimplifying study design in the majority of cases (Plassmann et al. 2007a). Technical methods are steadily improving (see section 12.4), but they still offer only a relatively indirect measurement of cortical activity changes, due to limitations in temporal and spatial resolution. Beyond this, all results provided by consumer neuroscience rely on three assumptions: that the measured activation is not the result only of noise or systematic errors, that a correct spatial and temporal assignment of measured quantities is possible, and that the supposition about typical functions of certain brain areas is valid in the actual case as well. Furthermore, it is presumed that the stimulus under investigation, and no confounder, leads to the cortical response of participating subjects (Kenning and Plassmann 2005; Huettel et al. 2009b).

Another limitation could be the generalizability of the studies, which is often called into question. High costs cause the use of a limited number of participating subjects, and a small sample size increases the possibility of false positives and presents a higher probability of committing a Type II error, that is, the error of failing to reject a null hypothesis when it is in fact not true (Tversky and Kahneman 1971). However, an argument supporting the validity of the results could be that several researchers investigating relevant marketing questions – in different national or cultural settings, applying various experimental approaches, and with the help of brain research methods – have arrived at very similar results concerning the specific brain activation (Ambler et al. 2000; Dimoka et al. 2011; McClure et al. 2004; Koenigs and Tranel 2008; Plassmann et al. 2007a; see Hubert and Kenning 2008 for an overview from an economic perspective). On the other hand, the robustness of neuroeconomic and consumer neuroscience findings may also constitute a counterargument for the validity. For example, there are both semantic and phenomenological variations between different brands, but the brain seems to process them in a very similar way, as can be deduced by observing the specific activation pattern with fMRI. Thus, it could be possible that the research method is still too inaccurate to measure weak activations in the brain (Savoy 2005).

12.7　CONCLUSION AND OUTLOOK

The selected overview of research in consumer neuroscience shows that a wide spectrum of traditional marketing-mix components and brand research has already been investigated in this new area (Hubert 2010; Hubert and Kenning 2008; Perrachione and Perrachione 2008). The application of neuroscience methods to marketing and consumption-relevant problems has yielded a number of theoretical contributions. First, neuroscience tools potentially lead to "objective" results, so that researchers can hope to gain specific new insights into unconscious and automatic processes that influence human behaviour. Second, neuroeconomics and consumer neuroscience emerged from the consolidation of economics, neuroscience, and psychology. This transdisciplinary approach may assist all aforementioned disciplines in gaining innovative perspectives and in generating new ideas. In particular, it offers the opportunity for consumer neuroscience to confirm, reconfigure, or improve conventional theories of marketing theory (Fugate 2007, 2008). Therefore, one important contribution of consumer neuroscience is awareness of the influence of emotions and biology on decision-making. At this point, the research has shown that, with emotions and unconscious processes playing a central role in generating behaviour, consumers cannot be considered as completely rational in decision-making (Bechara and Damasio 2005; Camerer et al. 2005). Another example of a contributing aspect is the strict distinction of marketing-mix instruments that is challenged by some of the studies presented. The exploration of the "framing effect" (Deppe et al. 2007; Deppe et al. 2005a) yields important insights not only for distribution policy, but also for communication policy. As the consumer perceives the classical marketing-mix instruments simultaneously (Plassmann et al. 2008), there is a strong interaction between these elements. Thus, findings of consumer neuroscience support recent tendencies in marketing research to reconceptualize the classical approach of strictly separated marketing-mix instruments.

As outlined in section 12.2, consumer neuroscience evolved alongside wide-ranging developments in behavioural decision-making research and cognitive neuroscience. The incremental hope is to better understand various elements of consumers' evaluation and purchase decision processes (Kenning and Plassmann 2008). In sum, neuroscience has received considerable attention in consumer research for at least two reasons. First, neuroscience can be viewed as a new methodological tool, a magnifying glass to get a closer look at decision-making processes without asking consumers directly for their thoughts, evaluations, or strategies. Second, neuroscience can be viewed as a source of theory generation, supplementing traditional ones from psychology and economics.

In this chapter we introduced the emergence, the basis, relevant methods, theories, concepts and preliminary findings of the field of consumer neuroscience. The future and its final acceptance will depend on the benefits it can generate in concert with other disciplines. The hype of using different neuroscientific tools will not suffice to generate added value, and it will be crucial that it is complemented by more traditional behavioural and field experiments. Such a multi-method approach could transcend the limitations of mere correlational results subject to problems of causation or inverse reference. With the proper use of a variety of methodological approaches from neuroscience, statistical modelling and social science, consumer neuroscience has the potential to continue to become an exciting, growing area of inquiry. Although an old saying goes that predictions about the future are especially difficult, we anticipate that consumer neuroscience will produce a solid and continuing interest in understanding the neural mechanisms and correlates of consumer behaviour.

REFERENCES

Aaker, J.L. (1997), 'Dimensions of brand personality', *Journal of Marketing Research*, **34** (3), 347–356.

Aharon, I., N. Etcoff, D. Ariely, C.F. Chabris, E. O'Conner and H.C. Breiter (2001), 'Beautiful faces have variable reward value: fMRI and behavioral evidence', *Neuron*, **32** (3), 537–551.

Ailawadi, K.L. and K.L. Keller (2004), 'Understanding retail branding: conceptual insights and research priorities', *Journal of Retailing*, **80** (4), 331–342.

Ambler, T., A. Ioannides and S. Rose (2000), 'Brands on the brain: neuro-images of advertising', *Business Strategy Review*, **11** (3), 17–30.

Ariely, D. and G.S. Berns (2010), 'Neuromarketing: the hope and hype of neuroimaging in business', *Nature Reviews Neuroscience*, **11** (4), 284–292.

Backhaus, K., K. Mühlfeld and J. Van Doorn (2001), 'Consumer perspectives on standardization in international advertising: a student sample', *Journal of Advertising Research*, **41** (5), 53–61.

Bagozzi, R.P. (1991), 'The role of psychophysiology in consumer research', in T.S. Robertson and H.H. Kassarjian (eds), *Handbook of Consumer Behavior*, Englewood Cliffs, NY: Prentice Hall, pp. 124–161.

Bailetti, A.J. and P.F. Litva (1995), 'Integrating customer requirements into product designs', *Journal of Product Innovation Management*, **12** (1), 3–15.

Basso, D., M. Lotze, L. Vitale, F. Ferreri, P. Bisiacchi, M.O. Belardinelli, P.M. Rossini and N. Birbaumer (2006), 'The role of prefrontal cortex in visuo-spatial planning: a repetitive TMS study', *Experimental Brain Research*, **171** (3), 411–415.

Bechara, A. (2005), 'Decision making, impulse control and loss of willpower to resist drugs: a neurocognitive perspective', *Nature Neuroscience*, **8** (11), 1458–1463.

Bechara, A. and A.R. Damasio (2005), 'The somatic marker hypothesis: a neural theory of economic decision', *Games and Economic Behavior*, **52** (2), 336–372.

Bechara, A., A.R. Damasio, H. Damasio and S.W. Anderson (1994), 'Insensitivity to future consequences following damage to human prefrontal cortex', *Cognition*, **50** (1–3), 7–15.

Bechara, A., D. Tranel and H. Damasio (2000a), 'Characterization of the decision-making deficit of patients with ventromedial prefrontal cortex lesions', *Brain*, **123** (Pt 11), 2189–2202.

Bechara, A., H. Damasio and A.R. Damasio (2000b), 'Emotion, decision making and the orbitofrontal cortex', *Cerebral Cortex*, **10** (3), 295–307.

Bettman, J.R. (1974), 'Toward a statistics for consumer decision net models', *Journal of Consumer Research*, **1** (1), 71–80.

Bettmann, J.R., M.F. Luce and J.W. Payne (1998), 'Constructive consumer choice processes', *Journal of Consumer Research*, **25** (December), 187–217.

Bhatt, M. and C.F. Camerer (2005), 'Self-referential thinking and equilibrium as states of mind in games: fMRI evidence', *Games and Economic Behavior*, **52** (2), 424–459.

Bloch, P.H. (1995), 'Seeking the ideal form: product design and consumer response', *Journal of Marketing*, **59** (3), 16–29.

Brandstätter, E., G. Gigerenzer and R. Hertwig (2006), 'The priority heuristic: making choices without trade-offs', *Psychological Review*, **113** (2), 409–432.

Braver, T.S., J.D. Cohen, L.E. Nystrom, J. Jonides, E.E. Smith and D.C. Noll (1997), 'A parametric study of prefrontal cortex involvement in human working memory', *Neuroimage*, **5** (1), 49–62.

Breiter, H.C., I. Aharon, D. Kahnemann, A. Dale and P. Shizgal (2001), 'Functional imaging of neural responses to expectancy and experience of monetary gains and losses', *Neuron*, **30** (2), 619–639.

Brodmann, K. (ed.) (1909), *Vergleichende Lokalisationslehre der Großhirnrinde in ihren Prinzipien dargestellt auf Grund des Zellenbaues*, Leipzig, Germany: Johann Ambrosius Barth.

Camerer, C.F. (2003), 'Psychology and economics. Strategizing in the brain', *Science*, **300** (5626), 1673–1675.

Camerer, C., G. Loewenstein and D. Prelec (2005), 'Neuroeconomics: how neuroscience can inform economics', *Journal of Economic Literature*, **43** (1), 9–64.

Carlson, N.R. (ed.) (2004), *Physiology of Behavior*, Boston, MA: pearson Education Inc.

Choi, S.C. (1991), 'Price competition in a channel structure with a common retailer', *Marketing Science*, **10** (4), 271.

Constantinides, E. (2006), 'The marketing mix revisited: Towards the 21st century marketing', *Journal of Marketing Management*, **22** (3/4), 407–438.

Cooper, R.G. (1979), 'The dimensions of industrial new product success and failure', *Journal of Marketing*, **43** (3), 93–103.

Damasio, A.R. (2001), 'Fundamental feelings', *Nature*, **413** (6858), 781.

Debener, S., M. Ullsperger, M. Siegel and A.K. Engel (2006), 'Single-trial EEG-fMRI reveals the dynamics of cognitive function', *Trends in Cognitive Sciences*, **10** (12), 558–563.

Deppe, M., W. Schwindt, J. Krämer, H. Kugel, H. Plassmann, P. Kenning and E.B. Ringelstein (2005a), 'Evidence for a neural correlate of a framing effect: bias-specific activity in the ventromedial prefrontal cortex during credibility judgments', *Brain Research Bulletin*, **67** (5), 413–421.

Deppe, M., W. Schwindt, H. Kugel, H. Plassmann and P. Kenning (2005b), 'Nonlinear responses within the medial prefrontal cortex reveal when specific implicit information influences economic decision making', *Journal of Neuroimaging*, **15** (2), 171–182.

Deppe, M., W. Schwindt, A. Pieper, H. Kugel, H. Plassmann, P. Kenning, K. Deppe and E.B. Ringelstein (2007), 'Anterior cingulate reflects susceptibility to framing during attractiveness evaluation', *NeuroReport*, **18** (11), 1119–1123.

Dimoka, A., P.A. Pavlou and F. Davis (2010), 'NeuroIS: the potential of cognitive neuroscience for information systems research', *Information Systems Research*.

Dimoka, A., R.D. Banker, I. Benbasat, F.D. Davis, A.R. Dennis, D. Gefen, A. Gupta, A. Ischebeck, P. Kenning, G. Müller-Putz, P.A. Pavlou, R. Riedl, J. Vom Brocke and B. Weber (2011), 'On the use of neurophysiological tools in information systems research: developing a research agenda for neuroIS', *Management Information Systems Quarterly (MISQ)*.

Eliashberg, J. and R. Steinberg (1987), 'Marketing-production decisions in an industrial channel of distribution', *Management Science*, **33** (8), 981–1000.

Engel, J.F., D.T. Kollat and R.D. Blackwell (eds) (1968), *Consumer Behavior*, New York, NY: Holt Rinehart and Winston.

Engel, J.F., R.D. Blackwell and D.T. Kollat (eds) (1978), *Consumer Behavior*, Hinsdale, IL: Dryden Press.

Engel, J.F., R.D. Blackwell and P.W. Miniard (eds) (1995), *Customer Behavior*, Fort Worth, TX: Dryden Press.

Erk, S., M. Spitzer, A.P. Wunderlich, L. Galley and H. Walter (2002), 'Cultural objects modulate reward circuitry', *NeuroReport*, **13** (18), 2499–2503.

Ernst, M. and M.P. Paulus (2005), 'Neurobiology of decision making: a selective review from a neurocognitive and clinical perspective', *Biological Psychiatry*, **58** (8), 597–604.

Ernst, H., W.D. Hoyer, M. Krafft and K. Krieger (2011), 'Customer relationship management and company performance – the mediating role of new product performance', *Journal of the Academy of Marketing Science*, **39** (2), 290–306.

Evanschitzky, H., P. Kenning and V. Vogel (2004), 'Consumer price knowledge in the German retail market', *Journal of Product & Brand Management*, **13** (6), 390–405.

Evanschitzky, H., G.R. Iyer, H. Plassmann, J. Niessing and H. Meffert (2006), 'The relative strength of affective commitment in securing loyalty in service relationships', *Journal of Business Research*, **59** (12), 1207–1213.

Farah, M.J. (2002), 'Emerging ethical issues in neuroscience', *Nature Neuroscience*, **5** (11), 1123–1129.

Farah, M.J. (2007), 'Social, legal, and ethical implications of cognitive neuroscience: "neuroethics" for short', *Journal of Cognitive Neuroscience*, **19** (3), 363–364.

Farah, M.J. and P.R. Wolpe (2004), 'Monitoring and manipulating brain function: new neuroscience technologies and their ethical implications', *Hastings Cent Rep*, **34** (3), 35–45.

Ferstl, C., M. Rinck and D.Y. von Cramon (2005), 'Emotional and temporal aspects of situation model processing during text comprehension: an event-related fMRI study', *Cognitive Neuroscience*, **17** (5), 724–739.

Fletcher, P.C., F. Happe, U. Frith, S.C. Baker, R.J. Dolan, R.S.J. Frackowiak and C.D. Frith (1995), 'Other minds in the brain: a functional imaging study of "theory of mind" in story comprehension', *Cognition*, **57** (2), 109–128.

Foxall, G.R. (1981), *Strategic Marketing Management*, London/New York: Routledge/Wiley.

Foxall, G.R. (1983), *Consumer Choice*, London: Macmillan Press.

Foxall, G.R. (2005), *Understanding Consumer Choice*, London and New York: Palgrave Macmillan.

Foxall, G.R. (2007), *Explaining Consumer Choice*, London and New York: Palgrave Macmillan.

Foxall, G.R. (2008), 'Reward, emotion and consumer choice: from neuroeconomics to neurophilosophy', *Journal of Consumer Behavior*, **7** (4–5), 368–396.

Foxall, G.R., R.E. Goldsmith and S. Brown (1998), *Consumer Psychology for Marketing*, International Thomson Business Press.

Fugate, D.L. (2007), 'Neuromarketing: a layman's look at neuroscience and its potential application to marketing practice', *Journal of Consumer Marketing*, **24** (7), 385–394.

Fugate, D.L. (2008), 'Marketing services more effectively with neuromarketing research: a look into the future', *Journal of Services Marketing*, **22** (2), 170–173.

Gallagher, H.L. and C.D. Frith (2003), 'Functional imaging of "theory of mind"', *Trends in Cognitive Sciences*, **7** (2), 77–83.

Gigerenzer, G. (1991), 'From tools to theories: a heuristic of discovery in cognitive psychology', *Psychological Review*, **98** (2), 254–267.

Glimcher, P.W. and A. Rustichini (2004), 'Neuroeconomics: the consilience of brain and decision', *Science*, **306** (5695), 447–452.

Glimcher, P.W., C.F. Camerer, E. Fehr and R.A. Poldrack (eds) (2008), *Neuroeconomics: Decision Making and the Brain*, London/New York: Elsevier Academic Press.

Goldstein, D.G. and G. Gigerenzer (2002), 'Models of ecological rationality: the recognition heuristic', *Psychological Review*, **109** (1), 75–90.

Grezes, J. and J. Decety (2001), 'Functional anatomy of execution, mental simulation, observation, and verb generation of actions: a meta-analysis', *Human Brain Mapping*, **12** (1), 1–19.

Groeppel-Klein, A. (2005), 'Arousal and consumer in-store behavior', *Brain Research Bulletin*, **67** (5), 428–437.

Grosenick, L., S. Greer and B. Knutson (2008), 'Interpretable classifiers for FMRI improve prediction of purchases', *IEEE Trans Neural Syst Rehabil Eng*, **16** (6), 539–548.

Hansen, F. (1976), 'Psychological theories of consumer choice', *Journal of Consumer Research*, **3** (3), 117–142.

Hansen, F. (1981), 'Hemispheral lateralization: implications for understanding consumer behavior', *Journal of Consumer Research*, **8** (1), 23–36.

Hansen, F. (2005), 'Distinguishing between feelings and emotions in understanding communication effects', *Journal of Business Research*, **58** (10), 1426–1436.

Hansen, F. (2007), *Emotions, Advertising and Consumer Choice*, Copenhagen: Copenhagen Business School Press.

Hansen, F., S. Christensen, S. Lundsteen and L. Perry (2007), 'Emotional responses: a new paradigm in communication research', *Advances in International Marketing*, **18**, 93–114.

Heckman, K.E. and M.D. Happel (2006), 'Mechanical detection of deception: a short review', in *Educing Information – Interrogation: Science and Art. P.R. Foundations for the Future*, Intelligence Science Board, National Defense Intelligence College (NDIC) (ed.), Washington, DC: NDIC Press, pp. 63–93.

Hedgcock, W. and A.R. Rao (2009), 'Trade-off aversion as an explanation for the attraction effect: a functional magnetic resonance imaging study', *Journal of Marketing Research*, **46** (1), 1–13.

Howard, J.A. and J.N. Sheth (eds) (1969), *The Theory of Buyer Behavior*, New York, US: John Wiley & Sons.

Hsu, M., M. Bhatt, R. Adolphs, D. Tranel and C.F. Camerer (2005), 'Neural systems responding to degrees of uncertainty in human decision-making', *Science*, **310** (5754), 1680–1683.

Hubert, M. (2010), 'Does neuroeconomics give new impetus to economic and consumer research', *Journal of Economic Psychology*, **31** (5), 812–817.

Hubert, M. and P. Kenning (2008), 'A current overview of consumer neuroscience', *Journal of Consumer Behavior*, **7** (4), 272–292.

Hubert, M., M. Hubert, J. Sommer and P. Kenning (2009), 'Consumer neuroscience: the effect of retail brands on the perception of product packaging', *Marketing Review St. Gallen*, **26** (4), 28–33.

Huesing, B., L. Jäncke and B. Tag (eds) (2006), *Impact Assessment of Neuroimaging*, Zuerich, CH: vdf Hochschulverlag.

Huettel, S.A., A.W. Song and G. McCarthy (2005), 'Decisions under uncertainty: probabilistic context influences activation of prefrontal and parietal cortices', *Journal of Neuroscience*, **25** (13), 3304–3311.

Huettel, S.A., A.W. Song and G. McCarthy (eds) (2009a), *Functional Magnetic Resonance Imaging*, Sunderland, MA: Sinauer Associates, Inc.

Huettel, S.A., J.W. Payne, C. Yoon, R. Gonzalez, J.R. Bettman, W. Hedgecock and A.R. Rao (2009b), 'Commentaries and rejoinder to "Trade-off aversion as an explanation for the attraction effect: a functional magnetic resonance imaging study"', *Journal of Marketing Research*, **46**, 14–24.

Iacoboni, M. and M. Dapretto (2006), 'The mirror neuron system and the consequences of its dysfunction', *Nature Reviews Neuroscience*, **7** (12), 942–951.

Iacoboni, M., R.P. Woods, M. Brass, H. Bekkering, J.C. Mazziotta and G. Rizzolatti (1999), 'Cortical mechanisms of human imitation', *Science*, **286** (5449), 2526–2528.

Jacoby, J. (2002), 'Stimulus-organism-response reconsidered: an evolutionary step in modeling (consumer) behavior', *Journal of Consumer Psychology*, **12** (1), 51–57.

Jones, L.S. (2007), 'The ethics of transcranial magnetic stimulation', *Science*, **315** (5819), 1663–1664.

Kandel, E.R., J.H. Schwartz and T.M. Jessell (eds) (1995), *Essentials of Neural Science and Behavior*, Stanford: Appleton & Lange.

Kassarjian, H. and T.S. Robertson (eds) (1968), *Perspectives in Consumer Behavior*, Glenview: Scott, Foresman and Company.

Kenning, P. and H. Plassmann (2005), 'NeuroEconomics: an overview from an economic perspective', *Brain Research Bulletin*, **67** (5), 343–354.

Kenning, P. and H. Plassmann (2008), 'How neuroscience can inform consumer research', *IEEE Trans Neural Syst Rehabil Eng*, **16** (6), 532–538.

Kenning, P. and H. Plassmann (2009), 'How recent neuroscientific research could enhance marketing theory', *IEEE Transactions*, **16**, 532–538.

Kenning, P., H. Plassmann, M. Deppe, H. Kugel and W. Schwindt (2002), 'The discovery of cortical relief', *Field of Research: Neuromarketing*, **1**, 1–26.

Kenning, P., H. Plassmann and D. Ahlert (2007), 'Applications of functional magnetic resonance imaging for market research', *Qualitative Market Research: An International Journal*, **10** (2), 135–152.

Kenning, P., M. Deppe, W. Schwindt, H. Kugel and H. Plassmann (2009), 'The good, the bad and the forgotten – an fMRI study on ad liking and ad memory', *Advances in Consumer Research*, **36**, p. 4.

Knutson, B. and R. Peterson (2005), 'Neurally reconstructing expected utility', *Games and Economic Behavior*, **52** (2), 305–315.

Knutson, B., S. Rick, G.E. Wimmer, D. Prelec and G. Loewenstein (2007), 'Neural predictors of purchases', *Neuron*, **53** (1), 147–156.

Koenigs, M. and D. Tranel (2008), 'Prefrontal cortex damage abolishes brand-cued changes in cola preference', *Social Cognitive and Affective Neuroscience*, **3** (1), 1–6.

Kotler, P. (ed.) (1976), *Marketing Management. Analysis, Planning and Control*, New Jersey: US: Prentice Hall.

Kotler, P. and G. Armstrong (eds) (2009), *Principles of Marketing*, New Jersey: Prentice Hall.

Kotler, P. and K.L. Keller (eds) (2005), *Marketing Management*, New Jersey: Prentice Hall International.

Krain, A.L., A.M. Wilson, R. Arbuckle, F.X. Castellanos and M.P. Milham (2006), 'Distinct neural mechanisms of risk and ambiguity: a meta-analysis of decision-making', *Neuroimage*, **32** (1), 477–484.

Kroeber-Riel, W. (1979), 'Activation research: psychobiological approaches in consumer research', *Journal of Consumer Research*, **5** (4), 240–250.

Krugman, H.E. (1971), 'Brain waves measures of media involvement', *Journal of Advertising Research*, **20**, 65–68.

LeDoux, J.E. (1995), 'Emotion: clues from the brain', *Annual Review of Psychology*, **46**, 209–235.

Lee, E. and R. Staelin (1997), 'Vertical strategic interaction: implications for channel pricing strategy', *Marketing Science*, **16** (3), 185.

Lee, N., A.J. Broderick and L. Chamberlain (2007), 'What is "neuromarketing"? A discussion and agenda for future research', *International Journal of Psychophysiology*, **63** (2), 199–204.

Lewis, D. and D. Bridger (2005), 'Market researchers make increasing use of brain imaging', *Special Feature ACNR*, **5** (3), 36–37.

Lichtenstein, D.R., N.M. Ridgway and R.G. Netemeyer (1993), 'Price perceptions and consumer shopping behavior: a field study', *Journal of Marketing Research*, **30** (2), 234–245.

Linden, D.E.J., R.A. Bittner, L. Muckli, J.A. Waltz, N. Kriegeskorte, R. Goebel, W. Singer and M.H.J. Munk (2003), 'Cortical capacity constraints for visual working memory: dissociation of fMRI load effects in a fronto-parietal network', *Neuroimage*, **20** (3), 1518–1530.

Logothetis, N.K. (2008), 'What we can do and what we cannot do with fMRI', *Nature*, **453** (7197), 869–878.

McCabe, K., D. Houser, L. Ryan, V. Smith and T. Trouard (2001), 'A functional imaging study of cooperation in two-person reciprocal exchange', *Proc Natl Acad Sci USA*, **98** (20), 11832–11835.

McCarthy, E.J. (ed.) (1960), *Basic Marketing*, Homewood: Irwin.

McClure, S.M., M.K. York and P.R. Montague (2004a), 'The neural substrates of reward processing in humans: the modern role of fMRI', *Neuroscientist*, **10** (3), 260–268.

McClure, S.M., J. Li, D. Tomlin, K.S. Cypert, L.M. Montague and P.R. Montague (2004b), 'Neural correlates of behavioral preference for culturally familiar drinks', *Neuron*, **44** (2), 379–387.

Meenaghan, T. (1995), 'The role of advertising in brand image development', *Journal of Product & Brand Management*, **4** (4), 23.

Milgrom, P. and J. Roberts (1986), 'Price and advertising signals of product quality', *Journal of Political Economy*, **94** (4), 796–821.

Mitchell, J.P., M.R. Banaji and C.N. Macrae (2005), 'The link between social cognition and self-referential thought in the medial prefrontal cortex', *Journal of Cognitive Neuroscience*, **17** (8), 1306–1315.

Murphy, E.R., J. Illes and P.B. Reiner (2008), 'Neuroethics of neuromarketing', *Journal of Consumer Behaviour*, **7** (4–5), 293–302.

Newland, M.C., H.S. Pennypacker, W.K. Anger and P. Mele (2003), 'Transferring behavioral technology across applications', *Neurotoxicology and Teratology*, **25** (5), 529–542.

Nicosia, F.M. (ed.) (1966), *Consumer Decision Processes: Marketing and Advertising Implications*, Englewoods Cliffs, NJ: Prentice-Hall.

O'Doherty, J.P. (2004), 'Reward representations and reward-related learning in the human brain: insights from neuroimaging', *Current Opinion in Neurobiology*, **14** (6), 769–776.

Ofir, C., P. Raghubir, G. Brosh, K.B. Monroe and A. Heiman (2008), 'Memory-based store price judgments: the role of knowledge and shopping experience', *Journal of Retailing*, **84** (4), 414–423.

Owen, A.M., K.M. McMillan, A.R. Laird and E. Bullmore (2005), 'N-back working memory paradigm: a meta-analysis of normative functional neuroimaging studies', *Human Brain Mapping*, **25** (1), 46–59.

Pasternack, B.A. (2008), 'Optimal pricing and return policies for perishable commodities', *Marketing Science*, **27** (1), 133–140.

Perrachione, T.K. and J.R. Perrachione (2008), 'Brains and brands: developing mutually informative research in neuroscience and marketing', *Journal of Consumer Behaviour*, **7** (4–5), 303–318.

Pitt, Leyland F., P. Berthon, A. Caruana and J.–P. Berthon (2005), 'The state of theory in three premier advertising journals: a research note', *International Journal of Advertising*, **24** (2), 241–249.

Plassmann, H. (2008), 'Deal or no deal? The neural basis of decision utility and loss aversion during consumer decision-making', *Advances in Consumer Research*, **35**, 129–132.

Plassmann, H. (2010), 'Neuromarketing: hope or hype', International Marketing Program, INSEAD Executive Education (unpublished data from presentation).

Plassmann, H., T. Ambler, S. Braeutigam and P. Kenning (2007a), 'What can advertisers learn from neuroscience?', *International Journal of Advertising*, **26** (2), 151–175.

Plassmann, H., P. Kenning and D. Ahlert (2007b), 'Why companies should make their customers happy: the neural correlates of customer loyalty', *Advances in Consumer Research*, **34**, 1–5.

Plassmann, H., P. Kenning, A. Pieper, W. Schwindt, H. Kugel and M. Deppe (2007c), 'Neural correlates of ad liking', *Proceedings of the Society for Consumer Psychology Conference*, Las Vegas, 155.

Plassmann, H., J. O'Doherty and A. Rangel (2007d), 'Orbitofrontal cortex encodes willingness to pay in everyday economic transactions', *Journal of Neuroscience*, **27** (37), 9984–9988.

Plassmann, H., J. O'Doherty, B. Shiv and A. Rangel (2008), 'Marketing actions can modulate neural representations of experienced pleasantness', *Proceedings of the National Academy of Sciences*, **105** (3), 1050–1054.

Plomin, R., J.C. DeFries and G.E. MacClearn (eds) (1990), *Behavioral Genetics – A Primer*, New York, US: Freeman and Company.

Purves, D., G.J. Augustine, D. Fitzpatrick, L.C. Katz, A.-S. La Mantia and J.O. McNamara (eds) (2001), *Neuroscience*, Sunderland, MA: Sinauer Associates, Inc.

Rao, V.R. (1984), 'Pricing research in marketing: the state of the art', *Journal of Business*, **57** (1), 39–60.

Reimann, M., O. Schilke, B. Weber, C. Neuhaus and J. Zaichkowsky (2011), 'Functional magnetic resonance imaging in consumer research: a review and application', *Psychology and Marketing*, **28** (6), 608–637.

Riedl, R., R.D. Banker, I. Benbasat, F.D. Davis, A.R. Dennis, A. Dimoka, D. Gefen, A. Gupta, A. Ischebeck, P. Kenning, G. Müller-Putz, P. Pavlou, D.W. Straub, J. vom Brocke and B. Weber (2010a), 'On the foundations of neuroIS: reflections on the Gmunden Retreat 2009', *Communications of the Association for Information Systems (CAIS)*, **27** (15), 243–264.

Riedl, R., M. Hubert and P. Kenning (2010b), 'Are there neural gender differences in online trust? an fMRI study on the perceived trustworthiness of eBay offers', *MIS Quarterly*, **34** (2), 397–428.

Rizzolatti, G., L. Fadiga, V. Gallese and L. Fogassi (1996), 'Premotor cortex and the recognition of motor actions', *Cognitive Brain Research*, **3** (2), 131–41.

Rolls, E.T. (1999), *The Brain and Emotion*, Oxford: Oxford University Press.

Ruff, C.C., S. Bestmann, F. Blankenburg, O. Bjoertomt, O. Josephs, N. Weiskopf, R. Deichmann and J. Driver (2008), 'Distinct causal influences of parietal versus frontal areas on human visual cortex: evidence from concurrent TMS–fMRI', *Cerebral Cortex*, **18** (4), 817–827.

Rypma, B. and M. D'Esposito (1999), 'The roles of prefrontal brain regions in components of working memory: effects of memory load and individual differences', *Proceedings of the National Academy of Sciences USA*, **96** (11), 6558–6563.

Saad, G. (2008), 'The collective amnesia of marketing scholars regarding consumers' biological and evolutionary roots', *Marketing Theory*, **8** (4), 425–448.

Samanez-Larkin, G.R., S.E.B. Gibbs, K. Khanna, L. Nielsen, L.L. Carstensen and B. Knutson (2007), 'Anticipation of monetary gain but not loss in healthy older adults', *Nature Neuroscience*, **10** (6), 787–791.

Sanfey, A.G., J.K. Rilling, J.A. Aronson, L.E. Nystrom and J.D. Cohen (2003), 'The neural basis of economic decision-making in the ultimatum game', *Science*, **300** (5626), 1755–1758.

Sanfey, A.G., G. Loewenstein, S.M. McClure and J.D. Cohen (2006), 'Neuroeconomics: cross-currents in research on decision-making', *Trends in Cognitive Sciences*, **10** (3), 108–116.

Savoy, R. (2005), 'Experimental design in brain activation MRI: cautionary tales', *Brain Research Bulletin*, **67** (5), 361–367.

Saxe, R. (2005), 'Against simulation: the argument from error', *Trends in Cognitive Sciences*, **9** (4), 174–179.

Selnes, F. (1993), 'An examination of the effect of product performance on brand reputation, satisfaction and loyalty', *European Journal of Marketing*, **27** (9), 19–35.

Shamoo, A.E. (2010), 'Ethical and regulatory challenges in psychophysiology and neuroscience-based technology for determining behavior', *Accountability in Research: Policies & Quality Assurance*, **17** (1), 8–29.

Shamoo, A.E. and D.B. Resnik (eds) (2009), *Responsible Conduct of Research*, New York, US: Oxford University Press.

Shamoo, A.E. and J. Schwartz (2008), 'Universal and uniform protections of human subjects in research', *American Journal of Bioethics*, **8** (11), 3–5.

Sharot, T., M.R. Delgado and E.A. Phelps (2004), 'How emotion enhances the feeling of remembering', *Nature Neuroscience*, **7** (12), 1376–1380.

Shiv, B., A. Bechara, I. Levin, J.W. Alba, J.R. Bettman, L. Dube, A. Isen, B. Mellers, A. Smidts, S.J. Grant and A.P. McGraw (2005), 'Decision neuroscience', *Marketing Letters*, **16** (3), 375–386.

Shocker, A.D., M. Ben-Akiva, B. Boccara and P. Nedungadi (1991), 'Consideration set influences on consumer decision-making and choice: issues, models, and suggestions', *Marketing Letters*, **2** (3), 181–197.

Silayoi, P. and M. Speece (2007), 'The importance of packaging attributes: a conjoint analysis approach', *European Journal of Marketing*, **41** (11/12), 1495–1517.

Singer, T. (2009), 'Understanding others: brain mechanisms of theory of mind and empathy', in P.W. Glimcher, C.F. Camerer, E. Fehr and R.A. Poldrack (eds), *Neuroeconomics: Decision Making and the Brain*, London/New York: Elsevier Academic Press, pp. 251–268.

Singer, T. and C. Lamm (2009), 'The social neuroscience of empathy', *Annals of the New York Academy of Sciences*, **1156**, 81–96.

Stoll, M., S. Baecke and P. Kenning (2008), 'What they see is what they get? An fMRI-study on neural correlates of attractive packaging', *Journal of Consumer Behaviour*, **7** (4/5), 342–359.

Talairach, J. and P. Tournoux (eds) (1888), *Co-Planar Stereotaxic Atlas of the Human Brain*, New York, US: Thieme Medical Publishers, Inc.

Tortora, G.J. and Bryan H. Derrickson (2006), *Introduction to the Human Body: The Essentials of Anatomy and Physiology*, Wiley.

Tversky, A. and D. Kahnemann (1971), 'Belief in the law of small numbers', *Psychological Bulletin*, **76**, 105–110.

Vanhuele, M. and X. Drèze (2002), 'Measuring the price knowledge shoppers bring to the store', *Journal of Marketing*, **66** (4), 72–85.

Völckner, F. (2008), 'The dual role of price: decomposing consumers' reactions to price', *Journal of the Academy of Marketing Science*, **36** (3), 359–377.

Völckner, F. and J. Hofmann (2007), 'The price-perceived quality relationship: a meta-analytic review and assessment of its determinants', *Marketing Letters*, **18** (3), 181–196.

Vul, E., C. Harris, P. Winkielman and H. Pashler (2009), 'Puzzling high correlations in fMRI studies of emotion, personality, and social cognition', *Perspectives on Psychological Science*, **4** (3), 274–290.

Wilkie, W.L. and E.S. Moore (2003), 'Scholarly research in marketing: exploring the "4 Eras" of thought development', *Journal of Public Policy & Marketing*, **22** (2), 116–146.

Wilson, R.M., J. Gaines and R.P. Hill (2008), 'Neuromarketing and consumer free will', *Journal of Consumer Affairs*, **42** (3), 389–410.

Winer, R.S. (1986), 'A reference price model of brand choice for frequently purchased products', *Journal of Consumer Research*, **13** (2), 250–256.

Woodworth, R.S. (ed.) (1921), *Psychology: A Study of Mental Life*, Henry Holt and Company.

Yoo, B., N. Donthu and S. Lee (2000), 'An examination of selected marketing mix elements and brand equity', *Journal of the Academy of Marketing Science*, **28** (2), 195–211.

Yoon, C., A.H. Gutchess, F. Feinberg and T.A. Polk (2006), 'A functional magnetic resonance imaging study of neural dissociations between brand and person judgments', *Journal of Consumer Research*, **33** (1), 31–40.

Zak, P.J. (2004), 'Neuroeconomics', *Philosophical Transactions: Biological Sciences*, **359** (1451), 1737–1748.

13 The role of neurophysiology, emotion and contingency in the explanation of consumer choice[1]

Gordon R. Foxall, Mirella Yani-de-Soriano, Shumaila Y. Yousafzai and Uzma Javed

13.1 INTRODUCTION

The Behavioral Perspective Model (BPM) of purchase and consumption (Foxall, 1990) aims to improve understanding of behaviourism, intentionality and cognition in the explanation of consumer choice. The initial phase of the BPM research programme has been to examine an extensional explanation of choice (based on radical behaviourism). This perspective has been adopted in order, first, to establish the boundaries of so parsimonious an approach to explanation and, secondly, to identify the scope for intentional and cognitive explanations of consumer choice. Empirical work demonstrates the value of the extensional construal in explaining the nature of consumer brand and product choices and the interpretation of consumer behaviour in relation to the situations in which it occurs. A limitation of this approach arises from the attempt to account in purely extensional terms for the continuity of consumer behaviour over situations. This makes the use of intentional language an inevitable part of the explanation of consumer behaviour but there remains the problem of employing intentionality in a logical and scientifically consistent manner rather than opportunistically. This chapter is concerned with the role of one aspect of intentionality, emotion, in the explanation of consumer choice in order to comprehend behavioural continuity. It draws upon the philosophy of psychology known as intentional behaviourism (Foxall, 2004) in order to ascribe intentionality in accordance with scientific canons of procedure that are consistent with evolutionary reasoning. This methodology extends Dennett's (1969) emphasis on the role of evolutionarily consistent neuronal activity in the adoption of intentional explanations of behaviour by using the BPM to relate emotionality to the contingencies of reinforcement that are responsible for the shaping and maintenance of consumer choice.

13.2   THE BEHAVIOURAL PERSPECTIVE MODEL

All too often consumer behaviour texts portray emotions as causes of behaviour which can be manipulated for managerial purposes rather than as elements of experience that participate in the social-scientific explanation of choice. There is a particular gap in our knowledge of the way in which emotions are related to publicly available influences on behaviour, the 'contingencies of reward (or reinforcement) and punishment', that are the most apparent determinants of choice in the contemporary marketplace. This chapter relates emotion to the environmental contingencies of which consumer choice is demonstrably a function and suggests how both the contingencies and the emotions related to them contribute to the explanation of consumer behaviour.

Foxall (1997a) presented a critique of the social cognitive approach to the attitude-intention-behaviour sequence that remains a prevalent feature of models of consumer behaviour in the marketing literature. Finding a lack of empirical support for such a relationship, except where measures of emotion, cognition and response reflected high levels of situational correspondence, the chapter argued in favour of an alternative, behaviour-analytical model of purchase and consumption, the Behavioural Perspective Model (BPM). The BPM was proposed as a means of systematizing the likely effects of those situational influences, conceptualized in terms of contingencies of reinforcement and punishment. This obviated the need to demonstrate attitude-intention-behaviour consistency on the understanding that all three were the result of underlying cognitive events; instead it enabled the verbal behaviours involved in the expression of attitudes and intentions and the overt behaviours involved in purchase and consumption to be differentially explained in terms of the contingencies of reinforcement and punishment to which each was uniquely subject. The overall aims of the model and the research programme in which it features has been to ascertain the feasibility of constructing a radical behaviourist model of consumer choice and, if this proves possible, to examine the epistemological status of such a model in order to build and test more complex theories of consumer behaviour.

The underlying philosophical basis of the model has evolved (e.g. Foxall, 2004, 2007b) and empirical work has been generated which supports its underlying approach to the explanation of such aspects of consumer choice as produce and brand selection (Foxall et al., 2007). One strand of empirical research indicates how reported emotional responses to consumer situations are related to specific patterns of environmental contingency (Foxall and Greenley, 1998, 1999, 2000; Foxall and Yani-de-Soriano, 2005) and the results of this work are applied in this chapter to illustrate and extend the theoretical developments that have taken place over the last dozen or so years. Recent developments in the theoretical portrayal of emotion and contingency, and its relationship to brain processes involved in the evaluation of alternative courses of action, have increased the relevance of neuroscience to consumer choice; this emphasis is reflected in both the progression of the BPM approach generally (Foxall, 2008a) and the discussion in this chapter of the explanation of consumer behaviour.

The chapter first reviews the BPM as a means of predicting such aspects of consumer behaviour as brand and product choice and examines the (extensional) nature of its explanation, going on to argue that, although this is sufficient for the prediction and control of its subject matter, it is not able to account for some aspects of behaviour such as its continuity. That emotion provides a means by which this gap can be filled permits an interpretation of consumer behaviour derived from the extensional behavioural- and neuro-sciences. 'Emotion', understood as consisting in subjective experience and as intentional, can then be employed in the explanation of consumer behaviour in the rigorous terms proposed by 'intentional behaviourism' (Foxall, 2007b). Intentional behaviourism involves the responsible ascription of emotions on the basis of molar patterns of operant behaviour and related afferent–efferent linkages at the neuronal level. The BPM contingency matrix offers an alternative, empirically based, means of categorizing patterns of contingency in relation to emotional responses to consumer environments to that, say, of Rolls (1999). Mehrabian and Russell's (1974) depiction of emotionality in terms of pleasure, arousal and dominance is evaluated as a framework for the empirical investigation of contingency and emotion. The chapter continues with a discussion of the extent to which the intentionally construed model accounts for behavioural continuity and the personal level, whilst indicating how a behavioural interpretation can be bounded. It concludes by considering briefly the emerging theoretical synthesis among these variables and cognition.

13.2.1   The Generic Model

Consumer behaviour is influenced by both the economic and technical properties of goods on the one hand and the social meaning of acquiring, owning and using them on the other. People drive cars in order to get around and in order to be seen getting around, wear clothes for protection from the elements and to signal to everyone how well they are doing at work, adorn themselves with jewellery not only to impress their fellows or fit in with their expectations but to raise or confirm their own self-esteem.

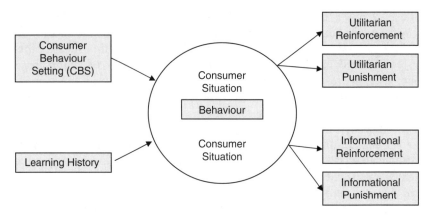

Figure 13.1   Generic Behavioural Perspective Model (BPM)

To the extent that consumption is influenced by these consequences, it is operant; to the extent that it reflects both the functional and the symbolic, it is under the influence of a complex of utilitarian and informational reinforcers. Businesses meet these consumer wants by offering marketing mixes that stress product attributes of both kinds, advertising and distribution channels that complement and enhance them, and price levels that are consonant with both the technical-economic purposes and the social-psychological meanings that the resulting brands address. Both sources of reinforcement must be included in a behaviour-analytic model of consumer choice. So must the punishing consequences associated with each, for every economic transaction meets with aversive outcomes as well as those that reward. These consequential causes of behaviour are depicted on the right-hand side of the BPM (Figure 13.1).

Shown on the left are the stimuli that set the occasion for these causal consequences should particular acts of purchase and consumption be enacted. The consumer behaviour setting (CBS) is composed of stimuli that signal the outcomes of behaviour – the availability of particular brands, for instance, within a supermarket – and stimuli that motivate the behaviour – say a point-of-sale advertisement that emphasizes the unique taste or value-for-money that buying the item will generate. Open settings permit a wider range of behaviours to be enacted ('offer more choice') than closed settings in which just one or a few behaviours are possible. CBSs can be described on a continuum from relatively open to relatively closed. This conceptualization is especially relevant to the study of consumer behaviour, and particularly, retail research. Generally, though not inevitably, in the relatively closed setting, persons other than the consumer arrange the discriminative stimuli that compose the setting in a way that compels conformity to the desired behaviour. Such conformity is achieved by making reinforcement contingent on such conformity. The open setting, however, is marked by a relative absence of physical, social and verbal pressures to conform to a pattern of activity that is determined by others (what ecological psychologists call a behaviour programme: Schoggen, 1989); it is comparatively free of constraints on the consumer, who, thus, has an increased range of choices. He or she has some ability to determine personal rules for choosing among the products and brands on offer, which stores to visit, and so on. A typical open setting is represented by a departmental store in which the consumer can move from section to section, browsing here, considering there, making a purchase or leaving altogether to find another store or even giving up on shopping and going home.

In contrast, extremely closed CBSs are exemplified by the dental surgery or the gymnasium where only one course of action is reinforced and removing oneself from the situation, while not impossible, is fraught with social and, ultimately, health-related costs. Less extreme but still distinctly closed for the consumer behaviour context, a bank is usually a physically closed setting, arranged to encourage orderly queuing by customers and to discourage behaviour that detracts from the efficient execution of transactions. Social and verbal elements also enter into the closed nature of the setting: the single-file line that leads to the teller window does not encourage conversation, at least not to the point where the business of the bank is likely to be delayed. Social and regulatory aspects of the CBS are also apparent in less formal contexts such as having to purchase a birthday gift for a friend, which is closer to the centre of the open-closed continuum. The setting is closed insofar as the consumer conforms to social rules that describe moral or material rewards for reciprocity or punishments for ignoring generosity in others, though it has facets of openness stemming from the capacity of friends to depart from social norms or even break the rules on occasion, not only without censure but with a strengthening of the relationship.

Also on the left of the BPM shown in Figure 13.1 is the consumer's learning history for this and similar products, what he or she has done in the past and the reinforcing and punishing outcomes this has had. The learning history primes the discriminative stimuli (S^D) and motivating operations (MO) that make up the CBS and evokes the behaviour that will generate or avoid the consequences on offer. S^D are stimuli in the presence of which the individual discriminates behaviourally by performing a response that has previously been reinforced in these or similar circumstances; MO are stimuli that enhance the ability of a reinforcer to strengthen a response. For instance, while the wording of an advertisement,

'Persil washes whiter!' may be an S^D for buying this product, the accompanying picture of a child wearing pristine, clean clothes might enhance the efficacy of the reinforcer if this symbol has previously been associated with sound parenting (Fagerstrom et al., 2010). It is the consumer situation that results from the interaction learning history and CBS that is the immediate precursor of consumer behaviour. The consumer situation induces or inhibits particular consumer behaviours depending on whether the consumer behaviour analysis is relatively open or relatively closed. In this non-intentional construal of the BPM, the consumer situation thus amounts to the *scope* of the setting, i.e. its degree of openness or closedness weighted by the individual's consumption history directly impacts upon the probability that particular consumer behaviours will occur.

The stimuli that comprise the CBS and that enter into the consumer situation induce the consumer to discriminate his or her behaviour by purchasing or consuming certain products and services, marques and brands rather than others. The behaviours performed are those that have been reinforced in the past and the discriminative stimuli, motivating operations and learning history that interact to form the consumer situation are associated with utilitarian or functional and informational or symbolic reinforcements that will result from current behaviours. These consequences of behaviour, shown on the right-hand side of the model in Figure 13.1, may be positive or aversive, reinforcing or punishing in their effects on future consumer choice. Utilitarian reinforcers, which are mediated by the products themselves, are associated with the technical and operational qualities of the item bought and consumed. Informational reinforcers are socially mediated, however, and consist in performance feedback on the consumer behaviour in question or other behaviours instrumental in making it possible. Almost any car will provide the utilitarian benefits of transporting its owner or driver, 'getting from A to B', that is. But a Porsche usually delivers the performance feedback that comes from recognition of the owner's occupational status, social position, and other sources of honour and prestige. Like other socially constructed, symbolic outcomes of behaviour, informational reinforcers are relative to the values of the community: in a social system conscious of CO_2 emission or fossil fuel consumption, a prestige car might not confer the positive social feedback just assumed.

Consumers acquire combinations of utilitarian and informational benefits in the course of buying and using products, represented as a pattern of low/high utilitarian reinforcement and low/high informational reinforcement. The idea of a pattern of reinforcement replaces that of schedule of reinforcement, something applicable more to the precision of the laboratory than interpreting complex choices in the market place. Defined in terms of pattern of reinforcement, consumer behaviour falls into one of

	Low utilitarian reinforcement	High utilitarian reinforcement
Low informational reinforcement	MAINTENANCE	HEDONISM
High informational reinforcement	ACCUMULATION	ACCOMPLISHMENT

Figure 13.2   Patterns of reinforcement and operant classes of consumer behaviour

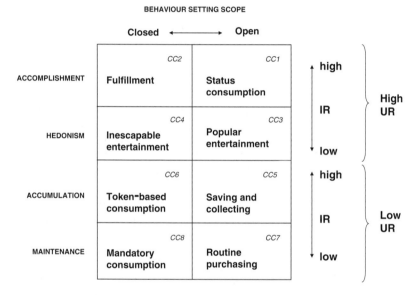

Figure 13.3   The BPM contingency matrix

four operant classes: maintenance, accumulation, hedonism and accomplishment (Figure 13.2). The BPM Contingency Matrix (Figure 13.3) comprises eight distinct categories of contingencies, the outcome of combining CBS-scope and reinforcement patterns (Foxall, 2010a). The following sections reveal that the generic BPM shown in Figure 13.1 can be construed in both extensional and intentional forms and that these offer different levels of explanation of consumer behaviour. Thus far, empirical work has emphasized the extensional construal of the model; this chapter argues for an intentional construal based on research into the role of emotionality in consumer choice.

13.2.2 Empirical Research

What kind of model is the BPM and what confidence may we have that its explanatory categories actually relate consistently to consumer behaviour? The model was devised to overcome the drawbacks of a social cognitive portrayal of choice by examining the possibility that a model of consumer choice devoid of unobservables could be constructed and employed in the interpretation of purchase and consumption. The aim was then to test this model to destruction. Two outcomes of this procedure were possible. Either an entirely non-intentional approach would be shown adequate for the explanation of consumer behaviour or, more probably, the necessity of employing intentional terminology and therefore intentional explanation would become evident. These founding objectives guided the BPM research programme since its inception (Foxall, 1988). When the earlier chapter in this series was published (Foxall, 1997a), the BPM had been used solely as an interpretive device, a means of recasting familiar themes in consumer research in behavioural terms in order to demonstrate that this portrayal accounted for the empirical data at least as well as did cognitive theories and to suggest alternative avenues for research not included in the social cognitive paradigm. Hence, attitude-behaviour relationships, consumer innovativeness, 'green' purchasing and consumption, as well as general purchasing, consumption and saving behaviours were re-examined from this antithetical perspective. At that point little more was expected of the BPM approach than its contribution to the growth of knowledge in a Feyerabendian manner (Feyerabend, 1975) through a clash of competing interpretations.

The interim has been marked by a large volume of empirical research intended to test the predictive capacity of the BPM. This work has increasingly incorporated techniques pioneered in behaviour analysis and, especially, behavioural economics (Hursh, 1984) in order to investigate behaviour in the non-intentional terms that are the hallmark of operant psychology and experimental economics. Defining economic choice as the allocation of behaviour within a framework of costs and benefits (Staddon, 1980), this perspective adopted matching and maximization techniques to the study of consumers' brand and product choices (Foxall, 1999; Foxall and James, 2002, 2003; Foxall and Schrezenmaier, 2003; cf. Curry et al., 2010). This translational research programme has demonstrated that the matching phenomena explored by Herrnstein (1961, 1970, 1997) provide psychological measures of standard microeconomic variables such as product and brand substitutability, complementarity and independence (Foxall et al., 2010b; Romero et al., 2006) which also serve to define product categories, subcategories and brands (Foxall et al., 2010a).

Further behavioural economics research has involved the operational measurement of utilitarian and informational reinforcement, and the estimation of price elasticity of demand coefficients for brands feature varying combinations of these elements of reward (Foxall et al., 2004, 2007, 2010a; Oliveira-Castro et al., 2006, 2008a, 2008b). This work underpins the BPM approach by showing that consumer demand is a function not only of price but of the pattern of reinforcement delivered by goods.

13.2.3   An Extensional Construal

Extensional language
Theories of behaviour are a matter of how language is deployed to make a subject matter intelligible: they are methodological devices rather than ontological descriptions. We understand behaviour in daily life by reference to a person's intentions: he or she did that because they *expected* to, *desired* the outcome, or *believed* it was morally incumbent. Such intentional explanation is also at the heart of social and behavioural science: If A *desires* x and *believes* that doing y will lead to x, he or she will do y (e.g., Rosenberg, 1988) and economics (Rosenberg, 1992). The essence of the 'attitudes' represented by the italicized words is that they form sentences that are about something other than themselves: we do not simply 'expect' or 'desire' or 'like' per se; we 'expect that p', 'desire that p' or 'believe that p'. Rediscovering the scholastic philosophers' analysis of aboutness or intentionality, Brentano (1874) took it to be the mark of the mental, that which distinguished the substances that composed the world. The modern interpretation of intentionality inheres however in the recognition that the attitudes and the proposition they take as their predicates (hence, 'propositional attitudes') serve only to distinguish one kind of sentence, one kind of explanation, from another (Chisholm, 1957; Dennett, 1969; Russell, 1912).

The radical behaviourist explanation that the BPM research programme seeks to evaluate is wholly different from an intentional explanation. First, it consists of the identification of the environmental stimuli that control behaviour; when these have been identified and described (in non-intentional terms), the behaviour has been explained. Second, it resolutely adheres to a form of explanation that strenuously avoids intentional terms such as 'believes' and 'desires' – it is extensional. The essence of behaviourism is the avoidance of intentionality in its scientific discourse (Foxall, 2004). As the founder of radical behaviourism, Skinner (1945) strove to avoid intentional terms in scientific discourse. His meticulous standards of linguistic expression inhere in his later writing that, 'We say that spiders spin webs in order to catch flies and that men set nets in order to catch fish. The "order" is temporal' (Skinner, 1969, p. 193). That is, we are saying simply that *first* the spider spins and *then* it catches flies, that men *first* set their nets and *then* catch fish. Neither the spider nor the men pursue a purpose or seek to fulfil an intention when spinning or setting. Skinner (1971, p. 18) is also scrupulously careful to avoid intentional language in defining operant behaviour as 'behaviour that *operates* on the environment to produce consequences'. There is now no suggestion that the operation is performed 'in order' to produce consequences, emphasizing that the order implied is just that of temporal sequence. Extensional linguistic convention is the heart of radical behaviourism, the locutionary style that defines it as a philosophy of psychology (Foxall, 2004).

More technically, extensional language consists in sentences whose truth value lies in the substitutability of coextensive terms: our rephrasing, *salve veritate*, 'This consumer has purchased Brand X' as 'This consumer has purchased Product Y' when X is the sole member of the Y product category is an example of extensionality. This is the language which is generally taken to be that of hypothetico-deductive science: it leads directly to statements that can be tested by comparison with empirical evidence (Chisholm, 1957; Dennett, 1969; Quine, 1960). By extensional language is meant, therefore, sentences that are referentially transparent, that conform to the normal usages of science, contain no intentional terms: sentences that allow substitution of identicals. Extensional language is a means to express statements that met the truth value of science devised by Quine (1960) who argues (p. 151): 'All failures of extensionality are failures of substitutability of identity.' Terms which have the same extension can be substituted for one another in extensional sentences *salve veritate* but such substitutability of identity is not possible *salve veritate* in intensional sentences. In the latter, the terms have different intentions or meanings in the individual's mental or subjective or private life (or at least that which is being attributed to him or her). These two expressions nevertheless have different *intentions* or meanings and are not therefore substitutable if the truth value of the sentence is to be preserved.

The extensional construal of the BPM

The structure of the extensionally conceived model is such that consumer behaviour is portrayed as the outcome of functional relationships between a consumer situation and a response, where the consumer situation is the intersection of a CBS and a learning history of reinforcement and punishment by utilitarian and informational consequences. CBS-scope, insofar as it contains the consequences of behaviour that have formed the individual's learning history, can thus be said to be the 'cause' of consumer behaviour, in the sense that the behaviour is a function of the stimuli that compose CBS-scope. The consumer situation is thus understood in the extensional model solely in terms of the scope of the CBS.

An extensional model incorporates causal influences but does not employ intentional idioms or reasoning to explain its dependent variable(s). As such, the Behavioural Perspective Model locates consumer choice at the intersection of the consumer's learning history and the current CBS, i.e., where the experience of consumption meets an opportunity to consume anew. This intersection of time and space forms the *consumer situation*, the immediate shaper of approach–avoidance responses involved in purchase and consumption. We have already seen that in line with a theory that takes the prediction and control of behaviour as its raison d'etre, the extensionally defined consumer situation is coterminous with the scope of the CBS. The consumer situation is defined in terms of the range of options available to the consumer as determined by the stimulus antecedents of feasible behaviours, some of which will have been present on earlier consumption occasions; in the presence of the individual's learning history, these initially neutral stimuli are transformed into the discriminative stimuli and motivating operations that set the occasion for current choice. The consumer's consumption history invests the initially neutral stimuli with a kind of meaning, which consists in no more than the capacity to generate specific kinds of approach and or avoidance behaviours that produce consequences to regulate the rate of recurrence of the behaviours that produced them. Thus both CBS and consumer situation simply set the occasion for three types of behavioural consequence: utilitarian reinforcement which consists in the functional outcomes of behaviour, informational reinforcement, which stems from the symbolic outcomes, principally performance feedback, and aversive/punishing consequences, the costs of purchase and consumption. Such aversive outcomes can themselves be subdivided into those that are utilitarian in nature and those that are symbolic. The components of the model are operationally defined, specified in terms of the functional relationships that stem from their observable impacts upon behaviour. Hence, an *operant response*, one which operates on the environment to produce the consequences that govern its subsequent rate of emission, 'is not simply a response that the organism thinks will have a certain effect, it does have that effect' (Smith, 1994, pp. 127–128). Further, a *reinforcer* 'is not simply a stimulus that the organism desires to occur. It is a stimulus that will alter the rate of behaviour upon which its occurrence is contingent' (ibid.). And a *discriminative stimulus* 'is not simply a stimulus that has been correlated with a certain contingency in the organism's experience. It is one that successfully alters the organism's operant behaviour with respect to that contingency' (Smith, 1994, p. 129). It does not signal, refer to or represent the utilitarian and informational reinforcers or punishers likely to be contingent on the performance of particular responses: it simply 'sets the occasion' for these consequences.

The rationale for building a model of consumer behaviour in these terms derives not from the conventional wisdom of hypothetico-deductive scientific methodology but from the need to examine whether a theory of choice can avoid the intentional language of beliefs and desires, i.e., statements that do not permit the substitutability of co-extensives. The key motivation for this is the finding that both cognitive and behaviourist accounts of consumer choice are equally supported by the empirical evidence on attitudinal–behavioural correspondence (Foxall, 1997c, 2005): to favour the former whilst ignoring the latter represents not only a slavish adherence of an applied field to the prevailing paradigm of the disciplines from which it derives, in this case cognitive psychology, but an intellectually closed perspective which will not conceive of explanation in terms not belonging to this framework of conceptualization and analysis. But why radical behaviourism? The central fact in the delineation of radical behaviourism is its conceptual avoidance of propositional content. This eschewal of the intentional stance sets it apart not only from cognitivism but from other neo-behaviourisms. Indeed, the defining characteristic of radical behaviourism is not that it avoids mediating processes per se but that it sets out to account for behaviour without recourse to propositional attitudes. Based rather on the contextual stance, it provides definitions of contingency-shaped, rule-governed, verbal and private behaviours which are non-intentional. For reasons of disinterested curiosity, therefore, as well as the more pragmatic search for a general explanation of choice, a research program based on the development and evaluation of an extensional model of consumer choice becomes inevitable. This is what the extensional construal of the BPM attempts.

The extensional model has made considerable advances in the interpretation and prediction of complex human choice, some of which were reviewed above. But there are limits to extensionality as a result of which it is necessary to incorporate intentional language into the model (Foxall, 2004, 2007c). Indeed, radical behaviourists already use such language when they are faced with the limitations of extensionality. What is essential to the BPM research programme is to understand why radical behaviourists do this and, if it is necessary, to do it rigorously and consistently. The evolution of the BPM as a generic portrayal of consumer choice which includes extensional, intentional, and cognitive theories elucidates the kind of theoretical development required by applied behaviour analysis in order to make comprehensive sense of its subject matter. We shall argue that emotion is an example of intentionality that provides a missing link in the attempt to account for the continuity of behaviour. An interesting parallel development is that of cognitive psychologists who have also shifted their focus to emotion in recent years, though for rather different reasons (see, for instance, Hodgkinson and Healey, 2008, in press). What is being emphasized here is that the philosophically legitimate ascription of intentionality requires great care if it is to avoid being a mere convenience. There needs, first, to be a solid rationale for the emergence of intentional language in the BPM account of consumer behaviour, followed by a reasoned understanding of why emotion has assumed an essential role in the explanation of behaviour. These are pursued below in terms of the inability of the extensional model to explain behavioural continuity and the exposition of why a particular conception of emotionality can fill this gap. The logic by which the ascription of emotion can be justified is discussed in terms of neurobiology and environment–behaviour relationships and the resulting philosophy of psychology, intentional behaviourism, is outlined.

13.2.4   Accounting for Behavioural Continuity

Although an extensional account facilitates prediction and control by reference to the stimuli that determine the rate of recurrence of behaviour, it cannot explain the *continuity of behaviour over settings and situations.* As the consumer moves from setting to setting, they may be faced with stimuli that differ from those previously encountered; yet they act in a manner consistent with the behaviours displayed in those rather different settings. In contrast, there are other occasions when the pattern of behaviour displayed by the consumer in familiar settings deviates markedly from what might be expected, as for example, when a lazy glutton starts to eat only less fattening foods and to take up exercise. What accounts for such deviations from patterns of behaviour that have hitherto remained constant over time? It is beyond the capacity of a purely extensional model to explain the continuity of behaviour across settings or the discontinuity of behaviour that occurs when the consumer switches to a new pattern of choice that has not previously been reinforced. The recurrence of the same or similar stimuli in a succession of settings is not generally sufficient for such explanation: only in the most closed experimental setting could it be taken as such. In complex situations of purchase and consumption, it is usually impossible to isolate the stimuli that are responsible for consumer responses with the precision available in the laboratory and without interpretation based on the ascription of intentionality. Moreover, most stimuli differ somewhat from setting to setting. Physiological changes resulting from behaving once in one setting cannot be shown to explain the continuity of behaviour even across settings that exhibit stimulus similarities let alone among divergent stimulus contexts. Rules cannot account for behavioural continuity or pattern shifts unless some mechanism of perception, encoding, interpreting can be identified. (Rules may be MO in an extensional account, but while they may predict or control behaviour they cannot explain behavioural continuity or deviations from established behaviour patterns.) Only by employing intentional language can we provide an explanatory account.

Foxall (2007b) presented the argument for incorporating intentionality into theories of choice on the grounds that an extensional theory could not of itself account for the continuity/discontinuity of behaviour (see also Foxall, 2004, 2007c, 2008b). Some examples may make this argument more concrete. First, take a person whom we have observed drink alcohol heavily on a daily basis but who, we note, now drinks only on Friday evenings and confines himself to two drinks. As Rachlin (1995) says, we might explain this behaviour by saying that the individual concerned has 'decided' on this change. The use of intentional language appears inevitable if we are to account for this behavioural discontinuity. Second, consider a heavy user of the four brands, A, B, C, and D, that comprise this individual's consideration set for a particular consumer nondurable, who now includes a new brand, E, in their repertoire. As is the case for many consumers in affluent societies, we cannot assume anything about the individual's learning history except that they are a heavy user of the product category. It seems impossible to account for their inclusion of the new brand without referring to the individual's beliefs and desires. Finally, let us consider the case of a participant in an operant experiment who maintains their behaviour pattern even though the contingencies governing reinforcement of that behaviour have changed. Again, there is little we can say about the individual's learning history. It seems reasonable to assume some control of their overt behaviour by their private verbal behaviour especially since we have no evidence of prior control of overt behaviour via instructions. It does not seem that behaviour such as this can be explained other than by ascribing certain beliefs and desires to the experimental participant.

These examples of behavioural continuity/discontinuity define a continuum of behavioural change which relates the sequence of observed behaviour to changes in the attendant sequence of reinforcement. The behaviour of the heavy user of alcohol which reflects some early signs of addiction (such as bingeing followed by remorse which is not sufficient to allay further bouts of heavy drinking) but whose behaviour changes to a more restrained pattern of moderated drinking cannot be explained in terms of the contingencies alone. The initial phase leads to aversive consequences which do not reduce the level of alcohol consumption; the subsequent behaviour pattern is adopted before the novel consequences of restrained consumption have had time to exert an effect on choice. The abrupt change in the first molar pattern of behaviour can be explained only in terms of the individual's having made a decision to try a different style of behaviour. Such change is described as *major* or *discontinuous*.

The consumer who adopts a new brand also exhibits a change in their sequence of behaviour, not by abandoning the existing pattern of choice but by supplementing and extending it. There is a change in behaviour but it amounts to no more than trying a new brand in a product category of which the consumer has much experience, i.e., a novel version of a familiar pattern of reinforcement. Most consumers of a product category purchase within a small consideration set of tried and tested brands; many, especially the heavier users of the product, try new brands that appear to contain the characteristics of the product class; some of those who try it incorporate the new brand into their future consideration set (Ehrenberg, 1972). Most consumers who select a new brand in this way or change to another in their existing consideration set choose one that contains a similar combination of functional and symbolic benefits (the pattern of reinforcement) as existing members of the set (Foxall et al., 2004). The prediction of such behaviour follows easily enough from consideration of the contingencies alone (at least for aggregates, not necessarily for individuals) but an explanation of the change itself requires consideration of the processes of comparison and recognition that must precede the change. How are the verbal stimuli (e.g., advertisements) translated into the new pattern of consumer behaviour via comparison with the characteristics of the brands already in the consumer's repertoire? Selective perception, beliefs and desires must be used as part of the explanation of such behaviour. It is not sufficient, therefore, to say that more continuous change of this sort, even though it may be readily related to the contingencies, is 'explained' by its embodiment of stimulus or reinforcer discrimination and generalization. Use of such terminology merely redescribes the observed choices.

Finally, the behaviour of the experimental participant who exhibits rigidity in the face of changing contingencies is an example of behavioural continuity that cannot be explained in terms of the contingencies themselves (Lowe, 1983). The situation is exemplified by the consumer who continues to purchase and use a particular brand of razor blades even though the quality of the shave obtained from them has markedly diminished. Why is human behaviour so insensitive to changes in contingencies when this is not true of nonhumans? The person presumably has not perceived the change in contingencies and is operating according to a self-generated rule reached in decision making prior to the contingency change. The behaviour of persons in this situation often comes to conform to the contingencies after time. How does this change in perception occur? Is there further decision making?

13.3　INTENTIONAL BEHAVIOURISM

13.3.1　'Neural Intentionality'

It is one thing to accept the need to incorporate intentional terms into an explanation of consumer choice, quite another to propose a legitimate means by which this might be accomplished without succumbing to the temptation to base intentional inferences naively on the behaviour to be explained. Intentional behaviourism proposes reasoned criteria for attributing intentionality in a manner consistent with evolutionary criteria. The starting point is Dennett's (1969) suggestion that intentionality be ascribed on the basis of evolutionarily consistent afferent–efferent neural links that account for how organisms select a particular behaviour (reaching out) as the appropriate response to a given internal state of deprivation (hunger) and a given environmental context (availability of alternative food sources, each with its own costs of procurement). 'Afferent' and 'efferent' denote functions of neurons which are cells in the nervous system that transmit impulses to other neurons. Dendrites, of which there are a number to each cell, receive signals from other neurons and are accordingly known as *afferent*. Axons, of which each cell has only one, transmit signals to other neurons and are, therefore, known as *efferent*. These terms are used to denote the functions of neurons by reference to the direction in which they transmit impulses: towards the central nervous system (CNS) in the case of afferent or sensory neurons, away from the CNS in the case of efferent or motor neurons. The thrust of Dennett's (1969) system appears on first reading to be that intentionality can be ascribed at the personal level (that of people and minds) on the basis of considerations that arise at the sub-personal level (that of brains and neuronal functioning). As his work developed, however, Dennett (1978a, 1987) increasingly sought method for ascribing intentionality at sub-personal levels, a complicating factor that a keener reading of his earliest work reveals to be an underlying current.

At the heart of his method of using extensional sentences as the basis of ascribing intentionality, is Dennett's linking of basic biological facts with their evolutionary history: 'Intentional description *presupposes* the environmental appropriateness of antecedent-consequent connections; natural selection guarantees, over the long run, the environmental appropriateness of what it produces' (Dennett, 1969, p. 41).

Dennett (1969) portrays the peripheralist approach of the behaviourists as incapable of producing a coherent science of behaviour because of its inability to incorporate the use of intentional language in everyday discourse. He assumes as evidence for the existence of entities described intentionally the fact that people speak as though these things existed. Above all, Dennett berates the behaviourists for being unable to produce an account of human behaviour including verbal behaviour that proceeds in the absence of intentional terms. The behaviourist paradigm, parsimoniously reduced to observable stimuli and responses, is sufficient to predict and control learning but is incapable of explicating in non-intentional language what is learned. Dennett's solution is to offer first intentional characterizations of behavioural events and their causes and then to seek extensional justifications for doing so. He seeks ground rules for this translation from the intentional to the extensional in the logic of evolution by natural selection. His argument is that the brain must have evolved in a way that enables it to discriminate the significance of afferent stimuli in terms of the effectiveness of efferent responses on the environment on which the organism depends for its survival and biological fitness. However, this argument anticipates a resolution of the very problem Dennett is trying to solve by arbitrarily ascribing intentionality to neural systems in the form of their intuiting the 'significance' of afferent stimuli. Dennett's project fails by dint of its circularity and by not recognizing that evolution is a process of elimination rather than of insight.

Three methodological points emerge from this consideration, all of which entail breaks with Dennett's centralist approach. First, intentionality can be responsibly ascribed only at the personal level. Secondly, intentionality can be ascribed only to entities whose behaviour can reasonably be ascribed to intentional functioning – computers, incapable of feeling pain, are eliminated (Dennett, 1978b). Thirdly, intentionality can be ascribed only on the basis of demonstrated causal relationships between behaviour and the products of evolution by natural selection (i.e. appropriate neural functioning) and, as is argued below, environment–behaviour connections established by operant learning.

In view of this, intentional behaviourism applies to patterns of molar operant behaviour rather than single instances of choice. Intentional behaviourism (Foxall, 2007b) rests on the premise that intentionality can be legitimately ascribed to the individual in order to explain his or her behaviour on the following bases. First, in line with Dennett's thinking, it must be possible to show afferent–efferent linkages at the neuronal level that are logically consistent with both the behaviour to be explained and the intentionality to be ascribed in explaining it. However, the means of making such ascriptions is more complicated than in Dennett's original treatise (Dennett, 1969). These linkages must, as was mentioned above, be shown to have evolved through natural selection; but neuronal plasticity occurring during the lifetime of the individual must also be related to the contingencies responsible for it. Secondly, it must be possible to demonstrate that the pattern of behaviour to be explained is a molar sequence of operant choice rather than a single instance. Dennett's concentration on the molecular level, which refers to the explanation of a single instance of behaviour, makes no contribution to our primary concern to explain the continuity of behaviour. After all, the task we have set ourselves is the elucidation of the means by which such continuity can be explained in behavioural science (including occasions of discontinuity).

The argument that the ascription of intentionality relies on demonstrating appropriate afferent–efferent links (Dennett, 1969) can be conveniently called the 'neuro-intentional approach', though this is not Dennett's term. It is a necessary though insufficient element of the explanatory method of intentional behaviourism. Dennett's (1969) argument that content may be reliably ascribed on the basis of evolutionarily consistent afferent–efferent linkages is consistent with the view that such content belongs at the personal level of explanation while the extensional neuroscience from which it derives is part of the sub-personal level. As long as these levels are kept separate, the use of both intentional and extensional routes to knowledge can be legitimized within the same framework of exposition.

13.3.2   Intentionality and Contingency

Intentionality is to be ascribed based on evolutionarily consistent afferent–efferent linkages identified by neuroscience (Dennett, 1969). Neuroscience is an extensional science that is concerned with the sub-personal level of explanation. Intentionality is ascribed at the personal level. The consideration of afferent–efferent neuronal links justifies the role of neuroscience in the explanation of behaviour through the ascription of intentionality. Another extensional approach to knowledge, behavioural science, is also involved and, within that, the demonstration that molar patterns of the behaviour that is to be explained can be functionally related to their consequences. This requirement has two implications. First, we are dealing with operant relationships, that is, with the assumption that the behaviour under investigation is explicable in terms of the patterns of reinforcement and punishment associated with it. The insistence on operant behaviour is particularly justified in that reinforcement and punishment are clearly implemented in the brain (Rolls, 2005). This is presumably an evolutionary endowment and makes the identification of relevant afferent–efferent links of the kind Dennett insisted upon. Second, we are concerned not with the interpretation of single instances of behaviour but with sequences of choice that correlate with sequences of consequences.

The necessity of demonstrating a molar pattern of operant behaviour is, therefore, twofold: (1) knowing what we want to explain, and (2) including ontogenetic as well as phylogenetically shaped afferent–efferent links in the process of ascribing intentionality, i.e., incorporating development as well as evolution. In terms of the first requirement, Dennett is sketchy on what behaviour is, why it matters, and how it enters into the explanation. The intentional stance approach does not show how behaviour is to be included in the ascription of intentionality. Dennett says that the system to be predicted must be invested with the beliefs and desires it *ought* to have given its history and position. Only if we know its behavioural learning history and its current behaviour setting can this be done. This requires something closely akin to the BPM: the elements entering in to the consumer situation and the consumer situation itself, including the various consequences of behaviour that are (i) signalled by the discriminative stimuli and motivating operations that compose the setting and which have (ii) previously enabled a learning history to be established. One way of getting at this information is through consideration of the molar pattern of choice. A more refined approach is yet to be established in which we can appreciate more fully the contingent consequences of behaviour (informational reinforcement and utilitarian reinforcement and the pattern of reinforcement to which they give rise) so that the attitudinal and propositional components of intentionality can be properly adjudged and ascribed.

In order to meet the second requirement, we must reach an understanding of how afferent–efferent links are formed and strengthened by ontogenetic development as opposed to the phylogenetic processes to which Dennett alludes. Natural selection is not the only source of afferent–efferent linkages that influence behaviour. In the course of individual development, synaptic strength is affected by the effects of reinforcement on the firing rate of neurons making particular responses more or less probable in the future (Hebb, 1949; Knorski, 1948).

> Just like the muscles of your body, connections in the brain will strengthen and grow as they are exercised . . . The brain cells that are involved in the activities that occur most frequently will have extensive connections, whereas those that are used less frequently will be pushed out of the way, and their targets will be taken over by their more hardworking neighbours. (Greenfield, 2000, p. 62; for further discussion, see Frey, 1997)

These processes are themselves the result of natural selection of course but they represent the effects of voluntary or operant behaviour on synaptic strength, an additional influence to that produced phylogenetically and which is largely responsible for involuntary or reflexive behaviour. In defining voluntary and involuntary responses, Skinner (1953, pp. 110–113) is careful to emphasize that they are equally determined by environmental events and that neither implies free will. Such synaptic strength is brought about in the course of the organism's lifetime as a result of cumulative behavioural repetitions. The resulting efficacy of the afferent–efferent links involved should be taken into consideration in the ascription of intentionality just as those which evolved in the lifetime of the species deserve notice. In fact, given the importance of voluntary behaviour to human behaviour, it is likely that such influences may be the greater not only in determining choice but in allocating intentionality to it.

13.4   THE ASCRIPTION OF EMOTION

13.4.1   Salient Facets of Emotion

Emotions do not constitute a uniquely definable class of entities and an absolute definition seems impossible. Philosophers and psychologists differ considerably in defining emotion (Frijda, 2008; Solomon, 2008). Even separating emotion from other sensational states demands intense precision (Bennett and Hacker, 2003). Price (2005, p. 11) distinguishes emotions from bodily feelings (nausea), reflex responses (startle), moods (persistent anger), character traits (such as cowardice and possibly also depression and anxiety), emotional attitudes (love which manifests as other emotions such as pride or sadness depending on the occasion and what happens to the object of love). What is especially germane to the discussion of emotion in the current context, however, are the understandings that emotions manifest as subjective feelings based on physiological events, that they are intentional, may have a cognitive component (depending on what we believe, e.g. about the likelihood that a tiger will attack us), and may seem to play a causative role in directing behavioural responses (Roberts, 1988). In this section, we pay particular attention to the first two of these, briefly returning later to questions of cognitive content and causation.

Emotion as subjective experience
Whatever view is taken of the causes and components of emotion, subjective feelings are especially relevant to the mode of explanation pursued here. The theoretical basis of the present argument emphasizes the evolutionary logic by which felt emotion arises from behaviour that

is performed in a particular context of contingent reinforcement and punishment. We may add that felt emotion influences learning history to guide further behavioural choices in similar contexts. Unless this minimal assumption is made, it is difficult to appreciate why strong and insistent emotional responses evolved. Emotional feelings undoubtedly are caused by neurophysiological processes but it is important (as Barrett et al., 2007, who adopt Searle's (2000) 'biological naturalism' approach, argue) to keep separate the phenomenological experience of an event and its causation (cf. Izard, 2009). The fact that emotional feelings are instantiated at the sub-personal level of neurophysiological processing is not sufficient to define emotion; equally important is the content of emotion, the subjective experience which is the outcome of both neural firings and contextualized behaviour. It is a reasonable assumption that emotion, however it is defined, will not influence further behaviour unless something is felt, even though the feeling itself, as an entity that cannot be subjected to direct laboratory investigation, may not be a demonstrable cause of that behaviour.

Having argued that an account of emotion must treat both its causes and its content, Barrett et al. (2007) abstract two further principles of biological naturalism that relate to the role of emotional feelings in the explanation of behaviour. First, they note that a wholly causal account of emotional content may not be feasible. In wider philosophical terms we may note that there are two levels of explanation involved here, the personal and sub-personal which may not be conflated (see the discussion of Dennett's development of the intentional stance in Foxall, 2007a). McGinn (1991, 2004) points out that conscious experience is not and may never be reducible to physiological operations. It is, as Barrett et al. (2007, p. 376) point out, the scientist's work to supply the means of bridging these levels, which is precisely the task adopted by intentional behaviourism (Foxall, 2004), which as noted earlier is the primary explanatory device adopted in this chapter. Secondly, they point out that the ontological subjectivity of emotional feelings refers to their unique, personal and private nature. The ontological status of emotion feelings cannot be abrogated by measures of behaviour, physiology, or neural functioning even if these are reliable indices of felt emotion. Barrett et al.'s solution inheres in the dictum that 'To know what emotion feels like, it is necessary to ask people what they experience' (2007, p. 376; see also Barrett et al., 2005). However, while the truth of this is unassailable, in itself it brings us no closer to understanding the nature of explanatory significance of felt emotion than the attempt to reduce it to its physiological causes. Biological naturalism lacks an account of how emotional verbalizations are linked to the appetitive and aversive contingencies that control them and, therefore, of the role of emotional feelings in learning history and subsequent behaviour.

Verbal reports do not stem directly from feelings but are the products of patterns of reinforcement and punishment (Foxall and Greenley, 1999; Foxall and Yani-de-Soriano, 2005). Intentional behaviourism supplies this understanding based on some of the methodological imperatives set by the private nature of emotionality and the methodological limitations posed by the inability to subject emotionality to a direct experimental analysis.

The subjective nature of emotional feeling carries further methodological implications. No matter how real an individual's emotional feelings are to that person, the subjective experience of emotion in others is, for that person, no more than an inference. Emotions themselves, whatever ontological status we assign them, cannot enter directly into experimental analyses and it is therefore impossible to identify exactly their influences on behaviour. A scientist making ascriptions of emotion in order to interpret consumer behaviour must therefore justify these ascriptions by means of empirical findings of systematic relationships between that behaviour and its neurophysiological causes on the one hand and its contextual causes on the other. This requires a means of adding meaning to verbal reports of privately experienced emotion. Biological naturalism also lacks an understanding of why and how explanation in terms of emotional feelings becomes necessary. Although psychologists and philosophers are quick to dismiss behaviourism as a relic of the past which has been superseded by the cognitive revolution, they do not point out what was specifically lacking in its explanations that makes a role for experienced emotion necessary. Finally, there may be something to be gained from the pursuit of an emotion-based explanation of behaviour in the confines of a specific range of behaviour.

Rather than plot a way through the myriad of available definitions of emotion, the present context emphasizes two implications of emotion for the explanation of behaviour. First, emotion embodies characteristic feelings that are mediated by neurobiological and/or experiential events, but emotion is not to be identified with either neuronal activity or overt behaviour. 'Insofar as emotion is at bottom sensation, then generating a feeling ipso facto generates a state of consciousness. Thus, an emotion feeling always registers in phenomenal consciousness' (Izard, 2009, p. 12). Understanding emotion requires recognition that, except for what each of us takes to be his or her own subjectively felt emotions, emotion is not empirically available for a third-person scientific analysis. What we take, with varying degrees of validation, to be reliable correlates of emotion (e.g. verbal and nonverbal behaviours, neuronal activities) are not the emotions themselves, not even emotion feelings. Although an individual may appear to have emotion feelings of their own and be willing to attribute these also to others on the basis of their similar behaviours and physiologies, that individual cannot adduce these feelings as material for an experimental analysis. In that respect, an attempt to extend the extensional explanation of behaviour by reference to emotion feelings depends on (a) reconstructing a plausible set of felt emotions for another person—what Dennett calls heterophenomenology—as a means of making the data intelligible, and (b) recognizing that this is a matter of supplementing rather than replicating scientific analysis. (Compare, however, Lowenstein et al., 2008, for an account of the expanding treatment of emotion in neuroeconomics which posits hot and cold cognition – a standpoint that contrasts markedly with the heterophenomenological approach.)

Emotion and intentionality
Secondly, in ascribing emotions to others in order to make their behaviour intelligible, we take emotions to be intentional (about or directed towards something other than themselves) and express statements about them in terms of propositional attitudes (Solomon, 1973). They are not to be identified with their physiological or behavioural correlates even though these causal factors are the basis of their formal attribution to others. What role do emotions play in explanation? Specific emotions often accompany specific behaviours: even the most irascible person only throws shoes at the TV when feeling angry with the programmes. But it is not possible to use emotional feelings experimentally in order to demonstrate their necessary or sufficient status in bringing about this behaviour. Since emotional feelings cannot be shown to be causal, how can they enter into explanations of overt behaviour? It is not a matter of showing that they are ontologically causal; they are methodologically necessary because we have to adopt the intentional language of emotion to account for the continuity of behaviour. Having established that some operant behaviour is shaped and maintained by its environmental consequences, we are unable to account for its continuity or discontinuity in operant terms. The only way to proceed (and behaviour analysts do this all the time) is to speak of the organism in terms of its beliefs and desires, i.e. to adopt the language of intentionality: propositional attitudes. The ontological implications of this are Rylean: it would amount to a category mistake to assume that speaking in terms of beliefs and desires meant that entities of a different order existed over and above the contingencies of reinforcement that are the stock in trade of extensional behavioural science and the afferent–efferent neural links that are part and parcel of extensional neuroscience (Ryle, 1949). But the methodological implications accord more with Dennett (1969): the intentional attributions are a necessary linguistic means of coping with the lacunae found in the extensional accounts.

'Emotion' as it is used here is, then, an inference of a potentially felt state that accounts for the continuity of behaviour. No ontological claims are made for this construct: it is ascribed on the basis of neurophysiological and behavioural evidence to provide for gaps in the attribution of behavioural causation based on contingencies of reinforcement and neural functioning. While there is no means of discovering the nature of a subjective emotion or its actual effect on behaviour, our inferences are based on personal experience with respect to the naming and functional attribution of emotions. There remains, nevertheless, a need to ascribe intentionality to actors in order to complete the explanation of their behaviour. Behaviour analysis would do this via the concept of the learning history but this is usually an empirically unavailable entity that itself requires explication at neurophysiological and intentional levels. It is here that emotional ascription can provide an augmented explanation that is consistent with the behaviour analytical framework without being confined to its restrictively extensional language.

Since emotions are intentional, they are inferences and the product of linguistic usage; they are not something that, in themselves, can enter into a scientific experiment. The physical and behavioural correlates of emotions, from which emotions are inferred, are not the emotions themselves. The ascription of an emotion to another requires a more sophisticated rationale than an everyday, folk-psychological inference from his or her behaviour. What we are seeking to do is to create an interpretation of a consumer's observed behaviour: first, by identifying the environmental consequences of that behaviour, reinforcers and punishers that can be shown empirically to be causal elements at the operant level; secondly, by identifying the neural structures and functions that are causal as a result of natural selection; and, thirdly, by using these causal elements to justify an intentional interpretation that supplements them by providing a language in which to describe the aspects of behaviour such as its continuity, discontinuity and cross-situational consistency that are not amenable to a causal analysis.

Emotion and explanation

An intentional behaviourist account of emotion makes three demands. The first is a definition and measure of emotionally expressive behaviour. Such behaviour might in principle be verbal or non-verbal. However, it is important to separate such behaviour from physiological indices of emotion which might be conflated with other neurological data employed in intentional behaviourism. The requirement is, therefore, for an empirical measure of verbal reactions to felt emotion based on a well-reasoned and research-based typology of human emotionality. A suitable measure would be a psychometrically well-founded instrument for the assessment of fundamental emotional feelings based on verbal responses to settings. The second and third are empirical evidence that neuronal activity and environment–behaviour links are respectively and consistently related to the self-reported behaviour revealed by the psychometric measure. These correlates of self-reported emotion with molar sequences of consumer behaviour provide the rationale for the ascription of emotion feeling. Let us look at these three requirements in turn.

13.4.2 Behavioural Expression of Emotion

While several typologies of emotion have been employed in consumer research (Havlena and Holbrook, 1986; Havlena et al., 1989; Holbrook and Batra, 1987; Huang, 2001; Sherman et al., 1997; Sweeney and Wyber, 2002), many investigators have employed the pleasure, arousal and dominance (PAD) scales devised by Mehrabian and Russell (1974). This approach is especially relevant to the present project in that these authors focus on the physical and social stimuli that influence an individual's emotional state and behaviours within a specific environment. This environment corresponds to the consumer behaviour setting defined in the BPM as comprising physical and social S^D and MO. Mehrabian and Russell (1974) argue on the basis of a thorough literature review (see also Mehrabian, 1980) that pleasure, arousal and dominance capture the emotion-eliciting qualities of environments and mediate approach-avoidance behaviours such as preference, exploration, affiliation, and work performance. These dimensions of emotional response are measured questionnaire-based self reports of respondents' verbal reactions to descriptions of situations elicited by semantic differential scales (Mehrabian and Russell, 1974). Mehrabian (1980) defends the selection of pleasure, arousal and dominance on the basis of their multi-modal (synesthetic) effects, reports of physiological reactions to such intermodal stimulation, and the findings of work using the semantic differential method of verbal scaling (Osgood et al., 1957, 1975) which established evaluation, activity, and potency as the basic dimensions in terms of which the meanings of concepts are delineable.

Pleasure-displeasure is a feeling state measured as a continuum ranging from extreme pain or unhappiness to extreme happiness that can be assessed readily with self-report, such as semantic differential measures or with behavioural indicators, such as smiles, laughter and, in general, positive versus negative facial expressions. Arousal-nonarousal is a feeling state varying along a single dimension ranging from sleep to frantic excitement which is most directly assessed by verbal report or with behavioural indicators such as vocal activity (positive and negative), facial activity (positive and negative expressions), speech rate, and speech volume. Dominance-submissiveness ranges from extreme feelings of being influenced and controlled by one's environment to feelings of mastery and control over it; it is also a feeling state that can be assessed from verbal reports using the semantic differential method. It is assumed that there is an inverse relationship between dominance and the judged potency of the environment. Behaviourally, dominance is measured in terms of postural relaxation, i.e., body lean and asymmetrical positioning of the limbs. An individual's feeling of dominion in a situation is based on the extent to which he feels unrestricted or free to act in a variety of ways (Mehrabian and Russell, 1974).

13.4.3   Neurobiological Basis of Pleasure, Arousal and Dominance

Mehrabian (1980) argues that pleasure, arousal and dominance are primary adaptations, a contention which entails the identification of these emotions' neural substrates and relatedness to adaptive behaviours. Accordingly, Barrett et al. (2007) confirm Mehrabian and Russell's judgment that these three emotions are fundamental to the mental representation of emotion and relate them to reinforcement and punishment (see also Barrett, 2005; Russell and Barrett, 1999). Foxall (2008a) suggests that Panksepp's (1998, 2005, 2007) seven core emotional systems – SEEKING, RAGE, FEAR, LUST, CARE, PANIC, PLAY – correspond at a general level to the three emotions adopted by Mehrabian and Russell (1974). (Panskepp employs uppercase letters for these core emotions which represent complex propositional systems in terms of 'convenient vernacular heuristics'.) The approximation is strengthened if, following Toronchuk and Ellis (2010), PLEASURE and POWER/DOMINANCE are also included as core emotions (Figure 13.4).

Pleasure
Barrett et al. (2007) specifically link 'core affect', pleasure-displeasure, with the helpfulness or harmfulness of stimulus events, the likelihood that these outcomes will lead to rewarding or aversive consequences, and their consequent acceptance or rejection (Barrett et al., 2007, p. 377). They thereby corroborate the conclusion that these hedonic considerations indicate utilitarian reinforcement, a view expressed also by Panksepp (1998, p. 112) who argues that such positive feelings indicate to the organism that biologically useful consequences are contingent upon its responses to the stimuli in question: '"Useful" stimuli . . . inform the brain of their potential to restore the body toward homeostatic equilibrium when it has

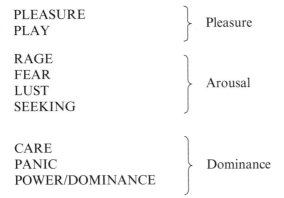

*Figure 13.4   Panskepp's (1998) seven core emotional systems, augmented
by PLEASURE AND POWER/DOMINANCE (after
Toronchuk and Ellis, 2010) and related to Mehrabian and
Russell's (1974) tripartite classification of emotions*

deviated from its biologically dictated "set point" level'. Affective processes are central to the homeostatic process: the experience of pleasure
denotes that equilibrium has been restored, e.g., because hunger or thirst
has been assuaged. As an index of material, biological equilibrium, mediated by tangible physical events, and based on the biogenic influences on
behaviour that give rise to primary reinforcement, the occurrence of pleasure is consistent with what consumer behaviour analysis understands as
utilitarian reinforcement. Pleasure is intrinsically involved in the setting of
goals, in evaluating the means available for their achievement, monitoring
progress towards them and judging accomplishment (Politser, 2008). And
what can be assumed to follow in the case of primary reinforcers can also
be expected to hold for their associated secondary reinforcers. It is encouraging also to note that research on the 'evolutionary substrates of socio-
emotional processes' provides a bridge between the neurochemical level
and the human social and cultural context. The connection between the
opioids, in particular, pleasure, and appetitive seeking behaviour strongly
supports the current interpretation of the nature of consumer choice and
its explanation.

While the experience of emotion cannot be reduced to neural substrates
(McGinn, 1996; Strawson, 1994), it is possible to identify the neurophysiological correlates of reported mental representation of emotion. In the
case of pleasure-displeasure, this involves the amygdala, orbito-frontal
cortex (OFC), and the ventromedial prefrontal cortex (vmPFC) (see,
inter alia, Rolls et al., 2009; see also Cardinal et al., 2002). In line with

this, Wager et al. (2008) conclude from a meta-analysis that increased activation in the brainstem areas ventral tegmental area (VTA), and the subcortical telencephalon areas nucleus accumbens (NAC) and portions of the ventral striatum (vStr), all of which are rich in dopamine (DA), is associated with pleasant experiences which also correlate with activity in the hypothalamus (Hy), vmPFC, and right OFC. In contrast, unpleasant experience is associated with activation in amygdala, anteria insula (aINS), periaqueductal gray (PAG), left OFC and more posterior portions of the vStr and ventral globus pallidus (vGP). 'The results provide a promising indication that different gross anatomical areas may be differentially sensitive to pleasant and unpleasant stimuli, although they do not imply that activation in any of these regions is uniquely associated with either category' (Wager et al., 2008, p. 259). These areas, associated closely with pleasure-displeasure, form a brain region 'that is involved in establishing the threat or reward value of a stimulus' (Barrett et al., 2007, p. 382). This is related to representations of core affect that has been the consequence of prior behaviour with respect to the stimulus in question: i.e., it is a representation of learning history.

Arousal

The elements of emotion, other than pleasure, that Mehrabian and Russell identify as central – namely, arousal and dominance – suggest the content of core emotion (the propositional component of its intentionality), of which Barrett et al. (2007) speak in terms of arousal-based content, relational content, and situational content. Arousal signifies activeness and is manifest in reports of being active, attentive, wound-up; while unarousal manifests in stillness, reported as being still, quiet, sleepy. This active-versus-still dimension corresponds with Mehrabian and Russell's arousal and incorporates the affective effects of informational reinforcement. Relational content is social and reflects the degree of domination or submissiveness that is felt in the presence of others. Situational content reflects the extent to which a setting is novel or unexpected, conducive to or obstructive of a goal, compatible or not with norms and values, and confers responsibility or agency. These considerations call forth maintenance of or change in the individual's behavioural stance, his or her readiness for action.

These content-conferring dimensions of emotion are environmentally determined and Barrett et al. (2007) point out that it may not be so easy to point to specific neural substrates in their cases as for core affect. Nevertheless, we can make some suggestions. The capacity of humans to consistently and communicatively make the mental state attributions on which depictions of emotional content are based is indicative of both biological and cultural mechanisms for this function. The ascription of content to one's core affect is ostensibly a matter of interpreting subjective experiences of emotion, which process includes the appraisal of the social and physical situations in which the individual finds him or herself. Barrett and her colleagues proceed from these considerations to the observation that experienced emotion correlates with activation of medial prefrontal cortex (MPFC) and the anterior cingulate cortex (ACC). These and other results confirm the case for the attribution of content to experienced emotion based on neurophysiological reasoning (see also Coull, 1998; Lewis et al., 2007; Paul et al., 2006; Rauch et al., 1999). The concern here is with an interaction of emotional and cognitive functions to produce content attributions appropriate to the situation in which the person and his or her behaviour are located. Barrett and her colleagues draw attention also to the operation of the ventrolateral prefrontal cortex (VLPFC) in generating the selection and inhibition of responses, and working memory; these are in turn implicated in the retrieval and integration of cognitive elements of memory processing such as the interpretation and evaluation of conceptual knowledge.

Specifically with respect to arousal and dominance, we can make some general observations on the likely brain areas and physiological functions associated with the ascription of appropriate content to core affect. Neuroscientists' frequent definition of arousal in terms of anxiety, fear, and anger chimes with Mehrabian's (1980) understanding of the term. Environments that signal or encourage competitiveness and uncertainty as to the outcomes of behaviour are most likely to engender arousal. Sex differences in arousal seeking tendency have evolutionary support and, expressed in terms of aggression vs. inhibition and flight vs. fight, manifest well-established sex differences in behaviour (Campbell, 2007; Taylor et al., 2000). Hormones such as oxytocin and testosterone play a role in the regulation of fear and aggression and nurturance and affiliation. Among the neurotransmitters, serotonin is associated not (as in popular imagination) with pleasure but with the reduction of anxiety. Reduced functioning of CNS serotonin underlies impaired impulse control and is further implicated in violence, impatience, and the assumption of risks of punishment or injury (Higley et al., 1996). The administration of serotonin, in contrast, as in SSRI medication, modulates antisocial tendencies (Knutson et al., 1998). These are behaviours closely connected with feelings of arousal and, although they are too extreme to find a place in most consumption activities and research, they are indicative of a role for arousal at all points along the consumer continuum. Arousal and impulsivity are clearly seen in everyday consumer behaviours such as innovativeness, novelty-seeking and unplanned purchasing; compulsiveness is at the root of unregulated consumption and addiction (Foxall, 2010b). Finally, while dopamine plays a general role in the anticipation of rewarded behaviour, it has a particular affinity with behaviour that eventuates in (reported) arousal. Dopamine is associated with feelings of excitement, engagement and the involved pursuit of primary reinforcers; it is responsible for the energization of higher areas of the motor cortex that is essential to SEEKING (Panksepp, 1998, p. 144).

The biochemical bases of behavioural responses link also to the arousal seeking tendencies evoked by environments that provide varying information rates (Mehrabian and Russell, 1974), i.e. the rate at which stimuli impinge upon the individual to create excitatory or inhibitory reactions. This is the basis of feelings of arousal, some of which reflect environmental dynamism which in turn can and often does provide the individual with performance feedback on the behaviour that he or she is enacting (Foxall, 2005).

The role of dopamine in pleasure and arousal is subtle. Berridge and Robinson (1998, 2003) do not confine their analysis of reward to learning processes in which the consequences of action are associated with the stimulus context in which behaviour has taken place. Rather, they call attention to both a hedonic or affective element (that denotes 'liking' or pleasure), and a motivational element (reflecting 'wanting' or incentive salience). 'Liking' is associated with opioid transmission on to GABAergic neurons in the nucleus accumbens (Winkielman et al., 2005). 'Wanting' or incentive salience, the motivational element in reward, is a separate process, that is more likely associated with dopamine release and retention. Hence, in contradistinction to some early views, dopamine is not an instigator of pleasure: it is in fact neither necessary nor sufficient for 'liking'. Manipulation of the dopamine system does, however, change motivated behaviour by increasing instrumental responses and the consumption of rewards; incentive salience is a motivational rather than an affective component of reward that transforms neutral stimuli into compelling incentives (see also Berridge, 2004; Robinson and Berridge, 2003).

In line with Berridge's (2000) argument that liking and wanting should be separated, Toronchuk and Ellis (2010) contrast PLEASURE which is relevant to consummatory behaviours and associated with opioid and GABA release, and Panskepp's (1998) SEEKING which is associated with dopamine release and which marks appetitive responses. This dichotomy is well-accommodated to the distinction drawn here since the wanting which is inherent in SEEKING is indicated by arousal rather than pleasure. Toronchuk and Ellis also note that social dominance is related to hedonic experience (pleasure-displeasure), which leads to the final dimension of emotion considered central by Mehrabian and Russell (1974).

Dominance

The term 'dominance' is frequently employed in social psychology to refer to interpersonal control, a behaviour known to be context-specific (Sulloway, 2007). The dominance to which Mehrabian and Russell (1974) drew attention is an emotional response to both physical and social environments and differs with the extent to which the consumer setting permits autonomy or induces conformity. This latter definition includes but is broader than the former. Barrett et al. (2007) include dominance in their model of emotion, associating it with the autonomy that is an American value and contrasting it with the submissiveness and harmoniousness that are often thought to be more highly valued in eastern societies such as Japan (p. 380). At the social psychological level, dominance undoubtedly is connected with some of the traits we have considered to constitute arousal. Dopamine and opioids are associated with sociability, prosocial behaviour, and affiliation; the neuropeptide oxytocin increases feelings of trust. Moreover, the reward-centered dopamine promotes social preferences; but the attractiveness of psychostimulants like cocaine increases with dopamine deficit (Panksepp, 2007, p. 156). Hence, submissiveness rather than dominance is associated with cocaine consumption. Both the neurotransmitter serotonin and the hormone testosterone are associated with high social status and feelings of dominance; challenges to status and increased stress are associated with higher cortisol levels (Buss, 2004, 2005; Cummins, 2005; Foxall, 2007b). The relationship between dominance and the BPM resides in a tendency of consumers to report high levels of this emotional response in more open settings, those that provide a wider range of behavioural outcomes, and which are usually under the control of the consumer herself rather than another agent such as a marketer or government department.

In a study that addressed the neurophysiology basis of pleasure, arousal and dominance in the context of consumer behaviour, Morris et al. (2008) sought to relate brain regions to PAD in the context of exposure to a TV commercial (see also Bernat et al., 2006). Their study revealed bilateral activations in the inferior frontal gyri and middle temporal gyri for pleasure, activations on the right superior temporal gyrus for arousal. No significant differences were found for dominance which the authors argue is unsurprising since dominance accounts for much less variance in emotional responses than pleasure or arousal 'and is often not a factor in vicarious experiences such as watching a television commercial' (Morris et al., p. 795). However, after positively reviewing the evidence for a model of emotionality that includes dominance as well as pleasure and arousal, Demaree et al. (2005) propose that 'the lateralization of emotional "dominance" be explored with the hypothesis that relative left- and right-frontal activation would be associated with feelings of dominance and submissiveness, respectively' (p. 3). Figure 13.5 summarizes the relationships among core emotions, their putative neurophysiological bases, and the patterns of contingency with which they are associated as defined by the BPM.

13.4.4   Linking Emotion and Contingency

The importance of emotion–contingency links

That emotion is consistently related to contingencies of reinforcement and punishment is a recurring theme in modern theories including Damasio's (1994) somatic marker hypothesis, Ledoux's (1996, 2000) emotional brain perspective, and Rolls's (1999) neurophysiological approach. But it is the last of these that makes the relationship most explicit and systematic. Rolls (1999) integrates classical (or respondent) and operant conditioning, and links the acquisition of behaviour and the generation of emotion to genetic factors, by proposing that emotions are states elicited by the reinforcing stimuli that condition instrumental behaviour. Genes specify not individual behaviours but the goals that will serve as reinforcers, i.e. influence the performance of operant responses, those whose rate of repetition is influenced by their consequences. The process is even more flexible than this, however, since an operant is not a single response but a class of behaviours that lead to and are selected and maintained by a common set of reinforcers or goals. This proposition is derived from a broader biological purview of emotionality and behaviour based on evolutionary considerations. The adaptive propensity of genes stems not from their leading to the elicitation of fixed action patterns but from the specification of goals (related to the enhancement of survival and fitness) towards which many behaviours will be directed and in the process selected (Rolls, 2005). Genes do not determine particular behaviours but something rather more general: the goals or consequences that stem from a number of functionally (though not topographically) equivalent responses each of which is a flexible adaptation to an appropriate set of environmental contingencies of reinforcement and punishment. Gene-specified primary reinforcers can in this process become arbitrarily related to a wide range of secondary reinforcers, producing patterns of contingency that are the proximal determinants of which operant responses are selected in particular circumstances. The ultimate agent of selection is biological, however: the emotional experience evoked by the contingencies of reinforcement and punishment. The relatively small number of specifications required at the genetic level by Rolls's (2005) theory is balanced in the lifetime of an organism by the learning of secondary reinforcers; instead of encoding an incalculable number of stimulus-response associations, the genes perform the restricted function of encoding relationships between goals and the variety of means by which they may be achieved. What is crucial is that the genes specify goals (behaviour-contingent consequences) which elicit particular emotions. It is the relationship between these emotions and the selection of behaviour that is of primary interest to us here. Hence, the conclusion that '. . . the heritability of behaviour is best understood as the heritability of reinforcers' and, therefore, of the emotions they elicit; the outcome is an adaptive construal of emotion which has implications for the genetic specification of synaptic structure and function (Rolls, 2005, p. 61). It is necessary to note here for later reference, the sort of mechanism that Rolls proposes for this example of genetic specification. It requires that synapses be specified across the nervous system from the point of sensory input to whatever region(s) of the brain at which the reinforcing or punishing value of the reinforcing stimulus (goal) is explicitly represented (ibid.). He proposes neural activity in the amygdala and orbitofrontal cortex (OFC) as defining the site(s) where such explicit representation may be located, and exemplifies the process in terms of sweet taste receptors on the tongue being connected to neurons that specify food reward, the actions of which are modulated by hunger signals (Rolls, 2005, p. 61, 2006).

Rolls (1995, 2005) proposes that increases in intensity of positive reinforcement are associated with increases in pleasure leading on to elation and ecstasy while the increasing intensity of aversive stimuli (the reception of which punish behaviour) is associated with increasing apprehension leading on to fear and terror. When, as in the processes of behavioural extinction and time out, respectively, a reinforcer is omitted or terminated, the emotional outcome is sadness and frustration leading on to anger and grief and ultimately rage. However, if an aversive consequence is omitted or terminated, as in the processes of avoidance and escape, respectively, the emotion felt is increasing relief. For all its logical insight, however, Roll's classification of emotions in relation to contingencies of reinforcement appears to reflect more the a priori reasoning of a generally informed account of emotion and behaviour rather than a framework based on empirical research specifically tailored to the study of economic behaviour with its dual sources of reinforcement and its sensitivity to the scope of consumer behaviour settings.

PAD and consumer behaviour

Systematic relationships between the emotional variables identified by Mehrabian and Russell (1974) and consumer behaviour emerge from a number of studies. Pleasure, arousal and dominance mediate more overt consumer behaviour such as desire to affiliate with others in the setting, desire to stay in or escape from the setting, and willingness to spend money and consume (Donovan and Rossiter, 1982; Donovan et al., 1994; Foxall, 1997d; Foxall and Yani-de-Soriano, 2005; Gilboa and Rafaeli, 2003; Groeppel-Klein, 2005; Mehrabian, 1979; Mehrabian and Riccioni, 1986; Mehrabian and de Wetter, 1987; Mehrabian and Russell, 1975; Russell and Mehrabian, 1976, 1978; Tai and Fung, 1997; Van Kenhove and Desrumaux, 1997). Donovan and Rossiter (1982) used the Mehrabian-Russell (1974) model in retail settings, focusing on store atmosphere, that is, within-store variables that influence shopping behaviour (Kotler, 1973–74). They report pleasure to be a very powerful determinant of approach-avoidance behaviours within the retail environment, including the tendency of the consumer to spend beyond his or her original expectations. Arousal similarly increased time spent on in-store browsing and exploring and willingness to interact with sales personnel. Bright lighting and upbeat music were noted as stimuli that induce arousal. Dominance, however, exerted little influence on consumer behaviour, to the extent that a second study (Donovan et al., 1994) incorporated only the pleasure and arousal of shoppers during the shopping experience. The results confirmed that pleasure predicted consumer behaviour such as extra time spent in the store and overspending; arousal did not predict overspending, failing to support the earlier research, but arousal predicted underspending in unpleasant store environments, something not revealed by the earlier study. These and other studies have focused mainly on understanding the role of pleasure and arousal in shaping consumer choice, while the role of dominance has been ignored or controlled (Biggers, 1981; Biggers and Pryor, 1982; Biggers and Rankins, 1983; Groeppel-Klein, 2005; Yani-de-Soriano and Foxall, 2006).

Moreover, in research involving the Behavioural Perspective Model dominance has proved to discriminate very effectively between open/closed CBSs. The identification of differences in dominance among consumer settings requires a model capable of generating consumer situations that discriminate adequately between varying levels of situational inducement (Foxall, 1990). Several investigations employing the BPM reveal that the influence of dominance on approach-avoidance behaviour is more clearly apparent from an array of consumer situations that distinguish open from closed CBSs than by the use of haphazardly developed consumer situations (Foxall 1997d, 2005). Discriminant analyses showed the significantly high power of the dominance dimension in discriminating between open/closed settings (Foxall and Greenley, 1999, 2000). Similar results were obtained in subsequent studies in Venezuela (Foxall and Yani-de-Soriano, 2005).

The BPM basis of emotion–contingency links

The wording of the items that Mehrabian and Russell (1974) employ in their scales to measure pleasure, arousal and dominance, plus the neurobiological considerations described above, suggest that these emotions can each be associated with particular structural variables of the BPM (Seva et al., 2010). By emphasizing the satisfaction and pleasure consumers are likely to receive from certain purchase and consumption environments, plus the usefulness of this emotion in indicating the presence of positively reinforcing behavioural outcomes that will eventuate in enhanced survival potential and biological fitness, pleasure is redolent of utilitarian reinforcement. Pleasure, therefore, should be expected to be a disproportionately encountered response to consumer situations that result in utilitarian (functional) consequences. This does not mean that it will be exclusively the emotional response reported for such consumer situations: each consumer situation is defined in terms of relative contributions from utilitarian and informational reinforcement and CBS-scope. But situations that are defined as relatively high in utilitarian reinforcement should produce relatively high pleasure reactions.

Inasmuch as it is defined primarily in terms of performance feedback, informational reinforcement can be expected to co-occur with reactions of arousal, which is often associated with the identification of discrepancies between current and indicated performance. To illustrate, road markings that indicate one's excess speed, for instance, are presumably intended to embody such feedback and to engender perceptual responses that bring drivers' behaviour into line with socially accepted norms. Mehrabian and Russell (1974) define a measure of the information rate of environments, scores on which correlate significantly with arousal scores; this idea of information rate provides an indication of the variation from norms present in environmental stimuli such as noise, crowdedness, temperature, lighting, and social interaction rates and thus includes the criteria of informational reinforcement without being coterminous with it. The expectation, therefore, is that consumer situations that are relatively high in informational reinforcement will be those for which reports of arousal are also disproportionately high.

Open CBSs are by definition those in which the consumer has relatively large numbers of behavioural options (sources of reinforcement) and hence those in which he or she can be predicted to experience a higher degree of dominance than in closed settings in which behavioural choices are severely limited perhaps to a single option. In the former, the consumer is more likely to be a determinant of the range of options available (through choice of store, time of shopping, lack of external compulsion) whereas in the latter agents other than the consumer are likely to arrange

BEHAVIOUR SETTING SCOPE

Closed ◄————► Open

	CC2	*CC1*
ACCOMPLISHMENT	PLEASURE AROUSAL dominance	PLEASURE AROUSAL DOMINANCE
	CC4	*CC3*
HEDONISM	PLEASURE arousal dominance	PLEASURE arousal DOMINANCE
	CC6	*CC5*
ACCUMULATION	pleasure AROUSAL dominance	pleasure AROUSAL DOMINANCE
	CC8	*CC7*
MAINTENANCE	pleasure arousal dominance	pleasure arousal DOMINANCE

Note: Studies show that (i) pleasure scores for contingency categories (CCs) 1, 2, 3 and 4 each exceed those of CCs 5, 6, 7 and 8; (ii) arousal scores for CCs 1, 2, 5 and 6 each exceed those of CCs 3, 4, 7 and 8; (iii) dominance scores for CCs 1, 3, 5 and 7 each exceed those for CCs 2, 4, 6 and 8. Moreover, (iv) approach-avoidance (aminusa) scores for CCs 1, 2, 3 and 4 each exceed those for CCs 5, 6, 7 and 8; and (v) approach-avoidance (aminusa) scores for CCs 1 and 3 each exceed those for CCs 2, 4, 5, 6, 7 and 8. (For explication, see text and Foxall et al., 2010).

Figure 13.5   Contingencies and emotions: research hypotheses and summary of findings

these matters. It is probable, therefore, that consumer situations which are relatively open will engender higher feelings of dominance than those which are relatively closed.

Eight studies have shown strong consistency of results in showing that pleasure scores are higher for consumer situations marked by higher utilitarian reinforcement; arousal scores, for consumer situations marked by higher informational reinforcement; and dominance scores, for situations marked by greater openness (Foxall, 1997a, 1997b; Foxall and Yani-de-Soriano, 2005; Yani-de-Soriano et al., in press). The hypothesized patterns of emotional reaction to consumer situations defined in terms of the structural variables of the BPM shown in Figure 13.5 are also those identified by these empirical studies (Foxall et al., 2010).

Table 13.1 *Means and standard deviations for the independent and*
dependent variables by contingency category (CC)
(N = 7479)

CC	Pleasure	Arousal	Dominance	Approach	Avoidance	Aminusa
1	47.39	41.49	39.86	14.48	4.82	9.49
	(5.73)	(12.48)	(7.52)	(5.29)	(4.39)	(7.39)
2	43.30	40.20	29.40	13.14	5.80	7.22
	(7.02)	(6.74)	(8.91)	(5.42)	(5.03)	(8.26)
3	44.04	31.69	36.34	11.93	5.98	5.96
	(7.67)	(8.14)	(7.38)	(3.64)	(4.82)	(7.39)
4	34.51	26.78	25.73	5.88	9.86	−3.88
	(10.72)	(7.30)	(7.39)	(3.73)	(5.57)	(8.01)
5	37.05	37.93	36.37	7.08	8.60	−1.50
	(98.67)	(6.69)	(7.23)	(3.79)	(5.33)	(7.54)
6	33.82	35.67	29.44	6.83	8.92	−2.18
	(8.38)	(8.08)	(6.95)	(3.78)	(5.42)	(8.70)
7	32.53	27.56	35.41	7.53	8.15	−.47
	(7.85)	(6.97)	(7.06)	(3.77)	(5.14)	(7.66)
8	25.31	27.14	24.77	6.04	10.16	−4.13
	(8.78)	(6.81)	(7.45)	(3.67)	(5.40)	(7.85)

Note: The results for multiple regression analysis are shown in Table 13.3. Main effects
are apparent for all three affective variables for each of the dependent variables, approach,
avoidance and aminusa.

13.4.5 The Relationship between Emotions and Consumer Behaviour

Eight studies – five in England (Foxall, 1997c, 1997d), two in Venezuela
(Soriano et al., 2002; Foxall and Yani-de-Soriano, 2005), one in Wales
(Foxall and Yani-de-Soriano, 2011) – tested the emotion–contingency
relationship; here we review the merged findings. The chapter does not
offer new data, therefore, but employs further statistical analyses in order
to review the evidence for the emotion-contingency link. Table 13.1 shows
the means, standard deviations and Pearson correlations for the affective
and behavioural variables. As expected, approach and avoidance are negatively related to each other; while approach is positively and significantly
associated with all three emotional variables, avoidance is negatively
related to these variables. All the affective variables were positively and
significantly correlated with the composite behavioural measure 'aminusa'
(approach minus avoidance). All correlations between the affective and
behavioural variables were in the 0.3 to 0.9 range which is what was
expected in this type of research (Sirkin, 1999).

Table 13.2   Means, standard deviations and correlation coefficients for the affective and behavioural variables (N = 7479)

Variable	Mean	SD	1	2	3	4	5	6
1. Pleasure	37.24	10.66		.44	.44	.50	−.38	.50
2. Arousal	33.56	9.89			.29	.37	−.25	.35
3. Dominance	32.16	9.05				.26	−.24	.29
4. Approach	9.12	5.30					−.52	.81
5. Avoidance	7.79	5.48						−.88
6. Aminusa	1.32	9.34						

Note: All correlations are significant at p < .01, two-tailed.

Since Mehrabian and Russell claim that pleasure, arousal and dominance are orthogonal variables, the inter-correlations between pleasure and arousal, and pleasure and dominance were taken into consideration in the analysis of the data. Moderate correlations (0.5) exist among pleasure, arousal, and dominance, indicating a level I of collinearity. However, this level of collinearity is not unacceptable on the basis of the conventional cut-off values of tolerance (T) .01 and Variance Inflation Factor (VIF) < 10 (Hair et al., 1998; Mason and Perreault, 1991). Table 13.2 shows that no tolerance value falls below 0.67, nor did VIF exceed 1.49. This level of collinearity is typical of behavioural studies in marketing research, especially when the predictors are multi-item composite scales (Mason and Perreault, 1991), which indicates that the inter-relations found are not sufficiently high to breach Mehrabian and Russell's assumptions of orthogonality of the three affective variables. Table 13.2 also shows that collectively, pleasure arousal and dominance explain 28% of the variance in approach, 16% in avoidance, and 28% in 'aminusa'. Pleasure has the greatest influence on the prediction of the dependent variables, followed by arousal and dominance.

Patterns of affect and behaviour by contingency category

Table 13.3 presents the means and standard deviations of the affective and behavioural measures for each of the eight contingency categories. One-way ANOVA was employed to assess the assumption that the means of pleasure, arousal, dominance, approach, avoidance and aminusa would differ for each of the eight contingency categories (CCs) as predicted by the BPM. Mean scores for pleasure, arousal, dominance, approach, avoidance and aminusa for each of the eight BPM's contingency categories (CCs) differ significantly (p < .01). Results of post-hoc tests to test the pleasure, arousal, dominance and approach-avoidance hypotheses are shown in Table 13.4.

Table 13.3 *Multiple regression analysis for variables predicting approach, avoidance and approach-avoidance (N = 7479)*

Model	F (3,7476)	Adjusted R Square	β	t-value	Tolerance	VIF
Approach =	961.70***	0.28				
Pleasure +			0.41	34.61***	0.71	1.42
Arousal +			0.19	16.83***	0.80	1.26
Dominance			0.03	2.78**	0.80	1.26
Avoidance =	473.19***	0.16				
Pleasure +			−0.30	−23.90***	0.71	1.42
Arousal +			−0.10	−8.11***	0.80	1.26
Dominance			−0.08	−7.10***	0.80	1.26
Approach- Avoidance =	967.32***	0.28				
Pleasure +			0.41	34.70***	0.67	1.42
Arousal +			0.16	14.14***	0.76	1.26
Dominance			0.07	6.37***	0.78	1.26

Note: ** $p < .01$; *** $p < .001$.

Pleasure The 'pleasure hypothesis', which states that pleasure mean scores for contingency categories (CCs) 1, 2, 3 and 4 will each exceed those of CCs 5, 6, 7 and 8, is supported: each of the pleasure means for CCs 1, 2, 3 and 4 is greater than those of CCs 5, 6, 7 and 8, except for CC4 = CC6 and < CC5.

Arousal The 'arousal hypothesis', which states that the arousal mean scores for CCs 1, 2, 5 and 6 will each exceed those of CCs 3, 4, 7 and 8, is supported: each of the arousal means for CC1, 2, 5 and 6 is greater than those for CCs 3, 4, 7 and 8.

Dominance The 'dominance hypothesis', which states that dominance mean scores for CCs 1, 3, 5 and 7 will each exceed those of CCs 2, 4, 6 and 8, is also supported: each of the dominance means for CCs 1, 3, 5 and 7 is greater than each of those for CCs 2, 4, 6 and 8.

Approach-Avoidance The 'approach-avoidance hypothesis', which states that approach-avoidance mean scores for CCs 1, 2, 3 and 4 will each exceed those of CCs 5, 6, 7 and 8 is supported: each of the approach-avoidance means for CCs 1, 2, 3 and 4 is greater than those for CCs 5, 6, 7 and 8, except for CC4 = 8 and < 5, 6, 7.

Table 13.4   Results of ANOVA's and Tukey's HSD tests for Pleasure, Arousal, Dominance and Approach-Avoidance by Contingency Category (CC)

CC	1	2	3	4	5	6	7	8
Pleasure Hypothesis: 1, 2, 3, 4 > 5, 6, 7, 8; $F_{(7,7472)} = 731.04$ p =.000								
1					10.3	13.6	14.9	22.1
2					6.2	9.5	10.8	18.0
3					7.0	10.2	11.5	18.7
4					−2.5	n.s	2.0	9.2
Arousal Hypothesis: 1, 2, 5, 6 > 3, 4, 7, 8; $F_{(7,7472)} = 522.90$ p =.000								
1		9.8	14.7				13.9	14.4
2		8.5	13.4				12.6	13.1
5		6.2	11.1				10.4	10.8
6		4.0	8.9				8.1	8.5
Dominance Hypothesis: 1, 3, 5, 7 > 2, 4, 6, 8; $F_{(7,7472)} = 524.39$ p =.000								
1	10.5			14.1		10.4		15.1
3	6.9			10.6		6.9		11.6
5	7.0			10.6		6.9		11.6
7	6.0			9.7		6.0		10.7
Approach-Avoidance Hypothesis: 1, 2, 3, 4 > 5, 6, 7, 8; $F_{(7,7472)} = 439.38$ p =.000								
1					11.0	11.7	10.0	13.6
2					8.7	9.4	7.7	11.3
3					7.5	8.1	6.4	10.1
4					−2.4	−1.7	−3.4	n.s
Approach-Avoidance in Open Settings: 1, 3 > 2, 4, 5, 6, 7, 8; $F_{(7,7472)} = 439.38$ p =.000								
1		2.3		13.4	11.0	11.7	10.0	13.6
3		−1.3		9.8	7.5	8.1	6.4	10.1

Approach-Avoidance and setting scope   The 'approach-avoidance for open settings hypothesis' which states that approach-avoidance mean scores for CCs 1 and 3 will each exceed those of CCs 2, 4, 5, 6, 7, and 8 is also supported: each of the approach-avoidance means for CCs 1 and 3 is greater than those for CCs 2, 4, 5, 6, 7, 8, except for CC3 < 2.

Interaction effects

On the basis of the general pattern of consumers' verbal/affective responses revealed by the eight studies, we now consider the nature of the interactions among the three dimensions, pleasure, arousal and dominance, and their effect on consumer behaviour. Theoretical considerations (Foxall, 1990/2004; Yani-de-Soriano et al., in press) suggest that pleasure would have a stronger effect on behaviour than arousal, and that high arousal would have a stronger effect on behaviour than a combination of low pleasure and low arousal. These expectations are in also in line with the literature on PAD (Biggers, 1981; Biggers and Pryor, 1982; Biggers and Rankis, 1983; Mehrabian and Russell, 1974). Four general propositions follow from this reasoning.

The first is that approach in situations marked by high levels of utilitarian reinforcement (Accomplishment and Hedonism) will be higher when informational reinforcement is also high (Accomplishment) than when it is low (Hedonism). Translating this into the terminology of the PAD approach yields the specific expectation (E1) that *approach will be higher when both pleasure and arousal are high than when pleasure is high but arousal is low*. The second proposition is that approach in situations marked by low utilitarian reinforcement (Accumulation and Maintenance) will be higher when informational reinforcement is high (Accumulation) rather than low (Maintenance). This leads to the expectation (E2) that *approach will be higher when arousal is high but pleasure is low than when both are low*. In the intermediate cases (Hedonism and Accumulation), it is proposed that approach will be higher in situations marked by high levels of utilitarian reinforcement but low levels of informational reinforcement (Hedonism) than in those marked by high levels of informational reinforcement but low levels of utilitarian reinforcement (Accumulation). This suggests the specific expectation (E3) that *approach will be higher when pleasure is high but arousal is low than when arousal is high but pleasure is low*. The final proposition entails that CBS-scope will have an effect on the way in which utilitarian reinforcement and informational reinforcement influence approach; and this leads to several expectations: in general (E4) that *dominance will have an effect on the way in which pleasure and arousal determine approach*; and more specifically that (E4a) *approach will be higher when both pleasure and dominance are high than when pleasure is high but dominance is low*, (E4b) *approach will be higher when dominance is high but pleasure is low than when both are low*; (E4c) *approach will be higher when both arousal and dominance are high than when arousal is high but dominance is low*; and (E4d) *approach will be higher when dominance is high but arousal is low than when both are low*.

The results show significant main effects for pleasure, arousal and dominance and enable us to interpret two- and three-way interactions among these affective variables, thus allowing us to confirm the presence of synergistic relations amongst the BPM structural dimensions. Approach-Avoidance mean scores for the High, Moderate and Low Pleasure

Table 13.5   Pleasure × Arousal interaction: cell means for Approach-Avoidance

	Arousal		
	Low	Moderate	High
High pleasure	Group 3	Group 2	Group 1
	x = 1.77	x = 4.48	x = 7.86
	s = 8.56	S = 8.05	s = 7.96
	n = 581	n = 1375	n = 1726
Moderate pleasure	Group 6	Group 5	Group 4
	x = −2.61	x = −1.20	x = −.73
	S = 7.54	s = 7.42	s = 8.48
	n = 684	n = 1199	n = 543
Low pleasure	Group 9	Group 8	Group 7
	x = −6.32	x = −4.24	x = −2.67
	S = 7.72	s = 9.81	s = 7.89
	n = 819	n = 403	n = 150

conditions differed significantly: $F(2, 7453) = 422.91$, p < .001; $F(2, 7453) = 71.99$, p < .001; $F(2, 7453) = 36.58$, p < .001, respectively.

Approach-Avoidance mean scores for the interaction of Pleasure and Arousal; Pleasure and Dominance, and Arousal and Dominance differed significantly: $F(4, 7453) = 15.12$, p < .001; $F(4, 7453) = 2.98$; p < .05; and $F(4, 7453) = 2.69$, p < .05, respectively. Finally, Approach-Avoidance mean scores for the interaction of Pleasure, Arousal and Dominance differed significantly: $F(8, 7453) = 4.71$; p < .001. In summary, in addition to the three significant main effects, we found three significant double interactions, pleasure × arousal, pleasure × dominance, and arousal × dominance. A significant triple interaction pleasure × arousal × dominance is also apparent. Partial eta squared for the various measures ranged from 0.01 to 0.10, representing small to medium sizes (Cohen, 1988). In order to test the research hypotheses, the ANOVA results of the interactions were followed by Tukey's HSD, and are explained subsequently.

Two-way interaction between pleasure and arousal   Tables 13.5 and 13.6 indicate that approach is higher when pleasure is high and arousal is also high or moderate than when it is low (group 1 > 3 and group 2 > 3, p = .000); hence, E1 is confirmed. When pleasure is moderate, higher levels of arousal dampen avoidance (4 > 6, p = .000). When pleasure is low, higher levels of arousal also dampen avoidance and (7 > 9, p = .000). Therefore, E2 is also supported. The results indicate, moreover, that approach is

Table 13.6   Significant differences between pleasure × arousal groups (Tukey HSD)

Group	Mean	1	2	3	4	5	6	7	8	9
1	7.86									
2	4.48	*								
3	1.77	*	*							
4	−.73	*	*	*						
5	−1.20	*	*	*						
6	−2.61	*	*	*	*					
7	−2.67	*	*	*	*					
8	−4.34	*	*	*	*	*	*			
9	−6.32	*	*	*	*	*	*		*	*

Note: * p < .05.

Table 13.7   Pleasure × dominance interaction: cell means for Approach-Avoidance

	Dominance		
	Low	Moderate	High
High Pleasure	Group 3 x = 4.40 s = 9.41 n = 826	Group 2 x = 5.31 s = 8.06 n = 1472	Group 1 x = 6.72 s = 7.99 n = 1384
Moderate Pleasure	Group 6 x = −2.50 S = 8.16 n = 728	Group 5 x = −1.39 s = 7.34 n = 1320	Group 4 x = .10 s = 7.95 n = 378
Low Pleasure	Group 9 x = −6.29 s = 8.77 n = 847	Group 8 x = −3.91 s = 7.70 n = 409	Group 7 x = −3.08 s = 8.15 n = 116

higher when pleasure is high but arousal is low than when arousal is high but pleasure is low (3 > 7, p = .000). Furthermore, approach is also higher when pleasure is high but arousal is low than when pleasure is high but arousal is moderate (group 3 > 8, p = .000); thus E3 is supported.

Two-way interaction between pleasure and dominance   Tables 13.7 and 13.8 indicate that approach is higher when pleasure is high and dominance

Table 13.8   Significant differences between pleasure × dominance groups (Tukey HSD)

Group	Mean	1	2	3	4	5	6	7	8	9
1	6.72									
2	5.31	*								
3	4.40	*								
4	.10	*	*	*						
5	−1.39	*	*	*	*					
6	−2.50	*	*	*	*					
7	−3.08	*	*	*	*					
8	−3.91	*	*	*	*		*			
9	−6.29	*	*	*	*		*	*	*	*

Note: * p < .05.

is also high than when it is low (1 > 3, p = .000); as a result, E4a is confirmed. When pleasure is moderate, higher levels of dominance dampen avoidance (4 > 5, 6 and 7 > 9, p = .000). When pleasure is low, higher levels of dominance also dampen avoidance (7 > 9, p = .000). Therefore, E4b is accepted.

Two-way interaction between arousal and dominance   Tables 13.9 and 13.10 indicate that approach is higher when arousal is high and dominance is also high than when it is low (1 > 3, p = .000); hence, E4c is confirmed. When arousal is moderate, approach is higher when dominance is high than when it is low (4 > 5, 6, p = .000). When arousal is low, higher levels of dominance dampen avoidance (7 > 9, p = .000). Therefore, E4d is upheld.

Three-way interaction effects among pleasure, arousal and dominance   Tables 13.11 and 13.12 show the following results for H4: (a) in high-pleasure-high-arousal environments, dominance has shown no significant effect on behaviour (group 1 = 2, 3); (b) in low-pleasure-low arousal environments, dominance has shown no significant effect on behaviour (group 25 = 26, 27); (c) in high-pleasure-moderate-arousal environments, dominance has shown no significant effect on behaviour (group 4 = 5, 6); and in high-pleasure-low-arousal environments, approach is higher when dominance is high or moderate than when it is low (group 7, 8 > 9, p = .000); and low dominance leads to avoidance behaviour; (d) when pleasure is moderate, approach is higher when dominance is high than when it is low, at any given levels of arousal (10, 13, 16 > 18, p = .000). In low

Table 13.9 *Arousal × Dominance interaction: cell means for Approach-Avoidance*

	Dominance		
	Low	Moderate	High
High Arousal	Group 3 x = 4.30 s = 9.80 n = 560	Group 2 x = 4.24 s = 8.98 n = 882	Group 1 x = 6.77 s = 8.45 n = 977
Moderate Arousal	Group 6 x = −1.02 S = 9.89 n = 849	Group 5 x = 1.10 s = 7.90 n = 1525	Group 4 x = 3.67 s = 8.29 n = 603
Low Arousal	Group 9 x = −5.10 s = 8.21 n = 992	Group 8 x = −1.29 s = 8.41 n = 794	Group 7 x = .51 s = 8.04 n = 298

Table 13.10 *Significant differences between arousal × dominance groups (Tukey HSD)*

Group	Mean	1	3	2	4	5	7	6	8	9
1	6.77									
3	4.30	*								
2	4.24	*	*							
4	3.67	*	*							
5	1.10	*	*	*	*					
7	.51	*	*	*	*					
6	−1.02	*	*	*	*	*				
8	−1.29	*	*	*	*	*				
9	−5.10	*	*	*	*	*	*	*	*	

Note: * p < .05.

pleasure-high or moderate arousal, higher dominance dampens avoidance (19 > 24, p = .000). Therefore, H4 is accepted.

The results show significant main effects for all the independent variables and significant interactions between pleasure and arousal, pleasure and dominance, arousal and dominance, and among pleasure, arousal and dominance. Because of the very large size of the sample in this study

Table 13.11   Pleasure × Arousal × Dominance interaction: cell means for Approach-Avoidance

| | Dominance | | |
	Low	Moderate	High
High Pleasure – High Arousal	Group 3 x =8.00 s = 8.40 n = 350	Group 2 x = 7.64 s = 7.76 n = 549	Group 1 x = 7.94 s = 7.90 n = 827
High Pleasure – Moderate Arousal	Group 6 x = 3.66 s = 8.90 n = 295	Group 5 x = 4.31 s = 7.65 n = 665	Group 4 x = 5.34 s = 7.98 n = 415
High Pleasure – Low Arousal	Group 9 x = −1.39 s = 8.92 n = 181	Group 8 x = 2.96 s = 8.50 n = 258	Group 7 x = 3.63 s = 7.00 n = 142
Moderate Pleasure – High Arousal	Group 12 x = −.21 s = 8.88 n = 136	Group 11 x = −1.33 s = 8.18 n = 281	Group 10 x = .06 s = 8.64 n = 126
Moderate Pleasure – Moderate Arousal	Group 15 x = −1.90 s = 8.02 n = 310	Group 14 x = −1.16 s = 7.05 n = 731	Group 13 x = −.01 s = 7.74 n = 158
Moderate Pleasure – Low Arousal	Group 18 x = −4.26 s = 7.59 n = 282	Group 17 x = −1.99 s = 7.20 n = 308	Group 16 x = .32 s = 7.37 n = 94
Low Pleasure – High Arousal	Group 21 x = −4.95 s = 7.86 n = 74	Group 20 x = −1.46 s = 6.95 n = 52	Group 19 x = 1.71 s = 7.74 n = 24
Low Pleasure – Moderate Arousal	Group 24 x = −5.56 s = −10.74 n = 244	Group 23 x = −2.70 s = 7.68 n = 129	Group 22 x = −.13 s = 8.03 n = 30
Low Pleasure – Low Arousal	Group 27 x = −6.82 s = 7.79 n = 529	Group 26 x = −5.15 s = 7.66 n = 228	Group 25 x = −6.35 s = 6.91 n = 62

Table 13.12 Significant differences amongst pleasure × arousal × dominance groups (Tukey HSD)

Group	Mean	3	1	2	4	5	6	7	8	19	16	10	13	22	12	14	11	9	20	15	17	23	18	21	26	24	25	27
3	8.00																											
1	7.94																											
2	7.64																											
4	5.34	*																										
5	4.31	*	*																									
6	3.66	*	*	*																								
7	3.63	*	*	*																								
8	2.96	*	*	*	*																							
19	1.71	*	*	*																								
16	.32	*	*	*	*	*																						
10	.06	*	*	*	*	*																						
13	-.01	*	*	*	*	*	*																					
22	-.13	*	*	*	*	*	*	*																				
12	-.21	*	*	*	*	*	*	*	*																			
14	-1.16	*	*	*	*	*	*	*	*																			
11	-1.33	*	*	*	*	*	*	*	*																			
9	-1.39	*	*	*	*	*	*	*	*																			
20	-1.46	*	*	*	*	*	*	*	*																			
15	-1.90	*	*	*	*	*	*	*	*	*																		
17	-1.99	*	*	*	*	*	*	*	*	*																		
23	-2.70	*	*	*	*	*	*	*	*	*	*	*	*	*	*	*	*	*	*									
18	-4.26	*	*	*	*	*	*	*	*	*	*	*	*	*	*	*	*	*	*									
21	-4.95	*	*	*	*	*	*	*	*	*	*	*	*	*	*	*	*	*	*	*	*	*						
26	-5.15	*	*	*	*	*	*	*	*	*	*	*	*	*	*	*	*	*	*	*	*	*						
24	-5.56	*	*	*	*	*	*	*	*	*	*	*	*	*	*	*	*	*	*	*	*	*						
25	-6.35	*	*	*	*	*	*	*	*	*	*	*	*	*	*	*	*	*	*	*	*	*	*					
27	-6.82	*	*	*	*	*	*	*	*	*	*	*	*	*	*	*	*	*	*	*	*	*	*	*				

Note: * p< .05.

507

(N = 7480), the expected frequencies are in all cases sufficiently large, validating the assumption that frequencies in each of the cells would be normally distributed (Howell, 1997, p. 628).

Two-way interaction effects between pleasure and arousal Analysis of the significant interaction between pleasure and arousal shows that approach is higher when pleasure is high and arousal is high or moderate than when arousal is low. These results are consistent with previous research (Sweeney and Wyber, 2002; Foxall and Greenley, 1998; Dube et al., 1995; Donovan and Rossiter, 1982; Biggers and Pryor, 1982; Mehrabian and Stanton-Mohr, 1985; Russell and Mehrabian, 1976, 1978; Mehrabian and Russell, 1974). These findings provide support for the first proposition. In situations marked by high levels of utilitarian reinforcement, i.e., Accomplishment and Hedonism, approach is higher when informational reinforcement is also high, i.e., Accomplishment, than when it is low, i.e., Hedonism.

Conversely, in low and moderate pleasure environments higher arousal dampens avoidance. The results are consistent with those from Van Kenhove and Desrumaux (1997) who argued that an attempt to dampen arousal in a low-pleasure store environment would create more avoidance behaviour (though in the right direction, this finding was nonsignificant); the results are partially consistent with Russell and Mehrabian's (1978) finding that in low pleasure states approach increased as arousal increased from moderate to high but declined as arousal increased from low to moderate. Conversely, Foxall and Greenley (1998) found that in low-pleasure environments, the moderate and high levels of arousal were associated with greater avoidance than was found in the low arousal condition. Biggers (1981), moreover, revealed that in low-pleasure situations, arousal had no effect on approach means and, similarly, Yani-de-Soriano et al. (in press) found no support for this relationship.

These findings reinforce the second proposition: in situations marked by low utilitarian reinforcement, i.e., Accumulation and Maintenance, approach is higher when informational reinforcement is high, i.e., Accumulation, than when it is low, i.e., Maintenance. Although both Accumulation and Maintenance are characterized by 'relatively low levels of utilitarian reinforcement', this may not mean precisely the same thing in each case. This is hinted at by Foxall (1997c, p. 144) when he argues that Accumulation is a consumer behaviour in which informational reinforcement is ultimately dependent upon utilitarian reinforcement, e.g., air miles lead to air travel and other benefits. By contrast, in Maintenance the relatively low levels of both utilitarian reinforcement and informational reinforcement are more independent of one another and both are lower than for other consumer behaviours. In line with this, the results show that avoidance is significantly lower when pleasure is moderate and arousal is high than when both pleasure and arousal are low. These results suggest an improvement in this kind of environment, which is not inherently *un*pleasant, but is not pleasant either. The findings are consistent with those from Foxall and Greenley (1998), who found that in moderate-pleasure environments, low arousal is associated with greater avoidance than is moderate arousal. This corroborates Van Kenhove and Desrumaux (1997) who report that very high arousal does not lead to greater avoidance. The results are partially consistent with Mehrabian and Russell (1974) who affirmed that in moderate-pleasure environments, moderate arousal enhances approach while very low or very high arousal leads to avoidance.

The results also suggest that approach is higher when pleasure is high but arousal is low than vice versa (when arousal is high but pleasure is low). This finding is consistent with those of Dube et al. (1995) and Foxall and Greenley (1998) and supports the third proposition. In the intermediate cases (Hedonism and Accumulation), approach is higher in situations marked by high levels of utilitarian reinforcement but low levels of informational reinforcement (Hedonism) than in those marked by high levels of informational reinforcement but low levels of utilitarian reinforcement (Accumulation).

Three-way interaction effects among pleasure, arousal and dominance Within the framework of the BPM, dominance has been shown to discriminate between open and closed consumer situations (Foxall, 1997a; Foxall and Greenley, 1998; Foxall and Yani-de-Soriano, 2005). However, at the aggregate level made possible by this review, the four operant classes of consumer behaviour show some key differences with respect to the role of dominance and its impact on approach-avoidance behaviour. In high-pleasure-high-arousal environments, dominance exerts no significant effect on approach. This is inconsistent with Biggers and Rankins's (1983) finding of higher approach in the high-pleasure-high-arousal-low-dominance condition than in the high-pleasure-high-arousal-high-dominance condition. This means that the approach exhibited by Status Consumption, CC1 (e.g., exotic holiday (relatively open setting)) is not significantly different from Fulfilment, CC2 (e.g., being on a training course to acquire a new skill for work or hobby (relatively closed)). As noted, Accomplishment, to which these two contingency categories belong, is defined by a combination of utilitarian reinforcement and informational reinforcement which is sufficiently strong to maintain the highest level of approach behaviour.

Similarly, in low-pleasure-low arousal environments, dominance shows no significant effect on behaviour. This result is consistent with Biggers and Rankins's (1983) findings but differs from those of Mehrabian and Stanton-Mohr (1985) who report that the combination of unpleasant, low-arousal and dominant feelings diminishes sexual desire and/or increases sexual problems. This implies that avoidance behaviour was not significantly different in the relatively open setting CC7, Routine Purchasing (e.g., weekly shopping), than in the relatively closed setting CC8, Mandatory Consumption (e.g., waiting at the terminal to catch a flight). The explanation is apparently that since avoidance is explained by the lack of pleasantness in a consumer setting, an environment that is inherently unpleasant cannot be made more attractive by increasing arousal or dominance (Foxall, 1997b).

However, the role of CBS-scope is stronger in the intermediate situations, Hedonism and Accumulation. In high-pleasure-moderate-arousal environments, approach is higher when dominance is high than when it is low; though in the right direction, however, this result is nonsignificant. In high-pleasure-low-arousal environments, approach is higher when dominance is high or moderate than when it is low, and low dominance leads to avoidance behaviour. These results are consistent with previous research (Biggers and Rankins, 1983; Mehrabian and Stanton-Mohr, 1985). Hence, for Hedonism behaviour, approach is significantly higher in the open than in the closed setting as proposed by the BPM. Popular Entertainment, CC3, e.g., being at a party, exhibits significantly higher approach than that in the Inescapable Entertainment, CC4, e.g., watching advertisements at the cinema. When pleasure is moderate, approach is higher when dominance is high than when it is low; at any level of arousal, and in low pleasure-high or moderate arousal, higher dominance dampens avoidance. Biggers and Rankins (1983) obtained similar results. This suggests that for Accumulation behaviour, approach is greater in an open than in a closed setting, as proposed by the BPM; therefore, Collecting and Saving, CC5, e.g., collecting issues of a magazine, exhibits greater approach than does Token-Based Consumption, CC6, e.g., collecting credit card points. Therefore, the fourth proposition is supported. Overall the results of the three-way interaction corroborate previous research involving the BPM's structural components reported by Yani-de-Soriano et al. (in press).

13.5   BEHAVIOURAL CONTINUITY REVISITED

The aim of intentional behaviourism is to ascribe intentionality (in this case emotionality) on the basis of evolutionarily consistent neuronal functioning and molar behaviour-environment relationships. The language of intentionality has become necessary in order to explain aspects of behaviour (the present account concentrates on its continuity or discontinuity) that cannot be explained solely in extensional terms. Although the extensional account identifies environmental stimuli that normally allow the behaviour in question to be predicted and controlled, it is not possible to locate stimuli that account for changes in behaviour or persistence when the contingencies of reinforcement have changed. It is therefore impossible to construct a consumer behaviour setting to aid the explanation of the behaviour because the S^D and MO cannot be ascertained. It is clear from the examples presented above (the experimental participant who is insensitive to changing schedule parameters, the addict who changes behaviour pattern, and the consumer who expands the choice set of brands considered for purchase) that some discriminative, motivating and/or reinforcing stimuli cannot be located.

An extensional account requires, moreover, that these stimuli be incorporated into a learning history that accounts for the observed pattern of behaviour in the past. While learning histories may be easily constructed for laboratory animals, it is a different matter to find one for the average consumer wandering around a large departmental store. Not only is such a learning history not immediately available to the consumer researcher: it is never likely to be empirically available in non-intentional terms. That is, the attempt to reconstruct a learning history for a consumer entails verbal interactions between that consumer and an investigator which inevitably means that it is expressed intentionally. One answer to this problem is to assume that a learning history that explains current behaviour is somewhere available and that until it can be specified scientifically it must be assumed to effect some kind of 'action-at-a-distance' on behaviour (Baum, 2007; Baum and Heath, 1982). However, to speak as though a learning history were available in the face of an inability to specify it with the precision required of a scientific account is misleading to say the least. The point at which the use of intentional language becomes inevitable is that at which an extensional account has become unfeasible. The use of the language of intentionality demarcates this impasse (Foxall, 2008b, 2009).

Why does finding afferent–efferent links and environment–behaviour links justify the use of intentionality? In the case of emotion, we cannot investigate the subjective experience of a consumer and relate this to his behaviour simply because the subjective experience is not publicly available. We are assuming, however, on the basis of Rolls's kind of reasoning, that felt emotion is a necessary link in a sequence from reinforced behaviour to learning history. That is, the emotion is the result of reinforcing stimuli evoking emotion feelings by respondent conditioning and that these feelings act as rewards that are connected in some way with the continuity of behaviour since they make the re-enactment of the behaviour more probable. We cannot reconstruct the processes whereby respondent conditioning produces emotion feelings in the individual, but we can find general criteria for the ascription of emotion feelings based on the general operation of biological and environmental procedures. That is, we can isolate the afferent–efferent and environment–behaviour links that are associated with people's verbal (and feasible nonverbal) expressions of specific emotions. From these we can attribute specific emotions, the content of which is judged from the verbal responses, to individuals in order to explain their behaviour in the absence of specific stimuli to which to attribute it.

The use of emotion-related words and facial expressions are among the means by which emotion feelings are indexed in experiments relating emotion to behaviour (e.g., in pain research; see inter alia Flor et al., 2002). It is clear from the above review of the neural correlates of pleasure, arousal and dominance that neuroanatomy and neurophysiology are closely related to the verbal and nonverbal expression of emotion feelings. And it is clear from the review of environment–behaviour relationships also reviewed that patterns of contingency are systematically related to verbal expressions of emotion feelings. It is the establishment of these relationships by the procedures of extensional sciences that gives confidence that the ascription of intentionality (in lieu of a learning history) is a justified part of the explanation of behaviour. This is a different kind of justification for the use of intentional language than that presented by Dennett (1969) who relies on the pre-emptive assumption of intentionality at the level of the neuron. In contrast, intentional behaviourism ascribes intentionality only at the personal level of explanation and only on the basis of the evidence of extensional neuroscience and behavioural science.

13.6   CONCLUSIONS

One strategy for coping with the limitations of an extensional account of such aspects of behaviour as its continuity is to manufacture a fictitious learning history, which, however plausible, cannot be subjected to a scientific analysis and is never likely to become available to the empirical investigator. An alternative is to recognize that a different way of talking about the causes of such behaviour is required and to substitute the beliefs and desires that can be ascribed to the consumer. If this ascription is to carry reasonable legitimacy, it must be founded on inferences that can be reasonably made from the extensional sciences which reflect evolutionary logic.

The use of language relating to emotions, for instance, must be securely founded upon the operation of a nervous system that has evolved to enable the organism to solve the kinds of problem posed by the behaviour, a problem that is related to its individual survival and biological fitness. The means of solving problems of obtaining food and other primary reinforcers are assumed to be hard-wired into the genetic composition of the consumer which specifies the goals necessary to optimize fitness. A second source of afferent–efferent support for the ascription of emotionality derives from the neuronal plasticity that is the result of behaviour that secures secondary reinforcers which contribute to the individual's survival and fitness. In both cases, the operant processes that eventuate in obtaining the reinforcer are the prelude to classical or respondent conditioning which engenders emotional feeling. Pleasure, arousal and dominance are subjective emotional feelings that have been shown to have a role in the phylogenetic history of the species and in the ontogentic learning of the individual. They are, therefore, indicated as outcomes of the processes of selection by consequences that inhere in natural and environmental selection. This seems a far surer basis for the linguistic ascription of at least a quasi-causal mechanism to account for behavioural continuity than the imagination of a learning history.

By incorporating intentional language, by speaking of quasi-causation in the case of intentional inferences, this approach is also intellectually honest in its demarcation of a sphere of behaviour that cannot be accounted for by extensional science alone. It makes clear, for instance, that the linguistic entities to which appeal is made in order to explain behaviour are not of the kind that are amenable to an experimental analysis, and are not empirically available, nor likely to become so. The faux-extensional approach that involves the fabrication of a learning history to account for continuity is subject to all of these limitations but its vulnerability is not obvious given the language in which it is expressed. The intentional terms are not inferred from the very behaviour they are said to explain (a practice that has marked social science at some stages of its development); rather they are founded upon the very extensional considerations that an entirely scientific account would embrace were the evidence available. By saying that the experimental subject believes that the contingencies operate in a particular way and pitches his behaviour accordingly, that the addict has decided to change her behaviour, that the buyer of consumer nondurables desires an alternative source of product category benefits, we are not providing the sort of evidence that the establishment of causal relationships via experimentation delivers. But we are acknowledging a gap in our extensionally expressible knowledge

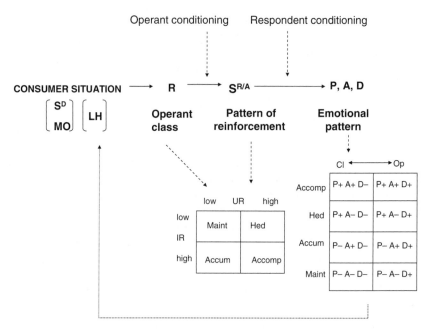

Note: S^D = discriminative stimuli, MO = motivating operations, LH = learning history, R = response, S^{R/A} = reinforcing and aversive consequences, P = pleasure, A = arousal, D = dominance, Accomp = Accomplishment, Hed = Hedonism, Accum = Accumulation, Maint = Maintenance, Cl = closed consumer behaviour setting, Op = open consumer behaviour setting.

Figure 13.6   Behavioural contingencies and patterns of emotion

and indicating that we can fill it only by the adoption of intentionality. By surmising that felt emotions produced via operant and respondent processes contribute to the consumer's learning history by providing a priming mechanism for the evaluation of stimuli that constitute the CBS, we are linking the intentional explanation proposed with the radical behaviourist approach which provides the general framework for investigation.

Figure 13.6 summarizes the development of the BPM framework in view of the relationships between reinforcement contingencies and emotion feeling that have been explored. Rolls's (1999) argument that emotions are states elicited by reinforcers is made explicit, and the classification of consumer behaviours and patterns of emotion identified in empirical research are drawn out for further study. The next stage in the research programme, suggested by the dotted arrow, aims to clarify the contribution of the felt emotions of pleasure, arousal and dominance to learning history. This is likely to rest upon the identification of brain regions such as the amygdala which are related not only to emotional processing but to behavioural reinforcement and memory. Further research is also directed towards understanding better the relationship between emotionality and propositional knowledge. Such enquiry recognizes that emotional events are closely allied with cognitive processing. The fact that emotion, cognition and approach-avoidance dispositions seem to occupy identical brain regions in terms of their physiological grounding (Barrett et al., 2007; Gray and Braver, 2002; Phelps, 2005, 2006; Spielberg et al., 2008) suggests that the attribution of propositional attitudes to consumers is closely related to the emotional experiences that we ascribe to them (see also Whalen and Phelps, 2009).

Emotion and cognition may be separate only phenomenologically, not causally (Barrett et al., 2007); they may not exist as independent systems since 'the separation does not seem to be respected by the brain' (p. 390). Brain structures involved in the neural circuitry for emotion such as the amygdala are also implicated in such cognitive activities as the allocation of attention, perceptual processing and memory. Moreover, cognitively embedded brain structures such as DMPFC and VLPFC are involved in the expression of emotion; decision processes with respect to moral reasoning are founded in core emotion; and economic decisions are emotionally coloured (Hodgkinson and Healey, 2008, in press; Lowenstein et al., 2008).

Finally it is important to recognize that in our role as psychological theorists, we are not here doing the work of the neuroscientist or behavioural scientist. We are using their work to show that in terms of current canons of scientific practice within those extensional sciences, it is possible to identify a sufficiently convincing empirical relationship between the dependent variable, behaviour, and the independent environmental and biological variables of which it is a function. Science is never static; in time, new results will clarify and perhaps even make redundant the relationships we have posited; new paradigms will alter the theoretical bases of sciences and the extensional understanding of the findings they generate. The extensional explanations will change and the intentional interpretation of behaviour will alter accordingly. We can only work where we are. We accept that behaviour is a function directly and proximally of neuronal processing and directly, indirectly and distally of patterns of environmental contingency. Even here, however, we are not attempting *qua* psychological theorists to be at the leading edge of either neuro- or behavioural science. But we acknowledge the imperative of supplementing the extensional language of these sciences and seek a logical rationale for resorting to the intentional.

ACKNOWLEDGEMENTS

The authors are grateful to Dr. Helen Hancocks, Professor Gerard Hodgkinson and Professor Leonard Minkes for helpful comments on earlier drafts.

NOTE

1. This chapter extends and updates Foxall (2011), reproduced by kind permission of the editors and publisher, with the addition of statistical analyses of the empirical work carried out by members of the Consumer Behaviour Analysis Research Group.

REFERENCES

Barrett, L.F. (2005), 'Feeling is perceiving: core affect and conceptualization in the experience of emotion', in L.F. Barrett, P.M. Niedenthal and P. Winkielman (eds) , *Emotion and Consciousness*, New York: Guilford, pp. 255–284.

Barrett, L.F., P.M. Niedenthal and P. Winkielman (eds) (2005), *Emotion and Consciousness*, New York: Guilford.

Barrett, L.F., B. Mesquita, K.N. Ochsner and J.J. Gross (2007), 'The experience of emotion', *Annual Review of Psychology*, **38**, 173–401.

Baum, W.M. (2007), 'Commentary on Foxall "Intentional Behaviourism"', *Behaviour and Philosophy*, **35**, 57–60.

Baum, W.M. and J.L. Heath, (1982), 'Behavioural explanations and intentional explanations in psychology', *American Psychologist*, **47**, 1312–1317.

Bennett, M.R. and P.M.S. Hacker, (2003), *Philosophical Foundations of Neuroscience*, Oxford: Blackwell.

Bernat, E., C.J. Patrick, S.D. Benning and A. Tellegen (2006), 'Effects of picture content and intensity on affective physiological response', *Psychophysiology*, **43**, 93–103.

Berridge, K.C. (2000), 'Reward learning: reinforcement, incentives, and expectations', in D.L. Medin (ed.), *The Psychology of Learning and Motivation, 49*, San Diego: Academic Press, pp. 223–278.

Berridge, K.C. (2004), 'Motivation concepts in behavioural neuroscience', *Physiology and Behaviour*, **81**, 179–209.

Berridge, K.C. and T.E. Robinson (1998), 'What is the role of dopamine in reward: hedonic impact, reward learning, or incentive salience?', *Brain Research Reviews*, **28**, 309–369.

Berridge, K.C. and T.E. Robinson (2003), 'Parsing reward', *TRENDS in Neuroscience*, **26**, 507–512.

Biggers, T. (1981), 'The function of dominance-submissiveness within Mehrabian's theory of emotion', unpublished PhD thesis, Florida State University.

Biggers, T. and B. Pryor (1982), 'Attitude change: a function of emotion-eliciting qualities of environment', *Personality and Social Psychology Bulletin*, **8**, 94–99.

Biggers, T. and O.E. Rankins (1983), 'Dominance-submissiveness as an effective response to situations and as a predictor of approach-avoidance', *Social Behaviour and Personality*, **11** (2), 61–69.

Brentano, F. (1874), *Psychology from an Empirical Standpoint*, Leipsig: Meiner.

Buss, D.M. (2004), *Evolutionary Psychology*, Boston, MA: Pearson.

Buss, D.M. (ed.) (2005), *The Handbook of Evolutionary Psychology*, Hoboken, NJ: Wiley.

Campbell, A. (2007), 'Sex differences in aggression', in R.I.M. Dunbar and L. Barrett (eds),

The Oxford Handbook of Evolutionary Psychology, Oxford: Oxford University Press, pp. 365–382.

Cardinal, R.N., J.A. Parkinson, J. Hall and B.J. Everitt (2002), 'Emotion and motivation: the role of the amygdala, central striatum, and prefrontal cortex', *Neuroscience and Biobehavioural Reviews*, **26**, 321–352.

Chisholm, R. (1957), *Perceiving: A Philosophical Study*, Ithaca, NY: Cornell University Press.

Cohen, J. (1988), *Statistical Power Analysis for the Behavioral Sciences*, 2nd edn, Hillsdale, NJ: Lawrence Erlbaum Associates.

Coull, J.T. (1998), 'Neural correlates of attention and arousal: insights from electrophysiology, functional neuroimaging and psychopharmacology', *Progress in Neurobiology*, **55**, 343–361.

Cummins, D.D. (2005), 'Dominance, status, and social hierarchies', in D.M. Buss (ed.), *The Handbook of Evolutionary Psychology*, Hoboken, NJ: Wiley, pp. 676–697.

Curry, B., G.R. Foxall and V. Sigurdsson (2010), 'On the tautology of the matching law in consumer behaviour analysis', *Behavioural Processes*, **84**, 390–399.

Damasio, A. (1994), *Descarte's Error*, New York: Putnam.

Demaree, H.A., D.E. Everhart, E.A. Youngstrom and D.W. Harrison (2005), 'Brain lateralization of emotional processing: historical roots and a future incorporating "dominance"', *Behavioural and Cognitive Neuroscience Reviews*, **4**, 3–20.

Dennett, D.C. (1969), *Content and Consciousness*, London: Routledge and Kegan Paul.

Dennett, D.C. (1978a), *Brainstorms: Philosophical Essays on Mind and Psychology*, Montgomery, VT: Bradford Books.

Dennett, D.C. (1978b), 'Why you can't make a computer that feels pain', in D.C. Dennett (ed.), *Brainstorms: Philosophical Essays on Mind and Psychology*, Montgomery, VT: Bradford Books, pp. 190–229.

Dennett, D.C. (1987), *The Intentional Stance*, Cambridge, MA: MIT Press.

Donovan, R.J. and J.R. Rossiter (1982), 'Store atmosphere: an environmental psychology approach', *Journal of Retailing*, **58** (1), 34–57.

Donovan, R.J., J.R. Rossiter, G. Marcoolyn and A. Nesale (1994), 'Store atmosphere and purchasing behaviour', *Journal of Retailing*, **70** (3), 283–294.

Dube, L., J.C. Chebat and S. Morin (1995), 'The effects of background music on consumers' desire to affiliate in buyer-seller interactions', *Psychology & Marketing*, **12**, 305–319.

Ehrenberg, A.S.C. (1972), *Repeat Buying*, Amsterdam: North Holland.

Fagerstrom, A., G.R. Foxall and E. Arntzen (2010), 'Implications of motivating operations for the functional analysis of consumer behaviour', *Journal of Organizational Behavior Management*, **30**, 110–126.

Feyerabend, P. (1975), *Against Method*, London: Verso.

Flor, H., B. Knost and N. Birbaumer (2002), 'The role of operant conditioning in chronic pain: an experimental investigation', *Pain*, **95**, 111–118.

Foxall, G.R. (1988), 'The behavioural analysis of consumer choice: issues for theory and research', *Proceedings of the European Institute for Advanced Studies in Management Conference 'New Challenges in Management Research'*, Leuven, The Netherlands. (reprinted in Foxall, 1996, Chapter 5).

Foxall, G.R. (1990/2004), *Consumer Psychology in Behavioural Perspective*, London and New York: Routledge (reprinted 2004 by Beard Books, Frederick, MD).

Foxall, G.R. (1996), *Consumers in Context: The BPM Research Program*, London and New York: Routledge.

Foxall, G.R. (1997a), 'Explaining consumer behaviour: from social cognition to environmental control', in C.L. Cooper and I.T. Robertson (eds), *International Review of Industrial and Organisational Psychology*, Volume 12, Chichester, UK: Wiley, pp. 229–287.

Foxall, G.R. (1997b), *Marketing Psychology*, London and New York: Macmillan.

Foxall, G.R. (1997c), 'Affective responses to consumer situations', *International Review of Retail, Distribution and Consumer Research*, **7**, 191–225.

Foxall, G.R. (1997d), 'The emotional texture of consumer environments: a systematic approach to atmospherics', *Journal of Economic Psychology*, **18**, 505–523.

Foxall, G.R. (1999), 'The substitutability of brands', *Managerial and Decision Economics*, **20**, 241–57.

Foxall, G.R. (2004), *Context and Cognition: Interpreting Complex Behaviour*, Reno, NV: Context Press.

Foxall, G.R. (2005), *Understanding Consumer Choice*, London and New York: Palgrave Macmillan.

Foxall, G.R. (2007a), *Explaining Consumer Choice*, New York and London: Palgrave Macmillan.

Foxall, G.R. (2007b), 'Intentional behaviorism', *Behavior and Philosophy*, **35**, 1–56.

Foxall, G.R. (2007c), 'Explaining consumer choice: coming to terms with intentionality', *Behavioural Processes*, **75**, 129–145.

Foxall, G.R. (2008a), 'Reward, emotion and consumer choice: from neuroeconomics to neurophilosophy', *Journal of Consumer Behaviour*, **7**, 368–396.

Foxall, G.R. (2008b), 'Intentional behaviourism revisited', *Behavior and Philosophy*, **37**, 113–156.

Foxall, G.R. (2009), 'Ascribing intentionality', *Behavior and Philosophy*, **38**, 1–6.

Foxall, G.R. (2010a), *Interpreting Consumer Choice: The Behavioural Perspective Model*, New York and London: Routledge.

Foxall, G.R. (2010b), 'Accounting for consumer choice: inter-temporal decision-making in behavioural perspective', *Marketing Theory*, **10**, 315–45.

Foxall, G.R. (2011), 'Brain, emotion and contingency in the explanation of consumer behaviour', in G.P. Hodgkinson and J.K. Ford (eds), *International Review of Industrial and Organisational Psychology*, Volume 26, Chichester, UK: Wiley, pp. 47–92.

Foxall, G.R. and G.E. Greenley (1998), 'The affective structure of consumer situations', *Environment and Behaviour*, **30**, 781–798.

Foxall, G.R. and G.E. Greenley (1999), 'Consumers' emotional responses to service environments', *Journal of Business Research*, **46**, 149–58.

Foxall, G.R. and G.E. Greenley (2000), 'Predicting and explaining responses to consumer environments: an empirical test and theoretical extension of the Behavioural Perspective Model', *Service Industries Journal*, **20**, 39–63.

Foxall, G.R. and V.K. James (2002), 'Behavior analysis of consumer brand choice: a preliminary analysis', *European Journal of Behavior Analysis*, **2**, 209–220.

Foxall, G.R. and V. James (2003), 'The behavioral ecology of brand choice: how and what do consumers maximize?', *Psychology and Marketing*, **20**, 811–836.

Foxall, G.R. and T.C. Schrezenmaier (2003), 'The behavioural economics of consumer brand choice: establishing a methodology', *Journal of Economic Psychology*, **24**, 675–695.

Foxall, G.R. and M.M. Yani-de-Soriano (2005), 'Situational influences on consumers' attitudes and behavior', *Journal of Business Research*, **58**, 518–525.

Foxall, G.R. and M. Yani-de-Soriano (2011), 'Influence of reinforcement contingencies and cognitive styles on affective responses: an examination of Rolls's theory of emotion in the context of consumer choice', *Journal of Applied Social Psychology*, **41** (10), 2508–2535.

Foxall, G.R., J.M. Oliveira-Castro and T.C. Schrezenmaier (2004), 'The behavioral economics of consumer brand choice: patterns of reinforcement and utility maximization', *Behavioural Processes*, **65**, 235–260.

Foxall, G.R., J.M. Oliveira-Castro, V.K. James and T.C.M. Schrezenmaier (2007), *The Behavioral Economics of Brand Choice*, London and New York: Palgrave Macmillan.

Foxall, G.R., V.K. James, J. Chang and J.M. Oliveira-Castro (2010a), 'Substitutability and complementarity: matching analyses of brands and products', *Journal of Organizational Behavior Management*, **30**, 145–160.

Foxall, G.R., V.K. James, J. M. Oliveira-Castro and S. Ribier (2010b), 'Product substitutability and the matching law', *Psychological Record*, **60**, 185–216.

Foxall, G.R., M. Yani-de-Soriano, S. Yousafzai and U. Javed (2010c), 'Emotion, contingency, and neuroeconomics in the explanation of consumer choice', Working Paper, Cardiff Business School, Cardiff University, UK.

Frey, U. (1997), 'Cellular mechanisms of long-term potentiation: late maintenance', in J.W. Donahoe and V.P. Dorsel (eds), *Neural-Network Models of Cognition: Biobehavioral Foundations*, Amsterdam: North-Holland, pp. 105–128.

Frijda, N.H. (2008), 'The psychologist's point of view', in M. Lewis, J.M. Haviland-Jones and L.F. Barrett (eds), *Handbook of Emotion*, 3rd edn, New York: The Guilford Press, pp. 68–87.

Gilboa, S. and A. Rafaeli (2003), 'Store environment, emotions and approach behavior: applying environmental aesthetics to retailing', *International Review of Retail, Distribution and Consumer Research*, **13**, 195–211.

Gray, J.R. and T.S. Braver (2002), 'Integration of emotion and cognitive control: a neuro-computational hypothesis of dynamic goal representation', in S. Moore and M. Oaksford (eds), *Emotional Cognition*, Amsterdam: John Bejamins, pp. 289–316.

Greenfield, S. (2000), *The Secret Life of the Brain*, London: Penguin.

Groeppel-Klein, A. (2005), 'Arousal and consumer in-store behavior', *Brain Research Bulletin*, **67**, 428–437.

Hair, J.F., R.E. Anderson, R.L. Tatham and W.C. Black (1998), *Multivariate Data Analysis*, fifth edition, Upper Saddle River, NJ: Prentice-Hall.

Havlena, W.J. and M.B. Holbrook (1986), 'The varieties of consumption experience: comparing two typologies of emotion in consumer behavior', *Journal of Consumer Research*, **13**, 394–404.

Havlena, W.J., M.B. Holbrook and D.R. Lehmann (1989), 'Assessing the validity of emotional typologies', *Psychology and Marketing*, **6**, 97–112.

Hebb, D.O. (1949), *The Organization of Behavior: A Neurophysiological Theory*, New York: Wiley.

Herrnstein, R.J. (1961), 'Relative and absolute strength of response as a function of frequency of reinforcement', *Journal of the Experimental Analysis of Behavior*, **4**, 267–272.

Herrnstein, R.J. (1970), 'On the law of effect', *Journal of the Experimental Analysis of Behavior*, **13**, 243–266.

Herrnstein, R.J. (1997), *The Matching Law: Papers in Psychology and Economics* (edited by H. Rachlin and D.I. Laibson), New York/Cambridge, MA: Russell Sage Foundation/ Harvard University Press.

Higley, J.D., P.T. Mehlman, R.E. Poland, D.M. Taub, J. Vickers, S.J. Suomi and M. Linnoila (1996), 'CSF testosterone and 5-H1AA correlate with different types of aggressive behaviors', *Biological Psychiatry*, **40**, 1067–1082.

Hodgkinson, G.P. and G.P. Healey (2008), 'Cognition in organizations', *Annual Review of Psychology*, **59**, 387–417.

Hodgkinson, G.P. and M.P. Healey (in press), 'Psychological foundations of dynamic capabilities: reflexion and reflection in strategic management', *Strategic Management Journal*.

Holbrook, M. and R. Batra (1987), 'Assessing the role of emotions as mediators of consumer responses to advertising', *Journal of Consumer Research*, **14**, 404–420.

Howell, D. (1997), *Statistical Methods for Psychology*, 4th edn, Belmont, CA: Duxbury Press.

Huang, H.M. (2001), 'The theory of emotions in marketing', *Journal of Business and Psychology*, **16**, 239–247.

Hursh, S.R. (1984), 'Behavioral economics', *Journal of the Experimental Analysis of Behavior*, **42**, 435–452.

Izard, C.E. (2009), 'Emotion theory and research: highlights, unanswered questions, and emerging issues', *Annual Review of Psychology*, **60**, 1–25.

Knorski, J. (1948), *Conditioned Reflexes and Neuron Organization*, Cambridge: Cambridge University Press.

Knutson, B., O. Wolkowitz, S.W. Cole, T. Chan, E. Moore, R. Johnson, J. Terpstra, R.A. Turner and V.I. Reus (1998), 'Selective alteration of personality and social behavior by serotonergic intervention', *American Journal of Psychiatry*, **155**, 373–379.

Kotler, P. (1973–74), 'Atmospherics as a marketing tool', *Journal of Retailing*, **49** (4) (Winter), 48–65.

LeDoux, J. (1996), *The Emotional Brain*, New York: Simon and Shuster.

LeDoux, J. (1998), *The Emotional Brain*, New York: Simon and Shuster.

LeDoux, J.E. (2000), 'Emotional circuits in the brain', *Annual Review of Neuroscience*, **23**, 155–184.

Lewis, P.A., H.D. Critchley, P. Rothstein and R.J. Dolan (2007), 'Neural correlates of processing valence and arousal in affective words', *Cerebral Cortex*, **17**, 742–748.

Loewenstein, G., S. Rick and J.D. Cohen (2008), 'Neuroeconomics', *Annual Review of Psychology*, **59**, 647–672.

Lowe, C.F. (1983), 'Radical behaviorism and human psychology', in G.C.L. Davey (ed.), *Animal Models of Human Behavior*, Chichester: Wiley, pp. 71–93.

Mason, C. and W.D. Perreault, Jr. (1991), 'Collinearity, power, and interpretation of multiple regression analysis', *Journal of Marketing Research*, **28** (August), 268–280.

McGinn, C. (1991), *The Problem of Consciousness*, Oxford: Blackwell.

McGinn, C. (1996), *The Character of Mind*, 2nd edn, Oxford: Oxford University Press.

McGinn, C. (2004), *Consciousness and its Objects*, Oxford: Oxford University Press.

Mehrabian, A. (1979), 'Effect of emotional state on alcohol consumption', *Psychological Reports*, **44**, 271–282.

Mehrabian, A. (1980), *Basic Dimensions for a General Psychological Theory: Implications for Personality, Social, Environmental, and Developmental Studies*, Cambridge, MA: Oelgeschlager, Gunn & Hain.

Mehrabian, A. and R. de Wetter (1987), 'Experimental test of an emotion-based approach to fitting brand names to products', *Journal of Applied Psychology*, **72**, 125–130.

Mehrabian, A. and M. Riccioni (1986), 'Measures of eating-related characteristics for the general population: relationships with temperament', *Journal of Personality Assessment*, **50**, 610–629.

Mehrabian, A. and J.A. Russell (1974), *An Approach to Environmental Psychology*, Cambridge, MA: MIT press.

Mehrabian, A. and J.A. Russell (1975), 'Environmental effects on affiliation among strangers', *Humanitas*, **11**, 219–230.

Mehrabian, A. and L. Stanton-Mohr (1985), 'Effects of emotional state on sexual desire and sexual dysfunction', *Motivation and Emotion*, **8**, 315–330.

Morris, J.D., N.J. Klahr, F. Shen, J. Villegas, P. Wright, G. He and Y. Liu (2008), 'Mapping a multidimensional emotion in response to television commercials', *Human Mind Mapping*, **30**, 789–796.

Oliveira-Castro, J.M., G.R. Foxall and T.C. Schrezenmaier (2006), 'Consumer brand choice: individual and group analyses of demand elasticity', *Journal of the Experimental Analysis of Behavior*, **85**, 147–166.

Oliveira-Castro, J.M., G.R. Foxall and V.K. James (2008a), 'Individual differences in price responsiveness within and across food brands', *Service Industries Journal*, **28**, 733–753.

Oliveira-Castro, J.M., G.R. Foxall and V.K. James, R.H.B.F. Pohl, M.B. Dias and S.W. Chang (2008b), 'Consumer-based brand equity and brand performance', *Service Industries Journal*, **28**, 445–461.

Oliveira-Castro, J.M., G.R. Foxall and V.K. James (2010), 'Consumer brand choice: allocation of expenditure as a function of pattern of reinforcement and response cost', *Journal of Organizational Behavior Management*, **30**, 161–175.

Osgood, C.E., G.J. Suci and P.H. Tannenbaum (1957), *The Measurement of Meaning*, Urbana, IL: University of Illinois Press.

Osgood, C.E., W.H. May and M.S. Miron (1975), *Cross-cultural Universals of Affective Meaning*, Urbana, IL: University of Illinois Press.

Panksepp, J. (1998), *Affective Neuroscience: The Foundations of Human and Animal Emotions*, New York: Oxford University Press.

Panksepp, J. (2005), 'On the embodied neural nature of core emotional effects', *Journal of Consciousness Studies*, **12**, 158–184.

Panksepp, J. (2007), 'The neuroevolutionary and neuroaffective psychobiology of the prosocial brain', in R.I.M. Dunbar and L. Barrett (eds), *The Oxford Handbook of Evolutionary Psychology*, Oxford: Oxford University Press, pp. 145–162.

Paul, L.K., A. Lautzenhiser, W.S. Brown, A. Hart, D. Neuman, M. Spezio and R. Adolphs (2006), 'Emotional arousal in agenesis of the corpus callosum', *International Journal of Psychophysiology*, **61**, 47–56.

Phelps, E.A. (2005), 'The interaction of emotion and amygdala: insights from studies of the human amygdala', in L.F. Barrett, P.M. Niedenthal and P. Winkielman (eds), *Emotion and Consciousness*, New York: Guilford Press, pp. 51–66.

Phelps, E.A. (2006), 'Emotion and cognition: insights from studies of the human amygdala', *Annual Review of Psychology*, **57**, 27–53.

Politser, P. (2008), *Neuroeconomics*, New York: Oxford University Press.

Price, C. (2005), *Emotion*, Milton Keynes: Open University.

Quine, W.V.O. (1960), *Word and Object*, Cambridge, MA: MIT Press.

Rachlin, H. (1995), 'Self-control: beyond commitment', *Behavioral and Brain Sciences*, **18**, 109–159.

Rauch, S.L., L.M. Shin, D.D. Dougherty, N.M. Alpert, S.P. Orr, M. Lasko, M.L. Macklin, A.J. Fischman and R.K. Pitman (1999), 'Neural activation during sexual and competitive arousal in healthy men', *Psychiatry Research Neuroimaging*, **91**, 1–10.

Roberts, R.C. (1988), 'What an emotion is: a sketch', *Philosophical Review*, **97**, 202–203.

Robinson, T.E. and K.C. Berridge (2003), 'Addiction', *Annual Review of Psychology*, **54**, 25–53.

Rolls, E.T. (1995), 'What are emotions, why do we have emotions and what is their computational basis in the brain?', in J.-M. Fellous and M.A. Arbib (eds), *Who Needs Emotions? The Brain Meets the Robot*, New York: Oxford University Press, pp. 117–146.

Rolls, E.T. (1999), *The Brain and Emotion*, Oxford: Oxford University Press.

Rolls, E.T. (2005), *Emotion Explained*, Oxford: Oxford University Press.

Rolls, E.T. (2006), 'The neurophysiology and functions of the orbitofrontal cortex', in D.H. Zald and S.L. Rauch (eds), *The Orbitofrontal Cortex*, Oxford: Oxford University Press, pp. 95–124.

Rolls, E.T., F. Grabenhorst and F. Leonardo (2009), 'Prediction of subjective affective state from brain activations', *Journal of Neurophysiology*, **101**, 1294–1308,

Romero, S., G.R. Foxall, T.C. Schrezenmaier, J. Oliveira-Castro and V.K. James (2006), 'Deviations from matching in consumer choice', *European Journal of Behavior Analysis*, **7**, 15–40.

Rosenberg, A. (1988), *The Philosophy of Social Science*, Oxford: Clarendon.

Rosenberg, A. (1992), *Economics – Mathematical Politics or Science of Diminishing Returns?* Chicago, IL: Chicago University Press.

Russell, B. (1912), *The Problems of Philosophy*, London: Home University Library.

Russell, B. (1967), *The Problems of Philosophy*, Oxford University Press (first published 1912).

Russell, J.A. and L.B. Barrett (1999), 'Core affect, prototypical emotional episodes, and other things called *emotion*: dissecting the elephant', *Journal of Personality and Social Psychology*, **76**, 805–819.

Russell, J.A. and A. Mehrabian (1976), 'Environmental variables in consumer research', *Journal of Consumer Research*, **3**, 62–63.

Russell, J.A. and A. Mehrabian (1978), 'Approach-avoidance and affiliation as functions of the emotion-eliciting quality of an environment', *Environment and Behavior*, **10**, 355–387.

Ryle, G. (1949), *The Concept of Mind*, Oxford: Oxford University Press.

Schoggen, P. (1989), *Behavior Settings*, Stanford, CA: Stanford University Press.

Searle, J.R. (2000), 'Consciousness', *Annual Review of Neuroscience*, **23**, 557–578

Seva, R.R., H.B.L. Duh and M.G. Helander (2010), 'Structural analysis of affect in the pre-purchase context', *DLSU Business and Economics Review*, **19**, 43–52.

Sherman, E., A. Mathur and R.B. Smith (1997), 'Store environment and consumer purchase behavior: mediating role of consumer emotions', *Psychology and Marketing*, **14**, 361–378.

Sirkin, M. (1999), *Statistics for the Social Sciences*, 2nd edn, Thousand Oaks, CA: Sage Publications.

Skinner, B.F. (1945), 'The operational analysis of psychological terms', *Psychological Review*, **52**, 270–277.

Skinner, B.F. (1953), *Science and Human Behavior*, New York: Macmillan.

Skinner, B.F. (1969), *Contingencies of Reinforcement: A Theoretical Analysis*, Englewood Cliffs, NJ: Prentice-Hall.

Skinner, B.F. (1971), *Beyond Freedom and Dignity*, New York: Knopf.

Smith, T.L. (1994), *Behaviour and its Causes: Philosophical Foundations of Operant Psychology*, Dordrecht: Kluwer.

Solomon, R.C. (1973), 'Emotions and choice', *Review of Metaphysics*, **27**, 20–41.

Solomon, R.C. (2008), 'The philosophy of emotions', in M. Lewis, J.M. Haviland-Jones and L.F. Barrett (eds), *Handbook of Emotions*, 3rd edn, New York: The Guilford Press, pp. 3–16.

Soriano, M.Y., G.R. Foxall and G. Pearson (2002), 'Emotional responses to consumers' environments: an empirical examination of the behavioural perspective model in a Latin American context', *Journal of Consumer Behaviour*, **2**, 138–154.

Spielberg, J.M., J.L. Stewart, R.L. Levin, G.A. Miller and W. Heller (2008), 'Prefrontal cortex, emotion, and approach/withdrawal motivation', *Social and Personality Psychology Compass*, **2**, 135–153.

Staddon, J.E.R. (ed.) (1980), *The Limits to Action: The Allocation of Individual Behavior*, New York: Academic Press.

Strawson, G. (1994), *Mental Reality*, Cambridge, MA: MIT Press.

Sulloway, F.J. (2007), 'Birth order and sibling competition', in R.I.M. Dunbar and L. Barrett (eds), *The Oxford Handbook of Evolutionary Psychology*, Oxford: Oxford University Press, pp. 297–310.

Sweeney, J.C. and F. Wyber (2002), 'The role of cognitions and emotions in the music-approach-avoidance behavior relationship', *Journal of Services Marketing*, **16**, 51–69.

Tai, S.H.C. and A.M.C. Fung (1997), 'Application of an environmental psychology model to in-store buying behavior', *International Review of Retail, Distribution and Consumer Research*, **7**, 311–337.

Taylor, S.E., L.C. Klein, B.P. Lewis, T.L. Gruenewald, R.A.R. Gurung and J.A. Updegraff (2000), 'Biobehavioral responses to stress in females: tend-and-befriend, not fight-or-flight', *Psychological Review*, **107**, 411–429.

Toronchuk, J.A. and G.F.R. Ellis (2010), *Affective Neuronal Darwinism: The Nature of the Primary Emotional Systems*, http://www.mth.uct.ac.za/~ellis/ToronchuK%20&%20 Ellis,%202010.pdf (accessed 26.06.10).

Van Kenhove, P. and P. Desrumaux (1997), 'The relationship between emotional states and approach or avoidance responses in a retail environment', *International Review of Retail, Distribution and Consumer Research*, **7**, 351–368.

Wager, T.D., L. Feldman Barrett, E. Bliss-Moreau, K.A. Lindquist, S. Duncan, H. Kober, J. Joseph, M. Davidson and J. Mize (2008), 'The neuroimaging of emotion', in M. Lewis, J.M. Haviland-Jones and L.F. Barrett (eds), *Handbook of Emotions*, 3rd edn, New York: The Guilford Press, pp. 249–271.

Whalen, P.J. and E.A. Phelps (eds) (2009), *The Human Amygdala*, New York: Guildford.

Winkielman, P., K.C. Berridge and J.L. Wilbarger (2005), 'Emotion, behavior, and conscious experience', in L.F. Barrett, P.M. Niedenthal and P. Winkielman (eds), *Emotion and Consciousness*, New York: The Guilford Press, pp. 335–362.

Yani-de-Soriano, M. and G.R. Foxall (2006), 'The emotional power of place: the fall and rise of dominance in retail research', *Journal of Retailing and Consumer Services*, **13**, 403–416.

Yani-de-Soriano, M., G.R. Foxall and A. Newman (in press), 'Interactive effects of the determinants of consumer response', *Psychology and Marketing*.

14 Consumer involvement: review, update and links to decision neuroscience
Judith Lynne Zaichkowsky

14.1 CONSUMER INVOLVEMENT: THE BIRTH IN CONSUMER BEHAVIOUR

The date was October 1980, the place was Arlington, Virginia, the venue was the eleventh annual conference of the Association for Consumer Research. It was 8 a.m. and the first session of the conference was entitled: "Emerging Issues in Low Involvement Theory", a special session involving the who's who of consumer behaviour researchers of the era. The chairs for the session were Rich Lutz of the University of California, Los Angeles and John Cacioppo of the University of Iowa. The goal of the session was to clarify the conceptual properties of the low involvement construct and to provide direction for future research.

Four papers were presented to address the implications of involvement for understanding consumer behaviour:

(1) "What is Low Involvement Low in?" by Clark Leavitt, Anthony Greenwald and Carl Obermiller, Ohio State University
(2) "Issue Involvement as a Moderator of the Effects on Attitude of Advertising Content and Context" by Richard Petty, University of Missouri and John Cacioppo, University of Iowa.
(3) "The Dimensions of Advertising Involvement" by Andrew Mitchell, Carnegie Mellon University
(4) "Reconceptualising Involvement" by Richard Lutz, University of California, Los Angeles.[1]

The discussant was Hal Kassarjian of U.C.L.A. who, a year later, became the co-editor of the *Journal of Consumer Research.* The room was packed and there was nary a place to stand.

The papers inspired great debate and interest from the audience about the theoretical issues and implications for consumer behaviour thought. As the discussion raged, and it actually raged, new doctoral students wondered what all the fuss was about. At that time the literature was heavily influenced by work in the 1970s which focused on information processing. Tangible elements like pricing were the focus of good PhD efforts.

Many found the session both amusing and puzzling in the debate to define and capture a theoretical construct. It seemed these people were talking in circles. In their theoretical review, Leavitt, Greenwald and Obermiller (1981) stated there was no agreement on what constituted high involvement, therefore low involvement was ambiguous. They offered a three stage processing model, with one type of high involvement (elaborated encoding) and two types of low involvement (attentive and inattentive).

Petty and Cacioppo (1981) reported results of an experiment which manipulated the personal relevance of the message, quality of arguments, and the source of the message. They hypothesized "involvement" accounted for the influence of the different factors for persuasion. Andrew Mitchell (1981) then offered yet another conceptual model, of how involvement affects information acquisition, resulting in three different types of information acquisition patterns. His conceptualization was close to Leavitt et al.'s and Petty and Cacioppo's in that he offered a high involvement process, where individuals devote all their attention to advertising and brand strategy and then two low involvement conditions. His first low involvement condition stated that consumers used a brand strategy with reduced attention, whereas in the second low involvement condition consumers had a non-brand strategy or severe attention deficit.

In the summarization and discussion of these papers, it was clear that low involvement decision making seriously challenged the cognitive orientation of present thinking of consumer research which developed in the 1970s. Kassarjian (1981) stated that it was "unfortunate that a simple instrument or tool has not yet been developed to measure the concept of involvement but if 'necessity is the mother of invention' that will come in time – for the measure of levels of involvement is unquestionably a necessity – one that can no longer be ignored" (p. 31).

He further predicted that the simple concept of involvement, introduced in the television advertising domain by Krugman in 1965, may be one of the more important scientific ideas to emerge in consumer behaviour. The topic would alter many, if not most of the conceptions of cognitive theory in consumer behaviour dominant at that time and this was indeed a great turning point in consumer behaviour and marketing research.

The starting point of Zaichkowsky (1985) was to read every academic publication in advertising, marketing, and consumer research containing the construct of involvement. The contribution was not to create something new, but more make sense and order, and link together what was already written in the literature. This reading created a theoretical structure of the

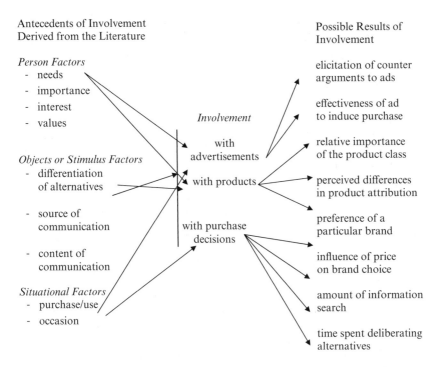

Antecedents of Involvement
Derived from the Literature

Possible Results of
Involvement

Person Factors
- needs
- importance
- interest
- values

Objects or Stimulus Factors
- differentiation
  of alternatives

- source of
  communication

- content of
  communication

Situational Factors
- purchase/use
- occasion

Involvement

with
advertisements

with products

with purchase
decisions

elicitation of counter
arguments to ads

effectiveness of ad
to induce purchase

relative importance
of the product class

perceived differences
in product attribution

preference of a
particular brand

influence of price
on brand choice

amount of information
search

time spent deliberating
alternatives

Note: Involvement = f (Person, Situation, Object). The level of involvement may be influenced by one or more of these three factors. Interaction among persons, situations and objects factors are likely to occur.

Source: Zaichkowsky, 1986b.

Figure 14.1   A framework for the involvement construct

antecedents and consequences of involvement (see Figure 14.1). It covered products, advertisements, and purchase situations. It was a conclusion of all previous research using the term involvement as applied to consumer behaviour.

14.2   THE PII MEASURE OF INVOLVEMENT

The original published measure of involvement, by Zaichkowsky (1985), continues to be used successfully by researchers looking to capture and categorize motivations to explain differences in individual consumer behaviour (e.g., Peck and Wiggens Johnson 2011). However this measure contained a questionable aspect that was not recognized during the completion of the dissertation by the author or by any of the PhD committee. There were 20 semantic differential items in the original measure. These items had been carefully screened and tested for validity and reliability over many different subjects and many different contexts. However, upon publication of the article, it was clear that there was imbalance and redundancy in the 20 item scale.

While all the literature on test development at that time suggested a minimum number of items, these procedures were rooted in psychology and education (French and Michael 1966; Nunnally 1978) and pertained to IQ tests or measures of personality traits. Churchill (1979) had also published an article on developing better measures for marketing and there were no insights to the potential overkill measurement problem in his writings. The construct which was conceptualized, and was trying to be captured, was a little different than the constructs for which the education test taking, personality trait, or marketing construct measure guidelines were developed. The involvement construct was fleeting, variable, and meant to capture a motivation, not an innate personal trait.

Another point was that many of the techniques, at that time for measurement of traits, only became quite feasible with the development of computers and computer aided statistical procedures, such as factor analyses (e.g., Cattell et al. 1970). These rules were published for IQ tests and personality traits, which had many different possible facets, and the involvement concept was actually much narrower than the broad test scales developed for education or psychology.

The dissertation stated that a fewer number of items might be appropriate, but deciding which of those 20 items would stay and which would go seemed to be yet another dissertation at the time. The decision to create the scale with 20 items was based on the ability to make fine distinctions between individual levels of involvement and also, on a practical level, to have the measure fit on one page. However, 20 items were really an overkill of reliability, not to mention the broader and more recent identification that involvement could be more cognitive or affective in nature (Park and Young 1986), and the individual PII items were not defined nor selected along those two dimensions.

Some years later the original Personal Involvement Scale which was published in the *Journal of Consumer Research* in 1985 was improved upon, and a 10 item scale (Revised Personal Involvement Inventory: RPII) was published in the *Journal of Advertising* (Zaichkowsky 1994). This new scale had a balance of cognitive and affective items and was easily applied to measuring involvement with advertising, products, or purchase situations. The RPII measure now corresponded to and linked the published ideas of the advertising industry in the Foote, Cone, and Belding Grid

To me XXXXX is

Important __:__:__:__:__:__:__ Unimportant[1]

Boring __:__:__:__:__:__:__ Interesting[2] (R)

Relevant __:__:__:__:__:__:__ Irrelevant[1]

Exciting __:__:__:__:__:__:__ Unexciting[2]

Means nothing to me __:__:__:__:__:__:__Means a lot to me[1] (R)

Appealing __:__:__:__:__:__:__ Unappealing[2]

Fascinating __:__:__:__:__:__:__ Mundane[2]

Worthless __:__:__:__:__:__:__ Valuable[1] (R)

Involving __:__:__:__:__:__:__ Uninvolving[2]

Not needed __:__:__:__:__:__:__ Needed[1] (R)

Note: (R) reverse coded (7–1); 1 indicates a cognitive involvement measure; 2 indicates an affective involvement measure.

Figure 14.2   Revised Personal Involvement Inventory

(Vaughn 1980, 1986) of high versus low involvement and affective and cognitive types of products. So ideally the type and the amount of involvement could be measured at the same time (Zaichkowsky 1986a). The items are randomly reversed and also randomly interspersed with one another. This randomization is important for the reliability and validity of the test taking (see Figure 14.2). Respondents are less likely to blindly tick down a column, they are led, by the random format, to actually think and register the word they are responding to. Granted that there is likely more measurement error in data using randomly reversed items, but this type of error is more desirable than error due to validity.

An example of the plot of the affective scores and cognitive scores to the rated involvement of an English print ad for trousers (Figure 14.3) evaluated by native Danish speakers is in Figure 14.4 (Norgaard 2011). The reader can see that while the scores are generally correlated, one can identify a couple of individuals who are quite affectively involved with the advertisement, but rated it very low in the cognitive descriptors. Then there are a group of respondents for whom the cognitive items are rated much higher than the affective dimension. And furthermore, there is a group

Figure 14.3   Jeans advertisements rated by Danish subjects

for whom the total scores on both dimensions were much higher than another group that was generally very low in both types of involvement. Depending upon the objective of the study, one might be able to identify segments of consumers on how differentially involved they are with the stimulus in question, as there are some obvious individual differences.

14.2.1   Issues of Scale Modification

Some readers of Zaichkowsky (1985) also identified the flaw of item redundancy and published many variations of the measure with fewer items (e.g., McQuarrie and Munson 1987, 1992). Other authors still pick and choose among the individual scale items of the RPII and also add other items when they want to measure involvement. For example, Xue and Zhou (2011) only used one item from that scale: important–unimportant,

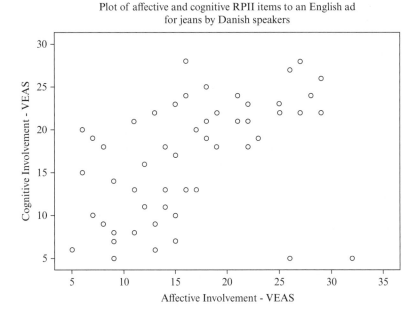

*Figure 14.4   Cognitive and affective involvement to a stimulus may be
measured and then plotted to identify market segments*

then added four other totally different items (convincing/unconvincing;
reasonable/unreasonable; useful/useless; likely/unlikely), and they say they
have used the RPII measure of involvement. These five items were never
tested to the 10 item RPII (which balances affect and cognition), so the
validity or reliability to the motivational construct of involvement might
need to be checked. It may be unclear what kind of construct their findings
refer to and if they are really capturing product involvement as a motivational construct. Convincing, reasonable, likely, and useful may not be so
motivational.

Other research may just cite the Zaichkowsky (1985) paper and then
ask respondents "Are you involved with XXX?" (e.g., Delezie et al. 2006).
This procedure may seem fine and easy to use by researchers, but all the
theory to affective and cognitive motivation is blurred. The attention to
content validity to the theoretical construct of involvement remains at
the integrity of the measure. If researchers are going to shorten the 10
item scale or convert it to a one item Likert scale, then there needs to be
some investigation to reliability and validity of their adapted measure
before use. In many ways researchers are reverting back to the single item
untested measures used in the 1970s. Their reasons may be the perceived

unimportance of the measure; their belief that this type of single item measure is just as "good" as a multiple measure (e.g., Bergkvist and Rossiter 2007); the desire to be as terse as possible, without believing there are measurement consequences; or they are sure their adapted measure is better in some way than the RPII.

Besides reducing the scale length, other changes to the scale use include transforming the semantic differential measure to a Likert scale with one direction. Or, in other words, taking one end of the bi-polar semantic scale and then asking the extent to which a respondent agrees or disagrees on a seven or five point scale to a statement like "watches are important to me". This form of a question is great for measuring opinions, but may not be so suitable to measure a motivation. One thinks about opinions, but motivations might be more subconscious and not get the same careful thought. Motivations may be hard for the individual to define and grasp. Perhaps they need to be reacted to, not necessarily thought about in the way a Likert scale is prone to probe. Making all the questions positive, when trying to measure a motivation, is also not very conducive to getting a respondent to pay attention to the task. Especially when their "involvement" level may be very low to begin with, or they are just filling out the questionnaire to receive a reward for their participation.

In addition to only giving one end of the scale to measure amount of the construct, Bian and Moutinho (2011) used five of the items from the McQuarrie and Munson (1992) measure to investigate behaviour towards purchasing counterfeit products. They then repeated some of these five items and added other items to make a 10 item measure. Their research found no significant effects for involvement with the product category of watches to the intended purchase of a counterfeit Rolex watch. Because the measure on involvement used in their study is on a Likert scale; (one sided; all positive; and has adapted items rather than items already tested for validity), it may be their hypotheses are not supported because of the measure. One cannot tell. Unsupported hypotheses are due to something about the theory, the data, or the measures.

14.3   THE SCOPE OF APPLICATION

In the 1980s, and before, researchers used to keep the letters they received from other researchers which asked for a copy of their work. That's how researchers knew the scope of their academic impact and level of interest other people had in their work. This, in addition to the lagged citation counts which were looked up in a heavy book in the library, was crucial information for promotion and tenure. The internet has changed research and science forever, and for the better. Exchange of information and the growth of new ideas and applications are now almost instantaneous. The internet keeps track of the network and history of thought. One can see where information came from and where new ideas are spreading. Many of the cites of Zaichkowsky (1985) are not in English publications, but are represented by scholarly publications from all over the world, e.g., Japan, Korea, Turkey, Germany, Spain, Austria, Brazil, and Taiwan. This motivational construct called involvement seems to be easily understood and the measure has been translated to many different languages for data collection.

Since the publication and subsequent papers on conceptualizing and measuring involvement there have been well over 3,000 citations of the Zaichkowsky (1985) article noted by Google Scholar, but only about 600 in the Business Source Complete data base. The concept and construct of involvement and its applications seem to know no discipline boundaries. For example scholarly researchers are using it to study innovative behaviour ("Characteristics and Values of Innovative Consumers: A Case from the Music Industry", Katsumata and Ichikohji, 2010); understand how consumers buy sports products on-line (Kim et al. (2010) *Journal of Sport and Leisure Studies*); and even what accounts for different approaches to meat consumption and catching poultry (Verbeke and Vackier 2004; Delezie et al. 2006 published in *Poultry Science* and *Meat Science*). A master's student in the English department, at the Copenhagen University, is asking "Are advertisements which contain English more involving than those which do not?" So students who were yet to be born when the 1985 JCR piece was published, are still finding the construct of involvement interesting and useful to their current research questions. It appears to be timeless and widely applicable.

The last time a meta analysis was carried out on the construct of involvement was in 1988 by Carolyn Costley. She looked at publications from 1976 to 1986 in *Advances in Consumer Research, Journal of Consumer Research, Journal of Marketing* and *Journal of Marketing Research*. Her total sum of published papers to work with was 18. From the analyses, a chart was prepared which summarized relationships and constructs in the literature. The object of involvement under investigation was always an ad, product or situation. The nature of the response was always affective, functional (cognitive) or both. Furthermore, the intensity of the affective response was high, low or continuous and allowed for classification of individuals. Significant relationships for the intensity and affective and cognitive involvement were undisputed. Therefore the literature was unequivocal that no matter what the context (stimuli/object), the response always could be functional (cognitive) and/or affective (emotional) in nature.

A new meta analysis on the over 600 citations in business journals or the over 2,000 citations by Google Scholar may be a challenge for today's researcher. This work would likely be difficult as the individual papers and authors do not always use the construct and measures as they are proposed. Researchers are a little entrepreneurial in their approach and even though papers use the same broad constructs, sometimes they are applied differently. The accurate documentation of the flow and spread of ideas and information about the construct of involvement in the published literature to show where the construct is applied may be a bit easier with content analysis software. These might be good ideas for a doctoral student project.

But it cannot be denied that involvement, as a motivational variable, predicts future behaviour. And predicting future behaviour is what everyone is interested in. Therefore the future of the involvement construct appears to be healthy. It should not die out soon.

14.4   EARLY LINKS OF BRAIN RESEARCH TO CONSUMER BEHAVIOUR

In the late 19070s two European consumer behaviour researchers were focusing on the brain and psychobiological approaches to understanding consumer choice: Werner Kroeber-Riel[2] (1979) of the Institute for Consumer and Behavioural Research at the University of Saarland, Germany; and Flemming Hansen[3] (1981) of the Copenhagen Business School. Kroeber-Riel's work focused on the relationship between behaviour and physiological processes of the nervous system, particularly those taking place in the brain. He speculated that, to a large extent, consumers respond automatically according to biologically determined patterns of behaviour.

Kroeber-Riel employed various physiological methods, such as EDR (electro dermal response), commonly termed GSR or galvanic skin response or SRR (skin resistance reaction) to measure arousal and also CLEM (conjunctive lateral eye movements) monitors to measure attention and information search. Using experimental settings to study the effectiveness of advertising, he postulated that advertising which does not arouse will have no effect because the information conveyed in the advertisement will not be processed. The questions that arose from his work were "How do you create a situation (advertising) that leads people to actively process what they are exposed to?"; or, "How do you involve people when they are exposed to advertising?"

Flemming Hansen's work specifically focussed on the notion of high and low involvement being tied to right and left brain activity. At that time, the thought among brain researchers was that human right and left hemispheres of the brain had different functions. The left hemisphere was thought to be responsible for traditional cognitive activities relying on verbal information, symbolic representation, sequential analyses and the ability to consciously report on what is going on. The right hemisphere of the brain was thought to be mainly for processing of pictorial, geometric, timeless and non-verbal information, and was also subconscious.

Hansen (1981) hypothesized that in low involvement situations the right brain processes dominate while in higher degrees of involvement, the left brain is activated. Thus, under high involvement, information processing and deliberate choice occur. Under low involvement, information is received holistically and choices are made without awareness. He also speculated that under low involvement, the number of exposures needed before a sufficient amount of learning occurred may be greater due to the dominance of the right brain processes. Another aspect of the theory was that there were individual differences for right versus left brain dominance. That is, there are types of people for whom thinking dominates and there are other types of people for whom emotion dominates. And, therefore, different types of advertising messages would appeal to left brain or right brain dominated people. To my knowledge there has been no test of this proposition in the literature.

14.5   ADVANCES IN TECHNOLOGY AND UNDERSTANDING OF BRAIN FUNCTIONS

The 1970s style brain research, or the separation of right brain and left brain as it leads to either cognitive or affective stimulation, has been replaced by updated theories. New technology has emerged and fields called cognitive neuroscience and affective neuroscience have been established. Consumer researchers have taken up decision neuroscience (Shiv et al. 2005) and the term to the lay person commonly used in the media is neuromarketing. However, the term neuromarketing is seen by some as "too commercial" and the preferred term among academics seems to be decision neuroscience.

There are various technical methods used in consumer/decision neuroscience. Brain activity can be measured by EEG (electroencephalogram), which documents the amount and pattern of electrical activity in the cerebral cortex (e.g., Thompson and Zola 2003). An individual might display changes in activation in certain parts of the cerebral cortex when looking at a picture they find very interesting over one they find bland or boring. With increasing attention, such measures often display faster (i.e., higher frequency) and lower amplitude waves (beta waves) which are observed in the EEG. This indicates more frequent information transfer between neurons and may serve as an index of processing load (brain activity). When brain activities increase, there is also an increase in blood circulation of the active part, measured by the Emisionstomgraph technique (advanced computer imaging) (Lassen et al. 1978). The application of EEG in academic consumer behaviour research appears in the advertising domain (Rothschild and Hyun 1990). But its use applied to measuring effectiveness of advertising is limited because the technique needs to be carried out in a laboratory setting and involves some complex attachments to the subjects. One major drawback of any neuroimaging tool is mobility, as motion itself induces some activation that must be accounted for.

On the other hand, arousal measured through the skin, phasic electrodermal reaction (EDR), continues to be a useful tool to understand consumer behaviour because it can easily be brought to the field and consumer arousal can be measured at the point of sale (Groeppel-Klein 2005). Consumer arousal is the precursor to the activation of buying behaviour, as it is an indicator of an affective reaction. It is the basis of emotions, motivation, information processing and finally behaviour. Arousal is the effect of emotional responses, in how the brain labels certain kinds of information as salient and important. This labelling of something as very relevant (both positive and negative) leads to higher arousal, more attention (bottom-up driven) and through this, increases in information processing. So arousal comes some place in the midst of the process, not in the initiation. Nevertheless, arousal measures during exposure to choices can predict subsequent choice behaviour, even if there is a long delay between exposure and choice (minutes, hours, days) (Falk et al. 2011). The measurement of arousal through skin reactance tells us there are hypothalamic reactions and some activity in the amygdala, which processes emotions. The reason this stream of research relates to involvement is motivational. Humans need to be aroused before they behave in a certain manner, and that emotional arousal can be linked to the activation of thought and subsequent decision making. Hence the link between cognition and emotion is almost inseparable.

Research on store atmosphere tells us that sensual cues have a significant impact on consumers' perception and buying behaviour (Donovan and Rossiter 1982). Kroeber-Riel (1979) identified three types of arousal inducing stimuli in the shopping environment: (1) innate stimuli, such as scents, colours, or plants; (2) intense stimuli controlled by the retailer such as intense lighting, motion, contrasting colours, music; (3) unusual and appealing decorations. These types of hedonic or highly affective shopping environments are said to increase arousal, heighten involvement, and create a valuable and entertaining shopping experience (Babin et al. 1994).

Using an experimental approach of a control (low aesthetic) situation and a second shopping environment following spatial layout, lighting, and colours to a highly aesthetic shopping experience, Groeppel-Klien (2005) found EDR arousal measures to be twice as strong in the highly aesthetically designed experimental condition. Also twice as many purchases were made in the aesthetic store environment over the control store. In addition, a triangulation of a paper and pencil measure of "joy" while shopping correlated .46 with the amplitude of EDR and .42 with its frequency. Hence, store aesthetics were a critical stimulator of good feelings, emotional response, arousal, and finally purchase behaviour. So the atmosphere with good aesthetics created more arousal, or more emotional involvement, and resulted in more purchases (cognitive response). It is clear the various aesthetics stimulate our senses and then activate the emotional arousal and hence the objects within the aesthetic environment become more "involving".

Other research documenting the impact of aesthetic displays on consumer purchase in shopping environments shows that a highly aesthetic display will help an unknown brand outsell a known brand, especially with an "emotional or affective" type of product like chocolate (Esch et al. 2003). Using coffee and chocolate as stimulus products, the researchers found the greatest increase in sales with the aesthetic displays, and the most increase in sales with the product category of chocolates. Therefore good aesthetics and design can be said to stimulate the brain into activation, which then can lead to a positive response toward the object around or in the aesthetic stimuli.

One of the current trends in decision neuroscience is the discussion about "common currency" in the brain. That is, to what extent is there a common valuation system that labels options using a similar metric across different domains? Sometimes diverse rewards such as food, money and even sex tap into the same reward mechanisms of the brain (Plassmann et al. 2011). This could mean that a positive aesthetic experience will affect the subsequent responses to a product/brand the aesthetics are attached to. It might be called a "contagion effect", where high reward expectancy leads to a positive shift in evaluation of images, and image evaluation is positively related to reward expectancy. This seems to be modulated through the basic parts of the brain's reward structures such as the striatum (Ramzoy and Skov 2010).

Perhaps, now, the most frequently used technique to research brain activity in consumer behaviour research applications is functional magnetic resonance imaging (fMRI). The procedure involves sampling signal intensities from thousands of voxels (three-dimensional boxes) in the brain every two seconds or so. For each measured voxel, comparisons are made between conditions (often through univariate analyses), and these statistical values are plotted onto a heat map in 3D. Thus the display from fMRI is a statistical representation of the univariate analysis for each of the thousands of voxels. This measurement allows the researcher to generate statistical representations of the underlying intensities and processes during perception, affect and cognition related to various stimuli. A detailed review of the fMRI and its applications to consumer research can be found in Reimann et al. (2011).

Through the use of the fMRI, one actually sees the processes of the brain as they are happening. This leads to a situation where "seeing is believing" in terms of brain activity. However "seeing is only believing", and the understanding of what is seen and documented through the fMRI technique, and its relevance to consumer reactions/decisions, is still in its infancy. For example, one might say fMRI is "just" another way to statistically test a priori hypotheses whether stimuli/products are processed differently through emotional responses or attention aspects. General and explorative brain mapping are not really telling us much, and trying to interpret reasons for brain activation after doing the analyses leads to logical fallacies or reverse inference (Plassmann et al. 2011).

With these advances in technology to view brain activity came a rewriting of theory pertaining to the idea of an emotional versus a cognitive side to the brain. Work in the area of memory laid out two central memory networks that operate simultaneously and in parallel. One memory system was mediated by the hippocampus and dealt with facts or declarative knowledge. The second memory system was mediated by the amygdala and processed emotions or affect (Le Doux 1994). These two parts of the brain co-exist in an intertwined fashion as mirror images of each other in the center of the brain (limbic system) at the base of the skull, above the spinal cord. So the notion of left brain–right brain exists, but the emotional and cognitive memory systems of the amygdala and hippocampus are both on each side of the human brain.

Today this view is further complicated by the fact that emotional/saliency responses found in the amygdala lead to stronger hippocampal memory (Murray et al. 2005). There still may be people who are more affective-emotional in their reactions to objects and people who are more cognitive and perhaps rational and hence look for information about the object. But this is not necessarily a right brain or a left brain activity.

In general, humans repeat behaviour that maximizes rewards or feelings of enjoyment. That is, we like it when the reward center of our brain is stimulated because dopamine is released by this stimulation and we feel a heightened feeling of pleasure. The current thinking is that reward expectancy and reward experience rely on separate systems in the brain. Neurally, reward expectancy seems to rely on increased activation in the striatum (and to some extent the amygdala), while the pleasurable experience of an outcome engages the medial orbitofrontal cortex (Berridge 2009). So the question as applied to consumer behaviour and marketing becomes "What products/brands/advertisements/purchase situations make the reward center of the brain release dopamine?".

Early work using fMRI to understand consumer decision making was carried out at the Social Cognitive Neuroscience Laboratory at the California Institute of Technology in Pasadena by Steve Quartz, a professor of Philosophy. Initial fMRI experiments (reported mainly through the media, e.g., Mahoney 2005) exposed subjects to 140 pictures of products and tried to answer the question: "Why are people willing to pay a premium for a product when that premium isn't buying them anything extra in terms of functionality?" Personality tests were also administered to see if there was some segmentation of brain reaction by personality. Each subject generated several hundred brain maps over the products they were exposed to. The analyses of the data from scanning brains showed that different people reacted differently to different images/products, or they had different activity levels in the various brain regions associated with emotion and reasoning. Furthermore subjects were not always conscious of their preferences, which the brain activity seemed to indicate.

If researchers in the field of consumer behaviour had carried out the Cal Tech research they would have identified, a priori, a myriad of variables such as brand equity, peer influence, etc., to explain this basic question of "willingness to pay a premium". Marketing academics know individual differences are the basic premise behind market segmentation. The marketing goal is to make sure that groups of consumers with similar responses are large enough to be a profitable segment. Then different stimuli and marketing techniques are targeted at each segment.

The interpretation of the picture of the brain provided by the fMRI scan may not be the same interpretation as the researcher theorizes. Current theory is that positive affect or positive emotions lead one to be able to be a more fluent processor. Thus the right and left brain are not separate systems but intertwined. FMRI may be an expensive method to study the effect of an ad or a package design. In some ways it is perhaps frivolous, when the medical applications to health of individuals are compared. However science knows no boundaries and as long as the technology is available, and there are people willing and able to be studied, research funds, and trained researchers eager to carry out experiments, these types of research studies with small samples will continue to flourish. This is the current future of understanding decision making.

14.6   RECENT THEORETICAL INVESTIGATIONS TO INVOLVEMENT

Basically the framework for involvement hypothesizes that there are inherent personal elements that attach the individual to the object. There can also be something about the object characteristics that causes the involvement, and additionally a situational effect may cause an involvement response to the object. Manipulating any or all of these aspects is what leads one to be more involved with an object. The first part of the structure, which just includes the link between the person and the object, has been termed enduring involvement in the literature (e.g., Higie and Fieck 1989; Richens et al. 1992). However, this early structure made no distinction for affective and cognitive involvement. Other researchers (e.g., Petty and Cacioppo 1986) developed the Elaboration Likelihood Model (ELM) where the role of emotion was only evident in the low involvement or peripheral route to persuasion. The simultaneous occurrence of emotion and cognition with a highly involving situation or object did not become the subject of many academic articles until well into the 1990s (Chaudhuri 1993).

The inseparability, or high correlation, of cognitive and affective involvement was theorized in the literature by Buck et al. (2004). They state emotional reactions and rational cognition are two persuasion processes that take place simultaneously and interactively. Their conceptual model to understand consumer behaviour joins affect, reason and involvement to a three dimensional diagram. The base of their model is an affective response upon which reason is built to a second dimension. The third dimension is involvement and is said to be a combination of affective and rational processing, or both thinking and feeling. This third dimension is a ratio of the affective and cognitive (reason) measure (Chaudhuri 2006). A final score for influence is calculated by adding the affect and the reason and dividing by two. Applying this model to many product categories provides a grid of high and low involvement products by affect to reason ratio (see Buck et al. 2004 for a diagrammatic representation). This approach explicitly considers emotion/affect to be a type of cognition different than analytical cognition, but the two are highly correlated (Buck et al. 2004).

Recent research has explored the roots of enduring involvement (Bloch et al. 2009). The research questions investigated were "What are the origins of product involvement", and "How do people become highly involved with a product category in the first place?" Furthermore, "What are the conditions under which high involvement with the product category thrives?" To answer these questions the authors undertook a qualitative approach with in-depth narratives of consumers and their autobiographical recollection of when their love, or high involvement, for certain product categories began. They chose four different product categories as stimuli: cars, fashion, photography and jazz. The data was collected via the internet, and a total of 57 people recollected 292 different episodes of their first and enduring interactions with these products.

The attributions given to self-understanding of the respondents' current involvement levels could be categorized into two major broad areas: (1) social influence and (2) exceptional product design. The social influence category contained four subsections: parents; extended family; close friends; and other peers. Parents were often the first influencers and the involvement around the object in question allowed a private bond between family members. For example if a father was a major car enthusiast, he was likely to pass that passion on to his sons. Very out of the ordinary behaviour was reported by those highly involved with the product, such as owning 20 plus automobiles, or allowing one's child to purchase their first car at the age of 12.

Involvement in fashion was likely to come from a family social influence once removed, such as a grandmother or aunt. Members of the extended family were thought to be inspirational because they were close enough to be aspirational, but distant enough to be novel. Therefore special relationships were formed with objects based on influence from a family member who did not live with the individual, but was highly regarded and looked up to.

In addition to family members, close friends and other peers facilitated the development of involvement with products. They helped identify important brands and pointed out nuances and innovations in product categories. This product related enthusiasm provided a means of generating friendships and social connections for the individual. Therefore the involvement with the product may begin as a necessary adjunct to desired social rewards and only later evolve into a deeper interest in the product class (Bloch et al. 2009).

The second major creator of enduring product involvement was an exceptional product design. Exposure to a captivating product exemplar, one that triggers a deep interest or "love at first sight", was a dramatic and compelling causal influence in all four product classes investigated. This fits the Zaichkowsky (1986b) framework where the differences within the product were hypothesized to lead to involvement. However the fact that these differences were based on exceptional product design adds an important link to emotional arousal and affect. Great aesthetics, functional superiority and excellent craftsmanship all had the ability to differentiate the object from others and move the consumer from an uninterested state into a lifelong passion or enduring involvement with the product class. What is associated with this exemplar in aesthetic product design is strong emotion or excitement.

The final contribution of the qualitative research to understanding enduring involvement is the idea that the brain needs to be fed over time to sustain the high levels of involvement with the object. This means the individual needs and seeks exposure to new applications; receiving new information; or creative new product designs. It is like fuel for the fire.

14.7   LINKING QUALITATIVE, QUANTITATIVE AND DECISION NEUROSCIENCE RESEARCH PERTAINING TO INVOLVEMENT

The common element among recent quantitative research paradigms in the study of involvement is the link between aesthetics, emotional arousal in the brain and motivation or involvement, which leads to a behavioural response. The use of unusual and appealing decorations in a shopping environment leads to a higher emotional arousal (Kroeber-Riel 1979), which has been shown to lead to increased purchase behaviour (Esch et al. 2003). The highly aesthetic shopping environment not only leads to increased purchase behaviour, but an increase in electrodermal reaction (EDR), completing the cycle from creative aesthetics to stimulating the brain to purchase the object (Groeppel Klein 2005). Hence there is a physiological reaction to the pleasing environment activated through the senses.

The qualitative research by Bloch et al. (2009) explicitly confirms the importance of exceptional creative design (fashion) or a creative sensual experience (jazz) in triggering an enduring involvement with the product category. Strong emotions were activated by sight and sound which led to the experiences being recalled with not only great emotion, but also great detail by the respondents. This can be explained and linked to brain research of the amygdala which plays a primary role in the processing and memory of emotional reactions.

A basic question that arose when reading about the fMRI study from Cal Tech (Mahoney 2005) was "What would be the scores of consumer rated involvement with the object in question, and how would these scores correlate with the brain activity?"; "Would the affective items correlate with areas of the brain that indicate emotional response and would the cognitive items correlate with a different area?" If the paper and pencil measure of involvement, as measured by the RPPI, correlates with certain brain activity, there may be much more confidence and also understanding of exactly what processes are at work when filling out the involvement measure in relation to an object.

To date research that explicitly measures superior design and involvement has not been carried out. However, Franke et al. (2009) carried out a study where consumers could actively custom design their own product, and they found involvement with the object to be greatly increased after the process. The relationship between aesthetically designed packages, brain activity and involvement is documented by Reimann et al. (2010). In experimental settings, decision making and choice among standardized and novel packages, within a series of low involvement product categories, were investigated. Known and unknown brands, as well as high and low price points, were manipulated. The results showed that a novel package with an unknown brand can be more attractive than a known brand with a standardized package. Furthermore novel packaging can lower price sensitivity.

The experiment was then repeated while subjects underwent fMRI scanning. After the scan participants filled out the RPII for the different products they were exposed to. Significant differences in brain activation were found between the aesthetic and standardized packaging. Significantly stronger brain activation was found in the ventromedial prefrontal cortex (vmPFC) for aesthetic versus standardized product packages, mainly for unknown brands.

To investigate the link between product involvement and brain activation during product perception, the affective and cognitive involvement scores (RPII) were triangulated with the beta value of brain activation. The scores were correlated with activation differences in the striatum, as the striatum is found to be important in goal directed evaluation of affective stimuli (Delgado 2007). There were strong positive correlations between the affective involvement items and activation difference between aesthetic and standardized packaging (r = .69). An opposite effect was observed for the cognitive involvement items (r = –.52). Further analyses did not reveal any other correlations between brain activation and the paper and pencil measure of involvement.

While this type of scale validation is in its infancy, some explanation is speculated. In terms of the concept or construct of involvement, as measured by the RPII, the affective items relate to feeling of emotional states. For example, this is captured by the reaction to and evaluation of the item "exciting-unexciting" which respondents cognitively appraise then remember when responding to the scale. The cognitive items are more factual, e.g., "relevant-irrelevant", and have little to do with emotion. There are many parts of the brain involved when one is exposed to stimuli and reacts to them. The amygdala plays a primary role in the processing and memory of emotional reactions. The ventromedial prefrontal cortex of the brain is an area to which dopamine (the rewarding neurotransmitter) is projected. The vmPFC is said to evaluate the emotional situation and subsequently give a "go" or "no go" signal for further action or behaviour. Thus a correlation between the affective items on the RPII and activation differences in the striatum would make sense, because respondents appraise "exciting" and the other affective word items as they relate to the stimuli. Also when our emotional reactions are heightened, events are remembered more vividly, especially when the emotion is negative (Kensinger and Schacter 2008).

The hippocampus area of the brain plays an important role in long-term memory and spatial navigation. A negative correlation for the cognitive items to this area of activation could mean that there is not a cognitive appraisal of emotional states as for the affective items, because the cognitive items are more factual i.e., relevant-irrelevant. Stimulation of the ventromedial prefrontal cortex was found to be positively related to the affective items.

14.8   SUMMARY

Historically emotion and cognition have been treated somewhat separately by academics. However current models and many researchers now question this assumption of separate areas of the brain for emotional and cognitive processes. Areas of the brain which are thought of as "emotional" or "motivational" are also engaged in cognitive tasks such as problem solving, memory, or attention (e.g., Pessoa and Adolphs 2010). It also may be difficult to find purely "cognitive" tasks that do not hold any emotional components.[4] Therefore if these processes are intertwined, then perhaps the measurements of the emotional and cognitive responses to the stimuli in question should be simultaneously carried out. The results from various fMRI studies show the links between emotional responses found in the amygdala lead to stronger hippocampal memory. Or, in other words, good feelings (possibly from aesthetics) facilitate better information processing.

The different approaches to the study of involvement have nicely converged or triangulated in a way that leads to great confidence in the construct and measures. It has also created a different way of thinking about involvement and also measuring it. Instead of high and low involvement being one dimension and cognitive and affective being the other dimension, the literature suggests thinking of involvement in terms of intensity (high versus low) on a continuum and simultaneously as cognitive and emotional/affective, also on a continuum. One might think of the possibility of four quadrants: low affective involvement and low cognitive involvement; low affective involvement and high cognitive involvement; low cognitive involvement and high affective involvement; and high cognitive involvement and high affective involvement. Therefore the cognition and affect may be activated together, rather than being one or the other. Perhaps as cognitive and affective involvement are measured together, the two dimensions can be plotted together (as in Figure 14.4).

From the initial framework for understanding of what causes involvement (see Figure 14.1), recent research has highlighted the importance of exceptional product design and aesthetics as the triggers for a more motivated behaviour towards the object. The importance of aesthetics for purchase intentions or actual behaviour is well documented in the consumer behaviour literature, and recent fMRI and EEG studies have supplied explanations for this behaviour through arousal and brain activation data. The notion that design and aesthetics create involvement that may be enduring in nature forms the basis for company product design strategy and consumer commitment in various retail establishments. Certainly hotels have embraced this differentiation to give guests an aesthetic experience above and beyond the usual. For example, Art'otel (www.artotels. dk) offers a unique total aesthetic experience that perhaps leads customers to be loyal. One can think of many more instances (such as Apple computers and phones) where good design has led to consumer commitment.

ACKNOWLEDGEMENTS

The author is indebted to Martin Reimann for his research collaboration on fMRI studies; Thomas Ramzoy, who heads the Decision Neuroscience group at CBS, for his comments and research guidance; Hal Kassarjian and Larry Percy for helpful comments on an earlier draft. Thanks to all for their time and effort. Any errors or omissions are the responsibility of the author.

NOTES

1. Richard Lutz did not publish his comments, so he is not referenced in the chapter.
2. Werner Kroeber-Riel passed away in January 1995 at the age of 65. His research is still relevant today; Andrea Groppel Klein has taken his place at Saarland.

3. Flemming Hansen passed away in June 2010 at the age of 72. His last endeavor at the Copenhagen Business School was to establish a neuroscience group, within the department of marketing, dedicated to studying the link between brain functions and consumer choice.
4. The author would like to thank Thomas Ramzoy for these words and thoughts.

REFERENCES

Babin, B.J., W.R. Darden and M. Griffin (1994), 'Work and/or fun: measuring hedonic and utilitarian shopping value', *Journal of Consumer Research*, **20** (4), 644–656.

Bergkvist, L. and J.R. Rossiter (2007), 'The predictive validity of multiple item versus single item measures of the same constructs', *Journal of Marketing Research*, **44** (2), 175–184.

Berridge, K.C. (2009), 'Wanting and liking: observations from the neuroscience and psychology laboratory', *Inquiry (Oslo)*, **52** (4), 378.

Bian, X. and L. Moutinho (2011), 'The role of brand image, product involvement, and knowledge in explaining consumer purchase behavior of counterfeits', *European Journal of Marketing*, **45**, 191–216

Bloch, P., S. Commuri and T. Arnold (2009), 'Exploring the origins of enduring product involvement', *Qualitative Marketing Research: An International Journal*, **12** (1), 49–69.

Buck, R., E. Anderson, A. Chauhuri and I. Ray (2004), 'Emotion and reason in persuasion applying the ARI model and the CASC scale', *Journal of Business Research*, **57**, 647–656.

Cattell, R.B., H.W. Eber and M.M. Tatsouka (1970), *Handbook for the Sixteen Personality Factor Questionnaire*, Illinois: Institute for Personality and Ability Testing.

Chaudhuri, A. (1993), 'Advertising implications of the pleasure principle in the classification of products', in W.F. van Raay and Gary J. Bamossy (eds), *European Advances in Consumer Research*, Vol. 1, Provo UT: Association for Consumer Research, pp. 154–159.

Chaudhuri, A. (2006), 'Involvement', in *Emotion and Reason in Consumer Behavior*, London: Elsevier, pp. 55–70.

Churchill, G. (1979), 'A paradigm for developing better measures of marketing constructs', *Journal of Marketing Research*, **16** (February), 64–73.

Costley, C.L. (1988), 'Meta analysis of involvement research', in Michael J. Houston (ed.), *Advances in Consumer Research*, **15**, Association for Consumer Research, Provo UT, pp. 554–562.

Delezie, E., W. Verbeke, J. De Tavernier and E. Decuypere (2006), 'Consumers' preferences toward techniques for improving manual catching of poultry', *Poultry Science*, **85**, 2019–2027.

Delgado, M.R. (2007), 'Reward-related responses in the human striatum', *Annals of the New York Academy of Sciences*, **1104** (1), 70–88.

Donovan, R.J. and J.R. Rossiter (1982), 'Store atmosphere: an environmental psychology approach', *Journal of Retailing*, **28**, 34–57.

Esch, Franz-Rudolf, Joern Redler and Tobias Langer (2003), 'Effects of product category, brand strength, and visual presentation formation of the efficiency of display promotion', in *ANZMAC Conference Proceedings*, Adelaide (December), pp. 1831–1837.

Falk, E.B., E.T. Berkman, D. Whalen and M.D. Lieberman (2011), 'Neural activity during health messaging predicts reductions in smoking above and beyond self-report', *Health Psychology*, **30** (2), 177–185.

Franke, N., P. Keinz and C.J. Steger (2009), 'Testing the value of customization: when do customers really prefer products tailored to their preferences', *Journal of Marketing*, **73** (September), 103–121.

French, John W. and William B. Michael (1966), *Standards for Educational and Psychological Tests and Manuals*, Washington, DC: American Psychological Association.

Groeppel-Klein, A. (2005), 'Arousal and in-store behavior', *Brain Research Bulletin*, **67**, 428–437.

Hansen, F. (1981), 'Hemispheral lateralization: implications for understanding consumer behavior', *Journal of Consumer Research*, **8** (1) (June), 23–36.

Higie, R.A. and L.F. Feick (1989), 'Enduring involvement; conceptual and measurement issues', in Tom Srull (ed.), *Advances in Consumer Research*, Vol. 16, Ann Arbor: Association for Consumer Research, pp. 690–696.

Kassarjian, H.H. (1981), 'Low involvement: a second look', in Kent B. Monroe (ed.), *Advances in Consumer Research*, Vol. 8, Ann Arbor: Association for Consumer Research, pp. 31–34.

Katsumata, S. and T. Ichikohji (2010), 'Characteristics and values of innovative consumers: a case from the music industry', working paper Manufacturing Management Research Center, Graduate School of Economics, The University of Tokyo.

Kensinger, E.A. and D.L. Schacter (2008), 'Memory and emotion', in Michael Lewis, Jeannette M. Haviland-Jones and Lisa Feldman Barrett (eds), *Handbook of Emotion*, New York: Guilford.

Kim, D., S. Lee and J. Han (2010), 'A confirmatory factor analysis for generation Y's online consumption on sport products', *Journal of Sport and Leisure Studies*, **40**, 163–172.

Kroeber-Riel, W. (1979), 'Activation research: psychobiological approaches to consumer research', *Journal of Consumer Research*, **5** (4) (March), 240–250.

Krugman, H.E. (1965), 'The impact of television advertising: learning without involvement', *Public Opinion Quarterly*, **29** (Fall), 349–356.

Lassen, N.A., D.H. Ingvar and E. Skinhoj (1978), 'Brain function and blood flow', *Scientific American*, **239** (4), 50–59.

Le Doux, J. (1994), 'Memory versus emotional memory in the brain', in P. Ekman and R. Davidson (eds), *The Nature of Emotion*, New York: Oxford, pp. 311–312.

Leavitt, Clark, Anthony Greenwald and Carl Obermiller (1981), 'What is low involvement low in?', in Kent B. Monroe (ed.), *Advances in Consumer Research*, Vol. 8, Ann Arbor: Association for Consumer Research, pp. 15–19.

Mahoney, Jill (2005), 'The brave new world of neuromarketing', *Globe and Mail*, 10 September, pp. A10–11.

McQuarrie, Edward F. and J. Michael Munson (1987), 'The Zaichkowsky Personal Involvement Inventory: modification and extension', in M. Wallendorf and P.E. Anderson (eds), *Advances in Consumer Research*, Vol. 14, Ann Arbor: Association for Consumer Research, pp. 36–40.

McQuarrie, Edward and J. Michael Munson (1992), 'A revised product involvement inventory', in J.F. Sherry and B. Sternthal (eds), *Advances in Consumer Research*, Vol. 19, Ann Arbor: Association for Consumer Research, pp. 108–115.

Mitchell, Andrew (1981), 'The dimensions of advertising involvement', in Kent B. Monroe (ed.), *Advances in Consumer Research*, Vol. 8, Ann Arbor: Association for Consumer Research, pp. 25–30.

Murray, E.A., K.S. Graham and D. Gaffan (2005), 'Perirhinal cortex and its neighbours in the medial temporal lobe: contributions to memory and perception', *Quarterly Journal of Experimental Psychology*, section B, **58** (3), 378–396.

Norgaard, Carsten (2011), 'English: Probably the best brand in the world', unpublished master's thesis, English Department, University of Copenhagen.

Nunnally, J.C. (1978), *Psychometric Theory*, 2nd edition, New York: McGraw-Hill.

Park, C.W. and S.M. Young (1986), 'Consumer response to television commercials: the impact of involvement and background music on brand attitude formation', *Journal of Marketing Research*, **23** (1), 11–24.

Peck, J. and J. Wiggens Johnson (2011), 'Autotelic need for touch, haptics, and persuasion: the role of involvement', *Psychology and Marketing*, **28** (3), 222–239.

Pessoa, L. and R. Adolphs (2010), 'Emotion processing and the amygdala: from a low road to "many roads" of evaluating biological significance', *National Review of Neuroscience*, November, **11** (11), 773–783.

Petty, Richard and John Cacioppo (1981), 'Issue involvement as a moderator of the effects on attitude of advertising content and context', in Kent B. Monroe (ed.), *Advances in Consumer Research*, Vol. 8, Ann Arbor: Association for Consumer Research, pp. 20–24.

Petty, Richard and John Cacioppo (1986), *Communication and Persuasion: Central and Peripheral Routes to Attitude Change*, New York: Springer-Verlag.

Plassmann, Hilke, Thomas Zoega Ramsoy and Milica Milosavljevic (2011), 'Branding the brain: a critical review', Faculty and Research Working Paper, INSEAD, France.

Ramzoy, Thomas and Martin Skov (2010), 'The insentience of brand equity – two studies of consciousness and brands', *Proceedings of the Consumer NeuroEconomics Conference*, Copenhagen, 1 June, p. 22.

Reimann, M., J.L. Zaichkowsky, C. Neuhaus, T. Bender and B. Weber (2010), 'Aesthetic package design: a behavioral, neural, and psychological investigation', *Journal of Consumer Psychology*, **20** (4), 431–441.

Reimann, M., O. Schilke, B. Weber, C. Neuhaus and J.L. Zaichkowsky (2011), 'Functional magnetic resonance imaging in consumer research: A review and application', *Psychology and Marketing*, forthcoming.

Richens, Marsha L., Peter H. Bloch and Edward McQuarrie (1992), 'How enduring and situational involvement combine to create involvement responses', *Journal of Consumer Psychology*, **1** (2), 143–154.

Rothschild, M.L. and Y.J. Hyun (1990), 'Predicting memory for components of TV commercials from EEG', *Journal of Consumer Research*, **16** (4), 472–479.

Shiv, B., A. Bechera, I. Levin, J. Bettman, L. Dube, A. Isen, B. Mellers, A. Smidts, S. Grant and A. McGraw (2005), 'Decision neuroscience', *Marketing Letters*, **16** (3/4), 375–386.

Thompson, R.F. and S.M. Zola (2003), 'Biological psychology', in D.K. Freedheim and I.B. Weiner (eds), *Handbook of Psychology: History of Psychology*, New York, NY: Wiley, pp. 37–66.

Vaughn, R. (1980), 'How advertising works: a planning model', *Journal of Advertising Research*, **20** (5), 27–33.

Vaughn, R. (1986), 'How advertising works: a planning model: revisited', *Journal of Advertising Research*, February/March, pp. 57–66.

Verbeke, W. and I. Vackier (2004), 'Profile and effects of consumer involvement in fresh meat', *Meat Science*, **67**, 159–168.

Xue, F. and P. Zhou (2011), 'The effects of product involvement and prior experience on Chinese consumers' responses to online word of mouth', *Journal of International Consumer Marketing*, **23**, pp. 45–58.

Zaichkowsky, J.L. (1985), 'Measuring the involvement construct', *Journal of Consumer Research*, **12** (December), 341–352.

Zaichkowsky, J.L. (1986a), 'The emotional side of product involvement', in Paul Anderson and Melanie Walendorf (eds), *Advances in Consumer Research*, Vol. 14, Provo UT: Association for Consumer Research, pp. 32–35.

Zaichkowsky, J.L. (1986b), 'Conceptualizing involvement', *Journal of Advertising*, **15** (2), 4–14.

Zaichkowsky, J.L. (1994), 'The personal involvement inventory: reduction, revision, and application to advertising', *Journal of Advertising*, **23** (4), 59–70.

Zaichkowsky, J.L. (2011), 'Consumer involvement', in Richard Bagozzi and Ayalla A. Ruvio (eds), *Wiley International Encyclopedia of Marketing, Vol. 3, Consumer Behavior*, Chichester: John Wiley & Sons Ltd, pp. 110–111.

PART V

CONSUMER BEHAVIOUR IN EVOLUTIONARY PERSPECTIVE

15 Consumers are foragers, not rational actors: towards a behavioral ecology of consumer choice

Donald A. Hantula

The most fundamental challenge for humans, or any other sentient creature, is the problem of finding, securing, and using resources; or in more general terms, foraging. Without regular access to resources such as food, water and other goods, any living being will soon perish. In the behavioral ecology literature, "foraging" is a concept that incorporates a variety of theoretical propositions and empirical models addressing common questions about decision rules for predators. However, foraging is not limited solely to decisions about edible prey items per se, but rather is a general purpose set of rules and strategies for adapting to environmental risk and uncertainty, yielding both prey items and information (Stephens et al., 2007). Though foraging is sometimes mischaracterized in terms of relatively restricted behaviors (e.g., foraging is simply searching for food), it is best conceptualized in more general terms of acquisition and exchange. Indeed, the prey items modeled in foraging theory are not confined solely to food, but also include commodities as diverse as nesting materials, territory, information, access to mates, and opportunities for social behavior. Similarly, human foraging is neither constrained to our ancestral environments nor to subsistence economics; it is the naturally selected way in which we manage patchy and stochastic environments, even today. Just as we once foraged in forests and savannas we now forage in grocery stores and websites. Foraging is more than a metaphor.

This chapter presents a behavioral ecology of modern human consumer choice situated in a post-industrial information-based economy. After first differentiating a behavioral ecology approach to choice and decision making from other models, the chapter explains foraging theory in greater detail and makes the case that it is essentially an economic theory. The fundamental importance of temporal constraints in foraging decisions is established, and parallels between fundamental foraging theory concepts such as the lazy-L model and marginal value theorem, and basic behavior analytic concepts such as delay discounting and matching are used as a foundation to extend foraging to choices made in the marketplace. Current information foraging and consumer foraging research is reviewed and a behavioral ecology of consumption is advanced. The chapter then explains some allegedly "irrational" consumer choices from a foraging perspective, and ends with provisional practical and policy recommendations that follow from a behavioral ecology of consumer choice.

The behavioral ecology stance taken in this chapter is distinctively different from evolutionary psychology. Evolutionary psychology has garnered much attention in the popular press and in various areas of psychology; however, notoriety is not necessarily veracity. At a surface level the basic claims of evolutionary psychology seem to hold some validity and make for interesting discussion, but biological and philosophical scholars of evolution raise serious questions about its major tenets and theories (Buller, 2005; McKinnon and Silverman, 2005). The entire evolutionary psychology program is called into question for ignoring modern research and theory in fields such as anthropology, cognitive neuroscience, developmental psychology, evolutionary biology, human genetics, and paleoecology (Bolhuis et al., 2011). Further, evolutionary psychology's massive modularity hypothesis (the idea that the mind consists of a number of evolved cognitive modules), which is the most "psychological" of its major tenets, is unsupported. Based on the now discredited artificial intelligence work of the 1970s (that domain specificity is critical to "intelligent" behavior) and a Chomskian view of humanity (such as the "language acquisition device"), Fodor (1983) asserted that the mind is composed of input or sensory "modules" that operate independently from one another. Information from these modules is then transferred to central processing units such as thought or reason (that are not modular). Evolutionary psychology extended this modularity hypothesis to cognitive processes at large. Fodor (2001) repudiated the "massively modular mind idea", and as Bolhuis et al. (2011) observe, evidence in comparative psychology and neuroscience points to more general processes. In particular they cite Pavlovian conditioning, operant conditioning, and foraging as robust cross-species examples that counter any modularity ideas. A behavioral ecology perspective on decision-making rejects the mind as massively modular machine metaphor.

Behavioral ecology differs from evolutionary psychology in other important ways. Behavioral ecology is an inductive perspective; evolutionary psychology is a deductive perspective. A behavioral ecology perspective asks us to question assumptions about the nature of human decision-making, and provides insights into new answers, telling us to look outside in the environment, not inside the organism, to determine how and why decisions are made. It is an ecological account, not a meditational account of behavior. The features of the environment that may select for or against particular decisions or decision strategies are what are important. Behavioral ecology views choice as a process resulting from naturally selected generally applicable decision rules, not discrete decision modules. Conversely, while evolutionary psychology has no quarrel with natural selection, it indiscriminately invents and invokes "Darwinian algorithms", psychological mechanisms, mental organs, modular minds and the like to explain choices. However it is never clear whether these explanatory devices refer to processes, mechanisms, states, or reifications. Finally a behavioral ecology perspective is economical and parsimonious, working from a few simple, yet powerful principles – much like evolution itself. The modular mind posited in evolutionary psychology would be massively maladaptive.

15.1 FORAGING AND RATIONAL CHOICE

Foraging research is voluminous, cutting across anthropology, biology, computer science, library science, marketing, and different areas of psychology. For example, quantitative work in foraging spans species from wasps to humans, and disciplines such as Behavioral Ecology (Stephens et al., 2007), Operant Psychology (Fantino, 1985; Fantino and Abarca, 1985), Cognitive Psychology (Rode et al., 1999), Information Systems (Pirolli, 2007), and Consumer Psychology (Rajala and Hantula, 2000). Illustrative qualitative foraging work is found in Anthropology (Winterhalder et al., 1999) and in Library Science (Sandstrom, 1994).

Thus, the term "foraging" is not used solely in the metaphorical sense as a synonym for "search" but instead refers to a dynamic transactional process. Such activity involves exchanging time and somatic energy for resources, and thus is essentially economic in nature. Because organisms are assumed to have finite time and energy to use in acquiring resources, models of foraging are predicated upon the assumption that organisms work toward maximally efficient commodity intake relative to time spent foraging (E/T). Put another way, the more efficient the forager, the more adaptive its behaviors within its environment, and, presumably, the greater its reproductive success. Foraging is an "economic theory" but it should not be confused with a rational choice perspective. Modern foraging theory clearly departs from economic rationality in its expectations for behavior and decision-making. Foraging is economic in the sense that it concerns what organisms choose to do with the resources with which they are presented. However, in terms of modeling behavior, it more closely resembles the theories of modern behavioral economists than classical optimization theory (Fisher, 1930; Jevons, 1871).

Table 15.1 An evolution of consumer decision making

	Rational choice	Heuristics & biases	Behavioral ecology
Discipline	Economics	Cognitive psychology	Evolutionary theory
Focus	Prescriptive	Descriptive	Descriptive
Reasoning	Deductive	Deductive	Inductive
Role of emotion	Emotion ignored	Emotion is error	Emotion is information
Research program	Develop rules for optimal choice	Compare choice to rational model & catalog errors	Analyze choice as adaptation
View of humanity	People are irrational	People are foolish	People are biological

Indeed, a behavioral ecology perspective on decision-making challenges both traditional rational choice theory, and quasi-rational choice cognitive models that sprang up in the latter part of the 20th century. As Table 15.1 illustrates, rational choice models of consumer decision-making are prescriptive theories based in classical economics that delineate optimal choices. However, challenges to fundamental assumptions of the rational choice model from cognitive psychology, such as complete access to information and unbiased uses of information, led to a quasi-rational choice model based on empirical observations of heuristics, errors, and biases. Whereas a rational choice model presumed that because people do not obey rules of rationality they are irrational, the errors and biases perspective agrees that while people do not choose rationally, they want to be rational actors but are limited by their cognitive capacity. This perspective launched a large research program dedicated to identifying and cataloging the myriad human decision foibles. In contrast, a behavioral ecology account of consumer decision-making is arational, taking no stance on the issue. Instead, it follows from evolutionary theory's focus on adaptation and views consumers as foragers.

15.2 FORAGING THEORY

Foraging is a biobasic behavior. All organisms are on the prowl for goods such as food, nesting materials and rudimentary tools in their environments. Some organisms even seek out gifts, as gift giving occurs across a wide spectrum of species from spiders to chimpanzees (Jonason et al., 2009). Foraging yields more than these commodities; it also provides rich information about the forager's environment, including distance between patches, prey density, and presence of other foragers or predators (the term "patch" refers to any bounded spatial or temporal co-location of prey items). Hence, foraging is the common mechanism for finding goods and information about goods in an uncertain environment. The famous "4Fs" (feeding, fighting, fleeing, and fornicating) of fitness may perhaps be modified. "Feeding" may be changed to "foraging" in this quadruplet because foraging includes, but encompasses more than, feeding. The first three are directed towards surviving and thriving so that the organism has an opportunity to engage in the fourth.

Foraging theory is a descriptive and inductive framework. Its fundamental assumption is that foraging is not random action, but rather is strategic behavior. Researchers have built elegant mathematical models of forager decision-making that have inspired much laboratory and field research. The resulting data strengthened the field to the point that the cutting edge of foraging theory is comparison of quantitative models. Foraging is explicitly viewed as behavior distributed across time, therefore temporal components are important in its models. All foraging models presuppose that the forager has a finite amount of energy that must support basic metabolic activities, foraging, and other behaviors throughout the day. Further, the forager is attempting to momentarily maximize energy intake per unit time or energy expenditure, within certain constraints. Foraging models are classified as prey or patch models. Prey models concern the decision to capture or not capture a prey item; patch models concern the decision to stay in a patch or leave it. The major variables in foraging models are probability (e.g., of prey encounter, capture), delay (in patch travel, to consume prey), and cost (e.g., to procure or consume).

Foraging theory delineates three major phases of foraging, namely searching, handling, and consumption (Stephens et al., 2007; Stephens and Krebs, 1986). In foraging theory, searching describes the time and energy devoted to finding patches and prey items, and handling denotes time and energy devoted to a prey item after it has already been acquired or captured and before any energy can be derived from it. For herbivores, this might involve cracking the shell of a seed or nut; for predators, this might involve transporting a prey item to a safe location and cleaning it before consumption. It is important to note that handling does not guarantee consumption; the prey item may be abandoned, stolen, or lost during handling. A nut or other food item may be dropped or discarded during shelling; a prey animal may be abandoned to escape a predator.

Foraging theorists recognize two major assumptions about any foraging species that must be considered. The first is a currency assumption. It is assumed that all foragers "spend" energy and time as currency while foraging. Foragers also spend energy and time for other "commodities" such as basic somatic functions (essentially "overhead" expenses), grooming, avoiding predation, nesting, and mating. Foragers also "earn" in the form of energy. The particular form of currency varies according to the forager's species; for example flesh would not be a form of currency for a herbivore. The second assumption is a constraint assumption. All foragers have limitations that constrain their ability to forage, and a successful forager is one that works within its constraints. Constraints are generally conceptualized as interactions between the forager and its environment; the forager's phylogenic endowments dictate its capabilities while the environment limits the availability of prey and information. This interactionist idea is important in understanding foraging; for example although there may be an abundance of prey in a patch, if the prey is out of the forager's reach, or too fast for the forager, that prey is functionally non-existent for that forager.

This conceptual focus is also a good example of the difference between the behavioral ecology approach taken in this chapter and the more common evolutionary psychology approach. Rather than positing several "modules" for feeding, consuming other goods, finding information, and managing risk as is done in evolutionary psychology, a behavioral ecology approach works inductively from phylogenic and environmental constraints to identify a more general constellation of adaptive behavior. Given the stochastic nature of the foraging environment, risk and uncertainty are ubiquitous. It is more efficient or economical from an evolutionary perspective to have a flexible and adaptable means for managing uncertainty than to have many modules for the different assumed components of foraging, all of which are steeped in uncertainty. It should also be clear from the foregoing discussion that modern foraging theory takes the concept of foraging a few steps further, casting foraging not so much as an issue of feeding per se, but as one of a more general adaptation to an equivocal environment. The successful forager is the forager that can not only consume calories while expending minimal energy, but can also glean information from the environment, and make choices. Indeed, "foraging" may probably be best understood as the naturally selected way in which an organism navigates the rocky shoals of a constantly shifting risky, scanty and equivocal environment.

15.2.1   Foragers are Financiers

A particularly straightforward way to understand foraging theory is to view foragers as finned, feathered and furry financiers. The currency and momentary maximization assumptions, and temporal perspective in foraging theory depict foraging as an economic system or system of exchange between the forager and the environment. For example, at the beginning of each day (for a diurnal forager), the forager spends energy to maintain its basic functions, and invests additional time and energy in foraging activities. The forager must turn a profit – that is, take in more energy than is expended overall. If the forager makes a sufficient profit, it may then have the time and energy to spend on other costly behaviors such as grooming, socializing, and perhaps even attracting, competing for, and securing a mate. If the forager does not turn a profit, it may be able to survive until the next day, but if it runs too large an energy deficit, it may perish by nightfall. Thus, in terms of evolutionary fitness, it is only the shrewd investor whose hereditary portfolio grows and whose genes are passed on to the next generation.

15.2.2   Time is Tight

Time-extended, or macro-level modeling to predict behavior has always been at the root of foraging theory (Stephens and Krebs, 1986). Foraging theory is inherently focused on molar explanations of behavior, and almost always seems to assume that behavior is only important and informative when seen over relatively broad time intervals. Time-extended models are the basic conceptual tools used to assess the long-term eco-logical costs and benefits of an organism's activities. For some organisms this will be a diurnal threshold, while for others the underlying temporal unit may be longer or shorter. The time horizon for foraging is central to developing hypotheses about behavior. For example, traditional time allo-cation models were based on the assumption that foraging choices lead to an optimization of total energy intake relative to foraging time (Lea, 1979; Stephens and Krebs, 1986). In contrast, more recent models, such as the energy-budget models, predict only that the organism will behave so as to minimize the possibility of an energy shortfall for the foraging period. Although energy is fungible (to a point), time is not. For a forager, time is a continually decreasing resource that cannot be replenished.

If it is assumed that a forager is attempting to momentarily maximize energy intake per unit time, the temporal dimensions of any decision will be more important than any potential energy intake. For a diurnal forager, this becomes especially important as nightfall approaches and the foraging window draws to a close. Counterintuitively, the forager who has the good fortune of an energy surplus will become increasingly risk-averse, preferring low variance prey items over those with a higher variance. Conversely, the forager running an energy deficit will become increas-ingly risk-seeking, choosing higher variance prey items over low variance prey items, and displaying choices that in a very real way, "go for broke" (Stephens and Charnov, 1982).

Foraging models generally do not provide specific predictions about molecular foraging behavior (i.e., one-shot choices), but rather predict patterns of behavior allocation, as illustrated by Stephens and Krebs' (1986) Lazy-L model for foraging intervals. Within the Lazy-L framework, it is assumed that energy intake is stochastic, and will fluctuate above or below the minimum energy requirement at points during the interval in response to the moment-to-moment foraging decisions. At the outset of a foraging interval, the significance of the daily threshold is minimal, and thus the results of molecular foraging decisions are inconsequential. As the interval elapses, the significance of the threshold for molecular decisions becomes more critical. In this way, the model accounts for the control of foraging by molecular temporal contingencies, and simultaneous control by the energy budget, which is an inherently molar feature of the decision-making environment.

Consideration of the effects of delay under molar constraints on decision-making obviously has a precedent in risk-sensitive foraging research (Winterhalder et al., 1999). If temporal discounting functions as a foraging rule, one basic question is whether or not the rule can be modified according to different foraging scenarios (Charnov, 1976; Stephens and Krebs, 1986). To address this question, we should first note Stephens and Krebs' (1986) assertion that foraging rules having to do with rate of energy intake (i.e., energy intake from foraging in a depleting patch) are meaningless without a specified time interval. Winterhalder (1980) explains that for a time interval, T, the energy acquired from foraging must be equivalent to the energy expended. For the interval T, the total energy acquired is

$$E_a = R(T - T_{nf}) \tag{15.1}$$

where E_a is total energy acquired through foraging, R is the rate of energy intake, and T_{nf} is total time allocated to non-foraging activities. This is consistent with the premise of a minimum daily energy requirement and the Lazy-L model. Rearranging this equation also demonstrates that the salience of time on foraging activity can also be a function of the relative availability of energy in the foraging environment, normally modeled as the average value of encountered prey items (Stephens and Charnov, 1982; Winterhalder et al., 1999). Thus, in terms of molar controls on foraging, time and energy are reciprocally related, and equally salient.

Figure 15.1 illustrates how Equation 15.1 relates to foraging decisions under molar time constraints in environments that are more or less "energy rich". It models behavioral allocation according to indifference curves (**fl**

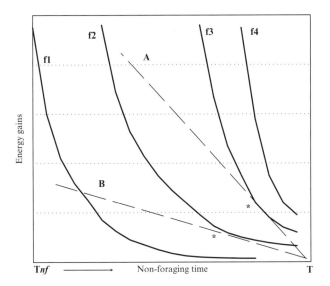

Figure 15.1   Indifference curves of a time-constrained forager

through **f4**), which treat energy and non-foraging time as fungible commodities. Here, non-foraging time includes all behaviors not associated with currency acquisition (Kacelnik et al., 1987). An organism devoting all of its time to foraging would be located at the point where curve **f1** intersects with the ordinate. From left to right, each curve represents a more favorable foraging environment (i.e., better overall rate of energy intake within-patch – potentially from larger prey items or from greater prey density). A forager will be indifferent to any point on any of the curves. Lines **A** and **B** represent habitat energy budgets, and * indicates points of optimization between energy intake and benefits derived from non-foraging activity. The slopes of the indifference curves illustrate the influence of molar time constraints on the forager. For this organism, even a slight increase in T_{nf} will result in a substantial drop in energy intake. In terms of decision-making this model shows the forager when to discontinue energy acquisition. The value of the different commodities (energy vs. non-foraging activities) is functionally related to the specified time constraints.

15.2.3   From Marginal Values to Matching

Marginal value theorem
The marginal value theorem (Charnov, 1976) is a foundation of modern foraging theory. According to the marginal value theorem, all prey occurs

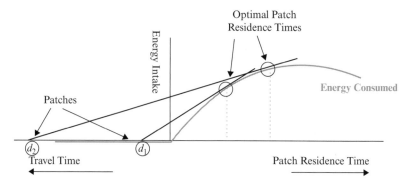

Note: The abscissa represents time. The left side of the figure shows travel times to two different patches (d₁ and d₂), while the right side of the figure shows patch residence time. The ordinate represents energy intake, depicted by the curve on the right side.

Source: Redrawn from Charnov, 1976.

Figure 15.2   The marginal value theorem

in a patch. When a forager is in a patch, it balances the yield of that patch against the yield of other available patches, if the forager were to leave and move to another patch. The first important insight from the marginal value theorem is that foragers do not find a patch and remain in it until all prey items are depleted and then move on to the next patch. Rather foragers will "leave some money on the table" and depart a patch when the rate of return of prey in the patch falls below the average rate of return available from other patches in the environment. The second important insight is that the travel time between patches is a critical variable in determining how long a forager will remain in a depleting patch. The more prolonged the travel time, the longer the forager will endure a scarce and spotty patch. As shown in Figure 15.2, the value of any patch or prey item is not an intrinsic property of that particular patch or prey item, but is a relativistic assessment in the dynamic context of the patch, prey item, depletion rate, and travel time.

Matching

The marginal value theorem is useful in understanding many different aspects of foraging such as patch sampling, patch switching, and the effects of travel time (Stephens et al., 2007). However, it begs an important question: how does the forager "know" or learn the average rate of return provided by patches in the environment? A central information archive or daily update that foragers may access does not exist; although foraging is in essence a financial phenomenon, there is no *Wall Street*

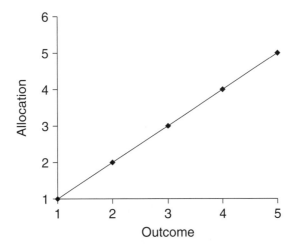

Note: Abscissa and ordinate are arbitrary units.

Figure 15.3 Illustration of the functional relation between behavioral allocation and received outcome in matching

Journal in the wild. At first glance it may appear that the marginal value theorem, just like classical rational choice theory, assumes the question away by positing access to perfect information and errorless processing of this information. Instead, the answer comes from the matching law (Herrnstein et al., 1997). Simply stated, the matching law holds that in any choice situation, behavior will be allocated between alternatives in a fairly close "match" to their relative rates of return. Foragers will allocate their behavior among options in proportion to the outcomes obtained as shown in Figure 15.3.

Quantitatively, the matching law is represented in Equation 15.2 (Davison and McCarthy, 1988)

$$B_1 = \frac{R_1}{R_1 + R_2 + R_e} \tag{15.2}$$

where B_1 is foraging behavior and the terms R_2 through R_e are returns from non-foraging activities. The total benefit from foraging (R_1) depends upon how much time is allocated to the remaining alternatives. When multiple alternatives are available, an individual distributes behavior, effort, time, or resources across the multiple alternatives in proportion to the relative rates of return associated with each alternative in a given period of time as shown in Equation 15.3

$$\frac{B_1}{B_1 + B_2 + \ldots + B_n} = \frac{R_1}{R_1 + R_2 + \ldots + R_n} \qquad (15.3)$$

where B_n are response alternatives and R_n are rates of relative rates of reinforcement on each of those alternatives. This process can only be understood as a molar phenomenon. Baum (2002) further argues that the concept of choice, or decision-making, can be described more accurately as allocating behaviors among response alternatives, rather than as a single decision. Because all the apportionment of behavior can be seen as a proportion of total behavior for some period, all choice behavior must be extended in time.

Based on Equation 15.3, an alternative form of this model could be constructed using energy as the constraining variable in a foraging scenario. If energy available for foraging is constrained, the trade-offs depicted by the slope of the indifference curves **f1** to **f4** in Figure 15.1 will change (Stephens and Krebs, 1986). In such a case, less time spent foraging will result in smaller decrements in *Ea* (from Equation 15.1) because the foraging activity is producing a low rate of energy intake. Again, this shows how the value of competing commodities is influenced by extended rather than local environmental contingencies. This simple example illustrates the potential effects of two important molar constraint variables on foraging activity relative to other types of activity. These models illustrate the point that the molecular decisions of the organism have no meaning unless these broader variables are specified. Nevertheless, the manner in which real decision-making might change under such constraints remains an empirical question.

Matching is ubiquitous, found in nearly all sentient species (Davison and McCarthy, 1988; Herrnstein et al., 1997) and may be innate (Gallistel et al., 2007). Matching shares an important feature with the marginal value theorem: predictions that a forager will not deplete a patch entirely (or maximize) but rather will depart a patch before depletion, and engage in patch sampling. Matching and the resulting patch sampling guarantees that the forager will contact other patches in the environment over time; thus it is the mechanism by which the organism learns the average rate of return in the environment and the existence of alternative patches. Although matching may appear to be sub-optimal at first glance, a more nuanced look at matching in terms of overall fitness tells a different story: matching is a long-term optimal strategy (Sakai and Fukai, 2008). In a stochastic and scarce environment, patches may disappear without warning, and prey items in patches may deplete quickly due to competing foragers or environmental changes. The forager who stayed exclusively in a "rich" patch (or a maximizer) would be at an incredible survival disadvantage if that patch or its prey vanished; however, the forager that matches will have a ready alternative.

Delay discounting

Research in both behavioral ecology and in behavior analysis shows clearly that matching is a naturally selected, innate, long-term optimal choice strategy for foragers. However, this conclusion begs another question: how does matching occur, or is there a particular decision rule that would produce matching? From the marginal value theorem, it is reasonable to expect that such a decision rule would be temporally based and would be as ever-present as matching. Given the strong departure from both classical economic as well as cognitive accounts of choice, such a decision rule would most likely appear to be sub-optimal at first glance. Delay (or temporal) discounting is the mechanism by which matching occurs. For any forager, the value of a prey item is a decreasing function of delay to that prey item; or in more quotidian terms, a dollar today is worth more than a dollar tomorrow. The fact that value is a function of delay is not controversial, however the shape of the discount function is the subject of much contention. Classical economic and rational choice theories hold that such a discount function would be exponential, as shown in Equation 15.4:

$$V = Ae^{-rD} \tag{15.4}$$

where V represents the time-discounted value of the outcome, A is the non-time discounted value of the outcome, e is the base of the natural logarithm and D is the delay between a choice and the outcome. However, research has now clearly established that the discount function is in fact hyperbolic (Ainslie and Haslam, 1992; Green and Myerson, 1996; McKerchar et al., 2009; Smith and Hantula, 2008) as shown in Equation 15.5:

$$V = A/(1+kD) \tag{15.5}$$

where V equals the value of the delayed outcome, A equals the non-time discounted amount of the outcome, D is the intertemporal delay between choice and outcome, and k is an index of sensitivity to delay.

Hyperbolic discounting differs from exponential discounting in many important ways. First and most importantly is the shape of the discount curve. A hyperbolic discount curve is more steeply bowed than an exponential curve with a rapid decrement in value as a function of time at the beginning of the curve and a gradual decrease afterwards. Second, while exponential curves are parallel across time, hyperbolic curves will cross, predicting preference reversals and violating the stationarity axiom of classical economics. Third, like matching, hyperbolic discount curves are found across species; exponential discount curves are not normally found in nature. The hyperbolic curve's steep discount function yields a very strong preference for immediate outcomes and a diminished preference for delayed outcomes. Whenever faced with a decision to pursue a prey item, stay in or leave a patch, a forager will choose the alternative with the least delay to a prey item. This over-sensitivity to, and preference for, more immediate outcomes leads to matching (Shimp, 1966). Essentially, the forager chooses the most valuable outcome on a moment-by-moment basis in a momentary maximizing process called melioration (Herrnstein et al., 1993; Herrnstein and Prelec, 1992). For a forager, delay is not simply exasperating – delay is deadly.

15.3   CONSUMERS ARE FORAGERS

Foraging theory accounts for human behavior in ancestral environments and subsistence economies. It also accounts for human behaviou in highly technologized, post-industrial, market-oriented economies. Ironically, the most direct tests of this seemingly primordial behavior have been accomplished in the context of the currently most advanced environment: online work and commerce. Hantula (2010) reviewed the extant literature on human foraging online as descending from two research themes: information foraging theory and the behavioral ecology of consumption.

15.3.1   Information Foraging Theory

According to information foraging theory, we are informavores. Sandstrom (1994) and Pirolli (2005, 2006, 2007) note the functional similarity between arboreal foragers and humans searching for information. Pirolli and Card's (1999) information foraging theory views information as a resource, or prey item. Humans searching for information in an online environment do so in a way that follows from foraging, attempting to optimize the utility of the information gained relative to the cost of obtaining it. Just as foraging theory assumes overall maximization of E/T, information theory assumes maximization of I/T (information per unit time). Information foraging theory relies on the concept of "information diet". An important component of information foraging theory is the SNIF-ACT model (Fu and Pirolli, 2007). According to the SNIF-ACT model, people use "information scents" to determine which links to follow on a web page, and use the mean information scent value to determine whether to stay on a particular website (information patch) or to travel to another website, consistent with the marginal value theorem's (Charnov, 1976) predictions regarding foragers in the physical environment. In Pirolli's studies, information foragers did not use or consume every piece of information encountered; much like an aboreal forager does not capture and consume every prey item encountered. Instead they discarded much of the information, even relevant information, after a quick scan, opting for short reports that contained much information for their size and rejecting larger, but potentially more information-rich reports, momentarily maximizing I/T.

Other studies of information foraging found results similar to Pirolli and Card (1999) in an analog online search task (Dennis and Taylor, 2006), and data consistent with the marginal value theorem (Charnov, 1976) and matching (Herrnstein et al., 1997) with adult humans switching between various word puzzles (Payne et al., 2007) and word search tasks (Wilke et al., 2009). A series of studies manipulating time pressure, text skimming and information linkages found that skimming the text, rather than reading half of it, improved memory for important ideas in the text but not for unimportant ideas (Duggan and Payne, 2009) – a result akin to a forager searching through prey items and discarding all but the most nutritious.

15.3.2   The Behavioral Ecology of Consumption

The behavioral ecology of consumption (Hantula et al., 2001; Rajala and Hantula, 2000) builds on behavior analytic research in behavioral economics (Hursh, 1980, 1984) by applying foraging theory to consumer behavior. It posits that the multiple phases of foraging activities, including searching, choosing between alternatives, and handling items are mirrored in human consumption decisions, and assumes that consumption behaviors emerge because of their adaptive characteristics, consistent with evolutionary theory. Online shopping is a natural modern day analogue to foraging in the savannah. In an online shopping environment, consumer items are prey, stores are patches, and travel time between patches is a function of connection speed, system speed, website design, and other delays between leaving an online store and entering another one. This analogue was the basis for a series of experiments on the effects of handling time (operationalized as feedback delay to item availability) in online shopping. Experiments using a range of delay values found strong quantitative fits to the hyperbolic discount function in Equation 15.5 (DiClemente and Hantula, 2003; Rajala and Hantula, 2000; Hantula et al., 2008); also each of these studies evidenced patch sampling as predicted by foraging theory, not maximizing by exclusively choosing of the richest patch as expected from rational and quasi-rational choice models.

Energy is the currency in foraging. However, humans in affluent market oriented economies are not as concerned with energy intake and outflow per se as they are with money intake and outflow. For humans, monetary budgets are accumulated through time and effort allocated to labor in exchange for wages. A foraging animal's energy budget is accumulated through foraging activities, and total accumulated energy is analogous to cash accrual. In both cases, the accumulation of resources represents expenditure of somatic effort and time by the organism. A major temporal component of human commodity acquisition is comprised of working for tokens, or monetary accrual. Before any goods are purchased and consequences are experienced, tokens must be accumulated and exchanged. Thus, the cost of a commodity may be regarded as a component of the total foraging time associated with a particular prey item (commodity) because its purchase represents an exchange for temporally extended responding on some type of monetary pay schedule. In literal terms, the time spent working for money is a phase of foraging, analogous to the handling phase. Framed in this way, the effects of price on preference should conform to the same hyperbolic discount function as delay shown in Equation 15.5. To test this idea, Smith and Hantula (2003) varied prices in online stores according to the hyperbolic discount function. Purchase data fit the hyperbolic decay function well. In a very real sense – time is money. Again, patch sampling occurred and individuals sometimes bought items in more expensive stores, even while the same item was available in a less expensive store.

15.3.3   Consumers Foraging in the Wild

A behavioral ecology account of consumer choice supplies logical explanations for seemingly "irrational" behavior in the marketplace. Rather than viewing us as coldly calculating utility maximizers or as fundamentally flawed information processors, a behavioral ecology account sees our choices in the marketplace as products of the same naturally selected decision strategies that have served us well for eons. We remain foragers: hunters and gatherers. The hyperbolic discount function as delay shown in Equation 15.5 can account for impulse purchases and other small consumer decisions that may put us on the primrose path to perdition (Foxall, 2010a). Understanding how such choices arise from evolved preferences, rather than from errors or moral failures will cast new light on some seemingly intractable consumer choice issues ranging from use of sunblock (Saad and Peng, 2006) to the august issue of conspicuous consumption (Saad and Vongas, 2009).

Preference inconsistencies

Consumers do not display consistent preferences as a rational choice model dictates. For example, a study of employees choosing monthly rewards among a set of substitutable, inexpensive consumer items found virtually no constant preferences over several months (Wine et al., 2012). The patch sampling found in previous online shopping experiments (DiClemente and Hantula, 2003; Rajala and Hantula, 2000; Smith and Hantula, 2003; Hantula et al., 2008) is another example of matching. Further, Foxall and colleagues studied large consumer panel data from fast-moving grocery purchases in the UK and found that consistent with laboratory studies of consumer foraging, consumers rarely buy only the least expensive product (maximize) or the same product (brand loyalty), but instead brand sample in the same manner as other foragers patch sample (Foxall and James, 2003; Foxall et al., 2010a; Foxall et al., 2004; Foxall and Schrezenmaier, 2003; Foxall et al., 2010b). That is, in the case of fast moving, substitutable consumer goods, matching, i.e., brand sampling is the norm. Qualitative work performed in conjunction with one of the quantitative studies (Foxall and James, 2003) revealed that although shoppers recognized the fact that they brand sampled, they were not able to explain their behavior in any way other than appeals to "Just for variety" (p. 828). From a rational choice perspective, such an explanation would be seen as further evidence of consumer capriciousness (Stigler and Becker, 1977), however from a behavioral ecology perspective this explanation is seen as a rough description of the effects of patch sampling. People are not necessarily cognizant of the reasons for their choices, and these sorts of explanations are more of a post-hoc rationalization than a causal statement. Consumers will stray from "choice" brands and stores; patch sampling is not a function of flightiness but one of natural selection.

Temporal preference reversals

Consistency in choice is seen as a hallmark of rationality. According to the stationarity axiom preferences should be stable across time; however according to data they are not (Kirby and Herrnstein, 1995). For example, a consumer may prefer to receive a watch rather than a sports radio in three days, but would prefer to receive the sports radio to the watch in four months. Contrasting the deductively dictated exponential discount model shown in Equation 15.4 and the inductively derived hyperbolic discount model in Equation 15.5 shows clearly that discount rates not only differ, but that a hyperbolic model predicts temporal preference reversals. Further, discount rates for a given individual are not constant, but differ within individuals (Schoenfelder and Hantula, 2003). Discount rates differ within individuals as a function of the metabolic function of the prey item (Charlton and Fantino, 2008), which is of particular interest in consumer foraging. That is, food is discounted more steeply than other consumer goods such as books and DVDs. Such metabolically attuned discounting suggests that differentiated discount rates are not a function of impetuosity or irrationality, but rather a result of natural selection.

(In)transitivity in choice

If consumers are rational actors, which this chapter suggests they are not, attraction and decoy effects (Fasolo et al., 2006; Pechtl, 2009) are preference anomalies. However, if consumers are foragers, as is suggested in this chapter, these are to be expected. These effects are defined as an inconsistent choice that occurs when consumers are presented with two desirable products (target and competitor), and a worse "decoy" such that if a consumer prefers desirable product A to desirable product B, introducing less desirable product C as a decoy will often reverse preferences. It is related to the economic concept of transitive choice, that is, if a consumer prefers A to B and B to C, then A should be preferred over C. However, human choices are often intransitive, which from a quasi-rational choice perspective is often attributed to heuristics that engender cognitive illusions or faulty calculations (Buschena and Zilberman, 1999; Kalenscher et al., 2010; Kivetz and Simonson, 2000). Intransitivity in preferences is not limited to humans; non-human animals such as Gray Jays exhibit such intransitive choices while foraging (Waite, 2001). These choices are neither irrational nor suboptimal, and closer analysis reveals that they are a product of the current foraging context, including time horizon and encounter rate, following from the marginal value theorem (Charnov, 1976).

Diet and nutrition

Worldwide, there is a curious correlation between obesity and socio-economic status (SES) (McLaren, 2007). In countries that rank low on the United Nation's Human Development Index (HDI), there is a positive association between obesity and SES: wealthier citizens are more likely to be obese. Conversely, in countries that rank high on the HDI, there is a negative association between obesity and SES: those living in poverty are more likely to be obese. Recent data from the USA (Townsend et al., 2009) and France (Maillot et al., 2007) are two examples of this larger trend.

A behavioral ecology account of consumer choice explains this seeming paradox. In low HDI countries, food is scarce and increased body weight is a signal of fitness, in terms of access to resources. Less energy dense foods (those that are high in water content and low in protein; e.g. fresh fruits and vegetables) are most readily available, but must be consumed in large quantities to maintain and gain body weight. In high HDI countries, high energy dense foods (those that are high in refined grains, added salt, sugars, or fats, e.g. processed prepackaged foods) are more readily available and less expensive than low energy dense foods; however, these foods are also much lower in necessary vitamins. Indeed, foods such as oils, margarine, cookies and bread have 10 to 40 times the energy density of fresh fruits and vegetables, which have 10 times the energy cost of processed foods (Drewnowski and Specter, 2004).

Social class predicts diet quality (Darmon and Drewnowski, 2008). High HDI countries are obesogenic environments. A foraging perspective takes this analysis further by explaining why these environments are so nutritionally toxic. The well known evolved preference for foods that are sweet, salty and high in fats is the first step, the relative low cost of these foods is the second step as identified by a preliminary foraging analysis (Lieberman, 2006). Matching analyses of grocery purchases in the UK (Foxall et al., 2010a; Foxall et al., 2004; Foxall and Schrezenmaier, 2003; Foxall et al., 2010b; Oliveira-Castro et al., 2006; Oliveira-Castro et al., 2010) provide strong evidence that food shoppers are acting as foragers. Foraging is not only about the benefits obtained; it is also about the costs incurred in searching, handling and consuming a good.

Consider the case of a person of low SES in the USA. In general, this individual not only has little money to spend on food; full-service grocery stores and purveyors of fresh fruits and vegetables are rare in impoverished areas, so accessing these foods is very costly in terms of time and transportation (Wiig and Smith, 2009). Further, little food preparation time is available for low-SES individuals (Dammann and Smith, 2009). A forager seeks to maximize E/T. The most energy dense foods are also often the least costly; a forager with limited resources would choose such foods that are exponentially more energy dense and less expensive, even though they are nutritionally poor in many other aspects. Ironically, because preprocessed foods contain large amounts of sodium, they serve as a motivating operation to make artificially sweetened, caloric beverages all the more reinforcing. Further, even if less energy dense but nutritionally rich foods are available at the same monetary and temporal costs, they will be less preferred due to the comparatively high handling costs. Unprocessed meats must be cooked; few fruits and vegetables are consumed without preparation. For example, high SES households consume more chicken while low SES households consume more processed pork products (Guenther et al., 2005). Unprocessed chicken is bland and must be cooked; seasoning is often added during cooking to make it appetizing. In contrast, processed pork products are often pre-seasoned and many may be eaten with little or no cooking or additional preparation. Similarly, using spices and flavoring agents while preparing many fruits and vegetables to make them more palatable imposes additional handling and economic costs. Put plainly, it is exponentially easier to open a box of salty snack crackers than it is to prepare more nutritious foods. From a foraging perspective, these consumers are neither irrational nor ignorant; they are behaving in exactly the way that has served our species well for many millennia.

15.3.4   Practical Management, Marketing and Policy Issues

Viewing consumers as foragers rather than rational actors necessitates that the assumed rational or quasi-rational viewpoint that undergirds marketing and policy choices will have to shift to a more ecological perspective. Because a behavioral ecology of consumption is still in its infancy, few of its possible applied implications have been attempted or realized. Its heterodox stance in contrast to rational and quasi-rational choice models suggests that any applications will not be incremental improvements to current practical and policy decisions grounded in classical rationality. Instead, a behavioral ecology of consumption questions conventional wisdom and suggests solutions that may at times appear to be radically different, and perhaps much more effective. Some selected implications for marketing strategy, sustainability, and public health are outlined below.

Implications for marketing strategy

Research in online shopping (DiClemente and Hantula, 2003; Hantula et al., 2008; Rajala and Hantula, 2000) suggests that the best investments e-commerce sites can make are those that result in decreasing delays to service, product availability feedback and other features of actually buying the good. Delay degrades value quickly, as the hyperbolic discount function shows. Flashy websites that take too long to load or to navigate may decrease sales. This can also be extended to physical delivery of goods ordered online; a similar discount function describes preferences for delivery options (Hantula and Bryant, 2005). Similarly, information foraging research (Pirolli, 2007) suggests that websites providing consumer information will be most useful if the information is available in smaller, easier to "digest" units. The SNIF-ACT model (Fu and Pirolli, 2007) takes this a step further. Informavores use information scents, or clues about existence of information that are easily accessible, such as on the top or right corner of a website. Information on websites that require scrolling to navigate may never be noticed. Bringing the marginal value theorem into play, the quicker and easier it is for consumers to leave one website and enter another, the less likely they are to spend much time on any one particular website. Fast and efficient search engines such as Google exacerbate the importance of speed in the online environment. If an online forager can more quickly locate, and navigate to another patch than the time it takes for a webshop to provide service, the total time to prey is reduced by leaving, rather than staying. Thus, less tolerance for delay, and more frequent store switching would be expected.

Patch and prey sampling is the norm (Foxall et al., 2010a; Foxall et al., 2004; Foxall and Schrezenmaier, 2003; Foxall et al., 2010b; Oliveira-Castro et al., 2006; Oliveira-Castro et al., 2010; Wine et al., 2012), which makes brand loyalty truly the holy grail of marketing practice: venerable, desirable but never obtainable. Efforts at securing brand loyalty are most likely misdirected. Instead, decomposing the economic concept of "utility" into utilitarian and informational reinforcement (Foxall, 2010b), and then applying matching analyses, should result in better product placement and market segmentation (Nicholson and Xiao, 2010; Wells et al., 2010). That is, rather than searching for a sustainable competitive advantage in the marketplace, regularly scanning the other patches and prey, and adjusting product features to make the product more comparatively desirable may be a better course of action.

Implications for sustainability
The steep discounting predicted by the hyperbolic model may inform the poor results of efforts to increase "green" consumption or decrease energy use. The central problem in this realm is that the benefits of any green consumer choices will occur far in the future, sometimes after the consumer's demise, yet the behavior changes are needed in the present (Arbuthnott, 2010; Carson and Roth Tran, 2009). Initiatives directed toward education, information and persuasion are not likely to have large or enduring effects. Taxing energy consumption and less green products will make the costs larger and more immediate and decrease consumption, but such taxes are often regressive and politically unfeasible. Following a behavioral approach to green consumption, standard "marketing mix" approaches may not be very effective. Instead, behaviorally inspired programs that employ either reinforcement or aversive contingencies, depending on the class of behavior in question, may be more effective. For example, reinforcement may be more effective to reduce home energy use, but punishment may be more effective to reduce water consumption (Foxall et al., 2006). Indeed it is more likely that informational reinforcers will be much more effective in increasing consumption of "green" goods. Paradoxically, if green goods are more expensive than their less environmentally friendly counterparts (and thus a sign of fitness and increased resources), they may become more widely adopted than if they are less expensive.

Implications for public health

Obesity has deleterious consequences for both individuals and society. In high HDI countries, obesity has become a disease of the poor. Indeed individuals receiving USA food stamps[1] have a higher BMI than those of the same SES not in the program (Kupillas and Nies, 2007). Given income and time constraints, the marked preference for processed energy dense foods is reasonable from a foraging perspective. This suggests that initiatives built on providing information and education are doomed to fail. Obesity reduction programs that instruct low SES individuals to spend more money on less energy dense foods may be seen as insulting and elitist. Small reductions in the price of fresh fruits and vegetables will also have little effect. Given the exponential differences in energy density and energy cost between processed foods and fresh foods, substantial price reductions or subsidies along with greatly decreased travel time will be necessary to increase intake of healthier foods. If such subsidies are not practicable, providing low cost complements to healthier foods may serve to increase their consumption. Decreasing the handling costs of healthier foods such as providing ready to eat or "prep cook" versions of fresh fruits and vegetables may be a more promising strategy to pursue. Similarly, raising the "price" for less healthy foods, in terms of increasing effort or time to consumption, while providing readily available substitutes is a promising strategy.

The preference reversals predicted by hyperbolic discounting provide a method to combat obesity. Not surprisingly, body mass index (BMI) correlates with discounting. Individuals with high BMI have a markedly strong preference for immediate outcomes (Zhang and Rashad, 2008), and are more likely to choose the present pleasure of more tasty food than the future fitness of a lower BMI. However, the timing of a choice here is critical; if individuals choose food before they enter a cafeteria or restaurant, they may make healthier choices. For example, employing a pre-commitment response (Ainslie, 1992) in which a patron pre-orders food (perhaps via a website) before entering an eating establishment may diminish the immediate temptation of less healthy foods upon arrival.

Drugs and alcohol are consumer products that present current challenges resembling those of obesity. Addictive substances and food alike activate the reward circuitry of the brain, largely through the release of dopamine. *Homo sapiens* evolved in a time of scarce and unpredictable food, which made a strong preference for fats, sweets and salt an important contributor to fitness. In addition this environment was nearly bereft of intoxicating substances, and those that were available (e.g. coca leaves) were of relatively low potency and caused illness when overindulged, so adaptations to these substances were not an important part of natural selection. In contrast the current environment is one of readily available and highly potent intoxicants. Foraging theory explains choices that addicts make, showing that consumption decisions regarding heroin are similar to those decisions made about any other prey item (Bickel et al., 2004). Drug use is not a moral failure; rather it is a by-product of a very well attuned reward recognition system. Not surprisingly, it is now recognized internationally that efforts focused on legally restricting access to drugs, i.e., the "war on drugs" have failed despite four decades of effort (Global Commission on Drug Policy, 2011). The global war on drugs sought to curb drug use by raising the price of drugs through eradication, interdiction and arrest. However, because the demand for drugs is highly inelastic (Hursh, 1991) and few suitable substitutes are readily available, such a supply-side strategy should not be expected to be very effective. Although no research on drug use from a consumer foraging perspective exists, foraging theory would predict that a drug control strategy focused on either providing substitutes for drug use, or even more easily available highly reinforcing goods may be particularly successful. Indeed, the contingency management approach to substance abuse treatment, which pays addicts to refrain from drug use, is known to be very efficacious (Higgins et al., 2008).

15.4 CONCLUSIONS

Contemporary humans who live in a highly technologized market oriented society are not so far removed from the plains and savannas of our ancestral past. We face the same functional problems, only their structure has changed. We use the same strategies to solve these problems as have served us well over the millennia; we still need to eat. Whether we are hunting a waterbird and plucking berries from a bush, or buying a packaged chicken and a pint of blueberries from a grocer, the basic challenges remain the same. Foraging has been the foundation of our (and many other) species' survival. Foraging allows us to transact with the environment, and secure food, other goods and information. Our species has not changed much, but the environment, and the ways in which we talk and think about it, have changed drastically.

The ways in which we think about ourselves have also changed. We began to see ourselves in a more exalted light – as *Homo economicus*, the rational thinker. Rational choice theory and its precepts followed. However, as Herrnstein (1990) observes, rational choice theory fails as a descriptive account of human choice, although it may serve as a prescriptive account of choice. This begs the question of who, and on what justification, would rational choice theory's prescriptions be determined to be "correct". In a sense, rational choice theory may have failed on both grounds. From a Kuhnian point of view, the quasi-rational perspective arose as a way for the reigning rational choice model to defend itself against many observed anomalies in choice and decision-making. It attempted to rescue rational choice theory by accepting its prescriptive component and adding a descriptive component focused on determining why we do not choose rationally, assuming that it was not for lack of trying. Various exceptions to rational choice precepts were not seen as challenges but were incorporated into the model by re-asserting that it was decision-makers, not decision rules, that were faulty. Ultimately, both rational choice and errors and biases approaches present a dismal view of humanity.

This quasi-rational choice perspective is also challenged empirically and conceptually. Some of the basic findings in the quasi-rational errors and biases literature were questioned from an evolutionary perspective, and a series of experiments showed that the "biases" found in previous studies were artifacts of the language used to describe choices in these experiments: studies using language that was more aligned with evolved ways of solving problems did not show any "biased" effects (Cosmides and Tooby, 1996). Foraging theory can easily explain prospect theory's precepts (the major quasi-rational choice theory) and account for the data collected under the errors and biases research program (McDermott et al., 2008). Foraging theory has expanded beyond its beginnings to explain human choice and decision in environments ranging from the arboreal to the technological. It also can both encompass the findings of the quasi-rational choice perspective and replace rational choice theory.

Ideas have consequences. Theories and models shape how we think of ourselves, and also what we should do about ourselves, for example in terms of business and policy decisions. Rational choice and quasi-rational choice models point toward marketing strategies and social policy interventions that assume a cold calculus drives decisions. Given these theories' bleak view of human nature, failure to adhere to prescribed choices is often described in pejorative terms – blaming the decision-maker, or in some cases the information provided. Policy initiatives are information laden and are structured such that systematic deviations from a plan are treated as additional obstacles to be overcome; such initiatives can also quickly become unnecessarily punitive. A behavior ecologic theory, in contrast, points toward marketing strategies and social policy interventions that assume naturally selected strategies drive decisions. Incongruence between the theory and individual choices is a failure of the theory, or maybe the environment, not the person. Policy initiatives would be more cost and benefit oriented from the perspective of the individual consumer, concerned more with how a decision or an environment can be restructured to produce a desired outcome rather than with finding another way to educate, inform or persuade people. A behavior ecologic view of humanity is positive and hopeful, seeing us as highly adaptable creatures who have overcome many formidable challenges in the past, and are equipped to survive in the future. Foraging theory may seem simplistic and to pale in comparison to the high level processes invoked by rational choice and quasi-rational choice theories, but from natural selection to a computer's binary code, it is only from simplicity that functional complexity may emerge.

NOTE

1. Food stamps are USA government supplied coupons that can be exchanged for food at retail stores. "Food stamps" is also a colloquial term for the Supplemental Nutrition Assistance Program (SNAP) that helps low-income people buy food (United States Department of Agriculture, 2011). The program name was changed to SNAP in 2008 to reflect a new focus on nutrition, including educational efforts, as well as an increase in benefits. Although it is a Federal program, it is administered by the states and each state may have different regulations, and even a unique name for the program (Social Security Administration, 2008).

REFERENCES

Ainslie, G. (1992), *Picoeconomics. The Strategic Interaction of Successive Motivational States Within the Person*, New York: Cambridge University Press.

Ainslie, G., and N. Haslam (1992), 'Hyperbolic discounting', in G. Loewenstein and J. Elster (eds), *Choice Over Time*, New York, NY: Russell Sage Foundation, pp. 57–92.

Arbuthnott, K.D. (2010), 'Taking the long view: environmental sustainability and delay of gratification', *Analyses of Social Issues and Public Policy (ASAP)*, **10** (1), 4–22.

Baum, W.M. (2002), 'From molecular to molar: a paradigm shift in behavior analysis', *Journal of the Experimental Analysis of Behavior*, **78**, 95–116.

Bickel, W.K., L.A. Giordano, and G.J. Badger (2004), 'Risk-sensitive foraging theory elucidates risky choices made by heroin addicts', *Addiction*, **99** (7), 855–861.

Bolhuis, J.J., G.R. Brown, R.C. Richardson, and K.N. Laland (2011), 'Darwin in mind: new opportunities for evolutionary psychology', *PLoS Biol*, **9** (7), e1001109.

Buller, D.J. (2005), *Adapting Minds: Evolutionary Psychology and the Persistent Quest for Human Nature*, Cambridge, MA: MIT Press.

Buschena, D.E., and D. Zilberman (1999), 'Testing the effects of similarity on risky choice: implications for violations of expected utility', *Theory and Decision*, **46** (3), 251–276.

Carson, R.T., and B. Roth Tran (2009) 'Discounting behavior and environmental decisions', *Journal of Neuroscience, Psychology, and Economics*, **2** (2), 112–130.

Charlton, S.R., and E. Fantino (2008), 'Commodity specific rates of temporal discounting: does metabolic function underlie differences in rates of discounting?', *Behavioural Processes*, **77** (3), 334–342.

Charnov, E.L. (1976), 'Optimal foraging: the marginal value theorem', *Theoretical Population Biology*, **9**, 129–136.

Cosmides, L., and J. Tooby (1996), 'Are humans good intuitive statisticians after all? Rethinking some conclusions from the literature on judgment under uncertainty', *Cognition*, **58** (1), 1–73.

Dammann, K.W., and C. Smith (2009), 'Factors affecting low-income women's food choices and the perceived impact of dietary intake and socioeconomic status on their health and weight', *Journal of Nutrition Education and Behavior*, **41** (4), 242–253.

Darmon, N., and A. Drewnowski (2008), 'Does social class predict diet quality?', *American Journal of Clinical Nutrition*, **87** (5), 1107–1117.

Davison, M., and D. McCarthy (1988), *The Matching Law: A Research Review*, Hillsdale, NJ: Lawrence Erlbaum Associates, Inc.

Dennis, A.R., and N.J. Taylor (2006), 'Information foraging on the web: the effects of "acceptable" Internet delays on multi-page information search behavior', *Decision Support Systems*, **42** (2), 810–824.

DiClemente, D.F., and D.A. Hantula (2003), 'Optimal foraging online; increasing sensitivity to delay', *Psychology & Marketing*, **20** (9), 785–809.

Drewnowski, A., and S.E. Specter (2004), 'Poverty and obesity: the role of energy density and energy costs', *American Journal of Clinical Nutrition*, **79** (1), 6–16.

Duggan, G.B., and S.J. Payne (2009), 'Text skimming: the process and effectiveness of foraging through text under time pressure', *Journal of Experimental Psychology: Applied*, **15** (3), 228–242.

Fantino, E. (1985), 'Behavior analysis and behavioral ecology: a synergistic coupling', *The Behavior Analyst*, **8** (2), 151–157.

Fantino, E., and N. Abarca (1985), 'Choice, optimal foraging, and the delay-reduction hypothesis', *Behavioral and Brain Sciences*, **8** (2), 315–362.

Fasolo, B., R. Misuraca, McClelland, and M. Cardaci (2006), 'Animation attracts: the attraction effect in an on-line shopping environment', *Psychology & Marketing*, **23** (10), 799–811.

Fisher, I. (1930), *The Theory of Interest*, New York: Macmillan.

Fodor, J.A. (1983), *The Modularity of Mind. An Essay on Faculty Psychology*, Cambridge, MA: MIT Press.

Fodor, J.A. (2001), *The Mind Doesn't Work That Way: The Scope and Limits of Computational Psychology*, Cambridge, MA: MIT Press.

Foxall, G.R. (2010a), 'Accounting for consumer choice: inter-temporal decision making in behavioural perspective', *Marketing Theory*, **10** (4), 315–345.

Foxall, G.R. (2010b), 'Invitation to consumer behavior analysis', *Journal of Organizational Behavior Management*, **30** (2), 92–109.

Foxall, G.R., and V.K. James (2003), 'The behavioral ecology of brand choice: how and what do consumers maximize?', *Psychology & Marketing*, **20** (9), 811–836.

Foxall, G.R., and T.C. Schrezenmaier (2003), 'The behavioral economics of consumer brand choice: establishing a methodology', *Journal of Economic Psychology*, **24** (5), 675–695.

Foxall, G.R., J.M. Oliveira-Castro, and T.C. Schrezenmaier (2004), 'The behavioral economics of consumer brand choice: patterns of reinforcement and utility maximization', *Behavioural Processes*, **66** (3), 235–260.

Foxall, G.R., J.M. Oliveira-Castro, V.K. James, M.M. Yani-de-Soriano, and V. Sigurdsson (2006), 'Consumer behavior analysis and social marketing: the case of environmental conservation', *Behavior and Social Issues*, **15** (1), 101–124.

Foxall, G.R., V.K. James, J.M. Oliveira-Casd, and S.Ribier (2010a), 'Product substitutability and the matching law', *The Psychological Record*, **60** (2), 185–216.

Foxall, G.R., V.K. Wells, S.W. Chang, and J.M. Oliveira-Castro (2010b), 'Substitutability and independence: matching analyses of brands and products', *Journal of Organizational Behavior Management*, **30** (2), 145–160.

Fu, W.-T., and P. Pirolli (2007), 'SNIF-ACT: a cognitive model of user navigation on the World Wide Web', *Human-Computer Interaction*, **22** (4), 355–412.

Gallistel, C.R., A.P. King, D. Gottlieb, F. Balci, E.B. Papachristos, M. Szalecki, et al. (2007), 'Is matching innate?', *Journal of the Experimental Analysis of Behavior*, **87** (2), 161–199.

Global Commission on Drug Policy (2011), *War on Drugs*, http://www.globalcommissionon drugs.org/Report.

Green, L., and J. Myerson (1996), 'Exponential versus hyperbolic discounting of delayed outcomes: risk and waiting time', *American Zoologist*, **36** (4), 496.

Guenther, P.M., H.H. Jensen, S.P. Batres-Marquez, and C.-F. Chen (2005), 'Sociodemographic, knowledge, and attitudinal factors related to meat consumption in the United States', *Journal of The American Dietetic Association*, **105** (8), 1266–1274.

Hantula, D.A. (2010), 'The behavioral ecology of human foraging in an online environment: of omnivores, informavores and hunter-gatherers', in N. Kock (ed.), *Evolutionary Psychology and Information Systems Research: A New Approach to Studying the Effects of Modern Technologies on Human Behavior*, NY: Springer, pp. 85–99.

Hantula, D.A., and K. Bryant (2005), 'Delay discounting determines delivery fees in an e-commerce simulation: a behavioral economic perspective', *Psychology & Marketing*, **22** (2), 153–161.

Hantula, D.A., D.F. DiClemente, and A.K. Rajala (2001), 'Outside the box: the analysis of consumer behavior', in L. Hayes, J. Austin, R. Houmanfar, and M. Clayton (eds), *Organizational Change*, Reno, NV: Context Press, pp. 203–223.

Hantula, D.A., D.D. Brockman, and C.L. Smith (2008), 'Online shopping as foraging: the effects of increasing delays on purchasing and patch residence', *IEEE Transactions on Professional Communication*, **51** (2), 147–154.

Herrnstein, R.J. (1990), 'Rational choice theory: necessary but not sufficient', *American Psychologist*, **45** (3), 356–367.

Herrnstein, R.J., and D. Prelec (1992), 'Melioration', in G. Loewenstein and J. Elster (eds), *Choice Over Time*, New York: Russell Sage Foundation, pp. 235–263.

Herrnstein, R.J., G.F. Loewenstein, D. Prelec, and W. Vaughan (1993), 'Utility maximization and melioration: internalities in individual choice', *Journal of Behavioral Decision Making*, **6** (3), 149–185.

Herrnstein, R.J., H. Rachlin, and D.I. Laibson (1997), *The Matching Law: Papers in Psychology and Economics*, New York, NY and Cambridge, MA: Russell Sage Foundation and Harvard University Press.

Higgins, S.T., K. Silverman, and S.H. Heil (2008), *Contingency Management in Substance Abuse Treatment*, New York, NY: Guilford Press.

Hursh, S.R. (1980), 'Economic concepts for the analysis of behavior', *Journal of the Experimental Analysis of Behavior*, **34** (2), 219–238.

Hursh, S.R. (1984), 'Behavioral economics', *Journal of the Experimental Analysis of Behavior*, **42** (3), 435–452.

Hursh, S.R. (1991), 'Behavioral economics of drug self-administration and drug abuse policy', *Journal of the Experimental Analysis of Behavior*, **56** (2), 377–393.

Jevons, W.S. (1871), *The Theory of Political Economy*, London: Macmillan.

Jonason, P., J. Cetrulo, J. Madrid, and C. Morrison (2009), 'Gift-giving as a courtship or mate-retention tactic? Insights from non-human models', *Evolutionary Psychology*, **7** (1), 89–103.

Kacelnik, A., J.R. Krebs, and B. Ens (1987), 'Foraging in a changing environment: an experiment with starlings (*Sturnus vulgaris*)', in M.L. Commons, A. Kacelnik and S.J. Shettleworth (eds), *Quantitative Analyses of Behavior Vol. 6*, Hillsdale, NJ: Lawrence Erlbaum Associates, pp. 63–87.

Kaenscher, T., P.N. Tobler, W. Huijbers, S.M. Daselaar, and C.M.A. Pennartz (2010), 'Neural signatures of intransitive preferences', *Frontiers in Human Neuroscience*, **4**.

Kirby, K.N., and R.J. Herrnstein (1995), 'Preference reversals due to myopic discounting of delayed reward', *Psychological Science*, **6** (2), 83–89.

Kivetz, R., and I. Simonson (2000), 'The effects of incomplete information on consumer choice', *Journal of Marketing Research*, **37** (4), 427–448.

Kupillas, L.M., and M.A. Niles (2007), 'Obesity and poverty: are food stamps to blame?', *Home Health Care Management & Practice*, **20** (1), 41–49.

Lea, S.E. (1979), 'Foraging and reinforcement schedules in the pigeon: optimal and non-optimal aspects of choice', *Animal Behavior*, **27** (3), 875–886.

Lieberman, L.S. (2006), 'Evolutionary and anthropological perspectives on optimal foraging in obesogenic environments', *Appetite*, **47** (1), 3–9.

Maillot, M., N. Darmon, F. Vieux, and A. Drewnowski (2007), 'Low energy density and high nutritional quality are each associated with higher diet costs in French adults', *American Journal of Clinical Nutrition*, **86** (3), 690–696.

McDermott, R., J.W. Fowler, and O. Smirnov (2008), 'On the evolutionary origin of prospect theory preferences', *Journal of Politics*, **70** (2), 335–350.

McKerchar, T.L., L. Green, J. Myerson, T.S. Pickford, J.C. Hill, and S.C. Stout (2009), 'A comparison of four models of delay discounting in humans', *Behavioural Processes*, **81** (2), 256–259.

McKinnon, S., and S. Silverman (eds) (2005), *Complexities: Beyond Nature and Nurture*, Chicago: University of Chicago Press.

McLaren, L. (2007), 'Socioeconomic status and obesity', *Epidemiologic Reviews*, **29**, 29–48.

Nicholson, M., and S.H. Xiao (2010), 'On the evolutionary bases of consumer reinforcement', *Journal of Organizational Behavior Management*, **30** (2), 127–144.

Oliveira-Castro, J.M., G.R. Foxall, and T.C. Schrezenmaier (2006), 'Consumer brand choice: individual and group analyses of demand elasticity', *Journal of the Experimental Analysis of Behavior*, **85** (2), 147–166.

Oliveira-Castro, J.M., G.R. Foxall, and V.K. Wells (2010), 'Consumer brand choice: money allocation as a function of brand reinforcing attributes', *Journal of Organizational Behavior Management*, **30** (2), 161–175.

Payne, S.J., G.B. Duggan, and H. Neth (2007), 'Discretionary task interleaving: heuristics for time allocation in cognitive foraging', *Journal of Experimental Psychology: General*, **136** (3), 370–388.

Pechtl, H. (2009), 'Value structures in a decoy and compromise effect experiment', *Psychology & Marketing*, **26** (8), 736–759.

Pirolli, P. (2005), 'Rational analyses of information foraging on the web', *Cognitive Science: A Multidisciplinary Journal*, **29** (3), 343–373.

Pirolli, P. (2006), 'The use of proximal information scent to forage for distal content on the world wide web', in A. Kirlik (ed.), *Adaptive Perspectives on Human-Technology Interaction: Methods and Models for Cognitive Engineering and Human-Computer Interaction*, New York, NY: Oxford University Press, pp. 247–266.

Pirolli, P. (2007), *Information Foraging Theory: Adaptive Interaction with Information*, New York, NY: Oxford University Press.

Pirolli, P., and S. Card (1999), 'Information foraging', *Psychological Review*, **106** (4), 643–675.

Rajala, A.K., and D.A. Hantula (2000), 'Towards a behavioral ecology of consumption: delay-reduction effects on foraging in a simulated internet mall', *Managerial and Decision Economics*, **21**, 145–158.

Rode, C., L. Cosmides, W. Hell, and J. Tooby (1999), 'When and why do people avoid unknown probabilities in decisions under uncertainty? Testing some predictions from optimal foraging theory', *Cognition*, **72** (3), 269–304.

Saad, G. (2006), 'Applying evolutionary psychology in understanding the Darwinian roots of consumption phenomena', *Managerial & Decision Economics*, **27** (2/3), 189–201.

Saad, G. (2007), *The Evolutionary Bases of Consumption*, Mahwah, NJ: Lawrence Erlbaum Associates.

Saad, G. (2008), 'The collective amnesia of marketing scholars regarding consumers' biological and evolutionary roots', *Marketing Theory*, **8** (4), 425–448.

Saad, G., and A. Peng (2006), 'Applying Darwinian principles in designing effective intervention strategies: the case of sun tanning', *Psychology and Marketing*, **23**, 617–638.

Saad, G., and J.G. Vongas (2009), 'The effect of conspicuous consumption on men's testosterone levels', *Organizational Behavior & Human Decision Processes*, **110** (2), 80–92.

Sakai, Y., and T. Fukai (2008), 'The actor-critic learning is behind the matching law: matching versus optimal behaviors', *Neural Computation*, **20** (1), 227–251.

Sandstrom, P.E. (1994), 'An optimal foraging approach to information seeking and use', *Library Quarterly*, **64** (4), 414.

Schoenfelder, T.E., and D.A. Hantula (2003), 'A job with a future? Delay discounting, magnitude effects, and domain independence of utility for career decisions', *Journal of Vocational Behavior*, **62** (1), 43–55.

Shimp, C.P. (1966), 'Probabilistically reinforced choice behavior in pigeons', *Journal of the Experimental Analysis of Behavior*, **9** (4), 443–455.

Smith, C.L., and D.A. Hantula (2003), 'Pricing effects on foraging in a simulated Internet shopping mall', *Journal of Economic Psychology*, **24** (5), 653–674.

Smith, C.L., and D.A. Hantula (2008), 'Methodological considerations in the study of delay discounting in intertemporal choice: a comparison of tasks and modes', *Behavior Research Methods*, **40** (4), 940–953.

Social Security Administration (2008), 'Food stamp facts', from http://ssa.gov/pubs/10101.html

Stephens, D.W., and E.L. Charnov (1982), 'Optimal foraging: some simple stochastic models', *Behavioral Ecology and Sociobiology*, **10**, 251–263.

Stephens, D.W., and J.R. Krebs (1986), *Foraging Theory*, Princeton, NJ: Princeton University Press.

Stephens, D.W., J.S. Brown, and R.C. Ydenberg (2007), *Foraging: Behavior and Ecology*, Chicago: University of Chicago Press.

Stigler, G.J., and G.S. Becker (1977), 'De gustibus non est disputandum', *American Economic Review*, **67** (2), 76–90.

Townsend, M.S., G.J. Aaron, P. Monsivais, N.L. Keim, and A. Drewnowski (2009), 'Less-energy-dense diets of low-income women in California are associated with higher energy-adjusted diet costs', *The American Journal of Clinical Nutrition*, **89** (4), 1220–1226.

United States Department of Agriculture (2011), 'Supplemental Nutrition Assistance Program (SNAP)', from http://www.fns.usda.gov/snap/

Waite, T.A. (2001), 'Intransitive preferences in hoarding gray jays (Perisoreus canadensis)', *Behavioral Ecology and Sociobiology*, **50** (2), 116–121.

Wells, V.K., S.W. Chang, J. Oliveira-Castro, and J. Pallister (2010), 'Market segmentation from a behavioural perspective', *Journal of Organizational Behavior Management*, **30** (2), 176–198.

Wiig, K., and C. Smith (2009), 'The art of grocery shopping on a food stamp budget: factors influencing the food choices of low-income women as they try to make ends meet', *Public Health Nutrition*, **12** (10), 1726–1734.

Wilke, A., J.M.C. Hutchinson, P.M. Todd, and U. Czienskowski (2009), 'Fishing for the right words: decision rules for human foraging behavior in internal search tasks', *Cognitive Science: A Multidisciplinary Journal*, **33** (3), 497–529.

Wine, B., S. Gilroy, and D.A. Hantula (2012), 'Temporal (in)stability of employee preference for rewards', *Journal of Organizational Behavior Management*, **32**(1), 58–64.

Winterhalder, B. (1980), 'Environmental analysis in human evolution and adaptation research', *Human Ecology*, **8**, 135–170.

Winterhalder, B., F. hu, and B. Tucker (1999), 'Risk-sensitive adaptive tactics: models and evidence from subsistence studies in biology and anthropology', *Journal of Archaeological Research*, **7**, 301–348.

Zhang, L., and I. Rashad (2008), 'Obesity and time preference: the health consequences of discounting the future', *Journal of Biosocial Science*, **40** (1), 97–113.

Index

Aaker, J.L. 50, 54, 64, 449
Abbas, A. 34
Abelson, R.P. 23
Absolut vodka ad 95–6
Adams, R. 20
addictive, impulsive and other counter-
    normative consumption 276, 304,
    316, 323–4
  'behavioral addiction' and
    pathological gambling 345–52
  drug addiction 303, 305, 308, 327–8,
    334–44, 570–571
  foraging theory 570–571
  internalized norms and paternalism
    352–5
  microeconomics of consumption
    324–34
  see also discounting and impulsivity
Adidas 70
adoption of innovations see innovation
    diffusion
Adorno, T.W. 52
advertising 65, 71, 73, 86, 88, 208
  addicted consumers 338
  advertising humor and culture see
    separate entry
  celebrity 27
  emotional responses 222
  individualist or collectivist societies
    54, 60–61
  innovation diffusion 271
  involvement 524, 526–30, 531, 532,
    533, 534, 537
  meaning of consumer goods 55
  neuroscience 446, 449, 464, 465–6,
    475, 491, 532, 533, 534, 537
  stores and shopping centres 135
advertising humor and culture 83–4,
    85–9, 112–14
  background: theories of humor
    89
    humor style 89–91
    perception of humor 91–2

crossing boundaries and humour
    92–7
  outdoor advertising 97–102, 113
  model: Challenge Model 84–5, 92,
    102, 112, 113
  violence, gender and humor
    102–105, 110, 113–14
    cultural implications 111–12
    male denigration 110–111
    men: inflated view of their worth
      108–9
    men are animals 105–6
    men are childish 106–7
    men are incompetent and ignorant
      108
    men are lazy 107
    patronizing men 107
    violence against men 109–10
aesthetics 535, 540, 541, 543
affluence and culture 69–71
Africa 75, 205
age 329, 337
  innovation diffusion 255, 256, 257,
    259, 263, 275
  self-control 310
Aggarwal, P. 19
Agnew, J.-C. 25, 204
Aharon, I. 446
Ahmed, S. 208, 336
Ahuvia, A.C. 182
Ailawadi, K.L. 447, 448
Ainslie, G. 292, 299, 305, 310, 329, 330,
    341, 342, 343, 344, 561, 570
Ajzen, I. 226, 274
Akhtar, S. 23
Akhter, S.H. 167, 169
Aksoy, L. 152, 153
Alba, J.W. 150, 152
Albanese, P.J. 362, 398, 403, 404, 412
Albert, N. 181, 182
Albinsson, P.A. 220
Alden, D.L. 73, 91, 93, 94
Alekshin, V.A. 23